SecondPerson

Second Person

Role-Playing and Story in Games and Playable Media

Edited by Pat Harrigan and Noah Wardrip-Fruin

Designed by Michael Crumpton

The MIT Press

Cambridge, Massachusetts

London, England

MIT Press books may be purchased at special quantity discounts for
business or sales promotional use. For information, please e-mail
<special_sales@mitpress.mit.edu> or write to Special Sales Department,
The MIT Press, 55 Hayward Street, Cambridge, MA 02142..

This book was set in Adobe Chapparal and ITC Officina
by Michael Crumpton and printed and bound
in the United States of America.

Second person : role-playing and story in games and playable media /
edited by Pat Harrigan and Noah Wardrip-Fruin.

p.   cm.

Includes bibliographical references and index.
ISBN: 978-0-262-08356-0 (hc: alk. paper)
1. Electronic games. 2. Role playing. 3. Interactive multimedia.
I. Wardrip-Fruin, Noah. II. Harrigan, Pat.

GV1469.17.S63S43   2007
793.93'2—dc22
2006046216

frontispiece illustration by Gustav Doré

Contents

x. Dedication and Acknowledgments

xi. Contributors

xiii. Introduction

 I. Tabletop Systems

 II. Computational Fictions

 III. Real Worlds

 IV. Appendices

Contributor Biographies

Permissions

Index

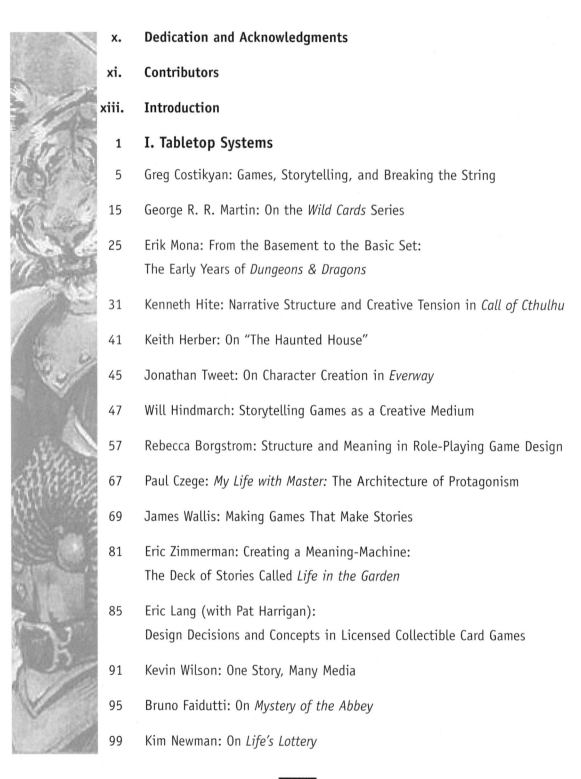

x. **Dedication and Acknowledgments**

xi. **Contributors**

xiii. **Introduction**

1 **I. Tabletop Systems**

5 Greg Costikyan: Games, Storytelling, and Breaking the String

15 George R. R. Martin: On the *Wild Cards* Series

25 Erik Mona: From the Basement to the Basic Set:
The Early Years of *Dungeons & Dragons*

31 Kenneth Hite: Narrative Structure and Creative Tension in *Call of Cthulhu*

41 Keith Herber: On "The Haunted House"

45 Jonathan Tweet: On Character Creation in *Everway*

47 Will Hindmarch: Storytelling Games as a Creative Medium

57 Rebecca Borgstrom: Structure and Meaning in Role-Playing Game Design

67 Paul Czege: *My Life with Master:* The Architecture of Protagonism

69 James Wallis: Making Games That Make Stories

81 Eric Zimmerman: Creating a Meaning-Machine:
The Deck of Stories Called *Life in the Garden*

85 Eric Lang (with Pat Harrigan):
Design Decisions and Concepts in Licensed Collectible Card Games

91 Kevin Wilson: One Story, Many Media

95 Bruno Faidutti: On *Mystery of the Abbey*

99 Kim Newman: On *Life's Lottery*

107   **II. Computational Fictions**

111   Jordan Mechner: *The Sands of Time*: Crafting a Video Game Story

121   Lee Sheldon: On *And Then There Were None*

125   Helen Thorington: On *Solitaire*

129   Jeremy Douglass: Enlightening Interactive Fiction:
      Andrew Plotkin's *Shade*

137   Steve Meretzky: The Creation of Floyd the Robot in *Planetfall*

139   Nick Montfort: Fretting the Player Character

147   Emily Short: On *Savoir-Faire*

149   Stuart Moulthrop: *Pax,* Writing, and Change

157   Talan Memmott: RE: Authoring Magritte: *The Brotherhood of Bent Billiard*

159   Lev Manovich: On Soft Cinema: *Mission to Earth*

163   Marie-Laure Ryan: On *Juvenate*

165   Mark C. Marino: On *Twelve Easy Lessons to Better Time Travel*

169   Chris Crawford: Deikto: A Language for Interactive Storytelling

177   D. Fox Harrell: GRIOT's Tales of Haints and Seraphs:
      A Computational Narrative Generation System

183   Michael Mateas and Andrew Stern: Writing *Façade:*
      A Case Study in Procedural Authorship

209   Robert Zubek: On *The Breakup Conversation*

213   Mark Keavney: On *The Archer's Flight*

217   III. Real Worlds

221   John Tynes: Prismatic Play: Games as Windows on the Real World

229   Sean Thorne: On John Tynes's *Puppetland*

233   Ian Bogost and Gonzalo Frasca: Video Games Go to Washington:
       The Story behind *The Howard Dean for Iowa Game*

247   Kevin Whelan: Political Activism: Bending the Rules

251   Jane McGonigal: The Puppet Master Problem:
       Design for Real-World, Mission-Based Gaming

265   Nick Fortugno: On *A Measure for Marriage*

269   Robert Nideffer: On *unexceptional.net*

273   Teri Rueb: On *Itinerant*

279   Tim Uren: Finding the Game in Improvised Theater

285   Joe Scrimshaw: On *Adventures in Mating*

289   Adriene Jenik: *Santaman's Harvest* Yields Questions, or
       Does a Performance Happen if It Exists in a Virtual Forest?

297   Torill Elvira Mortensen: Me, the Other

307   Jill Walker: A Network of Quests in *World of Warcraft*

311   Celia Pearce and Artemesia: Communities of Play:
       The Social Construction of Identity in Persistent Online Game Worlds

319   Adrianne Wortzel: *Eliza Redux*

331 IV. Appendices

333 Appendix A: *Puppetland* by John Tynes

349 Appendix B: *Bestial Acts* by Greg Costikyan

359 Appendix C: *The Extraordinary Adventures of Baron Munchausen*
        by James Wallis

383 Contributor Biographies

393 Permissions

395 Index

Dedication

Pat dedicates his work to his
mother, Beth, and his father, Todd.

Noah dedicates his work to his grandparents
Elma and Buford, Gertrude and Richard.

Michael dedicates his work to
his wife Marjetta.

Acknowledgments

As ever, there are more people to thank than can reasonably be represented here.
We hope we are not overly lax if we acknowledge only the following:

Doug Sery, Valerie Geary, Deborah Cantor-Adams, and everyone else at MIT Press; those who supported this work,
directly or indirectly, at Brown University, Hyperion Games, and the Johnston Center for Integrative Studies at the
University of Redlands; Carrie Rainey, Jennifer Mahal, Marjetta Geerling,
and others who made non-institutional contributions of time and support;
our contributors; our family and friends.

Thank you all,
Pat, Noah, and Michael

John Tynes would like to thank Jenny Scott for her meticulous scrutiny
and thoughtful criticism of "Prismatic Play."

Nick Montfort thanks J. Robinson Wheeler for his comments
on a draft of "Fretting the Player Character."

Contributors

Pat Harrigan (ed.)
Noah Wardrip-Fruin (ed.)

Ian Bogost
Rebecca Borgstrom
Greg Costikyan
Chris Crawford
Paul Czege
Jeremy Douglass
Bruno Faidutti
Nick Fortugno
Gonzalo Frasca
Fox Harrell
Pat Harrigan
Keith Herber
Will Hindmarch
Kenneth Hite
Adriene Jenik
Eric Lang
Lev Manovich
Mark C. Marino
George R. R. Martin
Michael Mateas
Jane McGonigal
Jordan Mechner
Talan Memmott
Steve Meretzky
Erik Mona
Nick Montfort
Torill Elvira Mortensen
Stuart Moulthrop
Kim Newman
Robert Nideffer
Celia Pearce
Teri Rueb
Marie-Laure Ryan
Joe Scrimshaw
Lee Sheldon
Emily Short
Andrew Stern
Helen Thorington
Sean Thorne
Jonathan Tweet
John Tynes
Tim Uren
James Wallis
Jill Walker
Noah Wardrip-Fruin
Kevin Whelan
Kevin Wilson
Adrianne Wortzel
Eric Zimmerman
Robert Zubek

Introduction
Pat Harrigan and Noah Wardrip-Fruin

How should we explain to someone what a game is?

I imagine that we should describe games to him, and we might add: "This and similar things are called 'games.'" And do we know any more about it ourselves? Is it only other people whom we cannot tell exactly what a game is?

But this is not ignorance. We do not know the boundaries because none have been drawn.

        —Ludwig Wittgenstein, *Philosophical Investigations*, aph. 69.

In fact, perhaps too many boundaries have been drawn. There are quite a few attempts to erect borders around the concept of *game*—especially now that games are increasingly recognized as a major cultural force, and as game studies emerges as an academic discipline (see sidebar).

However, in this volume the contributors are not interested in questions such as "What is a game?" This book is not concerned with questions of center and periphery. Rather, we are interested in questions such as "How is this played?"

For this reason we have adopted the term "playable media" to point toward our overarching concern. This includes games, as well as other forms that "invite and structure play" (Wardrip-Fruin 2005). This volume's contributors discuss role-playing games, board games, card games, computer games, interactive fictions, political simulations, improvisational theater, massively multiplayer games, locative media, live action role-playing, and more.

Of course, there are a variety of potential topics that one could pursue in relation to these forms. *Second Person* focuses on two interrelated strands: *role-playing* and *story*. These concepts run throughout this book, sometimes in parallel, sometimes in tension with each other. There is not always a happy marriage between something played and something told. If you are an actor in *King Lear*, Shakespeare has provided you with both a coherent story and a role to play within it—but your freedom of movement within your role is limited by the text. You may hiss or shout or whisper your lines; the director may choose to set the play on a Martian colony and portray Lear as a intelligent shape-changing fungus—but in the end, unless you are Thomas Bowdler, you will say, "My poor fool is dead," and sink into the fullness of the tragedy.

Conversely, as children you may have played "Cops and Robbers," or "Cowboys and Indians" (the examples of choice for a generation of tabletop role-playing game Introduction writers). In this case there is nothing to constrain what you say, where you run, who you shoot—but there is also no structure to speak of, nothing to ensure that the person you shoot falls down, that the villains wind up in jail. (This is what Rebecca Borgstrom calls the "nuh unh" factor.) The end of this sort of play, if it can even be said to

Putting forward a formal definition of "game" has become an area of major effort for the emerging field of game studies. Consider, for example, *Rules of Play*, a game design and theory text by Katie Salen and Eric Zimmerman (2003). This book's widely cited definition characterizes a game as "a system in which players engage in an artificial conflict, defined by rules, that results in a quantifiable outcome" (Salen and Zimmerman 2003, 80). Certainly there's nothing wrong with such attempts to define what we mean when we say "game"—but something is always made peripheral, something is always pushed to the border, or over it, when we engage in definition. In this case, the best-selling computer game of all time (*The Sims*) and all experiences like it—along with the immensely influential form of the tabletop role-playing game (e.g., *Dungeons & Dragons*) and its relatives—are pushed aside. According to Salen and Zimmerman, these experiences "have emergent quantifiable goals but usually no single overriding outcome" (83).

Jesper Juul, in his influential keynote address for the 2003 conference of the Digital Games Research Association, defines games differently. He contends:

A game is a rule-based formal system with a variable and quantifiable outcome, where different outcomes are assigned different values, the player exerts effort in order to influence the outcome, the player feels attached to the outcome, and the consequences of the activity are optional and negotiable. (Juul 2003)

Despite the differences in definition, however, Juul's border-drawing move has the same effect as Salen and Zimmerman's. The list of game forms pushed to the border of his model (it is represented as concentric circles) is a veritable canon, including those of: poker, blackjack, *The Sims, SimCity, Dungeons & Dragons, GURPS, EverQuest,* and *World of Warcraft.* Games that take place in the real world do not get a place on the diagram, but are later noted as border cases, and presumably this also places any forms of play that employ our bodies in performance on, or beyond, the border.

Perhaps all these games do belong on the border of any formal category of games. But we see here the lack of utility of a formal game definition for a book such as this one.

have an end, is not the ending of a coherent fiction. The events here are arbitrary and contingent, and therefore the opposite of what we call "story."

Beyond this there is the question of how the structures of story differ from one medium to another; telling a story in a novel is not the same as enacting it in a video game. Stories are experienced differently between the tabletop, the computer, and the stage. New forms of media not only require new approaches to story, but may even force us to re-examine our assumptions about how stories are told in more traditional forms.

By design, the subject of most of *Second Person's* contributors is, centrally, "you." This is because *you* are the person for whom the story is being told, and because the roles discussed in this book will, for the most part, be filled by you. *Colossal Cave Adventure*, the first computer text adventure, famously addresses the reader, "You are in a maze of twisty little passages, all alike." *The Cave of Time*, the first *Choose Your Own Adventure* book, announces that, "The adventures you take are a result of your *choice. You* are responsible because *you* choose!"[1] Jeremy Douglass, in his essay here, points out that even the most "first person" of game experiences— the 3D virtual reality that reaches its apotheosis in room-sized CAVE displays— serves the same function as the textual second person: simulated immediacy.[2]

Outside these caves, tabletop role-playing games speak directly to you as well; to pick only one example, Jonathan Tweet's *Over the Edge* tells us:

This game is a coded message. You will decode the message in your dreams and execute its instructions in the spaces between moments of will. Neither you nor I will ever know the contents of the message. (*Over the Edge* 1997, 2)

The authors, artists, and theoreticians in *Second Person* address the exigencies of playable media in a number of ways, and in a number of voices. Some essays are informal in tone, some academic, and some highly technical; this polyglot speaks to the varied disciplines from which our contributors are drawn.

For convenience the editors have arranged the essays into three sections.

Section I groups together essays about fictions playable on your tabletop, or in your easy chair, without aid of nonhuman calculation. Many of these, such as the tabletop role-playing games (RPGs) under discussion, have an explicit social component. Some, like Kim Newman's *Life's Lottery* and Zimmerman's *Life in the Garden*, can be seen as variations on traditional author-reader expectations.

Section II is concerned with computer-based playable structures. Here are Nick Montfort's and Jeremy Douglass's thoughts on Interactive Fiction (IF) and Michael Mateas and Andrew Stern's in-depth discussion of their interactive drama, *Façade*. Broadly speaking, the works discussed here are designed to be

1. The *Choose Your Own Adventure* series was an outgrowth of Edward Packard's *Adventures of You* books.

2. In the editors' opinion, the best novel to engage the VR CAVE technology is Richard Powers's *Plowing the Dark,* which makes heavy use of the second person form of address.

interacted with by one person: the singular, not plural, "you."

In section III we return to the social spaces of section I, but in a wider variety of ways. Our contributors discuss the virtual communities of massively multiplayer online role-playing games (MMORPGs, or MMOs); we see how digital media (as well as older role-playing techniques) inform political discourse; and we enter into multiple other theaters as well.

In addition, we have reprinted as appendixes three fully playable tabletop RPGs. Two of these (*Puppetland*, *The Adventures of Baron Munchausen*) are discussed in essays in this book. The other (*Bestial Acts*) is also written by one of our contributors, and as it explicitly tries to import Bertolt Brecht's theatrical concepts into a tabletop RPG format, it may prove somewhat more of a challenge to play, particularly for the faint of heart. These three RPGs provide not only an invitation to play, but demonstrate the wide variation possible in what many people still insist on seeing as a hidebound form.

Our hope is that this book will appeal to a wide variety of audiences. It discusses a number of playable forms, some of which have been unfortunately ignored by the academy, and all of which are important as we seek to understand our fields' presents and futures. For example, in the last few years there has been much academic discussion of video games and other forms of digital media, but little that acknowledges in any depth the debt many of these forms owe to tabletop role-playing games. Further, it is not too much to say that where academic discussion of tabletop RPGs exists, it is largely cursory—and, not infrequently, wrong.[3]

At the same time, the hobby game industry (of which tabletop RPGs are a part) has not, as a rule, examined its output in any thorough critical or analytic way—the companies that release RPGs preferring to concentrate on selling product rather than philosophizing about it. There are some exceptions, of course, particularly among the growing indie RPG movement, which we will have more to say about in our introduction to section I.

Second Person does not pretend to provide an exhaustive critical overview of tabletop RPGs, or of any of the other forms that bring together gameplay, roleplay, and story. But we hope it provides a framework for further examination of these forms, by placing these works into a continuum of artistic production and providing a sampling of approaches to them driven by game design, creative writing, and more traditional scholarly frameworks. The next step, as we understand it, is up to *you*.

References: Literature

Juul, Jesper (2003). "The Game, the Player, the World: Looking for a Heart of Gameness."
In *Level Up: Digital Games Research Conference Proceedings,* edited by Marinka Copier and Joost Raessens.
Utrecht: Utrecht University. <http://www.jesperjuul.net/text/gameplayerworld/>.

Salen, Katie, and Eric Zimmerman (2003). *Rules of Play: Game Design Fundamentals.* Cambridge, MA: MIT Press.

Stone, Allucquère Rosanne (1995). *The War of Desire and Technology at the Close of the Mechanical Age.* Cambridge, MA: MIT Press.

Wardrip-Fruin, Noah (2005). "Playable Media and Textual Instruments." Dichtung Digital 1 (2005).
<http://www.dichtung-digital.com/2005/1/Wardrip-Fruin>.

Wittgenstein, Ludwig (trans. G.E.M. Anscombe) (1999). *Philosophical Investigations.* Upper Saddle River, NJ: Prentice Hall.

Reference: Game

Over the Edge (Second edition). Jonathan Tweet with Robin D. Laws; Atlas Games. 1997.

3. As an example, an excerpt from Allucquère Rosanne Stone's *The War of Desire and Technology*:

> The first RPG was published as a set of rules and character descriptions in 1972 and was called, appropriately enough, Dungeons and Dragons. It was an extension, really, of SCA into a textual world. D&D, as it quickly became known, used a set of rules invented by the Austin game designer Steve Jackson called the Generic Universal Role Playing System, or GURPS. (Stone 1995, 68)

While it might be quibbling to point out that Stone has *D&D*'s publication date wrong (see Eric Mona's essay for an accurate account of this history), it is harder to overlook the fact that *The War of Desire and Technology* gets the relationship between *D&D* and *GURPS* exactly backwards. It was *D&D* that inspired *GURPS* (as it did every tabletop RPG), which appeared more than a decade afterward.

I. Tabletop Systems

Tabletop Systems

In the chapter that begins this section, Greg Costikyan elegantly outlines a spectrum of game-story forms—all of which are discussed, sometimes at length, by other contributors to this book. Costikyan, who began his career in tabletop game design before he became a respected designer and scholar of many different types of games, still retains a noticeable fondness for the tabletop role-playing game (RPG) form, as do the editors of this book.

But despite the soft spot that tabletop RPGs occupy in many hearts, at the time of this writing their commercial market is in bad shape. Just a few years ago this was not the case. For several years following industry leader Wizards of the Coast's release of the Open Gaming License,[1] supplements of all types based on the "d20" game system (as used in the popular RPG *Dungeons & Dragons*) flooded the market—and found many willing buyers. But before long, much as had happened in the collapse of the collectible card game (CCG) market in the 1990s, the bottom fell out of the d20 market, forcing RPG publishers to diversify or die.

Many surviving publishers responded by radically reducing their output, cutting staff, releasing "boutique" products (e.g., leather-bound, slip-cased editions of previous best-sellers) or focusing production on other types of games (often expensive board games).

This means that much of the most interesting work currently being done in tabletop RPGs is in the "indie RPG" movement, of which Ron Edwards of The Forge <http://www.indie-rpgs.com/> is the leading exponent. Edwards (*Sorcerer*, *Trollbabe*), Paul Czege (*My Life with Master*), Annie Rush (*The Secret Lives of Gingerbread Men*), Jared Sorensen (*Lacuna*), Matt Snyder (*Dust Devils*), John Wick (*Schauermärchen*), and many others have produced highly respected, innovative RPGs

The hobby game industry, of which tabletop RPGs are a part, can sometimes seem mystifying to those unfamiliar to it. The intricacies of publishing and distribution need not concern us here, but a few points are worth discussing.

Types of RPG Publications

For each tabletop role-playing game system (e.g., *Dungeons & Dragons*, *GURPS*) there will be one or more books (or at least, pamphlets).

Books central to the understanding of the system, which contain the specific rules and mechanics of the game, and which provide at least an overview of the game world, are generally referred to as *core rule books*. In some cases, there will be one book for the players and a separate one for the gamemaster (as in the *Advanced Dungeons & Dragons Player's Handbook* and *Dungeon Master's Guide*). In other cases (e.g., *Call of Cthulhu*) there will be only one core book per line, though certain sections may be intended for gamemaster eyes only. In still other cases (e.g., Matt Wilson's *PrimeTime Adventures*), there may be no part of the book that is kept secret from the players.

Sourcebooks provide further elaboration of the game world. This elaboration can take virtually any form, from books discussing advanced rules, to ones providing new areas of the game world for exploration and new characters for potential encounters, to books that provide new classes of characters that can be played. *GURPS*, a self-proclaimed "generic" system whose rules are designed to be able to accommodate any genre of role-playing (from Wild West to space opera, from epic fantasy to prehistoric man) has released a seemingly uncountable number of source books: *GURPS Horror*, *GURPS Aztecs*, *GURPS Ice Age*, *GURPS Illuminati*, *GURPS Cthulhupunk*, *GURPS Wild Cards*, *GURPS Camelot*, *GURPS High-Tech*, *GURPS SWAT*, *GURPS Who's Who*, etc.

---

1. Wizards of the Coast's OGL <http://www.opengamingfoundation.org/ogl.html> allows any other company to use their proprietary d20 system (used most famously in *Dungeons & Dragons*), provided they follow certain limitations and give clear acknowledgment to WotC. This produced a huge number of d20 supplements in a very short time, from all manner of publishers, on any number of topics, and helped to further cement WotC as the industry's leader and d20 as the system of choice for many tabletop role-players. Even after the d20 bust, WotC (a division of Hasbro) remains unrivalled as the 800-pound gorilla of the industry.

published independently by the authors without benefit of traditional distribution channels. In his contribution to *Second Person*, Czege discusses some of the indie RPG philosophy as it pertains to his design decisions for *My Life with Master*.

Web options, PDF, and recent advances in Print-On-Demand (POD) technologies have lowered the barrier to entry for aspiring RPG designers.[2] Many RPGs are available (sometimes exclusively) as PDF downloads from the author's sites or through small web-based companies such as Wicked Dead RPGs <http://wicked-dead.com/> or Indie Press Revolution <http://www.indiepressrevolution.com>. Within these channels, innovative publishing models are developing rapidly. For example, Dennis Detwiller, co-creator of *Delta Green*, has released quite a bit of new RPG material using the "ransom model." In these cases a product is released (as a PDF) only if visitors to his web site donate enough money in advance to finance its completion <http://www.detwillerdesign.com/>.

Naturally there are still the big players. *Dungeons & Dragons* is more popular than ever, and White Wolf's *World of Darkness* line runs a respectable second in industry popularity. In this book Erik Mona and Will Hindmarch give overviews of the early history of *D&D* and White Wolf's Storyteller system, respectively. Currently only Steve Jackson's *Generic Universal Role-Playing System* (*GURPS*) can claim to be as well-known as these two, although there are any number of notable other systems.

Ken Hite contributes a piece about one of these others, Chaosium's *Call of Cthulhu* (*CoC*) line. *CoC* has nothing like the player base of *D&D*, but is still one of the longest-running and most respected lines in the industry. Hite's chapter is accompanied by a short piece by one of *Call of Cthulhu*'s most accomplished designers, Keith Herber, discussing the unusual structure of his *Call of Cthulhu* scenario, "The Haunted House."

It should be noted that the big companies do continue to support a certain amount of innovation. Along these lines, Rebecca Borgstrom contributes a

Scenario books contain one or more pre-designed adventures or storylines for a gamemaster to play with his or her players. These are sometimes called *adventure books* or variations thereof, and in the early days of *D&D* were often called *modules*. It is not uncommon for sourcebooks to contain scenarios in addition to their other content.

The trend in mainstream RPG publishing in recent years is to release core books as hardbacks, and other types of books as either hardback or softcover, as determined by profit expectations. This has not always been the case: in the 1980s, there was a preponderance of games released in box sets containing softcover books, pamphlets, maps and other game aids. TSR (*D&D* Basic and Expert Sets, *Gangbusters*, *Boot Hill*) and Pacesetter (*Chill*, *Sandman*) released many products in this format.

Exceptions and contradictions to the above generalizations can easily be found. RPG publishing could be called (*pace* collectible card game jargon) an "exception-based" system, wherein the rules exist only to provide a framework for breaking them.

Terminology

Naturally, nearly all game systems have their own specific terminology. That said, certain terms have common currency.

LARP stands for a live-action role-playing game, in which players physically, and socially, act out their characters' roles (e.g., at a convention, or at a weekly gathering at a friend's house). They are not centered around the tabletop, and it can be argued that they are closer in form to improvisational theater than to their RPG cousins. LARPs are generally more focused on physical role-playing and storytelling rather than a complex system of game mechanics (there are usually no dice, for example); this transparency allows for a lower barrier to entry, and as a consequence LARP player groups tend to be larger than tabletop groups. Although LARPs are distinct from tabletop games, some systems (notably *Vampire: The Masquerade*) support both tabletop and LARP play.

A *PC* is a Player Character, an in-game character played by one of the players.

---

2. And established ones as well: Rebecca Borgstrom has released POD versions of some of her Hitherby Dragons fiction <http://rebecca.hitherby.com/>.

piece about her work for White Wolf's *Exalted* line, *The Fair Folk*. Her analysis is informed by both her work in the tabletop RPG field and her background as a computer scientist. Jonathan Tweet discusses the unique character creation system in his RPG, *Everway*, which was first published by Wizards of the Coast and is now supported by an indie community.

It is not uncommon for tabletop RPGs to be based on licensed properties (*Star Wars*, *The Lord of the Rings*) or for tabletop RPGs to make the jump to other media (*Vampire: The Masquerade*). It is not even uncommon for RPGs to generate novels and short stories based on their proprietary game world and characters (such novels are generally published by the same company that publishes the RPG). But it is rare for an entire RPG campaign to become a series of collaborative novels, freed from its RPG roots. This, however, is the case with the *Wild Cards* series, edited by George R. R. Martin. The evolution of these unusual books is described in Martin's piece, reprinted here with his permission from the ibooks editions of the first three *Wild Cards* books.

In James Wallis's chapter, the author provides a broad overview of several different types of non-RPG tabletop storytelling games, including his own *Once Upon a Time* and *Youdunnit* (and one arguable RPG: *The Extraordinary Adventures of Baron Munchausen*). In the process, he outlines a method for future storytelling game design.

Eric Lang (writing with one of this volume's editors) and Bruno Faidutti contribute pieces about games that fall on the extreme edge of our book's subject matter: Lang discusses two of his collectible card games (*A Game of Thrones* and *Call of Cthulhu*) and Faidutti discusses his board game *Mystery of the Abbey*. All of these games are based explicitly on works of fiction: George R. R. Martin's *A Song of Ice and Fire* series, the works of H. P. Lovecraft and other contributors to the "Cthulhu Mythos," and Umberto Eco's *The Name of the Rose*.[3]

Kevin Wilson writes about two of his board games as well: *Arkham Horror* and *Doom: The Board Game*. Wilson adapted both of these games from other

An *NPC* is a Non-Player Character. In tabletop RPGs, NPCs are played by the gamemaster. In video RPGs, NPCs are designed by the programmers and their actions executed by the game system.

Gamemaster (also *Game Master*; *referee*; *storyteller*; in *D&D*, *Dungeon Master*; and innumerable other terms). A player designated to administer the rules, and run the game world and NPCs; in contrast to the other players, who usually only play one character or a small number of characters and have no more agency in the game world than that provided to their characters.

Tabletop dice come in more varieties than the usual six-sided. Game rules often refer to them as d4, d6, d8, d10, and d20—in reference to the number of sides for each die. It is also not uncommon to use multiple dice to determine some value, which can also be preceded by "d." For example, "d100" (also called "percentile dice") usually refers to the process of rolling two 10-sided dice together to generate a random number between 1 and 100. Some games use "dice pools" or other methods of combining the random dice-generated numbers, and other games (e.g., Eric Wujcik's *Amber Diceless*) eschew randomness altogether.

Tolkien and Lovecraft

The influence of J. R. R. Tolkien's (1892–1973) The *Lord of the Rings* (LotR) on the works discussed in this book cannot be overestimated. The series was released in three hardback volumes in the United States in 1954 and 1955, and received a popular BBC radio adaptation in 1956, but did not truly capture the public's imagination until a paperback edition appeared in 1965.

With Jack Vance's *Dying Earth* series, Fritz Lieber's *Lankhmar* stories, Roger Zelazny's *Amber* novels, and the popular sword-and-sorcery stories best exemplified by Robert E. Howard's *Conan*, LotR strongly influenced the development of *Dungeons & Dragons*. *D&D* itself had a notable influence on William Crowther's computer text adventure, *Colossal Cave*. *LotR*'s quest structure can be detected in *World of Warcraft* as well as any number of

3. Lang's chapter (and Kevin Wilson's) also discusses the market considerations that enter into the creation and publication of a game—a topic of great interest in the hobby games industry and one that has a discernable effect on what games are actually produced. Faidutti touches on this point in a brief sidebar.

sources: *Arkham Horror* from Chaosium's *Call of Cthulhu* RPG and Richard Launius's original board game design, and *Doom* from the popular series of computer games. In his chapter, Wilson sketches some of the methods he used to successfully adapt these properties into the board game format.

Eric Zimmerman and Kim Newman discuss two unusual works of fiction (Zimmerman's is perhaps as much "book art" as "fiction"): *Life in the Garden* and *Life's Lottery*. *Life's Lottery* can be seen as a self-conscious updating of the *Choose Your Own Adventure* form, and *Life in the Garden* is part of a genre of recombinable fictions that also includes projects such as Robert Coover's "Heart Suit" and Helen Thorington's *Solitaire* (discussed elsewhere in this volume).

Zimmerman and Newman's pieces differ from the others in this section, in that they focus on the individual reading experience. Rather than, as with most RPGs, serving as a structure for harnessing creativity between players, these are unusual structures for relatively traditional artistic experiences. Not only do they focus audience experience on the individual appreciation of a pre-created work, they are also entirely pre-authored. The audience orders or operates their elements, but no new elements are introduced at the time of audience experience. Just this, as it turns out, can generate a rich tapestry of possible experiences. In this regard they serve as a good transition to our second section, which focuses on attempts to use the procedural power of the computer for such purposes.

other games. This influence will no doubt continue well into the foreseeable future, with the renewed popularity generated by Peter Jackson's movie trilogy.

A less obvious, but no less important, aesthetic influence on the playable media described in *Second Person* is the work of Rhode Island weird fiction author, H. P. Lovecraft (1890–1937).

Lovecraft's writing was virtually unknown during his lifetime, except to a small circle of admirers and fans of pulp magazines (notably *Weird Tales*), but in the decades since his death, his influence has crept far into popular culture. Aspiring occultists of the 1960s and 1970s spent many hours in vain searching for a copy of the infamous *Necronomicon*, not realizing that the existence of the book was a fiction created by Lovecraft. (Naturally hoaxsters and charlatans have since published quite a few *Necronomicons*, to take advantage of this fact.)

Lovecraft's posthumous literary influence is well-attested; authors such as Robert Bloch, Ramsey Campbell, Stephen King, Brian Lumley, T. E. D. Klein, and Thomas Ligotti, among others, have strong Lovecraftian elements in much of their work. Lovecraft's influence can be detected in films (*In the Mouth of Madness*) and television (the underlying cosmology of *Buffy the Vampire Slayer*). Hobby game shops sell cuddly plush versions of Lovecraft's malign alien entity Cthulhu.

In addition to the *Call of Cthulhu* RPG and CCG, Lovecraft's work has formed the basis for board games (*Arkham Horror*, *The Hills Rise Wild!*), video games (*Dark Corners of the Earth*, *Eternal Darkness: Sanity's Requiem*) and even a rock band (The Darkest of the Hillside Thickets <http://www.thickets.net/>) and a neo-silent film (the H. P. Lovecraft Historical Society's *The Call of Cthulhu* <http://www.cthulhulives.org/cocmovie/index.html>).

It is beyond the scope of this sidebar to go into detail about Lovecraft's work and the work of the other authors that have contributed to what has become known as the "Cthulhu Mythos" genre. But, like the sanity-destroying glimpses of the unknown that so often spell the ruin of Lovecraft's protagonists, you will find hints and allusions to it throughout this book.

Games, Storytelling, and Breaking the String
Greg Costikyan

Before 1973, if you had said something like "games are a storytelling medium," just about anyone would have looked at you like you were nuts—and anyone knowledgeable about games would have assumed you knew nothing about them.

Before 1973, the world had essentially four game styles: classic board games, classic card games, mass-market commercial board games, and the board wargame. None of these had any noticeable connection to story: There is no story in chess, bridge, *Monopoly,* or *Afrika Korps.*

But in the early 1970s, two things happened: Will Crowther's *Colossal Cave,*[1] and Gary Gygax and Dave Arneson's *Dungeons and Dragons.*[2]

Colossal Cave, and *Adventure,* the more refined form of that work that Don Woods created in 1976, were considered "interactive fiction" (IF) from the start, a term that creators of text adventures (no longer a commercial medium) still use today. When I first encountered *Adventure* (on minicomputers set up by MIT computer club members at the Boskone science fiction convention in the mid-1970s), *Adventure* was in a directory named "Interactive Fiction," which is why I started the application. I had no idea what "interactive fiction" was or could be, but I was interested in finding out. I quickly realized that, in fact, it was a pretentious way of referring to a new kind of game. I spent several hours playing before they kicked me off to make room for other people.

In fact, text adventures have real flaws both as games and as fiction—but they *are* games and *do* offer many of the aesthetic pleasures of fiction.

While the text adventure now survives only as the creation of hobbyists and digital artists, it spawned both graphic adventures (e.g., *Grim Fandango)* and the action/adventure hybrid (e.g., *Psychonauts),* which remain (to a greater or lesser degree) important genres today.

Dungeons & Dragons, originally created by Dave Arneson and refined by Gary Gygax, was an outgrowth of the *Chainmail* rules for playing fantasy battles with miniature figures. *Chainmail* already had rules for special "hero" characters on the battlefield, single individuals as (or more) powerful than a whole military unit. Arneson took those rules, elaborated them, and set the game, not on a battlefield, but in a "dungeon," an underground domain populated by monsters. In a sense, this was a simple extension of an existing game; but in another sense, it was a wholly novel form of game.

You played a single character with the ability to grow and gain in power over time; and while (initially) *Dungeons & Dragons,* as a rules set, did little to encourage plot complexity, true role playing, or anything like real storytelling, the mere fact of a character persisting in an imaginary world over multiple sessions of play offered a clear opportunity for a tighter connection between gameplay and story. *D&D* was innovative in another regard, too; it dispensed completely with the need for miniatures, a board, cards, or other physical game assets. It transpired entirely in the imagination— turning the tightly constrained nature of all previous games on its head. If you could imagine it, and the gamemaster was willing to go along, it could happen. This opened an exciting vista of vastly more free-form and flexible games.

Tabletop role-playing remains a vital and innovative commercial genre today and has directly influenced a whole slew of other genres, including computer/console RPGs, MMOs, LARPs, and the esoteric "indie" RPG movement (as discussed at The Forge: <http://www.indierpgs.com/forum/>).

The Clash of Games and Stories

Almost from the inception of "games with stories," there has been an ongoing culture clash between those who view story as perhaps important but tangential to understanding the nature of games, and those who view it as essential. In 1977,

---

1. The date of the original *Colossal Cave* is subject to some dispute. William Crowther has put the date at 1975, "give or take a year." <http://jerz.setonhill.edu/if/canon/Adventure.htm>.

2. The first commercial version of *D&D* was published in January 1974, but some pre-release copies were in circulation toward the end of 1973.

the Game Manufacturer's Association (GAMA) <http://www.gama.org>, a group of publishers of board wargames, tabletop RPGs, and other non-digital games aimed at an enthusiast audience, officially decided to name their industry the "adventure gaming industry" (something that later caused confusion for fans of text and graphic adventures). This decision was bitterly contested by some members of GAMA, including those companies whose main business was the publication of wargames; they did not see how *Third Reich* or *Napoleon at Waterloo* could remotely be called "adventure games." Redmond Simonsen,[3] then art director for SPI, a major wargame publisher, proposed "simulation games" as an alternative—but this proposition was soundly defeated.

The clash between those who viewed games as formal systems and those who viewed them as storytelling media persisted with the rise of digital games; if you view the program of any Game Developers Conference (or before it, the Computer Game Developers Conference), you will find panels or presentations debating the role of stories in games. You can even identify the proponents of opposing views clearly: Chris Crawford[4] and Dan Bunten in the "games as systems" camp, and Hal Barwood and Mark Barrett on the "games as story" side.

And of course, today there is an ongoing and contentious debate among game studies academics between "ludologists" and "narratologists"—a debate that recapitulates an argument developers have been having for decades (Wardrip-Fruin and Harrigan 2004).

Why does this debate exist? And why does it continue?

A story is linear. The events of a story occur in the same order, and in the same way, each time you read (or watch or listen to) it. A story is a controlled experience; the author consciously crafts it, choosing precisely these events, in this order, to create a story with maximum impact. If the events occurred in some other fashion, the impact of the story would be diminished—or if that isn't true, the author isn't doing a good job.

A game is nonlinear. Games must provide at least the

illusion of free will to the player; players must feel that they have freedom of action—not absolute freedom, but freedom within the structure of the system. The structure constrains what they can do, but they must feel they have options; if not, they are not actively engaged. Rather, they are merely passive recipients of the experience. If they are constrained to a linear path of events, unchangeable in order, they'll feel they're being railroaded through the game, that nothing they do has any impact, that they are not playing in any meaningful sense.

In other words, there's a direct, immediate conflict between the demands of story and the demands of a game. Divergence from a story's path is likely to make for a less satisfying story; restricting a player's freedom of action is likely to make for a less satisfying game. To the degree that you make a game more like a story—a controlled, predetermined experience with events occurring as the author wishes—you make it a less effective game. To the degree that you make a story more like a game—with alternative paths and outcomes—you make it a less effective story. It's not merely that games aren't stories, and vice versa; rather they are, in a sense, opposites.

Or at least so I argued in an article in *Game Developer* magazine back in 2000 (Costikyan 2000). But clearly, there are innumerable game styles that do combine stories and gameplay successfully, in ways that evidently appeal strongly to wide audiences. Perhaps a more sophisticated way of looking at the issue is this: To get a good story out of a game, you have to constrain gameplay in a way that ensures that a story is told through play. There are direct conflicts between the demands of story and the demands of gameplay, because constraints that benefit the story aspect of the game may sometimes make the game aspect less interesting; yet any game *is* a system of constraints. Players have free action only within those constraints; there are always limitations on behavior, and indeed, gameplay often emerges *precisely* because of those limitations.

To see this, consider chess (a game utterly lacking in

3. And not incidentally, the man who coined the term "game designer."

4. Paradoxically, since Crawford is now embarked on a quixotic attempt to develop what he views as true interactive fiction—which he nonetheless insists must be distinct from and quite different from "games."

story, and which would not be improved by, e.g., a cutscene explaining that it's a war between brothers or some such). If, in chess, every piece could move any distance in any direction, it would not be an interesting game. It is because the moves of each piece are highly constrained to specific patterns that the complex interplay of forces—making chess so fascinating a game—emerges.

In other words, since a game is a system of constraints, and since if we want a story to emerge from a game we must constrain it in such a way that it does, it is not a priori impossible to imagine constructing a set of constraints that both produces a story and also fosters interesting gameplay. Solving the problem is not easy, but it is conceptually possible.

And yet so far, almost all games that involve stories (or stories that involve some aspect of game) can be viewed along a single, linear axis, from those that are highly linear with minor gameplay to those that are quite open-ended but with story a minor appendage. Let's look at that spectrum—and then at some more recent games that may point the way to alternative approaches.

Cortázar's *Hopscotch*

Julio Cortázar's 1966 *La Rayuela* (published in English as *Hopscotch*) (Cortázar 1987) can be read in the same fashion as a conventional novel—from beginning to end—but in addition, in his front notes, Cortázar suggests an alternative reading: to read it in a different chapter order, which he provides. And indeed, if you read it in that fashion, you gain a rather different insight into the characters' motivations and the evolution of the story than if you read it in the normal order. In fact, to fully understand the novel, you need to read it both ways.

In other words, this is what you might consider the minimalist story-game hybrid: It's a branching narrative with one branch.

Of course, it's a hat-trick—it's interesting, but it's hard to imagine a whole genre of *Hopscotch*-like novels emerging. And while it's more gamelike than most stories, it's still a long way from a game.

Hypertext Fiction

From *Hopscotch*, we move up the spectrum to hypertext fiction, of the type promoted by Robert Coover at Brown University (Coover 1992), perhaps best exemplified by Michael Joyce's *afternoon: a story* (Joyce 1990).

While there are Web examples, the hypertext movement predates the Web, and most hypertexts are implemented in proprietary systems such as Eastgate's Storyspace engine <http://www.eastgate.com>. You begin by reading a text passage (perhaps with an accompanying image) within which there are (usually) multiple links. Selecting a link takes you to another passage. In other words, there are multiple paths at each node, creating a Web-like narrative.

Of course, any single exploration of the web is "linear," in the sense that you reach passages in an order determined by your selection of links—but unlike traditional narrative, you cannot sustain a single, linear, driving narrative arc. Instead, with the best hypertext fictions, you ultimately have explored enough of the narrative tree to reach some kind of epiphany.

While this is interesting, it is perhaps harder to create a satisfying story this way than with more traditional narrative—and from a gameplay perspective, it's not great. There are no trade-offs to be made, no reason to choose one link over another, no objective to pursue. The elements that make for interesting games are missing, other than some limited freedom of action.

Game Books

Game books (such as *Choose Your Own Adventure* and *Which Way* books) were most popular during the late 1980s, when the *Fighting Fantasy* game books from Ian Livingstone and Steve Jackson[5] were international best-sellers. In some ways, they're actually quite like hypertext fiction; you read a passage of text, at the end of which you are generally called upon to make a choice (the lady or the tiger), then turn to another passage elsewhere in the book that describes the outcome of the choice. In some game books, that's all there is; but in others (including the *Fighting Fantasy* books) there's a rudimentary game system to handle combat and some other actions—so that instead, the text might instruct you to resolve a battle with such-and-such a monster and turn to

---

5. The British Steve Jackson, not to be confused with the Texan Steve Jackson.

page X if you win and page Y if you lose.

This is certainly more gamelike; you do have some goal (there's at least one positive ending to work toward), and at least when there is a rudimentary system, outcomes are not arbitrary. There are problems, of course; many choices that are reasonable to offer the player lead to unsatisfying story outcomes (you plummet off the cliff and die), and repeat playability is minimal.

And in a way, it's almost identical to hypertext fiction (read a passage, select a link, read another passage) except that hypertext is the purview of the literati, and game books are viewed as degraded hackwork.

Paragraph-System Board Games and Solitaire RPG Adventures

Paragraph-system board games and solo RPG adventures are attempts to take the basic game book paradigm and push it toward deeper and more satisfying gameplay. A solitaire RPG adventure is essentially structured like a game book, but depends on the existence of a richer tabletop RPG system independent of the adventure booklet itself, which allows for more variety of outcome.

In a paragraph-system board game (Eric Goldberg's *Tales of the Arabian Nights* is the best example), the players move pieces about the board, and occasionally are called upon to turn to a passage of text in an accompanying book. This passage offers some sort of choice, possibly mediated through a game system—essentially leading the player through a brief game book-like scenario. Many such scenarios exist in the book, of which only a small fraction are used in a single session of play, and they may be encountered in any order, which makes the game quite replayable.

In other words, this is a step further along the axis from story to game.

Dragon's Lair

Just as there are tabletop analogs to the game book, there are arcade game ones. When *Dragon's Lair* was introduced in 1984, it was a smash hit at the arcade, because arcade game graphics were relatively primitive at the time, and it boasted cinematic-quality animation from Don Bluth—it

was perceived as an amazing visual experience. As a game qua game, however, it sucked. Essentially, you watched an animation clip lasting a few seconds, and had to quickly make a choice by moving a joystick in one direction or another. One choice led to death. The other triggered another few seconds of animation and another choice. You played by feeding in quarter after quarter and learning which choices didn't make you die through a process of rote memorization. Not surprisingly, the sequels failed.

Adventure Games

Text and graphic adventures are, in some ways, much like game books, too; you read a passage of text, or view an area of the gameworld, and often make a choice that leads you to another passage or area of the world. Rather than being an explicit branching narrative, however, players often return to areas in the world, and an inventory system and set of puzzles provides more gameplay. But the narrative is still quite linear; adventure games tend to be "beads-on-a-string": small areas where there is some freedom of action until some event occurs, at which point a transition to the next bead is opened. While there is some freedom within the beads, the overall game is a linear progress through the beads.

In principle, it would be possible to implement a game of this type that doesn't conform to the "beads-on-a-string" model; in practice, it makes little sense to do so. Content development is expensive, and if a player is only exposed to part of it in the course of a game, you've wasted development money. And the more branches you have, the less of the overall game a player will see.

In essence, adventure games are not all that dissimilar from game books—except that because they are digital, they can be more interactive, with new areas opening up and new items becoming available as the game progresses.

In graphic adventures, gameplay is often interrupted by cutscenes, and when skillfully used, this helps advance the story. In the worst cases (as with *Tex Avery: Overseer*), the result is essentially a lame movie interrupted by uninteresting bits of gameplay. But in the best cases (as with *Grim Fandango*), the net effect is perhaps among the best extant combinations of game and story.

Computer and Console RPGs

Adventure games are still quite limited in the freedom of action they offer players. Digital RPGs offer a bit more freedom; a richer character design and inventory system allows more options at each point, and quite often there is a choice of which path to take next, reducing the degree of linearity. They are still tied intimately to story—the story progresses during the game and reaches some eventual denouement—but there is more freedom on a moment-to-moment basis. Digital RPGs, however, have limited repeat playability because they are tied to an ultimately linear story.

MMOs

The line of descent from tabletop RPGs to massively multiplayer online games (MMOs) is clear—both have character design systems, elaborate variations in equipment, skills, and spells, and in both cases most games in these genres are built around killing monsters and taking their treasure, with a consequent advance in character power.

While tabletop RPGs have, over time, evolved more toward true role-playing and the telling of stories, MMOs are almost *devoid* of story. That's because these are "never-ending games": story ultimately depends on change, and players cannot be permitted to make real and meaningful changes to the game world.

Why is that? Imagine that an MMO comes to some sort of story climax, which could go either way, depending on the actions of the players. The live team must develop content to handle both outcomes. And on some servers, the event will go one way, and on others, the other. Suddenly, you have a fork in the game world—and your new content development problem is now compounded by the need to develop *different* new content for the two different worlds on an ongoing basis.

MMOs often *claim* to have stories: the manual might have badly written sword-and-sorcery at the front, and each new content update is supposed to "advance the story" in some fashion. But by and large, players don't give a crap about this; they're interested in the new content, new monsters, new areas to explore—but whatever supposed connection to an ongoing story is involved is irrelevant to the way they play. That there's a story is a conceit of the developers; it has no impact on actual play.

Interestingly, however, MMOs intersect with story in another fashion—via quests, which I'll discuss later.

In essence, MMOs are "story settings"—but have almost lost the connection to story in exchange for becoming good social environments as well as good games.

Tabletop RPGs

The game systems of tabletop RPGs are in some ways very similar to those of digital RPGs—sometimes identical, in fact, in the case of computer RPGs licensed from tabletop games. They are, however, vastly more free-form. The rules of the game provide a structure for resolving player actions: rules for combat, magic spells, skills, and so on. Unlike digital RPGs, there is no pre-established story line, although most paper RPG rule books contain one or several stories for new gamemasters to use. The expectation is that a gamemaster will invent his or her own stories for players, using the rules system as needed.

Paper RPGs, unlike electronic ones, are social affairs; players get together periodically to play, and spend at least as much time role-playing for their friends as they do trying to maximize their character's effectiveness in a purely structural context. It's common for a group of friends to get together for years, playing the same characters in the same game world with the same gamemaster. In the process, they establish long character histories, flesh out the world background, and so on. For long-term role-players, the stories they create through play can be as emotionally powerful and personally meaningful as anything you find in a novel or movie—perhaps more so because the players are personally involved in their creation.

These "stories" are meaningful to players precisely because they are intimately involved. Players frequently write "expedition reports," in which they retell the story of a particular session of play, or several sessions. Expedition reports almost invariably make dull reading for those who are not involved in the campaign, because they do not have the same intimate familiarity with the setting and the same long history with the players and their characters.

Many role-playing gamers never give "story" a second thought; they get their kicks from solving problems and playing roles, and they don't mind terribly whether the things they encounter knit together into some kind of coherent story. For them, that isn't their main interest in the game.

Additionally, traditional tabletop RPGs, while they often exhort players to roleplay and tell stories, don't generally provide a structure to shape them; their rules are concerned more with determining the success or failure of individual actions, and they leave it up to the gamemaster and players to shape the tale.

From *Hopscotch* to Tabletop

From *Hopscotch* to tabletop role-playing, we've moved along the spectrum I talked about: from a narrative with a single branch to the branching structures of hypertext, game books, solitaire role-playing adventures, and *Dragon's Lair*; to the beads-on-a-string of adventure games; to the slightly open-ended structures of digital RPGs; to the more free-form nature of tabletop. And in the process we've moved from stories with minor game elements to games that still have an attachment to story.

Only with the final game style, tabletop, do we escape the demands of linearity—and we do so, ultimately, only by relying on the creativity of a live gamemaster.

Clearly, one way to ensure that a story is told in a game is to make the game essentially linear, since after all, stories are by nature linear. And designers have found some compromises that allow reasonable freedom of action for players within the constraints of linearity. But are there ways of breaking out of those bounds?

Embedded Stories

One way is to embed stories in the game, rather than the game in a story. We saw this with *Tales of the Arabian Nights*: mini-stories told in the course of an encompassing board game. But we can see it today also in the quests of MMOs. A player encounters an NPC, is told the background of a story, is given a task to accomplish, does so, and returns for a reward (and quite often the next step in a story consisting of several quests). In the course of a character's career in an MMO, he may play through dozens, even hundreds of these mini-stories—and at least when they are well-written and implemented, they can be entertaining and greatly increase the appeal of playing. Indeed, the excellence of its quest

system is one of *World of Warcraft*'s greatest strengths.

Each of these mini-stories may itself be linear, but they are encountered by different players in different orders, so each player's experience is different. Moreover, since these stories are small, their individual development cost is also small, and there's no need to ensure that all players are exposed to all content—increasing repeat playability, something you basically don't get with any linear game.

It's a technique that can clearly be taken to game styles other than MMOs and board games—and an obvious area for designers to explore.

Algorithmic Systems + Multiple Approaches to Problems

Traditionally, both digital RPGs and adventure games present players with a series of challenges—with one, and only one, solution (generally hard-coded) for each. To open the gates to Hell, you must use the bell, the book, and the candle in a prescribed order. To get past the level boss, you must kill it, and there's some little trick to doing so.

As you move away from hard-coded systems to algorithmically driven ones (games set in 3D spaces with skill-driven combat, for instance, and games with physics engines), it becomes increasingly possible for players to discover ways to interact with the physical environment to solve problems, instead of relying on a single solution determined by the developers. Emergent complexity comes into play.

Naturally, developers will want to ensure that at least one solution for each problem exists—but an even better approach is to ensure that *more* than one solution exists for each problem. *Deus Ex* is an example here; in almost all cases, players can get through a level in at least three ways: by shooting everything in sight, by sneaking around, or by using cybernetic skills to hack through obstacles.

Deus Ex is still a "beads-on-a-string" game, with an invariant sequence of levels with predesigned obstacles. But it offers far more variety of play than most such games—and a degree of replayability, despite its linear story, since it can be interesting to try to complete the game with a different strategy the second time around.

This doesn't break us free of the tyranny of linearity—

and it's more work for developers, since they have to plan those multiple paths and potentially develop more content to allow for them. But from an artistic perspective, at least, it's clearly worthwhile.

Ending the MMO

I argued that an MMO cannot tell an overarching story because players cannot have a real impact on the gameworld. But that stops being true if the game itself has an end. *A Tale in the Desert* demonstrates this; it's now being run for the third time. It runs for one calendar year; during that time, the "people of Egypt" (the players) must assist Pharaoh in his struggle with "The Stranger" by completing certain tasks. If they succeed, Pharaoh (and by extension, all Egypt) "wins," and if they fail, they all fail. Some of these tasks, like building a pyramid, require a truly amazing amount of collaborative effort on the part of the player base. In the process, they materially affect the landscape of the game. And "Pharaoh" (Andy Tepper, the game's developer) often appears in-game.

The point is that you *can* impose a real narrative arc on an MMO—but only if the game, like all stories, comes to an end.

There are good business reasons not to do this; if you end a game, some portion of your subscribers will decide not to renew and play again. But again, from an artistic perspective, perhaps that loss is worthwhile.

Narrativist RPGs and Free-forms

Even as digital games have become more and more stereotyped, "indie" RPG designers and hobbyists have been exploring ways of creating games and scenarios that are designed specifically to produce well-defined story experiences, often by inverting or eliminating the rules conventions of older RPGs.

The indie RPG movement takes as its guidepost what they call "Gamist-Narrativist-Simulationist theory," which holds that role-playing gamers seek traditional gameplay experiences, excellent stories, or some form of realism. Though Ron Edwards, the theorist's leading exponent, claims not to give moral weight to one play style over another (Edwards 2001), it's clear that the whole "indie" project is aimed primarily at devising "narrativist" games.

One example is Paul Czege's *My Life with Master*. This game

has an invariant narrative arc; each player is a servant of "the Master," and by the end of the game, the Master will be destroyed, typically by enraged villagers but sometimes in some other fashion. In the course of the game, each player will either be destroyed by the self-loathing brought on by the tasks he is forced to perform by the Master, or will find some form of love or hope and escape the coming cataclysm.

Unlike conventional tabletop RPGs, *My Life with Master* does not have specific rules for task resolution; a character either succeeds or fails with a task, as the player wishes. The game is played in "scenes," and at the beginning of a scene, dice are rolled to determine whether the outcome of the scene is positive for the character or not. The player, with gamemaster assistance, narrates the scene and its outcome.

In other words, *My Life with Master* is not concerned with providing a system to resolve tasks; it is concerned with providing a system that results in narrative resolution. The details of the events within a scene are freed up, to be determined by the players as they wish—but the ultimate outcome is not.

In other words, *My Life with Master* is a perfect example of what I mean by "constraining" a game to produce a story.

Not all narrativist games take this approach—indeed, the appeal of this genre lies in the divergent and imaginative approaches taken by its practitioners. Another example is Ron Edward's *Sorcerer*, which *does* have rules for determining the outcomes of specific tasks, but whose primary focus is on individual psychology and a particular mood: a mood of subtle dread and ultimate horror. Its motto is "How far will you go to get what you want?"; each player character is a person with inner demons—literally so, for each is a sorcerer, living in the modern world, with a demon bound inside him or her. And each can draw on the demon to use paranormal powers, at a large personal cost.

While the indie RPG movement has taken conventional tabletop RPGs in the direction of games that shape narrative, a group of hobbyists, mostly in Scandinavia and Australia, have created a game style known as "the free-form," which can either be seen as taking RPG away from the tabletop and in the direction of improv theater, or as taking LARP and divorcing it from its fruity "dress up and hit each other with rattan sticks" origins.

Greg Costikyan

A free-form is a scenario for some number of players, ranging from a handful to several dozen, designed to be played in a few hours or (at most) days. Typically, it has no (or minimal) rules for task resolution, but does have one or more people who fulfill something of the same role as a gamemaster in a tabletop game (but may also have a literal role to play in the game). The free-form provides a setting and a structure for improvisational role-playing. The players take the role of characters, sometimes ones created in advance by the game operators, but more often ones improvised on the spot.

An excellent example is Thorbiörn Fritzon and Tobias Wrigstad's *The Upgrade,* which has been played at several events in Scandinavia. The conceit of *The Upgrade* is that each of the players is a contestant in a reality TV show called "The Upgrade," and each player is part of a couple, whether married or not. The couples are split up, and each assigned an alternative partner, with whom he or she spends time over the period of the reality show's filming. At the end of the final episode of the show, each player must decide whether to stick with his or her original partner, or "upgrade" to the person with whom he or she was paired. A typically degrading scenario, for reality TV, yes?

The gamemasters take the role of the producers of the show, and the players do not play out their full experience on the tropical island where *The Upgrade* is filmed; instead, the GMs sit them down and "introduce the next clip," saying something like, "Well, something very interesting happened when Hannah went for a stroll with Lars. Could you tell us about that, Hannah?"

At which point Hannah is expected to say a few words to the studio audience and we "cut to the clip," meaning that Hannah and Lars now roleplay a scene. The situation is made more complicated because any other player can stop the action to say, "Hannah at age twelve" or "Lars, three months after the show"—at which point that player (and any others she chooses) play out a mini-scene, not using Hannah's and Lars's players but taking the relevant roles themselves, either establishing something about the character (in the past scene) or imagining a "possible future." Thus, a player does not have complete control over the nature of his character; past scenes may establish things about the character that its

player then must accept and role-play. Similarly, the "hosts" can stop the action to role-play a little scene of their own (e.g., the two of them in the production trailer that evening, drunk and laughing about how they couldn't believe Lars had gotten tangled up in the fishing net), which event Lars then must role-play when we "cut back" to the "clip."

In other words, there is a structure here, and even what you might term "rules." But the main thrust is frenetic, on the edge, improvisational role-play—and the rules exist to shape that role-play into a coherent narrative arc rather than deal with the specifics of task resolution. Salen and Zimmerman would doubtless not consider this a "game" (no "quantifiable resolution," under their definition), but I surely do (Salen and Zimmerman 2003).

Transferring to Digital Media?

It's hard to see how the lessons learned from narrativist RPGs and free-forms can be brought to digital media since they depend so heavily on a gamemaster and player creativity—and "player creativity" doesn't generally work well in tandem with "limited, pregenerated digital assets." But perhaps a more generalized lesson can be learned: it's possible to constrain the narrative of a game if you free up constraints on player action in other regards, thus giving players the feeling that they still have a degree of freedom of action in the gamespace.

Breaking the String

While there is no dishonor in implementing an existing game style well, it seems to me that we've rung the basic changes on what's possible with the "beads-on-a-string" approach to combining games and narrative. If we want to get closer to games that also produce compelling stories, we're going to have to experiment with different approaches.

Some approaches to consider, as I've suggested, are embedded narratives and imposing a defined narrative arc on the game, but allowing a high degree of player freedom between those fixed points.

In general, it's important to think of story and game as discrete, if intertwined, entities, and look for novel ways of integrating them. And to find different ways to grant players "freedom of action" while working within a constrained narrative—or ways of constraining player freedom in one area while freeing it in another to produce an emergent narrative.

Precisely because there is a tension between the demands of game and the demands of story, the attempt to resolve that tension has spawned a number of interesting game styles. If, however, we are to get closer to something that deserves to be called "interactive fiction," we need to break the string of beads and find other approaches to pursue.

References: Literature

Coover, Robert (1992). "The End of Books." *The New York Times Book Review* 11 (June 1992): 23–25.

Cortázar, Julio (1987). *Hopscotch*. New York: Pantheon Books.

Costikyan, Greg (2000). "Where Stories End and Games Begin." *Game Developer* 7, no. 9 (2000): 44–53.

Edwards, Ron (2001). "GNS and Other Matters of Role-playing Theory." Chicago: Adept Press. <http://www.indie-rpgs.com/articles/1/>.

Joyce, Michael (1990). *afternoon: a story*. Watertown, MA: Eastgate Systems.

Salen, Katie, and Eric Zimmerman (2003). *Rules of Play: Game Design Fundamentals*. Cambridge, MA: MIT Press.

Wardrip-Fruin, Noah, and Pat Harrigan (2004). *First Person: New Media as Story, Performance, and Game*. Cambridge, MA: MIT Press.

References: Games

A Tale In the Desert. Andrew Tepper; eGenesis. 2003–2005.

Colossal Cave/Adventure. William Crowther (ca. 1975) and Don Woods (1976). ca. 1975/1976.

Dragon's Lair. Rick Dyer, Advanced Microcomputer Systems (AMS); Don Bluth, Bluth Studios; Cinematronics. 1983.

Dungeons & Dragons. Gary Gygax and Dave Arneson; Tactical Studies Rules (TSR). 1974

My Life With Master. Paul Czege; Half Meme Press. 2003.

Sorcerer. Ron Edwards; Adept Press. 2001.

Tales of the Arabian Nights. Eric Goldberg; West End Games. 1985.

The Upgrade. Thorbiörn Fritzon and Tobias Wrigstad. 2004–2005. <jeepen.olle.ter.dk/wiki/doku.php?id=theory:case_studies>

On the *Wild Cards* Series

George R. R. Martin

I.

In the books, Wild Cards Day is celebrated every September 15, in memory of September 15, 1946, the day that Jetboy spoke his immortal last words while Dr. Tod loosed an alien virus over Manhattan.

In real life, September 15, 1946 happens to be the day that Howard Waldrop was born . . . and Howard, coincidentally, wrote "Thirty Minutes Over Broadway," the opening story of the first *Wild Cards* book, wherein all these events take place.

In the books, September 20 is a day of no special note. In real life, however, it marks the day of *my* birth, two years and five days after H'ard. September 20 is the true Wild Cards Day. It was on that day in 1983 that Vic Milán gave me a role-playing game called *Superworld* as a birthday present, thereby unknowingly planting the first seed of the *Wild Cards* universe.

As I unwrapped that gift, I was still a relative innocent where role-playing games were concerned. Mind you, I had played plenty of games over the years. I had paid my bills directing chess tournaments in the early '70s, while trying to establish myself as an SF writer. Before that I had been captain of my college chess team, and of my high school chess team before *that*. Role-playing had not yet been invented when I was a kid, but we had checkers and *Sorry!* and *Parcheesi* for rainy days, and Hide and Seek and Ringoleavio and Oh O'Clock for warm summer evenings.

Although my parents never owned a house, that did not stop me from building vast real estate empires across a *Monopoly* board. There was *Broadside* and *Stratego* as well, and all through childhood I never lost a game of *Risk* (I always commanded the red armies, and refused to play if denied "my" color). After a while none of my friends dared to face me, so I'd set up the board in the bedroom and fight wars against myself, playing all six armies, inventing kings and generals to command them, merrily invading, attacking, and

betraying myself for hours. And maybe that was role-playing of a sorts, now that I come to think of it.

But it was not until I arrived in New Mexico in 1980 that I began to game regularly. Some of the Albuquerque writers had a small gaming group, and they invited me to come sit in on a session. I was pretty dubious at the time. I had seen kids playing *D&D* at cons, pretending to be Thongor the Barbarian and Pipsqueak the Hobbit while killing monsters and looking for treasure. I had read too much bad sword and sorcery in my youth for that to have much appeal. And there were all these weirdly shaped dice you had to roll to determine whether you lived or died. I would sooner have joined a weekly poker game or an ongoing game of

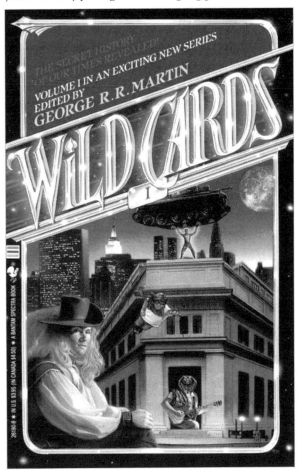

2.1) Cover of the first book in the *Wild Cards* series. (Bantam Spectra)

Diplomacy. I was much too old and sophisticated for this role-playing stuff, after all. Still, if this was what the local writers were into, I figured I might as well give it a try.

Famous last words, those.

This Albuquerque gaming group included Walter Jon Williams, Victor W. Milán, John J. Miller, his wife Gail Gerstner Miller, and Melinda M. Snodgrass, all of whom would eventually become important contributors to the *Wild Cards* anthologies. Royce Wideman and Jim Moore were also part of the group, and my own sweet lady Parris joined in with me. At the time we got involved, they were mostly playing a *Call of Cthulhu* campaign run by Walter, and less frequently Vic's *Morrow Project* scenario, so those were the first two games I sampled.

They were great fun . . . and nothing like I had imagined role-playing to be. I had fallen in with writers, and these games were *stories*. Playing Walter's game was like stepping into the pages of an H. P. Lovecraft story, except that the characters were more fully realized than Lovecraft's ever were. There was triumph and tragedy, heroism and cowardice, love affairs and betrayals, and every now and again a Shuggoth, too. Our weekly sessions were part communal storytelling and part improv theater, part group therapy and part mass psychosis, part adventure and part soap opera. We created some wonderful characters and lived inside them, and many a night never rolled those funny twenty-sided dice at all.

After a few months, I began to make noises about wanting to try and run a game myself. As much fun as the players were having, it seemed to me that the Game Master (GM) was having even more. He was the creator, the conductor leading the orchestra, the team captain and the opposing team rolled up in one omnipotent package. "God," the group called our GMs. Who doesn't want to play god? I finally succumbed to temptation and designed my own *Cthulhu* adventure for the gang. Once I had tasted the joys of godhood there was no turning back . . . even though this particular lot of players was so damned sharp that they unraveled the central mystery of my game about sixteen minutes into the action.

That was more or less where things stood when my birthday rolled around, and Vic gave me that fatal copy of

Superworld. The gang had tried another superhero game before my time and hadn't liked it much . . . but this was a new system, and Vic knew that I was a comic book fan from way back. I had cut my teeth on funny books while growing up in Bayonne, New Jersey. Superman and Batman had more to do with me learning to read than Dick and Jane ever did, and the first stories I ever published were amateur superhero "text stories" in the dittoed comics fanzines. *Superworld* seemed made for me, and me for *Superworld*.

What happened next was almost scary. I came up with a campaign and my friends came up with characters, and we began to play, and before any of us knew what was happening *Superworld* had swallowed us all. At first we were playing once a week, and alternating *Superworld* with sessions of Walter's game, or Vic's. But soon we stopped playing *Morrow Project* entirely, and then *Call of Cthulhu* as well. It was all *Superworld*. We would assemble at suppertime, play until two or sometimes three in the morning, and then postmortem the game we had just played for another hour or so. Many a time dawn caught me while I was driving home from Albuquerque to Santa Fe. Within half a year we were playing twice a week, with one campaign running in Albuquerque and a second in Santa Fe, and the same players participating in both. Once, at an especially dull SF con, we adjourned to my room and played *Superworld* all weekend, leaving the game to do our panels and readings and then rushing back.

A number of characters who would later grace the *Wild Cards* books made their first appearances in those games, albeit in early "rough draft" versions significantly different from their later selves. Melinda's first character was Topper, but a Topper who had only her costume in common with the bit player who would appear in *Ace in the Hole*. Walter's firstborn was Black Shadow, with powers and personality both rather different from his later *Wild Cards* incarnation. In the game, Shad was the brother of Vic's character, who would become the Harlem Hammer of the anthologies. Chip Wideman played a succession of surly antiheroes and the sweet-natured Toad Man before devising Cryptkicker, toxic shitkicker from hell. John Miller had Nightmare, who never did make it into the books. And Jim Moore . . . well, I could tell you about Jim Moore's characters, but if I did, the PC police would have to kill you. The first incarnation of Hiram Worchester was pure comic relief: a well-meaning oaf who fought crime from a blimp and called himself Fatman. And the primordial Turtle might have had Tom Tudbury's name, power, and shell, but he shared none of his history or personality.

Many of these early creations were retired when the players got a better feel for the campaign, and for the nuances of the *Superworld* roles. Topper hung up her top hat, Black Shadow faded back into the shadows, the Harlem Hammer went back to repairing motorcycles. In place of Shad, Walter introduced Modular Man and his mad creator. Vic Milán unveiled Cap'n Trips and all of his friends, and John Miller brought in Yeoman to displace Nightmare. Some of the gang had gotten it right on the first try, though; Gail never played anyone but Peregrine, and Parris was Elephant Girl from the start; the book version of Radha O'Reilly was pretty much a clone of the earlier game version.

The game was deeply and seriously addictive for all of us . . . but for me most of all. I was god, which meant I had lots of planning and preparation to do before the players even arrived. The game ate their nights and their weekends, but it ate my life. For more than a year, *Superworld* consumed me, and during that time I wrote almost nothing. Instead I spent my days coming up with ingenious new plot twists to frustrate and delight my players, and rolling up still more villains to bedevil them. Parris used to listen at my office door, hoping to hear the clicking of my keyboard from within, only to shudder at the ominous rattle of dice.

I told myself it was writer's block. My last book, an ambitious rock and roll fantasy called *The Armageddon Rag*, had failed dismally despite great reviews, and my career was in the dumps, enough to block anyone. Looking back now, though, it's plain to see that I wasn't blocked at all. I was creating characters and devising plots every day, like a man possessed. It was the opposite of being blocked. I was in a creative frenzy, of the sort I sometimes experienced on the home stretch of a novel, when the real world seems to fade away and nothing matters but the book that you are living by day and dreaming of by night. That was *exactly* what was happening here, only there was no book . . . yet. There was only the game.

I don't know just when my fever broke, or why. Maybe my steadily diminishing bank account and rapidly increasing debt had something to do with it. I loved the game. I loved all these wonderful characters that my friends and I had created, I loved the ego boost I got from my players after an especially exciting session . . . but I loved having a house to live in, too, which meant I had to keep making those pesky mortgage payments. And godhood, intoxicating as it was, did not pay.

Thus it was that one day, while rolling up yet another batch of really nifty villains, I said the magic words—"There's got to be some way to make some money from this."

II.

I knew we had some great characters. And I knew there were some great stories to be told about them; funny stories, sad stories, exciting stories. What was needed was a way to get the stories to an audience.

My first notion was to use my Turtle character as the basis for a stand-alone SF novel that I proposed to title *Shell Games*. It would have meant pulling him out of the game milieu and revamping the character thoroughly, but there was a strong story there—the tale of a projects kid from Bayonne, New Jersey, trying to be a superhero in a world where none exist.

That would have rescued one character, but would have meant discarding all the rest. Maybe that was why I found the approach ultimately unsatisfying. Besides, the game had been a group endeavor. Much of the fun of our *Superworld* games had come from the interactions *between* the characters. A novel about one telekinetic superhero wannabe in a mundane world was a very different thing, and somehow duller. This needed to be a group project, a collaborative endeavor.

It needed to be a shared world.

Shared world anthologies are an endangered species in today's market, but back in the '80s they were all the rage. The first modern shared world, the *Thieves' World* series edited by Bob Asprin and Lynn Abbey, had been a tremendous success, spawning not only games, comic books, and film options, but also a host of imitators. Most common were fantasy shared worlds like *Liavek* and *Ithkar* and *Borderlands*, but there were SF series like *The Fleet* and

George R. R. Martin

War World, and even an attempt to share a world of horror, called *Greystone Bay*. But there was nothing even remotely similar to what I had in mind—a shared world anthology series about a world in which superpowers are real, set on a present-day Earth and featuring the characters we'd created for the game.

I bounced my idea off Melinda M. Snodgrass, who ultimately became my assistant editor and strong right hand on the project. She was immediately enthusiastic. So were the rest of my gamers, when they heard the notion. All the writers in the gaming group were eager to contribute, and our friends who worked for a living were willing to sign up their characters, so they could be a part of the madness.

2.2) Cover of *Wild Cards: Aces High*. (Bantam Spectra)

For much of the previous decade I had been editing *New Voices*, an annual (in theory) anthology of original fiction by each year's John W. Campbell Award finalists, so I knew how to put together an anthology . . . but a shared world is a whole different animal. Fortunately, Bob Asprin and Lynn Abbey were extremely forthcoming when I quizzed them about their experiences with *Thieves' World*, as were Will Shetterly and Emma Bull of *Liavek*. With their help, and the Master Agreements that governed those two series, I was able to construct a Master Agreement that gave us firm legal basis to build our series on.

There is an undeniable stigma attached to game-related fiction. For the most part that stigma is well deserved. Thinly disguised *D&D* adventures have become as much a commonplace in today's slush piles as Adam and Eve stories were thirty years ago. Editors groan when they see them, with good reason. The truth is, the qualities that make for a good game do not necessarily make for good fiction, and in some cases are actually antithetical to it. My *Superworld* crew had enjoyed some splendid evenings, but if we simply wrote up our favorite adventures, as one of my players urged, we would have had nothing but a comic book in prose . . . and a pretty bad comic book at that, full of all the usual funny book clichés, costumes and superteams and secret identities, endless efforts by supervillains to conquer the world. Pretty silly stuff, when you stop to think about it. Fine for a game, maybe, but not for a book.

I wanted to do something better, and that meant stepping back for a moment to rethink certain aspects of our characters. Take my own Turtle, for instance. In the game, a player had a certain number of points to buy powers and skills, but the system allowed you to earn additional points by accepting disadvantages, be they mental, physical, or psychological. My players used to have a standing joke—if they came up against a young, handsome, intelligent foe bulging with muscles, no problem, but if a blind deaf pygmy with thalidomide flippers appeared on the scene, run for your lives. Well, the *Superworld* version of the Turtle was the genesis of that joke. To pay for such a high level of telekinesis and forty points of armor as well, I had needed to pile on just about every handicap in the book.[1] It made for a very formidable presence in our games, but in a book such an extreme character would have been ludicrous . . . and not much fun to read about, either.

I also felt we needed to rethink some fundamental aspects of our world itself. I had been reading comic books all my life, and loved them dearly . . . but even as a kid, I realized that certain comic book conventions were downright silly. All those skin-tight costumes, for instance. The way that people in comic books always decided to use their superpowers to fight crime. And the origins of those powers . . . that was a *huge* problem. In the funny books, and in our game as well, characters got their powers from a hundred and one different sources. X was hit by a lightning bolt, Y stumbled on a crashed alien spaceship, Z whipped up something in his lab, Q was bitten by a radioactive wombat, M unearthed the belt buckle of a forgotten deity . . . Any one of these would be a wondrous occurrence all by itself, and when you pile wonder upon wonder upon wonder you strain the willing suspension of disbelief to the breaking point. To make these characters work in a legitimate SF context, we needed a *single* plausible cause for all these superpowers.

Melinda Snodgrass was the one who provided it. "A *virus!*" she exclaimed one morning as we were drinking coffee in her old house on Second Street after a long night of gaming. An alien retrovirus that rewrites the genetic structure of its victims, changing them in unique and unpredictable ways. And her character could be the alien who brought it to Earth! Thus were born the xenovirus Takis-a and Dr. Tachyon, virtually in the same instant.

Melinda's virus not only solved the origin problem for us, but also turned out to have a *huge* and totally serendipitous side effect. We did not want a world in which *everyone* had superpowers—that might make for a wonderful premise, but not for the stories we wanted to tell. We had to limit its effects somehow. We considered restricting the experiment to a specific time and place— the aliens arrive one day, give superpowers to the

population of Dubuque, Iowa, and depart—but that would have made it hard to bring in some of our diverse lot of *Superworld* creations, not to mention severely limiting our ability to add new characters later in the series.

As we batted around the problem, the answer came to us. Not everyone gets the virus. Of those who do, most die from the violence of their transformations. And even the survivors are not home free. The vast majority of natural genetic mutations are harmful rather than beneficial. So would it be with the wild card; monsters and freaks would be much more likely to result than supermen.

Out of that came our jokers . . . and that made all the difference.[2] The game we had played had no jokers, no Jokertown, no Rox, no more than the funny books did.

In hindsight, it was the jokers who truly made the *Wild Card* universe unique. Our aces had their counterparts in the superheroes of the Marvel and DC universes; while we strove to make our versions grittier and more realistic, to portray them with more subtlety and depth, those are differences of tone, not of kind . . . and the comics themselves were becoming darker and grittier, too. In the end, what really set *Wild Cards* apart from all that had gone before were its jokers.

When Melinda and I told our notions to Vic Milán he grabbed the ball and ran with it, whipping up a lot of the pseudoscience of the wild card, the biogenetics and quantum physics that would eventually be published in the appendix to the first volume. At the same time Walter Jon Williams, unbeknownst to any of us, actually started writing a *story.*

Meanwhile, I was putting together a proposal to take to publishers . . . and recruiting other contributors as well. The Albuquerque gaming group had given me a superb core group of writers, but a *small* group. To sustain a long series, I would need a larger pool of potential contributors, writers who had *not* been a part of our marathon *Superworld* game. New writers would mean new characters, who might interact in unexpected ways with those carried over from the game. New writers would bring us fresh concepts and plot ideas, and would help lessen any lingering temptations

---

1. Tabletop role-players have since termed this sort of process "min-maxing."

2. In the *Wild Cards* universe, "Aces" are those whom the virus has mutated in a beneficial way—such as giving the Turtle his remarkable telekinetic ability. "Jokers" are those who have suffered some (often quite extreme) deformity from the virus—such as the transparent-skinned Chrysalis or the self-explanatory Snotman. Those unaffected by the virus are called "nats," while those killed by it are said to have "drawn the Black Queen."

to simply write up our games. Besides, there were a hell of a lot of fine SF writers out there who loved comic books and superheroes just as I did, and I knew many of them would jump at the chance to be part of a project like this.

Not everyone I contacted signed on, of course, but many did. Lewis Shiner was one of the first, and his character Fortunato became a key player right from the start. Ed Bryant brought us Sewer Jack, and also recruited his collaborator, Leanne C. Harper, while Lew brought in Walton (Bud) Simons. I signed on Arthur Byron Cover from L.A., *X-Men* scripter Chris Claremont from New York, George Alec Effinger from New Orleans. Stephen Leigh gave birth to Puppetman in Cincinnati, while back in New Mexico, Roger Zelazny gave us Croyd Crenson, the Sleeper, the most original concept of them all. And Howard Waldrop . . .

Howard Waldrop threw us a curve ball.

H'ard and I had known each other since 1963, when I bought *Brave & the Bold* #28 from him for a quarter and we started corresponding. We both had our roots in comics fandom, both published our first stories in the comic fanzines of the '60s. I knew Howard still had a lot of affection for "funny books." I also knew that he had a *character*. Howard always talks about his stories before he actually sits down to write them. Sometimes he talks about them for months, sometimes for years, occasionally for decades. Thus, if you knew Howard, you would have known about the dodo story, the zen sumo story, and the piss-drinking story long before he wrote word one of "The Ugly Chickens," "Man-Mountain Gentian," and "Flying Saucer Rock 'n Roll," respectively.

As it happened, Howard had been talking about something called the Jetboy story for a couple of years . . . though being Howard, he hadn't written it. It seemed to me that this "Jetboy" might be perfect for *Wild Cards,* so I invited H'ard to join the fun. And he accepted . . . sort of . . .

The thing is, Howard does things his own way. He'd write the Jetboy story for me, but he wasn't at all keen on this shared world stuff. So he'd write the first story for the first book, and kill Jetboy at the end of it. Oh, and by the way, his story took place right after World War II, and climaxed on September 15, 1946.

Up until then, we had planned to start the series with the virus arriving on Earth in 1985. And in fact Walter Jon Williams had already completed the story he had been writing in secret, a novelette called "Bag Lady," featuring two of his game characters, Black Shadow and Modular Man, chasing an art thief and dealing with an extraterrestrial menace called the Swarm.[3] Walter dropped the story in my lap one day at Melinda's house, savoring my surprise . . . and gloating over the fact that he'd already finished his story, while the rest of us hadn't even *started* ours.

Unfortunately, Howard Waldrop had just knocked Walter's plans—not to mention "Bag Lady"—into a cocked hat. Anyone who has ever dealt with Howard knows there is no stubborner man on this earth or the next one. If I wanted him in the book, it would have to be on his terms. That meant 1946.

And I *did* want him in the book, so . . .

We couldn't very well just open with Jetboy in 1946 and jump forward forty years to the present. An event as big as the release of the wild card was going to have huge repercussions. We had to dramatize the release of the virus and show what happened after Jetboy's death, and the readers would want to know about the intervening years as well. Thanks to Howard, we now had forty years of white space to fill in. All of a sudden the first volume of the series had become a "historical" . . . so "Bag Lady" no longer fit, and poor Walter had to hie back to his computer and start all over again (shows you what happens when you write stories in secret without informing your editor).

Sometimes the process pays you unexpected dividends. Howard's pig-headed insistence on 1946 not only gave us the Jetboy story to open the book, it forced those of us who followed to deal with themes and times we might otherwise have ignored . . . most particularly the era of HUAC and the McCarthy hearings, from which arose Dr. Tachyon's doomed love affair with Blythe van Rensselaer, and Jack Braun, the Golden Boy, the protagonist of "Witness," the story that Walter Jon Williams was forced to write to take the place of "Bag Lady." Both added immeasurable richness to our world and depth of our characters, and "Witness" went on to become the only shared world story ever to appear on the

---

3. The Swarm would turn up again as the primary menace in *Wild Cards II: Aces High*.

final ballot for a Nebula award.

Happenstance? Yes . . . and no. That's just the sort of thing that *should* happen in a good shared world. When writers work together, bouncing off of one another and reacting to each other's stories and characters like a group of talented musicians jamming, that sort of serendipity occurs more often than you'd think, as the subsequent history of the *Wild Cards* series was to prove over and over again.

III.

The great boom in shared world anthologies had begun in 1979, when Ace Books published Robert Asprin's *Thieves' World*, the first volume in a long-running fantasy series about the imaginary city of Sanctuary and the motley cast of swordsmen, sorcerers, princes, rogues, and thieves who roamed its streets, with occasional guest appearances by an equally motley assortment of gods.

Thieves' World had its precursors, to be sure. In comic books, both the Marvel and DC universes were shared worlds, wherein the heroes and villains lived in the same world, constantly crossed paths with one another, and had their friendships, feuds, and love affairs. In prose there was H. P. Lovecraft's Cthulhu Mythos. Lovecraft encouraged his writer friends to borrow elements from his stories, and to add their own, and Robert E. Howard, Clark Ashton Smith, Robert Bloch, August Derleth, and others gleefully took up the game. HPL himself would then make mention of the gods, cults, and accursed books the others had contributed, and the mythos became ever richer and more detailed.

Much later came *Medea: Harlan's World*, wherein Harlan Ellison assembled a group of top-rank science fiction writers to create an imaginary planet and work out all the details of its flora, fauna, geography, history, and orbital mechanics, whereupon each writer penned a story set on the world they had created together.

But *Thieves' World* was the breakthrough book that defined the modern shared world, and it proved so successful that it soon spawned a whole host of imitators. *Ithkar* and *Liavek* and *Merovingen Nights* had fantasy settings and the flavor of sword and sorcery, as did *Thieves' World* itself. *Borderlands* was more urban fantasy, with its punk elves and contemporary setting. *The Fleet* and *War World* brought the shared world

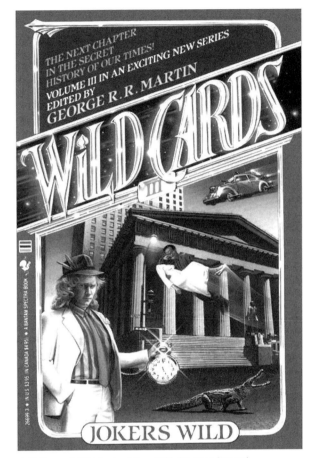

2.3) Cover of *Wild Cards: Jokers Wild*. (Bantam Spectra)

format to space opera, *Greystone Bay* extended it to horror, and *Heroes in Hell* took it to hell.

Some of these series came before ours; others followed us. Some had long runs; others only lasted for a book or two. In the end, *Wild Cards* would outlast all of them to become the longest-running shared world series of them all, with twelve volumes from Bantam, three from Baen, and, many years later, two more from ibooks. Which means that I now have more experience with shared worlds than any other editor, I suppose.

When *Wild Cards* was starting out, however, my editorial experience was limited to *New Voices*. I knew going in that a shared world was a very different sort of animal, and not one easily tamed.

A shared world poses some difficult artistic questions, the

most crucial one being the amount of sharing involved and the rules that govern it. All of the shared worlds of the '80s answered these questions in their own ways, I found, but some of the answers were more satisfactory than others. Some books shared only their settings; the characters never crossed paths, nor did the events of one story have any impact on those that followed. Each story existed in isolation, aside from a common geography and history. In other series, the characters did make "guest star" appearances in one another's tales, while the stories themselves continued to stand alone. But the *best* shared world anthologies, the ones that were the most entertaining and the most successful, were those that shared characters and plots as well as settings. In those books, and those alone, the whole was more than the sum of its parts. The "shared worlds" that minimized the sharing were missing the point of the exercise, it seemed to me.

Wild Cards would not make that mistake, I decided. We would maximize the sharing. More, we would strive to go well beyond what anyone else had ever done in the shared world game. So much so that when I drew up my "immodest proposal" for the first three *Wild Cards* books, I eschewed the old term "shared world" and promised the publishers a series of "mosaic novels."

That initial proposal was for three books, for no particular reason but that we wanted to do more than one, and no publisher was likely to buy twelve at a shot. That set a precedent, and later on we continued to plot, sell, and write the books in groups of three—"triads," as we called them, since they were not quite trilogies (the second triad turned into four books and the third one into five). The first two volumes of that first triad (which would eventually become *Wild Cards* and *Aces High*, though they had other titles in the proposal) would feature individual stories, each with its own plot and protagonist, a beginning, a middle, and an end. But all the stories would also advance what we called the "overplot." And between the stories we would add an interstitial narrative that would tie them all together and create the "mosaic novel" feel we wanted.

But the *true* mosaic novel would be the third book, wherein we brought our overplot to a smashing conclusion. No other shared world had ever attempted anything quite

like what we proposed to do with *Jokers Wild*: a single braided narrative, wherein all the characters, stories, and events were interwoven from start to finish in a sort of seven-handed collaboration. The end result, we hoped, would be a book that read like a novel with multiple viewpoints rather than simply a collection of related stories.

In my proposal I spoke of *Jokers Wild* as "a Robert Altman film in prose." Like *Nashville* and *A Wedding* and several other of Altman's trademark films, *Jokers Wild* would feature a large and varied cast of characters whose paths would cross and recross during the course of the book. The setting would be New York City on September 15, 1986— Wild Card Day, forty years after Jetboy's death and the release of the Takisian xenovirus over Manhattan. All the action would take place within twenty-four hours, giving us a strong chronological framework on which to hang our story threads. The first two *Wild Cards* books had featured the work of eleven writers and nine writers, respectively, but because of the complexity of what we were about to attempt, I decided to limit *Jokers Wild* to six stories (there are seven names on the title page, to be sure, but Edward Bryant and Leanne C. Harper were collaborating, as they had in Volume One). Each of the seven viewpoint characters had his dreams, his own demons, and his own goals, the pursuit of which would take him back and forth across the city, up skyscrapers and down into the sewers, bumping into other characters and other stories as he went.

It was seven stories and it was one story, but mostly it was an enormous headache. I did a lot of cutting and pasting and shuffling of sections as the manuscripts came in, striving for the perfect placement of all our cliffhangers, climaxes, and foreshadowing while simultaneously trying to keep chronology and geography firmly in mind. Half a hundred times I thought I had it, until noticing that Yeoman had taken six hours to get to Brooklyn, that Fortunato was in two places at once, that it had been three hundred pages since we'd last seen Demise. Then it was time to sigh and shuffle again. But I finally got it right. (I think.)

In truth, we were creating a new literary form of sorts, though none of us quite realized that at the time. We did realize that what we were doing was an experiment, and there were days when none of us were at all certain that that the beast was going to fly. It was the hardest, most challenging editing that I ever did, and the writing was no day at the beach either.

In the end, though, all the effort was worth it. Readers and reviewers both seemed to love the mosaic novel form (although one reviewer amused me vastly by making a point of how seamlessly I had blended the styles of such dissimilar writers, when of course I'd made no attempt to "blend" any styles whatsoever, preferring that each character retain his own distinctive individual voice).

And my writers and I agreed: *Jokers Wild* was the strongest volume in the series to date. The experiment had been a success, and the template was set. The full mosaic was too difficult and time-consuming a form to be used in every volume, but every third volume was just about right. So the template was set: all the *Wild Cards* triads to come would also conclude with a climactic mosaic, fully interwoven in the same manner as *Jokers Wild.*

References: Literature

Martin, George R. R., Edward Bryant, Leanne C. Harper, Stephen Leigh, Victor Milán, John J. Miller, Lewis Shiner, Melinda M. Snodgrass, Howard Waldrop, Walter Jon Williams, and Roger Zelazny (1987). *Wild Cards,* edited by George R. R. Martin. New York: Bantam Books.

Martin, George R. R., Lewis Shiner, Roger Zelazny, Walter Jon Williams, Melinda M. Snodgrass, Victor Milán, Pat Cadigan, John J. Miller, and Walton Simons (1987). *Wild Cards II: Aces High,* edited by George R. R. Martin. New York: Bantam Books.

Martin, George R. R., Melinda M. Snodgrass, Leanne C. Harper, Walton Simons, Lewis Shiner, John J. Miller, and Edward Bryant (1987). *Wild Cards III: Jokers Wild,* edited by George R. R. Martin. New York: Bantam Books.

Reference: Game

Superworld. Steve Perrin; Chaosium. 1983.

From the Basement to the Basic Set: The Early Years of *Dungeons & Dragons*

Erik Mona

Thirty-one years after the invention of *Dungeons & Dragons*, the original role-playing game remains the most popular and financially successful brand in the adventure gaming industry.[1] In that time, *D&D* has introduced millions of readers to the concept of role-playing. Even those who eventually move on to other systems usually get their start with *D&D*. Most gamers' understanding of "what happens" in a role-playing game is therefore defined by how *D&D* explains these concepts, and an analysis of how *D&D*'s rules manuals have explained the duties and roles of players throughout the game's many printings offers a glimpse at the evolution of the role-playing game itself. If *Dungeons & Dragons* is the lingua franca of most role-playing gamers, its definition of the role-playing experience defines an important touchstone helpful for critical study of the role-playing phenomenon.

This article gives a broad overview of *D&D* in its first era, from its origins in the basements of two Midwest game designers to its evolution into a boxed set of simplified rules aimed at the mass market. By the end of this period, *Dungeons & Dragons* had entered the common consciousness of the American public, and all subsequent revisions (and there have been many) can accurately be described as variations on the original. But how did the original come to take form?

On the Origin of *D&D*

The current version of *D&D* bills itself as edition 3.5, but several more significant revisions of the rules have appeared since the first *D&D* boxed set hit shelves in 1974.[2] Arcane differences between "basic" and "advanced" rules resulted in the current numbering system, but more than nine significant revisions of the game have appeared since 1974. The most primal form of *D&D* actually appeared three years earlier, as a fifteen-page "Fantasy Supplement" in the back of *Chainmail*, a medieval miniatures wargame written by Gary Gygax and Jeff Perren.

Chainmail certainly didn't invent the tabletop miniatures wargame (Gygax himself had been a member of the wargames-focused Castle & Crusade Society since 1968),[3] but it came along early enough in the popularity of that hobby that the authors devoted a four-page introduction explaining the concept.

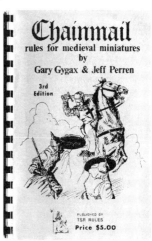

3.1) *Chainmail's* fifteen-page Fantasy Supplement formed the basis for *Dungeons & Dragons*. Third Edition ©1975 Tactical Studies Rules

While much of this text focused on the rudimentary requirements of play such as building a wargaming table and purchasing scaled-down miniature warriors, other passages reveal Gygax's interest in pushing the boundaries of immersive gaming experiences. "With no other form of wargaming—or nearly any other

1. This fact is so well established in the conventional wisdom of the adventure games industry that it's difficult to find adequate sourcing for the assertion, and it seems ridiculous to even try.

2. The most significant revisions of the *D&D* rules include *Dungeons & Dragons* (Gary Gygax and Dave Arneson, 1974), *D&D* Basic Set (1–7th printing, edited by J. Eric Holmes, 1977), *D&D* Basic Set (8–11th printing, edited by Tom Moldvay, 1981), *D&D* Basic Set (12–14th printing, edited by Frank Mentzer, 1983), *D&D Rules Cyclopedia* (Frank Mentzer, 1991), *Advanced Dungeons & Dragons*: First Edition (E. Gary Gygax, 1977–1979), *Advanced Dungeons & Dragons*: Second Edition (David "Zeb" Cook, 1989), *Dungeons & Dragons*: Third Edition (Monte Cook, Jonathan Tweet, and Skip Williams, 2000), and *Dungeons & Dragons*: Version 3.5 (Cook, Tweet, and Williams, revision by Andy Collins et al., 2003). All printing references are taken from The Acaeum <http://www.acaeum.com>, the most reliable source on vintage *Dungeons & Dragons* printings.

3. See <http://www.acaeum.com/Library/Domesday.html>.

form of game for that matter—is the player given the scope of choice and range for imagination that miniature warfare provides," he writes. "You have carte blanche to create or recreate fictional or historic battles and the following rules will, as closely as possible, simulate what would have happened if the battle had just been fought in reality" (*Chainmail* 1971, 7).[4]

Chainmail's Fantasy Supplement introduced many concepts that have endured through all editions of *Dungeons & Dragons*, including monsters like elementals and the chromatic dragons and spells like fireball, lightning bolt, and polymorph. Magical swords and arrows appear for the first time, as does the concept of dividing creatures by their philosophical alignment to law and chaos. Yet, despite these creative innovations, *Chainmail* is not a role-playing game, but rather a set of brief rules specifically meant to be used to simulate battles between large numbers of creatures. Brief rules for small battles and sieges suggest the idea of using

3.2) "Men & Magic," Volume I of the original *Dungeons & Dragons* game. ©1974 Tactical Studies Rules.

one miniature to represent a single character (rather than a whole unit), but the rules contain no suggestion that the player assume the role of these figures or establish any element of their "character" beyond the game statistics used to measure their combat effectiveness.

Three years later, Tactical Studies Rules released a massive expansion of the ideas outlined in *Chainmail*'s Fantasy Supplement in the form of three slim booklets entitled *Dungeons & Dragons: Rules for Fantastic Medieval Wargames Campaigns Playable with Paper and Pencil and Miniature Figures*. The title page of the first volume ("Men & Magic") clearly traces *D&D*'s origins back to *Chainmail*: "Dedicated to all the fantasy wargamers who have enthusiastically played and expanded upon the *Chainmail* Fantasy Rules, with thanks and gratitude. Here is something better!" (*Dungeons & Dragons*: "Men & Magic" 1974, 1)

Gygax's "something better" was nothing short of a completely new type of immersive play experience. The spark of genius came from Dave Arneson, a fellow Castle & Crusade Society member, who had expanded the Fantasy Supplement with rules for dungeon exploration in which each player represented a single character. Arneson's dungeon, set below Blackmoor Castle, originally contained the basic monsters in *Chainmail*, but the voracious appetite of his Twin Cities players spurred him to expand and innovate. "So even in the Dungeon it became quickly apparent that there was a need for a greater variety of monsters, more definition even within the type of monsters, and certainly a deeper Dungeon," he later recalled ("First Fantasy Campaign" 1980, 3). Reports from the Blackmoor campaign appeared in the *Domesday Book*, the official newsletter of the Castle & Crusade Society, and thus found their way to Gary Gygax. Arneson visited Gygax in Lake Geneva, Wisconsin in 1972 (Schick 1991, 132), and the two played a game using the modified and expanded rules. Gygax later wrote that Arneson's additions made *Chainmail* "a far more complex and exciting game" (*Dungeons & Dragons*: "Men & Magic" 1974, 3).

A few weeks after this historic meeting, Arneson sent Gygax a packet of rules and notes pertaining to the Blackmoor Campaign. "I immediately began work on a brand new manuscript," recalled Gygax. "About three weeks later, I had some 100 typewritten pages, and we began serious playtesting . . . *Dungeons & Dragons* had been born" (Gygax 1985b).

On the 1st of November, 1973, E. Gary Gygax penned the Forward (*sic*) of the very first *Dungeons & Dragons* rulebook. From the first page, he made clear that *D&D* was more than just another wargame. Gygax's description of this new concept in social interaction reads like a sales presentation:

3.3) "Monsters & Treasure," Volume II of the original *Dungeons & Dragons* game. ©1974 Tactical Studies Rules.

4. Page reference taken from the 1975 third printing by Tactical Studies Rules.

While it is possible to play a single game, unrelated to any other game events past or future, it is the campaign for which these rules are designed. It is relatively simple to set up a fantasy campaign, and better still, it will cost almost nothing. In fact you will not even need miniature figures, although their occasional employment is recommended for real spectacle when battles are fought. A quick glance at the Equipment section of this booklet will reveal just how little is required. The most extensive requirement is time. The campaign referee will have to have sufficient time to meet the demands of his players, he will have to devote a number of hours to laying out the maps of his "dungeons" and upper terrain before the affair begins. (*Dungeons & Dragons*: "Men & Magic" 1974, 3)

Despite the fact that the rules describe an essentially new experience, they are written with the assumption that the audience is already familiar with wargaming terms like "referee" and "campaign." Without discussing exactly what it is that *D&D* players do, Gygax's introduction hints at staggering possibilities. "There should be no want of players, for there is unquestionably a fascination in this fantasy game— evidenced even by those who could not by any stretch of the imagination be termed ardent wargamers" (Ibid.).

D&D's three rulebooks covered the spells, equipment, monsters, and combat system necessary to run a campaign centered around exploration of a giant dungeon similar to those of Arneson and Gygax (Blackmoor and Greyhawk, respectively[5]). Player characters gain experience points for defeating monsters

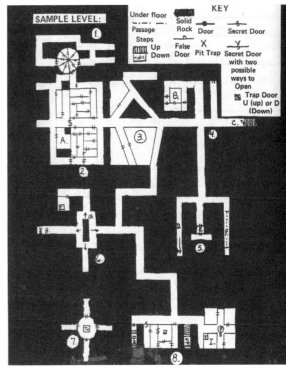

3.5) *D&D's* first sample dungeon. ©1974 Tactical Studies Rules.

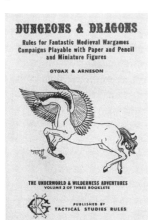

3.4) "The Underworld & Wilderness Adventures," Volume III of the original *Dungeons & Dragons* game. ©1974 Tactical Studies Rules.

in combat and gathering treasure, and in this manner they gain levels, with each level corresponding to an incremental increase in power and ability (*Dungeons & Dragons*: "Men & Magic" 1974, 18).[6]

Characters do not gain experience points for peacefully interacting with the world, but the rules do suggest a world beyond the dungeon, even if they don't spend an enormous amount of time offering suggestions to the referee regarding how to handle its exploration. To woo a hireling into service, for example, characters are expected to post notices at inns and taverns, send messengers to distant lands, or frequent public places, but the rules framework provided by the manuals focuses on the financial cost to the character rather than on social interaction (*Dungeons & Dragons*: "The Underworld & Wilderness Adventures" 1974, 23–24).

The most revealing window into the way *D&D* was meant

5. Follow-up volumes in the original *D&D* edition included *Greyhawk* (by Gary Gygax and Robert J. Kuntz) and *Blackmoor* (by Dave Arneson), notable for its inclusion of the first-published RPG scenario, "Temple of the Frog." Rather than expanding upon the mythoi of the two "official" *D&D* campaigns, the booklets mostly contain rules expansions such as new spells and classes. Other volumes included: *Eldritch Wizardry*; *Gods, Demigods, & Heroes*; and *Swords & Spells*.

6. The increase in abilities over time that would come to define D&D definitely came from Arneson's Blackmoor campaign.

3.7) The *D&D* Basic Set brought the game to a much wider audience with a larger format, simplified rules, and professional art. ©1978 Tactical Studies Rules.

to be played comes in the form of a two-page "Example of the Referee Moderating a Dungeon Expedition," presented as a dialogue between the referee and the caller, a player designated to speak for the group (Ibid., 12–14).

The following is a typical exchange:

CAL:The elf will check out the hollow sound, one of us will sort through the refuse, each trunk will be opened by one of us, and the remaining two (naming exactly who this is) will each guard a door, listening to get an advance warning if anything approaches.

REF:Another check on the hollow sound reveals a secret door which opens onto a flight of stairs down to the south. The refuse is nothing but sticks, bones, offal and old clothes. One chest is empty; the other had a poison needle on the lock. (Here a check to see if the character opening it makes his saving throw for poison.) The chest with the poison needle is full of

copper pieces—appears to be about 2,000 of them.

CAL:Empty out all of the copper pieces and check the trunk for secret drawers in the false bottom, and do the same with the empty one. Also, do there seem to be any old boots or cloaks among the old clothes in the rubbish pile? (Ibid., 14)

While the idea of a single player monopolizing the referee's time may seem strange from the perspective of a modern gamer, it must have been a necessity for a rules system that suggested an optimal player-to-referee ratio of 20:1 (*Dungeons & Dragons*: "Men & Magic" 1974, 5). The assumption of such a large group of players came partly from the game's wargaming roots, but also from the enormous popularity of Arneson's and Gygax's campaigns, each of which consisted of more than a dozen active players at their height. Shortly after the publication of the *D&D* rules, the game's popularity spread far beyond the campaigns of its creators. In part because the rules left a great deal up to the interpretation and whim of the referee, each *D&D* campaign was different, patched together with its own "house" rules and assumptions. Several versions of *D&D* appeared on college campuses across the United States, some of them prominent enough to warrant mentions in *The Dragon*, TSR's official magazine (itself launched in 1976) such as a reference to a CalTech high-level variant called *Dungeons & Beavers*. "Okay," Gygax remarked. "Different strokes for different folks, but that is not *D&D*" (Gygax 1985a, 26).

The somewhat nebulous nature of the *D&D* rules undoubtedly contributed to its early success, but Gygax remained unsatisfied. "*D&D* was released long before I was satisfied that it was actually ready," he wrote at the time. "You can, however, rest assured that work on a complete revision of the game is in progress, and I promise a far better product" (Gygax 1985b, 27).

Back to Basics

Gygax's "far better product" came in 1977 in the form of the *Dungeons & Dragons* Basic Set, a larger, more visually attractive boxed set that sought to introduce new players to the concept of role-playing by focusing on only the first three levels of play, thereafter directing interested players to the much more expansive *Advanced Dungeons & Dragons* game, forthcoming from Gary Gygax and TSR. Writer J. Eric Holmes revised the original Gygax and Arneson manuscript to make the rules far more accessible to children of age 12 and above. Unlike the arcane manila booklets of 1974, Holmes's attractive rulebook opens with a compelling description of play:

> Each player creates a character or characters who may be dwarves, elves, halflings or human fighting men, magic-users, pious clerics or wily thieves. The characters are then plunged into an adventure in a series of dungeons, tunnels, secret rooms and caverns run by another player: the referee, often called the Dungeon Master. The dungeons are filled with fearsome monsters, fabulous treasure, and frightful perils. As the players engage in game after game their characters grow in power and ability: the magic users learn more magic spells, the thieves increase in cunning and ability, the fighting men, halflings, elves and dwarves, fight with more deadly accuracy and are harder to kill. Soon the adventurers are daring to go deeper and deeper into the dungeons on each game, battling more terrible monsters, and, of course, recovering bigger and more fabulous treasure! The game is limited only by the inventiveness and imagination of the players, and, if a group is playing together, the characters can move from dungeon to dungeon within the same magical universe if game referees are approximately the same in their handling of play. (*Dungeons & Dragons* Basic Set (rulebook) 1977, 5)

The introduction carefully contextualizes the original rules and provides the best description to date of what happens in a *Dungeons & Dragons* game, limiting the focus exclusively to the dungeon environment. The 1974 edition's rudimentary guidelines for wilderness play are notably absent, along with the rules handling upkeep of baronies and strongholds (presumably made irrelevant by the game's focus on low-level characters). The Basic Set's rules for non-player characters parrot those of the original game, adding nothing to an element of gaming that would see great expansion with future editions.

If the Basic Set's innovation lacked breadth, it certainly delivered in depth. A section entitled "Dungeon Mastering as

a Fine Art" suggests using graph paper to map out vast dungeons composed of "interlocking corridors, passages, stairs, closed rooms, secret doors, traps, and surprises for the unwary" (Ibid., 39). A cutaway illustration depicts a seven-level dungeon built into a mountain carved into a giant stone skull. The rulebook also includes a brief sample dungeon (complete with a full-page map), and starting with the fourth printing in 1978, the boxed set replaced two booklets of maps, encounter tables, and treasure lists with *In Search of the Unknown*, a 32-page adventure "module" describing a dangerous cavern complex of empty rooms meant to be stocked by the Dungeon Master using provided random tables. The game might only be about dungeons, but at least the dungeons were getting a lot more interesting, and an element of play-acting first took stage.

"Dramatize the adventure as much as possible," suggests Holmes, "describe the scenery, if any. Non-player characters should have appropriate speech, orcs are gruff and

3.6) A typical image from the original *D&D*. © 1974 Tactical Studies Rules.

ungrammatical, knights talk in flowery phrases and always say 'thou' rather than 'you'" (Ibid., 40). The example of play shows these new suggestions in action:

> *D.M.:* Around the corner come four orcs. "Surface dwellers! Kill them, cut them to mincemeat! Pound them to hamburger!"

> *Caller:* The fighting man is ready. He swings (rolls die). An 18!

> *D.M.:* It's a hit. Roll your damage.

> *Caller:* (Rolls a six-sided die.) A four.

> *D.M.:* He's dead. You cut him in half. The second orc is on you. He swings . . . (The fight continues until all four orcs lie dead.)

Holmes retained the caller as the interlocutor between the players and the referee, but did so only out of reverence for the original *Dungeons & Dragons* game. "I have never seen a successful game where one of the players was elected caller and actually did all the talking to the DM," he said four years after the release of the Basic Set. "Usually everybody talks at once. The resulting confusion is much more lifelike; one can hear the characters dithering at the cross corridor as the monsters approach. 'Run this way!' 'Charge them!' 'Get out of the way, I'm throwing a spell . . .'" (Holmes and Moldvay 1981).

The caller (along with a host of other rules) would eventually fall from grace with *Advanced Dungeons & Dragons*, a three-hardcover overview and massive expansion on the original game written by Gygax and published concurrent to the Basic Set in 1977. The three volumes (the *Monster Manual*, *Player's Handbook*, and *Dungeon Master's Guide*),[7] comprising some 490 pages, laid out a much-expanded vision for the *D&D* game, ballooning the class and race options available to players and extending the implied duration of *D&D* campaigns by allowing characters to achieve the twentieth level of ability.[8] Holmes's *D&D* Basic Set was meant as a "feeder system" into the expanded *AD&D* game (*Dungeons & Dragons* Basic Set [rulebook] 1977, 2), and while many

technical differences exist between what ultimately became known as "Basic *D&D*" and *Advanced Dungeons & Dragons*, the two games are essentially identical in terms of the player's role and the role-playing experience.

Although much refinement would occur with new editions leading up to the present day, the formula for the success of *Dungeons & Dragons* and the impression it made on gamers (and future game designers) was well established by 1977's boxed set. At last, *D&D* had evolved from a niche product to a true mass-market phenomenon. The invention of the role-playing game was complete.

References: Literature

Holmes, J. Eric and Tom Moldvay (1981). "Basic *D&D* Points of View . . . From the Editors Old and New." *Dragon* 52 (August 1981).

Gygax, Gary (1985a). "*D&D* is Only as Good as the DM." In *Best of the Dragon Volume 1*. Lake Geneva, WI: TSR, Inc.

Gygax, Gary (1985b). "Gary Gygax on *Dungeons & Dragons*." In *Best of the Dragon Volume 1*. TSR, Inc.

Schick, Lawrence (1991). *Heroic Worlds*. Buffalo, NY: Prometheus Books.

References: Games

Advanced Dungeons & Dragons: First Edition. E. Gary Gygax; TSR Inc. 1977–1979.

Advanced Dungeons & Dragons: Second Edition. David "Zeb" Cook; TSR Inc. 1989.

Chainmail. Gary Gygax and Jeff Perren; Guiden Games. 1971. (3rd printing: TSR. 1975.)

Dungeons & Dragons. Gary Gygax and Dave Arneson; TSR Inc. 1974. (Includes "Men and Magic," "The Underworld & Wilderness Adventures," and "Monsters and Treasure.")

Dungeons & Dragons Basic Set (1–7th printing). Edited by J. Eric Holmes; TSR Inc. 1977.

Dungeons & Dragons Basic Set (8–11th printing). Edited by Tom Moldvay; TSR Inc. 1981.

Dungeons & Dragons Basic Set (12–14th printing). Edited by Frank Mentzer; TSR Inc. 1983.

Dungeons & Dragons: Third Edition. Monte Cook, Jonathan Tweet, and Skip Williams; Wizards of the Coast. 2000.

Dungeons & Dragons: Version 3.5. Monte Cook, Jonathan Tweet, and Skip Williams; revision by Andy Collins et al.; Wizards of the Coast. 2003.

Dungeons & Dragons Rules Cyclopedia. Frank Mentzer; TSR Inc. 1991.

"First Fantasy Campaign." Dave Arneson. 1980.

---

7. Only the *Monster Manual* appeared alongside the Basic Set in 1977. The *Player's Handbook* followed in 1978, and the *Dungeon Master's Guide*, nearly as large as the previous *AD&D* manuals put together, finally arrived in August 1979.

8. Gygax and Arneson's original *Dungeons & Dragons* presented classes that "topped out" at varying levels, from the fighter's 10 to the wizard's 16. Holmes's Basic Set focused exclusively on levels 1–3.

Narrative Structure and Creative Tension in *Call of Cthulhu*
Kenneth Hite

> Puerile though the story was, old Zadok's insane
> earnestness and horror had communicated to me a
> mounting unrest . . .
> —H. P. Lovecraft, "The Shadow Over Innsmouth"

Published adventures for the role-playing game *Call of Cthulhu* have remained unusually successful, both artistically and economically, in the role-playing game industry. Most role-playing supplements contain additional information on game rules or setting, or cover specific subjects such as weapons or genre emulation rather than present pre-scripted adventures or scenarios. Such adventure material is relatively rare, and "pure" adventure books rarer still. The conventional wisdom within the role-playing design field is that *Call of Cthulhu* is the only role-playing game aside from *Dungeons & Dragons* (the overwhelmingly most popular role-playing rules set) that can support a continuous stream of profitable adventures.

Like most conventional wisdom, this is not quite accurate. For example, White Wolf Publishing reliably produces one or two "chronicle" books a year designed for the various games using their Storyteller system (the second-most-popular role-playing rules set), and Palladium has four adventure books currently in print supporting *RIFTS* (the third-most-popular role-playing game rules set). However, for a relatively small company, Chaosium has a large adventure

4.1) Cover of the Sixth Edition *Call of Cthulhu* core rulebook. (Chaosium)

book "footprint." Eleven of twenty-one *Call of Cthulhu* supplements currently in print from Chaosium are adventure books; six of the others include adventures, a much larger ratio than more prolific companies such as White Wolf, despite a smaller player base.[1] Further, *Call of Cthulhu* adventures have won five Origins Awards for Best Roleplaying Game Adventure,[2] and three *Call of Cthulhu* sourcebooks with strong adventure content have won the Origins Award for Best Roleplaying Game Sourcebook.[3]

Two other *Call of Cthulhu* campaigns have won the Games

1. There is no current reliable player base data, but White Wolf game book sales, for example, are typically five to ten times those of Chaosium. According to a 1999 marketing study conducted by Wizards of the Coast, the publishers of *Dungeons & Dragons*, 8% of tabletop role-players played *Call of Cthulhu* at least once a month, compared with 40% for Storyteller system games (*Vampire: the Masquerade* and *Werewolf: the Apocalypse*) and 66% for *Dungeons & Dragons* (Dancey 2000). Dancey's study, and his summary of its results, have drawn criticism from many corners of the RPG industry and fan base on methodological and ideological grounds, but no better data has yet been released.

2. *The Great Old Ones* (1990), *Horror on the Orient Express* (1991), *Complete Masks of Nyarlathotep* (1996), *Beyond the Mountains of Madness* (1999), and *Unseen Masters* (2001).

3. *Cthulhu by Gaslight* (1987), *Delta Green* (1997), and *Delta Green: Countdown* (1999).

4.2) Cover of Sandy Petersen's *Shadows of Yog-Sothoth*. (Chaosium)

Day Award for Best Adventure.[4]

Aside from artistic merit, one key factor in both the marketability and the usability of *Call of Cthulhu* adventures (like *Dungeons & Dragons* adventures) is their high degree of standardization. Just as standard *Dungeons & Dragons* adventures present a geographically constricted series of gladiatorial contests in the typical dungeon adventure, standard *Call of Cthulhu* adventures present a dramatically constricted series of horrific discoveries in a mystery story plot. This pattern holds both in individual adventures and linked campaign series.

The key factor allowing this standardization in both *Dungeons & Dragons* and *Call of Cthulhu* is the assumption of a common motive for all potential player characters. All *Dungeons & Dragons* characters, regardless of species, alignment, or adventuring specialty, can be assumed (at least

by a publisher of *Dungeons & Dragons* adventures) to want to kill monsters and take their treasure as a means of increasing their own personal power. All *Call of Cthulhu* Investigators (player characters), likewise, can be assumed to be actively investigating, which is to say seeking out (or at least not actively avoiding) occult mysteries to solve as a means of defeating (or at least stalling) servants of the evil alien god Cthulhu or similar monstrosities.

The *Call of Cthulhu* rulebook has consistently affirmed this assumption. On the first text page of the first edition of *Call of Cthulhu* (1981), under the "Purpose of the Game" we read:

> Players in *Call of Cthulhu* will take the part of intrepid Investigators of the unknown, attempting to ferret out, understand, and occasionally destroy the horrors, mysteries, and secrets of the Cthulhu Mythos. (*Call of Cthulhu* 1981, 4)

Several pages later, under "Working for a Living":

> Characters need to have some reason for investigating the Cthulhu Mythos, and this may be provided by their occupation. (Ibid., 8)

In the "Keeper's Lore" ("Keeper" is the *Call of Cthulhu* term for Game Master) section further on, the would-be Keeper is advised:

> Your player should always have a motive to investigate a particular scenario. Perhaps it is tied into an old family secret of his? If he is a journalist, your problem is solved: the journal employing him simply sends him to investigate the story! (Ibid., 72)

Over twenty years later, the sixth edition (2004) of the rulebook reiterates similar assumptions:

> [Players] take the part of characters who attempt to solve some mystery or resolve some situation. (The rules call these characters "investigators" because that is what they do, not because they are professional investigators—player characters can have all kinds of occupations.) . . . The game is an evolving interaction between players (in the guise of characters unraveling a

4. *Shadows of Yog-Sothoth* (1982) and *Spawn of Azathoth* (1987).

mystery) and the keeper, who presents the world in which the mystery occurs. (*Call of Cthulhu* 2004, 24–25)

Both the first and sixth editions of the *Call of Cthulhu* rulebook offer nearly identical specific structural advice on constructing such a horror mystery story. From the first edition:

> Each scenario in *Call of Cthulhu* should be organized like the layers of an onion. As the characters uncover one layer, they should discover another. These layers should go on and on until the players themselves decide they are getting too deep and stop their investigations. On the surface, the scenario should look like it is no more than a conventional "haunted house," mystic cult, or even a hoax. As the players delve deeper in the mystery, hints and notes should be given showing the greater significance of this particular haunted house in the scheme of things. (*Call of Cthulhu* 1981, 71)

From the sixth edition:

> A scenario in *Call of Cthulhu* can be organized like the layers of an onion. On the surface, suppose that the scenario looks like it's about a conventional haunted house. It might even look like a hoax. As the investigators penetrate the first layer, they should discover another beneath. These layers might go on and on, until the investigators themselves decide they are getting too deep and stop their investigations. As the investigators delve more deeply into the mystery, hints and notes should situate the haunted house in some greater scheme. (*Call of Cthulhu* 2004, 135)[5]

The sixth edition also provides a sidebar with step-by-step guidelines for "Building a Scenario":

> Since most *Cthulhu* adventures are mysteries whose solutions lead to understanding, their structures are progressive and problem-solving, and in outline are much more alike than different. . . .
>
> 1) A mystery or crisis is posed. . .

2) The investigators become linked to the problem. . .

3) The investigators attempt to define the mystery. . .

4) The investigators use the clues and evidence to confront the danger. . .

5) The mystery or problem is solved. (Ibid., 136)

In *The Philosophy of Horror,* Noël Carroll (1990) not only notes a similar commonality between horror story plots and detective story plots but provides a very similar schema of horror plot structure—what Carroll calls the "complex discovery plot." Carroll provides four stages rather than five: "onset, discovery, confirmation, and confrontation," which map almost perfectly onto the first four steps from the *Call of Cthulhu* rulebook above (Carroll 1990, 99). (The fifth step, "resolution," is more essential to a role-playing game featuring continuing characters, than it is to horror stories in

4.3) Cover of Bruce Ballon's *Unseen Masters*. (Chaosium)

---

5. The sixth edition version is slightly less proscriptive than the first, substituting "can" for "should," and being headlined "An Example of A Plot" rather than the sterner "How to Set Up a Scenario" from the first edition.

general.) This understanding of horror narrative, then, is not unique to role-playing games or to *Call of Cthulhu*.[6]

The *Call of Cthulhu* rulebook, which bylines itself as "horror role-playing in the worlds of H. P. Lovecraft (*Call of Cthulhu* 2004, 3),"[7] represents horror mysteries, therefore, as paradigmatic of *Call of Cthulhu* adventures. It strongly implies that such narrative structures are likewise paradigmatic of the corpus of H. P. Lovecraft stories on which the game is based. As an example of such a horror mystery story, both the first and sixth editions of the *Call of Cthulhu* rulebook adduce H. P. Lovecraft's novel, *The Case of Charles Dexter Ward*, in nearly identical language (*Call of Cthulhu* 1981, 71; *Call of Cthulhu* 2004, 135).

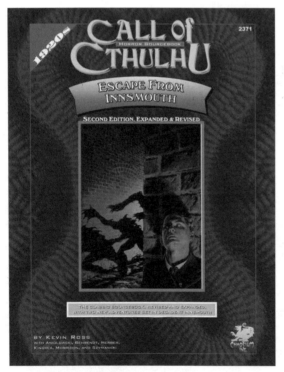

4.4) Cover of *Escape From Innsmouth*, which contains Keith Herber's "The Raid on Innsmouth." (Chaosium)

Prominent Lovecraft scholar S. T. Joshi concurs, calling *Ward* "the greatest supernatural detective story ever written," further noting that "the whole style and construction of the novel is that of a detective tale" (Joshi 1990, 195). Other Lovecraft stories likewise follow the general horror-mystery outlines of the complex discovery plot and the "Building a Scenario" sidebar. "The Shunned House," "The Dunwich Horror," "The Thing on the Doorstep," "The Lurking Fear," "The Horror at Red Hook," and "The Dreams in the Witch-House" can all be understood as horror mysteries, complete with the successful resolution of the monstrosity at the end, though often not without cost to the viewpoint characters. Charles Dexter Ward, for example, does not survive the novel, although the evil wizard who kills him is defeated.

Another set of Lovecraft stories, however, derive their power primarily from the *unsuccessful* resolution of the horror, despite the horrifyingly successful solution of the mystery. These include "The Rats in the Walls," "The Whisperer in Darkness," "Pickman's Model," "The Shadow Out of Time," *At the Mountains of Madness*, "The Shadow Over Innsmouth," "The Haunter of the Dark," and ironically "The Call of Cthulhu" itself. In all these narratives, the horrors survive, completely destroy the narrator, or both. Still another group of Lovecraft stories diverges further still from the horror mystery model, more closely matching what Carroll calls the "overreacher" plot structure (Carroll 1990, 118). In such stories as "The Statement of Randolph Carter," "From Beyond," "Imprisoned With the Pharaohs," and "Herbert West: Re-Animator," the quest for forbidden knowledge by an overreaching main character boomerangs horribly. There is some overlap; for example, "The Dreams in the Witch-House" can also be read as an overreacher plot, and Carroll reads "The Dunwich Horror" as a combination of the overreacher plot (about the evil sorcerer, Whateley) and the discovery plot (about the good scholar Dr. Armitage) (Ibid., 124). Similarly, a horror mystery that uncovers too much, such as *At the Mountains of Madness*, can also be read

---

6. This understanding of adventure construction is, however, not universal within role-playing, or even horror role-playing. For example, *Vampire: The Requiem* announces as its intention that the Storyteller "build chronicles that explore morality through the metaphor of vampirism," (*Vampire: The Requiem*, 14) emphasizing "Theme and Mood" (Ibid., 16) rather than plot in this introductory section. The discussion of "Plots" comes ten pages into the "Storytelling" chapter (Ibid., 208), well after "Characters," "Setting," "Xenophobia," and finally "Themes" (again). For further discussion of adventure construction in horror role-playing, see *Nightmares of Mine* (Hite 1999).

7. On page 1 of the first edition rulebook, the byline reads: "Fantasy role-playing in the worlds of H. P. Lovecraft."

as an overreacher story, in which the act of investigating the mystery is itself an overreaching act.

Although no published *Call of Cthulhu* scenario of which I am aware casts the players overtly as overreaching madmen,[8] the rules work to slowly enforce such a fate on all Investigators in a kind of metanarrative encompassing the entire course of the character's existence. According to the rules of *Call of Cthulhu*, learning more about the "Cthulhu Mythos" (whether by reading books, seeing monsters, or casting spells) costs Investigators their Sanity, which lowers permanently as their Cthulhu Mythos knowledge scores increase (*Call of Cthulhu* 2004, 40, 67, 75–76). Thus, every Investigator by definition becomes an overreacher, doomed to the same fate as the hapless narrators of "The Call of Cthulhu" or *At the Mountains of Madness*. As Sandy Petersen, the game's designer, writes: "The whole concept of Sanity permeates the game and makes it what it is." Although some concessions to playability demanded a mechanism to regain Sanity temporarily, "the tendency is still definitely towards Sanity loss rather than gain" (Petersen 1982, 8–13).[9]

That said, individual published *Call of Cthulhu* adventures more consistently follow the complex discovery plot structure than Lovecraft's stories do. However, many adventures manage to present overreachers as key elements (usually villains) of the mystery, in much the same way that Lovecraft combined the two forms in "The Dunwich Horror." An early version of this pattern appears in "Shadows Over Hollywood," a short adventure included in the first edition rulebook (in which the overreaching cult of Santa Maria de la Sombra Segunda wiped itself out before the adventure begins) (*Call of Cthulhu* 1981, 91–92). The first clear example of what we might call the "investigating the overreacher" plot in a published adventure appears in "The Asylum" (1983). Further examples include "The Curse of Chaugnar Faugn" (1984) and the culmination of the form, perhaps, in 1990 with *At Your Door*, which enmeshes hapless Investigators in a duel between two rival overreachers. Pagan Publishing's *Delta*

4.5) Cover of *Delta Green*. (Pagan Publishing)

Green (1997)[10] presented a conspiracy of overreachers (Majestic-12) as the Investigators' standard foes, and derived much of its uncanny frisson from the strong implication that the Investigators' parent agency, the titular Delta Green conspiracy, was likewise caught in an overreaching spiral. The Delta Green campaign frame (or "narrative structure," as John Tynes refers to it) (*Delta Green*, 4) thus manages to dramatically square the circle of complex discovery, overreaching, and noble doom for Investigators' personal narratives while inexorably linking them into the materialist maltheism of the Cthulhu Mythos.

Chaosium adventure writers also explored the boundaries of the role-playing adventure form. The horror mystery, as noted before, is dramatically constrained: the characters

---

8. At least two Pagan Publishing scenarios follow discovery plot structures, in which the characters are (unbeknownst to themselves) overreaching madmen. The two are *Devil's Children* (1993) and "In Media Res" (1993). Both began as convention scenarios; see note 17.

9. The quote on Sanity appears on page 11. A similar discussion of the inevitable doom of all Investigators appears in "Preparing for the End," on page 143 of *Call of Cthulhu* (2004).

10. The Delta Green conspiracy first appeared in "Convergence" (1993), in Pagan Publishing's magazine *The Unspeakable Oath*.

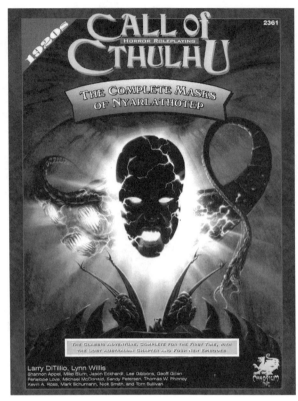

4.6) Cover of Larry DiTillio and Lynn Willis's *Masks of Nyarlathotep*. (Chaosium)

must discover the horror, uncover clues to the horror, confront the horror, and defeat the horror, in that order. The easiest way to structure such a story is to present clues that each lead to the next clue, like bread crumbs on a trail or beads-on-a-string. Some adventures experimented, instead, with the geographical constraint common to *Dungeons & Dragons* adventures. All that is necessary in those adventures is for the Investigators to enter the crypt, or haunted house, or ghoul warren; the act of confronting the individual horrors in each room or chamber—the order being unimportant—serves as sufficient clue fodder for the final confrontation. Such "dungeon crawl" design is clearly evident in "Black Devil Mountain" (1983), "The Haunted House" (1984), "Thoth's Dagger" (1984), "The City Without a Name" (1984), and in *Mansions of Madness* (1990), a

collection of haunted house adventures.

Going another direction, some writers crafted "gauntlet" scenarios in which the characters can do nothing except witness unimaginable horror, and hope to survive to tell the tale. Since these narratives lack much of a role for players, they tend to be embedded in larger campaigns. Examples include "The Rise of R'lyeh" in *Shadows of Yog-Sothoth* (1982), the Xura sections of "The Land of Lost Dreams" (1986), and "In a City of Bells and Towers" in *Horror on the Orient Express* (1991).[11] The closest to a paradigmatic example of this form is perhaps "The People of the Monolith" (1982),[12] closely based on a story by Robert E. Howard in which the uncharacteristically passive narrator falls asleep beneath a Hungarian monolith and dreams of an eldritch ceremony.

No discussion of narrative structure in *Call of Cthulhu* adventures is complete without mention of Larry diTillio's *Masks of Nyarlathotep* (1984) and Keith Herber's "The Raid on Innsmouth" (1992). Although like other campaigns (for *Call of Cthulhu* and other games), *Masks of Nyarlathotep* presented a linked set of adventures ending in a final confrontation and resolution, it departed radically from the "trail of bread crumbs" convention. Each adventure contained in the campaign leads to all the other adventures; the Investigators could pursue the adventures in any order.

The villains, meanwhile, were working to a specific calendar, with their great ceremony timed (by the designer) to occur after the Investigators completed all the "confirmation stage" adventures and gained the necessary knowledge to (hopefully) foil the plot. Within each adventure, diTillio combined geographical constraint (each adventure takes place in a single city) with open structure; some of the encounters were simple bloodbaths, others were fiendish traps or puzzles, some were "dungeon crawls," and still others were complete red herrings. The players could follow their own investigative instincts through a "target-rich" environment, with the extraordinary deadliness of the settings providing the constraint on player action that ordinarily flows solely from the written plot.

For some reason, despite overwhelming critical praise for this model, Chaosium returned to conventional campaign

11. This adventure originally appeared in *Dagon* 22/23 (1988): 47–54.

12. The original Robert E. Howard story is "The Black Stone."

structures thereafter, even going so far as to tweak critics of such "railroaded" campaigns by setting *Horror on the Orient Express* (1991) on a literal railroad. That year, designer Keith Herber plotted the wildly radical structure of "The Raid on Innsmouth." This adventure is divided into six mini-scenarios called "objectives." Each Investigator is assigned to one objective; during the other objectives, his player takes the role of an expendable cannon-fodder character. As the objectives rotate through their arc, the whole story of the raid is revealed to the players, though never to any one character. "The Raid on Innsmouth" is easily the most formally ambitious adventure ever published by Chaosium, and perhaps by any game company.[13] Like *Masks of Nyarlathotep*, it became an exemplar, but not a model, of the *Call of Cthulhu* adventure form.

Lovecraft's major influence on horror writing was thematic and mythic, rather than formal. The discovery plot (like the detective story) goes back to Poe, and the overreacher plot might well be called "the Frankenstein plot" after its most famous example. Although Lovecraft produced masterful versions of both, he did not create a new form. Lovecraft's great innovations in the genre were the "Copernican revolution" of scientific horror (in which the supernatural becomes, rather, the alien) (Leiber 1980) and his creation of the maltheistic mythology of Cthulhu and Yog-Sothoth and so forth, the "Cthulhu Mythos," as a single horrific backdrop that extends through all time and space (Joshi 1990, 190-193).[14] In addition to the larger concept of an "anti-mythology," many of Lovecraft's contemporaries and successors adopted the specific deities, grimoires, and so forth of the Cthulhu Mythos for their own fiction, often divorcing it from Lovecraft's stark scientific materialism in the process. These authors also added their own tomes, monsters, and gods to the Mythos, as have published *Call of Cthulhu* adventures.[15]

Chaosium and its licensees have used the Cthulhu Mythos more consistently than Lovecraft did; only a very few published adventures fail to invoke one or another of the Mythos' portentous magic books or alien pantheons. However, not all published *Call of Cthulhu* materials follow Lovecraft into complete materialism or into complete maltheism. Ghosts, vampires, and werewolves appear in the (non-Mythos) "Beasts & Monsters" section of the *Call of Cthulhu* rulebook (*Call of Cthulhu* 2004, 205, 209-210), and Healing spells appear in the "Mythos Grimoire" (Ibid., 237). Likewise, the plots of some published adventures more closely resemble those of Lovecraft's successors than his own—beginning with the first published *Call of Cthulhu* campaign, *Shadows of Yog-Sothoth*, a globe-trotting chase reminiscent in pace and flavor of August Derleth's linked story-series, *The Trail of Cthulhu*. Some adventures deliberately evoke Lovecraft's successors, of course, such as *Ramsey Campbell's Goatswood* (2001), an adventure collection based on Campbell's contributions to the Cthulhu Mythos.

Less explicitly, *Call of Cthulhu* adventures, like the larger post-Lovecraftian horror fiction field, have been exploring not just other facets of the Cthulhu Mythos but other facets of, and approaches to, horror. Keith Herber's portrait of a town far gone in decay in *Return to Dunwich* (1991) builds not on Ramsey Campbell's Cthulhu Mythos stories but on Campbell's bleak vision of social despair in such novels as *The Face That Must Die* (and perhaps on Stephen King's blue-collar New England horror). Clive Barker's emphasis on the physicality of horror is reflected in the themes of body modification (explicit sexuality remaining taboo in a product intended for sale to minors in the United States) and cannibalism emphasized in campaigns like *At Your Door* (1990) and *The Realm of Shadows* (1997).

Psychological, internalized horror fiction of the sort revitalized by Robert Bloch's novel *Psycho* and Thomas

---

13. The role-playing game *Ars Magica* (1988) is built on such "troupe-style" structure within campaigns—players take turns playing dominant Magi, as opposed to cannon-fodder Grogs or sidekick Consors, for each adventure—but no single published adventure that I know of expects players to rotate roles throughout. I do not know whether Herber was familiar with *Ars Magica* when he designed "The Raid on Innsmouth."

14. Lovecraft adapted the concept of a mythical pantheon from Lord Dunsany, but transposing imaginary deities to the modern world, and portraying them as unvaryingly dangerous, inimical, or malevolent, was his contribution.

15. The Cthulhu Mythos has infiltrated the works of such authors as Robert Bloch, Ramsey Campbell, August Derleth (who coined the phrase "Cthulhu Mythos"), Neil Gaiman, Robert E. Howard, Stephen King, and Colin Wilson. See Jarocha-Ernst (1999), or Harms (1998).

Harris's Hannibal Lecter series has steadily informed *Call of Cthulhu*'s treatment of insanity, culminating with Bruce Ballon's *Unseen Masters* (2001), which introduced the "unreliable narrator" to *Call of Cthulhu* adventure design and received the 2001 Mary Seeman Award for Outstanding Achievement in the Area of Psychiatry and the Humanities from the Psychology Department of the University of Toronto. Ballon also explicitly credits the works of M. R. James, Philip K. Dick, Umberto Eco, and "the child-demon films I watched in my youth" as influences on this campaign (*Unseen Masters*, 81, 127). Even more explicitly, "In a City of Bells and Towers" (1991) attempts to adapt the surreal, dreamlike horror of Thomas Ligotti[16] to a *Call of Cthulhu* adventure, setting the adventure (a nightmare sent to the Investigators) within a strange, Expressionist vision of the city of Zagreb. The scenario goes so far as to include Ligotti's short story, "The Journal of J. P. Drapeau," as a player handout. In short, the degree and diversity of thematic and mythic exploration in published *Call of Cthulhu* adventures over the last twenty-five years mirrors that of the horror fiction genre since Lovecraft's "Copernican Revolution" in horror.

It is difficult to assess whether styles of play have likewise changed since 1981, but personal experience and anecdotal evidence would tend to indicate otherwise. Gaming groups do not tend to adopt "Raid on Innsmouth"-style multiple-character play for *Call of Cthulhu* despite (or perhaps because of) the timid exhortation of the rulebook concerning the utility of multiple characters (*Call of Cthulhu* 2004, 28–29). Even scenarios designed to be run at gaming conventions, while allowing for wildly variant character groups or settings

(since they need not support an ongoing campaign) seldom tamper with the established "horror mystery" narrative structure, although they may compress it to fit in a four-hour time slot.[17] Although individual gaming groups may vary their styles, several factors likely tend to standardize and stabilize play styles across the *Call of Cthulhu* player population at large.

The first is the rapid turnover in the role-playing hobby as a whole. Role-playing gamers traditionally enter the hobby around ages 12 or 13, before high school. They play until age 16 (dropping out with the availability of a car, and the concomitant expansion of available competing activities), re-enter the hobby in college (when mobility and choice are artificially constrained again) and drift out of it after graduation, marriage, childbirth, or other life changes.[18] By this understanding, a typical gaming group lasts only four years at the most; even if the gamers in it play *Call of Cthulhu* for the entire length of their involvement in the hobby (unlikely), the traditional game structure will not pall.[19]

Another is Chaosium's institutional conservatism. The *Call of Cthulhu* rulebook, despite having gone through six editions (and numerous sub-editions) since 1981, has changed very little. The core game mechanics, institutional guidelines, and even much of the rulebook text have remained constant (and robust) throughout. Lynn Willis, who wrote portions of the insanity rules in 1981, has directed *Call of Cthulhu*'s development as editor in chief since 1993, and contributed to virtually every *Call of Cthulhu* product. Charlie Krank, the product developer and layout artist of the sixth edition rulebook, playtested the first edition rules. No other role-playing game line can make a similar claim to longevity and

---

16. For Ligotti's style and contributions to horror, see Joshi (2001).

17. One example of radical adventure design in convention gaming is John Tynes's "In Media Res," which contains no conventional Cthulhu Mythos elements, and centers on player characters with no memory who have apparently just escaped from an asylum for the criminally insane. I have seen in various convention program books occasional notices of games in which the players take the role of Cthulhu cultists; I cannot say whether the adventure plot structure remained conventional, although I would tend to guess so. See also the discussion of "Tournament Games" in *Call of Cthulhu* (2004, 146–147).

18. Again, this data is largely anecdotal, but Dancey (2000) supports them.

19. My own experience as a *Call of Cthulhu* Keeper may serve as an example. I have run *Call of Cthulhu* repeatedly since 1981, both as standard campaigns (1981–1988, 1997–1999, 2000-2002) and convention games (1989-1996). Despite my atypical background as a professional role-playing game designer, and my increasing tendency in other game systems to run character-driven dramatically open narratives, my *Call of Cthulhu* play has remained (with few exceptions in individual scenarios, including my second convention scenario, which was a pure "chase sequence") ruthlessly formally traditional throughout. From 1981 to 1988, especially, I primarily ran published adventures.

continuity in design staff. Further, Chaosium regularly reprints and repackages older adventures for new audiences. Eight of the eleven adventure books currently in print from Chaosium are reprints, including a reissue of the very first *Call of Cthulhu* campaign, *Shadows of Yog-Sothoth*. Two adventures from the original rulebook, "The Haunted House"[20] and "The Madman," are still in the sixth edition rulebook (*Call of Cthulhu* 1981, 74–77; *Call of Cthulhu* 2004, 250–255,[21] and 265–269).

Still another is the leveling influence of a common, unchanging, and relatively narrow set of ur-texts— Lovecraft's Cthulhu Mythos stories—upon which to base adventure games. Although *Call of Cthulhu* players may encounter Lovecraft by way of Stephen King or other modern writers, or "jump off" from Lovecraft into later (or earlier) horror fiction, the rulebook encourages a natural centripetal tendency to concentrate on Lovecraft's works as the core and model of *Call of Cthulhu* adventures (*Call of Cthulhu* 2004, 135). Chaosium further reinforces this tendency by publishing adventures that are pure remakes of, or sequels to, Lovecraft's stories, such as "Escape from Innsmouth" (1992), "Return to Dunwich" (1991), and *Beyond the Mountains of Madness* (1999). The nature of Lovecraft's work also cements this tendency. Lovecraft's fiction, of course, was written primarily for pulp magazine audiences, with a concomitantly strong appeal to adolescent males, who today make up the core role-playing gamer demographic.[22] The gamer's discoveries of role-playing and of Lovecraft quite likely often happen at the same age, which buttresses Lovecraft's already towering status as narrative scripture to *Call of Cthulhu* Keepers.

Thus, the standardized form of *Call of Cthulhu* adventures born in part of commercial necessity is identified with Lovecraft's narrative structure, which is then invoked (by players perhaps more than adventure designers) to justify standardizing play styles. The words of the *Call of Cthulhu* rulebook and the publishing choices of Chaosium reinforce all these tendencies, and have done so consistently since 1981. The result is a game in

constant creative tension between adventure narrative and larger character narrative, and between standard adventure narrative structure and trends in both role-playing game design and horror fiction at large. Given the longevity and artistic success enjoyed by Chaosium and by *Call of Cthulhu*, it would seem to be a productive tension.

References: Literature

Carroll, Noël (1990). *The Philosophy of Horror*. London: Routledge.

Dancey, Ryan S. (2000). "Adventure Game Industry Market Research Summary." <http://www.rpg.net/news+reviews/wotcdemo.html>.

Harms, Daniel (1998). *The Encyclopedia Cthulhiana* (2nd edition). Oakland, CA: Chaosium.

Hite, Kenneth (1999). *Nightmares of Mine*. Charlottesville, VA: Iron Crown Enterprises.

Jarocha-Ernst, Chris (1999). *A Cthulhu Mythos Bibliography & Concordance*. Seattle, WA: Armitage House.

Joshi, S. T. (1990). *The Weird Tale*. Austin, TX: University of Texas Press.

Joshi, S. T. (2001). *The Modern Weird Tale*. Jefferson, NC: McFarland.

Leiber, Fritz Jr. (1980). "A Literary Copernicus." In *H. P. Lovecraft: Four Decades of Criticism*, edited by S. T. Joshi. Athens, OH: Ohio University Press.

Petersen, Sandy (1982). "*Call of Cthulhu* Designer's Notes." *Different Worlds* 19 (1982): 8–13.

References: Games

Ars Magica. Jonathan Tweet and Mark Rein-Hagen; Lion Rampant. 1988.

"The Asylum." In *The Asylum & Other Tales*. Randy McCall, Sandy Petersen (editor); Chaosium. 1983.

At Your Door. L.N. Isinwyll, Mark Morrison, Barbara Manui, Chris Adams, Scott D. Aniolowski, and Herbert Hike; Chaosium. 1990.

Beyond the Mountains of Madness. Charles Engan and Janyce Engan; Chaosium. 1999.

"Black Devil Mountain." In *The Asylum & Other Tales*. David A. Hargrave and Sandy Petersen (editors); Chaosium. 1983.

Call of Cthulhu (1st edition). Sandy Petersen; Chaosium. 1981.

Call of Cthulhu (6th edition). Sandy Petersen and Lynn Willis; Chaosium. 2004.

"The City Without a Name." In *Curse of the Chthonians*. William Hamblin; Chaosium. 1984.

Complete Masks of Nyarlathotep. Larry DiTillio and Lynn Willis; Chaosium. 1996.

20. Not Keith Herber's scenario, described elsewhere in this volume, but the mini-adventure found in the *CoC* rulebook throughout its editions.

21. In the sixth-edition rulebook, the scenario is retitled "The Haunting."

22. Per Dancey (2000), 19% of role-playing gamers are female.

"Convergence." In *The Unspeakable Oath* 7 (1992): 58-77. John Tynes; Pagan Publishing. 1992.

Cthulhu by Gaslight. William A. Barton; Chaosium. 1987.

"The Curse of Chaugnar Faugn." In *Curse of the Chthonians*. William A. Barton and Sandy Petersen (editors); Chaosium. 1984.

Delta Green. Dennis Detwiller, Adam Scott Glancy, and John Tynes; Pagan Publishing. 1997.

Delta Green: Countdown. Dennis Detwiller, Adam Scott Glancy, and John Tynes; Pagan Publishing. 1999.

Devil's Children. David Conyers, David Godley, and David Witteeven; Pagan Publishing. 1993.

The Great Old Ones. Marcus L. Rowland, Kevin A. Ross, Harry Cleaver, Doug Lyons, and L. N. Isinwyll; Chaosium. 1990.

"Escape From Innsmouth." In *Escape From Innsmouth*. Kevin Ross; Chaosium. 1992.

"The Haunted House." In *The Trail of Tsathoggua*. Keith Herber; Chaosium. 1984.

Horror on the Orient Express. Geoff Gillan, Mark Morrison, Nick Hagger, Bernard Caleo, Penelope Love, Russell Waters, Marion Anderson, Phil Anderson, Richard Watts, Peter F. Jeffery, Christian Lehmann, L. N. Isinwyll, and Thomas Ligotti; Chaosium. 1991.

"In a City of Bells and Towers." In *Horror on the Orient Express*. Mark Morrison; Chaosium. 1991. Original appearance in *Dagon* 22/23 (1988): 47–54.

"In Media Res." In *The Unspeakable Oath* 10 (1993). John Tynes; Pagan Publishing. 1993.

"The Land of Lost Dreams." In *H.P. Lovecraft's Dreamlands*. Mark Morrison and Sandy Petersen (editors); Chaosium. 1986.

Mansions of Madness. Fred Behrendt, Michael DeWolfe, Keith Herber, Wesley Martin, and Mark Morrison; Chaosium. 1990.

Masks of Nyarlathotep. Larry diTillio; Chaosium. 1984.

"The People of the Monolith." In *Shadows of Yog-Sothoth*. Ted Shelton; Chaosium. 1982.

"The Raid on Innsmouth." In *Escape From Innsmouth*. Keith Herber et al.; Chaosium. 1992.

Ramsey Campbell's Goatswood and Less Pleasant Places. Scott David Aniolowski, Gary Sumpter, Richard Watts, J. Todd Kingrea, Clifton Ganyard, Rob Malkovich, Steve Spisak, Mike Mason, and David Mitchell; Chaosium. 2001.

Realm of Shadows. John H. Crowe III; Pagan Publishing. 1997.

Return to Dunwich. Keith Herber; Chaosium. 1991.

"The Rise of R'lyeh." In *Shadows of Yog-Sothoth*. Sandy Petersen; Chaosium. 1982.

Shadows of Yog-Sothoth. John Carnahan, John Scott Clegg, Ed Gore, Marc Hutchison, Randy McCall, and Sandy Petersen; Chaosium. 1982.

Spawn of Azathoth. Keith Herber; Chaosium. 1987.

"Thoth's Dagger." In *Curse of the Chthonians*. William Hamblin; Chaosium. 1984.

Unseen Masters. Bruce Ballon; Chaosium. 2001.

Vampire: The Requiem. Justin Achilli, Ari Marmell, Dean Shomshak and C. A. Suleiman; White Wolf Publishing. 2004.

On "The Haunted House"
Keith Herber

The original *Call of Cthulhu* "Haunted House" scenario that appeared in the book *Trail of Tsathoggua* was written in 1983, when *Call of Cthulhu* was still a relatively new game and role-playing was still in its early stages. Seeing the light of day in 1981, *Call of Cthulhu* was unique to RPGs in that it didn't rely on experience points, treasure, or other tangible rewards to induce players to participate. *CoC* investigators would not find hordes of gold or powerful weapons, nor would they gain fame or respect for their daring exploits. Quite the opposite, in fact. Investigators usually finish adventures in worse shape than they began, with less money, less sanity, and possibly a lowered social standing. Like cats, investigators are driven by curiosity, not by material gain.

One of the concepts of "The Haunted House" was to expand upon the original Haunted House mini-adventure that has been included as part of the rules package since the game's first printing. This one small scenario has done more to draw role-players to *Call of Cthulhu* than anything ever published for *CoC*, and I had the desire to exploit the concept to the max. By moving the idea to a very large house (a mansion typical of the Hollywood haunted house movie) every conceivable detail could be provided. Most *CoC* scenarios take place in towns, or open woods, or across several different locations. By necessity, not everything can be detailed, leaving it to the Keeper to be fast on his or her feet, and improvise information for curious investigators. "The Haunted House" was completely contained in one location, every room described in detail, every conceivable clue provided, and the scenario even included specific room–by–room suggestions about what the haunt might do to frighten investigators visiting a certain area. Unlike many *CoC* scenarios that tend to unfold of themselves regardless of player actions, the Haunted House is designed so the antagonist responds directly to player actions and little else.

5.1) Cover of *Trail of Tsathoggua,* which contains Keith Herber's "The Haunted House." (Chaosium)

I also wanted to create a scenario that avoided combat as much as possible. Prior to *Call of Cthulhu*, almost all RPGs were combat-oriented, as befitting a hobby with its roots in wargaming. But *CoC* offered something different, and the insidious Sanity rules were at the heart of that experience. Not only do investigators run the risk of being torn limb from limb, eviscerated, or swallowed whole, but may lose their minds as well. The whole underpinning of the game depends on the threat to one's sanity, one's sense of well–being and security.

While earlier games had invoked various saving throw rules to simulate fear or terror in a character, they were never very effective:

Gamemaster: "You open the door and see something awful. Make your Fear saving throw."

Player: "I rolled a sixteen. I needed a fourteen or less."

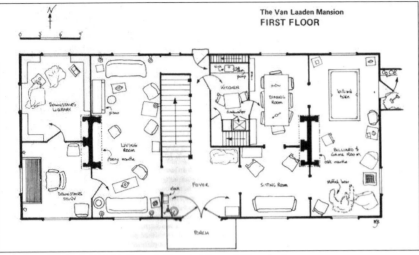

5.2) First Floor map of Keith Herber's "Haunted House." (Chaosium)

> *Gamemaster:* "You're so horrified by what you see, you can't act."
>
> *Player:* "Oh, okay."

The Sanity rules of *Call of Cthulhu*, on the other hand, manage to reflect the deteriorating sanity of many of the protagonists of the stories on which the game is based. Continued exploration of the Mythos tends to lower a player's SAN rating, making it continually harder to maintain one's sanity, leading to greater SAN losses, which it turn makes it harder to maintain control in the next sanity-threatening situation, and so on. It actually has a rather unsettling way of replicating real-life emotional problems and the way they feed upon themselves. It's possibly the most effective and realistic set of rules ever created for a role-playing game. A player creeping around any *CoC* scenario who has a current SAN rating of 33 (or possibly less) is usually ready to jump out of his skin at the first sign of anything unusual. He knows he's teetering on the brink of madness, and even a small shock may send him over the edge, leaving him permanently insane.

I wanted a scenario that threatened to drive investigators mad, rather than simply tearing them to pieces. I also wanted to see if I could create a scenario so difficult to unravel that most investigating parties would eventually give up and leave without solving the mystery, without destroying the haunt that inhabited the house. I wanted an adventure that would leave players with stories to tell. Best of all, it utilized the moral ambiguity inherent to Lovecraft and *CoC*. The haunt isn't really bothering anyone—save the rich man who inherited the house. The investigators—who generally assume themselves to be "good"— are actually there to evict the supernatural tenant and will be paid money for destroying a creature who is actually bothering almost no one.

As a personal RPG philosophy, I believe that most players want to relive adventures and stories of the type they've read in books, or seen in movies or on television. Consequently, I've always made heavy use of established dramatic clichés, either presented

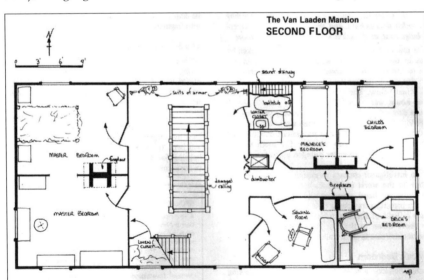

5.3) Second Floor map of Keith Herber's "Haunted House." (Chaosium)

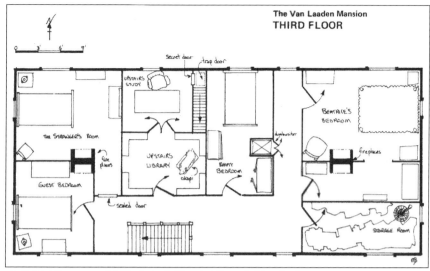

The Van Laaden Mansion
THIRD FLOOR

5.4) Third Floor map of Keith Herber's "Haunted House." (Chaosium)

an uncommon amount of restraint, or run the risk of destroying the entire party on first encounter.

The haunt is far less dangerous than most Mythos creatures, and this allows the Keeper to settle into the scenario and actually play against the investigators on a more-or-less even playing field, utilizing the haunt's resources to frustrate and terrify them, rather than simply destroying them. Although the haunt has a wide variety of powers to use against the investigators, they drain the creature's power, which then must regenerate over a period of time. This requires the Keeper to refrain from simply hurling everything at the investigators at once. The most powerful effects not only drain the haunt completely, leaving it temporarily defenseless, but can also threaten the haunt's own existence and so must be used with care.

The adventure abounds with red herrings. I included every possible haunted house cliché I could think of, most intended to lead the investigators down fruitless paths. There are numerous clues that point to the actual haunt, but the haunt is totally atypical, and the solution to the haunting doesn't offer itself on a silver platter. Players generally keep coming back to one particular set of intriguing clues, but often don't follow up on them as they get distracted by other red herrings that promise more straightforward solutions.

It's a relatively benign scenario, intended to drive you mad, not kill you. In the several times I ran the adventure, no investigators were killed, nor were any driven permanently insane. At the same time, no one ever solved the adventure, or even came very close to a solution. All retired from the scenario, mostly unharmed, with a little less sanity then they began with, but almost all had good stories to tell the next few years.

Reference

"The Haunted House," in *Trail of Tsathoggua*. Keith Herber; Chaosium. 1983.

straightforwardly or turned on their ear. Like any pop culture form of entertainment, you want a mix of the familiar combined with something new. I started the Haunted House design by making a list of all the spooky events I could remember from movies like *Poltergeist, House on Haunted Hill, The Haunting of Hill House*, and every other haunted house movie or story I could remember: flying knives, mysterious cold spots, chairs that rocked without an occupant, and anything else I could thing of. I adapted some whole cloth, while others I reworked to either fit the situation or to put a new twist on them. Then I added ideas of my own. It was only after compiling this initial list that I gave any thought to creating the haunt's powers, and then they were custom-designed to allow the haunt to create the effects I wanted.

The haunt was given powers and abilities that allowed it to terrify the investigators, and even inflict minor wounds, but for the most part kept it from actually killing or maiming anyone. Most of the creatures in the *Call of Cthulhu* world are exceptionally powerful and dangerous, and the Keeper needs be watchful he doesn't overwhelm the players with Sanity losses, or wipe out the entire party in their first encounter. While earlier games followed the example set by *Dungeons & Dragons*, using an intricate rule balance to try to keep the players on a level footing with the challenges, the terrors of the Mythos are so overwhelming and powerful that a Keeper is required to use

On Character Creation in *Everway*
Jonathan Tweet

Everway is a free-form tabletop fantasy RPG in which players take the roles of heroic figures that travel among countless parallel worlds. Action resolution uses cards drawn from a Tarotlike deck rather than dice. Character stats determine the likely outcome of an action, and the card draw provides a conceptual result that the gamemaster interprets creatively to determine the actual result.

Accommodating Free-form Character Creation in *Everway*

When creating a character for *Everway*, the first thing a player does is select from a deck of several trading-card size "vision cards." These cards depict warriors, monsters, temples, magicians, exotic animals, and other fantastic characters, creatures and settings. Each player chooses five cards and invents a character based on them. In general, the cards represent the character and scenes from the character's life, but they can also represent visions, goals, enemies, etc. The challenge in designing *Everway* was helping the gamemaster be ready to accommodate any possible character that players could dream up.

6.1) Two examples of *Everway* fortune cards. (Gaslight Press)

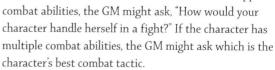

6.2) Two examples of *Everway* vision cards. (Gaslight Press)

Question and Answer

During character creation, players show each other their vision cards and explain who their characters are. Then they take turns asking questions about the other players' characters. This step helps players develop their characters more thoroughly and engages the whole group in each player's story. For the gamemaster, however, it's an opportunity to be sure that the free-form nature of character creation hasn't left the character missing important details. Question and answer is important for:

Engagement: Listening to a player talk about their character is widely recognized as dull. It's like listening to someone recount a dream: it means a lot more to the talker than to the listener. The Q&A process, however, turns the monologue into a dialogue. It makes character exposition much more engaging.

Combat Abilities: Standard RPG characters have their combat abilities finely detailed, but free-form characters can have poorly defined combat capabilities. If the character has no apparent combat abilities, the GM might ask, "How would your character handle herself in a fight?" If the character has multiple combat abilities, the GM might ask which is the character's best combat tactic.

Motivation: Standard RPG characters come with built-in motives, such as "find treasure" or "defeat supervillains." Free-form characters, however, are sometimes conceived as unlikely to get involved in the plots that are going to drive the campaign. In such a case, the gamemaster can ask, "What sort of circumstances would motivate your character to get involved in trouble or danger?"

Personality Traits

Everway has four "personality" traits to ensure that the free-form character has direction:

Motive: A common flaw in free-form character concepts is that the character has no motivation. The player, in order to play "in character," avoids conflicts, and a character that avoids conflicts is boring. In *Everway*, each player chooses a motivation so that each character has some reason to get involved in the conflicts that are going to make the campaign interesting.

Virtue, Fault, and Fate: Each player chooses three cards from the Fortune deck to represent a personal strength, a personal weakness, and some personal conflict to be resolved. This step helps the player take the broad character concept and sum it up. This step is also a hook for the gamemaster, who uses it to see what is central to each character's personal story.

Character Powers

Everway has no list of special powers from which players choose. The system has to be able to take any power that a player has dreamed up and assign a "value" or "power level" to it, so that it can be balanced in the overall character equation. Powers I've seen in play include prophetic visions, the ability to drain life energy from others, and the posession of the mummified hand of the character's dead lover (a fetish that channels fiery attacks). Each power is rated on whether it's versatile, whether it's potent, and whether it frequently makes a difference in play. For each answer Yes, the power costs 1 point, with a maximum of 3. It's a grainy measure of power level, but it's precise enough for free-form play. The gamemaster takes character powers into account when adjudicating actions, but there is no separate mechanic for using powers.

Reference
Everway. Jonathan Tweet; Wizards of the Coast. 1995.

Storytelling Games as a Creative Medium
Will Hindmarch

White Wolf Publishing's *Vampire: The Requiem* is the boy king of storytelling games, successor to father and founder *Vampire: The Masquerade*. For fifteen years, *Vampire* in its various editions has been one of the most successful paper-based role-playing game properties, second only to the *lingua franca* of the hobby, *Dungeons & Dragons*. *Vampire* is perhaps best known for attracting large numbers of new players to the role-playing game hobby with its dramatic, modern gothic style and emphasis on narrative rather than game mechanics.[1] *Vampire: The Requiem* describes itself as a modern gothic storytelling game in which players "play the monster" and "explore morality through the metaphor of vampirism" (*Vampire: The Requiem*, 14).

But what is a storytelling game? How can gameplay create a story? Superficially, a storytelling game is like a kind of role-playing game, but that description is, at best, insufficient. To identify storytelling games, we have to first understand why their identity is confusing. What makes a storytelling game more than an RPG, and what even makes storytelling a game?

Greg Costikyan, creator of the seminal role-playing game *Paranoia* and a prolific writer on numerous game design topics, has described stories and games as "antitheses" (Costikyan 2000). In his article, "Where Stories End and Games Begin," he supposes that "there's a direct, immediate conflict between the demands of story and the demands of a game." If this is true, how is a storytelling game played?

7.1) Cover of *Vampire: The Masquerade*. (White Wolf Publishing)

The argument against the mingling of stories and games is not new. Ludologists like Costikyan have been fighting against the union of the two for years. In 1994, he wrote:

> Again and again we hear about story; interactive literature; creating a story through role-play. The idea that games have something to do with stories has such a hold on designers' and gamers' imagination that it probably can't be expunged. It deserves at least to be challenged. (Costikyan 1994)

Vampire was only three years old when Costikyan wrote this challenge to the idea that games have "something to do

---

1. Owing to the company's almost sole use of the phrase "storytelling game" in marketing, one might presume that a storytelling game is simply any role-playing game published by White Wolf, but that's not strictly accurate. In the Storytelling System rulebook, "Storytelling System" is claimed as a trademark of White Wolf Publishing, Inc., but "storytelling game" is not (*The World of Darkness*, 10).

Many other pen-and-paper RPGs that could also classify as storytelling games, using our definitions in this article, do not advertise or label themselves as such. In truth, most don't. A whole subset of "independent," small-press RPGs also focus on story over simulation and power advancement, such as *Dogs in the Vineyard* and *My Life With Master*, but these games avoid the storytelling game label, presumably to distance themselves from White Wolf's perceived ownership over the term. In some ways, these small-press RPGs have the same kind of "indie cred" that independent films do in relationship to studio pictures. As with films, it's often only subject matter and financing that truly separate the two. Despite the fact that only White Wolf products are currently labeled as storytelling games, any RPG that shares the same emphasis and reliance on story could be called such.

7.2) Cover of *Vampire: The Requiem*. (White Wolf Publishing)

with stories," but its popularity continued to grow throughout the '90s, as did the popularity of other story-intensive games, such as "interactive movies" utilizing full-motion video and such recognizable properties as *Star Trek* and *The X-Files*. Costikyan's emphatic desire to separate stories from games didn't waver, however. In 2000, the very same language appears in his article "Where Stories End and Games Begin," for *Game Developer* magazine.[2] *Vampire* was in its third edition.

To understand how storytelling games reconcile the theoretically antithetical relationship between their two halves—story and game—we'll challenge Costikyan's supposition that games are not a storytelling medium.

The Self-Image of Storytelling Games

Before we examine the two halves of storytelling games, however, let's look at their history and language. The idea that storytelling games and role-playing games are separate entities was put forth in 1991, in the first edition of *Vampire: The Masquerade*:

> *Vampire* is not only a storytelling game, but a role-playing game as well. You not only tell stories, but you also act through them. Role-playing is a kind of interactive storytelling. (*Vampire: The Masquerade*, 1991, 20)

This definition—fifteen years old, now—is out of date. It suggests that a storytelling game is one in which the players narrate stories, while an RPG is one in which the stories are acted out. Even if that were accurate in 1991, it's not how the games are categorized now. Today, with computer- and console-based RPG players outnumbering pen-and-paper players, the RPG category describes games in which players control individual characters in the game world and develop those characters' traits and abilities over the course of play. The acting or role-playing element isn't even essential to the application of the label today. Additionally, the storytelling involved in most electronic RPGs, such as *Knights of the Old Republic*, is barely interactive, limited to a few decision points. The player controls the development of her character, but not how the story is told. Likewise, although the player is in control of a single character, selecting and advancing his traits and buying him equipment, she is not acting through the story as a feature of the gameplay.

By contrast, in 2004, White Wolf's Storytelling System rulebook states that "Storytelling is a type of role-playing game," implying that storytelling games are a subset of RPGs (*The World of Darkness*, 188).[3] That is certainly true inasmuch as storytelling games are rightly filed on the store shelf with RPGs, but storytelling games don't refine the core ideas of RPG gameplay—they expand on them. A storytelling game is a collaborative narrative game built around an RPG.

2. Strictly speaking, the punctuation changed. But Costikyan continues to challenge the idea even though it "probably can't be expunged"—but, he implies, should be.

3. *The World of Darkness* is the formal title of the Storytelling System rulebook, named for the game world in which *Vampire: The Requiem* and its sister games, *Werewolf: The Forsaken* and *Mage: The Awakening* are set.

Vampire, for example, is an RPG *plus* a storytelling game. It can be (and is often) played solely as an RPG, in which the advancement of a character's supernatural powers is the player's only goal, but that is not the goal stressed by the game itself. As it says in *Vampire: The Requiem*, "It's about stories" (*Vampire: The Requiem*, 198). The RPG element of the game is present because it's entertaining, but also because it's functional:

> The only reason to have rules in a game, especially a storytelling game like *Vampire*, is to more or less level the playing field. The Storyteller can adjudicate most things in her *Vampire* game, deciding on her own whether or not the characters accomplish the actions they attempt. But truly unbiased rulings need some sort of standard or precedent, just so everybody knows that everyone's getting the same treatment. (*Vampire: The Masquerade* 3rd ed., 1998, 190)

Perhaps the most evocative description of *Vampire*'s gameplay dynamic comes from the third edition of *Vampire: The Masquerade* (1998):

> Forget about the pages of rules and the handfuls of dice. Close the book, turn out the lights, and tell a story about dark desires and relentless hunger. I'll tell you about a vampire, about her talents and her weaknesses, and you tell me what kind of challenges she faces, what rewards or perils come her way. You plan the twists and turns the story will take, and I will tell you how the vampire navigates them. Only you know how the story ultimately ends, but only I know how the vampire will arrive there. Along the way, the work you put into the story gives my vampire the chance to grow and develop, and her actions breathe life in the world you have created. (*Vampire: The Masquerade* 3rd ed., 1998, 254)

In the preceding quote, the speaker is a player in the game and "you" are the Storyteller. RPGs customarily discriminate between Storytellers and players, though the Storyteller is actually a player in the game, too. The Storyteller can be

7.3) Cover of the Storyteller System core rulebook *The World of Darkness*. (White Wolf Publishing)

considered a kind of specialized player with responsibilities and authorities inherited from the needs of the game.[4] According to the first edition of *Vampire* (1991):

> One of the players is the Storyteller, who creates and guides the story. The Storyteller describes what happens as a result of what the players say and [their characters] do. It is the Storyteller who decides if the characters succeed or fail, suffer or prosper, live or die.

> The Storyteller's primary duty is to make sure the other players have a good time. The way to do that is to tell a good story. (*Vampire: The Masquerade*, 1991, 20–21)

The power structure at the game table is uneven by design—the Storyteller has more authority and more responsibility

---

4. The term Storyteller is not standard outside of White Wolf games. The most common name for the game's "referee" is Gamemaster (GM), though many games use their own distinctive names as well. *Dungeons & Dragons* uses the familiar, often-maligned, term Dungeon Master, while Decipher's *Star Trek Role-Playing Game* uses the title Narrator. Because the GM's job in every game is to make the game session a success, his duties are necessarily different depending on the goals of the particular game.

7.4) Cover of *VII*, a *Vampire: The Requiem* sourcebook.
(White Wolf Publishing)

than the other players. With that imbalance comes the expectation of a greater reward for many Storytellers. Implicit in that description of the Storyteller's role is an affirmation of his power over the players and over the story.

By the third edition in 1998, the description of the Storyteller's relationship with the players had changed to something less uneven:

> Fulfilling the expectations and interests of [the] players is the first trick to creating the game's setting. Then—if the chronicle and its overall story have been carefully developed—the actions of the characters, both good and bad, will have consequences that in turn spawn further stories. Never forget: The more the players are involved with what happens in a chronicle, the less work you, the Storyteller, must take upon yourself. You aren't supposed to do it all alone. The Storyteller should have as much fun with the game as the players.
> (*Vampire: The Masquerade* 3rd ed., 1998, 254)

From all of this we can infer, as many have, that "a good story" is one of the goals of a storytelling game. It shouldn't be. "Good storytelling" should be the goal of a storytelling game.

Telling Stories Based on Random Numbers

A brief primer on the Storytelling System: Every character in the game is described by mental, physical, social, and supernatural traits, representing things like natural aptitude, training, mystical spells, and earthly possessions. Each trait is measured on a scale from zero to five by a number of dots (e.g., Strength •• or Wits ••••). Each dot represents one ten-sided die.

When a character, at the behest of the player, attempts significant actions that could change the course of the story or the state of the game world, dice are used to randomly determine the outcome of that action. Two traits are combined to form a "dice pool"—a collection of ten-sided dice based on the values of those two traits—which is rolled and examined. Every die that comes up 8 or higher is considered "a success." If the dice pool yields successes, the action is performed successfully. If every die comes up 7 or lower, the action fails.

The Storyteller can add or subtract dice from a player's dice pool by describing aspects of the game world that aid or hinder her character's action. These factors are also typically rated from zero to five. A good car adds dice to dice pools based on the traits Dexterity and Drive, while rain-slick roads could subtract dice from the pool.

That's it. As with many RPGs, the basic rules are simple but the game also gives Storytellers mechanisms that alter the basic rules to create suspense or an atmosphere of danger. In the Storytelling System, for example, a player may be required to accumulate a target number of successes before a time limit expires, or a poison might wither the character's traits as he slowly sickens.

Narrative information travels into and out of the game mechanics. The Storyteller contextualizes die rolls by framing them with descriptive narration, possibly emphasized with a dice pool bonus or penalty. It's also the Storyteller's job to translate the data generated by the dice—often as simple as "succeed" or "fail"—into an exciting bit of narration. When the dice say that a gunshot misses a player's character, the Storyteller says, "You hear the drywall behind you crack like a bat and taste plaster in the air when the shot lands behind you."

RPG rules help the players and the Storyteller understand and explain how their characters, as their agents in the game world, affect and respond to the actions that unfold in the story. The game world exists only in an imaginary space created and shared between the players, including the Storyteller, and the game mechanics carry their agency into the game world in a quantifiable way that other players can't ignore. Each player is free to visualize details about the game world and the characters in it without the approval or additional input of other players or the Storyteller.

The Storyteller may describe a nighttime cemetery as being foggy and cold, with slick and slippery grass underfoot between the weather-worn Victorian headstones, but each player is free to add more details—deliberately or spontaneously—to the image in her own mind. One player may visualize the Victorian headstones as tall family stones draped with angelic statuary, while another player imagines the headstones barely visible above the grass and through tangling vines. Until or unless these details are challenged, and it becomes necessary for all of the players to agree on them for the sake of the action, each player's mental image goes untransmitted and exists only in their own imaginary space.

Let's say one player wants her prowling vampire to hide in the cemetery. In her mind, the cemetery is populated by those large familial headstones, so hiding should be relatively easy. The Storyteller, however, imagined the headstones as being low and lost amid the grass. He decides that movement through the tall grass is likely to make noise and disturb the scenery enough to attract attention to the hiding character. He describes these facts mechanically as a −2 dice penalty to the prowling vampire's dice pool. New features of the game world have now moved into the shared imagination of the players— the headstones are small and hiding in the cemetery is difficult—and the mechanical representation of these details gives them added meaning. If any other player attempts to have her character hide, she will be subject to the same dice pool penalty.

The rules represent a kind of social contract between the players. If a player chooses to ignore a penalty or injury to her

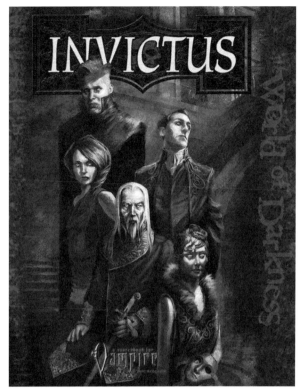

7.5) Cover of *Invictus*, a *Vampire: The Requiem* sourcebook. (White Wolf Publishing)

character that comes from the game world, then she is plainly not participating in the game. If one player declares, "I shot you!" another player cannot simply insist, "You missed!" unless the dice back her up.

The random element also creates real suspense for the player, who makes choices based on her character's best interests and her own dramatic intent without knowing for certain how those choices will play out. The Storyteller must take the sudden, and potentially substantial, changes to the action that occur as a result of those random results and integrate them into the story as it is being told, without breaking the audience of players' suspension of disbelief or investment in the developing story. Managing even that difficult task is often easier than integrating the input of multiple contributing interactors in the same developing story as it is being told, but that is the challenge of being the Storyteller.[5] That's the game the Storyteller is playing.

5. The term "interactor" is borrowed from Janet H. Murray's *Hamlet on the Holodeck*.

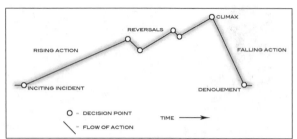

7.6) A traditional plot diagram showing dramatic tension rising vertically as the story unfolds horizontally from left to right. Though major incidents, such as reversals and setbacks, change the level of drama in the story, the story itself never truly branches. Only one path leads from the beginning to the end—the path written in the book or shown in the movie.

Storytelling in Action

The goal of a storytelling game isn't to produce a good story; it's to participate in good storytelling. Storytelling games are about the challenge of conceiving and telling stories, not the enjoyment of having a story or reading one. The process is the point, not the output.

This is the key difference between gaming as a storytelling medium and, for example, fiction. A novel is already complete when it is read, the story has been told, the game is over. That's what makes the reader a passive participant in the story rather than an agent in its telling; she's arrived too late to participate—the interactive part of the storytelling process has ended.

The point of fiction as a medium is to yield a product—a story—worthy of being read. That is not a kind of storytelling that most games are good at, as a medium. Games are good in the moment. Games are anecdotal. Stories that develop over the course of gameplay are personally exciting and meaningful in a way that movies and novels aren't, but they achieve this level of personal meaning at the expense of secondhand meaning. No one but the players are included in the excitement. The story of your stellar Crazy King match in *Halo 2* means a lot to you, but no one else is going to get excited about it.

Storytelling games, and potentially any paper RPG played with an emphasis on narrative, are especially good at enabling multiple players to share in the challenge and entertainment of the storytelling process. Players enjoy the total narrative and creative freedom of writing their own novel, and it's the fun that comes with that freedom that's

important, not the ultimate quality of the tale told. An RPG-originated story worthy of being read by a second party is a lucky by-product, not an essential product.

One of the usual pills in the ludologist's medicine bag is the conflict between the inherent linearity of a story versus the essential non-linearity of a game. Greg Costikyan, for example, writes:

> A story is linear. The events of a story occur in the same order, and in the same way, each time you read (or watch or listen to) it. A story is a controlled experience; the author consciously crafts it, choosing precisely these events, in this order, to create a story with maximum impact. (Costikyan 2000)

Costikyan is clearly writing about finished stories. A completed novel is the same each time it's read. The linearity he's writing about isn't presumably just a feature of the novel being written already, but an expectation based on the idea that a story is carefully plotted and calculated, with one particular course that makes the story *that* story. A story's linear nature can be seen in traditional plot diagrams (figure 7.6).

A story is, traditionally, the linear course from the beginning of the story to its dramatic, consciously crafted ending. It is not the level of drama (measured by rising action) that is linear on a plot diagram, but the temporal course of the story from beginning to end. Every time the story is read, the same events happen in the same order, from the inciting incident through the denouement. The story is fixed.

The *finished* story is fixed. When the story is being written—being told—Costikyan's linearity doesn't exist yet. Storytelling often is not linear. Prolific horror writer Stephen King makes choices as he reaches decision points in his own novels. He describes himself as the "first reader" of his novels, but in a sense he's also the only player in the interactive game of their telling:

> I lean more heavily on intuition [than plot when writing] and have been able to do that because my books tend to be based on situation rather than story. . . . I want to put a group of characters (perhaps a pair; perhaps even just one) in some of predicament and then watch them try to work

themselves free. My job isn't to *help* them work their way free, or manipulate them to safety—those are jobs which require the noisy jackhammer of plot. (King 2000, 160–161)

Still, King is a lone writer, with total control over the outcome of his story. Many Storytellers fancy themselves to be a kind of "performance novelist," acting out their tales for the enjoyment of an audience of gamers. Wholly concerned with story over game and enchanted with the idea of garnering reputations as talented writers or would-be directors, they create rich, controlled experiences for players to travel through with an absolute minimum of interactivity, like a video game that's mostly cutscenes.

For a storytelling game to be successful, it cannot neglect one of its halves for the others. If the interactors lose their agency in the story, they cease to be players in a game and become the passive (and likely bored) audience of a one-man show. Costikyan warns about the necessity of player freedom:

> A game is non-linear. Games must provide at least the illusion of free will to the player; players must feel that they have freedom of action within the structure of the game. They must not be constrained to a linear path of events, unchangeable in order, or they'll feel they're being railroaded through the game, that nothing they do has any impact, that they are not playing in any meaningful sense. (Costikyan 2000)

This degree of freedom is possible in storytelling games without sacrificing the story. Character (and therefore player) freedom is metaphorically possible in fiction. It is really possible in storytelling games. Stephen King describes his writing process:

> The situation comes first. The characters—always flat and unfeatured, to begin with—come next. Once these things are fixed in my mind, I begin to narrate. I often have an idea of what the outcome may be, but I have never demanded of a set of characters that they do things my way. On the contrary, I want them to do things *their* way. In some instances, the outcome is what I visualized. In most, however, it's something I never expected. (King 2000, 161)

By defining a situation that's ripe for drama, King is

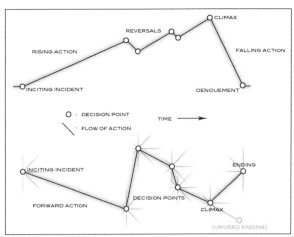

7.7) The same plot diagram from figure 7.6, with each reversal or potential setback turned into a decision point wherein the players might alter the course of the story. The drama continues to rise as the story moves towards its climax, despite temporary setbacks (top). By "tipping" the diagram and looking at it from "above," the multitude of possible choices, and therefore outcomes, stemming from each decision point are visible (bottom). Though only one outcome is experienced from each decision point, the course of the story from beginning to end isn't actually linear until all of the decisions have been made. The course of the story isn't fixed.

creating what Henry Jenkins calls "narrative architecture" (Jenkins 2004, 121). The boundaries of the situation become the edges of the stage on which the story is played out. The situation might be controlled strictly by physical boundaries, like the walls of a English manor house, or it might be subtly marked by the detectable subject of the tale, such as a manhunt. A whole city might be the stage for a manhunt, but the players can be reasonably expected to stay within the boundaries of the situation by staying on the trail of their target, thereby keeping the Storyteller's job manageable—he won't have to devise scenes and characters on the fly for every corner of the city if the players don't wander outside the stage he's set.

The key to maintaining player freedom in a storytelling game is the abandonment of expectation. The Storyteller designates a setting for the game that is "rich with narrative potential" and creates a collection of dramatic conflicts and decision points to use within that space as they become necessary during play (Jenkins 2004, 129). The Storyteller then lets the players loose within the game world, trusting that genre and subject matter will instinctively show the players the boundaries of the game space. As the players explore the game world, which is constantly being colored and informed by the Storyteller to reinforce the themes and atmosphere of his story, a narrative naturally emerges.

During play, the Storyteller simultaneously manages three interconnected tasks (figure 7.7):

1. Contextualizing, adjudicating and narrating the circumstances and outcomes of every die roll.

2. Maintaining a constant (but not necessarily steady) increase in dramatic tension as rising action climbs toward climax.

3. Subtly but firmly guiding the course of the story from each decision point toward a satisfying conclusion to the story.

The Storyteller may have an ending in mind for his story—ideally he should have a few—but he must abandon the expectation that a particular ending be fulfilled. Predetermined endings are an aspect of storytelling in other mediums. The Storyteller has a degree of input into the nature of the story's ending, but should not necessarily have more input than the players. The Storytelling System rulebook explains,

> The Storyteller's job isn't to defend his story from any attempt to change it, but to help create the story as events unfold, reacting to the players' choices and weaving them into a greater whole, introducing secondary characters and exotic settings. (*The World of Darkness*, 22)

In the hands of an unresponsive Storyteller with a specific story already in mind, a storytelling game rapidly becomes a stiff, awkward hybrid of interactive fiction (IF) and RPG. Interactive fiction presents the reader with a small selection of possible choices for the characters and the story to pursue, but the list of choices necessarily restricts the reader to the choices on the list. And the outcome of each choice has already been written—that next branch of the story has already been told—so the reader isn't really influencing how the story is told, only how it is read by her. The fiction may be interactive but the creation of the story is not.

Storytellers running pre-scripted stories are giving up the best aspects of both hobbies, the freedom of storytelling and the puzzle-like layered narrative of IF, for the sake of feeling like a writer. The Storyteller sits, frustrated, and players attempt to fulfill expectations they cannot identify by wandering without dramatic momentum through a potentially infinite game world in search of an invisible hotspot. The players are stuck trying to collaborate on a story that's already been finished, trying to play a game where none exists.

Chris Crawford's describes interactive fiction this way:

> Interactive fiction is certainly interactive, and it's fictional in the sense of being made up, but it's certainly not storytelling. Some practitioners of the field write eloquently of the glorious narrative possibilities, but the actual creations remain elaborate puzzles. (Crawford 2005, 337)

To be fair, Crawford seems to mean that interactive fiction is "not storytelling" on the part of the reader, who is an interactor with no real influence on the story. Certainly many interactive stories are well told, but the rearranging of jigsawed chapters is still a puzzle activity, not gameplay, no matter how handsome the picture looks when it's finished. Crawford maintains that interactive fiction will always be limited in this way. Finished stories cannot include "creative options"—the unexpected actions players inevitably think up and want to attempt, but which weren't included in the potential courses of action by the writer because they cannot react to the immediate, unforeseen input of the player.

Emily Short, a prolific and respected writer in the IF hobby, meditating on some ways that interactive fiction might deal with the challenge of providing creative options in her review of Crawford's book, described this solution:

> The trick lies, I think, in providing a simulation for whatever aspect of the world the player uses to express his choices. This is impossible if the player is expressing choice via an option list. It is possible with a world model and [text] parser, though, to give the player several ways to achieve the same outcome, and even (with a sufficient simulation under the surface) for that list of ways to include some unexpected by the author. (Short 2005)

Short might as well be describing a human Storyteller. A Storyteller parses the inputs of the player, who may attempt any action she can imagine. A Storyteller models the game world with words and dice at the moment the story is being told, in reaction to the actions of the player's character, expected or not.

A human Storyteller is still the machine best suited to the job of understanding, reacting to and influencing the dramatic choices of human players. The role-playing game is merely an interface, connecting players across psychic distances like Xbox Live connects us across miles. You say your character is clever, but if and when it becomes necessary to be more precise while telling our story, we have a common language that enables us to understand exactly what you mean by "clever"—your character has four dots in Wits.

Interactive, electronic Storytellers are gaming's City of Gold, even in the face of human counterparts, for a sadly simple reason: capable, engaging Storytellers are few, especially relative to the number of would-be players online and at the game table. The number of Storytellers who can raise fear like fog with nothing but dialogue, blot out the sun with improvised narration, and hatch whole characters from dice is smaller still.

References: Literature

Costikyan, Greg (1994). "I Have No Words and I Must Design." *Interactive Fantasy* 2 (1994): 22-38. <http://www.costik.com/nowords.html>.

Costikyan, Greg (1998). "Don't Be a Vidiot." Presented at Game Developers Conference (1998). <http://www.costik.com/vidiot.html>.

Costikyan, Greg (2000). "Where Stories End and Games Begin." <http://www.costik.com/gamnstry.html>.

Crawford, Chris (2005). *Chris Crawford on Interactive Storytelling*. Berkeley: New Riders.

Jenkins, Henry (2004). "Game Design as Narrative Architecture." In *First Person: New Media as Story, Performance, and Game*, edited by Noah Wardrip-Fruin and Pat Harrigan. Cambridge, MA: MIT Press.

King, Stephen (2000). *On Writing*. New York: Scribner.

Murray, Janet H. (1997). *Hamlet on the Holodeck: The Future of Narrative in Cyberspace*. Cambridge, MA: MIT Press.

Short, Emily (2005). "On *Chris Crawford on Interactive Storytelling*." <http://emshort.home.mindspring.com/CCReview.html>.

Sutherland, John (2005). "What Every Game Developer Needs to Know About Story." *Gamasutra* (July 27, 2005). <http://www.gamasutra.com/features/20050727/sutherland_01.shtml>.

Sylvester, Tynan (2005). "Decision-Based Gameplay Design." *Gamasutra* (March 21, 2005). <http://www.gamasutra.com/features/20050321/sylvester_01.shtml>.

References: Games

Vampire: The Masquerade. Mark Rein-Hagen, et al.; White Wolf Publishing. 1991.

Vampire: The Masquerade 3rd ed. (aka *Vampire: The Masquerade Revised*). Robert Hatch, et al.; White Wolf Publishing. 1998.

Vampire: The Requiem. Justin Achilli, et al.; White Wolf Publishing. 2004.

The World of Darkness. Bill Bridges, et al.; White Wolf Publishing. 2004.

Structure and Meaning in Role-Playing Game Design
Rebecca Borgstrom

1. Introduction

Every role-playing game takes place in a fictional world—a setting.

In a session of play, players typically generate more information about the setting than they find in the canonical game materials. They may also create new rules or change canonical rules and setting elements to suit their tastes. Even if they use the game material without modifications, they choose how to assign importance to the various rules and setting elements.

Players often extrapolate connections between small details in the provided world. This creates content that they consider implicit to the canonical game. Other groups may possess a fundamentally different understanding of the setting that is equally consistent with the information the game provides.

For these reasons, the setting that one group plays in is not the setting that another group plays in. In effect, role-playing games in their static published form do not describe a specific fictional world or story. They describe a large multidimensional space of fictional worlds and stories organized by unifying data.

Here is an example.

In the canonical *Exalted* setting, the Scarlet Empress disappeared in Realm Year (R.Y.) 763, five years before the story begins. Every group using the canonical *Exalted* setting stipulates this datum. This is a constraint on all of the fictional worlds in which such groups play, but it is not a specific fictional event. There are valid instantiations of the *Exalted* setting in which demons kidnapped her in R.Y. 763 and other valid worlds in which she retreated, voluntarily, to the Heavenly City of Yu-Shan. Even though it is commonly understood as a specific event in a single fictional world, it is actually a constraint that some event in the world must fit.

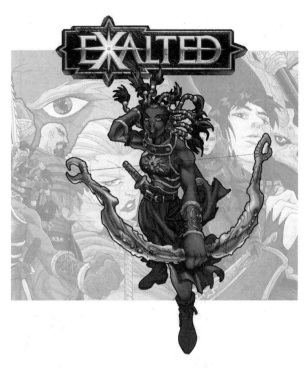

8.1) Cover of *Exalted*. (White Wolf Publishing)

1.1 Motivation

This chapter studies the design of the "Traits," "Character Creation," and "Magic" chapters of *Exalted: The Fair Folk*.

Exalted: The Fair Folk is set in the Wyld, a primal Ginnungagap of myth in which quite literally anything can happen. This is the void outside the canonical game world for *Exalted*, a place where chaos casts up fragments of stories and events. This setting does not stipulate as absolute the default assumptions for a role-playing setting, such as gravity and linear causality.

Designing the ground rules for this setting raised the question: how can one provide useful information about a setting without constraining the world presented therein?

1.2 Methodology

This chapter presents a new analytical model for role-playing games.

This model looks at the structural effects of rules and setting statements without reference to their proposed meaning in the game world. This is most useful in two cases:

8.2) Cover of *Exalted: The Fair Folk*. (White Wolf Publishing)

for evaluating abstract rules and setting elements, and for thinking about the game world as an object independent of the events of play.

This chapter then explores how the desire to provide useful structural support shaped the design of *Exalted: The Fair Folk*. It discusses key elements of the aforementioned three chapters in light of this design goal and the analytical model provided.

For convenience, since *Exalted: The Fair Folk* is already a cumbersome name, further mentions will omit the reference to the specific chapters under discussion.

1.3 Core Concept

Each datum provided by a role-playing game is a trade-off between lost possibility—the stories you can no longer tell—and structure, which helps tell the stories that remain.

1.4 Overview

In section 2, this chapter defines the analytical model used thereafter. This model defines the story the players tell as the outcome of a computation performed on the space of possible stories. Game data are beneficial if the structure provided allows the players to take the "right" length of time computing a satisfying series of events.

In section 3, this chapter discusses the *Exalted: The Fair Folk* project.

In sections 4 through 6, this chapter discusses the inherent structure of a role-playing game session and the stories that the players tell. It explains how *Exalted: The Fair Folk* uses this structure to facilitate play.

In section 7, the author presents a short summary, conclusions, and directions for future work.

2. The Model

Consider a typical situation in *Exalted*: three characters, having recently arrived in the capital city of a corrupt principality, set out to reform or destroy it.

The events of the story are undefined until the characters experience them in play. They could topple the Prince from his throne or save him from wicked ministers who have led him astray. They could seize command of the principality's army to defend against an as-yet-unknown threat, or encounter an old nemesis working behind the throne and have that enemy drive them from the region.

Before the game begins there is a large space of possible stories defined by the initial premise. During the process of gaming the players progressively reduce the space of possible stories down to a single story—one set of things "happened," while all other sets did not.

"Fun" and "satisfaction" are byproducts of this computation. This model treats them as a function of time and work—we assume that players receive maximum fun and satisfaction when the amount of time and work spent on any given part of the story is close to some optimum defined by the players' interests.

Other sources of fun and satisfaction—gaming material that inspires the players, game books that are good reads, and so forth—are not dealt with here.

2.1 Structure and Meaning

Every time the players agree on something—implicitly or explicitly—regarding the story, that provides *structure*. For example, when the players agree to set their game in Germany but decide to make up the various locales and characters rather than researching them, this imposes structure on the story.

When there is sufficient structure for the players to answer a specific question regarding the imaginary world, that creates *meaning*. For example, when the players conclude that Mayor Franz of their characters' hometown is corrupt, Franz's corruption is a shared meaning that emerges from the game. If one player decides that Franz is nevertheless worthy of trust, his integrity is a personal meaning for that player that emerges from the game.

Meaning is a form of structure, but the converse is not true. If the players agree to play for exactly an hour, as in *Puppetland*, this imposes massive structural constraints on their game but has no specific meaning in play. It does not define any single detail of the setting or story, although it influences how each develops.

Structure in a game restricts the field of possible stories and limits the set of potentially emergent meanings. Stories are most structured after they are told.

2.2 Stories

This chapter defines a story as the final resolution of a specific premise, such as the typical premise mentioned above ("Three characters arrive . . .").

When the players are satisfied with their ability to answer the question, "What happened regarding that premise?" their answer forms the story.

This chapter focuses its attention on stories that are also traditional narratives—that is, single large-scale consistent stories defined over the course of multiple hours or even multiple sessions of play.

2.3 Gaming

This chapter views gaming as a computational process.

Gaming is work, in the sense of effort over time. That work takes the form of processing the raw data—the set of possible stories applicable to the story's premise. The players generate additional structure until a single story remains.[1]

> **Structure and Meaning: An Example**
>
> The Storyteller proposes a premise for a new game: three characters travel to Low Fires, the capital city of a corrupt principality, and reform or destroy its corrupt government. The players agree and create three characters—Sour, Lily, and Morgan. This is structure.
>
> The players create backgrounds for their characters. Lily has family in Low Fires. She fled the region to avoid conscription into its workforce. In the course of many adventures, she cultivated her strength and found two powerful allies. Now she can return and redeem her homeland. This narrative provides additional structure and gives meaning to the events that Lily experiences. Sour and Morgan also have backgrounds that add structure to the game.

> **Gaming: An Example**
>
> The three characters arrive in Low Fires. At this point the Storyteller does not know what will happen. In one possible story, the characters make for the Prince's palace and launch an immediate offensive. In another, they scout the outskirts of society first, gathering data on the state of affairs.
>
> The players develop their plan: the characters will impersonate foreign dignitaries from a distant, powerful court and use this imaginary influence as leverage. Their first actions in Low Fires are to spread rumors that three great and powerful nobles will soon arrive. They sell this information to the information brokers of Low Fires society.
>
> The space of stories is now much diminished. Just as the first chapter of *The Lord of the Rings* cannot reasonably lead in to the second and later chapters of either *The Shining* or *Gone with the Wind*, the events now established have made their mark on the rest of the game, with permanent implications on how the story will develop.

---

1. That is, until they can answer "what happened?" in a fashion complete enough to satisfy them.

2.4 Game Material

The rules and setting for a game facilitate play by generating some of this structure in advance.

In classic "Cops and Robbers," it is traditionally difficult to determine whether one character has successfully shot another. The "nuh unh" factor[2] obstructs simple methods of resolution. In many modern role-playing games, it is equally difficult to determine whether one character's argument successfully convinces another; there is a similar "nuh unh" factor at work.

Exalted provides rules for combat and social situations. These allow impartial arbitration of a character's success. Numeric character traits determine the base probability of success and dice rolls collapse that probability in practice. If the players can use these rules without contradicting their own ideas of genre, the rules structure the development of the story. They facilitate play because deciding between the stories of a character's success and the stories of a character's failure is quicker and less stressful.

In a similar fashion, descriptions of regions, people, cultures, and other setting details do some of a game's storytelling work in advance.

2.5 Genre and Play Contract

The players' ideas regarding the game and its genre also provide structure. In a game of *Exalted*, players generally commit to playing characters in an epic swords and sorcery saga. What this actually says about the story depends on the individual players in question, but it always says something, and it helps decide which way the story goes.

In a similar fashion players can facilitate play by making rules regarding how they'll play the game. They may define one player as the Storyteller, whose authority on most game events is final, or decide aspects of the story they *want* to tell before play begins.

2.6 How Good Games Go Bad

There is a certain "natural length" for a set of events in a role-playing game. This is the time frame that maximizes the players' fun and satisfaction.

If the game has too much structure, events will proceed

Game Material: An Example

The Storyteller does not know if the information brokers believe the characters. Referring to the *Exalted* rules, the Storyteller has the players make Manipulation + Socialize rolls—rolling a handful of 10-sided dice and referring to the characters' established Traits—to determine if the characters succeed or fail.

The result is success, further shaping the story.

Genre and Play Contract: An Example

At this point, it is up to the Storyteller to decide how the government reacts to the rumor that the characters have spread. In the abstract, there is no reason to think that anything in particular happens as a result. Unless the player group has a commitment to realism, there is no reason for the government to react realistically. Unless the player group has a commitment to drama, there is no reason for it to react in an interesting fashion.

In practice, the player group as a whole and the Storyteller in particular have specific ideas about the kinds of stories that are interesting to tell. In almost any game, accordingly, the Storyteller reacts by processing the new information in context of the desire to tell the right kind of story and looks for "what happens next."

In this case, the Storyteller observes the players to figure out what they think is likely to happen. The players feel that the next step is to send Morgan ahead as a messenger, formally announcing their presence. The Storyteller concludes from this that the players are still working on establishing legitimacy, so she decides that no one in Low Fires has particularly strong reactions yet—but she begins working on how people will react when faced with mysterious emissaries from an unknown region.

How Good Games Go Bad: An Example

During this process, the Storyteller might read official game material regarding Low Fires. She discovers that the government of Low Fires has officially grown increasingly xenophobic and has been turning away most emissaries. She reads descriptions of the people and institutions responsible for this policy.

---

2. People saying "nuh unh!" when shot.

too quickly. For example, if a player is interested in the resolution of an epic long-term conflict, and the game rules suggest resolving it with a single Long-Term Conflict roll, the player might not have fun.

If the game has too little structure, players have to spend large amounts of time resolving questions and events that don't interest them. For example, in games like "Cops and Robbers," arguing over whether a robber was successfully shot is not necessarily fun for all players involved.

In practice, most games have a tiered resolution system. The amount of structure scales up or down, depending on how much time the players want to spend. *Exalted* is one of a large class of games where the impact of a single roll varies and the number of situations played strictly by the book varies, based on the player group's tastes.

In games like this, where the amount of structure is scalable, there are two common failure modes for the game.

In the first failure mode, something happens for which the game can't provide scalable structure. In a game of *Dungeons & Dragons* modeled on *Much Ado about Nothing*, the rules are almost no help. They do not speak to the matter of who finds love with whom, or when. Similarly, in *Exalted*, the game provides no information on how to permanently destroy the setting's most dangerous antagonists. To matchmake in *Dungeons & Dragons*, or kill a Deathlord in *Exalted*, the player group must have a strong and shared vision of the relevant genre. If they do, or if they *want* to spend a long time hashing out the relevant issues, there's no problem. If they don't, the necessary structure isn't present and figuring out what happens takes too long.

In the second failure mode, the structure in the game contradicts itself. The available data actually eliminates all the possible stories. This is most common when the rules demand one resolution and the players' expectations demand another—e.g., the rules make it clear that an antagonist can kill all the protagonists and that isn't the story that the players want to tell.

2.7 Commentary

This model focuses solely on the amount of effort gaming requires, with the presumption that this effort is fulfilling up to a point. Other factors are studied only as they

> This is a large unexpected dose of additional structure surrounding the resolution of the players' plan. Discovering this structure has two possible effects.
>
> If the material is worded in such a way as to be compatible with the current direction of the story, it reduces the Storyteller's work. There is an impending point of conflict: the emissaries risk being turned away, and the Storyteller already knows the important details of the opposition's force.
>
> If the material totally shuts down the current story—that is, the characters *will* be turned away, and the entire fake-emissaries plan *will* fall flat—the Storyteller might have to abandon some of that structure. This is a stressor on the game itself, possibly forcing the Storyteller to spend time improvising material that she'd hoped to derive directly from the Low Fires book.

manifest in this model—for instance, disputes between players increase the work of a game, while a shared sense of genre adds structure and reduces the amount of necessary work. The quality of the game experience is outside the model's scope.

3. The Project

Exalted: The Fair Folk is set in the void beyond the world. This void is called the Wyld. It is a mystery. It is outside the world, outside traditional rules. It is not bound by the laws we know.

In the broader narrative of *Exalted*, stories of the Wyld are stories about impossible, indescribable places and things beyond the boundaries of the known. More important, they are stories about how more ordinary characters deal with those things. For this reason, the Wyld is "about" exploration, and spirituality, and mystery, and limitless possibility, and hope, and the recognition that people never know quite as much as they think they do.

Exalted: The Fair Folk is a game set in the same place as all the things you can't quite make out in the corner of your eye. It's about that place where words on the tip of your tongue live, where the ideas you'll have tomorrow come from. It's about knowing that no matter how much you know about the world, something could come from outside that world tomorrow and change everything.

3.1 Challenges

In *Exalted: The Fair Folk* anything can happen, and almost everything does. This puts the game at large natural risk for each of the two failure modes.

To avoid the first failure mode, the game must provide significant structure for any describable event. If, for example, zombie philosophers burst from the soil and deconstruct the characters' worldview—hoping, no doubt, to devour their dazed victims' brains—the game's rules must handle these events smoothly.

To avoid the second failure mode, the game's structure must not conflict with the player group's expectations for how such an event plays out, *even though the game cannot isolate those expectations before publication.* Some player groups may think of zombies as unstoppable horrors; others as the grist for dark comedy. The game's model for the zombies must support the appropriate outcome in either case.

3.2 Approach

The approach taken in *Exalted: The Fair Folk* is to model in the setting the mechanisms by which the player group determines the story. The low-level physics provided for the Wyld focuses on providing layers of additional structure to support the storytelling process instead of providing meaning or data in advance.

4. Something from Nothing

In a session of *Exalted: The Fair Folk*, the players play out the story of events in an indescribable world—a world that is functionally a mystery, still a magical thing outside the normal bounds of reality and comprehension, even after a session of play.

To do this, players need a base assumption set about the world that allows sessions of play to occur.

These are the assumptions that *Exalted: The Fair Folk* assumes that the players will probably want to make:

For the purpose of play:

Characters exist.

Characters are distinct.

Characters can act.

Characters can interact.

Characters have motivation for conflict.

The concept of a setting exists.

The concept of a story exists.

Players each have a defined role in the process of storytelling.

Setting constraints:

The setting is meaningfully "outside" the normal world.

The setting is meaningfully "chaotic."

The setting is meaningfully "indescribable."

The setting has a meaningful "fairy tale feel."[3]

These tenets are the building blocks for an *Exalted: The Fair Folk* setting. To facilitate player agreement on these tenets, seven of them are listed explicitly in the book and the existence of other tenets is noted.

In addition, to give them more structural depth, these tenets are recognized explicitly as key concepts and assigned a large number of connotative qualities. The premise here is that a working vocabulary facilitates the construction of a mental model for the world. It helps determine which questions are worth asking, so that players can derive meaning from the answers. This technique is used repeatedly in *Exalted: The Fair Folk*.

Specifically, the tenets are described as *shinma*. They are anthropomorphized as beings, terrible god-monsters from whom the tenets' existence flows.

Something from Nothing: An Example

Let us imagine that the Storyteller decides to run a game of *Exalted: The Fair Folk* set in the Wyld beyond the world.

The players might reasonably ask: "what do you mean 'set in'? How can there even be a *place* beyond the world?"

To this, the Storyteller can now reply: through the grace of the shinma.

If the players or characters need to know more than that, they can figure it out during the course of play.

---

3. This is a structural decision made by Geoff Grabowski on behalf of the publisher, not an intrinsic characteristic of places beyond the known.

One such shinma is Nirguna. The term is a Hindu word meaning "without attributes." Nirguna defines existence. Through Nirguna, things exist. Insofar as things fail to exist, this is a failing of Nirguna.

Nirguna is also described as "the nothing and everything dream, the raw beating heart at the core of the Wyld." It has aspects such as "Namadiksha, the gift of names" and "Neti Neti." The first refers to the ceremony by which parents name a child. The second means "not this, not that," and is a Upanisadic formula indicating through negation the undefinable nature of the universe.

Nirguna is written to keep players from worrying about why there is a "something" to exist in the Wyld at all. If they do not care, they may shrug and say, "Nirguna." If they do care, the list of connotative meanings is a springboard for exploration of these matters.

5. Context

Having established the existence of a world, it is useful to delimit the context of play. For the purposes of this chapter, this refers to time and space.

Distance in the Wyld is mutable. The Wyld is inherently unmappable. This means that the book cannot provide a simple comprehensive atlas for the characters' travels. Tactical movement is also complicated—it may, in one story, be reasonable to measure each step carefully and, in another, to travel in one jump from an earthbound plane to the distant sun.

However, the context of the Wyld is not entirely unapproachable. In telling a story that involves distance or time, the players must assign each event in the game world a rough time and place. Only the times and places where events happen are relevant to the story. These times and places are distinct only to the extent that the story differentiates between them. In short, distance and time exist only insofar as the players have information about them.

This frees *Exalted: The Fair Folk* to organize the spatial context into *waypoints* and *journeys*. Each waypoint is a place in which events happen. Characters can travel between the waypoints, taking journeys, but no real details are known. In short, unaccounted-for time during travel is spent on a journey, where the only meaning is that travel happened.

> **Context: An Example**
> Having determined that there is a place beyond the world, by the grace of the shinma, the Storyteller sets up a waypoint space. This is a set of waypoints, journeys, and the connections between them. This is the setting of the game. Each scene of play takes place in a waypoint; unremarkable travel occurs on the journeys.

Everything else happens in a waypoint.

This structure imposes no additional constraints on the Wyld itself. Waypoints can move in the Wyld and their physical size varies. At the same time, the waypoint structure creates a loose grid-like system for the Wyld that allows the players to think about questions of distance.

Similarly, *Exalted: The Fair Folk* organizes time in terms of *scenes* and *stories*. During scenes, events happen, with "downtime" between them. These scenes group naturally to form stories, delimiting a meaningful series of events.

6. Game Structure

Having defined the Wyld as a waypoint space abiding by certain tenets, the players need the following additional information to proceed to creating the story:

Specific defined methodology for proposing new events and situations;

Motivation for picking certain events over others;

Resolution mechanisms for disputes regarding the story's direction; and

Ways to assess the story's meaning in the broader context of the fictional world.

6.1 Methodology

The method for shaping events in the Wyld is *in-character action*. Each player takes on the role of a character who is an agent of change in the void beyond the world.

Exalted: The Fair Folk defines its principal characters, the raksha or Fair Folk, to have the following key characteristics:

They can shape reality to cause any event appropriate to the story to occur.

They display apparent awareness, intelligence, and personhood.

They are susceptible to tactical measures of performance and player evaluations of personality.

In theory, the latter two measures are subjective. One can therefore model any setting that allows the meaningful exploration of premises as including these creatures—for example, when a rock rolls down a hill, declaring, "a raksha caused that rock to roll down the hill," or, "that rock was secretly a raksha that chose to roll down the hill."

In practice, due to other design constraints, the raksha are not the perfectly abstract templates for action presented here.

6.2 Motivation

In order to have a game, the raksha must prefer some events over others. This is a weak point in the *Exalted: The Fair Folk* rules. The set of motivations chosen is not an "ideal and minimal" set taken from the study of narrative, psychology, or game theory. Instead, the rules model four specific tactical rewards:

Emotional advantage, specifically, weakening another raksha's self-control;

Authority and power, specifically, imposing obligations on other raksha;

Control over resources, specifically, claiming the possessions of another raksha;

Higher-level goals, specifically, achieving something that makes another raksha more vulnerable to manipulation of other sorts.

In general, players are driven to the tactical behavior that a system rewards. They also have a drive to tell the "correct" story. The game cannot predict the players' concept of a correct story. Thus, to keep these two drives from conflicting, *Exalted: The Fair Folk* must separate tactical rewards from game events. The connections between the events in play and the tactical actions taken by the raksha are almost entirely descriptive. The only solid connection is that shaping "appropriate" events, that is, events that fit the descriptive templates provided, gives a bonus toward success on the tactical action. Thus, raksha seeking to earn one of the tactical rewards are drawn to a set of story types appropriate to the tactical reward.

Methodology: An Example

To shape the story, the players create three raksha—lords of the madness beyond the world.

The first is a warrior. He is addicted, despite his distaste for them, to such orderly things as "events" and "places." He chooses a body and a role that expresses his nature—Sour, an older man prone to ranting.

The second is a visionary. She has dreams for what the Wyld should become. She also manifests a body and a role—Lily, a lean woman with a mysterious past. Lily does not deign to define the mystery at present; beyond the edges of the world, the requirement that a mystery must exist for one to be mysterious does not apply.

The third is an artisan. He gives the name Morgan. Sometimes he manifests in stories as a tall human and sometimes as a bear.

Motivation: An Example

The Storyteller creates an antagonist—the Prince of Low Fires. Since he is their antagonist, it falls to Lily, Sour, and Morgan to do something about him. They decide to set out to his location in the waypoint space and impose such obligations on him as to restrain his malice.

"What kind of place does he live in?" one player asks.

To answer this question, the Storyteller creates the city of Low Fires and the principality around it. She decides that the Prince's will has shaped most of the surrounding waypoint space into a corrupt principality, giving it a reasonably solid and predictable form.

Dispute Resolution: An Example

The raksha launch their attack on the Prince of Low Fires. Lily, Morgan, and Sour travel to Low Fires and use various tricks to present themselves as emissaries of a distant foreign power. As they do so, they lure the Prince into participating in the story that they tell.

These events "hook" the Prince of Low Fires into the story. It becomes possible to win tactical advantage against him by cleansing the government of the city that previously existed only as an instrument of his will.

The story plays out much as it would in a normal setting, but the edifice of normalcy is provided entirely by the players' acceptance of the shinma, the limits of the waypoint space, and the will of the raksha involved. To the extent that these things shift—that the shinma

6.3 Dispute Resolution

Exalted: The Fair Folk uses a turn-based system for shaping reality. This is a standard approach to resolving large-scale conflicts in role-playing games. Since it is difficult to reach consensus if the players all talk at once, their individual contributions to a conflict are studied in order, organized, and sequenced by the game's initiative system—its rules for breaking larger goals into atomic actions, which the players take in sequence.

In practice, this seems to work well for *Exalted: The Fair Folk* but could benefit from a shift in focus. The rules on shaping reality assume that each raksha is telling a story of their own, and these stories interweave to form the larger whole. However, this makes the events of the game dependent on which raksha is shaping them at any given time. Future versions of *Exalted: The Fair Folk* would benefit from treating each raksha's contribution as something closer to the corresponding player's contribution—"story elements" or "narrative threads" or other things that rise temporarily to prominence within a larger story framework.

6.4 Integration with Creation

Exalted comes with an existing universe—Creation, the world shaped by the Primordials and inhabited by humans, spirits, and the eponymous Exalted. This is a highly structured world about which much is known. Creation and the Wyld regularly interact—not directly, but through the raksha visiting Creation or the people of Creation visiting the Wyld.

Previous material about Creation and Creation-Wyld interactions suggest that Creation is "more real" than the Wyld and its powerful figures "more powerful" than the raksha, but that the raksha were powerful enough to pose a threat to the world. In short, the raksha's ability to overwrite reality should be a notable edge when facing Creation opposition—but not the overwhelming advantage that "the ability to overwrite reality" suggests.

To translate the effects of the raksha's shaping into Creation terms, *Exalted: The Fair Folk* provides a palette of "naked" mechanical effects. "Naked" effects are game mechanics that have a meaning in the world but for which that meaning is not provided—such as the rules for magic in *Sorcerer*, where the same rules apply whether one's power

> prove unreliable, the characters leave the waypoint space, or the rules by which the raksha choose to play their game change—that edifice collapses and play takes a different direction.
>
> In this fashion *Exalted: The Fair Folk* attempts to support the events the players have chosen to focus on—three characters traveling to a corrupt principality to reform it—without imposing a fixed structure on the setting itself. If the players change course and decide that the Wyld spontaneously gives birth to giant monsters that attack Low Fires, the rules support these new ideas as well.

comes from inner demons, hermetic magic, or selling out to one's corporate masters.

Specifically, when mortals find themselves opposing a raksha's shaped reality, they suffer penalties to their dice pools (their probabilistic chances of success) and a reduction in Willpower—not the real-world concept of determination and skill but a system trait that shares some of its qualities. The events that cause these penalties, and what they mean at the time, are not specified. They are simply structure that helps measure the overall impact of the raksha's shaping.

Current feedback suggests that providing structure with the connotative meanings of existing mechanics (dice pools and Willpower) is not as useful to players as creating setting-based connotation such as the shinma. Players are more likely to look for an existing, defined meaning for game mechanics and more willing to impose their own meanings on setting material.

7. Conclusions

Exalted: The Fair Folk attempts to model in its Wyld the meaning of "this is a world in which sessions of a role-playing game take place." This concept turns out to have substantial intrinsic and explicit meaning that a game can exploit to facilitate play.

In creating a structure to support these meanings, *Exalted: The Fair Folk* replaces an essentially unplayable premise— "you are entities in a place where anything can happen, and nothing means anything"—with a game of competitive storytelling that players describe as difficult to fully wrap their heads around but rewarding to play.

7.1 Directions for Future Work

In the course of a role-playing game session, players use the existing structure of the game world to generate new information. Understanding this process falls within the domain of epistemology (what does it mean to know something about the game world?) and information theory (what does it mean to derive new information from existing structure?). It is the author's conclusion that it is possible to go significantly further in developing a formal language for studying this process in a rigorous fashion, and that this would facilitate more efficient role-playing game design.

Reference

Exalted: The Fair Folk. Rebecca Borgstrom, Genevieve Cogman, Michael Goodwin, John Snead, and W. Van Meter; White Wolf. 2004.

My Life with Master: The Architecture of Protagonism
Paul Czege

My Life with Master is a role-playing game about the horrific and dysfunctional ties that bind a monstrous Master and his or her minions. Its mechanical core was designed over several mornings in the summer of 2002—but it was a decade of dissatisfaction with published role-playing games, and then a year of experimental play, which made that possible.

The Dissatisfaction

Telling stories about your experiences is a process of selecting, organizing, and presenting a relevant subset of the superset of all possible information you could include in the story. And the organizing principle is your purpose for telling the story, the message you want to convey to the audience; you organize and present your information around that theme. As such, storytelling is a retroactive process. And traditional RPGs are storytelling like that. Their focus is on architecting events for throwing at the player characters. Story only happens in retrospect, when you pick from all the details of the game session and organize them for yourself in service to theme, character protagonism, and the dramatic. But when you're in it, generating the non-thematic noise, and your interest is story, you're not having much fun.

And so, ten years of clueless dissatisfaction, of not recognizing that a character needs the efforts of an active author if his emergence from noise as the protagonist of a story is to be anything other than retroactive construction (or railroading on the part of the gamemaster, which is actually a form of active authorship—just a socially dishonest one).

The Education

It was online conversations with Ron Edwards and others <http://www.indie-rpgs.com/about> in 2000 that introduced me to Ron's ideas about why people play, and how traditional game mechanics can disappoint or actively frustrate those priorities. I credit Ron for a dramatic renewal of my

9.1) *My Life with Master* (Half Meme Press)

appreciation for the role-playing hobby. I began to play, widely, regularly, and experimentally, mostly free and self-published games. And from this I began to understand how powerful role-playing experiences that produce story with less noise could be delivered by game rules that consciously mediate play as an endeavor of collaborative authorship.

The Architecture of Protagonism

Traditional role-playing games fail consistently as engines of story creation from their relentless doubting of the protagonism of the player characters. A character can generally suffer an ignominious demise at any turn. No author of fiction would be so cavalier. And so neither is *My Life with Master*. Antagonism in traditional games is merely a continuous questioning of the survival and thematic credibility of the player character. No author of fiction would be so self-defeating of his storytelling effort. And so neither is *My Life with Master*.

The protagonism of the player character minion in *My Life with Master* is presumed, not earned. This presumption of protagonism is partly mechanical, in that game events threaten the fate of the character, but don't impose that fate until the game's denouement. And it is partly social, in that setup for play consists of a structure for conversation that collaboratively creates an antagonist (the Master), who all participants can love to hate, as well as a player character workshop that produces minions who thematically benefit from this antagonism. So, *My Life with Master*'s formula for play is simply a social and mechanical structure in which the other players are an interested audience to the struggles of a given player character, because they have creative investment in the character and the antagonist, and the game rules can be trusted to not disappoint that interest.

Reference

My Life with Master. Paul Czege; Half Meme Press. 2003.

Making Games That Make Stories
James Wallis

In the ongoing debates about storytelling and narrative in games, the various commentators often overlook a key point: even in the most cutting-edge examples of the state of the art, it is not the players who tell the story, it is the game. Whether computer games with a narrative element, board games, card games, or face-to-face role-playing games, the essential plot and structure of the narrative is predetermined before the game begins, and cannot be altered.

This style of game is interactive storytelling only in the sense that the story is told. The plot is not interactive. It may contain variables, most notably multiple endings, but the basic shape of the story is fixed in advance and the only way the player can divert the storyline away from its pre-set path or prevent it from reaching one of its predetermined conclusions is to not finish the game. The player may have the illusion of being in control, but this is usually down to clever game design hiding the rails to give the impression of an open-ended narrative.

In many narrative games the plot is so untouchable that the players must watch it unfold in cutscenes or between non-player characters, while the gameplay consists of grunt-work that adds little to story or plot and would be elided in a novel or film—journeying from place to place, exploring buildings, locating objects, killing monsters, shopping, and deciding what to wear. Replay the game and the same story will be revealed in essentially the same way. Even in titles like *Knights of the Old Republic*, a *Star Wars*-themed console RPG hailed for letting players choose whether to embrace the light side or the dark side of the Force, one must still play through the same key encounters in the same order. In a slightly different vein, *Fable* allows players to craft their own story-path and customize their character, but while many of the game's encounters can be played in any order or even omitted, they are all pre-scripted around a central narrative.

Thankfully this is not the only way that games can handle stories. There is a small but growing number of titles that use the creation and telling of a new story (or in some cases, several stories) as an integral part of the gameplay. These are more than systems for group storytelling: they combine narrative elements with standard game features including competitive play, a clear ending point and a winner. For the purposes of this article I will refer to them as *story-making games*. Some significant examples in the field include *Dark Cults* (1983), *Tales of the Arabian Nights* (1985), *Once Upon a Time* (1993/1996), *The Extraordinary Adventures of Baron Munchausen* (1998), and *Pantheon* (2000).

Of those five I designed two and published a third, and this is not a coincidence. I think story-creation as a part of gameplay is important and under-explored. Books, films, and TV have conditioned us to be passive consumers of stories, not active participants in their creation, and games have gone the same path. Story-making games, by contrast, offer a way of creating a story within the structure of a game, which not only helps to structure the narrative but adds interaction and competition.

Some critics have complained that the act of storytelling is intrinsically cooperative and at odds with the competitive element of gameplay. But balancing the two sides of that dichotomy is one of the things that makes it such an interesting field. The challenge of simultaneously telling a story and playing a game—or if you prefer, telling a story while thinking not only of plot and character but also of tactics, strategy, and how to avoid the other players derailing you—is exhilarating.

Story-Making

Human beings like stories. Our brains have a natural affinity not only for enjoying narratives and learning from them, but also for creating them. In the same way that your mind sees an abstract pattern and resolves it into a face, your imagination sees a pattern of events and resolves it into a story.

Games have always had a close affinity with story-making. Adding a few lines of description to a video game or a background and artwork to an abstract board game gives dramatic context and an added sense of depth, allowing the player to create an internal narrative as the game progresses. To take an example, chess is primarily an abstract game but has pieces with titles that help in their anthropomorphization, and it is possible to create complete narratives based on chess games, as several authors have done.[1]

The gameplay of most face-to-face games involving some element of strategy breaks down into a structure that looks a lot like that of a conventional story: setup, opening, middle section, endgame. That implies that mapping a story structure on top of standard gameplay, or at least fitting a game to a genre, is a fairly trivial job. It's not.

Take, for example, *Cluedo* (retitled *Clue* for the U.S. market), which describes itself as "the classic detective game" and is based on the classic English country house murder mystery story, as popularized by Agatha Christie. In most of these detective stories a crime is committed and subsequently analyzed, suspects are questioned, evidence discovered and analyzed, alibis examined and motives revealed, until in a thrilling climax the villain is unmasked. In *Cluedo*, you wander aimlessly around a board, not following clues but hazarding guesses at three unrelated elements of a murder. Not only can you win by proving that you committed the crime, you can accuse yourself and be wrong, and will lose the game as a result. As a game mechanic this works, but in story and genre terms it is a tale told by an idiot.

Cluedo is not, of course, a game that sets out to create or tell a story, though one might hope the best-selling murder mystery game in the world would make at least a token effort to be true to its genre.[2] Instead, it attaches the tropes of its chosen genre to aspects of its gameplay, to create the illusion of a whodunit.

It is possible to create a story-making game about murder mysteries. In my forthcoming title, *Youdunnit*, currently doing the dance of the many publishers, players play characters who must work together to solve a murder that one of them committed. The members of the group are assigned characters, each of whom knows certain key facts about the others. They take turns to present pieces of evidence that can be canceled out or combined to form chains of means, motive, and opportunity, until one character has their guilt "proven" to the satisfaction of the group. Each *Youdunnit* case is about a specific murder—the specifics of the crime and the various potential murderers are all detailed—but can be played multiple times with different outcomes, using the same elements to create different stories. *Youdunnit* demonstrates many of the principles described in this article, and I will return to it.

In fact, designing a story-making game in which the story created and the gameplay used to create it are equal, which is both fun and creates a satisfying story, requires a synergy between the two forms that is not easy to achieve.

What Makes a Story?

To understand what makes a story-making game work or not, we must first consider what makes a story work. Like a good game, it needs to have a beginning, a middle, and an end. It needs characters who interact and do things, and things that happen to the characters. And it needs a story—a plot that runs from beginning to end and then stops. This is not as simple as it sounds. We all know how to tell stories, though as we grow older many of us forget that we know.

When small children begin to tell their own stories, these may consist only of characters, and this is enough for them. Chicago educationalist Vivian Gussin Paley describes an early story by Mollie, a three-year-old: "Once upon a time there lived a horse and a chicken and a dog. And the next morning there was a robber in the house. That's Frederick. He's the robber. That was scary." Frederick, one of Mollie's friends, has an even shorter story: "Frederick." Paley questions the fact that the story has only one word, but John, a five-year-old, corrects her: "It's not one word. It's one person" (Paley 1986).

Before long, as the teller grows in confidence and familiarity with the art of manipulating narrative elements, their stories acquire a setting and then sequences of events, and finally the coherent unity that identifies what we think of as a story. Within a few months of her first story, Mollie's storytelling skills have mushroomed:

My story is about a little girl who goes to the park to see her mother. And a little boy wild thing comes. Then a monster comes. The girl was bleeding

1. Examples include *The Squares of the City* (John Brunner 1965) and *Alice Through the Looking Glass* (Lewis Carroll, 1871).

2. On the subject of *Clue Dungeons & Dragons* (2001)—in which the murder-mystery is combined with a wandering-monster mechanic, so players are trying to solve a killing while killing things—the less said the better.

10.1.1) Cards from *The Helpless Doorknob,* Edward Gorey.

because the monster hit her. So her mother told her she was Fire Star. Fire Star fixed the monster on fire and the monster couldn't get out of the fire. Then the little boy wild thing was friends with all the friends they ate with. They all went to bed and slept. (Paley 1986)

What makes these early stages of storytelling interesting is the degree that they resemble the results of some of the more rudimentary story-making games like *Story Blocks* (1990), the *Goosebumps Storytelling Card Game* (1996), and *The Helpless Doorknob* (1989), which all involve laying a sequence of cards or blocks to make a narrative.

Story Blocks are wooden blocks with pictures and brief texts. Lining them up produces a sequence like: "This is a story about Sam / near the magic monster / beside the park playground / and a crawling caterpillar / walking with a white wolf / grinning grandly / and a goofy gorilla / trying to touch a turtle / beneath the blue moon / The End." It's clever, but it's not a story: there is no sequence of structure, events, cause and effect, or conclusion. In its defense, it is designed as a toy rather than a game, and it is meant for young children, but one might suggest that young children deserve better.

The *Goosebumps Storytelling Card Game* is a deck of fifty-four cards illustrated with characters, places, items and events. The rules say: "On your turn, repeat the story the others have created so far, and add to it with a card from your hand. For example, if the first set of cards creates 'We were in the GRAVEYARD' . . . then 'We were in the GRAVEYARD and the PIZZA arrived.' And on your turn 'We were in the

Alfred returned from Novaya Zemlya.

A disguised person came to one of the side doors.

10.1.2) Cards from *The Helpless Doorknob,* Edward Gorey.

GRAVEYARD and the PIZZA arrived—but was covered in RATS!' If you goof, you're out. The last player left is the winner." That's the entirety of the rules, and a sample of the cards. The onus of creating an actual story is left utterly on the players, while the gameplay is nothing more than a memory test. As with *Story Blocks*, the resulting narrative has no intrinsic structure. It's almost unnecessary to say that it's not an enjoyable game and does not produce satisfactory stories.

What these games create is a basic narrative, not a story. The key element they lack is a mechanic or device to create the structure that would turn the former into the latter. In fact, the only simple sequence-of-cards game I know of that actually works is *The Helpless Doorknob*, "a shuffled story by Edward Gorey," a set of twenty illustrated cards that can be

arranged in any order. The resulting story has no beginning, no ending, and a cast of characters whose motives and actions are inexplicable and unexplained: "Alfred returned from Novaya Zemlya / Adela became disoriented at Alaric's funeral / Alethea vanished from a picnic," and so on. While this narrative has the same structural problems as the "stories" produced by *Goosebumps* or *Story Blocks*, it is entirely in keeping with the style and atmosphere of a typical Edward Gorey story, with its themes of strange but unrelated actions hinting at dark, underlying plots, and therefore fits its genre and its purpose perfectly.[3]

What does Gorey's shuffled story have that the others don't? Intentionally or not, it hits one of the four cornerstones that underlie any successful game or system that allows players

3. More recently the card game *Gloom* (2004) combines Gorey-esque themes with a strategic card-game containing story-making elements. Although amusing, the story is not, however, an intrinsic element of the gameplay.

to actively manipulate a story: a clear understanding, encapsulation, and communication of its *genre*. The other three cornerstones, which I will come to shortly, are *structure*, *rules*, and *story/game balance*.

Genre

The current generation of story-making games do not create a fully-fleshed story, which is one of the reasons they do not lend themselves to computer versions or computer-moderated play. Instead, they provide the pieces of the story's skeleton and the rules for assembling it. The players' interaction with the game builds these pieces into the framework of a story, while the players' imagination and improvisation simultaneously add the flesh of the narrative, bouncing off the prompts and inspirations provided by the game engine.

This has three implications relevant to this piece. First of all, many of the story-making games we are considering depend to an extent on the players' ability and confidence in constructing and narrating stories. This is undeniably a weakness: none of them are necessarily won by the best storyteller, but weaker and less assured players may feel they are at a disadvantage.

Second, the game's mechanics must take into consideration the rules of the genre that it is trying to create: not just the relevant icons and tropes, but the nature of a story from that genre. A fairy tale has a very different structure and set of requirements than a horror story or a soap opera, and a game must work to replicate that. Skilled players can do some of the work, but the nature of games, particularly commercial ones, means that a designer cannot make any assumptions about the people who will play their design.

Third, for a group of players to be able to create the same story, they must all understand the basic rules that underlie what's acceptable within it and what isn't—in other words, the basic rules, tropes, and narrative structure of its genre.

The best demonstration of the strength of genre within story-making games is *Pantheon* by Robin D. Laws. *Pantheon* itself is only one of five game scenarios in the book, all of them driven by a system of rules called the Narrative Cage-Match system, which is tweaked for each scenario. Using this system, players create characters and

10.2) The cover of *Pantheon*. (Hogshead Publishing)

work together to tell a round-robin story about those characters within a preset genre. On her turn each player adds a sentence to the story, which must include her character and can include one other player's character. If a player objects to someone else's sentence, she can go head-to-head over changing it or letting it stand.

At its heart this is a very simple and familiar form of story-making, and Laws has the good sense to play to its proven strengths. What he adds is setup, characters, and a scoring system that doesn't kick in until the story-making part of the game is over.

Each of the five scenarios in *Pantheon* starts with a detailed genre-specific setup that most games-players will be familiar with: the crew of an undersea base are attacked by a monster; relatives battle for a deceased gazillionaire's estate; post-Tarantino gangsters feud over a safe of stolen cash; giant monsters destroy an Asian city; and the gods create the universe and mankind. These are the jumping-off points for

10.3.1) Cards from *Dark Cults*. (Dark House)

each story, and beyond that the players are on their own, using only their knowledge of the genre's conventions and tropes and the actions of the other players to construct the story. Usually the narrative created is convoluted but complete and entertaining.

Once the story is done, players are scored depending on how many genre tropes they hit. These can initially be counterintuitive: points are usually awarded for surviving the story, but in some cases you can score more by dying in a generically appropriate way—for example, in "Grave and Watery," the player of the lunatic mercenary scores big if his character is killed not by the monster but by another player. Players don't know in advance the specific tropes they're supposed to use, but it's astonishing how many will crop up in any given game, right down to specific phrases. Familiarity with genre is a powerful tool in story-making.

That doesn't mean that a story-making game has to come from a genre that's well known. *The Extraordinary Adventures of Baron Munchausen*, which I designed, challenges players to tell stories in the style of the late Baron, the eighteenth-century nobleman whose after-dinner descriptions of his singular exploits are still in print today. Not everyone is familiar with these tall tales or the distinctive overblown style in which they are told, and one

of my primary concerns when playtesting the game was whether new players would pick it up quickly enough, or at all. My fears were groundless: it seems there's something in the Baron's style, or in the style of larger-than-life stories generally, that is easily communicated or that people understand instinctively. During the game's first playtest, players were joined by a nine-year-old who had missed the explanation of the rules, but who listened intently to our boasting and tall tales. When his turn came, he spun a completely original story, perfectly in-genre and perfectly in-game.

Communicating genre across a group is one thing, but it's another to pass it on to people who have never seen the game in action—typically people who buy a game in a store. Written down, the rules of *Baron Munchausen* are about five hundred words long and boil down to: "One player is challenged to tell a story on a subject they've never heard before, and must start immediately, while fending off interruptions from the rest of the group." At first sight this appears terrifying, if not nigh-impossible. In fact almost everyone can do it, as long as they're shown in advance that it's possible. But how can a designer show a prospective player not only that the game is playable, but give them the right idiom for playing it?

the abandoned mansion

half real, half imagined flopping

a sobbing young woman

10.3.2) Cards from *Dark Cults*. (Dark House)

The solution I devised for *Baron Munchausen* had a useful side effect: it made it publishable. Nobody was going to pay for a few hundred words of rules, but the *Baron Munchausen* rulebook is written not by me but by the Baron himself—by charming coincidence, I discovered the long-lost manuscript of the game that my ancestor John Wallis, a games publisher in the late 1700s (true) had commissioned from Baron Munchausen (not quite as true). The Baron takes 14,000 words to explain the rules, with frequent humorous digressions, diversions, excursions to refill his glass, and anecdotes about his adventures. By the time the reader reaches the concise version of the rules on the inside back cover,[4] they understand the genre, idiom, and how to play it.

The same idea can also benefit conventional face-to-face role-playing games. The notorious complexity of the mix of ideas in R. Sean Borgstrom's[5] *Nobilis* is eased enormously by its 20-page example of play that demonstrates not only a number of the game's core rule mechanics in use, but also several types of character and how they should be played, the style of the game, and the structure and unfolding of a *Nobilis* adventure.

By contrast, the card game *Once Upon a Time* has a clear and immediately graspable genre: it is based explicitly on classic western European fairy tales. In the game players tell a story using elements from cards in their hands (for example: a Princess, a Forest, Two People Meet, a Sword, This Animal Can Talk), each Storyteller trying to steer the narrative so that she can play out her hand and win by finishing the story with her "Happy Ever After" card. However, other players can interrupt her and take over the story in midflow. These interruptions are the game's key mechanic: players can either interrupt using an Interrupt card, or if the Storyteller mentions a typical fairy tale trope for which another player holds the card.

When my co-designers and I were playtesting *OUaT*, we found that though people were creating great stories while playing the game, it was impossible to use some cards to interrupt because no player ever spontaneously introduced the fairy tale tropes on them into their stories. What was strange is that these cards related to what seemed to us to be standard elements from the best-known fairy tales:

---

4. Or in the current case, the final pages of this volume.

5. "R. Sean Borgstrom" is the same person as Rebecca Borgstrom, whose "Structure and Meaning in Role-Playing Game Design" appears earlier in this section.

10.4.1) Cards from *Once Upon a Time*. (Atlas Games)

dwarves, spinning-wheels, apples, frogs, woodsmen, genies, ghosts, and a sausage. Actually I'm not sure how the sausage got in there. But the players seemed to be in a general unconscious agreement that these elements were not part of the genre of fairy tales they wanted to tell. People don't always tell the sort of stories they like to hear, or the type of story they're familiar with.

Structure

Structure is something I stress a lot when talking about game design. It's a catch-all term to describe the underlying mechanics, the combination and interplay of the game's setting, rules, components, and players' thought processes, assumptions, and behavior that cause the game to work the way it does, and sometimes to work at all.

In most games, the structure is simply the way the game is played. In story-making games, it is also the principal way that the narrative shape of the story is formed, whether that means the overall arc of the story to be created, the nature and motivation of the character or characters at its center, the addition of difficulties for the protagonist to overcome, or the way it moves towards an endgame and satisfactory conclusion.

Structure is not the same thing as rules. The *Once Upon a*

Time rulebook is a handful of small pages, none of which describe the game's structure or explain how the story comes together in play. The rules of *The Extraordinary Adventures of Baron Munchausen*, as noted, boil down to "Each player tells a story while fending off interruptions from the others. Then everyone votes for their favorite story." That's how the game plays. It's not how the game works.

Improvising a story, telling it as fast as it occurs to you, is very not easy. Describing *Baron Munchausen* makes it sound like being constantly interrupted by the other players would make the job even harder, but in fact the opposite is true. Each interruption becomes a narrative rung that the storyteller can choose to reject or build into their story. The other players may think they're hindering the storyteller, but in fact they're doing a lot of the work of progressing the narrative. They are also introducing an important facet of stories: a succession of new difficulties and dangers that the protagonist—who in *Baron Munchausen* is also the storyteller, all stories in the game being told in the first person—must overcome to reach his goal and succeed. The game wouldn't work at all without the interruptions: they function on both a gameplay level and a structural narrative level, and they inject humorous and social elements into the game as well.

 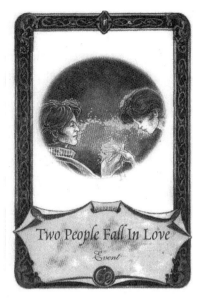 

This Animal Can Talk
Aspect

Two People Fall In Love
Event

Princess
Character

10.4.2) Cards from *Once Upon a Time*. (Atlas Games)

In many face-to-face games, RPGs in particular, structure comes through density of rules,[6] defining the in-game characters' possible and impossible actions with charts and tables. RPGs are an interesting case, because in theory a game-character's actions are limitless: they can go anywhere and do anything within the bounds of the game world, but that would often let them wander outside the scope of the story.

By defining the character's role within the world and giving them implicit goals—defeat things, gain rewards, advance in experience, power, and status—an RPG's rules make sure that characters and therefore players have a focus that allows the referee to create scenarios for them to play through. In a few RPGs that don't do this, usually the slightly more avant-garde ones in which players can create characters from many backgrounds without any shared goal (I'm thinking particularly of the otherwise superb *Over the Edge* by Jonathan Tweet), that focus is lost and scenario creation and play is noticeably less simple.

Story structure can also come from the game's setting and the assumptions that people take from a game's components and packaging. If you buy a game called "Kill the Dragon," you assume that there will be a dragon and to win you must kill it, and that is the direction your play will take. In fact there may be better ways to win the game.

Mertwig's Maze (1988)—not a story-making game, though each player's actions do create a narrative of sorts—presents itself as a humorous quest-style board game: players must undertake adventures to the far corners of the kingdom, beat monsters, recruit allies, and find treasures in order to inherit the throne. However, players can win *Mertwig's Maze* by spending most of the game in the central town, buying equipment and recruiting followers, while never being attacked by monsters, before attacking returning players who have already collected victory tokens, and stealing them. Not very heroic, though it explains a lot about the quality of rulership in fantasy kingdoms.

But very few people play the game like that, partly because the implicit structure angles them away from it, and partly because it's boring. In *Mertwig's Maze*, as in many games, entering into the "spirit of the game" is more enjoyable than playing to win, and in a story-making game that means the creation of a satisfactory story.

6. I treasure the review of *Once Upon a Time* from *Dragon* magazine (the house magazine of then-publisher of *Advanced Dungeons & Dragons*, TSR Inc.), which complained that the game didn't have enough rules (issue 204: April 1994).

Rules

Early role-playing games derived their structure almost entirely from their rules. The first editions of *Dungeons & Dragons* explain almost everything about the game's play by describing the rules by which it works—and by implication how the world the game is set in works. Additional background and setting came mostly from the game's artwork.

Focusing on rules rather than structure or genre to provide narrative shape is a perfectly reasonable approach. All stories must follow the rules of their genre and of storytelling in general if they are to satisfy an audience. However, in fiction and verbal storytelling those rules are concealed from that audience, and visible only to the writer or anyone who analyses the story. In a story-making game—as in games in general—the rules are front and center, and every player has to know them.

A story-making game that uses rules to impose structure is the granddaddy of the field, *Dark Cults* (1983). Based on the stories of horror author H. P. Lovecraft, or more accurately on the atmosphere of stories by H. P. Lovecraft, *Dark Cults* is a card game in which Life and Death—represented by two teams of players—battle for control of the fate of a single protagonist as he takes a sinister late-night excursion. Each player plays a card in turn, either pushing the protagonist into greater danger or offering him a way to safety, and tells a section of the story as she does so. There are several categories of cards, and each one says what other categories can be played after it. This structures the story, creating situations of impending and deepening peril that end either with the character surviving or meeting a grisly fate.

Dark Cults illustrates one of the perils of using rules to give narrative structure. While it works reasonably well as a game *qua* game—its strategy is not sophisticated and its tactics depend on the luck of the card-draw, but it is easy to learn, fun to play, and at the end one side has clearly won— it has two problems.

In the game every card played scores a different number of points depending on which team played it. This has to be tracked turn-by-turn, so attention is constantly drawn away from the story to check the card's point value and write it down. This might not be a problem with many genres of

story-making, but horror stories depend greatly on the creation and maintenance of an atmosphere of dread. *Dark Cults* does this with suitably dark card art and a game mechanic that replicates the style of its genre, but the point-scoring constantly breaks its atmosphere. And in a game that finishes when one side has won control of the character's destiny, why then decide the victor on who did better overall?

I've tried to avoid this pitfall in the design of *Youdunnit* by keeping the rules as stripped-down as possible. The genre of murder mysteries is well understood, so players do not need additional rules to prompt them toward discovering the murderer, and the winner is obviously going to be the person who uncovers the murderer's identity first. There is a bidding mechanism similar to the one in *Baron Munchausen* (q.v.) involving tokens to determine whether each piece of evidence revealed is true or false, but this is backed up by player rhetoric.

The only counterintuitive piece of *Youdunnit's* design, where the rules subsume the genre conventions, is that the identity of the murderer is not fixed at the start: the game's skill involves pinning the crime on another player before anyone can pin it on you. This awareness of the game-nature of the activity forces a detachment between the player and the character they are playing in the game (*Youdunnit* is at heart a role-playing game, though far removed from the Gygax-Arneson design paradigm that has defined the field since the mid-1970s), but it doesn't seem to impede anyone's enjoyment of the game, or their ability to play it to win.

Story and Game Balance

I mentioned before that *Dark Cults* had two significant problems. The first is with its rules, the second lies in the narrative it creates. Although its mechanics build the atmosphere of a classic horror story, it focuses entirely on what in fiction terms would be the midsection of the tale. The establishment of setting and character are perfunctory, as the character leaves his or her boardinghouse for a late-night walk, and the narrative ends either with the protagonist returning to the same location or meeting a suitably unpleasant doom. There's nothing in the cards, the rules or the structure of the gameplay that encourages the creation of an actual plot, and without plot a horror story is just a succession of scares.

For my money, *Dark Cults* depends too heavily on rules and not enough on implicit structure: its stories come secondary to its gameplay, and as a result are rarely satisfying in their own right. While it's fun enough to play, the end of the game usually leaves a somewhat hollow feeling, similar to a Hollywood movie that takes an intriguing premise and realizes somewhere in the third act that it doesn't know the answer to the question it posed at the beginning, or a whodunit in which the murderer is never found.

In defense of *Dark Cults*, I have spent years trying to create a story-making card game based on classic Victorian ghost stories, specifically the work of M. R. James. When this game is done it will be called *It Was a Dark and Stormy Night*, but as yet it doesn't exist. The structure of a ghost story is much more intricate and delicate than that of, say, a fairy tale or a murder mystery, and to capture it satisfactorily in a set of rules and game components has so far proved impossible. More than once I have come up with a new idea for making the game work, only to realize I have, in fact, replicated *Dark Cults'* core mechanic in different clothes.

By contrast, *Once Upon a Time* works well because the fairy tales and fairy tale archetypes on which it is based are universally known and very robust: in the course of one game elements can be introduced, switched around, transformed into a frog, and written out, and you've still produced a satisfactory story with a conclusion and a winner in 10–15 minutes. It works because people understand, not just the tropes of the genre, but the shape of a typical fairy tale. The game mechanics only structure the story in two principal ways: each player's "Happy Ever After" card gives them the ending they must reach; it, and the need to play all the cards in their hand, drives the content of the story they are trying to tell. The rest comes from the knowledge, learned at an early age, of how to assemble discrete elements into a story. I'd be the first to admit that the stories told in a session of *Once Upon a Time* lack depth or emotional resonance, but for the most part they're coherent and complete.

Any game that deals with the creation or telling of a story has to find a balance between its narrative and its gameplay, and the designer has to choose where the emphasis lies. Story-making games have an added difficulty in that, for the game to

work properly, the players have to be prepared to both play the game and tell the story, and give equal weight to both. *Once Upon a Time* has a bad reputation among games purists, because it can be won by gabbling out a nonsense story in order to play all your cards as quickly as possible. We were aware of this as a flaw in the design but couldn't find a way to prevent players like that from playing like that. It may be a victory, but as with the *Mertwig's Maze* "shopping" tactic or the first-turn victory in *Mornington Crescent*, it's not in the spirit of the game.

Once Upon a Time's mechanics are flexible and appear as if they ought to be portable to many other types of story. However, a ghost story told using the same game-engine would be a slapstick affair with nothing resembling the steady build of tension and horror that I'm trying to create with *A Dark and Stormy Night*. There have been fan-created games using *OUaT*'s game design, but with subjects ranging from comic book superheroes to fetish erotica. Most of them work passably well as games, but not well as engines for creating stories in their chosen genre.

No game can exist without rules, at least implicit ones. Many games have nothing else. But in story-making games, too great a density of rules or a single rule in the wrong place can destroy the cohesion or the effect of the story.

Conclusion

The key to a successful story-making game, at least in the ones that have been released so far, is simplicity of design. That doesn't necessarily mean a lack of complexity in its gameplay or narrative structure, but it does mean that rules have to be integrated with structure and genre to form a coherent package. I am a self-confessed proponent of "elegance through simplicity" in game design, and I realize that this doesn't fit every taste, or every style of game. However, if you're presenting a game in which players have to think simultaneously about gameplay, tactics, and creating a coherent story, then there aren't many mental processor-cycles left. In *Once Upon a Time*, a player who is interrupted must draw a new card. It's not a complex rule in a game that doesn't have many, but I've found that around one player in four must be constantly prompted to do it. They don't forget, they're just thinking about other things.

There are more complicated story-making games. *Tales of the Arabian Nights* has a different approach that derives in part from the solo-play adventure game books of the 1980s. Players take the part of Middle Eastern adventurers, exploring a mapboard and encountering all manner of characters, monsters, and hazards. These are determined by a combination of cards, die rolls, and a complex table of matrices, all of which direct the player to the "Book of Tales," which has over 1,300 numbered paragraphs, each one a short episode based on incidents from Middle Eastern folk tales: players are presented with a situation, choose an option, and are rewarded, punished, or thrown down a well as a result.

As the game continues, players mentally build these episodes into a continuing narrative that describes their progress through the game world. That's not the game's primary intention, but while in rules terms it is no different from any board game in which one's turn involves a move, an action, and an effect, the specifically narrative nature of each action, the sheer diversity of them, and their cumulative effect all give the game a unique flavor and add color, depth, and replayability. *Tales of the Arabian Nights* stands in a subtly different classification: the passive or unintentional story-making game.[7]

The bulk of its gameplay and its rules, however, are not concerned with the story, which gives it a curious split personality. On one level there is the strategic play concerned with gaining the money and status needed to win, and on another the amusing and often arbitrary story-fragments (brilliantly written and perfectly in-genre) that are clearly at the heart of the game and provide its major enjoyment.

All the games I've described above are competitive rather than collaborative: while the players may be collaborating on the creating the story, they are competing to win the game, either by manipulating their character into the optimum position (*Pantheon, Youdunnit*) or by controlling the narrative (*Once Upon a Time*). In the current generation of games the skill needed to create a convincing and enjoyable narrative has little overlap with the skill needed to win the game. Only in *Baron Munchausen* does the teller of the best story win. It's possible that in the future greater complexity—or more refined elegance—in the design of story-making games will produce games or at least game-engines that combine gameplay and story-making more closely, and which can create stories that carry greater emotional resonance or meaningful content.

Story-making games are not a major genre at the moment but they offer ideas and techniques relevant to in-game narrative that can, with some intelligent application, make beneficial contributions to any game, whether face-to-face or based on computer. Interactive entertainment does not have to mean the viewer should be a passive participant in the act of storytelling. Creating stories is an ability we all have, and constructing an exciting tale can be as exhilarating as the thrill of winning a tightly-fought game. Like their traditional cousins, story-making games have only one winner, but if the gameplay has created a story that is complete, enjoyable, and satisfying, then everybody wins.

Reference: Literature

Paley, Vivian Gussin (1986). *Mollie is Three: Growing Up in School*. Chicago: University of Chicago Press.

References: Games

City of Chaos. Colin Thornton and Martyn Oliver; Monocle Games. 1996.

Cluedo. Anthony Pratt; Waddington Games. 1948.

Clue Dungeons & Dragons. Hasbro. 2001.

Dark Cults. Kenneth Rahman; Dark House. 1983.

The Extraordinary Adventures of Baron Munchausen. James Wallis; Hogshead Publishing. 1998.

Fable. Peter Molyneux; Lionhead Studios; Microsoft Game Studios. 2004.

Gloom. Keith Baker; Atlas Games. 2004.

Goosebumps Storytelling Card Game. Waddingtons. 1996.

The Helpless Doorknob. Edward Gorey. 1989.

Knights of the Old Republic. Bioware; Lucasarts. 2003.

Lone Wolf and Cub. Matthew J. Costello; Mayfair Games. 1989.

Mertwig's Maze. Tom Wham; TSR Inc. 1988.

Nobilis. R. Sean Borgstrom; Hogshead Publishing. 2002.

Once Upon a Time. Richard Lambert, Andrew Rilstone, and James Wallis; Atlas Games. 1993, revised edition 1996.

Over the Edge. Jonathan Tweet; Atlas Games. 1992.

Pantheon. Robin D. Laws; Hogshead Publishing. 2000.

Star Trek: The Adventure Game. Greg Costikyan; West End Games. 1985.

Story Blocks. Mary Sinker and Robert Venditto; Rhyme & Reason Toys. 1990.

Tales of the Arabian Nights. Eric Goldberg; West End Games. 1985.

---

7. Other related games include *Star Trek: The Adventure Game* (1985), *City of Chaos* (1996), and the lamentably bad *Lone Wolf and Cub* (1989).

Creating a Meaning-Machine: The Deck of Stories Called *Life in the Garden*

Eric Zimmerman

INSTRUCTIONS
Shuffle the pages. Without looking,
Select five pages and place them
Between the covers of the book.
Then read the story.

—from *Life in the Garden*

Life in the Garden (1999) is an interactive paper book I created with graphic designer Nancy Nowacek. The fifty or so pages of the story are cardlike sheets to be shuffled, picked, and placed between the covers of a tiny book, temporarily creating a story. The first page ("Adam, Eve, and the serpent lived in the garden") and the final page ("The End") are always the same, but the rest of the text and images are selected and ordered randomly.

Coherence Out of Chance

For example, running along the bottom of these pages is a story that Nancy created (and then photographed) by following the prescribed instructions:Despite its randomizing mechanism, *Life in the Garden* creates a coherent tale with shape, focus, and closure nearly every time it is read. More than just sets of themed parts, the stories are narratively surprising, highly particular, and often read like philosophical fables, complete with a moralistic conclusion.

In this way, *Life in the Garden* is an inverted exquisite corpse. Instead of an open-ended rule set that produces "surreal" juxtapositions of unexpected content, *Life in the Garden* is a system intended to produce—against all expectations—a coherent narrative experience.

The text and format of *Life in the Garden* was written while I was in graduate school, and the book was published several years later. Even from my early handwritten prototypes on index cards, the project was conceived as an *experience*, and I was lucky enough to have Nancy Nowacek bring her visual and product design smarts to the endeavor. Our goal was to create a magical object that would feel like an artifact from the rabbit hole, a private and precious book in the fashion of Maurice Sendak's tiny volumes of the *Nutshell Library*.

Design Strategies

Life in the Garden was not the result of analytically plotting out content to form. It emerged organically through a process of constant prototyping and playtesting, modifying and refining the format and writing—and later, the images,

11.1) A story of *Life in the Garden*. (RSUB Press)

11.2) A story of *Life in the Garden*. (RSUB Press)

layout, and packaging. Some of my design strategies included the following:

1. Appropriating Eden

The garden of Eden is a set of characters, situations, themes, and ideas that are incredibly pregnant with meanings and possible interpretation. Members of the cast (Eve, God, Adam, the serpent, and the occasional anonymous angel) can be invoked without resorting to backstory exposition. By writing into a story-world that already exists, I take advantage of the reader's presumed knowledge of that world, and the personal meanings that the reader brings.

2. Strategic Writing

Creating the text for *Life in the Garden* was part storywriting and part building-block design. Like a set of LEGO bricks, the pages are modular and must work well in any configuration. Any individual page needs to be able to function as a first page, as an ending page, or as something in the middle. At the same time, the content of the pages must add up to an expressive and varied experience.

3. Thematic Coherence

Part of the "sense" of a *Life in the Garden* story results from a limited number of content themes that are repeated often. Sleeping and dreaming, the time-based processes of nature and their inevitable decay, and the mythologized origin of writing and naming occur throughout the pages. Chances are that in any given story, themes mentioned on some of the pages will overlap.

4. Size Mix

The pages are a set of ingredients for a procedural stew, and the parts had to be balanced to result in a properly variegated texture each time. My playtesting process resulted in a very specific ratio of "short" one-line pages, "medium" pages with two or three lines, and "long" pages of several lines. Themes and content were also parsed carefully into the mix. For example, by only including a handful of genuinely perverse incidents (such as the serpent crawling up Adam's anus) these pages retain their pleasurable surprise, even upon repeat reading.

A Garden of Meaning

I created *Life in the Garden* as an experiment in interactivity and narrative. As a system that sums to more than its set of parts, *Life in the Garden* is a meaning-machine, operating on several interrelated levels:

> one through the designed text and images;
> two as a system physically manipulated by players;
> three by way of the biblical myth that is the setting of the stories.

On all three of these levels (there are certainly many more), the player/reader actively participates in the creation of meaning. By "meaning" I am describing two things: first, the raw process of signification by which signs are given linguistic or other value; and second, the idea of "meaning" as heartfelt

11.3) A story of *Life in the Garden.* (RSUB Press)

11.4) A story of *Life in the Garden.* (RSUB Press)

or personally meaningful. These two senses of meaning for me are intertwined and simultaneous in the experience of *Life in the Garden*. They parallel the two understandings of meaning that Katie Salen and I explored in the concept of "meaningful play" in our book *Rules of Play* (2003).

As a handheld narrative system, *Life in the Garden* is reading as sleight-of-hand, a magic trick where the winking magician and the pleasantly deceived audience are one and the same. The player fills the gaps and ambiguities between the pages with meaning, completing and enlarging the statements that emerge from the designed elements.

For example, consider the text of the following two *Life in the Garden* pages:

So Eve tickled Adam and he laughed.
- and -
God was not pleased.

Encountered in succession, as they are here, it is nearly impossible for the reader *not* to create a causal relationship between the two statements. What was it that displeased God? Was it the tickling? The laughing? Something implied by such intimate behavior? Or perhaps the events on previous pages?

The reader, stumbling across these narrative fragments, invents ways to connect them, imparting to them additional meanings. Woven together with the pages that come before and after, the images that face each page, and the larger associations of the Eden myth, the experience of *Life in the Garden* takes shape as a dense net of signification that changes—literally—each time it is read.

The formal structures and content of *Life in the Garden* could easily be reproduced as a digital work—say, for a personal computer—but it would lose what makes it distinctively compelling. Projected on a monitor and manipulated by a mouse, without the ritual of shuffling and selecting cards, without the intuitively tactile understanding that comes from holding the entire system in-hand, it would simply not work. Excluded from the generation of meaning by hidden black boxes of algorithmic processes and content databases, the participant would no longer have the sense of *making* meaning, and would simply be a witness to a clever confection of randomized story. The failure of *Life in the Garden* in this hypothetical context is an essential lesson for digital media storytellers.

Life in the Garden is out of print. Although I often get inquiries about purchasing copies, they are simply not available. However, this story has not ended just yet. Nancy and I are, after many years, beginning to work on several more decks of stories for a future as-yet-to-be-determined publisher. As I write this, prototypes for future versions based on fairy tales, abstracted narratives, and stylized situations from everyday life are taking shape. From *Life in the Garden*, it seems, many more meanings have yet to emerge.

References

Salen, Katie, and Eric Zimmerman (2003). *Rules of Play: Game Design Fundamentals*. Cambridge, MA: MIT Press.

Zimmerman, Eric, and Nancy Nowacek (1999). *Life in the Garden: A Deck of Stories*. New York: RSUB Press.

11.5) A story of *Life in the Garden*.(RSUB Press)

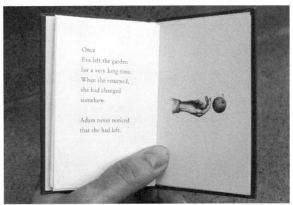

11.6) A story of *Life in the Garden*.(RSUB Press)

11.7) A story of *Life in the Garden.*(RSUB Press)

Design Decisions and Concepts in Licensed Collectible Card Games
Eric Lang (with Pat Harrigan)

There are a fair number of games in the hobby industry based on literary licenses. I've played most of them, and designed a certain number myself. For almost every license, there is a divergent theory about just how a design can capture the essence of the literary property while maintaining its integrity as a game.

The first collectible card game (CCG) I designed was based on Roger Zelazny's *Chronicles of Amber* novels, but unfortunately that design never made it to publication. My first published designs were the *A Game of Thrones* CCG and the *Call of Cthulhu* CCG, both by Fantasy Flight Games (FFG).[1]

Simulation and Evocation

I should note here that the theoretical positions in this chapter are written from the point of view of tabletop games (card, board, role-playing), although I find the principles to be fairly universal. And although there is a general consensus among designers as to the meaning of simulation in games, there are a few slightly different ideas about just what simulation actually means.

To many, simulation means using game mechanics as a set of tools to recreate a linear thread of events, one that mimics the source narrative as closely as possible. Such a design would be considered successful if it were possible for players to use the game to role-play the story (say, the entirety of *The Lord of the Rings* or *A Song of Ice and Fire*), while still being offered the option to diverge from the narrative for the sake of replayability.

12.1) An example of an *A Game of Thrones CCG* plot card. (Fantasy Flight Games)

It is my belief that simulation, as a means to an end, is often misused in games. Many believe that the player's motivation to immerse herself in the world informs every aspect of her play pattern. While it is true that her affinity for the literary property will most likely lead her to the game in the first place, and that a successful atmospheric *evocation* will enhance her experience, it rarely goes farther than this.

"Evocation," is what I have self-defined as the goal of a successful design based on a strong property. I believe that what players want is not so much to transpose themselves into the heart of the narrative through game play, but to enjoy a lateral experience that enhances their overall appreciation for the property.

One can evoke a theme or genre by taking a function-oriented design and priming the rules and components with strategically placed keywords and themes. Thus, the rules and components of a game based on *The Lord of the Rings* will, no doubt, make liberal use of hobbits, ringwraiths, Eyes of Sauron, etc.[2] A game based on *A Song of Ice and Fire* can be expected to involve sellswords, maesters, the Great Houses of Stark, Lannister, and Targaryen, and many other key concepts of George R. R. Martin's books.

This is one area where having a background in writing is a distinct advantage; good writers get the maximum effect

---

1. *A Game of Thrones* is based on George R. R. Martin's *A Song of Ice and Fire* series of fantasy novels, and *Call of Cthulhu* is based on the works of H. P. Lovecraft and other Cthulhu Mythos writers.

2. In fact, Reiner Knizia's excellent board game, *Lord of the Rings: The Confrontation,* is fundamentally such an abstract game, with a *Lord of the Rings* theme "spray-painted" onto it. It should be said that this in no way diminishes the quality of the game itself.

from a carefully chosen minimum of words.

Loaded words in games do double duty in this case: they both harness a player's intuition to evoke the mood or atmosphere of the setting, and ease the learning curve of the game itself (stories are easier to follow than a highly technical set of rules). The choice of which (and how many) terms to use is not trivial, of course. One cannot simply pepper a game with random fantasy jargon, lest it seem contrived and burdensome.

While it is true that tension exists between the authorial dictatorship of storytelling and the decision trees of game playing, games are not without narrative flow. Like stories, games have a beginning, middle, and end. The best games have an ebb and flow of tension that escalates between "plot points" (in games, these are what I refer to as the "payoff moments"—when the tide of strategy in a game has turned in a player's favor, and the action takes a new direction) until finally arriving at a climax.

While it is important to make sure a game is fair and balanced, it is equally important to engineer the experience such that the average game will follow such a narrative flow. If players are acutely aware of a beginning, middle, and end to their game experience, this will also serve to evoke the literary source material.

Respecting the Medium

As with all licenses, it must be recognized that a game set in a particular extra-game storyworld is an *adaptation* of the story experience. Games form their own paradigm, obviously, but even within the realm of games there exist several unique paradigms that must be understood and respected. Trying to create, for example, a "strategic game of spatial relations" as a collectible card game (and not, for

12.2) An example of an *A Game of Thrones* CCG character card. (Fantasy Flight Games)

instance, a board game, for which the concept might be better suited) will often lead to a subpar result.

For example, the creators of Guardians of Order's *A Game of Thrones* role-playing game undertook a drastically different design process than I did with the *AGOT* collectible card game. This much might seem obvious, but I have too often witnessed designers take a single approach to a property regardless of medium.

Creative Practicalities

The process of creating a CCG is not a solitary one. Although I created the game structures and rules for both the *A Game of Thrones* and *Call of Cthulhu* CCGs, FFG management advised at all stages of the initial development. After the games launched, I restricted myself to designing the mechanics of the individual cards, leaving much of the creative development (writing card names, assigning art descriptions to the artists, creating "flavor text") to the FFG staff developers (mostly staff CCG developer Casey Galvan and my studio partner Jonathan Moriarty) or freelancers. Teams of playtesters were also employed to identify potential problems with card interactions that were missed during design and development.

A Game of Thrones CCG

To my advantage, I had already read most of the *Song of Ice and Fire* series before being asked to lead the design of the collectible card game. I could have designed a game that simulated the events of the War of Five Kings effortlessly, but this was not the goal. Before the design period began, FFG had identified its target market: fantasy readers and collectible card game "fad players" (i.e., the pool of gamers in the hobby industry who drift from hot new game to hot new game—whose loyalty is invaluable but difficult to obtain).

Most of the players for the game would be familiar with collectible card games, but would only have dabbled in them at best. It was also crucial to the success of the game that it

12.3) An example of a *Call of Cthulhu CCG* story card.
(Fantasy Flight Games)

be playable without *any* knowledge of the property. At the time, Martin's series was very popular but had not quite peaked. It was at what we called a "latent" stage, where it still had the opportunity to significantly grow its fan base. This was important at the beginning stage of design, because it meant I also had to take into account that approximately half of our initial audience would not yet have read the books.

One of the decisions I made in the game design that truly paid off was the use of carefully chosen "loaded" terms. For example, I selected the term "kneel" to indicate that a particular card has been temporarily used (this is a standard CCG mechanic, normally called "tap" or "turn"). This strongly evoked a medieval air, and brought to mind the many occasions in the series where characters are said to "bend the knee" to signal obedience. The names of some of the phases of the game turn (Plot, Draw, Marshalling, Challenges, Dominance, Stand) strongly implied a narrative flow; the first card a player would see when he or she began the game would be a House card with these phases written on it. Without knowing a single thing about the game, a new player would subconsciously approach the game expecting medieval conflict and intrigue. This in turn would inform the remainder of their experience.

The *AGOT* gameplay breaks down to this: each player represents one of the Great Houses of Westeros, and competes to be the first player to reach 15 points of power. They do this by marshalling certain characters (sometimes specific characters from the books, such as Eddard Stark or

Collectible Card Games

The first collectible card game was Wizards of the Coast's *Magic: The Gathering*, still the most popular and profitable CCG in the world. All other CCGs inevitably descend from the *Magic* model.

Several of the larger publishers release collectible card games in "sets" or "blocks" of new cards several times a year. FFG releases three sets each of *AGOT* and *COC* every year: one "base set," consisting of 240-odd cards, and two "expansion sets" of 140-odd cards; the three annual sets are referred to collectively as a "block."

Each release consists of a certain number of new cards, some of which are more easily obtainable than others. FFG, following the model of most other hobby game companies, releases each new set in the form of packs of cards; each pack contains eleven cards randomly drawn from the new set, seven of which are "common" cards, three of which are "uncommon," and one of which is "rare." Consequently it is more difficult to collect the uncommon cards than the commons, and significantly more difficult to collect the rares.

Although it is practically and financially infeasible for most players to collect every card from a particular release, it is fortunately not necessary to try. Players are expected to construct playable "decks" of cards (usually of about 50–60 cards) from the pool of cards available to them; their opponents do the same. Players then square off, seeing who can construct the better deck and, once constructed, utilize it better.

What sets CCGs apart from other forms of hobby games is the on-the-fly customizability of each player's deck. While a typical board or card game (e.g., *Clue*, poker) utilizes a single unvarying set of game components (board and pieces, deck of fifty-two cards, etc.), players of a CCG have hundreds or thousands of cards to select from when constructing their decks. If a player is being routinely beaten by an opponent, she may revise or reconstruct her deck, using different cards from the available sets, in order to beat her opponent the next time she plays. That opponent may then find herself in the same position, and need to reconstruct her own deck—and so on ad infinitum.

Khal Drogo, and sometimes more generic types, such as "House Umber Knight" or "Sellsword"— but even most of the generic characters are named in accordance with the conventions George R. R. Martin laid out in his series) and competing with their opponents' characters in three types of challenges: military, intrigue, and power. Different challenges provide different benefits for the winner.

In addition to their primary deck of cards, players also have a seven-card "plot deck," one card of which each player reveals each round. The revealed plots have global effects (such as "Kill all characters in play") and identify other parameters for that round as well, such as how much gold the player will have to spend, in what order she takes her turn, etc. The plot cards were an attempt to reconstruct some of the larger trans-individual events in Martin's series, events that were not triggered solely by the actions of particular characters or Houses. On a gameplay level, they added another element of player strategy: in addition to selecting characters, locations, events, and items for their primary decks, players also had to decide which plots would most hinder their opponents and allow their own primary decks to work to their best advantage.

Even beyond the combinatorial aspects of the other cards, the plot cards added more potential variation to game events. In my early years as a designer I had learned a powerful lesson: part of what people enjoy about licensed properties is the ability to break the author's rules and create situations that break canon. Many designers might shy away from "ridiculous" situations within the game-sphere, but I embraced the possibilities.

A helpful mantra is: *Respect the medium*. Collectible card games are at their root combinatorial exercises; players fall in love with possibilities as much as they do strategies, and no other type of game offers more options. As long as players

12.4) An example of a *Call of Cthulhu CCG* character card. (Fantasy Flight Games)

could conceive of the possibility that an event might take place in the world of Westeros, I had to make sure it could be done in the game. And in many cases, things that could never happen in the books could also be done.

A Contrasting Design: *Call of Cthulhu CCG*

Designing FFG's follow-up to the *A Game of Thrones* CCG was a very different experience. The Cthulhu Mythos is a far more diffuse series of works than the three volumes of *A Song of Ice and Fire* that had then been published. The design mandate had limited our source material to those stories written by H. P. Lovecraft and those game materials published by Chaosium (excluding much contemporary Lovecraftian fiction and certain latter-day game properties to which we didn't have the rights, such as Pagan Publishing's *Delta Green*), but this was still a vast amount of material.

Complicating things even further was the nature of the Cthulhu Mythos itself. Martin's series was the creation of a single author, but the material of the Cthulhu Mythos was a patchwork of stories and game material from dozens of different authors, over the course of most of the twentieth century. Lovecraft himself wasn't interested in formalizing the background and concepts of the Cthulhu Mythos (in fact, the idea of doing so was arguably opposed to his aesthetic project), so there was no central authority to refer to as there was in the case of *A Game of Thrones*.

At the same time, this freed the creative team (mostly Pat Harrigan and Darrell Hardy) to get inventive with the material. George R. R. Martin had assembled a coherent fantasy world for *A Song of Ice and Fire* and was understandably protective about the liberties we could take with that world. But the loose, almost improvisational, nature of the Cthulhu Mythos allowed the design team a certain amount of artistic license.

On a design level though, this presented a problem. The

Chaosium RPG—which would be the reference point for most people in our industry familiar with the Mythos—had generally cast players as intrepid investigators fighting the forces of the Mythos, and this lent itself to a two-sided "asymmetrical design." Players would either play the investigators or the unspeakable horrors of the Mythos. However, feedback from hobby games retailers had convinced FFG that a game consisting of only two non-combinable sides was not a saleable product. There had to be more than two factions, and they had to be fully combinable. Therefore, we invented seven factions (the Blackwood Detective Agency, Miskatonic University, the Syndicate, the Cthulhu Cult, the Cult of Hastur, the Cult of Yog-Sothoth, and the Cult of Shub-Niggurath), any one of which could be combined with any other.[3]

The original *COC* design involved Investigators trying to complete "case" cards, and Mythos players trying to complete "conspiracy" cards, but this made no sense in the new seven-faction design. I collapsed the cases and conspiracies into one "story card" deck that was functionally distinct from the *AGOT* "plot" deck. Instead of each player bringing a customized plot deck, in *COC* the players would draw from a central deck of story cards, three of which would be drawn at the start of each game and placed between the players. When a story card was won, it would be replaced with the next card from the story deck.

The story deck would always consist of the same ten cards, but would be shuffled before each game so that players could not predict the order in which the cards would come up. Players would compete to place victory tokens on their side of the story. The first player to get five tokens on their side would win that story card; the first player to win three story cards would win the game.

Like *AGOT*'s plot cards, the story cards would have global effects (e.g., "Discard all characters in play"), but these effects would only trigger if the winner of the story card wanted them to. In other words, if you won a story, you had the option of enacting its effects.

This is the inverse of *AGOT*'s "plot" model. In Martin's *A Song of Ice and Fire* (still uncompleted at the time of this writing), the reader is privy to the complicated intrigues of the Great Houses, but not to their ultimate outcomes. In the heterogeneous stories of the Cthulhu Mythos, the resolution of any individual tale is often reliant on whether the forces of humanity or the abyss get the upper hand (and there are plenty of examples of both in Lovecraftian fiction and Chaosium's RPG). Therefore the resolution of *AGOT*'s plots is only a step on the road to victory, while the successful resolution of *COC* stories is an end in itself—in fact, it is the very way victory is achieved.

References

Call of Cthulhu CCG. Eric Lang; Fantasy Flight Games. 2004.

A Game of Thrones CCG. Eric Lang and Christian T. Petersen; Fantasy Flight Games. 2002.

Magic: The Gathering. Richard Garfield; Wizards of the Coast. 1994.

3. To avoid absurdities such as Professor Armitage teaming up with Cthulhu, we also introduced the keywords "Heroic" and "Villainous." A heroic character could not be in play on the same side as a villainous character, and vice versa.

One Story, Many Media
Kevin Wilson

Video Games	Board Games
Good at real-rime	Poor at real-rime
Orchestrated soundtrack	Sound effects difficult and expensive
Instant gratification	Slower playing experience
Lack of human interaction	Face-to-face (very social)
2D (visual elements only)	3D (tactile elements)

Thanks to modern licensing practices, it's not unusual to see one Intellectual Property (IP) translated into many different forms. Such conversions can prove extremely challenging, but they're also a good way to identify an IP's core "value proposition"—that is, the essential set of traits that allow the consumer to recognize the IP as being unique and valuable. It's also a good way to examine differences in storytelling across different media. During the last several years, I've created licensed board games from such diverse game media as video games (*Warcraft* and *Doom*) and pen-and-paper role-playing games (*Call of Cthulhu*). Each such conversion brings its own challenges, but at the core is a single task: How can I retell a story designed for an entirely different medium in a way that acknowledges the strengths and weaknesses of the medium I'm working in?

Perhaps the best illustration of this was the *Doom 3* conversion from video game to board game. In its original form, *Doom* relied on state-of-the-art rendered 3D graphics, a carefully orchestrated soundtrack, and hundreds of lighting and animation effects to deliver its story. Additionally, the play experience was one of total adrenaline and instant gratification, featuring online death matches and a dedicated modding community eager to use the graphics engine to create their own works of art. In fact, *Doom* effectively created the first-person shooter death match community when it first brought office LANs around the world to a standstill after its release.

However, it didn't seem like it was enough to simply simulate the video game in board game form. Doing that would deliver nothing new and exciting to the fan base and, worse, would ignore the strengths and weaknesses of the board game medium—effectively, the story would suffer. Struggling with the issue for a while, it was easiest to finally make a shopping list comparing video games to board games:

A list of the core elements of *Doom* was also created:
Doom weapons (Shotgun, BFG, Chainsaw, etc.)
Doom monsters (Imps, Mancubi, Pinky Demons, etc.)
Marines
Mars base
Moving through corridors
Opening doors
Color-Coded keycards
Triggered events
Different levels

With these lists, I was able to focus in on the things that board games were good and bad at, and the things I needed to retain the *Doom* "identity." Obviously the board game wasn't going to be able to rely on any sort of animated graphics or sound. Additionally, there was no way to capture the freewheeling adrenaline blast of the computer game—board games simply played too slowly for that. However, board games had their strengths. They were face-to-face, so the player communication issues that haunt video games even after the creation of such programs as Teamspeak were negligible. Better yet, they could use tactile elements, engaging a player's sense of touch in a way that video games couldn't. Armed with this information, it was much easier to determine what features to focus on and emphasize in the design.

First, it was determined that gameplay would be kept simple and fast, to get as close to simulating the speed of the video game as possible. A player's turn consisted of choosing one of four actions and carrying it out, while attacks were distilled to a single die roll that determined both range and damage. Large sculpted plastic miniatures would take advantage of the tactile strengths of the medium, and it was decided to pit a team of marines against a single monster player in order to maximize the social elements of the game.

13.1) The layout of *Doom: The Board Game*. (Fantasy Flight Games)

Finally, randomized special abilities were added to the marines to pigeonhole them into specific roles and enhance the need for teamwork. The story arc was effectively changed from a solitary marine facing hordes of monsters to a team of marines working together against an unseen menace controlling dozens of monsters. The monster player could threaten and bluster, while the marine players would need to discuss strategies in order to act as a team.

Once this was accomplished, it was a simple matter to import the core concepts of *Doom*—creating weapons and monsters using the attack dice system, and building changeable boards out of cardboard. A series of scenarios, or levels, were created for the marines to fight their way through, and triggered events were added both in the scenarios and in the form of event cards to keep things surprising even after the players had played through a level previously. In addition, the triggered events could allow me to tell stories through the board game that I wouldn't have previously thought possible. With them, I could create more effective foreshadowing, branching plotlines, and even more complicated player decision trees. I was also able to follow the storyline of the video game, but keep it different enough to surprise hardcore fans.

In the end, the finished result had some very distinct differences from its video game roots, but it still retained the "feel" of *Doom*, because the core elements were retained and adapted to the new medium. Better still, it delivered a play experience that was unique and different from the video game, allowing fans to experience one of their favorite stories in a

whole new way, and so I consider the design an artistic success.

The original board game *Arkham Horror* was designed by Richard Launius and published by Chaosium in 1984. In the two decades since the game's original publication, the hobby game market (and board game design philosophies) have changed drastically, so when Fantasy Flight Games acquired the license to republish *Arkham Horror*, a thorough overhaul of the game was necessary. Beyond simply commissioning new art and designing more modern-seeming game components, I fundamentally altered some of the core rules mechanics (e.g., instead of rolling dice for movement, each Player Character now has a "Speed" score that determines how far he or she can move).

This redesign was challenging, to be sure, but it also offered some exciting opportunities for storytelling, particularly because it allowed me to draw more deeply on some of the storytelling elements of the *Call of Cthulhu* role-playing game (the inspiration for Richard's original design). For example, I replaced the charts and tables in the original game with location-specific decks of cards, which are drawn from when a player moves to that location. Typically, these are short, self-contained encounters that tell a brief story. However, by carefully crafting these encounters for each location, it is possible to give each place a certain feel, with recurring characters and themes.

I also experimented with creating actual story arcs via the location decks. In one instance, a kindly old man named Harney Jones helps out the player during most of the encounters at a certain location. However, one encounter results in the death of the old man and the closure of that location for the rest of the game. Due to the random nature of the location decks, it's possible for the old man to die immediately the first time a player enters that location. However, with repeated plays, the players learn and remember the story as I intended it, because even if it doesn't work out every time, more often than not it occurs in the order I intended. The players meet kindly old Harney Jones, he helps them out somehow, and then later they find that he

able to create a story that feels dangerous and tense for the player who chooses to take a gamble and accept the deal.

The funny thing is, I only stumbled across these methods of storytelling for board games because I was attempting to convert a role-playing game

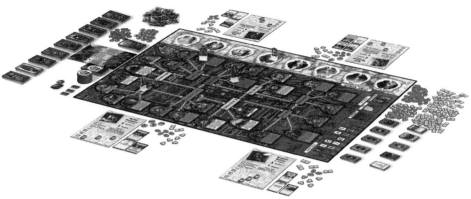

13.2) The layout of *Arkham Horror*. (Fantasy Flight Games)

has passed away while sitting in the rocking chair on his porch. It's not a complex story, but it's certainly more involved than players expect from a board game.

Another location features the possibility of accepting a deal from a dark stranger to gain some beneficial items now for an unspecified cost later. All that the player is told is that he should "remember that you have make a deal with the dark man of Wizard's Hill." He has to take the cost on faith unless he's played the game enough to learn what it is beforehand. There is a random event deck that is drawn from every turn, and in that deck is a single card that calls the debt due by killing every character that made a deal with the dark man. On the one hand, the card could never come up, and the player would receive a powerful reward for free. On the other hand, if the card does show up, it has a good chance of costing the players the game. In this way, I was

into one. Without the outside stimulus of the role-playing game, I wouldn't have noticed that it's possible to create fairly complex and interesting stories in the form of a board game. Similarly, the triggered events in *Doom* only came about because of similar triggered events that I've seen and programmed into video games, effectively an IF . . . THEN tree. So, I've found that by respecting a medium's strengths and weaknesses, but at the same time looking to see what storytelling techniques other media have to offer, I've been able to bring some genuinely new things to the world of board gaming.

References

Arkham Horror. Richard Launius and Kevin Wilson; Fantasy Flight Games. 2005.

Doom: The Board Game. Kevin Wilson; Fantasy Flight Games. 2004.

On *Mystery of the Abbey*
Bruno Faidutti

Every game tells a story, even the most abstract one. A game of chess or *Go* has a beginning, a development, an intrigue, characters and reversals, and a denouement, and can be retold as such. An abstract story, however, doesn't speak to one's imagination, and that's probably why I've always favored strongly themed games and still consider role-playing games—and specifically live action role-playing games (LARPs), which capture the theatrical essence of role-playing games—as the only real games, and all other kinds of games, be they abstract games, computer games, or board games, as merely substitutes.

The fact is, however, that I don't have the time and energy any longer to indulge in writing LARP scenarios and organizing such big events—and that I'm becoming a bit of a lazy homebody. That's probably why I've given up live-action role-playing, after about ten years of intensive practice, and moved to the calmer and smoother universe of board games.

14.1) *Mystery of the Abbey*. (Days of Wonder)

My LARP gamer history, however, as well as my interest in literature, is probably the reason why I try to give a strong theme to all my games and to have them tell something that feels like a story, something you can retell when the game is over—something you can dream of.

I always keep in mind when designing a game that it must have a kind of "story arc" (I hope I've understood this idea, since there's no equivalent for "story arc" in the French language), a thread that will both help players place themselves in the game, know where and when they are, and create some growing tension, some apprehension of what will happen later. A real story, in an evocative historical or fantasy setting, is one of the most efficient ways to suggest this story arc and the one I usually use when I design a game, but it's not the only one available since you can easily retell a game of chess or *Go* with the same tension and suspense as a whodunit.

Mystery of the Abbey is a whodunit board game for three to six players. It is derived from *Clue*, but is a kind of more fun, wild, and chaotic *Clue*. The setting is the abbey from Umberto Eco's *The Name of the Rose*, and players move about the abbey trying to find out who killed Brother Adelmo—which in game terms means determining which one of twenty-four suspect cards is missing (placed under the board at the start of the game, without any player looking at it). Step by step, or rather, mass after mass, players get clues about the murderer: Is he a father, a brother or a novice? A Franciscan, a Benedictine, or a Templar?[1] Clues can be found by asking other players about the suspect cards in their hands, or using the special abilities of the different buildings in the abbey.

The first version of what would later become *Mystery of the Abbey* was a science fiction game, *The Red Creature with One Eye and Eight Tentacles*. The story was a kind of second-degree whodunit, all about finding out which creature was missing from the space station by asking players about the number of one-eyed, three-tentacled, or green creature cards in their hand. It was fun, but a bit of a brain burner,[2] and the theme was not really suggestive. When Serge Laget and I decided to use this base system for a *Name of the Rose* game,

---

1. In the original version of the game, the third order was the Dominicans, and the French edition uses the Hospitallers. (See sidebar.)
2. A "brain burner" is a game that requires such deep strategic thinking that the theme, and sometimes the fun of the game, is forgotten.

14.1) Pawns for *Mystery of the Abbey*. (Days of Wonder)

it meant more than changing the setting, and it brought many new rules and elements to the game.

The rule stating that you can make a vow of silence (refuse to answer a question posed by another player) has a strong effect on the game and strongly contributes to the monastic ambiance. This is more allusion—in French we say a "wink"—than simulation. When someone states that he has made such a vow, you know you are in a monastery—even though it has nothing to do with the monastic orders used in the game, and even though in the real world you usually don't make such a vow for just a few hours.

It is the same with the masses that regulate the game. Every four turns, players are called to mass and their pawns gather in the abbey church. Players pass cards to their neighbors during the mass, suggesting the talking and whispering of monks at this occasion. Also, there is always some unexpected event occurring at the end of the mass— suggested by drawing an event card. Laget and I wanted action cards, and calling them "books" was an obvious move.

This shows clearly that there is no "first" and "second" between game systems and game setting, but that when the design flows well, as I like it to flow, systems and theme regularly generate each other in a dialectic process. Sometimes, a mechanism can induce a theme (a whodunit game where you look for the culprit can be set in the Cadfael/*Name of the Rose* universe); sometimes the setting

Meddling with Monks

When he painted the monk figures, Emmanuel Roudier took his inspiration from the character cards in the first edition of the game, and from a few monk figures he found here and there in his books. He made gray monks, brown ones, and white and black ones (the latter supposedly Dominicans, although they usually dress in plain white). Afraid that there could be confusion between the gray monks and the white ones, the publisher decided to change the white and black to white and red—easy to do with Photoshop. (The red monks indeed look nicer and are easy to distinguish from the others.) When I received the first files, I was shocked. I immediately protested that red Dominicans were something really strange and would not look serious, and asked to make them plain white. I was answered that they looked nicer in red (that's true) and that Days of Wonder's first market was American families, who don't care about the color of Dominican robes, since they have absolutely no idea about it, if they have ever even heard of Dominicans.

We had long phone and e-mail arguments about it, until I suggested a compromise: we keep the red monks, but we name them Hospitallers. Hospitallers are supposed to be in white, with a red Hospitaller cross, and are often figured in war costume. They were not only fighting monks, in fact some of their monasteries indeed used to provide food and shelter to pilgrims. I thought everything was okay, until someone found out that the same American families (see above) didn't know about Hospitallers and might think that the game had something to do with hospitals and medicine. . . . So we now have Hospitallers in the French version, and Templars in the American one!

This is a fun story, but I think it shows well the concern we all, designers and publishers, have both for the technical playability of the game and for its ability to generate the feeling of a story, a feeling that needs nothing in the game that will feel "out of place" to players and could destroy the magic—like the paratroopers' base in the Balearics in *El Grande*.

suggests a mechanism (if it's a monastery, there must be a rule about silence, and there must be masses).

The idea was to suggest both *Clue* and *The Name of the Rose*, so there had to be rooms, there had to be a murder, and there had to be monks. Our rooms not only have different names, but also different effects, selected both to be useful in the game and to suggest the story. A problem with *Clue* is that you can play Miss Scarlet without knowing that Miss Scarlet is the murderer, and we took care to avoid such incoherencies. To differentiate the monks, rank and order sounded obvious,

and combining those with a physical aspect gave a strong whodunit feel to the questions asked: "Have you seen a fat, bearded Benedictine . . ." Now you are in a whodunit.

Reference: Literature

Eco, Umberto (translated by William Weaver) (1983). *The Name of the Rose*. Orlando: Harcourt Books.

Reference: Games

Mystery of the Abbey. Bruno Faidutti and Serge Laget; Days of Wonder. 2003.

On *Life's Lottery*
Kim Newman

Life's Lottery is a *Choose Your Own Adventure*-style novel in 300 sections, which range from a few sentences to several pages each. The reader takes on the role of Keith Marion and, by making a series of choices, guides Keith throughout his life, from his birth (in Section 1) to a number of possible outcomes. Many of the important elements in Keith's later life are formed by childhood events: a deliberate decision to pass or fail an exam strongly influences Keith's later economic opportunities; the decision whether to participate in a cruel childhood game (catching and passing on "Timmy germs") affects the reader's perception of Keith's psychological makeup.

Structure and Design

I didn't have the idea of 300 sections at the very beginning, but it came up fairly early in the process, maybe even in the first week of actual writing. Limiting the number of sections to 300 had no particular significance (I can't even remember how I arrived at it), but had several practical uses, including keeping the novel to a manageable size.

I suspect I wrote the book the only way it could be written—much as it's usually read, by following particular threads and branches through. This means that early on, I was picking numbers for sections fairly arbitrarily and later filling in between sections already written. I wanted the book to read chronologically if a reader started at page one and proceeded as in a normal novel, and so there was a certain amount of provisionality (I had a lot of Post-It notes with numbers and arrows up on a paper flowchart as an outline) until everything was set.

Early in the process, I decided to limit in some ways the paths Keith, and thus the reader, took through life, to keep the word length practical but more importantly to concentrate on the central character rather than explore his world. Given that he was born about when I was (though his background and most of his lives are very unlike mine) and I didn't want to make the book too

science-fictional (in the sense of depicting the future, which I thought would distract from the focus on the personal), there isn't much about the character's life past early middle age. I have a token strand or two that take the story into the 2020s and beyond, but not many. I could have had Keith symbolically born in 1900 and taken him through to old age—but that would have made the book a historical novel, inevitably getting caught up in a couple of world wars, which would be a similar distraction. I've written quite a few books and stories with "big-picture settings," in which huge historical events are dealt with, and one of my self-set disciplines here was not to do that; there are lines in which Keith becomes powerful, but we don't go there much.

Although I didn't abandon anything I had written or outlined, I realized early on that the book was infinitely extensible. Even within the rules I'd set for myself, I could have continued forever with different timelines. In the book, the narrator's voice notes some things that might be stacking the odds—like the disproportionate number of early deaths that occur, mostly, to tie off branches, but also to emphasize the fragility of anyone's life. We all dodge death every day by crossing the road, and so the other possibility is always there.

Section 1

My friend, you have a choice. Of course, you have a choice. You can go this way or that. You can call heads or tails. You can have coffee or tea.

It's simple.

Except maybe you don't have a choice. Because of matters settled before your father's sperm met your mother's egg, you don't have a choice. You're set on this road. You always call heads. You must have tea.

Maybe that's the choice. To have a choice or not to have a choice. Free will or predestination.

You choose.

Think about it for a while. Use one side of the paper. Leave a wide margin. Don't skip on regardless, though. Really think. It's important. It affects everything.

Get back to me when you've made up your mind. When you've chosen.

When you've made your choice, go to 2.

Options

Certain of the book's themes became important because they came up while I was writing and seemed like useful fulcrums. I wanted to make some events trivial and some momentous. This is a lot like my usual process of writing fiction: recurring themes or images tend to arise early on and get used throughout. Some have a personal meaning for me (the story about the buried tin of marbles is something from my childhood) and some just come up in the process and are incorporated into the fictional lives (I don't know why there's a pirate theme in the book—unless it's a vague memory of the pirate theme in *Watchmen*).

I had a specific political purpose in the sections dealing with the British education system as it was in the 1970s—and which some people tend to agitate for a return to even now. I wanted to show the injustice of deciding a child's educational future on one exam taken at the age of ten or eleven—which is why I had a branch in which Keith fails the exam and then tries to catch up later but can't. I was aware that the book has to cheat a bit here, and assume the boy has a choice to pass or fail—but I didn't think I could get away with including an exam paper and asking the reader to take it, then self-assess which school they would have gone to. Apart from anything else, very few readers will be the actual age the exam was designed for.

An equivalent "game" like that of "Timmy germs" was played at my primary school, and I've no idea how it affected the girl (a gypsy, I think) who was its victim. I wanted to keep stressing choices between easy morality (we all think as adults we wouldn't have done things like that) and the pressure to take part in an unjust society (as children, we mostly did—all these years on, I can't even remember whether I did or not).

Here, my assumption was that most readers would "do the right thing" on the first run-through, whether they would have or not in real life; the point of a lot of these choices is multifold: first to make you ask what you would do in this situation, then to empathize with Keith and ask what he would do, and finally to read all the options and consider the consequences. This is a way in which the *LL* format differs from "normal" fiction—here, you are at once a reader and the main character, and so

the "Keith" of every person who reads the book is a different, unique character created in collaboration between the reader and the author.

Quite a few story possibilities also "double back" on themselves, merging with the outcomes of other possible choices. This is partly because I wanted to make it clear to the reader that it was all right to turn back the pages and explore different timelines—that their initial choices weren't definitive. I did hear of one person who read the book by making a series of choices, reading those sections, and thought he had finished when he came to a death or an "And so on"—then put it aside without considering the rest of the text, which is fair enough, but not what I hoped for. By including certain literal time travel elements, I assumed people would get the message that they *could* go back and start again, or read in parallel sections that show different outcomes from choices. One conception of the book is that it's de facto science fiction, since it deals with alternate realities (there are alien invasions and time travel and other things, but that's science fiction furniture rather than theme).

Novel or Game?

I think *LL* is designed to *seem* like a game, but not be one. There is no true or correct or winning path—the point is to consider all the losing options. The book is probably disproportionately downbeat, because happy, uneventful lives would have been dull to read about. Readers (and writers) are in a thorny relationship with fictional characters: in theory, they might like them, but in practice they want them to have difficult, often painful lives so they are interesting to read about. Here, I make more explicit this sadism—often, choosing a path that's bad for Keith makes for more fun for the reader. A great deal of Keith's character is provisional, dependent on choices the reader makes, which the author then shores up in the consequent section by making him (perhaps retroactively) the sort of person who would have taken that route.

All the possibilities were equally real to me, even the obviously fantastical ones (which are used quite sparingly). I deliberately incorporated strands that took us out of "social realism" into various forms of fantasy—for instance, if the reader commits Keith to a vigilante revenge storyline, the book turns into an action movie scenario that is probably less "convincing" than other paths, if more satisfying in some ways. I took care to work in a whodunit, horror stories, social satire, perilous journey, farce, *noir*-like crime, etc., because all of those are possible genres that a book could turn into. One of the things about the postmodern generation, of which Keith and I are members, is that we are aware of genre and pop culture, and that it shapes the way we see or label things, which is why there's so much discussion of films, TV, pop music, etc. in the book.

Arbitrariness and Socially Formed Character

When I set out to write the book, I was torn between believing that every little choice we make can have a butterfly effect and reshape our entire lives, and that nothing we do matters because blind chance can whisk us off on paths we didn't even consider. I tried to keep that balance in the book—partly because it seems that the balance exists in life, and partly because it made *LL* "work" better.

I did include deliberately misleading choices—like a bit about seat belts, where Keith ends up in one of those accidents where taking the safety precaution gets the passenger's neck broken. (I'm not sure of the statistics on this, but I suspect they're higher than the automobile industry would have you believe—though less so with the extensible belts now in use than back when this scene was set.)

I also decided that the narrator of this second-person book would not be me, but a fairly demonic, though mostly honest character, which means he's playing with the reader even as some readers are trying to "play" the book. The red wire/blue wire choice was an obvious one to put in, since it's in all those bomb disposal scenes in films—which rarely deal with the fact that people who build bombs (unlike those who build useful appliances) can use whatever color wires they like, and so disposal experts in real life have to ignore such signifiers.

One of Keith's unhappier storylines allows him a choice between a sad sexual fantasy involving *Star Trek*'s Lieutenant Uhura and one involving *Doctor Who*'s Jo Grant. I happen to prefer *Doctor Who* to *Star Trek*, for quite cogent reasons that are beside the point in the terms of the novel. (I've just done a book for the British Film Institute on *Doctor Who*, which goes a bit further into this.) This is why things work the way they do when the choice is made—but beyond that, both series had episodes with "evil alternate universe" doppelgangers.

This is something at the heart of *LL*, but still unusual in the alternate history sub-genre. In most AH novels, any real historical characters included—usually presidents, etc.—have recognizably the same characteristics they had in the real world (Adolf Hitler is a fascist bastard, etc.); but *Star Trek* and *Doctor Who*, in the "Mirror, Mirror" and "Inferno" stories, posit that if the world were different, people we know (recurring characters) would be different too, which suggests (bluntly) that if society were more rotten than it is, we would be more rotten too (and Spock would have a beard). Though *LL* isn't much concerned with changes in society, I did want to show character as defined by circumstance—things we think of as inherent and inbuilt, like sympathies or sexuality, might be up for grabs if our lives were radically different.

The Lottery

The book's recurrent lottery theme is partly topical—when I was writing the book, the United Kingdom had only recently introduced a national lottery and there was still a lot of fuss about it. It may even be arbitrary in that having decided this title (my alternate was *Choose Your Own Adventure*) I was more or less forced to put the real lottery into the storylines. Nevertheless, it does connect with the tension between the illusion of effort (picking "lucky" numbers, using "systems," as in roulette, etc.) and the reality of random chance. I was not aware when I wrote the book that the term *"life's lottery"* was used by right-wing Americans to caricature a liberal position on the underprivileged—suggesting that leftists feel whole segments of society are "losers in *life's lottery*" because they have been excluded by birth from all manner of advantages, whereas they themselves believe anyone can rise from anywhere and become an American success story (which usually has tragic connotations of its own).

I'd be interested to read an American version of *LL*, which might diverge in significant, interesting ways from the British. I'd also like to see an equivalent book written by a woman with a female protagonist—obviously, the choices women make or are faced with, and the interests they have, would be very different also.

Section 13

The second sidebar reprints Section 13 of *Life's Lottery*. This particular section crops up in Keith's life unexpectedly, in many of the storylines. The reader is instructed to read Section 13, and return to the storyline they came from. It's a bit of a cheat, I admit—but I thought it necessary, partly as a signpost for when we were entering more fantastical areas. (Some readers view this as similar to Freud's "uncanny," but I could as easily have pasted in Rod Serling's "Next stop . . . the Twilight Zone.") It was useful also partly to remind readers that this was not a story with one reality, but a book in which they were encouraged to take multiple passes through a multiple universe. I was also gluing this book to some of my earlier fictions, which have more supernatural material—in particular, my novels *The Quorum* and *Jago*, and the short story collection *Where the Bodies Are Buried*, feature some of the characters and settings (even events) of *LL*, and readers who'd been following me from book to book (as opposed to those who just picked up this one) would get another variant experience (for instance, knowing more about "Derek Leech," the actual narrator).

People and Places

There is a certain sense that Keith displaces quite a bit of water with the people he knows—so that they are different in his differing realities, but less extremely than he is. In almost all the branches, Keith meets most of the "important" people in his life as a child or a relatively young man, and I deliberately didn't do that much with his many possible children (who mostly seem like a phantasmal melange rather than discrete characters).

Certain places (such as Sutton Mallet) and events also take on multiple significances depending on the reader's choices. I was quite pleased with the way this turned out, since it was tricky to manage: the idea is that certain events or places in the novel should be mystifying or easy to overlook the first

Section 13

Sometimes, you step off the path, through the cobweb curtain, into the shade. This is where you meet me. This is where I live. Most people step off the path at one time or another. If you press them, they'll tell you their stories. But not willingly. It's private. Between me and them. You'd be surprised how many people you know who've stepped off the path and met me. That, though you don't quite realise it yet, is what's just happened to you. Can you feel the scuttling caress of tiny spider-legs on your hackles? Have you noticed time has changed, slowed to a tortoise-crawl or speeded up to a cheetah-run? The air in your nostrils and the water in your mouth taste different. There's an electric tang, a supple thickness, a kind of a rush. If you come through the shade whole, you'll want to scurry back to the light, back to the path. Most people have an amazing ability to pretend things didn't happen, to wish so fervently that things were otherwise they can make them so, unpicking elements from their past and forgetting them so thoroughly—at least, while they're awake—that they literally have not happened. All of you can affect the warp of the universe, just by wishing. But to wish, you need motivation. What has just happened might be motivation enough. At first, you won't be able to stop thinking about it, asking what has actually happened, looking for a comforting 'explanation'. Maybe it was mirrors, maybe you were given drugs, maybe aliens abducted you. Who knows? Maybe you're right. I don't know everything. From time to time, you run into me—sometimes because you get itchy and stray, sometimes by accident. From time to time, I like to catch up with you. I like to catch up with all my friends, Keith. For now, you're shaken. Perhaps you can't believe you're alive and sane. Perhaps you aren't. Whatever the case, you must put the shade behind you. For the moment. We'll meet again. Before you know it, you'll pass through the cobweb curtain and be back.

time you read about them, but increase greatly in meaning with each return. Sometimes, the reader learns more from multiple paths than Keith ever does from his single experiences—I think only the reader ever fully works out who kills who and what happens on that Welsh mountainside, for instance.

I went to Sutton Mallet in a key scene in *The Quorum* (which includes a semi-autobiographical account of the night I wound up in the real village while trying to find the much larger and more significant town of Shepton Mallet) and it made sense to me to go back there for added weirdness this time round (my as-yet-unpublished *An English Ghost Story* goes back again). Given that so many places are returned to in so many contexts in *LL*, I also wanted to leave areas mysterious—and that house in that village is one of them.

Reading *Life's Lottery*

I've not done any research on how people read the book, and I didn't want to dictate any correct way of reading it. I expect most people "explore" the book as much as they "play" it. The first readers of the manuscript dealt with it on disc, and could use the search function as a primitive hyperlink— which they seemed to like (they could also tick off the sections they'd read and consume the whole book piecemeal that way). Later an actual e-book edition was released. Besides the obvious advantage of being able to click to the section you've chosen and insert multiple bookmarks, the most interesting aspect of the e-book was putting in all the footnotes to explain "Britishisms" to American readers (or even British readers born much later than me). I've always

> Years may pass between your detours, but when you step off the path again those years will be as seconds. Maybe life is only truly lived in the shade. Well, enough deep thought for the moment. Get on with things. Try to pretend there is no shade. I'll see you soon.
>   Go on.

been dubious about e-books, but I could see the point of doing *LL* in that way, since it actually uses the electronic medium rather than simply being a book on a screen.

Of all my books, *LL* has probably got the most attention in the United Kingdom—in terms of media attention, reviews, reader feedback, etc. I've had people come up to me in the street to talk about it. It seems to have sold quite well. However, it's never been published in the United States, so there must be some sense that it's too strange or "British" to travel. What I wanted to do at the outset was write something that was at once experimental and accessible. Apart from the people who read it straight through (for whom I wrote some sections you can't get to any other way), I assume every reader's path through the book is unique. As usual with my stuff, some people love it, some people hate it, some are indifferent—you tend to hear word back from the folks at the extremes. It's certainly a book people are still interested in talking about.

Reference

Newman, Kim (1999). *Life's Lottery*. London: Simon & Schuster UK Ltd.

II. Computational Fictions

Computational Fictions

What makes computer games different from other games? What makes *Pong* different from tennis, video poker different from traditional poker, or one of EA's *Lord of the Rings* computer role-playing games different from *Dungeons & Dragons*?

Of course, the differences are many, when considering particular games—for example, whether referees are employed, cards are used, or hard cover rulebooks of hundreds of pages are regularly published. But another type of difference runs consistently through all of these examples.

If we play tennis, we expect that all players understand the structure of play (e.g., who serves, from which side, in which order); it is we, or an umpire, who judges balls in or out of bounds and keeps score. In *Pong*, however, this is all determined by computational processes. At our weekly poker nights, we shuffle the cards into a random order, deal them out as required by the game variant being played, and judge each player's hand according to the rules; but a video poker machine takes on all these tasks itself. Playing *Dungeons & Dragons*, we utilize maps, character documents, rulebooks, dice, and ongoing discussion to simulate a virtual world and adventure within it; EA's *Lord of the Rings* games simulate everything within the software.

This is to say, non-computer games require that people understand them as a system, make judgments, and keep track of the game state. They require that players operate the game mechanics; therefore, the game mechanics are an important part of player experience. By contrast, computer games take on at least part of the mechanics themselves. Many computer games continue to function appropriately as a system even if the players completely fail to understand them—it's possible to play some computer games successfully based on an entirely mistaken understanding of how they function internally, even while the games themselves

continue to enforce their own rules and structures. But players who significantly misunderstand non-computer games will almost invariably cause the game systems to operate incorrectly.

There are limits to what this proceduralism can accomplish. A competent group of *Dungeons & Dragons* players can simulate any eventuality and deal with any action or communication attempted by the players, while even the best computer RPG can barely prevent the dialogue of computer-controlled characters from becoming painfully repetitive. Any action too far outside those already imagined by a computer game's design team is usually either met with an uninteresting response or is simply impossible to carry out.

But this is only to say that given our current state of technological advancement, there are things that computers do poorly and things they do well. Take for example, Avalon Hill's *Squad Leader*, which simulates a WWII battle through a notoriously elaborate rules system. Although the game has its adherents, most would admit that it pushes the bounds of what human memory and patience can accommodate.

A computer, on the other hand, can easily handle *Squad Leader*'s complex mechanics (simulating terrain, movement, weapons accuracy and penetration, morale, line of sight, prep fire, defensive fire, advancing fire, close combat) and much more. A game like Gearbox's *Brothers in Arms* provides both a more complex simulation than *Squad Leader* and a player experience that requires no knowledge of how the simulation operates. Computer games can also surprise their players: rules can change, contents can be revealed, and other operations can take place without the players making them happen. The variety of contents can also be much greater than with non-computer games, as contents can be recombined (or even generated) algorithmically.

Of course, the real question is not, "Can computers reproduce or replace tabletop games?" Certainly computers can speed certain processes—*Diplomacy* may be easier to play by e-mail than by post—but that is not the limit of what can be done. Similarly, computer games may seem, at first blush, to be operating at a handicap: they lack the apparent access to human creativity and the context of social relations that contribute much of the power of non-computer games. But this is only as true as it is of other art forms—such as literature and film—which generally must create an audience experience on their own, rather than in combination with the efforts of a group of human players.

Rather than focus on comparisons between tabletop and computer games, the contributors to this section ask, "What types of new playable media are made possible through use of the computer?" In particular, they focus on playable experiences that develop characters and stories—undertakings that are usually considered the province of other primarily non-social art forms (again, such as literature and film). And this raises the necessity of seeing these works in more traditional aesthetic terms, rather than purely ludic ones.

That is to say, in addition to game design, in addition to interaction, in addition to the elegant design of their internal procedures, the works in this section demand we be prepared to consider them for their characters, fictional worlds, use of language, and so on. Helen Thorington's *Solitaire* may look like a card game, but it can't be played to win. Talan Memmott procedurally "re-authors" Rene Magritte, but not as a game license. And Stuart Moulthrop, in calling his *Pax* a "textual *instrument*," specifically points us toward an aesthetics of playing that isn't game-centric.

Of course, we can't ignore the fact that there are tabletop games that demand to be seen in these terms as well. The works discussed in this book's first section are examples, and there are many more. A game such as *Betrayal at the House on the Hill* isn't enjoyable because of its elegant gameplay. In fact, its many horror scenarios include some that are remarkably poorly balanced. Rather, the enjoyment comes from the way that its structures, as a work of playable media, are so well integrated with its horror genre content. It's not a finely structured game with horror

"spray-painted" on, any more than *The Maltese Falcon* is a novel with noir detection lathered over it.

For some of the works presented here, the most effective way to understand their procedural, interactive, and aesthetic dimensions may be to see them as hybrids between computer and non-computer forms, or as extensions of aesthetic traditions into the digital realm. *Juvenate,* discussed here by Marie-Laure Ryan, can be seen as bringing together the forms of the artist's book and the computer-driven flowchart or maze. Mark Marino's *Twelve Easy Lessons to Better Time Travel* brings together a *Tristram Shandy*–style narrative with the forms of cross-media learning modules. Lev Manovich utilizes digital procedures to combine and display traditional cinematic elements in new ways. D. Fox Harrell's GRIOT performances take place in both the digital and real worlds, using computational processes modeled on human conceptual blending to produce narrative poetry in response to user input.

An important component of almost any experience of story or role-playing, with or without a computer, is the presence of characters. As discussed in the introduction to the previous section, in a tabletop RPG, character is not a procedural issue. There are PCs, acted by players, and NPCs, acted by the gamemaster. On-the-fly interactions between these fictional characters is accomplished effortlessly, in what is for most of us the most user-friendly medium possible: human speech. Designers of computer playable media have to look for different solutions.

A brief example of one such approach is given here by Steve Meretzky. Meretzky has designed games for most conceivable media, but here revisits one of his most famous early creations, Floyd the robot, in Infocom's text adventure *Planetfall.* Floyd is arguably the first fully-realized NPC in a computer game; the nature of the character's scripting lent Floyd a perceived depth that had been lacking up to that point.

Further discussion of character comes from Lee Sheldon, who discusses the computer game adaptation of Agatha Christie's mystery novel *And Then There Were None.* In particular, he addresses the problem of how much information the suspects know, and how and why they might give it to the PC investigator. Sheldon's "suspicion meter" model is one method of addressing this need.

A longer discussion of a game scripting process can be found in Jordan Mechner's chapter on Ubisoft's story-rich platformer *Prince of Persia: The Sands of Time*. In scripting the events, dialogue, and characters for the game, Mechner drew on his experience as a screenwriter, and the result is, in fact, highly cinematic.

Michael Mateas and Andrew Stern, in their work *Façade*, have taken a different approach, attempting to be more "dramatic" than cinematic. *Façade* places the player in an awkward dinner party with a married couple, Grace and Trip, on the verge of a breakup.[1] What Grace and Trip say, and how they say it, is dependent on their "perception" of the player's attitude and what has already gone before in the conversation. This, in turn, feeds back into the continuing conversation and ultimately affects the outcome of the scenario; that is, whether Grace and Trip stay together or break up, and what they might learn about themselves and the relationship in the process. From the player's point of view (ideally), they are participating in a natural, if somewhat tense, conversation.

Another potential breakup is discussed in Robert Zubek's chapter on his *The Breakup Conversation*. Here, the user takes the role of one half of a relationship—the half that wants to break up, in fact. The game

system plays the user's partner, and tries to prevent the breakup. Success and failure are determined by the outcome of the conversation.

Chris Crawford also discusses an approach to programming conversation—along with other story-determining actions—into a playable, digital form. His solution is to create a "toy language," with which players and NPCs can interact. He also demonstrates how this stripped-down language can be used to enable story creation, providing one method of reconciling the fundamental concerns of this book: role-playing and story.

Two chapters, by Nick Montfort and Jeremy Douglass, point to the continuing interest in the Interactive Fiction (IF) form. With its roots in early text adventures like *Colossal Cave/Adventure* and the pioneering work of the Infocom writers, IF has evolved in a wide variety of directions. Montfort and Douglass provide close examinations of two works, and also address wider issues with this form. The questions they raise, of simulation and of playing the "player character," resonate with many other topics discussed in *Second Person*. Emily Short is also present, to discuss her celebrated work of IF, *Savoir-Faire*.

Our final contributor to this section, Mark Keavney, has created the "City of IF" web site, although his definition of IF is quite different from that of Montfort and Douglass. Stories at City of IF are generated through the human-to-human interaction of a community of authors and web visitors.[2]

---

1. In fact, the explicit model for *Façade* is Edward Albee's play *Who's Afraid of Virginia Woolf?*

2. Astute readers will notice that "City of IF" lacks the sort of procedurality that unites the other works in this section. As such, it could be argued that this chapter more properly belongs in part III of this book. But Keavney describes his project as IF, and so we have placed his chapter among those of the other IF writers. Happily, *Second Person* is not an interactive work, procedural or otherwise, and the authors of this introduction reserve for themselves this measure of editorial fiat.

The Sands of Time: Crafting a Video Game Story
Jordan Mechner

In 2001, a small team within Ubisoft's Montreal studio led by producer Yannis Mallat began concept development on the project that would become *Prince of Persia: The Sands of Time*. Initially a consultant, I later joined the team as writer and game designer. Being part of this project was a great experience and I'm glad to revisit it for this book.

By its nature, video game writing is inextricably bound up with game design, level design, and the other aspects of production. A film screenplay is a clean, written blueprint that serves as a starting point and reference for the director, actors, and the rest of the creative team. It's also a document that film scholars and critics can later read and discuss as a work distinct from the film itself. Video games have no such blueprint. The game design script created at the start of a production is often quickly rendered obsolete, its functions assumed by new tools created to fit the project's specific needs.

In this chapter I'll try to shed some light on the creative and technical decision-making processes that went into crafting the story and narrative elements of *Prince of Persia: The Sands of Time* (*POP* for short). The team's approach was practical, not literary; our challenge was to find the right story for a mass-market action video game. In the rapidly changing game industry, each project is unique and presents its own demands and opportunities, according to current technology and the nature of the particular game. What works for one game might not work for another.

Storytelling is, of course, just one aspect of game design. For those interested in reading more about the overall production process on *POP*, I recommend Yannis Mallat's postmortem article (Mallat 2004).

16.1) The Prince recharging the dagger in *Prince of Persia: The Sands of Time*. (Ubisoft)

Rule #1: Do It, Don't View It.

What kind of story does a video game need?

The traditional way to tell a story in a video game is to create a series of cinematic cutscenes that serve as "rewards"—transitions between gameplay levels. However, the *cool* way to tell a story in a video game is to eliminate or reduce the canned cutscenes as much as possible, and instead construct the game so that the most powerful and exciting moments of the story will occur within the gameplay itself.

The screenwriting maxim "actions speak louder than words" applies to video games as well as films, but in a different way. Video games, unlike movies, are interactive. Whereas in a film it's better to show than to tell, in a video game it's better to do than to watch. Give the story's best moments to the player, and he'll never forget them. Put them in a cutscene, and he'll yawn.

Philosophically, the *POP* team was pretty much united in our lack of enthusiasm for cutscenes. If we could have eliminated them altogether, we would have done so with pleasure. On the other hand, our mandate was to make a successful mainstream action-adventure game on a relatively tight budget and schedule. The game concept already called for pushing the envelope in a number of ways; an overambitious approach to storytelling could have sunk the ship.

Given that cutscenes were a realistic and efficient option, at least we could make them more palatable by observing a few do's and don'ts:

Good Cutscenes:

Are brief (30–60 seconds), well-written, and tightly edited.

Are visually consistent with the gameplay (ideally, using the same character models, environments, and graphic engine as the game itself).

Contain the same kind of action as the gameplay.

Flow naturally out of the preceding gameplay action and into the following action.

Tell a strong, simple story.

Bad Cutscenes:

Are several times longer than they need to be.

Are so visually splendid that they seem to belong to a different world from the rest of the game.

Are dialogue-heavy and exposition-heavy. Characters who are taciturn throughout the game suddenly open up and become blabbermouths.

Inadvertently call attention to the game design's limitations (e.g., if the hero can survive that jump, why couldn't he hop over a three-foot-high wall three levels back?).

Tell a story that has nothing to do with the game.

Close observers of *POP* may notice that we ended up breaking at least one of these guidelines: Several key cinematic cutscenes, including the opening and ending sequences, were pre-rendered in full motion video instead of using the real-time gameplay engine. The production, marketing, and other considerations that went into this decision are beyond the scope of this article. I mention it as a reminder that whatever theoretical game-design ideals we start out with are always subject to the actual, real-life production process. The design needs to be robust enough to withstand compromises and still make a good game.

Jordan Mechner

Rule #2:
Story Is Not King.

As the previous list of dos and don'ts suggests, many games hurt themselves by using (abusing?) cinematic cutscenes to try to tell a story that doesn't match the game. If the core component of the gameplay is "shoot every spaceship you see," is the game truly enhanced by weaving an epic tale of galactic political strife, interpersonal rivalry, and romantic subplots?

In film, story is king. Stunning cinematography and amazing action set pieces may help sell the movie—but if they're not working in the service of the story, the film will fall flat with viewers. Not so in video games. The gameplay isn't there to serve the story; it's the other way around. The purpose of the story is to support and enhance the gameplay.

POP's core gameplay is very simple. There is only one playable character (the Prince). The gameplay is a combination of acrobatic exploration (getting from point A to point B) and combat (killing everyone you meet), plus one cool, original feature: You can turn back time to undo your mistakes. The challenge for the writer is to invent a story that will fit this gameplay, making the most of its strengths without highlighting its limitations.

At first, the team started with a great title and core concept—the "Sands of Time." Unfortunately, the first pass at a game script succumbed to many of the "don'ts" listed above. It had a proliferation of characters representing various political factions, a hero whose goal was not always clear, and long, exposition-burdened dialogue scenes. The complex story setup failed to provide compelling answers to two key questions:

What is Point B and why do I need to get there?

Why do I need to kill everyone I meet?

Making the decision to scrap the existing storyline and start fresh from the "Sands of Time" concept gave the team the freedom to create a new story that would yield more bang for the buck. We took our new direction from the core features of the gameplay itself:

Unity of time and place: The action unfolds over the course of a single day and night, all within the

16.2) Know who's on the box. (Ubisoft)

grounds and gardens of the Palace of Azad.

Acrobatics: Much of the fun of the game lies in the Prince's extraordinary agility. For him to walk down hallways and open doors like a normal person wouldn't take advantage of what makes him special. So let's set the game in a *destroyed* palace—one that's been hit by a terrible cataclysm that has collapsed staircases and buried passageways under rubble, forcing the player to improvise new ways to get from point A to point B.

Combat: The game interface is designed for fight/flight—not for engaging other characters in conversation. So let's populate our palace with monsters, not people. Monsters so implacably determined to kill the Prince that the only meaningful ways he can interact with them are to kill them or run away.

Rewind: We want to make the player *work* for this cool ability to turn back time. The Sands of Time must function first of all as a reward, a substance that the player can collect, hoard, and spend.

Rule #3:
Maximize Efficiency.

Programming and screenwriting have at least one thing in common: Efficiency is a cardinal virtue. Whenever you can achieve the desired effect with the fewest moving parts, it yields all manner of benefits down the line. So, the Sands of Time became not only the valuable substance that the Prince spends his time collecting, but also the *cause* of the cataclysm that destroys the palace and creates the monsters. The Prince commits the terrible mistake of opening Pandora's Box, unleashing the plague of the Sands of Time on an unsuspecting world. His mission: Collect the Sands, put them back into Pandora's Box, and set the world right again.

The Dagger of Time is at once a weapon, a receptacle, and a MacGuffin: The Prince can fight the sand monsters with his sword, but like the undead zombies they are, they keep getting back up again and again—until he uses his magic dagger to suck the sand that runs in their veins in place of blood. In so doing, he both dispatches the monsters for good, and conveniently fills his dagger with sand. Which he can then use to rewind time.

I can't overstate the importance of simplifying the story as much as possible, especially in the beginning. Video game writers and designers are often tempted to start embroidering and elaborating on their ideas too early in the process. The reason this is a trap is that production resources are finite. Every character, object, and environment that can be eliminated at an early stage will increase the resources and opportunities available to enrich the characters, objects, and environments that remain.

Rule #4:
Know Who's on the Box.

Once the bones of the *POP* story felt solid, the next step was to flesh it out with a setup and a cast of characters. Notice the order of priorities: first gameplay, then story, then characters.

There is, however, one exception: The hero. The guy on the box. The Prince of Persia. Not every game needs a memorable main character, or even a main character at all (think *Civilization*)—but ours did. The gameplay and the character of the Prince were inseparable. Together, they constituted our "hook." A weak hook—one that players don't get excited

16.3) The giant hourglass that contains the Sands of Time. (Ubisoft)

about—can doom an otherwise excellent, well-reviewed, heavily marketed game to the bargain bin.

You might not think the character of the Prince needed much work. He was, after all, our franchise character, our brand name, the reason the project existed. We couldn't afford to take that attitude. Most of the design team were old enough to have played the original 1989 side-scrolling computer game, but a sizable portion of our target audience would be encountering the Prince for the first time. We needed to reinvent the Prince of Persia as if he had never existed before.

If the purpose of the story is to reveal the gameplay in its best light, then the purpose of the cast of characters is to reveal the hero in *his* best light. In building a cast of characters for *POP*, the question for the writer was: Who do we *need*?

The original draft of the story had nine characters, including two love interests, two villains, and two helper/mentor characters. We scrapped them all and started fresh with the simplest possible (remember Rule #3) configuration of characters: A hero, a villain, and a girl. The needs of the story helped us flesh out the three characters' roles:

> *The hero:* The young Prince who accidentally unleashes Armageddon through the sort of innocent mistake that could happen to anyone.
>
> *The villain:* The Vizier who manipulates the hero into

opening Pandora's Box (the giant hourglass that contains the Sands of Time) for his own nefarious ends. Having done this, he whisks the hourglass off to the top of the palace's most inaccessible tower, thus providing the player with a physical destination and goal to justify all the getting from Point A to Point B.

The girl: Farah is at once a love interest, an action sidekick, and the character who stands for what is good and right. As the only human survivor besides the villain, she becomes the Prince's companion in adversity. Of course their relationship is fraught with mistrust, because she and the hero are both after the same thing (the dagger).

Present in the story—but not in the gameplay—are two additional characters: the hero's father (the King of Persia), and his friend, the Sultan, in whose palace the action takes place. Benign authority figures, both are transformed into sand monsters in the opening cutscene, adding to the hero's grief and guilt without complicating the game design.

As to why our three main characters survive the cataclysm while everyone else is turned into sand zombies, we decided that each of them (for different reasons) possesses a special artifact that offers protection from the Sands of Time: the Prince, his dagger; the Vizier, his staff; and Farah, her medallion.

Rule #5:
Build a Playground for Your Hero.

In the original story, the action took place in the Prince's home palace, and the Dagger of Time was an old family treasure. For the new story, it seemed more useful to make the palace of Azad neutral ground, a place that both the Prince and Farah would be encountering for the first time. So we created a prologue in which the dagger and the Sands of Time are "liberated" by the Prince's victorious army from a conquered Indian palace.

The player's first goal in the game is to steal the dagger from the well-protected treasure vault—a setup modeled on the classic tomb-raiding opening sequence of *Raiders of the Lost Ark*. That movie was a primary inspiration for the original *Prince of Persia* game fifteen years earlier, so it seemed forgivable to draw on it yet again for the Prince's rebirth.

16.4) Farah, NPC combat partner and the story's romantic interest. (Ubisoft)

The prologue serves several important functions. It sets up the world of the game, the three main characters, and what they want. It showcases the Prince's character and abilities (a daredevil who races ahead of the attacking army in order to gain "honor and glory" by being the first to steal a valuable trophy of war). It establishes the two main artifacts, the hourglass and the dagger, and explains how they come into the hero's possession. It offers the player a manageable environment in which to practice the Prince's acrobatic and swordfighting abilities. Finally, it lays the groundwork for the anti-war theme that, though never stated outright, underlies the whole tale.

Rule #6:
Break as Many Rules as You Can Get Away With.

It should be noted that the hero's goals and actions in the prologue are, by most standards, wrong. The Prince's army attacks the Indian palace for no good reason other than greed and conquest. This point raised some concern during development: Might players not resist identification with such a hero? For whatever reason, I always liked this aspect of the story and felt confident it would not bother players in the least.

Remember the scene in *Psycho* where Anthony Perkins has to clean up the evidence of the horrific murder we've just

seen "Mother" commit? The victim is Janet Leigh, the heroine of the movie. We *liked* her. Yet no sooner is she dead than we shift our allegiance and start rooting for Perkins to succeed in covering up the evidence of the crime. Watching someone attempt to accomplish something difficult and dangerous usually causes us to empathize with them—even if we disagree morally with what they're doing. I felt sure this principle would apply to video games as well as movies. Because we control the Prince's actions and thus his fate, we're even more inclined to identify with him, and less inclined to judge him, than if it were a movie.

Later in *POP*, the player is asked to follow the elaborate verbal instructions of an exhausted, freaked-out guard to activate the palace's defense system. It's a long and challenging puzzle, and when he finally succeeds, what happens? A ghastly array of blades, slicers, and other traps spring out from the walls—causing the player to realize that (a) the guard was probably insane, come to think of it, and (b) now he has to spend the rest of the game evading these very traps. If you want to talk about mistakes committed by the hero, this one takes the prize. Unlike the big "Pandora's Box" mistake, which occurs in a cutscene (thus, one could argue, relieving the player of responsibility for the Prince's actions), this one occurs *in the game*. The game actually requires the player to accomplish a goal that will make things harder for him going forward. Logically, it should make him want to rip the CD out of the drive. But as a game/story twist, does it work? It seems to.

The great thing about video game writing is that as an industry, we're still in the process of figuring out what works and what doesn't. In studio film screenwriting, experimenting with the time-tested rules of dramatic construction is a lot harder to justify and get away with. Every video game project offers the writer opportunities to break new ground, even if only in small ways; it would be a shame if we didn't try.

Rule #7:
Combine Previously Uncombined Genres.

One of the classiest aspects of the 1940 *Thief of Baghdad* (another source of inspiration for the original *Prince of Persia*) is that it starts out with the hero telling his story to a mysterious woman in flashback. As he finishes his tale, we realize that the villain has been listening behind a curtain the whole time. Nesting stories within stories in this fashion is a signature device of the *1001 Nights*—the collection of medieval Islamic folk tales that is the *ur*-source material for *Thief of Baghdad* and *Prince of Persia*.

To our knowledge, voice-over narration as a framing device had yet to be tried in a video game. We decided to push the device to its limit by making the entire game a flashback, narrated by the hero in the past tense.

It was by no means clear that this would work. Voice-over narration has ruined more movies than it's helped. Dozens of good films, from *Blade Runner* to *Age of Innocence*, have (for me) been seriously marred by clunky or unnecessary voice-overs.

One could also argue that the idea itself is a contradiction in terms. The essence of a video game is that the action happens in the present tense, reacting to the player's improvisations from one moment to the next. Wouldn't a past-tense narration cheat the player of the feeling that he is shaping his own destiny?

Again, my memories as a filmgoer gave me confidence that it could work. Two of my favorite Hollywood *noir* films, *Double Indemnity* and *Sunset Boulevard* (both directed by Billy Wilder), are narrated by a hero who is fatally wounded or dead. Knowing the story will end badly doesn't seem to harm the sense of empathy or suspense we feel along the way. I felt that by using film noir as a model for an action-adventure video game set in ninth-century Persia, we would be getting away with something.

So, we open the game with the Prince telling his story, in flashback, to a person *we don't see*. Only at the end of the game is it revealed *who* this person is. The narration had to be crafted to work on two levels: It must make sense both the first time through the game, and then in retrospect, when the player knows who the Prince is actually telling his story to and why.

Finding the right tone for the narration was essential. The Prince telling his story in retrospect is a more mature and reflective character than the gung-ho Prince the player sees at the beginning of the game. His experience has made him sadder but wiser. We sought ways to express the Prince's evolution gradually throughout the game as well, in his physi-

cal appearance and movements. At the moment, near the end of the game, when the on-screen action catches up with the narration, the player should finally understand the full impact of the tragedy the Prince has suffered.

The voice-over narrations during the game play (as opposed to during cinematics) were among the most rewarding to implement. Some of them were purposefully added as guidance to clue the player in to what his next goal should be:

> And there it lay, just out of reach: The Dagger of Time. There was a treasure I could carry with pride as a trophy of our victory. If I could only get there.

(Hint: Notice, gentle player, that dagger on the far side of the room.)

> Try as I might, I could not break that crumbling stone wall. Perhaps a warrior with the strength of Rustam might have smashed through it; but I had not strength enough in my arm. . . . Nor in my sword. It was as if a magic charm protected it.

(Hint: There's a more powerful magic sword to be found somewhere around here. And when you find it, come back and try it on that section of the wall.)

Other voice-overs were added purely for atmosphere, to deepen the player's experience and add emotional layers to what would otherwise have been straight-ahead action:

> The fabled menagerie of Azad. . . . The Sultan's pride and joy. It had been one of the wonders of the world. As a child I had dreamed of it, and longed to see it with my own eyes. Now it was a place of terror, an abandoned ruin, laid waste by the Sands of Time.

> You think me mad. I can see it by the look in your eyes; you think my story is impossible. Perhaps I am mad. Who would not be driven mad by horrors such as I have lived? But I assure you, every word is true.

The tone of the narration obviously owes less to Billy Wilder than to Edgar Allan Poe (or maybe Vincent Price). For by this point it had become clear to us that, although *POP* was officially a "swashbuckling acrobatic action-adventure," we were, in fact, making a game in the "survival horror" genre.

This might sound like cause for concern, but it's a good thing. (Just be careful who you tell. Definitely don't mention it to the marketing department.) Many great successes—movies, video games, novels, whatever—result from the covert fusion of two hitherto separate genres. *Alien* looks like sci-fi but is really a horror movie. *The Sixth Sense* looks like a horror film but is actually a family tearjerker. And so on. On *POP*, we figured that if we did our job right, nobody would notice that it was a survival-horror game—not the game-playing public, and not the marketing department.

Anyway, the narration worked great. So satisfied were we with its effect that we went back and recorded additional dialogue for new situations, extending it even into the menu interface. For example, when the player presses pause, the Prince says in voice-over:

> Shall I go on with my story?

When the player presses resume:

> Now, where was I?

And when the Prince, as video game heroes are apt to do, is killed during gameplay, he hastily corrects himself:

> Wait, what did I just say? That didn't happen.
> Let me back up a bit.

And the "story" resumes from the last save point.

Rule #8:
A Memorable Character Is One You Can Play With.

By far the greatest storytelling challenge in *POP* was the relationship between the Prince and the female NPC-sidekick/romantic interest, Farah. (Game designers are fond of acronyms. This one refers to neither the National Press Club nor the National Petroleum Council, but to a "non-playable character"—one that engages with the player's character during the in-game action, but whom the player does not control.)

This relationship lies at the heart of the story. The cinematic cutscenes might be as well written, acted, and animated as we could make them, but they would never be enough to sell the relationship between Farah and the

16.5) Acrobatic combat in *Prince of Persia: The Sands of Time*. (Ubisoft)

Prince—unless it was present in the gameplay as well. Any emotional resonance our story managed to achieve would be, in large part, a function of how believable, likable, and well-developed a character Farah was.

We had to walk a fine line. On the one hand, we were aiming for a romantic-comedy-adventure structure like *Romancing the Stone* or *It Happened One Night,* where the hero and heroine get off on the wrong foot and proceed to argue and bicker their way through the movie, each too proud to be the first to suggest that they are falling in love. On the other hand, we were doing a video game, not a movie. A video game sidekick's primary role is to help the player win—by providing clues, opening doors he can't, fighting at his side. Farah needed to be a real help to the Prince; otherwise she'd be just a pain in the neck.

One of the places where it was important to strike the right balance is the cooperative combat system. When a gang of sand monsters attacks, Farah draws her bow and starts shooting. Usually, it's an advantage to have Farah on your side. If it should happen that you're down to your last hit point, at the mercy of a sand monster's raised axe, and Farah saves your life with a well-placed arrow—at that moment, you positively love her. (This is known as a "solid foundation for a relationship.") However, Farah's not perfect, and it can also happen that the Prince accidentally steps into her line of fire and catches an arrow in the buttocks. At which point he yells "Ow!" and Farah replies "Sorry!" (or variation thereof). We could, of course, have just as easily programmed Farah to be a perfect archery machine who never misses and never makes a mistake. But that wouldn't have been as much fun.

If you like the way Farah turned out in the game, that's great. Just know that she is about 20% of what was originally envisioned. Ultimately, having a well-developed secondary non-playable character took a back seat to having a playable game that we could ship for Christmas. Otherwise we'd still be working on her.

Rule #9:
Dialogue Is Not Precious.

Early on, we made the somewhat unorthodox decision that we would never interrupt the game to play in-game dialogue. The gameplay is paramount, and if the player doesn't want to listen to the dialogue, it shouldn't be forced on him. So, for example, if Farah starts talking to the Prince, there's nothing to stop him from running away and missing the rest of whatever she was saying.

We also decided that the dialogue should be treated as just another element of the soundtrack, so that if the Prince and Farah were far apart, their dialogue would be heard at a very faint level. This meant that in the recording session, the actors had to *really yell* for their dialogue to be audible when played back in the context of the game. A person shouting at the top of her lungs sounds totally different from a person speaking normally, even if the dialogues are equalized to play back at the same dB level.

There's a partial sample of the spreadsheet we used to

16.6) The Prince and Farah. (Ubisoft)

record the character dialogues at the bottom of this page.

Note that these dialogues are mutually exclusive. Only the final three are a series to be played in sequence (as indicated by asterisks on the left-hand side): Farah speaks, the Prince responds, then Farah again. The rest are alternative, stand-alone dialogues, each triggered by a different gameplay situation.

In all, we recorded nearly a thousand lines of dialogue. Less than half of them ended up in the game. That's OK. Dialogue is one of the cheapest elements in the game (assuming the actors are paid union scale) because creating it requires only a few people's time. Programming, by contrast, is one of the most expensive—not because programmers get paid so much, but because a programming delay takes *everyone's* time.

Context/Story	Filename (Wav)	Event	Character	Description/Intention	Dialogue: English
Prince drops down from top of wall onto wrong side of gate	FRIG240	FrVo_GP22PrinceScrewsUp	FARAH	Critical	Why didn't you open the gate?
Prince opens gate	FRIG241	FrVo_GP22PrinceOpensGate	FARAH	Mildly pleased	You did it!
Prince does not open gate right away	FRIG242	FrVo_GP22FarahLockedOut1	FARAH	Betrayed	Hey! Open the gate!
Prince still does not open gate	FRIG243	FrVo_GP22FarahLockedOut2	FARAH	Doesn't like him teasing her	Come on! This isn't funny!
Prince STILL does not open gate	FRIG244	FrVo_GP22FarahLockedOut3	FARAH	Pretending she doesn't care	All right, be that way. I can wait here all night.
Prince locks himself on other side of gate	FRIG245	FrVo_GP22PrinceLockedOut	FARAH	Feigned consternation	Oh no, the switch doesn't work any more! You'll have to go back around the long way!
*	PRIG091	PrVo_GP22PrinceLockedOut_Response	PRINCE	Outraged	WHAT?!
*	FRIG246	FrVo_GP22PrinceLockedOut_Kidding	FARAH	Sweet	Just kidding. [Steps on pressure plate to open gate]

All eight of the lines listed here were recorded, implemented, and turned out great. The last three were cut from the game in the final stages for lack of RAM and other considerations. Don't think we mourned the lost dialogue—we mourned the precious time the programmer had taken to implement them in the first place.

Rule #10:
Create the Tools You Need.

Everyone knows what a film screenplay looks like. The film screenwriter thus has the benefit (and the constraint) of filling a well-defined role. Not so the video game writer. Depending on the nature of the game and the organization of the team, the writer's role can be vastly different in nature and scope from one project to another.

What does a video game screenplay look like? On *POP*, the screenplay for the cinematic cutscenes looks a lot like a film screenplay:

> EXT. RAMPARTS - DAY
>
> As the Prince runs, the stone floor starts to crumble beneath his feet.
>
> He turns, runs back. Too late. Falling, he tries to grab the crumbling ledge. It breaks away.
>
> He plunges into the darkness of a stone shaft. A rain of rocks accompanies him. Falling past a ledge, he tries to grab it; his fingers slide off.

16.7) Farah firing arrows.

> INT. DUNGEON - DAY
>
> WHAM! The Prince hits the stone floor. As he is getting up, a ROCK falls on his back, knocking him flat.

Handy though it is for cutscenes, screenplay format is of limited use in describing in-game situations. The bulk of the writing work on *POP* involved not the screenplay, but other communication tools—most of which were created or improvised according to the demands of the production and might not work at all for a different game.

One such tool was the dialogue recording spreadsheet excerpted here. Another was the stack of "NPC Gameplay Design Documents" specifying when and in what circumstances the dialogues are to be played.

At the bottom of this page is an example from GP35

Farah does the rest

Context/Story	WAV	Event	Character	Description/Intention	Dialogue: English
Through the grill, we can see Farah emerge from the crack, jump and pull a lever. When the gate is open, she plays:	FRIG442	FrVo_GP35GateOpen	FARAH	Offhandedly (Calling to him in next room)	The gate's open!
5 seconds later, Farah plays:	FRIG443	FrVo_GP35AnotherCrack	FARAH	(Calling to him from next room)	There's another crack! I'll see where it goes!
She enters the crack and disappears for 15 seconds. *5 seconds after Farah has disappeared into the crack, Prince plays:*	PRIG159	PrVo_GP35AnotherCrack	FARAH	(To himself) Angry, mimicking her	"I'm afraid. What if I get into trouble?"
15 seconds after Farah entered the previous crack, she emerges into GP51. If Prince is not there yet, she plays:	FRIG444	FrVo_GP35Arrive	FARAH	(Calling to him from next room)-Letting him know where she is	Over here!

(Gameplay Unit 35, otherwise known as "The Harem")

The NPC design documents are written in "pseudo-code"—less precise than actual computer code, less poetic than a screenplay—for the AI programmer, who will use it as a sort of blueprint to write the actual code that will make the characters move and speak in the game.

Looking Back

Overall, I'm delighted with the way *POP* turned out and the various ways we succeeded in weaving the story into the gameplay. I'm particularly happy with the voice-over narration and story-within-a-story; they offer a special satisfaction and reward for those who play the game all the way through.

Because the storytelling innovations in *POP* were subtle, they attracted less attention than the game's more obvious "wow" features. The story quietly underlies the gameplay experience, enhancing without distracting from it, just as we hoped.

The techniques we tried out in *Prince of Persia: The Sands of Time* remain rich with unexplored potential. They offer intriguing possibilities that cry out to be pushed further. Perhaps in another game.

References: Literature

Mallat, Yannis (2004). "Postmortem: *Ubisoft's Prince of Persia: The Sands of Time.*" *Game Developer (April 2004)*.

References: Games

Prince of Persia. Jordan Mechner; Broderbund. 1989.

Prince of Persia: The Sands of Time. Ubisoft. 2003.

Jordan Mechner

On *And Then There Were None*
Lee Sheldon

Adapting anything from one medium to another offers many more challenges than an original work coming to life on the canvas for which it was intended. Retooling Agatha Christie's classic mystery novel *And Then There Were None* (*ATTWN*) as a game for the PC—the first time any Christie story has been made into a game—is a case in point.

ATTWN is a graphical adventure game set on a storm-swept island off the south coast of Devon, England. In the original novel, ten strangers, each harboring murderous secrets of their own, are lured here and killed off one by one. In a departure from the many adaptations of this famous story in other media, an integral eleventh character is also added to the game: the player character. This is the boatman, Patrick Narracott, who brings them to the island, a man with his own secrets. The gameplay consists of the player acting as amateur detective: attempting to find clues to the identity of the diabolical

killer, save as many of the intended victims as possible, and to either find a way off the island or to summon help.

The novel is filled with character interaction that needed to be replicated, both player-NPC and NPC-NPC. Much of this takes place in dialogue, as all of those trapped on the island take part in an increasingly frantic roundelay of interrogation, speculation, and accusation. While true to the original novel, this somewhat upset the balance between gameplay and story that I always strive to maintain. All I could do was try to make the talk as entertaining as possible, and hope the player didn't grow too restless.

I also added a romantic rivalry for the affections of the young former governess, Vera Claythorne, between the player character Narracott and adventurer Philip Lombard. As for the investigation, NPCs can aid the player, or thwart the player's efforts. In a nod to the infamous pirate from *Colossal Cave*, the first adventure game of them all, the fastidious butler may relieve the player of inventory items Narracott has collected that are not rightfully his. And the player must contend with attempts upon Narracott's life by a killer understandably annoyed by the presence of this outsider, who could wreck his carefully constructed plot built around a nursery rhyme that allows for only ten little victims.

For me, one of the most interesting challenges was creating gameplay that fit with the key conventions of Christie's particular brand of mystery story. Some translated easily to gameplay: surveillance, rifling through the belongings of suspects, examining fingerprints, and medical forensics (mercifully simple given the time period the story is set in— pre–World War II—and the isolation of the island). The presence in the cast of both a doctor and judge helped with questions medical and judicial. The requisite storm added to the

Once a bent copper, always a bent copper, right Fred?

17.1) Screenshot of the confrontation with Blore. (Awe Games)

atmosphere, as well as helping to limit the movements of the player character when necessary to the design. And I called upon Christie's brief historical footnotes to her fictional island, as well as the true history of that stretch of Devon coastline, to create a somewhat larger island with more interesting nooks and crannies to explore, and more obstacles to bedevil the player.

Other conventions needed a bit more thought. But I realized I had a golden opportunity to not only add a layer of gameplay that would be true to the story, but at the same time banish a personal bête noir of my own, common to adventure games.

Exploration is an essential element in many types of games, from solo shooters to massively multiplayer worlds. In adventure games the player character is often allowed to enter any room, either by wandering in, or first solving a puzzle to gain entry. Sometimes those rooms are occupied. Often they are occupied by NPCs, who have more right to be there than the player character. We know what would happen in a shooter: gunsmoke and blood sprays. In an adventure game, the NPCs (maybe fearing they're actually in a shooter) usually fidget in place with fixed smiles on their faces, while the player character paws through their most personal possessions under their very noses.

In *ATTWN*, NPCs react to the player character's invasion of their privacy. If Narracott creeps into a bedroom and begins going through someone's belongings, a confrontation may result:

> INT. BLORE'S ROOM—DAY
>
> Once the player has turned to the page in Blore's notebook where Blore describes recognizing Narracott and plans to scuttle the boat, Blore enters. (*-1 on suspicion meter*)
>
> Blore: Once a bent copper, always a bent copper, right Fred?
>
> Blore takes the notebook away.

After a brief dialogue, the player can choose to leave, or will be firmly escorted from the room. Notice that reference to a suspicion meter in italics?

In mystery stories, we have another convention: the shifting of suspicion from one suspect to another. This is easy to do in the game. But often, the suspicion also can fall on the investigator. If not suspected of the actual crime, the detective's motives can be murky. Suspects become less cooperative. It was the second case I wanted to play with, so I created a simple Suspicion Meter. This is not a part of the interface, but a behind-the-scenes method of tracking the relationship of Narracott to the others in the game. There are only three states, although obviously it could have been more elaborate. They are Positive (+1), Neutral (0), and Negative (-1). The player begins the game in the Neutral state. If Narracott is caught by an NPC doing something that would appear suspicious, the player loses a point with that NPC. If Narracott aids an NPC, the player gains a point.

The NPCs' answers to questions and willingness to cooperate with Narracott's plans depend on the state. Here are two possible replies to a question the player chooses to ask, depending upon his current standing with the NPC Lombard:

> You said you recognized Owen's voice?
>
> (*+1 on suspicion meter*)
>
> Lombard: Alright, Narracott, I'll tell you. I was hired by Archibald Morris, the non-existent Mr. Owen's attorney. He first made contact with me over the telephone. It was Morris' voice on that recording, I'd swear to it.
>
> (*0 on suspicion meter*)
>
> Lombard: I've had time to think it over and I'm sure I did. But I see no reason to share that information with *you*.

Since the -1 state can result in a refusal to answer questions or cooperate at all, and, as can be seen in the example, the 0 state is not always very satisfying. (and since the +1 state always provides more information), there is at all times a way to get back on an NPC's good side.

Here is an example from the design document page for one of the NPCs, Emily Brent:

Range

Emily can most often be found knitting on the front patio.

Suspicion Modifiers

+1 Obtain apple juice

+1 Quote from bible

-1 Caught in her room

-1 Caught in a lie

Useful Information

Emily knows quite a lot about Cyril Hamilton, the boy who died while Vera was his governess.

The result of NPCs reacting to the player character's actions, and the subsequent effect on the player's investigation, means that players cannot simply steamroll past the NPC encounters in the game. The NPCs are real characters with opinions of their own, and they must be treated accordingly.

Any attempt to use gameplay to bring NPCs more fully to life is a worthy one, in my opinion. I've presented here only one example of story and gameplay working together, instead of being segregated. Gameplay and story need not be at odds with one another. And story need not be confined to the ghetto of cinematics.

Reference

And Then There Were None. Awe Games. 2005.

On *Solitaire*
Helen Thorington

A collaboration between myself (idea and texts), Marianne Petit (drawings and Flash programming), and John Neilson (CGI programming), *Solitaire* combines the pleasure of a card game with the challenge of telling a story. Each *Solitaire* deck contains 54 cards picked randomly from a database. Fifty-two of these have drawings on one side and a line of prewritten text on the other. The remaining two are jokers or free cards on which the player can write his/her own text.

If the text on any one of the cards interests you, you can select it by clicking on the words "select this line." If not, you can "throw it away" and draw another card. Each time a text selection is made, the text automatically appears on the right side of the screen, making it possible to keep track of the progress of the developing story. When finished, you can name and sign your story and store it (or not) in the online gallery.

Using this combination of prewritten texts and texts written by the player in real time, any player can author a story.

How it works:
Go to the web site.
Click on the card.
Give yourself a name.

Give the deck a virtual shuffle.
Deal yourself a hand.

Draw one card, then another, and another.
Click on each card.
Black and white images appear.
They look like woodcuts: the face of a woman, a city in shadow, a dark figure fading in and out of focus.
Click on each card again. Short texts appear.

The following are examples of prewritten texts:

The landscape is vast and cold and lonely.
Hungry for human contact, he prowls the night.
He glides quietly among the ghostly buildings.
She remembers the dexterity of his hands, the swiftness
of their movements.

The prewritten texts are all geared to the notion of solitude: a lonely landscape, isolated characters, things remembered, the hope of finding another. "Shadows," by a player calling himself Spiv Vey, is an example of a player using both my texts and his own to create a story about a solitary person. The underlined words are Spiv Vey's contribution to the story.

> *He lies in wait . . .*
> *An eerie dark emptiness reigns*
> *Sometimes he sees a lifeless form*
> <u>*Sometimes a shadow turning*</u>
> *Echoey voices pursue him*
> *Among the abandoned brick buildings with their*
> *shattered windows, their rusted and broken fire escapes*
> *Disturbing thoughts poke around in the empty corners of*
> *his mind*
> *In the milky twilight he listens for a presence he knows he*
> *will never find again . . .*
> <u>*Still he waits, silently in the shadows . . .*</u>

"in the darkness, nothing," by Mary Trevor, is another example, this time one that focuses on the female character. For Mary, she is a person who wants to be alone.

> *she comes to believe that darkness is her natural habitat . . .*
> *she slips away . . .*
> <u>*she hopes never to see him again. She wants to be alone.*</u>
> *he glides quietly among the ghostly buildings . . .*
> *he pursues her, sensing her presence and her antipathy*
> *to him.*
> *in the instant of discovery, a thin cry breaks from her lips*
> *and her hands flutter up to cover her face . . .*
> *she kicks out, twisting her body in an effort to escape . . .*
> *she cannot breathe . . .*
>
> *in the milky light he listens for a presence he knows he*
> *will never find again . . .*

Long my favorite, "Errand," by "Hank," visits an unexpected transformation on my vague, gloomy texts by making them an occasion for the remembered grocery list.

> *A milky twilight settles over the city, tall buildings become*
> *ghostly shadows.*
> *As he slips through the night her thoughts unfold in him*
> *eggs, lettuce, cereal, cigarettes . . .*

Hundreds of stories have been written for *Solitaire*. Many are simply unrelated selections strung together. But others evidence an intelligence at work trying to shape a meaningful story from a series of more or less disparate parts. More

often than not the successful stories are short. They may be personal, as in the following:

WITH HIS MOTHER, WHOM HE KNOWS LITTLE ABOUT
by T

> *rich, goodlooking young man wishes to be in touch . . .*

Or they may encapsulate a fictional moment in which some future action is implied. "Missing myself," by "yoonyung," is an example.

> *In the instant of discovery a thin cry breaks from her lips*
> *and her hands flutter up to cover her face*
>
> *His grip is powerful*

A pulse of fear beats quietly in them both.

What would I do now if I were to create a second *Solitaire*? As the objective is to draw on the creativity of *Solitaire* players for the creation of stories, as many of the prepared texts as possible must be left open so that they combine with multiple other texts. To accomplish this, those things that limit what you have written to one use, or that close it to intervention, must be eliminated. Punctuation and capitalization may be perceived as limitations; complete sentences similarly.

For instance:

"Hungry for human contact, he prowls the night."

As is, this is a self-contained sentence relating only to the story's male figure. If it were broken apart so the phrase "hungry for human contact" were accessible by itself, the text might also relate to the female. It could then be followed by "he prowls the night," "she waits silently in the shadows," or any other appropriately gendered phrase. Remove the period from the same sentence and a phrase like "among the abandoned brick buildings with their shattered windows, their rusted and broken fire escapes" could be appended.

A sentence like "He listens to the silence, separating the silence of solitude from the silence of shared expectation" implies the known presence of another human being.

If you were to remove the punctuation and break the sentence up, "he listens to the silence" would be available to precede or follow "he is alone" or "hungry for human contact"; or it could be followed by "she is here," "his memory is clouded," or other phrases and sentences.

The current *Solitaire* has four intended stories (four suits):

about him
about her
about them
a second story about them

A second *Solitaire* would allow for a greater exchange of elements within these stories. Another thing I would do is provide a simple editing mechanism, one that would allow players to eliminate or rearrange the selections they have made before placing them in the gallery. And third, I would debate long and hard—should I reconfigure the work to accommodate the new content provided by players who make use of their jokers to write their own texts? Is it more interesting to the solitary player that the work is open (that it incorporates the thinking processes of multiple authors), or is it more interesting when greater restrictions are placed on how the work is played? How would a player feel who was interested in composing a story from existing texts (with a few additions of his/her own), if required to alternate red and black suits as he/she composed? In the past, I would have come down on the side of the open work. Today I waver, wondering if the greater challenge, for myself and for the player, wouldn't be in placing greater restrictions on the way the work is played.

Reference
Solitaire. Helen Thorington, Marianne Petit, and John Neilson. 1998. <http://turbulence.org/Works/solitaire/index.html>.

Enlightening Interactive Fiction: Andrew Plotkin's *Shade*

Jeremy Douglass

In Andrew Plotkin's interactive fiction *Shade* (Plotkin 2000), you are sitting up late on the night before a trip to a desert rave. At first you are preoccupied by the tedium of travel preparations and the stress of misplaced plane tickets. However, a growing unease sets in as the familiar landscape of your apartment begins to change—objects morph, break, and dissolve, while sand appears everywhere in patches, then piles, then avalanches. The arriving headlights of your airport taxi wash away the walls of your apartment and reveal the truth: you have already gone to your rave and wandered into the desert. Dying of exposure there in the harsh noon sun, you hallucinate your dim apartment, reliving the small choices leading up to the end.

A Brief History of IF

Shade is an interactive fiction (IF, or "text adventure game")—an object-oriented story simulation in which a command line is used to interact with a text parser. The parser prints text describing the situation to the player ("You are sprawled on the futon") and the player responds by typing ("> EXAMINE FUTON") to receive a response ("The futon is definitely on the downhill side of life's rolling knolls."). By convention, IF descriptions are generally written in the second person, while player responses are imperative statements.

Interactive Fiction computer games began with *Adventure*, a spelunking simulation written by Will Crowther in 1975, and later expanded by Don Woods into a Tolkien-esque fantasy in 1976. It inspired many variations, adaptations, and homages, including the first commercial computer game (*Adventure*) sold by Scott Adams in 1978, as well as the first personal computer game blockbuster

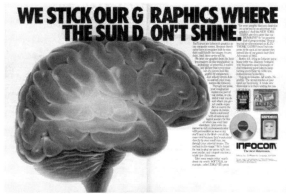

19.1) A 1983 Infocom advertisement. (Activision)

when MIT startup Infocom published *Zork* in 1980, helping to establish the first commercial PC games era (Nelson 2001; Montfort 2003).

While the second-person mode was present in IF from its first days as a simulated environment and through its period as Tolkien fan art on the mainframes of American campuses, it is Infocom whose marketing made the second-person mode synonymous with embodiment and immersion: "Interactive fiction is a story in which YOU are the main character." While it sounds as if the player was invited to step into the world of the story, it was just as often an invitation to step into a role on a stage. Rather than YOU being the main character, you had the opportunity to role-play the main character, exploring "your" personality as a detective, a spy, an AI, etc., even while exploring the environment . . . and there were many "you" roles to explore.

Infocom's catalog eventually encompassed a wide variety of genres, including detective fiction, espionage, fantasy, romance, science fiction, and space opera, often with corresponding characters to become. However, this genre explosion in IF coincided with the rise of the graphics card and a massive shift in the computer games marketplace. In advertisements, Infocom responded to the market threat of graphics by lauding the rich complexity of prose ("We draw our graphics from the limitless imagery of your imagination") and deploring the mindlessness of arcade shooters ("I was a Teenage Zombie!"). The company also experimented with multiple hybrid text-graphic forms; yet, like all text game companies of that era, Infocom eventually went out of business.

Yet the downfall of commercial IF in the late 1980s crystallized a grassroots art and design community around the emerging Usenet. In the 1990s, as graphical desktop computing entered the landmark era of Windows 3.0, Mosaic, and *Myst*, IF experienced a quiet renaissance, with languages, libraries, toolkits, and game files circulating freely among individual artist-practitioners on a growing number of groups, web sites, and forums, including rec.arts.int-fiction, the if-archive, and ifMUD. The strong retro aesthetic of the community was tempered by an interest in further developing the form, shaped by the practical necessities of doing independent, and often single-person, development on no budget. This led many new artists to turn away from sprawling mazes filled with puzzles, and reconceptualize IF design in contrast to the computer game industry as a craft of interactive dramatic short fiction.

In design and content, *Shade* is indebted to the original era, yet quintessentially a product of the later indie scene.

Light and Dark

> Odd, how the light just makes your apartment gloomier. Pre-dawn darkness pools in the corners and around the tops of walls. Your desk lamp glares yellow, but the shadows only draw your eyes and deepen. (Plotkin 2000)

Throughout *Shade*, you inhabit two worlds. In the first world, a vision of the apartment invites you to reflect on choices in your former life that lead to the second world, the reality of the desert and of the player's death. Although your apartment is brightly lit by a bulb, it is also a shadow world, the hallucination of a dead or dying shade. The question is not whether this death will happen, but when and how bad news will arrive.

> One window, whose shade is down, and the front door firmly shut.

> Your luggage is piled untidily by the door. A potted hyacinth sits beneath the window.

> You are sprawled on the futon, staring up into that gloom. Your eyes feel gritty. But it's too late—early—no time left for sleep, anyway. In a few hours your ride will arrive.

> On the desk are your to-do list and a travel book.

The drawn shade and the front door of the apartment are always there, and beyond them lie the desert of the real and the realization of death that end the story. Yet this realization must come slowly—the process cannot be short-circuited by opening the door early, as Plotkin's character is constitutionally unwilling to even look outside until the taxi arrives. The "firmly shut" door, the lamp bulb that "glares," and even the drawn shade hint at a fierce immutability.

> >OPEN DOOR

> The sun hasn't risen; what light you have would just leak out into the night. Anyway, the taxi hasn't arrived, so there's nowhere to go.

> >OPEN SHADE

> Darkness is already crawling around the edges of the windowshade. You have no desire to look night in the face.

> >TURN OFF LAMP

> You do not want the dark.

These responses are essentially error messages—no matter how many times you turn off the lamp, the requested interaction is politely refused, and the underlying world model is not changed. However, understanding of the work is advanced by reading these messages; indeed, trying to interact and failing is necessary, as their poetic menace puts much of the coming experience in context.

The style of these messages is particular to whoever "you" are supposed to be ("You have no desire," "You do not want"). They represent the normal constraints of the simulation on the player ("You can't do that") in terms of psychological characterization ("You won't do that"). Player input serves as id, parser response as superego, and the emerging character is a negotiation between play and design. For the player, the psychological error messages naturalize the limits of the simulation as merely the limits of a personality. Rather than being disciplined for attempting to explore the unimplemented reaches of the world, the player is invited to discover the inhibitions (and thus definitions) of a persona. Play is exploration—but it is also autobiographical archeology, holding bits of "yourself" up to the light.

Shade is a work of light, as a narrative and as a game. As a narrative, it tells a story of enlightenment—in this case, realizing your own death and understanding your complicity in causing it. As a game, it is a simulation almost totally defined by vision and perception—in IF, scope of interaction is largely determined by what you can and cannot "see." We can understand how Plotkin innovates and responds to the traditional use of light in IF by considering that the ur-text, Crowther's *Adventure*, was originally a spelunking simulation.

In *Adventure*, the presence of a light source was necessary for almost any activity—navigation, manipulation of objects, etc. Given the original context, this makes sense, as it is highly dangerous to wander around cave systems in the dark. The introduction of fantasy elements only increased the importance of using light to model glowing objects, fire, etc. Widespread reimplementation and later commoditization as the *Zork* series left the primacy of light firmly embedded in both the games and the development languages and tools. ("It is dark. You are likely to be eaten by a Grue.") Today, explicit illumination remains integral even to contemporary IF authoring systems like TADS ("lightsource") and Inform ("has light"), with light as a core attribute of every object.

Indeed, an examination of the source code of much contemporary IF can reveal odd vestigial light codes. According to the *Inform Beginner's Guide*, "There must be at least one light source in every room (unless you want the player to be told that 'It's pitch dark and you can't see a thing'); most commonly, that light source is the room itself" (Firth 2002, 32). For example:

```
Object hallway "Hallway"
  with
    description "A twisty little passage runs north
      to the bedroom and east to the bathroom.",
    n_to bedroom,
    e_to bathroom,
    has light;
```

Here, the hallway object itself emanates light. If it didn't, by default most IF player characters could not find their way from bedroom to bathroom with the lights out. "This illustrates one of the terrible things about darkness in a game. You can't see anything; you can do very little indeed.

All objects except those in your inventory are out of scope, unreachable, as if non-existent. Worse, if you DROP one of the objects you are carrying, it will be swallowed by the dark, never to be found until there is light to see by" (Ibid, 142).

Without vision, there is no agency. This may not seem so strange unless you consider interacting with such work from a radically different perspective. For example, because serially displayed text is highly accessible, the blind gaming community has long turned to interactive fiction as a mainstay of computer entertainment. The irony of designing such a medium around the indispensability of lamps is hard to miss.

In *Adventure*, *Zork*, and many more classic IF works, darkness kills (or at least incapacitates). In *Shade*, this situation is ironically reversed. You fear the darkness "crawling around the edges of the windowshade," and fear that precious light will "leak out into the night." Yet death has already arrived in the form of a light that cannot be escaped.

Other contemporary IFs have played with reversing expectations about light as well. "Enlightenment: an interactive one-room absurdity," by Taro Ogawa, uses the standard light model and turns the goal on its head. An adventurer of the classic *Zork* style is encumbered with an armload of glowing objects, yet is desperately trying to hide, lose, and break his plundered riches to gain a much-needed moment of darkness.

"Hunter in Darkness: A Cave Crawl," also by Andrew Plotkin, pitches a hunter headlong into a cave only moments after the story begins. Lost and injured, the player must feel and smell the way to freedom.

In its code, *Shade* simply opts out of light simulation entirely, overriding it in a single expression:

```
! Simple light function which says everything is lit.
[ OffersLight i;
  if (i == 0)
  rfalse;
  rtrue;
];
```

At the level of code, like the level of the story, everything is illuminated—although at neither level is this immediately apparent to the player.

The Source

Arguments for selecting *Shade* either as a case study or as a classroom example of IF might highlight its relatively short length, the high quality of the writing, and the availability of the code. The commented source code of *Shade* is, in fact, freely downloadable for noncommercial use, and is extremely edifying for anyone curious about (or confused by) the experience. The code is written in Inform, an object-oriented, C-like language, which can often be read like colloquial English even by non-programmers. However, in the case of *Shade*, the code is more intricately designed (and thus significantly less readable) than most IF. Yet even the complexities of *Shade* are often in pursuit of a simplified interface.

One example is the treatment of navigation. IFs are traditionally navigable by compass rose (N, S, E, W), with objects and events distributed in space as an exploration. *Shade*, by contrast, eschews navigation for a single location. Subtitled "a one-room game set in your apartment," *Shade* is playfully referring to the phenomenon of apartment pieces in IF—generally learner works in which authors new to the medium begin by scrupulously implementing a detailed model of everything within sight of their desks. Such pieces usually lack setting, conflict, and/or plot, tending instead to concentrate on the detailed execution of conventionally modeled IF objects—an interactive lamp, cabinet, closet, and so on.

Just as *Shade* opted out of conventional light modeling, it dispenses with conventional spatial navigation. Instead, the kitchen, bathroom, and bedroom of the apartment form one unified location—a contiguous "room" with several "nooks," whose objects are always in scope. The player location is indicated through nuance and shifting emphasis. Interacting with something in the one area automatically shifts the player to that area, while the view is reorganized to describe nearer objects before those further away. The net effect is a feeling of differentiated space without rigid underlying zones.

> You survey your one small room. The kitchen alcove has a refrigerator, a sink, a stove, and barely enough

space to stand between them. One wall projects out to form a counter, with a cupboard beneath it. The rest of the place is mostly filled by your futon, and the computer desk in the corner. The bathroom alcove is across from you, and the closet next to it....

> TURN OFF COMPUTER SCREEN

You step out of the kitchen nook, and sit down at the desk.

You hit the power key; the computer gives a tiny sigh and shuts down.

> LOOK

You survey your one small room. One desk, paper-piled, with a dusty computer shoved to the side. Your futon, upon which you sit. Second-hand stereo sitting on a cardboard crate. A kitchen nook one way and a bathroom nook the other, with a closet to the side....

Another way in which *Shade* simplifies through complicating is by providing stable references for series of objects—actually the same Platonic "object" in the code, changing names and representations gradually over time, as with the hyacinth that morphs into a cactus.

```
Object -> plant "plant"
with
name 'pot' 'potted' 'plant' 'soil',
short_name [;
switch (self.number) {
0: print "hyacinth";
1: print "spider plant";
2: print "palm plant";
3: print "cactus";
default: print "[BUG]";
}
rtrue;
],
```

While the hyacinth changes sequentially, another piece of code controlling the task list involves a group of selectively visible items that "jump out at you" only as they become pertinent or available in the loose progression of events. While this subtle effect naturalizes the progression through the IF, individual tasks disrupt and forestall progress—in particular, the bit of code behind the missing plane tickets.

```
Global ticket_counter = 0;
[ CheckTicket obj;
if (obj.ticket_search >= 2) {
if (obj.ticket_search == 3)
"No matter how often you look, the plane
tickets aren't there.";
obj.ticket_search = 3;
"The plane tickets still aren't there.";
}
obj.ticket_search = 2;
ticket_counter++;
if (ticket_counter < 3) {
"Nope. The tickets aren't there.";
}
Goaled(tickets);
move tickets to Apartment;
print_ret "Nope. The tickets aren't — ", (emph)
"Aha.",
"They are, after all. The tickets slide to the floor and
lie there, smirking at you.";
];
```

The tickets are not merely hidden, nor hidden randomly. The code declares them to be hidden in "the third hiding spot searched." Once the tickets turn up missing, Plotkin's code keeps a global counter on the number of hiding places checked, with a further counter for each individual place, so that response messages vary. Only when two of the appropriate places have been checked will the tickets turn up in the third.

One of the consequences of this hiding method is that the hunt for the tickets tends to familiarize the player with the environment by producing a thorough ransacking of the house. It also produces a moderate amount of frustration. Finding the tickets on the third try is unlikely, as not all locations in the house are hiding spots, but finding them on the first or second try is, in fact, impossible. Lost items, as *Shade* describes them, simply take longer to find.

Of course, this shaping of experience is not evident to the first-time player. Only upon replaying *Shade* and going immediately to the previously discovered hiding place (e.g., the jacket in the closet) will the player find no tickets, and

realize that the world model is not logical and deterministic in some straightforward way. This discovery on replay is virtually guaranteed, for unlike randomization, the tickets are defined such that they will not appear wherever the player knows them to be. Using outside knowledge from the last traversal, the re-player will go directly to the jacket or stack of papers where the tickets were last found, and in doing so change (but not shorten) the story of the search. The description approximates the real-world experience of a frustrating search, not through more detailed models of the hunting ground, but through a simulation that requires a similar process. When the sequence ends, picking up the tickets triggers another detail niggling towards revelation: "Taken. Something scrapes underfoot as you bend to pick the tickets up."

Not coincidentally, the inability to trust one's own eyes is the common thread in all the preceding examples. With the hyacinth/cactus, you learn that the connections between objects and their appearances are complex and mutable. With the task list, you learn that attention is fickle, and you will only perceive what "interests you." With the tickets, you learn (if you replay, if you notice at all) that unseen processes manipulate your experience. All is not as it seems.

In *Shade*, the textual aesthetics of light, with "crawling shadows" and "burning glare," are communicated directly to the player. The code aesthetics of light, however, occur at the disjunction between the player's mental model of the code as it is expected to be ("If I LOOK in a place, an object is either there or not, and if it is there, a description of the object will be printed") and the reality of the code as it actually functions. The implied code is wrong, and the virtual light entering the player's imaginary eye is to be mistrusted, if for no other reason than that the actual code is unconventional: what is seen is not always what is modeled, and what is modeled is not always seen.

For this among other reasons, *Shade* can be a frustrating experience. Concealing or misrepresenting the simulated world state seems to break the fundamental contract between the parser and the player: the parser providing a description of the world, and the player providing descriptions of actions in that world. After evidence of such a breach of faith, some players may no longer be interested in interacting.

Yet these frustrations are to a certain extent naturalized if we choose to either side with the player character against the illusions of a deceptive world or side with the "real" world against the illusions of a self-deceptive player character. In either case, there is a gap between vision and the world, between the code as we assumed it was and the code as we discover it must be. That gap is defined by what innovative or unexpected quality we encounter in the code itself, and one reads/plays the work by closing the gap—by solving, by revealing, by coming to understand.

Second Person in Context

While *Shade* is technically innovative in a number of ways, it is utterly conventional in one very important way—the use of the second-person mode of address.

IF works are overwhelmingly written in the second person. Over 90% of the IF currently listed in Baf's Guide are second-person works (2288/2510), with the remainder split between first person, third person, and various text-art experiments or "abuses." By contrast to IF, a vanishingly small number of novels are written using second person as the dominant mode—and most that do feature intercepted communication (e.g., the epistolary novel) rather than continuous direct address. Yet there are two other forms of entertainment in which use of second person predominates: game books, aka *Choose Your Own Adventure* books, and role-playing games (RPGs), whose gamemaster creates the world by directly addressing the players.

The precursors to contemporary game books may have been the nonfiction instructional series TutorText, whose first volume, "The Arithmetic of Computers," was printed in 1958. Fictional game books did not appear until 1967, when Raymond Queneau of the Oulipo published *Un conte à votre façon.* That same year saw the publication of E. W. Hildick and Peter Barrett's *Lucky Les,* the first illustrated children's game book, and the subsequent steady increase in game book publication until over a decade later when the first *Choose Your Own Adventure* appeared in 1979 and "almost single-handedly started the American game book boom of the eighties" (Katz 1998).

Just as TutorText predated game books, mass market wargaming of the kind popularized by Charles S. Roberts in his 1952 *Tactics* predated the ur-role-playing game *Dungeons & Dragons.* In 1968, the year after the publication of *Un conte à votre façon,* wargamers began a series of experiments with fiction and fantasy to alleviate growing boredom with historical reenactments and straight scenarios. The official TSR publication did not arrive, however, until 1974.

Like game books and RPGs, IF was arguably predated by simulation methods that emphasized fact over fantasy and system over story, one example being Terry Winograd's 1972 object modeling program "SHRDLU." In 1975, the year after *D&D* was released, IF first circulated in what rapidly became a fantastical form. IF was sold commercially as early as 1978; however, it did not reach a mass audience until 1981, when Infocom expanded on their initial PDP-11 release with new versions targeting the personal computer market.

Why did the 1970s see the rise of mass audiences for second-person simulations? RPG historians such as Gary Allan Fine lay credit for the flashpoint at the feet of Tolkien's 1965 U.S. paperback release of *The Lord of the Rings,* which shifted the interest of tabletop wargaming communities to fantasy role-playing (Fine 1983). In Tolkien, *Adventure* and early RPGs have a common ancestor, and out of common communities came a history of cross-influences. Many of these influences weave through MUDs, MOOs, and present-day MMORPGs. Yet the proximity of second-person simulations to contemporary computer games creates the possibility of slippage or misunderstanding in using the term "person," especially when shifting between discussion of language-based and visually-based simulations.

Strangely, the use of the term "person" in language studies does not correspond to its use in visual studies. Most games studies discussions use "person" in the visual style, corresponding to the viewpoint of the player. The first-person camera is the most immediate, providing a view from the eyes of the avatar with little more than a hand of the avatar-self encroaching on the image. The third person camera is more mediated and distancing, in that the separate self of Lara Croft or Master Chief is displayed on screen and followed through the game world by a cinematic crane shot. The function of this mediacy is complex (Bolter and Grusin 2000), but one effect is that greater immediacy imparts greater immersion.

In language simulations such as IF, game books, or RPGs, this process works differently. Rather than the process of simulation occurring as if from the player's viewpoint, the simulation is addressed to the player from the simulator ("You are in a maze of twisty little passages") creating complementary thoughts in the mind of the player ("I'm in a maze!"). Second-person narration ("You are") evokes first-person participation ("I am!"). Like the visual form of a first-person shooter, second-person text is the most immediate, with most of the "you" ("I!") being automatically cropped out of the mental image. Conversely, a 3D game with a first-person camera image of a field and a white house could be described as an assertion on the part of the simulator in the second-person mode of address: "You are standing in an open field west of a white house...."

In both the textual and visual case, the game system describes an inhabitable experience through assertion (second person) for the purpose of the player's participation, identification, or immersion (first person). We can conclude that the "first-person camera" as it is discussed in games studies and the "second-person narration" of RPGs and IF are not, in fact, two categories, but rather two perspectives on the same category of simulated immediacy.

This immediacy is distinct from the more mediated "first-person narration," which creates much the same distancing effect as a "third person camera." It does this in much the same way, by introducing a separate self into the frame. Upon reading "I am sitting at my desk," many IF players immediately think (and sometimes type) "> WHO ARE YOU?"

The odd category out in this typology of point-of-view is the "second-person camera," a phrase that only makes sense in interactive media and then only in the rare cases when the player can intentionally switch the camera to the first-person perspective of a non-controllable character, as in Julian Oliver's experimental game *Adventures in the Second Person*. As Oliver describes, "In this take on the 2nd Person Perspective, you control yourself through the eyes of the bot, but you do not control the bot; your eyes have effectively been switched. Naturally this makes action difficult when you aren't within the bot's field of view. So, both you and the bot (or other player) will need to work together, to combat each other."

I know of no equivalent in IF, nor in game books, in which the descriptive text simulates one point of view while player input controls a different character. Hypothetically, such an IF might look like "Hunter, In Darkness," still controlling the hunter, yet written from the point of view of the hunted Wumpus. How exactly might we implement such an external point of view in *Shade*, even if we chose to? Whose would it be? Our player character is the only "living" being in the story other than the hyacinth/cactus plant. And for good reason—*Shade* is a fundamentally introspective and contemplative work. There is only second-person address ... at least, only up until the final moments of the text, when "you" are finally addressed by a third, a person who is also you.

Beyond Yourself

Although the interface and description of *Shade* are rigorously constructed from the second-person point of view, from the outset there another perspective present in the room, a kind of IF play-within-a-play.

> Right now, however, there's a game on the screen—one of the text adventures, or interactive fictions, or whatever they are this month—the only kind of game your beige antique can run, anyway.

> The you-have-died message is blinking morosely at you. You started up Ready, Okay! last night, trying to distract yourself until morning. But you can't get even halfway through without running out of insulin.

The uncanny "you-have-died" foreshadows the end of *Shade*, and reads in retrospect like a message straight from the subconscious of the traveler. While *Shade* does not allow you to play "Ready, Okay!", Emily Short argues convincingly that the description signals a tragedy foretold: "Ready, Okay!" is the conventional novel of noted IF author Adam Cadre, and announces from its introduction that most of the high school cast of characters will be dead by the end of the book. What's more, Short points out that the insulin identifies which of Cadre's characters is the protagonist of Plotkin's imaginary IF—the spacey younger sister, a character coincidentally inclined towards events like the desert rave. The traveler may have been playing a game that can't be won. Regardless, our story of the prelude to *Shade* is that the traveler sat down at an IF and tried to pretend to be someone else, eventually giving up. The problem of being someone else returns in the conclusion.

The final scenes of *Shade* are marked by a tiny scurrying figure hiding at the edge of your vision. In the penultimate sequence, you interact away the last illusory artifacts of your old life, revealing radio, futon, etc. as nothing but sand. Throughout, the tiny figure hides until there is nowhere left to hide, at last emerging to trudge lost across the desert sands.

Shade is not a story about what is, but about how you come to know what you know. It is almost certain that the tiny figure is "you" and that the illusion of the apartment must be stripped away in order to contemplate this self. That the apartment is an illusion is re-emphasized by the lingering mirror, which can be re-entered after most of the apartment has been reduced to sand, restoring you suddenly to sunlit apartment and creating a moment of hope that it was all just a bad dream. But no. The apartment remains a lie—and it is a lie that you have been telling yourself.

It is here in the psychological bifurcation of "lying to yourself" that the stability of the second-person character, the traveler, breaks down. If the traveler is this tiny figure desperately struggling to hide from the sand and the light and the truth, then who are "you" now, this new point of view in the featureless desert, towering over the traveler and providing a third-person perspective? Are "you" a ghost? Nature? Death?

There is nothing left of your old illusion but the travel book, now changed: "The Desert Elemental's Handbook— you've been studying it for ages. Trace moisture segregation, arthropod ecocycles, sand/grit/fines sizing distributions. And, of course, the artistic aspects of heat, time, distance, and death." In the beginning of the story the book is perhaps most indicative of the traveler's failure to prepare properly for a desert trip—now it is a source of "tables of starvation," "chapters on bones," "a section on thirst," and so on.

With everything fallen before your Midas touch and dissolved to sand, the only thing remaining to interact with is the tiny figure. The player can struggle against the inevitable logic of the text, but the only remaining choice is not to play. Playing on, each touch fells the wandering figure with fatigue and heatstroke. On the final touch, the figure

finally lies still and is buried, only to return:

> The tiny figure crawls out from under the sands.
> It's dead.
> "You win," it says. "Okay, my turn again."
> >...
> Nothing left to do. Time passes.
> The sun crawls higher.

Interestingly, the prompt and ellipsis in the final quote is not player input—it is provided by the parser for you, and as such is the final replacement of you in your role as interactor. An ellipsis seems to be the only appropriate response to the dead figure's statement. What could winning mean anymore, and what are turns? *Shade* first dispensed with light, and space, and gradually with all the objects throughout it. Finally, here, it dispenses (and so dispenses with) time. By retelling a cross-country trip without ever leaving a small patch of sand, *Shade* presents a portrait of a personality even as the traveler unravels into nothing. By the time the second person has arrived on the scene, the first is no person at all.

References: Literature

Bolter, Jay David, and Richard Grusin (2000). *Remediation: Understanding New Media*. Cambridge, MA: MIT Press.

Fine, Gary Allan (1983). *Shared Fantasy: Role-Playing Games as Social Worlds*. Chicago: University of Chicago Press.

Firth, Roger, and Sonja Kesserich (2002). *The Inform Beginner's Guide*, 2nd edition. St. Charles, IL: The Interactive Fiction Library. <http://www.inform-fiction.org/manual/download_ibg.html>.

Katz, Demian (1998). "Gamebook Database." Gamebooks.org (August 1998). <http://www.gamebooks.org/list_years.php>.

Nelson, Graham (2001). *The Inform Designer's Manual,* 4th edition. St. Charles, Illinois: The Interactive Fiction Library. <http://www.inform-fiction.org/manual/html/>.

Montfort, Nick (2003). *Twisty Little Passages: An Approach to Interactive Fiction*. Cambridge, MA: MIT Press.

Plotkin, Andrew (2000). *Shade*. <http://wurb.com/if/game/918>.

Schick, Lawrence (1991). *Heroic Worlds: A History and Guide to Roleplaying Games*. Amherst, NY: Prometheus Books.

Schofield, Dennis (1998). "The Second Person: A Point of View? The Function of the Second-Person Pronoun in Narrative Prose Fiction." Ph.D. Thesis. Deakin University, Geelong, Australia.

Reference: Game

Adventures in the Second Person. Julian Oliver; Selectparks. 2005. <http://www.selectparks.net/modules.php?name=News&file=article&sid=284>.

The Creation of Floyd the Robot in *Planetfall*
Steve Meretzky

Planetfall was the first game that I wrote for Infocom, one of the leading computer game companies of the 1980s. It was an all-text adventure game, meaning that the player directed the actions of a player character in the game by typing commands to that character in plain English, such as "ENTER THE SPACESHIP" or "PICK UP THE ELVEN SWORD." The game would then respond with a sentence or two of text, describing what happened when the player character attempted that action. These games were typically a mix of a storyline, exploration of an interesting environment, and some puzzles—often quite hard—that needed to be solved to advance the game.

I began working on *Planetfall* in September 1982. At that point, Infocom had released five text adventures. These games were minuscule by today's standards, driven by the capacity of computer floppy drives; the original release of *Planetfall* was only 108 kilobytes—about as many bytes as a medium-sized image on a Web page.

In those early games, there were numerous NPCs (non-player characters), such as the Wizard and Demon in *Zork II* or the various suspects in the mystery game *Deadline*. One of my thoughts, going into the start of work on *Planetfall*, was to try to concentrate on a single NPC. By devoting the writing time—and more importantly, the precious disk space—to a single character, that NPC could be much deeper and more interesting.

Why a robot? For one thing, it fit the science-fictional setting of the game. But more important, I calculated that even with the concentration on a single NPC, the character would still fall far short of simulating a human being, but that players would have lesser expectations for a nonhuman character such as a robot.

There were essentially four components to writing the character. The first was direct interaction between the player and Floyd. (In the examples that follow, the all-caps text are commands to the game as typed by the player).

So:

>SEARCH FLOYD

Floyd giggles and pushes you away. "You're tickling Floyd!" He clutches at his side panels, laughing hysterically. Oil drops stream from his eyes.

The second component was when the player spoke to Floyd. These were traditionally the hardest player inputs to deal with, because there was only enough disk space to handle a fraction of the possible conversational gambits, so most inputs had to be covered by fairly general defaults. For example:

>FLOYD, WALK NORTH

Floyd looks slightly embarrassed. "You know me and my sense of direction." Then he looks up at you with wide, trusting eyes. "Tell Floyd a story?"

The third component was simply a list of actions that Floyd might perform at the end of a given turn, if he was in the same location as the player. For example:

Floyd rubs his head affectionately against your shoulder.

or

Floyd reminisces about his friend Lazarus, a medical robot.

The final component was when Floyd's actions would be triggered by something behind the scenes of the game, such as the player and Floyd entering a given location, or by an "interrupt routine" scheduled earlier in the game. Thus, entering the infirmary for the first time triggers Floyd's discovery of a robot breastplate labeled "Lazarus," poignantly informing Floyd that his best friend is no longer alive, and foreshadowing Floyd's own death.

My goals with Floyd were to make him cute and endearing, in the way that children and pets can be. My biggest surprise was that, unintentionally, Floyd also turned out to be a very humorous character. As some players began to point this out as the aspect they most enjoyed about Floyd, I played it up even more. For instance, when you save the game, normally an outside-the-gameworld activity, Floyd would respond:

>SAVE
Your game has been saved.
Floyd's eyes light up. "Oh boy! Are we gonna try
something dangerous now?"

Having made the decision to create such a single, deep
character, I thought there would be the potential for
emotional resonance with the player, which I could take
advantage of by putting this character in peril or even having
events lead to that character's destruction. This ultimately
led to Floyd's death scene, in which he courageously
volunteers to go into a dangerous location to retrieve an
important object, citing his metallic indestructibility. He
retrieves the object, but suffers serious damage, and dies in
your arms. This worked out better than my fondest hopes,
and numerous players over the intervening years have told
me that they cried at this point in the game. *Softline*, an early
computer game magazine, compared the moment to
Charlotte's death in *Charlotte's Web*.

Another interesting thing I discovered, talking to players
over the years, is the large number of players who *didn't* like
Floyd while he was alive, finding him annoying or distracting.

But once he was dead, they realized they missed him! They
weren't particularly moved by his death, but his absence
created a void in their gameworld akin to the loss of an
acquaintance in real life.

Perhaps the most amazing thing about the creation of
Floyd was how easy it was. The entire code and text for the
character, if printed out, would perhaps run to ten pages.
What's amazing is not that I was able to create a computer
game character that touched people so deeply, but how
infrequently the same thing has been accomplished in the
intervening two decades.

References: Literature

Saberhagen, Fred, Lafore, Robert, Prussing, Scott, Simonsen,
Redmond, Blank, Marc, and Berlyn, Mike (1983). "Call Yourself
Ishmael: Micros Get The Literary Itch." *Softline,* volume 3:
September–October 1983: Cover, 30–34.

White, E. B. (1952). *Charlotte's Web*. New York: Harper Bros.

References: Games

Deadline. Marc Blank; Infocom. 1981.
Planetfall. Steve Meretzky; Infocom. 1982.
Zork II. Dave Lebling; Infocom. 1981.

Fretting the Player Character
Nick Montfort

In interactive fiction, the "player character" is that character who the interactor (or player, or user) can direct with commands. The first example of interactive fiction, Will Crowther and Don Woods's *Adventure*, instructed the interactor: "I will be your eyes and hands. Direct me with commands of 1 or 2 words." In *Adventure* this *I* may seem to be the same as the narrator (Buckles 1985, 141–142), but the development of later interactive fiction has made it clear that this entity—the "eyes and hands" that focalize the description of the interactive fiction world and the narration of events in it, and the agent that the interactor can direct or command, through which the interactor can influence the simulated world—is best considered as a separate entity, the player character.

Given this particular name, this basic relationship, and the affinity that interactive fiction has with role-playing games, it may seem reasonable to imagine that the interactor "plays" the player character. However, the interactor actually is not playing a character in any usual way. That is, it is not at all useful to consider that the player character is played by the interactor in any literal, typical sense of play: not in the dramatic sense, not in the gaming sense, and not even exactly in the sense of many other multi-party role-playing contexts, from *Dungeons & Dragons* to multi-user online environments.

This chapter is meant to disturb the role-playing concept of the player character and the assumptions that are often brought to this element of interactive fiction. This fretting of the player character begins by examining the ordinary senses of play and considering how play of these sorts differs from the interactor's activity. The discussion continues to explain how the player character's *not* being played by the interactor has been important to several successful interactive fiction works—specifically, ones with well-defined, memorable player characters. Finally, I describe how this perspective on the player character has influenced me as I wrote and programmed *Book and Volume* (2005).

I.

The interactor commands the player character and apprehends the world mainly through the player character, but for the following reasons the interactor does not really play the player character, however generic or specific this player character is.

In considering the dramatic sense of play, it is reasonable to consider the basic techniques of such actors, or players, and to see that they have no straightforward relationship to the techniques of interactors. It is easy to find accomplished interactive fiction players who gain great enjoyment from their play, but who have never asked "what's my motivation?," who have never imagined childhood traumas in order to portray their player characters more naturally and emotionally, and who certainly do not focus on their own bodies in performing the physical actions that enact a character. To range beyond the tradition of the Actors Studio to the theater of Augusto Boal—whose practice is also grounded in the awareness of one's physical body and in the use of this body to enact characters—may provide rich ideas for how interactive situations relate to political engagement (Frasca 2001), but it still does not allow us to usefully describe the interactor's relationship to the player character in terms of dramatic play. Typically, the interactor is simply not working very hard to act in a manner particular to a character, as is done when playing a dramatic role. Instead, the interactor is putting on the character as a pair of eyes and a pair of hands—not as a human being with an emotional and cognitive existence, a physical body enacted by one's own physical body.

Although particular works of interactive fiction—indeed, the majority of such works—may be games, the interactor is also not "playing" the player character in the sense in which "play" is used in gaming. The interactor is playing the game. Someone who has enjoyed playing *Monopoly* might express this sentiment by saying "I enjoyed playing *Monopoly*" but it would be strange to hear someone say, "I enjoyed playing the car" or, "I enjoyed playing the hat." Similarly, people frequently say how much they like "playing *Zork*," but it is unusual to hear them explain how much they got out of "playing the nameless adventurer." Or, if that seems a straw-adventurer argument, consider that they might say, "I enjoyed playing *The Hitchhiker's Guide to the Galaxy*," but it would be much more unusual to hear them say, "I enjoyed playing Arthur Dent." Since we can play Infocom's version of *The Hitchhiker's Guide to the Galaxy* in the gaming sense, we can win it, but it isn't possible to win Arthur Dent, whatever the love-story subplot of a Disney movie would have us believe.

The play that is undertaken by the players of *Dungeons & Dragons*, a game that was influential in the genesis of interactive fiction and which was played by authors of both *Adventure* and *Zork*, seems closer to the activity of the interactor in many ways. (The term "player character" even made its way to interactive fiction from *D&D*.) A person who plays *D&D* in the gaming sense, unless he or she is the Dungeon Master, also plays a character. This character also serves as the "hands and eyes" of the player in the world of the *D&D* campaign, and is the agent by which puzzles in the world can be solved and mysteries can be unlocked. But there are a few important differences.

While theatrical modes of play are not always part of a *D&D* session, such play is undertaken at times, and some groups of players value making decisions that are "in character" even more than they do successful progress through a story, environment, or series of puzzles. A single character is typically played over the course of many adventures, and the players typically have some freedom to define their character's traits, although randomly determined abilities provide a basic idea of what the character is like. Also, a player character's relationship to other characters in the party is quite important. Similar sorts of play are seen in other fantasy role-playing games and in quest-based multiple-user dungeons (MUDs), the multi-player generalizations of single-player interactive fiction. Within all of these frameworks, though, the individual adventure or quest tends to exist on behalf of the character, which levels up and develops over time, and on behalf of the party and the dynamics of the group of players. These games and environments also offer the opportunity to determine what the character does and says in front of other people in a social setting, virtual or real, and so make the playing of the player character a social and not a purely personal experience.

There are some senses in which the interactor could be said to play the player character, but they are remote from the ordinary ones and fail to characterize the relationship very well. A chess player can play her bishop to b2, and an interactor might play a player character in a similar sense, deploying that character to a particular location for a purpose within a game. (In *Suspended*, which offers a board game-like map and tokens to keep track of the six robot player characters, this meaning seems particularly suitable.) However, the chess player does not sense the state of the game via the bishop, so one important purpose of the player character is overlooked in this comparison. The problem here is similar to the one we would encounter if we were to call the player character a puppet and imagine the interactor as operating the puppet (Sloane 2000). The limitation in this metaphor is that while it captures the player character as being that anthropomorphic entity that can be commanded and moved about, it fails to capture how the world is presented to the interactor from the perspective of this character.

Janet Murray notes that "[T]he lesson of *Zork* is that the first step in making an enticing narrative world is to script the interactor" (Murray 1997, 79). It is indeed essential to put the interactor into a situation where there is a reason to act, a reason to type something, but the "script" that is needed for the interactor in interactive fiction is more akin to the classic AI concept of a script (e.g., the basic knowledge of how to act when we enter a restaurant wanting to eat a meal) and not very related to a text meant to be read verbatim by an actor. Creating a good player character within an interactive fiction world involves putting this character in a situation that is motivating for the interactor—but not giving the interactor an actual dramatic script or a role to play.

So what does the interactor do with the player character, in a word? Perhaps it is interesting to say that the interactor steers the player character—"steer" being the English word for the Greek лщветоб, which by a twisty etymological path gave English the "cyber" prefix. To think of the interactor as steering, rather than playing, suggests that the player character is a sort of vehicle from which a world can be seen and otherwise experienced, and that this character both constrains us (we have to remain in the vehicle) and also opens up possibilities (we can use this vehicle to get around and even to effect changes in the world). This term may suggest too direct of a link between the interactor and the actions of the player character—the player character in many interactive fiction works is reticent and difficult to steer, and sometimes to good effect—but such lack of complete control is not really incompatible with this concept. The main deficiency of seeing the player character as steerable is that it does not highlight this vehicle's nature as a character—as an anthropomorphic, meaningful actor. The simple "man" or "ship" of early arcade games is also steerable, after all. But for now, why not exchange the flawed idea that the player character is played with the idea, perhaps less or at least differently flawed, that the player character is steered, so as to see where that leads?

II.

This section considers a few exemplary, memorable player characters, and suggests that they succeed more because they are good to steer than because they are good to play.

Ian Finley's *Babel* (1997) is set in a desolate research station and begins with the player character in an amnesiac state ("Even your mind is cold and empty. Where are you? Who are you?"), a condition that is sure to bring on déjà vu for many players. Interactive fiction authors have often robbed the player character of memory so that the player's awareness will initially match that of the player character; Thomas M. Disch's *Amnesia* (1986) was not the first to do it, and since then there have been many others, including Suzanne Britton's *Worlds Apart* (1999), Adam Cadre's *Shrapnel* (2000), and *Olvido Mortal* (2000) by Andrés Viedma Peláez.

While playing *Babel*, the player character's past history is slowly filled in, thanks to a startling "tellurgic" ability that allows events from the past to be replayed and re-experienced. While these revelations are compelling and it is interesting to unlock them by exploring the station, the interactor simply directs the player character to perform rather mechanical actions, inspections, and manipulations.

The player character's nature as a person is important to the charge of this interactive fiction experience and to the way the interactor reads and interprets the text that is produced, but there is no real role to play, only an existing history that waits to be discovered. The player character can be steered through the station to recover his memory. But the interactor does

little more than steer and sense. The author, not the player, is the one who decides when the player character will cry, the one who defines all the details of the player character's earlier and more expressive actions and reactions.

One of several nice flourishes in Adam Cadre's *Varicella* (1999) is that the personality of player character Primo Varicella is constantly being suggested and the image of this character is constantly being reinforced, almost always in amusing ways. *Varicella* also relates some things about the player character's past, albeit in more usual and subtle ways, many of the same ways that are often at work in literary narration. Even the most stereotypical adventure-game actions reinforce the player character's obsession with decorum (">JUMP You jump on the spot, achieving nothing. How unseemly!"). The player can choose one of three tones of voice (servile, cordial, and hostile) for Primo to use when addressing other characters, but the particular utterances, and how they are delivered, are chosen by Cadre and set in the program. To be sure, the successful interactor has to direct Primo to do evil things, as is this character's nature, but there is no need to really play the palace minister's part as an actor would. It is enough to figure out what "flawless plan" Primo has hatched and put that plan, sinister as it may be, into action.

Emily Short's *Savoir-Faire* (2002) provides a player character, Pierre, who seems a bit grasping and profligate but is not the purely reprehensible character that Primo Varicella is. Daphne Brinkerhoff (2002), reviewing this game, wrote, "I particularly enjoyed being hungry and eating. . . . there is evidence (especially if you play it right) that he has a strong sense of humor and self-mockery. Basically, I enjoyed being Pierre." This report is quite consistent with the idea that in *Savoir-Faire*, the interactor does not play Pierre. The reviewer states that she enjoyed not playing but "being" Pierre and notes, referring not to Pierre but to the game, that you can "play it right." The evidence of Pierre's humor and attitude was placed in the program by Short, not added by the interactor. The player, as in *Babel* and *Varicella*, can discover bits of Pierre's personal history; the REMEMBER command is supplied for this purpose in *Savoir-Faire*. The game's environment (an estate where Pierre grew up) is used, directly and indirectly, to supply more information about Pierre, up to the final revelation at the end of the game.

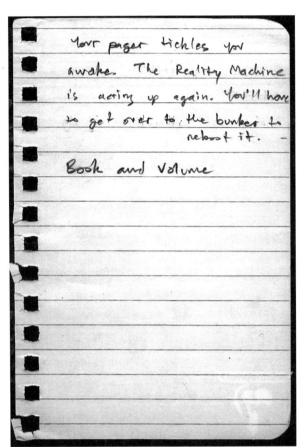

Your pager tickles you awake. The Reality Machine is acting up again. You'll have to get over to the bunker to reboot it. —

Book and Volume

21.1) Notes for *Book and Volume*.

Steering Pierre though this space is what reveals his background, along with a full understanding of the current situation, to the interactor.

Michael Gentry's *Anchorhead* (1998) differs from *Varicella* and *Savoir-Faire* in providing a world that is as strange to the interactor as it is to the player character. The player character has just moved into a small New England town named Anchorhead, and presumably discovers the place's ordinary and extraordinary attributes at the same time that the interactor does. But the player character's husband, Michael, comes along with her and is present at many times during the game. He is a history professor whose distant relatives lived for generations in a house that he has just inherited; he has just taken a job on the faculty of the local university. The player character's job or lack thereof, family history (apart from Michael's side of the family), and background (apart from being married to Michael) are all unknown, however.

The player character can move through the world, learning horrifying details that reveal things about the past, but these are all about Anchorhead's past—none are about her own background. The interactor does not even learn the player character's name in the course of completing the game. Again, the interactor must think of the right questions to ask, the right places to hide, and the right areas to search. The player certainly may feel fear and disquiet in sympathy with the player character, but it is hardly necessary that the interactor take on the role of Michael's wife in any dramatic sense.

While my focus here is not on graphical adventure games, these have player characters as well and this discussion should apply to the way the interactor and the player character relate in those games. Whether the game provides a player character who is a nameless blank, as in *Myst*, or a pair of well-defined characters, as in *Sam and Max Hit the Road*, the interactor is almost always asked less to play the roles of these characters and more to steer them through the world of the game.

An exception can be seen in Michael Mateas and Andrew Stern's *Façade* (2005), which is not billed as a graphical adventure game but as an interactive drama. In *Façade*, the interactor is invited to take on a role, naming the character one of many available names, and then encountering a situation in which it is possible to be flirtatious or grave, to side with one of the other characters or to try to play them against each other. Perhaps the disappointment of some interactive fiction and graphical adventure game fans with *Façade* is rooted in their unwillingness to play a role and their discomfort at finding a player character who is well-suited for playing but not amenable to the usual type of steering. While this sort of player character opens up new possibilities for interaction, it's clear that in this framework, Mateas and Stern have put almost all of their own character-building efforts into Grace and Trip. By leaving the player character in *Façade* wide open for the interactor, *Façade*'s player character is made a much less interesting element, per se, than are the player characters of *Babel*, *Varicella*, *Savoir-Faire*, and *Anchorhead*. There can be benefits to working in both sorts of frameworks, but it always seems to be helpful to know the difference between the two.

III.

My own interactive fiction work includes *Winchester's Nightmare* (1999), in which the player character is named after and based on a historical figure, and *Ad Verbum* (2000), which has a nameless adventurer/day laborer who is a sketchy parody of the typical nameless adventurer. In *Book and Volume*, I took a different tack and allowed the interactor to name the player character, although this character's occupation, place of residence, and basic personality remain the same whatever name is provided.

My work on *Book and Volume* first began when I jotted a short note that sounded like the prologue to some interesting interactive fiction piece, I believe sometime around the summer or fall of 2003. That short text, which begins "Your pager tickles you awake," set up a situation that seemed to motivate a character's rather routine action and yet leave some room for intrigue. I also wrote down the title itself, whatever exactly that was supposed to mean at the time. (I know now. The title comes from *Hamlet,* Act One, Scene Five; it is quite essential to the piece. I can think of no decent explanation for why this work of interactive fiction has this title, however, that would be shorter than the interactive fiction work itself.) I thought about the project on and off for several months and began seriously working on it near the end of April 2004. The first five words of that note survived through the completion of release one in November 2005 and are the first five diegetic words presented to the interactor at the beginning of *Book and Volume*.

I relate this creation myth because the player character's basic role in *Book and Volume* was the thing I imagined first. Thinking of the player character in complete isolation, or envisioning an IF world by itself, without the player character in it, does not really make for a complete thought. One of the important differences between recent interactive fiction works and early efforts such as *Adventure* and *Zork* is that the player character and the surrounding environment in contemporary IF tend to be integral. "A famous cave" or "a wacky Great Underground Empire" are adequate ways to characterize some early IF pieces, but saying that *Book and*

Book and Volume Transcript

Your pager tickles you awake.

Upstairs in the house of your childhood, in your room, and it must be time for school because—no, it's the weekend, you remember, but your alarm is going off anyway. You should have been awake already. You're going to miss the bus. Your mother climbs in the window. You're dreaming.

You're a grown-up: It opens to you again, a sluggish window summoned by a mouse click. Waking up now in your own apartment, your new apartment. Your pager is buzzing and vibrating both, serious. It is in fact the weekend, but you're not in elementary school. No one is crawling in through the window. You're a system administrator for nWare. Waking up urgently, here in nTopia.

Home

The constellations on the ceiling are as you left them: Pisces, Cetus, Aquarius, and the ones without celestial referent, left by some crazed astronomer in residence here before you. What could you call them? The Cradle, The Way, The Burning Book. . .

They're still glowing, too. Must not have napped for long.

>look at the constellations

If your milky memories of astronomy class serve, the glow-in-the-dark stars seem not just slapped on at random but willfully misconfigured. They lend the place some sort of character, though an Escher poster would be hip in comparison.

The pager buzzes and jars you, its motor driven to disrupt and demand attention. This is no Harry Potter broomstick.

>turn off the pager

If it were only so easy. You have to listen to whatever messages are on there to get the thing to stop.

The pager vibrates like it's repeatedly tapping you to get your attention, and it buzzes gratingly.

>look at the pager

It's too dark too see, like inside of a dog.

The buzzing of the pager continues. You are tooth to the dental drill of the device.

>turn on the light

You switch the light on.

MUEAAAAAHA THE PAGER THE PAGER THE PAGER MAKE IT STOP

Home

Although almost unfurnished, since you've been here only a few days and haven't had time to settle in, the place is more *Fight Club* than *Shade*: young, urbane, professional. It's yours, though. It's your residential canister. And it looks like we also have your nLap 500 and a heap of clothes.

>examine the pager

Cell phones are ubiquitous in nTopia, and your pager is a sort of

Volume takes place in a factory town run by a giant computer and media company does not really tell the whole story in the same way. The player character's standing, position, and perspective within this town is also essential. If the player character were a visitor, a prospective employee, an artist, a developer, a manager, a retail worker, or a city official, that character's perspective would be quite different. So as I developed the first sketch of the city's map, I also noted events, incidents, and aspects of the player character's experience.

It is often the case that the player character and the environment fit together in an essential way: in Graham Nelson's *Curses* and Andrew Plotkin's *Shade* it is important that the IF world involves the player character's own residence, not just any house or apartment, and that the player character is in a certain situation of searching for a map or of seeming to wait to leave on a trip. In *Anchorhead* and in Gareth Rees's *Christminster*, it is important that the player character is an outsider, a newcomer to a small town in the first case and a visitor to a college in the second. And similarly, in many other games, including *Babel*, *Varicella*, *Savoir-Faire*, and Dan Shiovitz's *Bad Machine*, the "rest of the world," without the player character in it, would not be nearly as interesting or compelling as that world is when encountered by the player character.

The interactor in *Book and Volume* is allowed to determine something about the player character: The interactor is asked at one point to type in the player character's name. (In testing, I noticed that interactors often type in their own name or handle, which was not too surprising, since most interactors are probably not ready to make up a name for their player character when this prompt appears.) *Book and Volume* discerns whether the name seems to be a male or female one, using a simple perceptron classifier whose weight vector has integer-valued components. The weight vector was learned by training, using the pocket perceptron algorithm, on the 500 most popular male and female names in U.S. census data. In the tradition of Infocom's *Moonmist* and *Leather Goddesses of Phobos*, this changes a few things about what is narrated, but the essential workings of the IF world and the important aspects of the player character's position in it remain the same. While the interactor is invited to

funky, retro sheriff's badge among them. Press the gray button there, and any voice messages you have will play; hold the button down to erase them. The vibration and buzzing mean that an urgent message, or one the sender thought was urgent, has arrived and has not yet been played.

Your nRich cybercash chip is installed in your pager, along with your nPediment identifier tag for keyless entry, the same one that most of your co-workers have installed in their phones, wallets, or upper arms.

You return to lucidity for what is going to be a very brief moment, unless you make the pager stop buzzing and vibrating.

>press the button

A beep issues from the pager, then a voice:

Net extremely hoseled. Engine team being hideously masticated by this outage. Demo rapidly approaching. Get to the cages. Reboot the servers. Hasten. Do not rest. Please. All five of them. Email me to confirm you're heading out to do this. Please. Engine boys are going to run off and leap the railing if the network isn't restored.

The frenetic voice is definitely that of your boss, Wilbur.

>get the nlap 500

You conduct the acquisition.

>open it

You open the nLap 500, which wakes the moment it begins to unfold. A window slams open. Ass. Complete ass. The red stapler appears.

Welcome to nSys! I'm Stan! Oop, I don't know your name yet! Please tell me your first name!

:Doug

The desktop flashes light blue for a moment.

Good to meet you, Doug! I'm here to help you work different! With nWare's nSys operating system, you don't have to think! You can just USE THE COMPUTER! Don't fret about what to click and what to type, just work better, faster, and more limberly! Just USE THE COMPUTER! I'll be back if you need help!

"Stan" steadies his metal jaw and winks out of sight.

Your boon companion "Stan" has somehow reset himself like that three times already. Fortunately he—it—only forgets your name in the process.

imagine the player character as male or female, the interactor is not called upon to perform masculinity or femininity by means of typed commands, as in *Façade*. Rather, the interactor is to use commands to have the player character perform the asexual, genderless functions of an alienated, introverted, recently arrived system administrator, and simply gets subtly different descriptions of the world and of the events in it—ones that many players may not even realize are "customized." The game never makes any explicit reference to the gender of the player character.

Book and Volume provides a series of tasks that are meant to offer some initial structure and motivation, but I hope that interactors discover during their efforts at these that such tasks are not the real point of the game. One of the challenges I had in "tuning" *Book and Volume*, near the end of the game's development, was in making it known that the player character could, if the interactor chooses, range beyond the job tasks that were assigned—without explicitly saying everything else that is to be done, which would be just another way of assigning tasks. Among other things, an interaction with *Book and Volume*, much like an interaction with Steven Meretzky's *A Mind Forever Voyaging*, can produce the story of a person who discovers how to do things that are not explicitly asked. In *Book and Volume*, unlike in *A Mind Forever Voyaging*, this does not save the country. But I believe that the player character—and the interactor—does something very important by making this discovery, whether or not a fictional country is saved as a result.

IV.

My concept is that the player character in interactive fiction is not played at all, but is a constraint and possibility defined by the author, within which the interactor is bound to a particular perspective and a particular set of capabilities, by means of which the interactor can explore everything in the work and figure everything that the interactive fiction holds and offers. The computer program itself, written by the author, carries the burden of defining the player character's personality, his or her attitudes, and the way in which actions are accomplished. The interactor is left to understand the strange world of the particular interactive fiction work— including the nature of the player character—through exploration and by demonstrating an understanding of the world's workings.

This perspective on the player character may seem to leave less of a place for the interactor. After all, the interactor, in this formulation, is unable to expressively enact a role, as many might have guessed was possible. But there are still substantial, important abilities and benefits that interactive fiction provides to interactors, who are

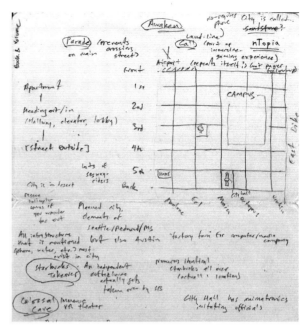

21.2) Notes and diagrams for *Book and Volume*.

capable of exploring the world in their own way, figuring out what schemes and principles underlie it and what mysteries it holds, and demonstrating their understanding of it by effecting changes.

By saying that the interactor "directs" the player character, there is the suggestion that some higher-level control, not over the particular manner of physical action but over the general intention of the character, is what is established by the interactor's input. While the typical dramatic player plays a character and is constrained by a (dramatic) script, the interactor does not get to play but has some ability to write the player character's script, a script that appears as part of the transcript that the game generates. The interactor is constrained by the interactive fiction world and by the nature and willingness of the player character, but there is considerable freedom in directing and commanding, and considerable engagement in seeing the world from the standpoint of the character that is under the interactor's control.

I have mentioned a different perspective, inadequate but provocative, that sees the interactor as steering the player character. I believe it is necessary to look beyond this concept and to also consider that the steerable thing being discussed is a character, with an anthropomorphic nature and a character's place within the interactive fiction world. The player character must be meaningful enough as a character but also be capable of being steered, and must be steerable enough so that everything important within the interactive fiction world can be explored. The interactor must have enough control over the player character to be able to express an understanding of this world though that character.

If we are willing to admit that dramatic role-playing is not done by the player, and that the definition of the player character is the work of the program, and thus the IF author, we can fully acknowledge a powerful, nuanced way in which a character can be represented and simulated within interactive fiction. The author forges the world and the vessel of the player character within it, fixing these in code. The interactor can steer or "be" this character, understanding the world through this character and configuring the world to unlock whatever secrets it may hold. A well-crafted player character in interactive fiction does not need to be the same sort of entity that a dramatic or literary character is; Varicella in the Palazzo may actually be a more suitable player

character than Hamlet on the Holodeck would be. But the vessel must be suited to the voyage, to the interactive fiction world as well as the overarching or underlying space of possible stories, the comprehending riddle. For interactive fiction to succeed, the player character must, in some sense, fit within the interactive fiction, and the interactor must fit within the player character.

References

Brinkerhoff, Daphne (2002). Review of *Savoir-Faire*. *SPAG (Society for the Promotion of Adventure Games)* 30 (September 20, 2002). <http://www.sparkynet.com/spag/s.html#savoir>.

Buckles, Mary Ann (1985). "Interactive Fiction: The Computer Storygame *Adventure*." Ph.D. Dissertation. University of California, San Diego.

Frasca, Gonzalo (2001). "Videogames of the Oppressed: Videogames as a Means for Critical Thinking and Debate." Master's Thesis. Georgia Institute of Technology.

Murray, Janet (1997). *Hamlet on the Holodeck*. New York: Free Press.

Schank, Roger C. and Robert P. Abelson (1977). *Scripts, Plans, Goals, and Understanding: An Inquiry into Human Knowledge Structures*. Hillsdale, NJ: Lawrence Erlbaum Associates.

Sloane, Sarah (2000). *Digital Fictions: Storytelling in a Material World*. Westport, CT: Ablex Publishing.

On *Savoir-Faire*
Emily Short

Savoir-Faire is an interactive fiction, set in an alternate France of the mid-1780s, about a nobleman who runs into debt. When he returns to his estate for help, he finds that his family is missing; he is forced to rely on the Lavori d'Aracne, a system of magic use, to solve his financial problems and discover what has gone wrong.

The game was designed to make the player competent in the role of Pierre, and especially to familiarize him with the system of magic. I had in mind the model of a calculus or classical mechanics text, the kind that introduces a few basic principles—seemingly so straightforward and innocuous—and then, through a series of rigorous exercises, forces the student to demonstrate to herself the

many, diverse, and occasionally mind-bending ways these principles play out in the real world.

The prologue introduces the basic element of in-game magic, a linking skill that allows one object in the game world to control another. Unlocking a box, for instance, would have the effect of unlocking a door to which the box is linked. Breaking an object will shatter its partner object. The player's first challenge is to link a pair of locked doors to something that he can open, forcing the doors to fly open as well. Until he has demonstrated this understanding of the way linking works, he is confined to the kitchen and garden, where he will find items his character remembers from past magical experiments. The descriptions of these are, in essence, worked sample problems demonstrating the fundamental functions of linking—and also retellings of the player character's personal history.

When the player gets past the locked doors, he learns about a variation on linking that blends the properties of two objects, usually with protective effects. A fragile item reverse-linked to a solid one will not break, even if it is

---

Example 1

>x snuffbox

A little pastel-colored metal box in which you keep your supply of snuff.

Something about the snuffbox tickles your recollection.

>remember snuffbox

. . .

"Don't play magic pranks on the guests," said the Count, confiscating the little box you had been using to control the Marquis' snuffbox (so it would refuse to open when he tried the little one-handed flick he was so fond of, and then pop open of its own when he set it down . . .).

"Why NOT?" you demanded, twisting under the painful grip he had on your shoulder. "You don't mind if I play with the servants."

"First," said the Count, clearing the links from the box with a brush of his fingers, "I hope you do not play anything malicious on the servants; it is only all right as long as it is games and they do not mind." He set the box down. "And second, the Marquis is nobility."

"I do not understand."

The Count sighed. "I thought you might not. Pierre, you are an—unusual case, being exempt from this rule, but you know that for the most part, only the nobility are able to perform the lavori d'Aracne; and of them, only the most noble families, who have access to the Honors of the Court. To play magic tricks on the Marquis, therefore, is to remind him that his lineage is not as good as ours. He will be insulted and grow angry, and I cannot afford to allow that to happen."

Example 2

>examine bauble

A delicate ornament made of glass, containing inside it a little sun and star that whirl infinitely in the hollow space. It was a plaything of Marie's, which (due to careful reverse linking to a perfectly round rock) she could hurl at walls and never break, drop down staircases and find intact at the bottom. But it is very doubtful that the link has lasted out the years.

>examine onion

The pale yellow skin is still tight and glossy.

>link onion to bauble

Bending your will, you form the link between the single yellow onion and the celestial bauble.

>throw bauble at wall

(the wall)

The celestial bauble arcs through the air, strikes the wall, smashes dramatically, and spills the tiny silver star and the tiny golden sun.

The onion does not fare well; it splits down the middle and then falls apart in pieces, as though chopped by a skillful invisible chef. When all is done, the chopped pieces lie in their own discarded skin.

mistreated; a book reverse-linked to another book will produce a blended text, neither entirely one nor the other. These two kinds of linking are the basis of nearly all the challenges in the game.

The more difficult puzzles of the midgame require lateral thinking about what linking can do: deciding which items can be linked, modifying objects to make them linkable, reactivating old links, and applying these rules to unusual objects. The challenges are roughly progressive, so that the player constructs a simple light source before gaining access to more complicated lighting puzzles. In many cases there are several routes to a given end, and I did my best to support all of the plausible options, since the world model can only be learned if it is relatively consistent.

Some of the effects of the Lavori are more obvious than others, and the player may not be able to guess what will happen if he links two mirrors together, or machines, or cups of water. So *Savoir-Faire* is not only textbook but also laboratory. A substantial portion of the code exists only to reward undirected play, and to give appropriate responses—character-appropriate responses, when possible—for all sorts of actions unrelated to specific puzzles. Because the wetness or dryness of objects is sometimes important, everything in the game responds to being wet: writing runs and becomes illegible, clothes go sodden, dirt turns to mud. Partly this is a stratagem to alleviate the boredom of a difficult puzzle game: inevitably there will be times when the player gets stuck, can make no direct progress, and begins, instead, to tinker with the environment. It is good if that tinkering is fun; better still if, subtly, it offers new perspective on the problem holding him up.

By the conclusion, the player has become a fairly good magician in his own right, and is fully able to act the role of Pierre. The endgame presents a simple but timed crisis, with no more opportunity for exploration and no tolerance for mistakes—but thanks to the lessons he has already had, the player is ready to save the day with the confidence and panache appropriate to his character.

Example 3

```
>i
You are carrying:
 four books:
 The Lavori d'Aracne
 Guide to Assorted Wines
 Clock Repair
 On Vegetable Dyes
>read lavori
```

On the subject of mirrors: Unusual and costly mirrors of special power exist which enhance the workings of the lavori d'Aracne; they may be recognized by their failure to reflect in the ordinary way. Some make it easier to form a link through the mirror than through open air, allowing the magician to reverse-link items that are otherwise too dissimilar to use. Likewise, such a mirror . . .

But then, unfortunately, it breaks off, the page apparently having been chewed out and carried away by something or other.

```
>read clock repair
```

A detailed discourse on how to take care of and repair an assortment of common and mechanical clocks. It begins with comprehensible matters, such as pulling up the weights to begin the operation of the pendulum when the clock has stopped, and other bits of routine maintenance; it finishes with diagrams of a clock's inner workings that are almost embarrassingly intimate and far too complex for you to follow.

```
>reverse link lavori to repair
```

Bending your will and all your attention, you manage to make a reverse-link between The Lavori d'Aracne and Clock Repair, feeling their properties begin to merge together.

```
>read repair
```

The book now turns out to be all about how to construct different types of time-keeping device and false clock using nothing more than household objects and the power of the Lavori. How often this is likely to come in handy is open to doubt, though you pause momentarily to be intrigued by the diagram of a cork that sinks or floats depending on the state of its linkage.

Reference

Short, Emily (2002–2004). *Savoir-Faire*.
<http://nickm.com/if/emshort/savoir_faire.html>.

Pax, Writing, and Change
Stuart Moulthrop

1.

These brief notes are offered in place of something longer and more fully considered, for which there will probably never be time. These days, reflection is a luxury in most working lives, and it comes particularly dear for those who work in cybertext, which can claim neither the high-cultural entitlements of literature nor the market appeal of video games, but subsists on the margins of those worlds, among others. Most who move in this edgy space are amateurs, obsessives, and/or academics, people driven by, if not to, distraction. We are always "of two minds," as Michael Joyce (1995) put it, though two is by no means a maximum.

While obsession and compulsion come with the territory, it seems impossible to be single-minded about cybertext. *Writing* in this context necessarily takes in more than traditional literary composition, so that staying alive in craft demands an ever expanding mastery of concepts, tools, and techniques, from object-oriented programming to database integration, from sampling and looping to 3D modeling and CAVE painting. In this sprawling poetics, grammar and rhetoric must make room for interaction design and information architecture, an adjustment that seems more accommodation than displacement. At the same time, though, earlier assumptions about voice and vision, narration and presentation collide with the ethos of play, as we find ourselves inevitably edging across the boundary between literature and ludology. In this case, compromise or "remediation" seem less eligible. It is tempting to say, always of course with a fortifying dose of postmodern irony, that we have reached the end of a certain literary history, if indeed we do not stand outside it altogether.

That history always had its problems. It was hard enough to be a writer in the old century, when cinema, radio, and television controlled the cultural agenda. Then, literary people could at least invoke a purity of critical detachment, lampooning the world of broadcast media and other Airborne Toxic Events as if these monstrosities could not touch the core concerns of writing. That was an illusion, to be sure, but like most magic tricks, no less powerful for its emptiness. Now, though, as the *mass* of media morphs in so many ways to multi-, this Puritanism seems harder to sustain, at least in my neck of the marches. Some of us think that writing itself has changed, transformed in far from superficial ways by its contact with digital culture. The change affects writers as well. Like Thomas Pynchon's Scurvhamites, we may find ourselves looking longingly into the machine, embracing its profane possibilities, choosing to defect from the Elect.

Increasingly, these moments of reflection when one writes about new media provide distinct relief from the main task of writing *in* the new media, in structures at once ominous and utopian. Lawrence Lessig describes the threshold of a new order in communication, one that might revise the balance between reception and production to create a new common ground for creativity, a "read-write" culture (Lessig 2005). At the same time, recall that *al Qaeda* means *the base*, as in *database*. One man's rhizome, another's tool for militant jihad.

Through all this turmoil runs the quicksilver essence of language, now as much performative as magical, adding to inspiration or incantation the banal sublime of cybernetics. John Cayley declares that "programming is writing," a proposition I hasten to endorse because I also believe in its converse, namely, the transformation of all words anywhere into cybernetic operators (Cayley 1999). But of course this maneuver raises no end of questions. What can it mean to write in dynamic and emergent systems, designing networks for playful readers who will twist, permute, and otherwise change all our clever regimes? Or to turn the lens outward, how can we continue to satisfy that irresistible critical impulse, situating ourselves within a moment, a history, and a history of resistance? How can the calling of the writer be responsible to a common experience that seems increasingly consumed by war, catastrophe, and indeed revolution, however we choose to define that most slippery term?

As always, questions are the simple part. Answers come harder, and as I have previously apologized, this piece is far too easy. The remarks that follow come at these big questions only in dim and cursory ways, and really only in respect of my cybertext called *Pax: An Instrument,* which no one could mistake for the best of its kind (Moulthrop 2003). Nonetheless, for what it is, *Pax* did emerge in large part from an attempt to frame and respond to large concerns like those named here; so perhaps the exercise can have at least some diagnostic value.

2.

Thematically, *Pax* traces back, like so much else these days, to the late summer of 2001, when agents of al Qaeda turned commercial airliners into terror weapons, touching off a panic about airline and "homeland" security,

05:28 PM | Home Land

PASSENGERS ARE ASKED TO REMAIN WHERE THEY ARE UNTIL THE AREA IS SECURE.

Wait there's more.

How can there be disbelief without chicken legs?

The more we comprehend, the more we truly know.

Rafe

I'll answer for all of this someday.

After this, the American century becomes meaningless.

Before the crows ate all the corn, this country never really dreamed.

Slowhand

Rosemary and sweetmeats tartine in port wine reduction (Bistro bistro, 1992).

23.1) *Pax* in process.

along with an interminable war against enemies to be named later. In other words, *Pax* began on that terrible day the world ended; or strictly speaking, several months into the end times that followed. As I say in the introduction: "'Pax' is a lesser apocalypse that began to unveil itself one stormy spring day near Dallas when someone closed the terminal and the guns came out."

The events behind this remark bear no comparison to the sufferings of 9/11 victims, or those caught up in the deadly hurricanes of 2005, or any calamities that may have ensued between this writing and your reading; but they will nonetheless be familiar to anyone who has been a frequent flyer in these first years of the new century. Passing through Dallas-Fort Worth International Airport in March 2002, I was among a large group of people stopped at gunpoint by National Guardsmen and prevented from entering a part of the terminal whose security had somehow been compromised. Possibly someone had run through a checkpoint or displayed other alarming behavior. There may have been a threatening phone call. For all we knew, someone may simply have ignored posted warnings and made a joke about a bomb. These were the days when irony was dead.

We never learned the particulars. Confusion was general. An hour or so into the incident, I watched a soldier call his girlfriend on his cell phone, asking if there was anything about us on CNN. There was not.

We were held up about four hours, all told, during which time the crowd grew larger and less patient. Various conflicting announcements were made in person and over the P.A. system. Buses were coming to take us to connecting flights, or to hotels. They never arrived. At one point we were told to exit the terminal. We could leave the airport, presumably on foot and without checked luggage, or we could stand on the sidewalk in the warm prairie rain, as most of us did, waiting to see what came next. I had a brief conversation with a couple of troopers who seemed as puzzled as the would-be travelers, though considerably more patient. This was good, because there remained between us the awkward fact of their orders, which probably included shooting us if we tried to re-enter the terminal.

Eventually the whole thing dissipated. The guards stood aside. Someone had resolved the problem, whatever it was, or erased it from the official version of the day. Nothing had happened, after all. We hurried off to our flights, which were ready for immediate departure. Everyone flew away.

By luck or grace, no one's world actually ended. The worst of my troubles amounted to temporary inconvenience, and I eventually made it home without so much as a lost bag— hardly an apocalypse, one might object. Still, if presidents can sideline the literal in search of a deeper truth, why not writers? I mean the term in its strict sense of revelation or unveiling, of the end of concealment, or nakedness. There is always a certain exposure or vulnerability in travel, particularly in flying; and this sense is all the more acute when my travels take me to Dallas, another place where the end of the world once played, where the curtains were pulled back, for a brief and fatal moment, then slyly restored. You can learn a lot there.

Transiting Dallas that particular day, I picked up some important lessons about the new America, with its penchant for armed response on the one hand and secrecy on the other, with its silent bureaucracies and its need not to know. *Pax* then was born as a meditation on flying and falling, on judgment and its lapses, and the terrible eschatology of airports; but above all, it configured itself as a system of imperfect information.

3.

Technically speaking, *Pax* is a relatively compact cybertext built in Macromedia's Shockwave Flash environment for delivery via the World Wide Web. Combining animations derived from rendered 3D graphics with written text, the project explores a space between hypertext on the one hand, and video games on the other. Its technical motivation came from a remark made in early 2001 by John Cayley, who noted that we *play* many things besides games, including musical instruments. What, he wondered, would textual instruments look like? One possible answer is *Pax*.

In this work, the reader/player elicits and assembles text by interacting with characters who drift through the main section of the screen. These floating figures cycle through animations that make them seem to spin through the air. At first the figures move from the bottom of the screen to the top, though later they reverse course. They appear only faintly until the player brings the mouse pointer close to them, when they become more substantial. Moving over the outline of a character arrests that character's progress and fixes the character within a superimposed clock face.

Clicking at this point causes the system to retrieve a passage of text and add it to a scrolling field on the right-hand side of the screen. The text comes in two flavors or types: a generalized, algorithmically generated near-nonsense that represents the random babble of the unconscious; or a more coherent prose passage that represents some focused comment on the character's predicament. The type of response is determined by the relative awareness of the

---

Excerpt from a *Pax* Transcript

SO . . .

Can you imagine emptiness without falling stars?

I.W.

. . . .

L'entre-jeu. The hand pauses in the arc of a million unmade moves. The mind overflows with emptiness.

The more we see, the less we understand.
Before the dogs began to bark, we didn't read much as a rule.
References: future, homeland, patriot, nowhere, watchword.
It has more and more been hard to embrace pain.

e*star

. . . .

This isn't what I expected . . . all this whiteness . . . so much nothing. Let me guess, the boys in black got it wrong—how totally not surprising.

With weapons like this, who needs leaders?
References: last call, more time, from hell, turbulence.

MM

. . . .

Dance macabre, dance bizarre, the greatest show not of this earth.

How can one think of belief without beer cans?

MM

. . . .

Like a bird she circles, like a fish; or like something she hasn't begun yet to imagine.

You have the money to descend.

03:44:26
PASSENGERS ARE ASKED TO REMAIN WHERE THEY ARE UNTIL THE AREA IS SECURE.

Wait there's more.
How can there be disbelief without chicken legs?
The more we comprehend, the more we truly know.

Rafe

. . . .

I'll answer for all of this someday.

After this, the American century becomes meaningless.
Before the crows ate all the corn, this country never really dreamed.

Slowhand

. . . .

Rosemary and sweetmeats tartine in port wine reduction (Bistro bistro, 1992).

Think about this: channel, state fear, uprising, company, precaution, official.

NGOfer

. . . .

character. When the player clicks on the floating figure, an image of the character's face appears toward the bottom of the screen. Initially the eyes are closed, but if the player clicks the floating body repeatedly, the eyes open and track the player's mouse movement. This change indicates that the character has become focused, so that a further query will call up some more coherent or meaningful text. Or perhaps it will not, because after a certain number of clicks, characters go dormant again and the player must re-engage them.

After text appears, the character drifts away, and the player may either let that character go or hold for further questioning. Once a character has been clicked, he or she will return within a few seconds. Since the number of characters who can appear at any given point is limited, engagement with one figure entails an opportunity cost, since others will remain offstage. Reading/playing thus becomes a matter of selection and filtering, a trait inherited both from hypertext and games.

There are strong temporal elements as well. Apocalypse implicates the clock as well as the calendar, as Alan Moore showed in *Watchmen*. While all this play of text and graphics unfolds in *Pax*, a clock is running. The time advances against real time at a standard multiplier, but jumps ahead whenever the player interrogates a character. Interaction carries a time cost. The current clock reading is displayed in various ways, including a digital timestamp that accompanies every bit of retrieved text, an analog clock face superimposed on the drifting characters when their progress is arrested, and a steady darkening of the graphical space on the screen as the time grows later. There are twelve hours to any full session with *Pax*, after which the system displays a final graphic and shuts down.

In addition to the temporal features, which probably show the strongest connection between *Pax* and games, the design also has two spatial registers, whose derivation owes more to hypertext fiction and its theory. One of these is the graphical space, the anomalous but steadily darkening blankness through which the characters rise and fall. The other is the text field, which displays items not in isolation but in a single, accreting scroll. This design feature responds to a challenge by the poet and theorist Jim Rosenberg, who has defined "spatial hypertext" as an attempt to build structures

Who made the world? I have no idea.

Before the mail arrived, I hardly saw into next week.
Before the shares were called in, America never thought about the matter.
You have the necessity to believe.

Di Laffing
. . . .
Once I did not believe in the concept of evil. That was before I got legal representation.

It has unluckily been necessary to live with falsehood.
Now this.
Before the mail arrived, this country knew nothing.

Blackbird
. . . .
What do you do about the blood?
Our concerns include: peace, annoyance, zero sum, suicide, war speak, suspect.

Di Laffing
. . . .
Fear no evil.

Can you conceive of fear without junk mail?

Di Laffing
. . . .
So maybe I am dead, and so are all those other confused-looking folks who by the way don't seem to have read the memo about casual dress in the afterlife. Did someone do this to us? Do I care?

After this, all they taught us comes to be radiant with hope.

mira
. . . .
Was there in fact always something terrible lurking here in this blank playground of empire's unspeakable fantasy?

It has often been conceivable to understand belief.
With enemies like this, who needs enemies?

Di Laffing
. . . .
I was never much for the physical stuff but I can do falls as well as the next girl, just you watch.

The less we learn about the struggle, the more we know what home is.
Life, liberty, and the pursuit of security.
A free people do not hide.

Nathan
. . . .
What if we're just going?

Before we knew, the subject never looked much into the sky.

Butcher
. . . .
He feels no more susceptible to this perception of 'falling' than he was to 'rising' before. The claim remains ungrounded; as the newspapermen say, an unsourced quote.

Items of interest: pass over, anxiety, nice day, struggle, interrupt, taken up.

Di Laffing
. . . .

of simultaneity and contiguity, instead of the binary replacement characteristic of the World Wide Web (Rosenberg 1996). On this level at least, *Pax* works by addition, not disjunction; though to be sure, its general architecture strongly emphasizes fragmentation.

In terms of its design pattern, *Pax* is a *sequencer:* a program that selects textual elements from a database and presents them to the player/reader in response to certain choices. When I was younger and yet more foolish, I once described Michael Joyce's *afternoon* as an invisible, automatic railroad (Moulthrop 1989). I suppose I meant this critically, but it did not keep me from hopping the next available freight. Thus, *Pax* is also a "robotic" textual system, and has its own set of invisible rails. Departing from the classic hypertext model, it adds two elements not available in Joyce's Storyspace environment: the progressive play clock, and a random value generator. Text is selected from a database identified with the character who is currently detained or in focus. The selection is based on a pseudo-random number. In turn, each character owns several source databases, which are rotated in and out of use as the play clock passes through six phases, each comprising two hours of the text's unreal time.

Thus, *Pax* is really not much like a musical instrument, but closer to a kind of 31st century dim sum joint run by a gang of vaguely malevolent robots. Imagine the text bits as covered plates, wheeled through the establishment by silent, glowering automata. The diners can stop the mechanical staff at any point to request a serving of the mystery dish, but they can never know exactly what they will find when the cover is removed. They can only be sure that the menu will shift gradually through six "movements": "Shaken Out of Time," "American Flyers," "Home Land," "Evil Ones," "Falling," and "Total Information." In each of these thematic clusters, the writing channeled through the characters falls into certain patterns or rhetorical positions. Though I have my own way of thinking about these patterns, I leave it to reader/players to find their own definitions. Hopefully, a certain broad, architectural outline should be evident. On any given run, the trajectory of the text is meant to display the parabolic symmetry of flying and falling, a pattern with a certain terrible necessity.

Reasons to suspect God doesn't have a very well developed ability to laugh at himself: (1) penises (2) uncircumcised penises (3) Tammy Faye is naked under her clothes (4) land mines (5) the city of Burbank.

Items of interest: thanks jc, going up, alliance, stormcloud, defend. After this, the American century gets empty as an old lost shoe. It has momentarily been conceivable to escape life.

Di Laffing

. . . .

Further evidence that Sigmund Freud did a better impression of God than George Burns ever could: (1) having to put condoms on sex toys (2) what can happen if you forget the condom (3) you can't call yourself Queer these days unless you've got a Theory (4) so-called celibate priests.

Items of interest: air miles, voicemail, live, innocence, bulletin, bulletin. Under the circumstances it seems best to look out.

END OF RUN

4.

Very little else about *Pax*, considered as a literary object, is likely to seem so formal or coherent. On most runs, the text might be described as a blog or wiki of the apocalypse. I will say more presently about this family resemblance, but first it bears noting that, like the text of most blogs, the words produced by *Pax* are meant for momentary consumption. They are not designed for permanence, or even much persistence. Cayley has asked why I did not enable the player/reader to save or print the results of a session. The omission was deliberate. I could have made the text field in *Pax* unselectable, but deliberately left it open to allow the possibility of copying output to an editor or word processor. The results of a run can in fact be preserved, should anyone want to. However, I do not point out this fact in the published instructions, and intentionally built no facilities for printing or file export, though the first at least was within my abilities. This decision has something to do with my feeling that *litterature potentielle* best deserves the name when it remains essentially fluid, evanescent, and unstable; but it also raises an important question about cybernetic writing, at least as I understand it.

To put this question plainly: if the text remains volatile or impermanent, why is there text in the first place? Joyce, John McDaid, and I once tried to distinguish our work by loudly repeating, *this is not a game*, but lately I have at least partly recanted. Many things are games, when you come down to it. So why not build an actual structure for play, following the main evolutionary line of motion graphics into some more familiar form of video interaction? Several innovative designers have done just this, most notably Ian Bogost of Persuasive Games. His microgame *Airport Insecurity*, designed to be played on a cell phone while standing in long security lines, lets the player simulate an attempt to smuggle a weapon past TSA screeners. The odds of success in the game are ostensibly based on the published records of security checks at various U.S. airports, giving frequent flyers something interesting to ponder as they wait to remove their shoes. Though this diabolically effective game does use text at various points, its primary medium is graphical. Using simple directional controls, the player maneuvers a low-resolution figure through a serpentine queue while trying to decide whether to leave the butcher knife in the carry-on, or slip it discreetly into the next trash bin.

Arguably, *Airport Insecurity* engages many of the same questions and social issues I claim for *Pax*. One might also say that it works much more subtly and elegantly, without having to haul (or discard) the clumsy baggage of literary convention. Take a few more steps in this direction, and we might well conclude that writing and gameplay need to remain clearly distinct: let writers do their thing and let the games be games, leaving each to its established rituals. There is a lot to be said for this position, but like all territorial barriers, it poses a danger. As I have argued elsewhere in more detail, segregating writing from game design could lead cybertext to a new "dissociation of sensibility," as the elders of our tribe once called it (Moulthrop 2005). It could encourage us to identify writing as the medium of reflection and argument, while graphical interaction becomes the exclusive domain of play. The outcome could be a significant restriction of horizons both for games and writing.

We have much to gain by keeping the borders free and the boglands open to smugglers and tramps. Much of this potential is already apparent in the work of people like Adam Cadre and Nick Montfort (literary smugglers, perhaps, but hardly tramps), who have brought the art of interactive fiction to a very high state of refinement. It is also evident in stranger parts of the creative landscape, in phenomena like

alternate-reality games, where what John McDaid used to call "modally appropriate" in-game communication often takes the form of e-mail, blog postings, and other forms of writing. Working a different angle, Jill Walker has recently coined the term "feral hypertext" to refer to similar forms of self-organizing text, and this category may be of great help in understanding the present evolution of writing (Walker 2005). All these developments suggest important new ways of understanding the structure of text in emergent systems, certainly including things like *Pax*.

Though text sequencers do not really belong in Walker's menagerie of untamed forms, their ability to mimic those species is at least suggestive. If we look beyond relatively crude attempts like *Pax* toward more ingenious conceptions— like the *News Reader* and *Regime Change* projects by Noah Wardrip-Fruin, David Durand, Brion Moss, and Elaine Froehlich—we may recognize a promising line of development (Wardrip-Fruin et al 2004). In *Pax*, the granularity of selection from the database is very coarse, often amounting to multiple sentences or entire paragraphs. In this respect, it does not differ all that much from node-link hypertext. Wardrip-Fruin and Durand's work, based on the much more dynamic construction of character strings or "N-grams," augurs a more genuine revolution in writing: not the composition of text, but the writing-as-programming of systems that themselves compose text—in other words, not writing by itself, but *the writing of artificial writers*. To be sure, this ground was well prepared decades ago in projects like ELIZA and Racter, but these precedents make current work all the more significant, suggesting that they may bring new advances to a neglected evolutionary line. Given a few more rev cycles, the intersection of artificial writers, games, and feral hypertext might bring us to an interesting place indeed.

It goes without saying that this unknown destination will be subject to the torque and stress of history, and that even self-organizing, "feral," and cybernetically programmed writers will need to respond to these forces as best they can. Apocalyptic wikis, textual marshlands where wild writing mixes with ghost words from the machine, may offer at least a possibility of new approaches. If nothing else, they suggest intriguing models of communication in a plenum of signs, or form out of noise; and in an age of read-write culture, this may well become the dominant paradigm.

For some, no doubt, these possibilities will look like nothing less than the ultimate collapse of structure, an end to the humanistic conversation, if not of legitimately human experience itself. But that experience has always been subject to punctuation. Our time has ever been about to end—or going about its ending. Deep in the machine, the wheels are always turning. The waters around us have grown, just as the prophet said they would, and so we will need to keep changing to ensure our place in new ecologies. This seems all the more reason to build channels and flow lines between writing and the moving image, to maintain crossing points from new media to old, and to keep the word in play.

References: Literature

Cayley, John (1999). "The Writing of Programming in the Age of Digital Transliteration." Cybertext Seminar. Jyvaskyla: University of Jyvaskyla. January 9, 1999.

Joyce, Michael (1995). *Of Two Minds: Hypertext Pedagogy and Politics*. Ann Arbor: University of Michigan Press.

Lessig, Lawrence (2005). *Free Culture: The Nature and Future of Creativity*. New York: Penguin.

Moulthrop, Stuart (1989). "Hypertext and 'the Hyperreal.'" *Proceedings of the Second ACM Conference on Hypertext and Hypermedia*. San Antonio, TX: ACM Press.

Moulthrop, Stuart (2003). *Pax: An Instrument. Iowa Review Web*. June 2003. <http://www.uiowa.edu/~iareview/tirweb/feature/moulthrop/moulthrop>.

Moulthrop, Stuart (2005). "After the Last Generation: Rethinking Scholarship in the Days of Serious Play." Forthcoming in *Proceedings of the Digital Arts and Culture Conference, Copenhagen, 2005*. <http://iat.ubalt.edu/moulthrop>.

Rosenberg, Jim (1996). "The Structure of Hypertext Activity." *Proceedings of the Seventh ACM Conference on Hypertext and Hypermedia*. New York: ACM Press.

Walker, Jill (2005). "Feral Hypertext." *Proceedings of the Sixteenth ACM Conference on Hypertext and Hypermedia*. September 6–9, 2005. New York: ACM Press.

Wardrip-Fruin, Noah, David Durand, Brion Moss, and Elaine Froehlich (2004). "Two Textual Instruments: *Regime Change* and *News Reader*." <http://www.turbulence.org/Works/twotxt>.

Reference: Game

Airport Insecurity. Ian Bogost; Water Cooler Games. 2005. <http://www.watercoolergames.org>.

RE: Authoring Magritte:
The Brotherhood of Bent Billiard
Talan Memmott

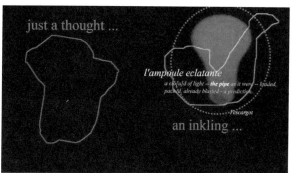

24.1) Many of the links in the piece are hidden and must be discovered by the user. Clicks may reveal certain text or graphical elements, while simply moving the mouse over certain objects may reveal entirely different information. Sometimes, once information is revealed and screen changes have occurred, there is no going back. Although the links and triggers may be variable, this gives the impression of linear continuity.

The Brotherhood of Bent Billiard is a hypermedia project concerned with the life and work of Surrealist painter Rene Magritte, dealing specifically with the many *pipe* paintings created during Magritte's lifetime. Inspiration for the project comes from an appreciation for Magritte's work, Michel Foucault's essay *This Is not a Pipe*, and Belgian poet-artist Marcel Broodthaers' response to Foucault's essay, titled *This Is a Pipe*. The term *Brotherhood* in the title is a play on Broodthaers' name, and a reference to the triangulation between Magritte, Foucault, and Broodthaers. *Bent Billiard* refers to the sort of pipe Magritte most often painted.

The project is not art history but hypermediated art historical fiction. A selection of twenty-nine Magritte paintings along with biographical information are re-collated and used as data for the re-authoring of Magritte, to form an alter(ed).na(rra)tive to/of Magritte's life and career. The *magritte* of *The Brotherhood of Bent Billiard*; this is not *Magritte*.

The twenty-nine paintings addressed in the project are presented in near chronological order, each "Book" of the project representing essentially a decade. Navigation through the piece is essentially linear but is still diverse. Explicit and implicit contextual and environmental links that require an exploration of the interface are put to use, while subtle cursor movements may sometimes affect navigation choices, trigger animations, or alter texts.

Through various contextual *'tweens* and *shapeshifts*, *Book One* of *The Brotherhood of Bent Billiard* traces the development of the pipe as emblem from its first abstract rendering in a little-known untitled painting of 1926 to perhaps Magritte's most recognizable work: *The Treachery of Images* (1929), the first of the famous *ceci n'est pas une pipe* paintings.

As the users move from one to another transformation of the pipe emblem, they navigate through environments inspired and adapted from Magritte works not necessarily related to the pipe theme. It is interesting to note that no actual images of Magritte paintings are used in the project; rather, the paintings provide stimulus for the development of narrative and interface assets. Sometimes certain colors from a work may be leveraged for the project; sometimes the influence is more concrete.

Environments for *Book I* are adapted from *Man with Newspaper* (1927), *The Threatened Assassin* (1926), and *The Lovers* (1928). At the opening of *Book I*, the round shapes and tangerine color of the interface are abstracted from *Man with*

24.2) Interaction with the two shadowy characters on this screen initiates textual commentary and variable audio dialog between the two characters. Moving the cursor over the punctuation in the voice bubble allows the user to remix musical fragments from various Brahms pieces.

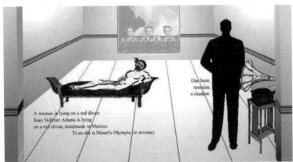

24.3) Cursor interaction with the various subjects in this screen reveals definitions and descriptions that may or may not have direct referability to Magritte's *Threatened Assassin*, upon which the screen is based. The sort of ludic semiosis that occurs on this screen includes references to Duchamp, the Marx Brothers, Manet's *Olympia,* and William Burroughs's famous "William Tell" act that lead to the death of his wife, Joan Vollmer Adams.

Newspaper. While the connection between source and interface may not be immediately obvious in this example, a later section of *Book I, The Threatened Assassin*, provides a more developed, straightforward environment, as well as a fictional scenario for *magritte* and his cohorts to perform.

The overall effect of *The Brotherhood of Bent Billiard* is something like a mystery or puzzle—built upon context and reference. Later Books in the project play with the idea

of the pipe as trademark for Magritte—along with the bowler hat, the dove, and a few other key icons. As redundancies of concept and repetition of signs build up in Magritte's work over his lifetime, so do the complexities of his emblematic and allegorical syntax. *The Brotherhood of Bent Billiard* plays with these mysterious complexities, building upon them. To a certain extent the project is a narrative hack of Magritte's symbolic calculus.

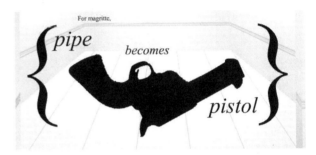

24.4) This screen combines three different Magritte works. The contexts of the original paintings are made mysterious by the morphing and repositioning of figures from one painting into the objects represented in another. As depicted here, the user may manipulate the pipe image, allowing it to oscillate between images of a pistol and a pipe, culminating in its transformation into the Nike Swoosh.

On Soft Cinema:
Mission to Earth
Lev Manovich

Cinema and Software

The twentieth-century cinema "machine" was born at the intersection of the two key technologies of the industrial era: the engine that drives movement and the electricity that powers it. While an engine moves film inside the projector at uniform speed, the electric bulb makes possible the projection of the film image on the screen.

The use of an engine makes the cinema machine similar to an industrial factory organized around an assembly line. A factory produces identical objects that are coming from the assembly line at regular intervals. Similarly, a film projector spits out images, all the same size, all moving at the same speed. As a result, the flickering irregularity typical of the moving image toys of the nineteenth century is replaced by the standardization and uniformity typical of all industrial products.

Cinema also reflects the logic of the industrial era in another way. Ford's assembly line, introduced in 1913, relied on the separation of the production process into a set of repetitive, sequential, simple activities. Similarly, cinema replaced previous modes of visual narration with a sequential narrative and an assembly line of shots that appear on the screen one at a time.

25.1) A database of 425 video clips used to generate *Texas* (a partial view).

Given that the logic of the cinema machine was closely linked to the logic of the industrial age, what kind of cinema can we expect in the information age? Rather than waiting for this new cinema to appear, the Soft Cinema project generates new cinema forms, using the key technology of the information society—a digital computer.

As I have already explained, the logic of twentieth-century cinema was not directly connected to the operation of an engine but instead reflected the industrial logic of mass production, which the engine made possible. Similarly, the Soft Cinema project is interested not in the digital computer per se, but rather in the new structures of production and consumption enabled by computing.

Our research follows four directions:

Following the standard convention of the human-computer interface, the display area is always divided into multiple frames.

Using a set of rules defined by the authors, the Soft Cinema software controls both the layout of the screen (number and position of frames) and the sequences of media elements that appear in these frames.

The media elements (video clips, sound, still images, text, etc.) arc selected from a large database to construct a potentially unlimited number of different films.

160

Lev Manovich

name	rank	activity	average greys	contrast	sub mot	cam motio	distand	geolocatio	typelocation	description	
001_016.mov	1	0,0123721	0,396306	0,305753	left	no	medium	berlin	pub_interior	berlin 1999 train station	
001_017.mov	2	0,0101112	0,363054	0,28031	left	no	far	berlin	city_view	berlin 1999 train station	
001_018.mov	1	0,00802633	0,439291	0,296975	forward	no	medium	berlin	city_view	train station	
001_021.mov	2	0,00750553	0,434836	0,296942	left	no	medium	berlin	city_view	people walking outside train station	
001_029.mov	1	0,00418441	0,386185	0,216594	no	no	medium	berlin	city_view	buildings	
001_030.mov	1	0,00527584	0,454169	0,276144	no	no	medium	berlin	city_view	post office	
001_031.mov	2	0,00588105	0,487063	0,291337	no	no	medium	berlin	city_view	water running in a river	
001_032.mov	2	0,00817064	0,475074	0,260974	no	no	medium	berlin	city_view	water running in a river	
001_033.mov	2	0,00692083	0,420145	0,222937	no	no	medium	berlin	city_view	water in a dar n/ river	
001_035.mov	2	0,00813276	0,437908	0,277298	no	no	medium	berlin	city_view	river/water	
ams.par.jap_002.mov	1	0,0046323	0,417986	0,317427	no	no	medium	europe	space_with_screen	city street wi people walking	
ams.par.jap_041.mov	1	0,0290042	0,259649	0,222506	no	panleft	medium	europe	space_with_screen	airport signs	
ams.par.jap_042.mov	1	0,00763042	0,343111	0,167343	no	no	close	europe	space_with_screen	airport with people	
ams.par.jap_043.mov	2	0,0180825	0,278841	0,250557	no	turning	medium	europe	privateinterior	hotel room	
ams.par.jap_044.mov	2	0,0112645	0,293447	0,220098	no	no	medium	japan	pub_interior	meeting room	
ams.par.jap_099.mov	1	0,0335198	0,474929	0,288257	no	trans_window	medium	japan	city_view	view out a tra n window	
ams.par.jap_101.mov	1	0,035681	0,417771	0,230665	no	trans_window	medium	japan	city_view	view out a tra n window	
ams.par.jap_102.mov	2	0,00979596	0,485448	0,282295	no	panleft	far	japan	city_view	river/water	
ams.par.jap_133.mov	1	0,00479121	0,469336	0,248959	no	panright	medium	japan	city_view	public sculptu e in the rain	
ams.par.jap_134.mov	1	0,00494727	0,42019	0,122982	no	no	medium	japan	city_view	rain	
ams.par.jap_135.mov	0	0,00956885	0,475699	0,193397	left	no	medium	japan	city_view	rain	
ams.par.jap_136.mov	1	0,00328248	0,439425	0,32863	no	no	close	japan	object	objects in a ca fé	
ams.par.jap_137.mov	1	0,00425654	0,379314	0,278743	no	no	close	japan	object	objects with r an walking in background	
ams.par.jap_138.mov	1	0,00787969	0,37695	0,318148	no	no	close	japan	pub_interior	man eating in café	
ams.par.jap_139.mov	1	0,00439859	0,404017	0,236849	no	no	close	japan	pub_interior	boy on chair i café	
ams.par.jap_140.mov	1	0,00745295	0,351694	0,274365	no	no	close	japan	tech	man with palm pilot	
ams.par.jap_141.mov	0	0,00861596	0,292875	0,190645	no	no	very_clos	japan	tech	close up of m n with palm pilot	
ams.par.jap_143.mov	1	0,00506803	0,401961	0,211791	left	no	medium	japan	space_with_screen	public building	
ams.par.jap_151.mov	1	0,00359668	0,102181	0,18936	no	panleft	close	japan	space	window to TV with excersize people	
Berlin_1.mov	1	0,0202419	0,417683	0,308701	right	no	medium	berlin	city_view	berlin s-bahn tation	
berlin_1_005.mov	1	0,00854281	0,412354	0,22013	no	no	close	germany	tech	girl at computer with purse	
berlin_1_006.mov	0	0,00730848	0,394761	0,205842	no	no	close	germany	tech	girl at computer with purse	
berlin_1_007.mov	1	0,00627681	0,393459	0,189203	no	no	close	germany	tech	boy at computer in thought	
berlin_1_008.mov	1	0,00632811	0,356293	0,169162	no	no	close	germany	tech	man at computer	
berlin_1_009.mov	1	0,00640958	0,454821	0,194305	no	no	close	germany	tech	hands using c mputer	
Berlin_1_01.mov	2	0,0175515	0,391472	0,312261	left	no	medium	berlin	city_view	berlin 1999 s-bahn station	
Berlin_1_010.mov	1	0,00654036	0,457076	0,195715	no	no	close	germany	tech	hands using c mputer	
Berlin_2.mov	0	0,0107685	0,44762	0,341623	left	no	medium	berlin	city_view	berlin street 999 - Checkpoint Charlie	
berlin_2_002.mov	1	0,0256468	0,438416	0,286065	no	right	medium	germany	pub_interior	chairs in an o fice room	
berlin_2_007.mov	1	0,0439538	0,397026	0,243651	no	trans_window	close	germany	city_view	graffiti from ut the bus window	
Berlin_2_01.mov	1	0,0145587	0,327971	0,298007	right	no	medium	berlin	city_view	berlin street 999 - Checkpoint Charlie	
berlin_2_010.mov	1	0,0491322	0,478167	0,144263	no	left	close	berlin	city_view	fast moving ju mbled street scene	
berlin_2_011.mov	2	0,00839755	0,211955	0,181606	no	no	medium	berlin	tech	2 Tvs flickeri g in a group of many TVs	
berlin_2_012.mov	2	0,00971161	0,247212	0,216543	no	no	medium	berlin	tech	2 Tvs flickeri g in a group of many TVs with re	
berlin_2_013.mov	1	0,00714188	0,489185	0,259785	no	no	medium	berlin	pub_interior	people standi g around meeting table	
berlin_2_014.mov	1	0,00692401	0,748701	0,343229	no	forward	medium	berlin	city_view	that monume t in berlin	
berlin_2_015.mov	1	0,00517316	0,385732	0,260506	no	left	medium	berlin	pub_interior	people in inter net café at night	
berlin_2_020.mov	1	0,0207006	0,488433	0,115437	no	no	close	berlin	pub_interior	water in wate fountain	
berlin_2_022.mov	2	0,00875125	0,452282	0,260013	no	no	medium	berlin	city_view	street corner in berlin	
berlin_2_023.mov	2	0,0142614	0,402402	0,333044	no	forward	medium	berlin	city_view	street corner in berlin	
berlin_2_024.mov	1	0,0477992	0,522573	0,126652	no	forward	close	berlin	city_view	feet walking o n sidewalk	
Berlin_3.mov	0	0,0107685	0,350407	0,244889	no	no	medium	berlin	city_view	berlin street 999 - Checkpoint Charlie	
berlin_3_001.mov	1	0,0118789	0,437505	0,274762	no	trans_window	far	berlin	city_view	driving in car	
berlin_3_002.mov	1	0,0372378	0,422829	0,196735	no	trans_window	medium	berlin	city_view	driving in car ooking out side window	

video_big_reduced

25.2) Same database with metadata describing the clips. Each row contains descriptions for one clip.

In Soft Cinema "films," video is used as only one type of representation among others: motion graphics, 3D animations, diagrams, etc.

Together, these directions define a new aesthetic territory. The three films presented on the Soft Cinema DVD—*Texas, Mission to Earth*, and *Absences*—explore some parts of this terrain.

Mission to Earth

Inga is an alien who comes to Earth from Alpha-1, a planet that is about twenty years behind Earth culturally and technologically. *Mission to Earth* is an allegory of both the Cold War era and of the contemporary immigrant experience that is so frequently the norm for inhabitants of "global cities." The film reminds us that while hybrid identity is often celebrated as progressive, it also entails psychological trauma.

One of the challenges in creating Soft Cinema films is to come up with narratives that have a structural relationship to the database aesthetics. If *Texas* uses semi-random database retrieval to represent "info-subjectivity," then *Mission to Earth* adopts the variable choices and multi-frame layout of the Soft Cinema system to represent "variable identity." That is, the trauma of immigration, the sense of living parallel lives, the feeling of being split between different realities. To this end, in generating every part of the film, the software chooses from among a number of alternative sequences that reflect Inga's variable identity. Other factors, such as the choice of a large or smaller window to display a particular sequence, and the number of windows (co-present realities) that appear in a layout, simultaneously tell us what the main character is seeing and represent her thoughts, memories, and feelings.

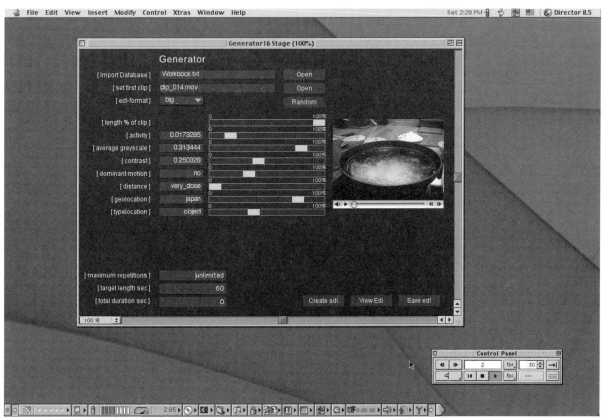

Figure 25.3) Interface of Generator software used to assemble sequences of clips.

One of the goals of this film was to visualize the narrative as much through motion graphics as through live-action video. Consequently, we invited Ross Cooper Studios to create a database of short motion-graphics clips, which would respond to the film's narrative and to the live video footage. In most parts of the film, you will see both video clips and motion-graphics clips appearing side by side. The motion graphics react to the video, but they also hold their own. In fact, they form a parallel film that follows the same narrative but visualizes its themes and the feelings of the characters through different means.

Authoring Process in Soft Cinema: Between Narrative and a Search Engine

Each video clip in a Soft Cinema film is described by ten parameters that can specify where the video was shot, the nature of its subject matter, its average brightness and contrast, the type of space, the degree and type of camera motion, and so on. These parameters are used by the software in assembling the movies. Starting with a particular clip, the software finds other clips that are similar to it on some dimensions. This is similar to the way in which we use web search engines such as Google. When Google returns a number of results for a particular search term, we can say that all these results are connected on a few dimensions: the search term, language, domains, etc.

In *Mission to Earth*, while I have exercised more control over what appears on the screen in particular moments, in *Texas* a larger part of authoring was delegated to a computer. What you see on screen while *Texas* is playing are multiple sequences generated in a manner described here. Each sequence is the result of a particular search through the Soft Cinema database. Each is perhaps equivalent to a "scene" in a normal film, while a series of such searches ("scenes") becomes equivalent to a traditional film. Film editing is thereby reinterpreted as the search through the database. Consequently, it is possible to describe a Soft Cinema film as a media object that exists "between narrative and a search engine."

Reference

Manovich, Lev, and Andreas Kratky (2005). *Soft Cinema: Navigating the Database*. Cambridge, MA: MIT Press.

On *Juvenate*
Marie-Laure Ryan

An audiovisual hypertext written with Director 7, *Juvenate* explores the inner life of a dying man haunted by the sounds and images of a world from which he is now physically isolated in his hospital bed. A quote from Charles Dickens on the exit screen weaves together life and death, suggesting that death is part of the fabric of life, but also framing the images of the mental journey of *Juvenate* as the poignant goodbyes of the dying man to the lifeworld and to those he loves, his son and his wife (or lover): "Life is made of many partings welded together."

A Chinese proverb on both the entrance and exit screens alludes to the mythical theme of the eternal return: "The beginning and the end reach out their hands to each other." The text concretizes this idea through the interleaved themes of childhood and illness, as well as through the recurrent visual motif of touching or reaching hands: the hand of the child on the face of the father; the hand of the woman on the hand of the man; and the hand of the man reaching out for a sunflower seed, which will sprout and blossom in front of barbed wire on the next screen.

"Heavily textured with supersaturated colors," as the authors describe them, the images convey "the intense sensory perception experienced by the terminally ill." Almost painful to contemplate, they refuse to aestheticize the experience of the dying. Some of the pictures can be interpreted as sensory perceptions, others as memories, and still others as dreams, visions, and fantasies. This is not a physical space experienced by a mobile body, but an alternative reality created by a feverish mind—the only space left open for exploration when the body is tied to a hospital bed.

Juvenate takes the user through a network of thirty-seven pictorial screens, each of which corresponds to a separate Director movie. The user navigates through an elegantly simple, natural interface: mousing over the screen until something happens. There is no need to click. For the reader who wants to visit the text systematically, rather than being carried around the inner world of the sick man by the random associations of the mind, a map accessible at any time gives direct access to every screen by clicking on its thumbnail image.

The movements of the cursor animate still pictures, make images emerge from the deep (an effect made possible by the layered structure of Director frames), and activate a variety of intradiegetic and extradiegetic sound effects: children's voices, bird songs, piano music, groans of a man trying to defecate in a hospital bed, and recordings of heartbeat by medical equipment. The juxtaposition of sound and pictures creates meanings that neither of these semiotic channels could convey by itself: for instance, a lawnmower sound threatens the radiant beauty of the sunflower.

The network and the map offer not only two alternative ways to navigate the text, but also two complementary ways to experience it. Some readers will regard the text as a game, and will give themselves a goal, such as visiting all the screens without consulting the map, or finding the way out of the labyrinth. (The exits are two screens that symbolize death.)

Other readers will rely heavily on the map, for instance to visit the sparsely connected screens of happy memories. These readers will travel in a manner much more leisurely through the network, taking the time to explore each picture

Figure 26.1) Screenshots from *Juvenate*.

in depth, attending to the musical structures of recurrent motifs that connect the various screens, breaking up the journey into small stages, and overall enjoying exploration more than destination. It is the rare merit of *Juvenate* to offer both a gamelike and an aesthetic experience, to reward both the goal-driven action of *ludus* and the free play of *paidia*.

Reference

Glaser, Michelle, Andrew Hutchison, and Marie-Louise Xavier (2001). *Juvenate: An Interactive Narrative* (CD-ROM). Produced in Association with the Australian Film Commission.

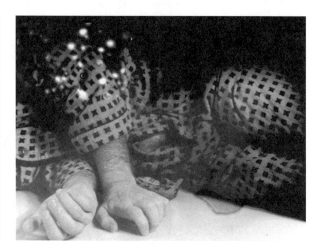

Figure 26.1) Screenshots from *Juvenate*.

On *Twelve Easy Lessons to Better Time Travel*
Mark C. Marino

"You appear to be time traveling. How can I help?"
—asks Ticky the Clock when you launch the chatbot assistant from *12 Easy Lessons to Better Time Travel*.

Ticky is just one of the interactive tools that interactors can use to overcome their time travel difficulties in this whimsical fictional cross-media learning module. The hosts or teachers, the forgetful Mr. Dr. Phebson and his lovely bride Mrs. Dr. Phebson, teach an advanced course in time-management techniques. Their case study: a tale of a forlorn time traveler, Barry Munz, who is caught by his past. Like meditating in a labyrinth, by navigating his story through hyperlinks, interactors will no doubt resolve their own issues. If that doesn't work, the Phebsons' course also offers other Internet modes of delivery, including an origami fortune-teller, a series of illustrated lessons, and even FAQs. *Twelve Easy Lessons* becomes an exploration of the aspect of narrative that has been most freed by new media: time itself.

27.1) Ticky the Clock, cousin of Clippy the Microsoft Paperclip.

The Lessons

Twelve Easy Lessons is a teaching system built around a series of instructional units. Mr. and Mrs. Dr. Phebson present the work as a cross-media interactive teaching module built for all types of learners, visual, interactive, depressed, and so forth. Among the teaching tools are a tutor chatbot, or conversation agent, named Ticky, twelve (quite easy) lessons, and a study case, focusing on Barry Munz and his problems with time travel. His story is navigable through hyperlinks.

In the Lessons, time travel has two basic rules. The first: Offenbach's Law: You are always going forward. And the second, Escher's Axiom, stems from the first: You can never go back

---

The Second Person Lesson

Mrs. Dr. Phebson: There is only one stupid question: "What time is it?"

Mr. Dr. Phebson: Er, It's nine o'clock.

Mrs. Dr. Phebson: Ha!

Mr. Dr. Phebson: Eight fifty-nine?

Mrs. Dr. Phebson: Nine o'clock is an artificial imposition! "O'Clock." Of the clock. The clock makes time.

Mr. Dr. Phebson: I see, and the imposition is arbitrary.

Mrs. Dr. Phebson: Well, not entirely arbitrary. It has *some* relationship to the Earth and the sun, but it *is* an artificial system that we collectively access on interfaces, such as watches. Now what's another set of information accessed via interfaces?

Mr. Dr. Phebson: Radio? TV?

Mrs. Dr. Phebson: And the Internet. The WWW is like time, except with a few more dials.

Mr. Dr. Phebson: Except, I can change what's on the Internet. I cannot change time, well, except through time travel. Ah-ha!

Mrs. Dr. Phebson: You see! Everything has changed. Time: analog, unidirectional, linear time marks one world, the world of obedience. The Internet marks a change in our relationship to information and interfaces and . . .

Mr. Dr. Phebson: Time! Thus, we no longer share received information, but can change it. So the Internet is like a window into time travel?

Mrs. Dr. Phebson: More than that, Phebby dear: The Internet is time travel!

27.2) The Drs. Phebson, your time travel hosts.

---

where you came from. With these two laws, the time traveler is armed with the disarming truths of time travel. Since most do not accept the basic laws, further instruction is necessary.

To time travel beyond the quotidian second-by-second business that we all participate in, the traveler must look at a picture and imagine what is missing beyond the edges. At the point at which he or she succeeds, time travel has been accomplished. (Of course, the story itself uses words instead of pictures, to prevent readers from actually time traveling away from their computers.)

The Phebsons present the case of Barry Munz to illustrate some of the difficulties that time travelers encounter.

The Case

Barry Munz is stuck in time, somewhere in the late 1980s, the infamous "End of History," even though his body continues to travel through time. He suffers from Time Discombobulation (chronus hemorrhoids), an ailment marked by a sense of dis-ease, or anxiety, in moments of low distraction, which prevents him from properly traveling through time. Of course, only one force is powerful enough to monkey with the great arrow of time: L-o-v-e.

Somewhere in his past, Barry has lost something to Molly Jones, his first love. As he travels back to encounter himself, he finds his Virgil, his guide, the nefarious Tab. With his parachute pants and feathered hair, like some trickster summoned from a John Hughes film, Tab runs amok in time. Needless to say, terribly sticky complications ensue.

Virtual Tutor

Ticky the Clock is a virtual tutor who will help travelers as they become lost or confused. Modeled on Clippy the Paperclip, Ticky answers not only the questions you ask, but even the questions you did not think could be asked. Ticky is a customized version of the Loebner-prize winning chatbot ALICE, which was designed by Dr. Richard Wallace.

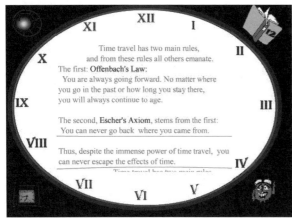

27.3) The clock portal identifies Internet browser windows as time travel technology.

Lesson Three. Instant Instances.

Rule: Changes in the past instantly alter the future.

Mrs. Dr. Phebson: Try to concentrate on the lesson this time, Phebby.

Mr. Dr. Phebson: Yes, my love. One popular time travel theory proposes: if you go back in time and make a change, the ramifications are instantaneously felt in the future. (See the A. Powers G-baby theory and the Butterfly-E Postulate.)

Mrs. Dr. Phebson: Thus, if Mr. Dr. Phebson were to go back in time and hide my keys to the car, I could not have driven here so would instantly disappear. [Mrs. Dr. Phebson disappears.]

Mr. Dr. Phebson: Or if she went back to when I was taking my Timology qualifying exam and performed an exotic jig, distracting me, I would instantly lose all my knowledge of time travel, or perhaps my ability to concentrate. Besides—

Ouch!—She has just gone back and pinched my posterior. She apparently found my magazine featured in Lesson 2. Ow. I can show you the welt.

The problem with this theory, obviously, is that it suggests that there is only one timeline. Also, it suggests time can be changed irreversibly, the very belief that the authorities used to rule time travel illegal in the middle of the third mislenia. Mislenia! Mrs. Phebson, what did I do to deserve this? Ouch!

10,000 Timepieces

This list falls a few thousand short of the promised 10K, but the meditation on the passage of time is important ballast for the turbulent tale of Barry Munz.

The portal to *Twelve Easy Lessons* is a clock face, which offers access to the twelve chapters of Barry Munz's tale. Four icons around the side of the clock offer access to the Lessons, Ticky, the 10,000 Timepieces, and the Megaclock, a time-based navigational device. Pressing the Megaclock will send the reader somewhere in the time of the tale. It is recommended for advanced travelers only.

Twelve Easy Lessons was written using a series of forty-two constraints, adapted from Oulipo (Ouvroir de Littérature Potentielle) practices. Inspired by Raymond Queneau's *Exercises in Style*, the episodes in time offer the same scene, encountered in new forms throughout the narrative. The primal scene eternally returns with variation throughout time periods, thanks to the persistence of memory and the obsessions of narrative. The graphical variations on the Megaclock icon, placed throughout the scenes, also constrained the selection of scenes. Other constraints used include color and number constraints, spawned from an origami fortune-teller. The 10,000 Timepieces continue this aesthetic of repetition with difference in its litany of clocks.

Twelve Easy Lessons follows a lineage of narratives that put time and textuality into play. From *Tristram Shandy* to Julio Cortázar's *Hopscotch*, the playful forerunners of electronic literature tried to shake time loose from the strictures of narrative. It draws upon the intertextuality of *Pale Fire* and the forking paths of *The Cave of Time*, the first *Choose Your Own Adventure* book.

Twelve Easy Lessons is an allegory that captures the major developments of time travel over the course of computer technology. In *afternoon*, Michael Joyce taught readers how to time travel electronically. Since then, time has continued

to be a central trope of electronic writing. Below is a key to help users decode the allegory, revealing the identity of several of the fictional characters.

Barry Munz: Nick Montfort
Doug: Alan Turing
Molly: Shelley Jackson
Vanity Plait: François Rabelais
Tab: Vladimir Nabokov
Chronic: Italo Calvino
Ticky: ELIZA

The piece employs HTML pages, Flash animations, and Artificial Intelligence Markup Language to deliver its multilinear stories. This cross-media training system can be licensed for corporate time-travel lessons, team building, and sensitivity training.

Reference

Twelve Easy Lessons to Better Time Travel (2006). Mark Marino. *Bunk Magazine*. <http://www.bunkmag.com>.

Deikto: A Language for Interactive Storytelling
Chris Crawford

The personal computer has been with us for twenty-five years now, and it has revolutionized the world around us. But in the arts, the computer has yet to approach its potential. Yes, the computer has dramatically changed the execution of existing artistic fields: movies, music, writing, and image creation will never be the same. These, however, are matters of applying the computer as a tool rather than exploiting it as a medium of expression. Yes, many artists have attempted to express themselves directly through the computer, but their efforts, while laudable extensions of existing artistic media, do not begin to use the computer as a medium in its own right.

Partly this is because so many artists fail to recognize that the essence of the computer as a medium of expression lies in the interactivity it makes possible. Yes, the computer is multitalented and can achieve great things as an image presentation medium or a sound presentation medium—but that is not its true genius. Movies can show text and play music, but text and music are not central to cinema as a medium of expression. Visual action is the essence of cinema; everything else is secondary. In the same fashion, interactivity is the essence of the computer; everything else is secondary.

I give interactivity this special place because interactivity is the one element that is unique to the computer. All of the other nice features of the computer—its graphics, its sound, its animation—are all offered by other media. Only the computer can provide interactivity. That is its strength. Using a computer for any purpose other than interactivity is like raising Arabian horses for any purpose other than riding.

The flip side of this emphasis on interactivity is a de-emphasis on the finer points of other media. Good literature lives or dies by the quality of the writing, the turns of phrase, the verbal imagery. Interactive art must sacrifice this kind of thing to concentrate on its strengths. Thus, it simply won't do to think of interactive art as "Old Art Form X with interactivity added." The phrases "interactive movie," "interactive literature," "interactive painting," "interactive novel," and so forth are all misleading. Interactivity is not a feature to be tacked onto an existing medium. It is the very essence of a new medium of expression. Interactive art, whatever form it takes, will most certainly not compete with or be seen as in any way related to any of the existing art forms. It is the first truly new artistic medium we have seen in a long time—and it cannot be extrapolated from any existing art form.

Of course, interactivity is difficult to understand, especially when we have so few models to guide us. Computer games offer lots of interactivity, but they are so drenched in violence and puerile fantasy that it's difficult to generalize from them.

Another reason for the dearth of artistic interactivity lies in the intrinsic abstractness of interactive design. Every other art form communicates its message through a specific instance of the message. Let's take the theme of pathos from loss of a child. Michelangelo created a magnificent instantiation of this theme in his Pietà. Countless paintings addressed the same theme, with imagery of the grief-stricken face of Mary. Some of the greatest works of modern photography are images of grief-stricken mothers burying their children. *The Lord of the Rings* uses this theme twice. It is an important and ever-present theme.

We know how to present this theme in images and stories—but how would we present it interactively? That would require us to create algorithms for the processes attending the loss of a child: the circumstances that created it, with possible parental culpability or inattention; the nature of the death and the intrinsic horror of all human loss; the means by which the news of the death is communicated to the parent; and the means by which a parent can express grief. All these factors must be determined at a level of abstraction previously unaddressed in art. How can we calculate the degree to which a parent's actions contribute to the probability of death of the child? The computation is conceivable, but immensely difficult.

How do we calculate the events that lead up to and follow the death? Again, this can be done but it requires a level of abstraction and complexity that boggles the mind. This is the challenge of interactive art; it is also its potential.

The Dearth of Tools

On top of all these obstacles, we have the greatest obstacle of all: the dearth of tools that give artists the power to express themselves in a manner both artistically meritorious and interactively substantial. Sure, there are plenty of level editors for creating your own blast-em-up, but they don't offer much artistic potential. There are plenty of wonderful tools for creating great images, music, novels, and movies— but nothing that gives an artist access to the interactive power of the computer. What we need is a programming language for artists.

Programming languages are created by programmers, mostly for programmers. They reflect the needs and interests of programmers, not artists. There have been a few programming languages designed for non-programmers, but none of these address the needs of artists.

What would a programming language for artists look like? I can assure you that it won't look like this:

NEW story =

a dusty western town
+ a boy and his dog
+ a man realizing that he is no longer what he once was
+ a prostitute with a heart of gold
+ a chase scene

The problem is that the computer is too dumb to understand any of these concepts. If you want a programming language that can add two numbers together, that's easy, because computers readily understand addition and numbers. But a programming language for artists cannot include most of the elements that artists consider fundamental to their work. We need to reduce artistic fundamentals to even smaller fundamentals, those of the computer: addition, subtraction, multiplication, and division with numbers. This is not a task for artists; it demands cerebration, not inspiration. It is instead a task for mutant

artist/programmers who unnaturally straddle the divide between the arts and the sciences. And what they produce will still demand that artists work hard to understand the mathematical constructs of the artistic programming language.

From Hot Air to Hot Circuits

At this point, I shall turn from concept to practice and describe my own work in this area: the *Erasmatron* <http://www.erasmatazz.com/>. Now in its fourth generation, the *Erasmatron* provides the artist with the means to create interactive storytelling products. This technology incorporates a great many ideas that have their own special terminology; that is the way of all technology. For example, the product of the artist's labors with the *Erasmatron* is called a storyworld. It's a complete dramatic environment, populated with characters possessed of personality traits, moods, and relationships. It has stages where action takes place and props for the actors to use. These elements are precisely defined so that the artist can manipulate them precisely; here is a brief description of the major elements in a storyworld:

Actors
An actor is a character in the storyworld, endowed with the following basic traits:

location (which stage the actor is occupying)
spying on (whom the actor is spying on, if anybody)
strength (overall physical strength)
wealth (how rich the actor is)
loquacity (how talkative the actor is)

There are also basic traits such as age, weight, height, and so forth. Next come the three basic moods that affect an actor's behavior:

arousal/disgust
joy/sadness
anger/fear

These moods are bipolar: the opposite of joy is sadness, so if an actor has joy/sadness equal to 0.0, then the actor is in a normal mood, but positive values indicate joy, and negative values indicate sadness.

Last come the personality traits. I spent many years honing this system and, while it isn't exactly what we'd want for good drama, it is (I think) the best compromise between dramatic requirements and computational capabilities.

> honest
> good
> dominating
> smart
> attractive

These are also bipolar traits, so that an actor with honesty equal to 0.0 is normal; an actor with a positive honesty is more honest than normal, and an actor with negative honesty is more dishonest than normal.

What makes this system special is that it directly leads to emotional relationships through what I call "perceived traits." This is easiest to understand when we talk about honesty. Suppose that Mary has an honesty value of −0.2; Mary is somewhat dishonest. But suppose also that Fred perceives Mary's honesty value as +0.3. Then Fred trusts Mary more than she deserves to be trusted. This discrepancy is, of course, the fodder on which drama feeds. Thus, for every actor, we have an honesty value, but we also have a value for how every other actor perceives the actor's honesty value—their trust in that actor.

But it goes even one step further in abstraction. We also keep track of how every actor perceives every other actor's perception of every actor's honesty. "Huh?" you stammer. "What's that?" Think of it in terms of this snippet of dialogue from a story:

> Don't ask Mary to borrow the money from Tom; you must not have known that Tom doesn't trust her. Ask Fred to borrow the money; Tom trusts Fred.

This atom of dramatic exchange relies on the fact that the speaker knows how Tom and Fred perceive Mary's honesty. It's a three-way relationship. Here's another example of the dramatic utility of this idea:

> You invited both Mary and Annabeth to your

party? How could you be so stupid? Don't you know they hate each other?

There are also stages, on which all events take place, and props, the objects that actors use during their interactions. I will skip the detailed specifications for these elements of the storyworld, as this kind of thing is common in the world of programming.

Deikto

The other major component of the *Erasmatron* technology is Deikto, a special language of interaction designed for interactive storytelling. We seldom realize it, but language controls the way we interact with others. That was the foundation for the idea of Newspeak in the novel *1984*; if the language lacked terms for freedom and justice, then nobody could express thoughts about those ideas and it would be easier to control the people. This concept, known in linguistics as the Sapir–Whorf hypothesis, has been disproved in its strongest form but confirmed in its softer applications. Basically, the Sapir–Whorf hypothesis addresses the influence that language has on our thinking. The strong version of the hypothesis, which never had many supporters, posits that language actually controls our thinking; it is impossible to think ideas that are not reflected in the language we use. This flavor of the hypothesis, as I said, has fallen into disfavor. The softer version of the hypothesis posits that language merely influences our thinking, and a variety of studies have supported this softer version of the hypothesis.

I decided to take advantage of this concept by creating my own little language that would express the concepts required for interactive storytelling. Any such language is necessarily limited; it is simply impossible to capture the richness of natural human language inside a computer. But if we tackle the much smaller problem of creating a narrow-purpose language, we bring the problem within reach of current computers. The trick here lies in keeping the language small and manageable; engaging in wild flights of fancy would surely doom any such effort to failure.

The most important reason for design parsimony in creating my toy language is the requirement that every single word used in this language must be fully computable. If I add the verb "give" to my toy language, then I must program the computer to understand everything about that verb: that it represents the transfer of an object from one person to another. The concept of ownership must be part of the program; and the program must understand that people can only give objects that they already own. That's a lot of programming—and that's only what's required for a simple verb such as "give."

Here is the list of verbs I have established so far in Deikto:

accept advice	hug
accept command	ignore
accept request	increase
advise for	injure
agree to deal	insult
answer	kill
ask (actor)	kiss
ask (prop)	laugh
ask (stage)	make
ask (gossip)	make love to
believe	meet
capture	open
command	play with
contradict	praise
deal	protect
destroy	request
drink	search for actor
eat	search for prop
empathize	seize
exclaim	sleep
find	small talk with
flatter	steal
flee from	report
get	take
give	tell (actor)
go	tell (prop)
gossip	tell (stage)
grab	threaten
greet	use
hide myself	verify
hide prop	wait
hit	what's new

You may find this list laughably short; how can one possibly tell a story using such a paucity of verbs? First, it is important to remember that in interactive storytelling, we

need expressive richness but not descriptive richness. We don't need the nuance and poetry that a truly gifted writer weaves into a good story. That's necessary for literature, but interactive storytelling is not literature and could never hope to compete with literature. We need the characters to be able to do things, but we don't need synonyms.

Even though this list is short, it imposes many complexities. Consider the difference between the verbs "advise," "command," and "request." Each of these verbs relies on a different relationship between the subject and the direct object. Advice relies on the advisee's respect for the wisdom of the advisor (his perceived value of the subject's Smart trait); commands rely on the direct object's deference to the subject (his perceived value of the subject's Dominating trait); and requests hinge on the good will that the direct object feels toward the subject (his perceived value of the subject's Good trait).

Worse, such verbs require multiple clauses, such as this:

Subject (advise/command/request) direct object that direct object (executes some verb) (to some other direct object).

As you can see, this can become quite messy.

This is where a second feature of Deikto comes into play. Deikto is a toy language that will never be spoken nor written; it will appear only on computer screens. Accordingly, it suffers none of the constraints—nor enjoys all the benefits—of speech and writing. In particular, Deikto can be displayed on the two-dimensional computer screen; why should such a language be restricted to the one-dimensional structure used in human languages? The result of this realization looks like this:

This Deikto sentences says, "I advise Mary (with medium urgency) that she should go somewhere." The last word in

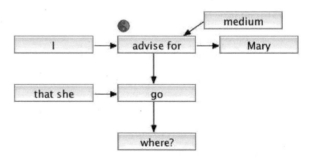

the sentence has not yet been filled in; this demonstrates the user interface for Deikto. The user builds sentences word by word, clicking on words like "where?," which brings up a pop-up menu showing a list of words appropriate for insertion into the blank spot.

Here's another, more complicated sentence showing off Deikto at its most complicated:

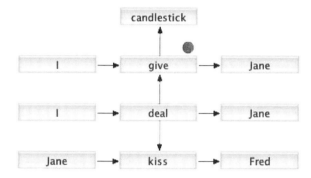

This sentence says, "I offer Jane a deal: if Jane will kiss Fred, then I will give Jane the candlestick."

The concept of a deal can be extended to a threat by use of the negation icon (the yin-yang symbol just above the verb). A version of this deal presenting a threat might read, "I offer Jane a deal: if Jane will kiss Fred, then I will not kill Jane."

However, I have drawn the line at the complexities of temporality in deal-making. How soon should Jane kiss Fred? Must I give her the candlestick before she kisses Fred, or vice versa? These matters are computationally simple, but expressively difficult: Deikto cannot express such considerations without undue complexity. I have decided to make all deals implicitly immediate; this is an example of the many trade-offs I had to make between dramatic completeness and artistic conciseness.

Of course, there's much more to creating a language than merely creating a list of verbs and designing a graphical scheme for displaying sentences. A huge pile of algorithms must be created for all the words in the language. I earlier mentioned the need to create algorithms reflecting the physical results of a sentence, such as transferring ownership of a given object. But there's much more to be put into algorithms. The most complicated problem arises from determining the reaction of characters to events. Will Jane

---

Expressing the Loss of a Child in an Imaginary Interaction via Deikto

Here I will use the space-saving convention of reducing Deikto sentences to linear structures. This is not the only way that an interaction involving the loss of a child could be handled; it is one of many thousands of possible ways. That's the beauty of interactivity: it addresses possibilities, not instances. That is also what makes interactivity so difficult to comprehend.

This is not a storyworld; it is a representation of a single journey through a storyworld. Interactive storyworlds offer the player zillions of possible stories; the player, in effect, builds a story in concert with the storybuilder. The storybuilder defines the content of the story while creating the storyworld; the player elicits that content in the playing of the storyworld, instantiating it into a single story. Thus, this presentation only offers a single possibility, not the full richness of the storyworld. To hint at the greater possibilities of such a storyworld, I have provided in italics a few alternative options that the player (playing Mom) could have chosen.

Billy request Mom that Mom permit that Billy go to town.
Mom permit that Billy go to town.

> *Mom not permit that Billy go to town.*
> *Mom require that Billy go to town with Mom.*
> *Mom offer deal Billy: Mom permit that Billy go to town if Billy promise Mom that Billy not go to lake.*
> *Mom offer deal Billy: Mom permit that Billy go to town if Billy promise Mom that Billy not play with Johnny.*

Mom command Billy that Billy not go to lake.
Billy go to town.
Billy meet Johnny.
Billy play with Johnny.
Johnny command Billy that Billy go to lake.
Billy slightly not accept command Johnny.
Johnny greatly insult Billy.
Billy slightly accept command Johnny that Billy go to lake.
Johnny go to lake.
Billy go to lake.
Johnny play with Billy.
Fate injure Billy.

173

Deikto

174

decide to accept my candlestick in return for kissing Fred? That depends on how much she wants the candlestick and how she feels about Fred. And she has more options than merely accepting or rejecting my offer. She might propose a counteroffer, or react angrily to my offer. All of these possibilities must be built directly into the language.

Trade-offs

The trade-offs between artistic power and manageability has been the most vexing problem in designing the *Erasmatron*. I solved the technical programs in the hidden areas of the program, and placed the means of solving the more artistic problems into the programming language I created. The separation of the artistic from the technical is not clean; I had to make some of the artistic decisions in building the *Erasmatron*, and the artist has to make some technical decisions in adjusting the language. Users always demand more power, but they seldom realize just how complicated a powerful program can be. Consider word processing. Perhaps you recall the clean and simple word processors of the early years. They were intuitive and easy to learn. Compare those word processors with a beast such as Microsoft Word. Yes, Word is certainly a powerful word processor—but do you know anybody who has truly mastered the program, who understands every nook and cranny of its capabilities? Consider the heavy books explaining how to use Microsoft Word. If interactive storytelling required the artist to master such books, do you think it could ever get off the ground?

The *Erasmatron* is not as easy to learn as the early word processors. It does require the equivalent of a book to explain its utilization. However, that book will be a hundred pages long, not a thousand. With the passage of time, as artists grow more comfortable with the *Erasmatron*, I will add more power to the program and its manual will someday challenge Word's manual in the World Heavyweight Manual championships—but not just yet.

The *Erasmatron* is an early effort, and as such it is flawed. Programmers and artists face a huge task in bringing computer technology within the reach of

artists. This task will require a great deal of trial and error. Both sides must stretch to the utmost to bring their fingertips within touching distance of each other. Artists must commit themselves to working with clumsy, weak, hard-to-learn software in order to show programmers how to make that software less clumsy, more powerful, and easier to use.

Johnny flee from Billy.
Billy exclaim greatly.
Sheriff find Billy.
Sheriff take Billy to home.
Sheriff tell Mom story.
Mom exclaim greatly.
Sheriff go to town.
Sheriff find Doc.
Sheriff tell Doc story.
Sheriff request Doc that Doc go to home.
Doc go to home.
Sheriff find Dad.
Sheriff tell Dad story.
Dad go to home.
Doc tell Mom that Billy health very negative.
Mom request Doc that Doc make Billy health positive.
Doc tell Mom that Doc not able make Billy health positive.
Doc advise Mom that Mom take Billy to city.
Mom accept advice.
Mom go to town.
Dad go to town.
Mom find Jethro.
Mom tell Jethro story.
Mom request Jethro that Jethro give Mom $300.
Jethro not accept request Mom.
Jethro offer deal that Jethro give Mom $300 and Mom give Jethro home.
Mom request urgently that Jethro give Mom $300.
    Mom accept deal.
Jethro refuse request.
Dad threaten Jethro that Jethro give Mom $300 lest Dad

injure Jethro.

> *Mom advise Dad that Dad not fight Jethro.*

Jethro insult Dad.

Dad hit Jethro with fist.

Jethro hit Dad with fist.

Sheriff take Dad to jail.

Mom go home.

> *Mom request Sheriff that Sheriff give Mom $300.*
>
> *Mom request Hank that Hank give Mom $300.*
>
> *Mom rob bank.*

Fate kill Billy.

The key point here is that, even though the language is skeletal, the story comes through quite clearly. This example demonstrates just how different interactive storytelling is from conventional storytelling. In terms of conventional storytelling, this story is wretched: there is no color, no subtlety, no nuance. However, this kind of storytelling boasts one advantage—and only one—over conventional storytelling: it is interactive. Mom could have made decisions that would have taken the story in different directions.

Another interesting point about this system is the role played by Fate in the story. Fate is an active character in the story who executes actions that are usually presented in passive form. The villain doesn't accidentally slip at the crucial moment and fall from the impossibly high precipice; Fate does that to the villain. Luke Skywalker didn't just accidentally run into Obi-Wan Kenobi; Fate made that happen. Fate is the most important character in interactive storyworlds, the direct representative of the storybuilder, who maintains the dramatic thrust of the story as it develops. The storybuilder must program Fate to watch over the story as it develops and keep everything moving in the proper direction. This most commonly takes the form of goosing up the action when the player manages to wander into a boring situation. The artist can program Fate to detect the loss of dramatic momentum and inject some new event guaranteed to get the story moving again.

I conclude with a small but critical observation. Most researchers working on interactive storytelling technology use the term "drama manager" for the system of algorithms that I call "Fate." Their term is technically superior, because it more precisely describes the function of this software. However, bridging the gap between artist and programmer will require terminological compromise, and I find "Fate" a snappier and more recognizable term than "drama manager." Here is a partial list of technical terms used by the *Erasmatron*; note how often I steal from the world of drama:

Fate

Actor (not "avatar")

Prop (not "object")

Role

Option

Plot Point

Event

History

Inclination (I might change this to "Preference")

GRIOT's Tales of Haints and Seraphs: A Computational Narrative Generation System
D. Fox Harrell

Within American culture there exist familiar depictions where Pan-African spiritual traditions such as Haitian Vodou or Brazilian Candomblé are presented as "evil." For example, the trickster Orixá Exu is conflated with the devil in some persecutorial Christian ideologies. By the same token, there exists within some African-based cultures the notion of the "white devil," or technology as the "unnatural fruit of Babylon." Demonization occurs from both sides of the dialectic, though power distribution is not equitable between them.

Tales of miscegenational diabolic power are common in contemporary cultural media as diverse as film, comics, popular music, and computer games: human mothers gave birth to Dante, the son of the demon knight Sparda in Capcom's *Devil May Cry* games series, Alucard ("Dracula" reversed) the son of Dracula in Konami's *Castlevania* game series, and Blade, the jazz trumpet-playing vampire hunter whose blood was tainted by a vampire's feasting on his mother at birth in Marv Wolfman's *Tomb of Dracula* comics series (Wolfman and Colan 1973). In the 1980s the Rastafarian hardcore/punk rock group Bad Brains described themselves as "Fearless Vampire Killers" as their singer intoned:

> The bourgeoisie had better watch out for me. All throughout this so-called nation, we don't want your filthy money, we don't need your innocent bloodshed. We just wanna end your world. Well my mind's made up. Yes, it's time for you to pay, better watch out for me. I'm a member of the F.V.K.

Imagery from the dark romance genre edged up against issues of identity, social inequity, and cultural

misrepresentation is a trope with a long history (Harrell 2005).

These are considered sensitive sociological and humanistic issues; more rarely are they considered cognitive issues, but seldom would anyone consider them *computational* issues (Ibid., 5). The GRIOT computational narrative system utilizes techniques suitable for representing meaning and expression such as the thoughts in the paragraph above. GRIOT is a computer program developed to implement systems that output narratives in response to user input. The first case studies built using GRIOT generate interactive poetry. GRIOT is based on an approach to computational narrative that builds on research from cognitive linguistics on metaphor and conceptual blending (Lakoff and Turner 1989; Fauconnier and Turner 2002), sociolinguistics on how humans structure narrative (Labov 1972; Linde 1993; Goguen 2003), computer science on algebraic semantics and semiotics (Goguen and Malcolm 1996; Goguen 1999).

A focus in the development of the GRIOT system was on developing computational techniques suitable for representing an author's intended subjective meaning and expression. Special attention was given to the generation of new concepts on the fly (by conceptual blending), and representing them for use in interactive and generative narrative artwork. An algorithm for conceptual blending called ALLOY lies at the heart of GRIOT. Gilles Fauconnier and Mark Turner's (2002, 8) conceptual blending theory describes the processes by which concepts are integrated, guided by "uniform structural and dynamic principles" both unconsciously in everyday thought and in more complex abstract thought such as in literary arts or rhetoric. A basic component of the theory is a conceptual space. Conceptual spaces, building upon Fauconnier's theory of mental spaces (Fauconnier 1994), are sets of "elements" and relations, "relatively small, transient collections of concepts, selected from larger domains for some purpose at hand, such as understanding a particular sentence" (Goguen and Harrell 2004).

A computational model of conceptual blending requires that conceptual spaces be formalized in a manner amenable to algorithmic generation, integration, media representation, and manipulation via user input. In GRIOT, conceptual spaces and mappings between them are represented using Joseph Goguen's algebraic semiotics (Ibid., 13). In algebraic semiotics the structure

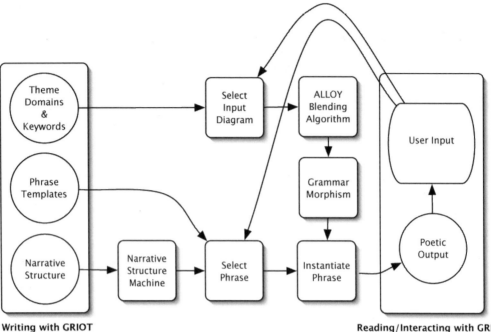

Writing with GRIOT
(Poetic System Designer Input)

Reading/Interacting with GRIOT
(Poetic System Output &
User Input Loop)

The GRIOT system:

(1) Writing with GRIOT: Initially a poetic system designer inputs the following components, which are processed by the system in preparation for user input:

    (1.1) A set of **Theme Domains** that provide information about a set of concepts (in "The Girl with Skin of Haints and Seraphs" the **Theme Domains** are: skin, angels, demons, old Europe, and old Africa, composed of sets of axioms),

    (1.2) A list of **Keywords** that access each theme domain,

    (1.3) A set of poetic narrative **Phrase Templates** (phrases organized by the type of clause they can compose, with wildcards that will be replaced on each execution), and

    (1.4) A **Narrative Structure** that defines how clauses can be composed (in "The Girl with Skin of Haints and Seraphs," these are based on a model from socio-linguistics research, a formalization of William Labov's structure of narratives of personal experience).

(2) Reading/Interacting with GRIOT: During the execution of **GRIOT**, each time the user enters a term it is scanned for a match with the domain **Keywords** and a response is produced as output to the screen. This process occurs a follows:

    (2.1) The system constructs conceptual spaces from the selected **Theme Domains** based upon the user's input. These conceptual spaces form an **Input Diagram** which describes two concepts that will be combined and the commonalities between them.

    (2.2) The core of the work is an algorithm called **ALLOY** that I implemented to model conceptual blending, not natural language processing. What comes out of it are conceptual spaces and axioms, not English sentences. The conceptual spaces in the **Input Diagram** are blended using **ALLOY** to construct new concepts.

    (2.3) The output from **ALLOY** is mapped to a grammatical form using a **Grammar Morphism**.

    (2.4) These grammatical blends then replace wildcards in the narrative **Phrase Template** to compose the appropriate clause type (as determined by the **Narrative Structure**). The Phrase Template is now said to be "instantiated," and is output.

(3) Input Loop: If the poem is not yet complete the system awaits new user input.

29.1) The GRIOT Architecture.

of complex signs, including multimedia signs (e.g., a film with closed captioning), and the blending of such structures are described using semiotic systems (also called sign systems) and semiotic morphisms (mappings between sign systems).

This does not imply a belief that meaning can be reduced to mathematical formalization; on the contrary, the underlying theories in cognitive linguistics assert that meaning is considered to be contextual and dynamic, and has a basis in embodied human experience. This means that meaning is "actively constructed by staggeringly complex mental operations" such as conceptual blending (Ibid., 8). Furthermore, meaning depends upon the fact that humans exist "in a world that is inseparable from our bodies, our language, and our social history" (Varela, Thompson and Rosch 1991). These underlying assumptions about the nature of meaning and the use of formalization are some of the characteristics that distinguish GRIOT from other work in poetry and narrative generation. Some implementation details for GRIOT can be found in Varela, Thompson and Rosch's *The Embodied Mind: Cognitive Science and Human Experience* and details for ALLOY can be found in Joseph Goguen and my "Style as Choice of Blending Principles." Figure 29.1 depicts the architecture of the GRIOT system and figures 29.2 and 29.3 illustrate the process of writing in GRIOT as an author and "reading/interacting" with GRIOT as a user.

The first poetic system implemented using GRIOT is entitled "The Girl with Skin of Haints and Seraphs." The system generates prose poems about a girl with skin of angels and demons in response to user input (via keywords as in figure 29.3 or a graphical user interface as in figure 29.4) that triggers the use of concepts from themes of Europe, Africa, skin, whiteness, devils, and angels. A poetic system is not the individual output of one execution of GRIOT, but rather the code that generates a variety of poems algorithmically. Templates and granular fragments of poetry organized by narrative clause type are combined with the output of ALLOY to result in poems that differ not only in how the templates are selected and configured, but in the meaning being expressed by the blended concepts.

Figure 29.2 provides a brief description of how a poetic system designer can input templates and theme domains (sets of relations that describe a theme). Concepts are combined

Angels Domain:
Keywords: angel, feather, wing, cloud,...
Axioms: (Person:cupid inspires Emotion:desire)
(Person:cherub strokes Object:harp)
...
Demons Domain:
Keywords: demon, pitchfork, devil, brimstone,...
Axioms: (Person:demon spawns Emotion:fear)
(Object:fire burns Person:soul)
...
Europe Domain:
Keywords: Europe, Greece, Viking,...
Axioms: (Person:Nordic-beauty inspires Emotion:awe)
...
Africa Domain:
...

Theme Domains & Keywords

Opening Phrases:
She begins her days (verb-clause)
Each morning foes called her (singular-noun)!
...
Narrative Phrases:
They would call her (singular-noun)
or (singular-noun)
(singular-noun)
...
Evaluative Phrases:
grave times indeed
she could cry
...
Closing Phrases:
...

Phrase Templates

Opening clause starts:
Consists of: +
<orientation phrase>

Narrative clause follows:
<opening clause>
<narrative clause>
<evaluative clause>

Evaluative clause follows:
<narrative clause>

Closing clause follows:
<evaluative clause>
...

Narrative Structure

29.2) Writing with GRIOT (Poetic System Designer Input).

according to principles that produce "optimal" blends. Typically this optimality results in "common sense" blends, but for particular poetic effects different, "dis-optimal" criteria can be utilized. In "The Girl with Skin of Haints and Seraphs,"

---

(1)
>Africa
her arrival onto this earth was marked when first-born and charcoal-girl transforms to impoverished-elder or charcoal-woman
>Europe
she worked raising snow-queen original-lady children of her own
>demon
the young lady would prevail
>demon
a caress across her skin scares up demon black
>angel
her failure was ignoring her wings and original-lady nature
>black
and she felt glad
>white
as she grew older she saw entitlement defiance wrinkles upon her face
>juju
ebony-wood-like brimstone defines fetish bedrock, the sign that let her know she finally really alive

(2)
>Europe
europeans and beauty create entitlement and cool ringing in the ears of the girl with skin of smugness and kindness blended with neck, red
>Europe
she worked raising imperialist, cherub children of her own
>Europe
death was better
>Europe
her spirit trusts that a nordic-beauty or epidermis arouses awe desire
>Europe
a spectral tone pervaded
>Europe
sunbather and first-born is now melaninated and impoverished-elder, causing her eyelids to droop
>Europe
she knows that childish reverence of contradiction days will fall further and further behind

(3)
>skin
she began her days looking in the mirror at her own pale-skinned death-figure face
>skin
she peeped out shame, hate
>skin
finally she fell from a cloud and skin and black drenched days were left behind

---

29.3) Reading/Interacting with GRIOT (The Girl with Skin of Haints and Seraphs: Three samples of user interaction and output).

each poem invokes similar core concepts and themes, and additional meaning emerges from the differences between the varying output poems.

The output from the "Girl with Skin of Haints and Seraphs" is meant to evoke the idea that identity is not based on static categories and classifications, but is rather dynamically changing and contingent upon social situations. A dynamic identity must take into account immediate social context. In the African Diaspora there are many artistic traditions that negotiate the disjunction between self-identity and social identity, between historical, traditional identities and identities of resistance. Dynamic improvisation and call-and-response structures are familiar aspects of pan-African narrative forms as diverse as the delta blues, Charles Mingus's calling out of the segregationist governor of Arkansas in "Fables of Faubus," the penetratingly satirical fiction and poetry of Ishmael Reed, hip-hop freestyle rhyming, and the African Brazilian martial art and dance Capoeira Angola (Downey 2005; Pequeno 2000).

Written prose poetry (Lehman 2003) and its more recent descendant flash fiction (Thomas, Thomas, and Hazuka 1992) ("short short" stories that encapsulate full narrative arcs within extremely abbreviated word counts) have not traditionally incorporated these techniques. On-the-fly improvisation has not often been incorporated for the simple reason that the nature of the printed text medium is not dynamically reconfigurable. Computational media have dynamic information structure and feedback loops built into the nature of the medium. The output of "The Girl with Skin of Haints and Seraphs," as shown in figure 29.3, combines prose poetry that is dynamically reconfigurable and founded in African and African-American vernacular traditions of signification (Gates 1988) with the use of algebraic techniques to construct imaginative metaphors on the fly.

I think of this work as development of improvisational texts (active media). Concepts and metaphors can change fluidly as a user engages a piece. From my vantage point, the cultural objects of most interest are GRIOT, ALLOY, and poetic systems themselves, not each individual poem or narrative as a cultural object on its own. The theoretical

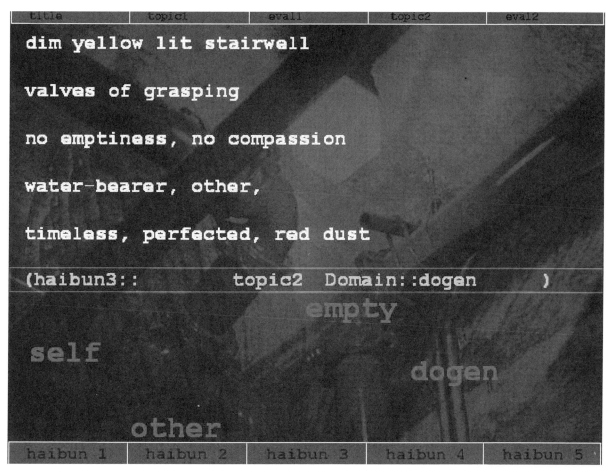

title   topic1   eval1   topic2   eval2

dim yellow lit stairwell

valves of grasping

no emptiness, no compassion

water-bearer, other,

timeless, perfected, red dust

(haibun3::   topic2 Domain::dogen   )

empty

self

dogen

other

haibun 1   haibun 2   haibun 3   haibun 4   haibun 5

29.4) GRIOT with graphical interface, generating haibun.

approach and technology used in GRIOT are not specifically suited to the subject matter of identity and improvisation; it is meant as a general framework for generating content by means of blending, and allowing narrative structure to be reconfigurable at the conceptual level.

The system has also been used with a graphical interface (depicted in figure 29.4) to generate haibun, a combination of prose and haiku poetry that is often used to narrate personal everyday experiences (Basho 1967), and beat poetry in a live performance with free jazz musicians (Harrell and Goguen 2005). My longer-term project involves using this technical and theoretical framework as a basis for creating further computational narrative artworks where in addition to textual input, users can interact with graphical or gamelike interfaces. This user interaction will still drive the generation of new metaphors and concepts, but along with text will also result in blends of graphical and/or audio media.

Reference: Literature

Bad Brains (1982). *Bad Brains* (LP). ROIR.

Basho, Matsuo (translated by Noboyuki Yuasa) (1967). *The Narrow Road to the Deep North and Other Travel Sketches*. New York: Penguin Classics.

Downey, Greg (2005). *Learning Capoeira: Lessons in Cunning from an Afro-Brazilian Art*. Oxford: Oxford University Press.

Fauconnier, Gilles (1994). *Mental Spaces*. New York: Cambridge University Press. (Originally published 1985. Cambridge, MA: MIT Press).

Fauconnier, Gilles and Mark Turner (2002). *The Way We Think: Conceptual Blending and the Mind's Hidden Complexities*. New York: Basic Books.

Gates, Jr., Henry Louis (1988). *The Signifying Monkey: A Theory of African-American Literary Criticism*. New York: Oxford University Press.

Goguen, Joseph (1999). "An Introduction to Algebraic Semiotics, with Application to User Interface Design." In *Computation for Metaphors, Analogy and Agents,* edited by Chrystopher Nehaniv. Berlin: Springer-Verlag.

Goguen, Joseph (2003). "Notes on Narrative." <http://www-cse.ucsd.edu/~goguen/papers/narr.html>.

Goguen, Joseph and D. Fox Harrell (2004). "Style as Choice of Blending Principles." In *Style and Meaning in Language, Art, Music and Design, Proceedings of a Symposium at the 2004 AAAI Fall Symposium Series*, Technical Report FS-04-07. October 21–24, 2004. Washington DC: AAAI Press.

Goguen, Joseph and Grant Malcolm (1996). *Algebraic Semantics of Imperative Programs*. Cambridge: MIT Press.

Harrell, D. Fox (2005). "Shades of Computational Evocation and Meaning: The GRIOT System and Improvisational Poetry Generation." Forthcoming in *Proceedings of the Digital Arts and Culture Conference*. November 30–December 3, 2005. Berlin: Springer-Verlag.

Harrell, D. Fox and Joseph Goguen (2005). (Music by Turetzky, Bertram, Borgo, David, and Goguen, Ryoko.) *The Griot Sings Haibun*. Performance at the California Institute for Telecommunications and Information Technology, Center for Research in Computing and the Arts. La Jolla, California (October 28, 2005).[1]

Labov, William (1972). "The Transformation of Experience in Narrative Syntax." In *Language in the Inner City*. Philadelphia: University of Pennsylvania.

Lakoff, George and Mark Turner (1989). *More Than Cool Reason—A Field Guide to Poetic Metaphor*. Chicago: University of Chicago Press.

Lehman, David, editor (2003). *Great American Prose Poems: From Poe to the Present*. New York: Scribner Book Co.

Linde, Charlotte (1993). *Life Stories: The Creation of Coherence*. Oxford: Oxford University Press.

Mingus, Charles (2000). *Charles Mingus Presents Charles Mingus* (compact disc). Candid Records. (Original session November 1960.)

Pequeno, Mestre João (2000). *Uma Vida de Capoeira*. Self-published.

Reed, Ishmael (1988). *New and Collected Poems*. New York: Atheneum Books.

Thomas, James, Denise Thomas, and Tom Hazuka, editors (1992). *Flash Fiction: Very Short Stories*. New York: W.W. Norton & Co.

Varela, Francisco J., Evan Thompson, Eleanor Rosch (1991). *The Embodied Mind: Cognitive Science and Human Experience*. Cambridge, MA: MIT Press.

Wolfman, Marv and Gene Colan (1973). *Tomb of Dracula* 10. New York: Marvel Comics.

Reference: Games

Castlevania: Symphony of the Night. Konami. 1997.

Devil May Cry. Capcom. 2001.

1. The full lineup for *The Griot Sings Haibun* was as follows:

D. Fox Harrell: GRIOT system design and implementation, *The Griot Sings Haibun* polypoem.

Joseph Goguen: Poetry performance, *The Griot Sings Haibun* polypoem, *November Qualia* (the poem that formed the template for the text of *The Griot Sings Haibun*).

Bertram Turetzky: Contrabass.

David Borgo: Saxophones and flutes.

Ryoko Amadee Goguen: Piano.

Writing *Façade*: A Case Study in Procedural Authorship
Michael Mateas and Andrew Stern

1. Introduction

The essence of the computer as a representational medium is procedurality—the ability of the computer to engage in arbitrary mechanical processes to which observers can ascribe meaning. Computers do, of course, participate in the production of imagery, support communication between people via the mediation of long-distance signals, control electromechanical devices, and support the storage and interlinking of large quantities of human-readable data. Many tools are available that allow users to engage these various capacities of the computer, such as image manipulation or Web page authoring, without requiring users to think procedurally. But it is precisely the computer's ability to morph into these special-purpose machines that highlights the computer's procedural nature. These special-purpose machines (e.g., tools) are made out of computational processes; the computer's ability to engage in arbitrary processes allows it to morph into arbitrary machines.

Taking full representational advantage of the computer thus requires procedurally literate authorship; that is, artists and writers who are able to think about and work within computational frameworks. By procedural literacy, we mean the ability to read and write processes, to engage in procedural representation and aesthetics, to understand the interplay between the culturally embedded practices of human meaning-making and technically mediated processes. Even for new media practitioners who don't themselves write much code, procedural literacy is necessary for successfully participating in interdisciplinary collaborative teams, and for understanding the space of possibility for digital works. Many authors find themselves engaged in some level of programming, especially for interactive work that, of necessity, requires conditional response to input, and thus the specification of a process. In the extreme case of developing new modes of computational expression, authors must be highly proficient in the use of general purpose programming languages, used to construct new languages and tools specialized for the new representational mode.

In this chapter, we provide a case study, using the interactive drama *Façade*, of this last type of procedural authorship. *Façade* represents a new mode of computational representation, *interactive drama*, combining the gamelike pleasure of moment-by-moment interaction with believable characters and the storylike pleasure of participating in and influencing a long-term, well-formed dramatic progression. As procedural authors, we undertook several design-plus-programming tasks: deconstructing a dramatic narrative into a hierarchy of story and behavior pieces; designing an AI (artificial intelligence) architecture and a collection of special-purpose languages within the architecture, which respond to and integrate the player's moment-by-moment interactions to reconstruct a real-time dramatic performance from those pieces; and writing an engaging, compelling story within this new framework.

This chapter makes a case for the importance of procedural authorship, describes the design goals of *Façade* and how these goals could only be met through a highly procedural approach to interactive narrative, and finally describes *Façade's* architecture, content organization, and the experience of authoring within this framework.

2. Procedurality

Janet Murray has identified four essential properties of the computer as a representational medium: that computers are procedural, participatory, encyclopedic, and spatial (Murray 1998). The *procedural*, of course, refers to the machinic nature of computers, that they embody complex causal processes, and in fact can be made to embody *any arbitrary* process. The *participatory* refers to the interactive nature of computers, that they can dynamically respond to outside signals, and be made to respond to those signals in a way that treats those signals as having the meaning ascribed to them by people (that is, nonarbitrary response). The *encyclopedic* refers to the vast storage capacity of digital computers, and their ability to organize, retrieve, and index stored material. The *spatial* refers to the ability of digital computers to represent space, whether that is the physical space of virtual reality and games or the abstract space of networks of information.

Various communities of practice tend to hold different properties as central. Here we provide a few examples of the privileging of various properties. For the Demoscene, a largely competition-oriented subculture with groups and individual artists competing against each other in technical and artistic excellence (Wikipedia 2005), procedurality is central; the aim is to procedurally generate as rich an audiovisual experience as possible using the minimum amount of stored content. The participatory is privileged in rhetorics of agency, control, and co-authorship, and has been adopted by communities as diverse as user-interface design, interactive art, and digital marketing. Database art privileges the encyclopedic, sometimes viewing all new media art practice as metaphorically related to the manipulation and resequencing of data stores. Spatiality is privileged by such diverse communities as virtual reality, game design, and hypertext.

While all of these properties play some role in various computational media, procedurality is the essential, defining property of computational media, without which the other properties could not exist.

Any participatory system requires the specification of potential action that is carried out in response to a stimulus. Capturing a space of potential action requires specifying a machine or process that can actualize the potential under different contingencies. In other words, participatory systems require procedurality. The converse is not true; there can be procedural systems that are not participatory, but rather execute a fixed process without accepting input. Many generative art systems, such as Aaron (McCorduck 1991), exhibit procedurality without being participatory.

Encyclopedic systems are similarly dependent on procedurality. Without the ability to perform operations on data, to be able to access, resequence, search, modify, index, and so forth, large data stores are useless. Without the

procedural competencies of Web search technologies, for instance, the Web literally could not exist at its current scale. There would be no reason to create a new Web page without the ability to relate the page to other, already published pages, and the ability for others to be able to find and view your page. Again, the converse is not true. Processes can create elaborate experiences from very small kernels; this capability is, in fact, the inspiration for the Demoscene.

The spatial is clearly a derivative property, a representational illusion actively maintained by a process. Graphical spatial representations make use of procedural models to compute and dynamically update the displayed space. Interactive spaces, which create the sense of space by supporting active navigation through the space, and which may not make use of 2D or 3D graphical representations at all, depend on the participatory, which in turn is dependent on procedurality.

The goal here is not simply to play a dominance game between the various representational properties of computers, but to avoid serious confusions that can arise in new media theory and practice from misunderstanding the central importance of procedurality. Without a deep understanding of the relationship between what lies on and beneath the screen, scholars are unable to deeply read new media work, while practitioners, living in the prison-house of "art-friendly" tools, are unable to tap the true representational power of computation as a medium.

Without an understanding of procedurality, of how code operates as an expressive medium, new media scholars are forced to treat the operation of the media artifacts they study as a black box, losing the crucial relationship between authorship, code, and audience reception. Code is a kind of writing; just as literary scholars wouldn't dream of reading only translated glosses of work, never reading the full work in its original language, so new media scholars must read code, not just at the simple level of primitive operations and control flow, but at the level of the procedural rhetoric, aesthetics and poetics encoded in a work.

New media practitioners without procedural literacy are confined to producing those interactive systems that happen to be possible to produce within existing authoring tools. To date, such tools tend to have an encyclopedic orientation; in the absence of significant support for procedural authorship (i.e., programming), authorship consists of the gathering together of numerous media assets (video, sound, text, image, etc.), and the spatial and temporal composition of those assets within the procedural framework supported by the tool (e.g., linking). This approach fundamentally limits the size and complexity of new media artifacts. For interactive works, this problem is especially severe, as it forces the author to pre-specify and explicitly author responses to all possible interactive situations.

2.1 Procedurality and Content

To describe the relationship between computation and media assets, Chris Crawford introduced the term *process intensity* (Crawford 1987). Process intensity is the "crunch per bit," the ratio of computation to the size of the media assets being manipulated by the system. If a game (or any interactive software) primarily triggers media playback in response to interaction, it has low process intensity. The code is doing very little work—it's essentially just shoveling bits from the hard drive or CD-ROM to the screen and speakers. As a game (or any interactive software) manipulates and combines media assets, its process intensity increases. Algorithmically generated images and sound that make no use of assets produced offline have maximum process intensity.

Process intensity directly enables richness of interactivity. As process intensity decreases, the author must produce a greater number of offline assets (e.g., pre-rendered chunks of text, animations or video) to respond to the different possible interactions. The number of offline assets required to maintain a given level of interactivity increases exponentially as process intensity decreases; therefore, in general, decreases in process intensity result in decreases in the richness of interactivity.

Although games have a relatively high process intensity within the space of new media artifacts, contemporary games are pushing against authoring limits caused by an overreliance on non-procedural, static assets. Contemporary games such as Electronic Arts' *The Lord of the Rings* franchise currently contain more media files than lines of code (Mateas 2005). Even open-world games such as the *Grand Theft Auto* franchise, lauded for their simulated, procedural

worlds, still use static assets for every vehicle, every type of person, every building, every weapon, and so forth.

Furthermore, developers at a recent Game Developers Conference voiced concern that next-generation console game hardware will only exacerbate this content crisis (Taylor 2005). The requirement for ever-more detailed graphics to entice consumers to purchase next-generation consoles means that assets become more expensive to produce, requiring ever-larger teams, making games more expensive. Consumers want more gameplay, meaning larger games, thus requiring even more assets to be produced; this all results in a positive-feedback loop that is considered by many to be unsustainable.

Where insufficient procedurality is creating a crisis in the authoring of traditional games, it has prevented some long sought-after genres of interactive art and entertainment, such as the high-agency interactive story, from even getting off the ground. Bringing process intensive, AI-based techniques to the problem of interactive story was one of the fundamental research goals of our interactive drama *Façade*.

3. Procedural Content in the Interactive Drama *Façade*
3.1 A Case Study for Procedural Content

Motivated by our belief that the research into highly procedural authoring methods will enable yet-to-be-realized genres of interactive art and entertainment, we undertook the development of the interactive drama *Façade*. The dream of interactive drama, perhaps best envisioned by the *Star Trek* Holodeck and first presented in an academic context by Brenda Laurel in *Computers as Theatre* (Laurel 1991), has players interacting with compelling, psychologically complex characters, and through these interactions having a real influence on a dynamically evolving storyline. Using a decade of prior research from the Carnegie Mellon Oz Project (Bates 1992; Loyall 1997) as a starting point and our belief that a fully realized interactive drama had not yet been built, we embarked on a five-year effort to develop procedural authoring methods for believable characters, natural language conversation, and a dynamic storyline, integrated into a small but complete, playable experience. Publicly released in July 2005, *Façade* has been downloaded by over

30.1) Grace and Trip in *Façade*, viewed from the player's first-person perspective.

150,000 players worldwide as of this writing, and has received widespread critical acclaim (Montfort 2005).

Enjoyable video games tend to be highly procedural in implementation, because among implementation methods, procedurality affords the greatest degree of dynamism and reactivity—features very satisfying to players. The best procedural video games excel at giving players high-agency experiences; that is, providing ample opportunities for the player to take action and receive immediate feedback. With *Façade*, we wanted to create an interactive drama that provides the level of immediate, moment-by-moment agency, that is, *local agency*, found in games. But unlike games, we want the player to experience *global agency*, that is, longer-term player influence on the overall story arc, over which topics get brought up, how the characters feel about the player over time, and how the story ends.

Like contemporary games, *Façade* is set in a simulated world with real-time 3D animation and sound, and offers the player a first-person, continuous, direct-interaction interface, with unconstrained navigation and the ability to pick up and use objects. But like drama, particularly theatrical drama about personal relationships such as *Who's Afraid of Virginia Woolf?* (Albee 1962), *Façade* uses unconstrained natural language and emotional gesture as a primary mode of expression for all characters, including the player. Rather than being about saving the world, fighting monsters, or rescuing princesses, the story is about the emotional entanglements of human relationships, specifically about the dissolution of a marriage. There is unity of time and space—all action takes

The following is an excerpt of a play session of *Façade*. Before this example began, the player chose the name Brenda. All she is told initially is that she is friends with Grace and Trip from college, hasn't seen them in a long time, and has been invited over for drinks. The drama begins with Brenda standing in a foyer at the front door of Grace and Trip's apartment.

From a first-person point of view, Brenda can freely walk and move about using the arrow keys, pick up objects and gesture using the mouse-controlled hand cursor, and speak at any time by typing and entering text, which is displayed at the bottom of the screen. Grace and Trip animate fluidly and speak their dialogue out loud.

A dialogue trace in the form of a stageplay, like the one below, is generated each time *Façade* is played.

GRACE (offscreen, audible behind the door)
Trip, when are you going to get rid of this?
TRIP (offscreen, audible behind the door)
What, Grace . . . this?
GRACE
Yes, you know how I feel about it—
TRIP
I know, I know, I'll do it right now, alright?!—(interrupted)
(Brenda knocks on the front door.)
TRIP
Oh, she's here!
GRACE
What?! You told me it'd be an hour from now!
TRIP
No, she's right on time!
GRACE
God . . . Trip!
(Trip opens the front door.)

TRIP
Brenda!! Ah, I'm so happy you could make it! We haven't seen you in so long, how's it going?
BRENDA
hi trip, how are you?

place in an apartment—and the overall event structure is modulated to align to a well-formed Aristotelian tension arc, that is, inciting incident, rising tension, crisis, climax, and denouement, independent of the details of exactly what events occur in any one run-through of the experience.

Additionally, the story-level choices in *Façade* are intended to not feel like obvious branch points. We believe that when a player is faced with obvious choice points consisting of a small number of choices (e.g., being given a menu of three different possible things to say), it detracts from the sense of agency; the player feels railroaded into doing what the designer has dictated. Instead, in *Façade*, the story progression changes in response to many small actions performed by the player throughout the experience. Later in this chapter we describe *Façade*'s procedural content in detail, and how it achieves these design goals.

3.2 Hindrances of Low- or Non-Procedural Content

Authors have faced a longtime conundrum when undertaking the construction of interactive stories: how can a story be structured to incorporate interaction, yet retain a satisfying, well-formed plot when experienced by the reader/player? Historically, the designs of low- or non-procedural interactive stories have been forced to make a trade-off between these two goals. The resulting "interactive story" may have a well-formed plot, but can only be minimally influenced by the reader/player, as seen in the linear narrative threads of most games and some text-adventure interactive fiction (IF).

Alternatively, the design trade-off may be made in the other direction, resulting in interactive experiences that can vary significantly as a result of player action, but lack the degree of coherence, pacing and focus that are pleasurable in well-constructed stories. A non-procedural, encyclopedic design approach, in which the author creates a large number of static story pieces (assets) that are sequenced by a simple system, inevitably forces this design trade-off. The author can choose to place minimal constraints on the ordering of story pieces, allowing the local sequencing of pieces to depend on the local player interaction. But then the sequences produced will lack the coherency of well-formed story arcs. Fragmented plots, or plots heavily diluted with unorganized or non-useful bits of

187

```
TRIP
Oh, we're great. I mean really, really great.
TRIP
Come on in!
BRENDA
great thanks
(Grace enters the living room.)
GRACE
Brenda, hi! How are you? God, it's been a while!
TRIP
Yeah, how—how are you doing?
GRACE
I just asked her that . . .
TRIP
Well, I'm asking her, too!
GRACE
(frustrated sigh)—(interrupted)
BRENDA
i'm good
GRACE
Oh, H-mmm (happy smile sound) . . . Well, come on in, make
yourself at home!
TRIP
So! Drinks!
(Trip closes the front door.)
TRIP
What would you like? How does a martini sound? Everybody
tells me I fix the best drinks, so I'm sure you're gonna love
this.
GRACE
Now Trip, don't get too worked up with the drinks tonight . . .
```

```
BRENDA
sure, a martini sounds great
```

action, are common in hypertext fiction as well as some IF, making them problematic to characterize as proper stories.

Within an encyclopedic design approach, the only way to increase interactivity is to author extraordinary amounts of content by brute force. This strategy has been borne out to be impractical; even the most successful *Choose Your Own Adventure* books or their digital equivalents, where the plot may vary significantly in response to reader's choices *and* be well-formed, necessarily offer an unsatisfyingly short series of infrequent, binary choices in order to avoid a combinatorial explosion of explicitly rendered (prewritten) plot directions. In such an approach, the limited and cumbersome nature of a non-procedural, encyclopedic approach is exposed.

The encyclopedic trade-off between coherency and the combinatorial explosion seen at the plot level is mirrored at the more detailed level of character dialogue. The low-coherency, simple-process approach to dialogue is exemplified by chatterbots, in which lines of dialogue are sequenced from a large pool in response to each player interaction, making use of little to no context, and depending primarily on simple stimulus/response rules. The high-coherency *Choose Your Own Adventure*-approach to dialogue is exemplified by dialogue trees, in which an author must explicitly and statically represent discourse context by pre-specifying all possible paths through the dialogue, resulting in the same combinatorial explosions suffered by story graphs.

Based on such frustrating limitations in prior approaches to interactive story, local and global agency have commonly been seen as incompatible.

3.3 Procedural Story Design

Our solution in *Façade* to this long-time conundrum is to recast player interactions within a story in terms of abstract *social games*. Games, which are procedural by nature, achieve the high degree of event variability and player agency that we desire; the challenge becomes how to design and structure games that reflect the particular meanings we wish our story to exhibit, and how to *dramatically perform* the games as coherent, focused, well-paced narratives.

Further, to be compatible with the procedural, simulation-oriented nature of games, the granularity of immutable story

TRIP
Beautiful!
(Trip trots over to the bar.)
GRACE
No no, Brenda, maybe you'd like some juice, or a mineral water?
TRIP
Oh come on . . .
BRENDA

what's wrong grace
GRACE
(anxious) What do you . . . No, we're fine, everything's fine . . . (clears throat)
BRENDA
ok
TRIP
Grace, I assume you want your usual . . . "a lovely, very cold glass of Chardonnay."
GRACE
(distant) Yes, a glass of Chardonnay sounds nice.
TRIP
Of course.
GRACE
(anxious) So, Brenda, I'm hoping you can help me understand where I went wrong with my new decorating, ha ha.
TRIP
Oh, Grace, let's not do that.
GRACE
(little sigh) You know, for this corner of the room, I had a desire for something . . . big . . . and bold . . .
TRIP
Yeah, this is a huge couch . . .
(Grace picks up her glass of wine from the bar.)
GRACE
. . . but now I can see how I should have chosen a simple, comfortable . . . love seat.
TRIP

content pieces must be made unusually small, on the order of individual and recombinable facial expressions, gestures and lines of dialogue, rather than multi-sentence lexias of text or extended cutscenes. As described in detail later, *Façade's* content pieces are organized into multiple, mixable hierarchical levels, sequenced by procedures written in multiple, mixable authoring languages.

At a high level, *Façade's* abstract social games are organized around a numeric "score," such as the affinity between a character and the player. However, unlike traditional video games where there is a fairly direct connection between player interaction (e.g., pushing a button to fire a gun) and score state (e.g., a decrease in the health of a monster), *Façade's* social games have several levels of abstraction separating atomic player interactions from changes in social "score." Instead of jumping over obstacles or firing a gun, in *Façade*, players fire off a variety of *discourse acts* in natural language, such as praise, criticism, flirtation, and provocation (see table 30.1). While these discourse acts will generate immediate reactions from the characters, it may take story-context-specific patterns of discourse acts to influence the social game score. Furthermore, the score is not directly communicated to the player via numbers or sliders, but rather via enriched, theatrically dramatic performance.

As a friend invited over for drinks at a make-or-break moment in the collapsing marriage of the protagonists Grace and Trip, the player unwittingly becomes an antagonist of sorts, forced by Grace and Trip into playing psychological "head games" with them (Berne 1964). During the first part of the story, Grace and Trip interpret all of the player's discourse acts in terms of a zero-sum *affinity game* that determines whose side Trip and Grace currently believe the player to be on. Simultaneously, the *hot-button game* is occurring, in which the player can trigger incendiary topics such as sex or divorce, progressing through tiers to gain more character and backstory information, and if pushed too far on a topic, affinity reversals. The second part of the story is organized around the *therapy game*, where the player is (purposefully or not) potentially increasing each characters' degree of self-realization about their own problems, represented internally as a series of counters. Additionally, the system keeps track of the overall story *tension level*, which

uhh . . .
(Trip hands Brenda her drink.)
TRIP
Here we are . . . hope you like it!
(Brenda takes her drink from Trip.)
BRENDA
Thanks, i'm thirsty.
GRACE
I'm sure I can return most of this, and try to—(interrupted)

no, I think it looks fine!

BRENDA
No, I think it looks fine.
GRACE
Really?
(Brenda sips her drink.)
TRIP
See, Grace, you're the only one unhappy with your decorating.
GRACE
(sarcastic) Oh well, I guess I'm wrong then. Ha ha. Thanks for clearing that up.
BRENDA
But it does look good, Grace.
(Grace sips her drink.)
GRACE
I can tell I'm going to need another one of these.
TRIP
(little sigh)
BRENDA
Well, the couch looks sexy.
TRIP
Oh! Brr, I'm going to have to turn up the thermostat if we're going to talk about sex.
GRACE
Trip, come on, that's not funny.
BRENDA
Oops.
TRIP
(sigh) Brenda, I should warn you, I never know how much of what I say is true.

Michael Mateas
and Andrew Stern

190

is affected by player moves in the various social games. Every change in each game's state is performed by Grace and Trip in emotionally expressive, dramatic ways. On the whole, because their attitudes, levels of self-awareness, and overall tension are regularly progressing, the experience takes on the form and aesthetic of a loosely plotted domestic drama.

As the granularity of the atomic pieces of story content (e.g., dialogue, emotion and gestural expression) becomes very small, and the procedures to sequence and combine them into a coherent narrative performance become primary to the realization of the experience for the player, the author's activity shifts from that of a writer of prose into a writer of procedures; that is, into becoming a programmer.

3.4 Richness Through Coherent Intermixing

To dramatically perform *Façade*'s social games as coherent, focused, well-paced narratives, an organizing principle is required that breaks away from the constraints of traditional branching narrative structures, to avoid the combinatorial explosion that occurs with complex causal event chains (Crawford 1989). Our approach to this in *Façade* is twofold: first, we divide the narrative into *multiple fronts of progression*, often causally independent, only occasionally interdependent. Second, we build a variety of *narrative sequencers* to sequence these multiple narrative progressions. These procedural sequencers, described next, operate in parallel and can coherently intermix their performances with one another.

Façade's architecture and content structure are two sides of the same coin, and will be described in tandem; along the way, we will describe how the coherent intermixing is achieved.

3.4.1 Architecture and Content Framework

The *Façade* system consists of several procedural subsystems that operate simultaneously and communicate with one another (Mateas and Stern 2000, 2003a, 2003b, 2004a, 2004b). Each is briefly described here.

The dynamic, moment-by-moment performance of the characters Grace and Trip—how they perform their dialogue, how they express emotion, how they follow the player around and use objects—are written as a vast collection of *behaviors*, which are short reactive procedures representing

numerous goals and sub-goals for the characters, arranged in a vast, hierarchical, dynamically changing tree structure. These behaviors are written in a reactive-planning language called "A Behavior Language" (ABL), developed as part of the *Façade* project, that manages both parallel and sequential behavior interrelations such as sub-goal success and failure, priority, conflict, preconditions, and context conditions.

The narrative sequencers for the social games are also written in ABL, taking advantage of ABL's ability to perform *meta-behaviors* that modify the runtime state of other behaviors.

The highest-level narrative sequencer, a subsystem called the *drama manager*, sequences dramatic *beats* according to specifications written in a custom drama management language. Beats in *Façade* are large groups of behaviors organized around a particular topic, described in the next section.

Another subsystem is a set of rules for understanding

agree	pacify
disagree	criticize
generalExclamation	oppose
positiveExclamation	greet
negativeExclamation	goodbye
express <emotion>	getAttention
maybeUnsure	inappropriateObscene
dontUnderstand	explain <explainAdviceDescriptor>
thank	advice <explainAdviceDescriptor>
apologize	
referTo <character> | <object> | <topic> | <theme>	explainRelationship <character1> <relationshipDescriptor> <character 2>
physicallyFavor <object>	
praise	leaveApartment
hugComfort	leaveForKitchen
flirt	
kiss	uncooperativeNotSpeaking
showConcern	uncooperativeNotMoving
howAreYou	uncooperativeFidgety
areYouOkay	
showSupport	systemDoesntUnderstand

30.1) *Façade*'s discourse acts.

and interpreting natural language (NL) and gestural input from the player. These rules are written in a custom language implemented with Jess, a forward-chaining rule language. When the player enters dialogue, these NL rules interpret one or more meanings (the aforementioned *discourse acts*). A second set of rules called *reaction proposers* further interpret these discourse acts in context-specific ways, such as agreement, disagreement, alliance, or provocation, and send this interpretation to the behaviors and drama manager to react to.

The final subsystem is a custom animation engine that performs character action, emotional expression, and spoken dialogue by way of real-time non-photorealistic procedural rendering, as well as music and sound. The animation engine is driven by the ABL behaviors; the engine also senses information about the location and actions of each character for the behaviors to use.

3.4.2 Beats, Beat Goals, and Beat Mix-ins

Façade's primary narrative sequencing occurs within a beat, inspired by the smallest unit of dramatic action in the theory of dramatic writing (McKee 1997). However, *Façade* beats ended up being larger structures than the canonical beats of dramatic writing. In dramatic writing, a beat tends to consist of just a few lines of dialogue that convey a single narrative action/reaction pair.[1] A *Façade* beat, however, is comprised of anywhere from 10 to 100 *joint dialogue behaviors* (JDBs), written in ABL. Each beat itself is a narrative sequencer, responsible for sequencing a subset of its JDBs in response to player interaction. Only one beat is active at any time. A JDB, *Façade*'s atomic unit of dramatic action (and closer to the canonical beat of dramatic writing), consists of a tightly coordinated, dramatic exchange of 1 to 5 lines of dialogue between Grace and Trip, typically lasting a few seconds. JDBs typically consist of 50 to 200 lines of ABL code. A beat's JDBs are organized around a common narrative goal, such as a

brief conflict about a topic, like Grace's obsession with redecorating, or the revelation of an important secret, like Trip's attempt to force Grace to enjoy their second honeymoon in Italy. Each JDB is capable of changing one or more values of story state, such as the affinity game's value, or any of the therapy game's self-revelation progression counters, or the overall story tension level. Within-beat narrative sequencers implement the affinity game; the topic of a beat is a particular instance of the affinity game.

Each beat can be viewed as a bag of procedural content, specifically JDBs, which are dynamically sequenced by the specific logic of each beat. The drama manager is, in turn, a bag of procedural content, specifically beats, which are dynamically sequenced by the general logic of the drama manager, as influenced by the preconditions, weights, priorities, etc. specified for each beat. The logic required to sequence individual lines of dialogue is more detailed and complex than can be easily described in the declarative annotations at the drama management level; this is precisely why our beats turned out to be larger than traditional beats of dramatic writing.[2]

There are two typical uses of JDBs within beats: as *beat goals* and *beat mix-ins*. A beat consists of a canonical sequence of narrative goals called beat goals. The typical canonical sequence consists of a transition-in goal that provides a narrative transition into the beat (e.g., bringing up a new topic, perhaps connecting it to the previous topic), several body goals that accomplish the beat (in affinity game beats, the body goals establish topic-specific conflicts between Grace and Trip that force the player to choose sides), a wait goal in which Grace and Trip wait for the player to respond to the head game established by the beat, and a default transition-out that transitions out of the beat in the event of no player interaction. In general, transition-out goals both reveal information and communicate how the player's action within the beat has changed the affinity dynamic.

1. For example, in the scene in Casablanca where Rick confronts Ilsa about why she returned, the following exchange forms a single beat: RICK: "Why'd you come back? To tell me why you ran out on me at the railway station?" ILSA: "Yes."

2. The detailed sequencing and coordination of individual lines of dialogue is more readily expressed in ABL than in the beat description language, and in fact changes enough from context to context within the drama that a generic decision-making process for sequencing lines of dialogue is not feasible (at least, not without much deeper knowledge representation, deep reasoning about human social interaction, including common-sense reasoning, etc.). Thus, we push that detailed logic into the custom narrative sequencers, written in ABL, that live within each beat, leaving the drama manager to sequence larger blocks of narrative content whose interrelationships are simple enough that they can be managed by the more generic decision-making process operating at this level.

A beat's canonical beat goal sequence captures how the beat would play out in the absence of interaction. In addition to the beat goals, there is a set of meta-behaviors, called *handlers*, which wait for specific interpretations of player dialogue (discourse acts), and modify the canonical sequence in response, typically using beat mix-ins. That is, the handler logic implements the custom narrative sequencer for the beat. Beat mix-in JDBs are beat-specific reactions used to respond to player actions and connect the interaction back to the canonical sequence. Handlers are responsible both for potentially adding, removing, and reordering future beat goals, as well as interjecting beat mix-ins into the canonical sequence. By factoring the narrative sequencing logic and the beat goals in this way, we avoid having to manually unwind the sequencing logic into the beat goal JDBs themselves, thus avoiding the dialogue tree problem mentioned earlier.

For *Façade*, an experience that lasts about 20 minutes and requires several replays to see all of the content available (any one run-through performs at most 25% of the total content available), we authored about 2,500 JDBs. Approximately 66% of those 2,500 are in beat goals and beat mix-ins, organized into 27 distinct beats, of which approximately 15 are encountered by the player in any one run-through (see the drama management section).

3.4.3 Global Mix-in Progressions

Another type of narrative sequencer, which operates in parallel to, and can intermix with, beat goals and beat mix-ins, are *global mix-ins*. (How coherent intermixing is achieved is described later.) Each category of global mix-in has three tiers, progressively digging deeper into a topic; advancement of tiers is caused by player interaction, such as referring to the topic. Each tier in the progression is constructed from one or more JDBs, just like beat goals or beat mix-ins. They are focused on satellite topics such as marriage, divorce, sex, and therapy; or about objects such as the furniture, drinks, their wedding photo, the brass bull, or the view; or as generic reactions to praise, criticism, flirtations, oppositions, and the like. Additionally, there are a variety of generic deflection and recovery global mix-ins for responding to overly confusing or inappropriate input from the player. In

PlayerArrives	TripStormsToKitchen
TripGreetsPlayer	PlayerFollowsTripToKitchen
PlayerEntersTripGetsGrace	TripReturnsFromKitchen
GraceGreetsPlayer	TripReenactsProposal
ArgueOverRedecorating	BlowupCrisis
ExplainDatingAnniversary	PostCrisis
ArgueOverItalyVacation	TherapyGame
FightOverFixingDrinks	RevelationsBuildup Revelations
PhoneCallFromParents	EndingNoRevelations
TransitionToTension2	EndingSelfRevelationsOnly
GraceStormsToKitchen	EndingRelationshipRevelationsOnly
PlayerFollowsGraceToKitchen	EndingBothNotFullySelfAware
GraceReturnsFromKitchen	EndingBothSelfAware

30.2) The names of *Façade*'s 27 beats.

total, there are about 20 instances of this type of narrative sequencer in *Façade*, comprising about 33% of the roughly 2,500 total JDBs.

3.4.4 Drama Management (Beat Sequencing)

The coarsest narrative sequencing in *Façade* occurs in the drama manager, or *beat sequencer*, as seen in table 30.2. This lies dormant most of the time, only active when the current beat is finished or is aborted (by the beat's own decision, or by a global mix-in). It is at the beat sequencing level where causal dependence between major events is handled—that is, where high-level plot decisions are made.

In a beat sequencing language, the author annotates each beat with selection knowledge consisting of preconditions, weights, weight tests, priorities, priority tests, and story value effects—the overall tension level, in *Façade*'s case. Given a collection of beats represented in the beat language, such as the twenty-seven listed in table 30.2, the beat sequencer selects the next beat to be performed. The unused beat whose preconditions are satisfied and whose story tension effects most closely match the near-term trajectory of an author-specified story tension arc (in *Façade*, an Aristotelian tension arc) is the one chosen; weights and priorities also influence the decision (Mateas and Stern 2003b).

Beat sequencing is further discussed in the Coherent Intermixing section, as well as that on Failures and Successes.

3.4.5 Long-term Autonomous Mix-in Behaviors

Long-term autonomous behaviors, such as fixing drinks and sipping them over time, or compulsively playing with an advice ball toy, last longer than a sixty-second beat or a ten-second global mix-in. While perhaps performing only a minor narrative function, occasionally mixing in a JDB into the current beat (comprising only 1% of *Façade*'s JDBs), they contribute a great deal to the appearance of intelligence in the characters, by having them perform extended, coherent series of low-level actions in the background over the course of many minutes, across several beat boundaries. By simultaneously performing completely autonomous behaviors and joint behaviors, *Façade* characters are a hybrid between the "one-mind" and "many-mind" extremes of approaches to agent coordination, becoming in effect "multi-mind" agents (Mateas and Stern 2004a).

3.5 Strategies for Coherent Intermixing

Since global mix-ins for the hot-button game are sequenced among beat goals/mix-ins for the affinity game, which both operate in parallel with the drama manager that is occasionally progressing overall story tension, several strategies are needed to maintain coherency, both in terms of discourse management and narrative flow.

First, global mix-in progressions are written to be causally independent of any beats' narrative flow. For example, while quibbling about their second honeymoon in Italy, or arguing about what type of drinks Trip should serve (affinity game beats, chosen by the drama manager), it is safe to mix in dialogue about, for example, sex, or the wedding photo (hot-button game mix-ins, triggered by a player's reference to their topics). Each mix-in's dialogue is written and voice-acted as if they are slightly tangential topics that are being jutted into the flow of conversation ("Oh, that photo, yeah, it's really . . .").

At the discourse level, mechanisms exist for smoothly handling such interruptions. During a beat goal, such as Trip's reminiscing about the food in Italy, if a global mix-in is triggered, such as the player picking up (thereby referring to) the brass bull, a gift from Trip's lover, the current Italy beat goal will immediately stop mid-performance, and the brass bull global mix-in will begin performing, at whichever

tier to which that hot-button game has already progressed. At the time of interruption, if the current Italy beat goal had not yet passed its *gist point*, which is an author-determined point in a beat goal's JDBs, it will need to be repeated when the global mix-in completes. Short alternate uninterruptible dialogue is authored for each beat goal for that purpose. Also, each beat goal has a *reestablish* JDB that gets performed if returning to the beat from a global mix-in ("So, I was going to say, about Italy . . ."). Mix-ins themselves can be interrupted by other mix-ins, but if so, are not repeated as beat goals are.

With only a few exceptions, the affinity game beats themselves are also designed to be causally independent of one another. For example, in terms of maintaining coherency, it does not matter in which order Grace and Trip argue about Italy, their parents, redecorating, fixing drinks, or their dating anniversary. When beat sequencing, this allows the drama manager to prefer sequencing any beats related to past topics brought up by the player. Likewise, hot-button mix-ins can be safely triggered in any order, into almost any beat at any time.

However, great authorial effort was taken to make the *tone* of each beat goal/mix-in and global mix-in match each other during performance. Most JDBs are authored with three to five alternates for expressing their narrative contents at different combinations of player affinity and tension level. These include variations in word choice, voice acting, emotion, gesture, and appropriate variation of information revealed. By having the tone of hot-button global mix-ins and affinity game beat goals/mix-ins always match each other, players often perceive them as causally related, even though they are not. Additionally, for any one tone, most JDBs are authored with two to four dialogue alternates, equivalent in narrative functionality but helping create a sense of freshness and non-roboticness in the characters between run-throughs of the drama.

4. Detailed Example of Authoring Procedural Content in *Façade*

To make concrete our discussion of authoring narrative and dialogue within a procedural framework, we will describe the process of authoring a specific story beat of the interactive drama *Façade*. Authoring a *Façade* beat involves a combination of interaction design, dialogue writing, and programming, summarized here.

4.1 Designing the Core Structure of a *Façade* Beat

Our example will be the beat "FightOverFixingDrinks," in which Trip and Grace argue over what kind of drink to make for the player, intended to reveal some of the underlying tension between them, and to further develop their characters. In the first half of the drama during which this beat can occur, the couple Grace and Trip, whose marriage has reached its breaking point, are trying their best to act like nothing is wrong. Specifically in this beat, we'll have Trip use fixing drinks as way to brag about how well-off and cultured he thinks they are. Grace, however, emboldened by the presence of the player, will counter Trip with an attempted attack on Trip about his materialism and faux-sophistication. Both Grace and Trip will challenge the player to take sides on these differences.

We will first lay out a relatively simple outline for the beat, to which we can add additional richness as we go. We designed a basic structure for this beat as follows, as a sequence of beat goals:

> Transition-in to the beat—Trip brings up the idea of drinks.

> Trip makes an initial suggestion, with bragging; Grace initially reacts to the brag. They wait for a few seconds for a player response, if any.

> Grace counters with her own suggestion based on what the player said, attacking Trip; Trip resists. They wait for a few seconds for another player response, if any.

> Transition-out of the beat—Trip and Grace each react to the player's decision, and Trip begins making the drinks.

It is important that each beat goal described here be relatively short, for example, no more than ten seconds each, ideally 5 seconds or less. A small granule size for beat goals allows other beat goals to be intermixed more easily into this sequence (as described next). If a beat goal were longer than ten seconds, we'd want to split it up into smaller multiple beat goals.

4.2 Reactivity Adds Richness

Next we will describe the additional reactivity requirements for this beat, which will add further richness to the interaction. These requirements include:

> At any time during the beat, the player should be able to interrupt what Grace and Trip are saying and get an immediate response of some sort. Whatever dialogue was interrupted should be re-spoken afterward in a believable way, as needed.

> At any time during the beat, the player should be able to bring up other topics or do actions that are not directly related to the topic of fixing drinks, and still get a response from Grace and Trip, as described earlier. These global mix-ins include progressing responses to tangential topics such as divorce, sex, or therapy, or about objects such as the furniture, their wedding photo, or the brass bull, or generic reactions to praise, criticism, flirtations, oppositions, and the like. After the response, Grace and Trip should return to progressing the original beat itself, in a coherent way.

> Any time *after* the beat, once in another beat, the player should be able to refer to what previously happened during this beat and get a response of some sort; we call this a post-beat mix-in.

To support these reactivity requirements, we will add the following specific features to the beat's structure:

Gist points: each beat goal needs to be annotated with a *gist point*, to know how far into a beat goal the player must have gotten to avoid needing to repeat it if interrupted to perform some other mix-in.

Repeat-dialogue: Each beat goal needs dialogue variation used in case the beat goal needs to be repeated, because it got interrupted in order to perform a mix-in.

Reestablish-dialogue: Each beat goal needs a prefatory line of dialogue that can re-establish its context, in case the previous beat goal was a global mix-in and the current beat goal is returning to what it was talking about. These often play as a prefix to the repeat-dialogue.

Local-deflect-dialogue: Each beat goal needs a small set of local deflect dialogue, to be used in case the player interrupts the beat goal with a very generic utterance, for which there is no appropriate global mix-in. These are essentially local mix-ins.

4.3 Performance in a Variety of Contexts Adds Richness

In addition to the reactivity requirements described thus far, we want this beat to operate in a variety of contexts. For example, its specific dialogue, and perhaps its structure, should vary if the beat is performed early in the drama when the tension is still low, versus a bit further along when the tension has increased. (Once the tension has reached a very high level, as authors we've decided that Trip won't be in the mood to fix anyone a drink, and this beat won't be allowed to occur.)

Also, the beat should vary in specific dialogue, and perhaps structure, if the player has been siding with Grace, or with Trip, or stayed neutral, independent of tension level. In fact, if the player's affinity changes *during* the beat, the beat should use its varying dialogue/structure appropriately.

Finally, this beat, by its nature, can be performed a second time, if enough time has passed since the first time it was performed. That is, if the player wants Trip to make a second drink for her, that should be possible. There needs to be enough internal dialogue and structure variation to avoid unbelievably repeating the same dialogue a second time.

To support such context variety, we will add the following specific features to our beat's structure:

> Each beat goal will be written with dialogue variations for each combination of tension level (low or medium) and each player affinity value (neutral, siding-with-Grace, siding-with-Trip), for a total of 2 x 3 = 6 variations.

> When the beat is occurring at the second (medium) tension level, we will author alternate transition-out beat goals (endings) for the beat, in which Grace reveals aloud one of Trip's façade-shattering alcohol-related secrets, such as a secret dislike of the taste of liquor, his secret job in college as a lowly bartender, or how he regularly sneaks off to a working-class sports bar down the street. We will divvy these up among the tension/affinity structure variations.

Meeting the requirements listed in this and the previous section contribute to creating *agency* for the player, because they allow the player to cause this beat to happen when she wishes. They also contribute to dramatic *believability*, because it only makes sense that drinks could be requested to be fixed at any time, at least until the tension level of the drama becomes too great. Without supporting these requirements, the timing and structure of the discourse and drama overall can seem arbitrarily and unnaturally constrained, significantly reducing agency and believability; that is, the aforementioned problems with the status quo of commercial and noncommercial interactive stories.

4.4 Alternate Dialogue Adds Richness

Ideally each line of dialogue has several variations; for example, three to five alternates, all with the same dramatic meaning but with different phrasings and word choice. While only one alternate will be heard for any line of dialogue per performance, the player will have the opportunity to notice this variation the next time she plays *Façade* and experiences this beat again, or if this beat happens a second time in the same session.

4.5 Parallel Behavior Adds Richness

Critical for lifelikeness and dramatic believability, Grace and Trip are required to perform expressive, parallel behavior as part of their beat goals:

> As Grace and Trip speak their dialogue, they should emote their current mood through facial expression, gaze and gesture. The specific dialogue they are speaking during the beat will affect their mood, of course, but overall mood can also be affected by whatever other events happened before this beat, as well as by whatever mix-ins may occur during the beat. For example, if a global mix-in occurs about divorce during this beat, that may sour Trip's mood, even if he started off somewhat chipper about fixing drinks. Additionally, while a character is speaking, all nonspeaking characters should react dynamically to the speaking character. This is why the author must write *joint* dialogue behaviors for each character; behavior must still be written for the nonspeaking

characters that control how they react to the dialogue being spoken by the speaking character.

As characters speak their dialogue, they should tend to follow the player to wherever she walks within the room. This means that, in general, the dialogue should be written to not depend on where the character is standing when it is spoken.[3]

At almost any time during this beat, we could have Trip autonomously decide to walk behind the bar and begin preparing drinking glasses as he speaks, in anticipation of pouring drinks. Like alternate-dialogue variation, this timing variation will be noticed in subsequent performances of this beat in this session or next. This requires the beat's dialogue to be written to be believable whether or not Trip is behind the bar.

4.6 Simplifications/Abstractions to Reduce Complexity

There are a few aspects of this design that can be simplified and/or abstracted to reduce the complexity of its implementation, while still achieving a satisfying level of agency and believability for the player.

Simplify the mapping of player utterances/actions to meanings, reducing the number of story reactions to author. Ideally, we would create a distinct reaction (plus alternate dialogue) for each discourse act the player could express, for each distinct context in a beat. However, there are dozens of supported discourse acts (see table 30.1), and potentially as many contexts within a beat as there are beat goals; for example, anywhere from five to ten per beat. The permutations would result in hundreds of reactions to author per beat. Instead, to make this tractable, we *grouped* related discourse acts together in context-specific ways. For example, if Trip suggests a martini and is hoping for agreement from the player, several similar discourse acts can be grouped together

to be interpreted as "agreement with Trip" in this context: agree ("yes"), positiveExclamation ("sweet!"), thank ("thanks"), express happy ("that makes me happy"), or a hug gesture. Although this requires authoring custom mappings per discourse context, it is less work than authoring dozens of individual reactions within every context.[4]

Reduce causal dependencies. Previously, we laid out the design goal of allowing tangential topic reactions to mix in at any time (aka global mix-ins, described earlier). For example, after Trip suggests a martini, if the player mentions divorce, Trip needs to respond about divorce, and hopefully return to his martini suggestion afterwards. But couldn't the mention of divorce, or anything else, change the situation enough that it doesn't make sense to continue suggesting martinis, or whatever was being talked about beforehand? To keep this tractable, we try to design the narrative and to write the specific dialogue to reduce such causal dependencies. Trip's dialogue responding to the topic of divorce, while subtly revealing some hidden tension or feeling about it, has him trying to sweep it under the rug, allowing him to believably return to what he was talking about. When re-suggesting martinis afterwards, Trip's mood may darken a bit, altering his facial expressions and body language from that point forward, but not necessarily requiring the FightOverFixingDrinks to alter its structure significantly. This strategy, of course, results in reducing global agency— although the player did cause an immediate local response (a reaction to the player's mention of divorce), that is, local agency, she causes fewer longer-term narrative effects (e.g., significantly changing the way drinks are discussed from that point onward). As authors we try to make up for that reduction in agency by *delaying* the narrative effect of having brought up divorce, responding to it later in the drama when it's easier to do so; for example, in a beat (such as the BlowupCrisis beat) that explicitly recounts the provocative

---

3. There are beats whose dialogue does depend on being performed in a specific location in the room; for example, the dialogue in ArgueOverItalyVacation requires Trip to stand near the Italy photo next to the bar and gesture towards it (or from behind the bar, as a special case, since the photo happens to be near the bar). The FightOverFixingDrinks beat, however, is one of the more common beat types that should be performable anywhere in the room.

4. Generally, each beat defines a discourse context, though there can be multiple distinct contexts within a single beat. The smallest discourse contexts are associated with individual beat goals, though beats may have sub-beat contexts that span several beat goals. Because we can't always group the same discourse acts together, in general each beat will need custom mappings from discourse acts to beat-specific meanings. For example, though "thank" and "positiveExclamation" both have the beat-specific meaning of agreement in the FightOverFixingDrinks beat, they may have distinct and different beat-specific meanings during other contexts in the drama.

things the player said earlier.

Collapse contexts together when possible. Previously, we set the design goal that each beat goal will be written with dialogue variations for each combination of tension level (low or medium) and each player affinity value (neutral, siding-with-Grace, siding-with-Trip), for a total of 2 x 3 = 6 variations. However some of these contexts are similar enough that they can be collapsed together. Specifically, in the case of a beat about Trip suggesting drinks to the player, as authors we could imagine that Trip would act with similar levels of braggadocio if he has affinity with the player, or if the affinity is neutral, while acting differently if Grace has affinity with the player. Furthermore, as authors we could decide that once the tension has increased to a "medium" level, it makes no sense for player affinity to be neutral; if the player is still neutral when the tension rises to medium, we will force player affinity toward Trip or Grace. Each of these simplifications removes a context from the list, reducing the total to four, thereby reducing the authoring burden for FightOverFixingDrinks by 33%.

Write the dialogue to allow for brief moments of uninterruptibility, reducing the need for repeat-dialogue in case of interruption. As described previously, each beat goal should have dialogue variation used, in case the beat goal was interrupted by a mix-in and needs to be repeated. However, we can eliminate the need for repeat dialogue for a beat goal if we can write the beat goal's dialogue to quickly communicate the gist of its meaning in its first few seconds, and annotate those first few seconds as *uninterruptible*. That is, if the player speaks during the first few seconds of such a beat goal, Grace and Trip's response is delayed until the beat goal's gist point is reached—a delay in reaction of a few seconds, which is just barely acceptable for believability. If the gist of the beat goal's meaning is communicated in those few seconds, we can interrupt the beat goal in order to perform a mix-in response to the interruption, and not bother repeating the interrupted beat goal later. This requires writing dialogue such that the minimum amount of content required for the beat's narrative progression to make sense is communicated close to the beginning of the beat goal, with the rest of the dialogue within the beat goal adding richness, color, and additional detail to the basic

content. As a general rule, the author must avoid long, complex lines of dialogue, instead breaking dialogue down into multiple lines that can be interrupted at line boundaries at a minimum (a fully interruptible line can of course be interrupted anywhere).

4.7 Authoring of a Beat Goal

Now that our design is in place, we are ready to author our beat goals. In the interest of space, we will only show the details of two beat goals for the FightOverFixingDrinks beat—the second and third beat goals listed in our core structure earlier, here given the names "TripSuggest" and "GraceCounterSuggest":

> *TripSuggest:* Trip makes an initial suggestion, with bragging; Grace initially reacts to the brag. They wait a few seconds for a player response, if any. (Grace and Trip's response to the player happens in the next beat goal, GraceCounterSuggest.)

> *GraceCounterSuggest:* Trip responds to the player, and Grace counters with her own suggestion, based on what the player said, attacking Trip; Trip resists. They wait a few seconds for another player response, if any. (Grace and Trip's response to the player happens in the next beat goal.)

We will write the dialogue in phases, starting off simple with just "TripSuggest," and adding richness as we go. In each phase of the authoring, **bold-italicized text** will denote changes from the previous phase. In the interest of space, we will show pseudocode between angle brackets, not actual ABL behavior code. "T." and "G." denote dialogue spoken by Trip and Grace, respectively. Where the word "Player" appears in the dialogue, the player's actual name is substituted, for example, "Brenda."

4.7.1 Scaffolding

Here are some basic lines of dialogue for "TripSuggest" that can serve as scaffolding for the authoring process.

"TripSuggest"

T: (cheery) What would you like?

T: (cheery) How about a martini?

T: (bragging) I'm a real expert at fixing these, at least that's what everybody tells me.

G: (a bit annoyed) Oh God, Trip, please . . . let's not go overboard with the drink preparation.

4.7.2 Uninterruptibility, Gist Point, and Reestablish-Dialogue

As described earlier we will set this beat goal to be uninterruptible at first, then set it to be interruptible and set its gist point a few seconds later. Also, we will prefix a line of reestablish-dialogue, to be played if the context of the beat needs to be re-established because of an interruption by a global mix-in.

"TripSuggest"

<set uninterruptible>

<if reestablish> T: (cheery) So! Drinks!

T: (cheery) What would you like?

T: (cheery) How about a martini?

<set interruptible>

<set gist point>

T: (bragging) I'm a real expert at fixing these, at least that's what everybody tells me.

G: (a bit annoyed) Oh God, Trip, please . . . let's not go overboard with the drink preparation.

This means that if the player speaks early on in the beat goal, Trip won't stop speaking until he's done saying, "How about a martini?" Then the reaction will occur (whatever it is), and the last two lines will go unheard.

4.7.3 Custom Reactivity

The "TripSuggest" beat goal we are authoring is the second beat goal in this beat; what if earlier, during the first beat goal, the transition-in, the player requested a specific drink; e.g., said "I'd like a beer"? We should have dialogue variation in "TripSuggest" to react to that.

"TripSuggest"

<set uninterruptible>

<if reestablish> *T:* (cheery) So! Drinks!

<if nothing suggested so far>

Extended Dialogue Listing

"TripSuggest" for TensionLow and PlayerAffinityNeutral/Trip

<set uninterruptible>

<if reestablish>
T: So! Drinks!

<if nothing suggested so far>
T: What would you like?
T: So, what's your poison?

T: How about something fun,
T: Let's have something fun,
T: We should have something fun,

T: How does a martini sound?
T: How about a martini?
T: Like a cosmopolitan?
T: Like margaritas?
T: Like sangria?
T: I've got the perfect bottle of cabernet I've been saving for just such an occasion.
T: Can I interest you in a single malt Scotch? It's primo.

<set interruptible>

<if a fancy drink was just requested>
T: Martinis . . . Great idea! Classic!
T: Ah, martinis . . . [Player], you've always had good taste.
T: Fabulous suggestion. I'll have the same.
T: Sure, that sounds great, I'll have one too!

<if a boring drink was just requested>
T: (wanting more) Oh, but we can do better than that . . .!
T: (wanting more) Oh, but let's enjoy ourselves tonight . . . !
T: (wanting more) Oh, but let's celebrate tonight . . .!
T: (wanting more) Oh, but let's live it up tonight . . .!

<brag>
T: I'm a real expert at fixing these, at least that's what everybody tells me.
T: Everybody tells me I fix the best drinks, so I'm sure you're gonna love this.
T: I just got a hold of this rare imported Icelandic vermouth I want you to try!
T: It's what we drink at these high-class poker games I go to with the execs at work.
T: Grace's dad taught me how to make these, it's a really classy drink.
T: The guy I play squash with introduced me to this drink, it's really amazing.
T: We went wine tasting last year in Napa with Grace's parents and discovered this stuff, it's exquisite.
T: I served these at our last party, they were a smash.

T: (cheery) What would you like?

T: (cheery) How about a martini?

<set interruptible>

<set gist point>

T: (bragging) I'm a real expert at fixing these, at least that's what everybody tells me.

<if a fancy drink was just requested>

T: (excited) Sure, that sounds great, I'll have one too!

<if a boring drink was just requested>

T: (a bit down) Oh, but let's enjoy ourselves tonight!

G: (a bit annoyed) Oh God, Trip, please . . . let's not go overboard with the drink preparation.

4.7.4 Map Player Utterances/Actions to Few Reactions

As described earlier for reacting to the player in our "TripSuggest" beat goal, we will group similar discourse acts together, and map them to a small set of reactions. Here, we map many of the discourse acts in table 30.1 to just five reaction types:

AgreeTrip: agree ("yes"), positiveExclamation ("sweet!"), thank ("thanks"), express happy ("that makes me happy"), hug.

DisagreeTrip: disagree ("nah"), negativeExclamation ("lame"), express angry ("I'm pissed"), express sad ("I'm suddenly bummed out").

SpecificFancyRequest: referTo <fancyDrink> ("how about a cosmo?", or "got any Scotch in there?").

SpecificBoringRequest: referTo <nonFancyDrink> ("just water for me," or "Coors Lite, if you have it").

NonAnswer: timeout (many seconds of silence from the player), referTo drink ("a drink sounds good"), express laugh ("ha ha"), maybe ("I guess so"), dontUnderstand ("I don't know what a martini is"), apologize ("sorry"), agree, etc. toward Grace ("sure Grace," "thanks Grace," etc.).

Note that the remaining discourse acts from table 30.1 not

T: It's the latest thing, you'll love it.

<Grace reaction to brag>
G: (a bit muted) Oh God, Trip, please . . . let's not go overboard with the drink preparation.
G: (a bit muted) (slightly annoyed) uhh . . . you and your 'high class' drinks . . .
G: (a bit muted) We don't need to make a big production out of this, Trip.
G: (a bit muted) Trip, let's not go crazy with the drinks, okay?
G: (a bit muted) Now Trip don't get too worked up with the drinks tonight . . .

"GraceCounterSuggest" for TensionLow and PlayerAffinityNeutral/Trip

<set uninterruptible>

<if AgreeTrip>
T: Beautiful!
T: Perfect!
T: Great! Martini it is.
T: Alright . . .! Cosmopolitans!
T: Ah margaritas! Yum yum!
T: Excellent. Mmm, mmm, sangria!
T: You got it. Scotch coming right up!

<if DisagreeTrip>
T: (dismayed) No . . . ?
T: (dismayed) What? Oh I thought you'd love that . . . !
T: (dismayed) Oh but we should enjoy ourselves tonight . . . !
T: (dismayed) Oh, but everybody loves that!

<if SpecificFancyRequest>
T: Oh, oh, yeah, that sounds even better! Great!
T: Oh yeah, great idea, great idea!
T: Oh yeah, that's even better!
T: Ooh, great, why didn't I think of that?

<if SpecificBoringRequest>
T: (let down) Oh, come on, let's enjoy ourselves tonight . . . !
T: (let down) Oh, but let's celebrate tonight . . . !
T: (let down) Oh, but let's live it up tonight . . . !
T: (let down) Oh, that's no fun . . . !

<if NonAnswer>
T: Uh, well, you know what, I'm just going to make you a martini.
T: Uh, well, you know what, I'm just going to make you a cosmopolitan.
T: Uh, well, I think I'll just make us all margaritas.
T: Uh, well, I'm just going to make us all some nice sangria.
T: Uh, well, I'm just going to pour you a glass of this wine.
T: Uh, well, I'm just going to make you a Scotch.

<if current drink suggestion is fancy>
G: No no, [Player], maybe you'd like some juice, or a mineral water?

handled by this local mapping will still be handled by the global context.[5] The reaction types listed here are implemented as dialogue variations in the beginning of the next beat goal, "GraceCounterSuggest":

"GraceCounterSuggest"

<set uninterruptible>

<if reestablish> *T:* About those drinks . . .

<if AgreeTrip> *T:* (excited) Good choice!

<if DisagreeTrip> *T:* (dismayed) What? Oh, I thought you'd love that . . . !

<if SpecificFancyRequest> *T:* (excited) Oh yeah, that's even better!

<if SpecificBoringRequest> *T:* (let down) Oh, but let's celebrate tonight . . . !

<if NonAnswer> *T:* (nervous) Uh, well, you know what, I'm just going to make you a martini.

<if current drink suggestion is fancy> *G:* No. no, Player, maybe you'd like some juice, or a mineral water?

<if current drink suggestion is not fancy, e.g., a beer>

G: Trip, we don't all share your infatuation with mixed drinks.

G: Player, you'd prefer just a beer, right?

<set interruptible>
<set gist point>

T: (dismayed, under breath) Oh come on . . .

4.7.5 Physical Performance

So far, our detailed beat goal authoring example has focused on the authoring of dialogue and dialogue logic. In addition, as mentioned previously, the author needs to specify physical performance. This includes deciding where the characters should stand in relation to the player's current position (staging), how close each character should be to the player (often determined by affinity), changes in mood (influences facial expression and body stance), any gestures the characters should perform, and how they are coordinated with the dialogue, base facial expression and

---

G: No no, [Player], maybe you'd like just a simple glass of white wine?
G: No no, [Player], how about something simple, like a nice glass of chardonnay?

<if current drink suggestion is not fancy, e.g., a beer>
G: Trip, that's not what [he|she] wants.
G: Trip, don't force your fancy drinks on [him|her].
G: Trip, don't pressure our friend, okay?
G: Trip, we don't all share your infatuation with mixed drinks.
G: Trip, maybe our friend isn't as excited by your suggestion as you are.

G: [Player], you'd prefer a simple glass of water, right?
G: [Player], you'd prefer a simple glass of juice, right?
G: [Player], you'd prefer a simple glass of soda, right?
G: [Player], you'd prefer just a beer, right?
G: [Player], you'd prefer a simple glass of white wine, right?
G: [Player], you'd prefer what you asked for, right?

<set interruptible>

<Trip final comment>
T: (dismayed, under breath) What . . . ?
T: (dismayed, under breath) Oh come on . . .
T: (dismayed, under breath) uhh . . .
T: (dismayed, under breath) but . . . uhh . . .

"TripSuggest" for TensionLow and PlayerAffinityGrace

<set uninterruptible>

<if reestablish>
T: (overly earnest, a bit desperate) So! Drinks!

<if nothing suggested so far>
T: (overly earnest, a bit desperate) What can I get you?
T: (overly earnest, a bit desperate) I want to fix you something special.
T: (overly earnest, a bit desperate) Anything you want!
T: (overly earnest, a bit desperate) I'll make us something really fun,
T: (overly earnest, a bit desperate) Let's have something really fun,
T: (overly earnest, a bit desperate) We need to have something really fun,

<reuse suggestions from PlayerAffinityNeutralTrip>

<set interruptible>

---

5. For example, if the player refers to sex during TripSuggest, since none of the TripSuggest-specific mappings handle references to sex, this context will suggest no reactions. The global context, on the other hand, will suggest a global mix-in reaction, which, since no more-specific context has a suggestion, will be selected as the reaction to perform. The global mix-in will be inserted between TripSuggest and GraceCounterSuggest; GraceCounterSuggest will then perform prefaced with its reestablish line. (Note that some other context in this or another beat might actually have a beat-specific response to a reference to sex, during which a global mix-in about sex would not be chosen to occur.)

momentary expressions (shock, surprise, etc.), and so forth. Besides participating in the dialogue logic, each JDB specifies procedural direction for how the character should perform its specific lines. The following is is some example ABL code for a single JDB, in this case the JDB for the "TripSuggest" case, where the player has not made any specific fancy drink request.

```
// ## if no specific fancy drink request (but includes
if we had gotten a specific non fancy request)
joint parallel behavior
bFAskDrinkT1NTPA_TripSuggest_BodyStuff() {
teammembers Trip Grace;
    precondition { StoryMemory
(BeatFAskDrinkT1WME bGotFancySpecificRequest
== false curDrinkIdea :: drink) }

        with (ignore_failure, property isStagingGoal true)
            spawngoal StagingConverse(40, player,
eConverseType_offCenterShared,
eWalkType_normal);
        with (persistent, team_effect_only) subgoal
TryToKeepFacingSprite(0, player);
        with (priority_modifier 1, ignore_failure,
team_effect_only)
            subgoal SetPerformanceInfo(40, 2,
eHeadEmphType_nodStrong,
eArmsEmphType_atSide,
                        startWith, -1,
eGazeType_normal, player, eFEBase_serious);
        with (priority_modifier 2) subgoal
SetMood(eMood_happy, eMoodStrength_barely, -1,
0);
        subgoal
bFAskDrinkT1NTPA_TripSuggest_BodyStuff_NoSp
Req_seq(drink);
        subgoal SetLetBeatGoalFinishFlag(true);
}
sequential behavior
bFAskDrinkT1NTPA_TripSuggest_BodyStuff_NoSp
Req_seq(int drink) {
    int doOptionalPreface;
```

```
<if a fancy drink was just requested>
T: (relieved, excited) Martinis . . . Perfect! Classic! Great idea!
T: (relieved, excited) Ah, martinis . . . Sweet! [Player], you've always
been a classy drinker.
T: (relieved, excited) Fabulous suggestion! I'll have the same.
T: (relieved, excited) Your suggestion is perfect! I'll have one too!

<if a boring drink was just requested>
T: (nervous, wanting more) But . . . I'm hoping we can have some
fun tonight . . .
T: (nervous, wanting more) But . . . I was hoping we'd enjoy
ourselves tonight . . .
T: (nervous, wanting more) But . . . I was hoping we would
celebrate tonight . . . !
T: (nervous, wanting more) But . . . I was hoping we'd live it up a
little tonight . . .

<brag>
<use dialogue from with NeutralTrip version>

<Grace reaction to brag>
G: (confident) Trip, Trip, Trip . . . don't go overboard with the drink
preparation tonight.
G: (confident) (slightly annoyed) Trip, you don't need to push the
'high class' drinks thing on our guests . . .
G: (confident) Trip, take it easy, don't make a big production out of
this.
G: (confident) Trip, don't go crazy with the drinks.
G: (confident) Trip don't get yourself worked up with the drinks.

T: (overly earnest, a bit desperate) Uh, [Player], come on, what do
you say?
T: (overly earnest, a bit desperate) Uh, [Player], it'll be great, what
do you say?
T: (overly earnest, a bit desperate) Uh, [Player], you'll love it, what
do you say?
T: (overly earnest, a bit desperate) Uh, [Player], let me make this for
you, what do you say?
```

"GraceCounterSuggest" for TensionLow and PlayerAffinityGrace

```
<set uninterruptible>

<if AgreeTrip>
T: (burst of relief, a bit desperate) Ah, I knew you'd agree!
T: (burst of relief, a bit desperate) Ah! I knew it.
T: (burst of relief, a bit desperate) Ahh, yes.
T: (burst of relief, a bit desperate) Ahh, I was right.

<if DisagreeTrip>
T: (dismayed, defeated) No . . . ?
T: (dismayed, defeated) Oh, I—I thought you'd love that . . .
T: (dismayed, defeated) Oh, but—but we should enjoy ourselves
tonight . . .
T: (dismayed, defeated) Oh, but everybody always likes my drinks . . .
```

```
// optional preface
    mental_act { doOptionalPreface =
randGen.nextInt(2); }
    with (ignore_failure) subgoal
bFAskDrinkT1NTPA_TripSuggest_BodyStuff_NoSp
Req_dia1(doOptionalPreface);

    // possible second preface
    with (ignore_failure) subgoal
bFAskDrinkT1NTPA_TripSuggest_BodyStuff_NoSp
Req_seq2(drink);

    // the drink suggestion
    with (ignore_failure) subgoal
DoFullExpressionBase(70, eFEBase_pleasant);
    with (ignore_failure) subgoal
bFAskDrinkT1NTPA_TripSuggest_BodyStuff_NoSp
Req_dia3(drink);
}
```

The purpose of showing a code snippet here is not to go
through the code in minute detail, but rather to point out a
few features of the ABL code for JDBs:

The first thing to note is that *it is* code; it is not some
static data structure or cutscene, but is rather a
dynamic little machine that knows how to perform
these particular lines, can perform them anywhere in
the room, even as the player walks around, can
perform them even if the character is engaged in
other long-term physical behaviors (e.g., Trip walking
around with his advice ball) and thus might require
substituting or suppressing physical movements.
This is not a cut-scene or statically prescribed
performance, but is rather a behavior that
dynamically adjusts the performance.

The joint parallel behavior (this one is for Trip)
automatically synchronizes with a paired behavior in
Grace, allowing them to tightly coordinate their
performance, even as they each simultaneously
engage in parallel, unsynchronized behavior. (Grace's
side of this joint behavior is not shown here.)

With the parallel behavior, the author is specifying a
bunch of action that should happen at the same time,
in this case that the character should initiate staging

```
<if SpecificFancyRequest>
T: (at first dismayed, then burst of relief) What . . . ? Oh, oh, yeah,
that's even better! Great!
T: (at first dismayed, then burst of relief) What . . . ? Oh yeah, great
idea, great idea!
T: (at first dismayed, then burst of relief) What . . . ? Oh yeah,
that's even better!
T: (at first dismayed, then burst of relief) What . . . ? Yeah! Ooh,
why didn't I think of that?

<if SpecificBoringRequest>
<choose one of the Disagree dismayed/defeated>

<if current drink suggestion is fancy>
G: (sweet) [Player], Trip's getting a little carried away . . . maybe
you just want some juice, or a mineral water?
G: (sweet) [Player], I think Trip is pressuring you too much . . . how
about just a simple glass of white wine?
G: (sweet) [Player], I think you'd prefer something simple and light,
like a nice glass of chardonnay, yes?

<if current drink suggestion is not fancy, e.g., a beer>
G: (cordial admonish) Trip, darling, that's not what [he|she] wants.
G: (cordial admonish) Trip, dear, don't force your fancy drinks on
[him|her].
G: (cordial admonish) Trip, Trip, you're pressuring our friend.
G: (cordial admonish) Trip, Trip, try to realize we don't all share your
infatuation with mixed drinks.
G: (cordial admonish) Trip, Trip, our friend isn't as excited by your
suggestion as you are.

G: (sweet) [Player], you'd prefer water, right?
G: (sweet) [Player], you'd prefer juice, right?
G: (sweet) [Player], you'd prefer soda, right?
G: (sweet) [Player], you'd prefer a beer, right?
G: (sweet) [Player], you'd prefer a glass of white wine, right?
G: (sweet) [Player], you simply want what you asked for, right?

<set interruptible>

<Trip final comment>
T: (impatient, a bit desperate) Grace . . . come on . . . !
T: (impatient, a bit desperate) Grace . . . !
T: (impatient, a bit desperate) uhh . . . Grace . . . !
T: (impatient, a bit desperate) but . . . uhh . . . Grace, come on . . .
```

"TripSuggest" for TensionMedium and PlayerAffinityTrip

```
<set uninterruptible>

<if reestablish>
T: (tense, crafty) So . . . drinks . . .

<brag 1>
T: (tense, bragging) This is great . . . For us I'm going to open an
amazing, I mean, exquisite Bordeaux.
```

to the center of the player's current view and share this position with another character, should try to keep facing the player as the player moves around, should perform their lines using strong head nods and arms-at-side gestures for dialogue emphasis, should be in a barely happy mood (this will combine with a serious base facial expression), and that they should perform a certain sequence of lines that start out uninterruptible (uninterruptibility will be turned off when the gist point is hit—this occurs in the details of dialogue behaviors that are not shown here).

At the beat-goal level, authoring for *Façade* combines being both a writer and a director, where both the dialogue logic and performance details are procedurally expressed.

4.7.6 Dialogue Variation for Tension Level, Player Affinity, and Alternate-Dialogue

To finish our authoring example, we need to fully list the dialogue of the remaining permutations of the two tension levels (low, medium) and three player affinities (neutral, Trip, Grace) for the "TripSuggest" and "GraceCounterSuggest" beat goals, including alternate-dialogue variation within each. As described earlier, the neutral and Trip affinities have been combined into one, thereby reducing the total number of permutations for this beat from 2 x 3 = 6, down to 2 x 2 = 4: TensionLow-AffinityNeutralTrip, TensionLow-AffinityGrace, TensionMedium-AffinityNeutralTrip, and TensionMedium-AffinityGrace. See the accompanying Extended Dialogue sidebar for this listing.

5. Evaluating *Façade*

In this section, we attempt to characterize the resulting degree of agency achieved in *Façade*, as well as failures and successes in terms of design, interface and system architecture.

5.1 Characterizing Agency

Creating player agency was a primary design goal for *Façade*, afforded by our approach of authoring highly procedural content.

5.1.1 Local Agency

When the player's actions cause immediate, context-specific,

T: (tense, bragging) Ah I know . . . I'm going to open us a magnificent, I mean, astounding Bordeaux

<local deflect dialogue: positive, negative, neutral>
T: (interrupted, smiling) Y—yeah, I'm going to open an exquisite Bordeaux!
T: (interrupted, puzzled, brow knit) N—no, I'm going to open an exquisite Bordeaux!
T: (interrupted, a bit puzzled) W—well, I'm going to open an exquisite Bordeaux!

<if reestablish>
T: (tense, bragging) So . . . I'm going to open an exquisite Bordeaux . . .

<set interruptible>

<brag 2>
T: (tense, bragging) Top of the line, very rare, very difficult to acquire —
T: (tense, bragging) Best of the best, you can't buy this in stores . . . Very, very special —

G: God, Trip, you are such a wine snob. Just like my dad.
G: God, Trip, you're just like my dad with the whole wine snob thing.

T: I'll take that as a compliment. [Player], what do you say?

"GraceCounterSuggest" for TensionMedium and PlayerAffinityTrip

<set uninterruptible>

<if AgreeTrip>
T: Excellent! You've got good taste.
T: Perfect! Ooh, you're going to love this.

<if DisagreeTrip>
T: (dismayed) Oh, but this is a very special bottle of wine . . . !
T: (dismayed) What? Oh, I thought you'd love that . . . !
T: (dismayed) Oh, but we should enjoy ourselves tonight . . . !

<if SpecificFancyRequest, SpecificBoringRequest, or NonAnswer>
T: No no, I really think we should have this wine, trust me, trust me!
T: Oh, come on, let's enjoy ourselves tonight, this wine will be so good. So good.

<if current drink suggestion is fancy>
G: (angry) No no, [Player], maybe you'd like some juice, or a mineral water?
G: (angry) No no, [Player], maybe you'd like just a simple glass of white wine?
G: (angry) No no, [Player], how about something simple, like a nice glass of chardonnay?

meaningful reactions from the system, we call this *local agency*. Furthermore, the greater the range of actions the player can take—that is, the more expressive the interface—then the richer the local agency (again, if the responses are meaningful).

Façade offers players a continuous, open-ended natural language interface, as well as physical actions and gestures such as navigation, picking up objects, hugging, and kissing. The millions of potential player inputs are mapped, using hundreds of the aforementioned NL rules, into one or more of approximately 30 parameterized discourse acts (DAs) such as praise, exclamation, topic references, and explanations; a second set of rules called reaction proposers interpret these DAs in context-specific ways, such as agreement, disagreement, alliance, or provocation.

Ideally, there would be immediate, meaningful, context-specific responses available at all times for all DAs. In the actual implementation of *Façade*, in our estimation, this ideal is reached about 25% of the time, where the player has a satisfying degree of real-time control over Grace and Trip's emotional state, affinity to the player, which topic is being debated, what information is being revealed, and the current tension level. But more often, about 40% of the time, only a partial ideal is reached: the mapping/interpretation from DA to reaction is coarser, the responses are more generic and/or not as immediate. Furthermore, roughly 25% of the time even shallower reactivity occurs, and about 10% of the time there is little or no reactivity. These varying levels of local agency are sometimes grouped together in temporal clusters, but also have the potential to shift on a moment-by-moment basis.

There are two main reasons for these varying levels of local agency. First, from a design perspective, at certain points in the overall experience it becomes necessary to funnel the potential directions of the narrative in authorially preferred directions, to ensure dramatic pacing and progress. Second, and more often the case, a lack of local agency is due to limitations in how much narrative content was authored (see the Failures section, later).

5.1.2 Global Agency

The player has *global agency* when the global shape of the experience is determined by player action. In *Façade* this

Michael Mateas
and Andrew Stern

204

```
<if current drink suggestion is not fancy, e.g., a beer>
G: (angry) Trip, that's not what [he|she] wants.
G: (angry) Trip, don't force your fancy wine on [him|her].
G: (angry) Trip, don't pressure our friend, okay?
G: (angry) Trip, we don't all share your infatuation with overpriced
wine.
G: (angry) Trip, our friend isn't as excited by your suggestion as you
are.

G: (angry) [Player], you just want water, right?
G: (angry) [Player], you just want juice, right?
G: (angry) [Player], you just want soda, right?
G: (angry) [Player], you just want a beer, right?
G: (angry) [Player], you just want a glass of white wine, right?
G: (angry) [Player], you just want what you asked for, right?

<set interruptible>

<Trip final comment>
T: (dismayed, under breath) What . . . ?
T: (dismayed, under breath) Oh come on . . .
```

"TripSuggest" for TensionMedium and PlayerAffinityGrace

```
<set uninterruptible>

<if reestablish>
T: (tense, desperate) So . . . drinks . . .

<grace comment 1>
G: (biting) Trip thinks he's at his classiest when he's on the serving
end of a swizzle stick.
G: (biting) Trip's favorite pastime is to get the blood alcohol
content of his guests higher than his golf score.
G: (biting) Trip would try to serve you one of his 'high class' drinks
before even saying hello if he could.
G: (biting) My dad bought Trip a silver-plated cocktail shaker for
Christmas a few years back—the rest is history.

T: (loud, angry, interrupting) Why don't I make us one of my new
drink inventions,

T: (desperate, biting) I call it Grace's Inner Soul. It's a mixture of
chardonnay, bitters, and lots of ice.

<set interruptible>

<local deflect dialogue: positive, negative, neutral>
T: (interrupted, smiling) W—wait, I want to make you one of my
drink inventions!
T: (interrupted, puzzled, brow knit) W—wait, I want to make you
one of my drink inventions!
T: (interrupted, a bit puzzled) W—wait, I want to make you one of
my drink inventions!
```

would mean that the final ending of the story, and the particulars of the narrative arc that lead to that ending, are determined in a smooth and continuous fashion by what the player does, and that at the end of the experience, the player can understand how her actions led to this storyline.

Façade attempts to achieve global agency in a few ways. First, beat sequencing (i.e., high-level plot) can be influenced by what topics the player refers to; the sequencing can vary within the number of allowed permutations of the beats' preconditions and tension-arc-matching requirements. Even with only twenty-seven beats in the system, technically there are thousands of different beat sequences possible; however, since most beats are causally independent, the number of *meaningfully different* beat sequences are few.

More significant than variations of beat sequences ("what" happened) are variations within beats and global mix-in progressions ("how" it happened). A variety of patterns and dynamics are possible within the affinity, hot-button, and therapy games over the course of the experience; in fact, these patterns are monitored by the system and remarked upon in dramatic recapitulations in the BlowupCrisis beat halfway through the drama, and in the RevelationsBuildup beat at the climax of the drama. A calculus of the final "scores" of the various social games is used to determine which of five ending beats gets sequenced, ranging from either Grace or Trip revealing one or more big hidden secrets and then deciding to break up and leave, or both of them too afraid to do anything, or both of them realizing so much about themselves and each other that they decide to stay together.

5.2 Failures and Successes of Façade

In this section we attempt to evaluate our results in creating the interactive drama *Façade*, whose design goals were strongly shaped by our procedural content-centric approach to implementation.

5.2.1 Agency

During the production of *Façade*, within our "limited" authoring effort (beyond the building of the architecture, *Façade* required about three person-years of just authoring, which is more than a typical art/research project but far less

---

```
<if reestablish>
T: (desperate, biting) >So . . . I should make you one of my drink inventions . . .

<grace comment 2>
G: (confident, pretending to be under breath, loud whisper) It's a secret—Trip doesn't even like the taste of alcohol.

T: (anxious, ignoring Grace) What?! So, [Player], how does that sound?
```

"GraceCounterSuggest" for TensionMedium and PlayerAffinityGrace

```
<set uninterruptible>

<if AgreeTrip>
T: Ah, [Player], you have deliciously wicked taste.
T: Ah, [Player], you are an adventurous drinker, like me.

<if DisagreeTrip>
T: (dismayed, anxious) No?

<if SpecificFancyRequest, SpecificBoringRequest, or NonAnswer>
T: (dismayed, anxious) You—you don't want my invention?

<if current drink suggestion is fancy>
G: (sweet) [Player], Trip's getting a little carried away . . . maybe you just want some juice, or a mineral water?
G: (sweet) [Player], I think Trip is pressuring you too much . . . how about just a simple glass of white wine?
G: (sweet) [Player], I think you'd prefer something simple and light, like a nice glass of chardonnay, yes?

<if current drink suggestion is not fancy, e.g., a beer>
G: (admonish) Trip, darling, that's not what [he|she] wants.
G: (admonish) Trip, dear, don't force your fancy drinks on [him|her].
G: (admonish) Trip, Trip, you're pressuring our friend.
G: (admonish) Trip, Trip, try to realize we don't all share your infatuation with mixed drinks.
G: (admonish) Trip, Trip, our friend isn't as excited by your suggestion as you are.

G: (sweet) [Player], you'd like water, right?
G: (sweet) [Player], you'd like juice, right?
G: (sweet) [Player], you'd like soda, right?
G: (sweet) [Player], you'd like a beer, right?
G: (sweet) [Player], you'd like a glass of white wine, right?
G: (sweet) [Player], you simply want what you asked for, right?

<set interruptible>

<Trip final comment>
T: (very tense exhale)
```

than a typical game industry project). We made the trade-off to support a significant degree of local agency, which came at the expense of not supporting as much global agency. Combined with the reality that the time required to design and author JDBs is substantial, only twenty-seven beats were created in the end, resulting in far lower global agency than we initially hoped for. As a result, we feel we did not take full advantage of the power of the drama manager's capabilities.

Furthermore, because the specification of each joint dialogue behavior—spoken dialogue, staging directions, emotion, and gesture performance—requires a great deal of authoring and is not automatically generated by higher-level behaviors or authoring tools, we are limited to the permutations of hand-authored, intermixable content. *Façade* is not generating sentences themselves—although it is generating sequences.

5.2.2 Feedback

A major challenge we encountered, at which we believe *Façade* falls short, is in always clearly communicating the state of the social games to the player. With traditional games, it is straightforward to tell players the game state: display a numeric score, or show the character physically at a higher platform, or display the current arrangement of game pieces. But when the "game" is ostensibly happening inside the characters' heads, and if we intend to maintain a theatrical, performative aesthetic (and not display internal feelings via stats and slider bars, à la *The Sims*), it becomes a significant challenge. In our estimation, *Façade* succeeds better at communicating the state of the simpler affinity and hot-button games than the more complex therapy game.

5.2.3 Interface

Another major challenge was managing the player's expectations, raised by the existence of an open-ended natural language interface. We anticipated natural language understanding failures, which in informal evaluations of *Façade* to date, occur about 30% of the time on average. This trade-off was intentional, since we wanted to better understand the new pleasures that natural language can offer when it *succeeds*, which in *Façade* we found occurs about 70% of the time, either partially or fully.

5.2.4 System Architecture

In our estimation, a success of *Façade* is the integration of the beat goal/mix-in, global mix-in, and drama manager narrative sequencers, with an expressive natural language interface, context-specific natural language processing, and expressive real-time rendered character animation. We feel the overall effect makes some progress toward our original design goals of creating a sense of the immediacy, presence, and aliveness in the characters required for theatrical drama.

As is evident from our authoring example, there is still significant effort in authoring an interactive drama within our architecture. Our architecture now makes authoring interactive drama possible, but not necessarily easy (it was extremely cumbersome or impossible using traditional finite state machine, dialogue tree, and story graph approaches).

It is unclear if there will ever be non-programming tools for authoring interactive drama; we believe it fundamentally requires procedural authorship. However, the idioms we have developed for structuring dialogue and using ABL within *Façade* can serve as a specification for a higher-level tool that facilitates authoring *Façade*-like experience. Even while authoring *Façade*, we were able to capture the general beat structure as an ABL code template that we could copy and modify for creating new beats. An obvious next step is to push these idioms as first-class language structures into ABL, or perhaps into a higher-level language that sits on top of ABL.

In general, our approach for architecting interactive drama systems is not to build a one-size-fits-all generic tool that tries to hide the fundamentally procedural nature of the medium, but rather to write languages for procedural authorship, build new experiences with those languages, and push the idioms and lessons learned from authoring prior experiences into first-class constructs in future languages.

5.2.5 Design

Certain aspects of our drama's design help make *Façade* a pleasurable interactive experience, while others hurt. It helps to have *two* tightly coordinated non-player characters who can believably keep dramatic action happening, in the event that the player stops interacting or acts uncooperatively. In fact, the fast pace of Grace and Trip's dialogue performance discourages lengthy natural language inputs from the player. By design, Grace and Trip are *self-absorbed*, allowing them to occasionally believably ignore unrecognized or unhandleable player actions. Creating a loose, sparsely plotted story afforded greater local agency, but provided fewer opportunities for global agency. However, the richness of content variation, and the (at least) moderate degree of global agency achieved, does encourage replay.

The huge domain of the drama, a marriage falling apart, arguably hurt the success of the overall experience, in that it overly raised players' expectations of the characters' intelligence, psychological complexity, and language competence. As expected, the system cannot understand, nor has authored reactions for, many reasonable player utterances. The large domain often requires mapping millions of potential surface texts to just a few discourse acts, which can feel muddy or overly coarse to the player. Also, continuous real-time interaction, versus discrete (turn-taking) and/or non–real-time interaction, added a great deal of additional complexity and authoring burden.

6. Conclusion

In this chapter, we have argued that procedural authorship is required to take full advantage of the representational power of the computer as an expressive medium. Procedurality is an underlying support for all modes of digital authorship; while procedural literacy is not required to create digital work, new media practitioners without procedural literacy are confined to producing those interactive works that happen to be possible to produce within existing authoring tools. We made a case for the importance of procedural authorship, describing the design goals of a case study, the interactive drama *Façade*, and how these goals could only be met through a highly procedural approach to interactive narrative. Based on our experience both architecting and authoring *Façade*, we have found that procedural authorship is essential for enabling yet-to-be-realized genres of interactive art and entertainment.

References: Literature

Albee, Edward (1962). *Who's Afraid of Virginia Woolf?* New York: Signet.

Bates, Joseph (1992). "Virtual Reality, Art, and Entertainment." *Presence: The Journal of Teleoperators and Virtual Environments* 1 (1992): 133–138.

Berne, Eric (1964). *Games People Play*. New York: Grove Press.

Crawford, Chris (1987). "Process Intensity." *The Journal of Computer Game Development* 2 (1987). <http://www.erasmatazz.com/library/JCGD_Volume_1/Process_Intensity.html>.

Crawford, Chris (1989). "Indirection." *The Journal of Computer Game Design* 3 (1989). <http://www.erasmatazz.com/library/JCGD_Volume_3/Indirection.html>.

Laurel, Brenda (1991). *Computers as Theatre*. Reading, MA: Addison-Wesley.

Loyall, Bryan (1997). *Believable Agents*. Ph.D. Thesis. Tech report CMU-CS-97-123. Carnegie Mellon University.

Mateas, Michael (2005). "Fever-Addled Impressions of GDC." *Grand Text Auto*. <http://grandtextauto.gatech.edu/2005/03/23/fever-addled-impressions-of-gdc>.

Mateas, Michael, and Andrew Stern (2000). "Towards Integrating Plot and Character for Interactive Drama." *Working Notes of the Social Intelligent Agents: The Human in the Loop Symposium*. AAAI Fall Symposium Series. Menlo Park, CA: AAAI Press.

Mateas, Michael, and Andrew Stern (2003a). "*Façade*: An Experiment in Building a Fully-Realized Interactive Drama." *Game Developers Conference* (*GDC*) 2003. San Jose, CA, USA.

Mateas, Michael, and Andrew Stern (2003b). "Integrating Plot, Character and Natural Language Processing in the Interactive Drama *Façade*." *Proceedings of the 1st International Conference on Technologies for Interactive Digital Storytelling and Entertainment* (*TIDSE*) *2003*. Darmstadt, Germany.

Mateas, Michael, and Andrew Stern (2004a). "A Behavior Language: Joint Action and Behavioral Idioms." In *Life-like Characters: Tools, Affective Functions and Applications*, edited by Helmut Predinger and Mitsuru Ishiuka. Berlin: Springer.

Mateas, Michael, and Andrew Stern (2004b). "Natural Language Understanding in *Façade*: Surface Text Processing." *Proceedings of Technologies for Interactive Digital Storytelling and Entertainment* (*TIDSE*) *2004*. Darmstadt, Germany.

McCorduck, Pamela (1991). *Aaron's Code: Meta-art, Artificial Intelligence, and the Work of Harold Cohen*. New York: W. H. Freeman and Co.

McKee, Robert (1997). *Story: Substance, Structure, Style, and the Principles of Screenwriting*. New York: HarperCollins.

Montfort, Nick (2005). "Finally, the Curtain Opens on *Façade*." *Grand Text Auto*. <http://grandtextauto.gatech.edu/2005/07/05/facade-is-released>.

Murray, Janet (1998). *Hamlet on the Holodeck*. Cambridge, MA: MIT Press.

Taylor, Alice (2005). "Burn the House Down." *Wonderland*. <http://crystaltips.typepad.com/wonderland/2005/03/burn_the_house_.html>.

Wikipedia (2005). "Demoscene." <http://en.wikipedia.org/wiki/Demoscene>.

Reference: Game

Façade, a One-Act Interactive Drama. Michael Mateas and Andrew Stern; Procedural Arts. 2005. <http://www.interactivestory.net>.

On *The Breakup Conversation*
Robert Zubek

The Breakup Conversation is a satirical simulation of the conversation at the end of a romantic relationship. The player is expected to perform a breakup over instant messenger, while the computer, playing the role of the soon-to-be-ex, will attempt to guilt and emotionally manipulate the player to give in and fail to break up. The title is a Windows-executable program, available for download at <http://robert.zubek.net/software/breakup>.

The player begins the interaction by selecting some personal information for the simulated soon-to-be-ex, after which an instant messenger window opens. The interaction mimics standard IM chat—it happens in real time via typed natural English text and emoticons (see figures 31.1 and 31.2).

The system does not attempt strong semantic processing of the player's utterances. Rather, it works by categorizing the utterances as situation-sensitive "moves" in an interaction space, whose significance depends not just on the text of the utterance, but also on the current position in the space. This was a deliberate design choice—after all, in situations such as a breakup, the context becomes pregnant with meaning: whether you address or ignore the developing issues, how strongly and quickly you respond to accusations, whether and how you play along with blame and guilt maneuvers—these are the kinds of pragmatic effects that become particularly meaningful.

To manage the complexity of such a conversation, the interaction space is actually decomposed into a large collection of small protocols—some are responsible for general conversational skills, while others are directly relevant to the breakup situation. In particular, the engine includes knowledge of numerous "guilt games" that could take place during a breakup, and some ways of getting through them—for example, the "it's not you, it's me" ritual, the "why are you doing this to me" blame, the refusals to discuss issues, and other ways in which people panic, reason, plead, lay guilt, and so on. These rituals are

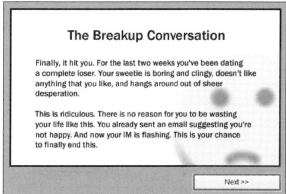

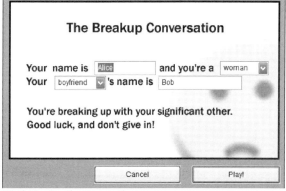

31.1) Starting the *Conversation*

treated informally, and meant to be exaggerated and entertaining, rather than psychologically felicitous—they were inspired by sitcoms, personal anecdotes, and popular self-help books on relationships.

Internally, the different components of the interaction are represented explicitly as small hidden Markov models, which

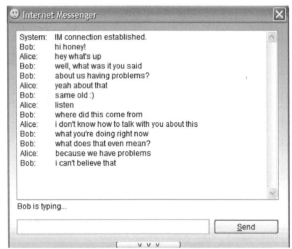

```
Internet Messenger                                    ☒
┌──────────────────────────────────────────────┐
│ System:   IM connection established.          ▲ │
│ Bob:      hi honey!                             │
│ Alice:    hey what's up                         │
│ Bob:      well, what was it you said            │
│ Bob:      about us having problems?             │
│ Alice:    yeah about that                       │
│ Bob:      same old :)                           │
│ Alice:    listen                                │
│ Bob:      where did this come from              │
│ Alice:    i don't know how to talk with you about this │
│ Bob:      what you're doing right now           │
│ Bob:      what does that even mean?             │
│ Alice:    because we have problems              │
│ Bob:      i can't believe that                  │
│                                                 │
│                                               ▼ │
└──────────────────────────────────────────────┘
 Bob is typing...

┌──────────────────────────────────┐  ┌────────┐
│                                  │  │  Send  │
└──────────────────────────────────┘  └────────┘
         [  ∨ ∨ ∨  ]
```

31.2) The IM window, where the conversation takes place.

are probabilistic finite-state representations, particularly good at estimating the state of the model from noisy and uncertain evidence information. The models are arranged in a tree-like control hierarchy, from general long-term models to specialized handlers: top-level elements influence the long-term development of the situation by enabling specialized situation controllers based on how the situation is going; those mid-level elements then drive the situation locally, by enabling and manipulating a number of specialized handlers, such as those responsible for very particular guilt-laying mini-games. Figure 31.3 presents a detail of the hierarchy.

In addition to the breakup-specific elements, the system also contains a number of more general models, responsible

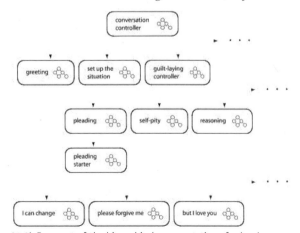

31.3) Fragment of the hierarchical representation of a breakup.

Breakup Conversation excerpt.
(Computer's utterances in **boldface**.)

Alice: hey there
Bob: how are you
Alice: not bad :)
Alice: and you?
Bob: what was that you said
Bob: that we should talk about the relationship?
Alice: yeah about that
Bob: :P
Alice: look
Bob: what did i do
Bob: look why wouldn't you just talk to me
Alice: no it's not you
Bob: oh really? then what?
Bob: what does that even mean?
Alice: it's me
Bob: i know it's me
Bob: why wouldn't you just talk to me about what's going on
Alice: i was thinking about us
Bob: it's because i stay at home
Bob: you loathe that i'm lazy
Bob: don't you
Alice: no i don't loathe you
Bob: it's not because of that?
Bob: how can you do this to me
Bob: then what is it?
Alice: i don't know
Bob: :(
Bob: i suppose i'm a naive loser
Alice: i'm feeling, well, like i'm suffocating
Bob: you're just messing with me
Alice: i need space
Bob: i can't believe that
. . .
Bob: you can't seriously be doing this
Bob: don't you love me?
Alice: i thought i did
Bob: but no longer?
Alice: i don't know
Bob: well then
Bob: do you hate me
Alice: you do things
Bob: do you despise me
Bob: did you really make up your mind?

for broader conversational competence; these include handlers for general greetings and pleasantries, dealing with requests, opinions, and especially insults (since players seem to really enjoy insulting computer agents). Figure 31.4 lists the different elements of the system—in the first column, general conversational elements shared among systems, in the second, elements specific to the *Breakup Conversation*, and in the third, elements used in *Xenos the Innkeeper*, a character for a fantasy game, also built using this technology.

Even though arranged in a control hierarchy, all of the active elements run in parallel, at the same time, monitoring the conversation for some evidence of whether they should try to do something about the situation. In effect, each element tries to process every utterance, and they all get a chance at updating themselves and producing a response.

First, the utterance is roughly preprocessed, translated into a probability distribution over the space of communicative acts (e.g., what is the probability that the utterance was a request, an insult, a compliment, etc.), and quick pattern matching is performed to pull out likely role bindings for the acts.

Second, the evidence distribution is passed to each of the active elements, which update themselves based on the evidence distribution, model parameters, and last known state probabilities. Each model's state is calculated by matching what was observed against what was expected given the situation, for every state in every model; this separation of observation and expectation simplified the task of knowledge representation, and improved the system's robustness.

Finally, all elements can propose responses, out of which one is selected and sent to the output production layer.

The resulting system is, at heart, a collection of numerous finite-state models, arranged in a control hierarchy but running in parallel. Each of them is only competent at a small fragment of the

interaction, but their aggregate and overlapping engagement results in a fluid overall interaction. The system works without being able to understand much language—but it is able to recognize the kinds of speech acts and utterance types it cares about, and match them against its multi-faceted representation of the evolving situation.

Shared Spaces	Breakup Specific	Xenos Specific
Low level monitors: Conversation timer Silence monitor Monologue monitor	**Breakup intro:** Allude to breakup Giving in monitor Guilting coordinator	**Quests:** Quest monitor Perform quest injection Deal with agreement Deal with rejection Rush the player
Ambient movement: Fidget machine Turn enforcement Ambient emote Stock response Turn monitor Topic monitor	**Guilting: Self-pity** Self-criticize Reject compliment "You must hate me" "Why are you mean" "Will you help me"	**Special routines:** Job request What question Where question Payment question Evaluate object Barter for object
Insult management: Direct insult Indirect insult Insult accumulation	**Guilting: Indignation** "I thought you loved me" "I thought you cared" "I don't deserve this" "How can you do this"	
General routines: Topic recognized but not the form Question recognized but not topic Question about object Question about health Request general Request item Disagreement Player evaluation Agent evaluation Condemnation monitor	**Guilting: Pleading** Beg for second chance Promise change "But I love you" **Guilting: Reasoning** Guess at reason Demand reason Evaluate reason Treat as excuse Deny reason	
Conversation structure: Greeting Intro conversation Outro conversation	**Panicking:** Silence Impatience monitor Resignation monitor Rejection monitor Start panic	

31.4) List of all the different mini-interactions implemented in *The Breakup Conversation*, and its sibling project, *Xenos the Innkeeper*.

211

On The Breakup Conversation

References

Zubek, Robert. (2004). "Character Participation in Social Interaction." Challenges in Game AI Workshop, AAAI-04. (AAAI Technical Report WS-04-04.)

Zubek, Robert. (2005). "Hierarchical Parallel Markov Models for Interactive Social Agents." Ph.D. Dissertation, Computer Science Department, Northwestern University.

Robert Zubek

On *The Archer's Flight*
Mark Keavney

For most of my life, role-playing games have been my passion. Nothing I knew had the same mix of spontaneity, mythic storytelling, and especially creative collaboration—the sense that together my fellow players and I were creating a story that no one of us could have created on his own. For over twenty years, I played and ran role-playing games, attended game conventions, and even wrote gaming magazine articles and game supplements.

The more I played, the more sophisticated my games became, with the emphasis shifting from killing monsters and gathering treasure to developing characters and telling a story. My last game, for example, was a quest for spiritual truth that explored themes of self-discovery, religion, and the nature of death.

But the more ambitious my games grew, the more frustrated I became with the form. For me, creating and playing these games was an art, but due to the nature of the form, that art could only be shared with a few people.

In 2002, I launched the web site City of IF <http://www.cityofif.com> to bring these kinds of interactive stories to a larger audience. I started by publishing the first chapter of a story called *The Archer's Flight*.

It described the character of Deica, a human girl raised in a village of centaurs, who grew up an outcast because of her strange form.

I told this story using a form of interactive storytelling that I now call "storygaming." The story had seventeen chapters, each published about two weeks apart. Each chapter ended in a "decision point" for Deica, and each decision was made collectively by the readers (i.e., players) rather than by me. Neither the players nor I owned the story completely: the players chose Deica's actions without knowing how they'd turn out, and I wrote how they turned out without choosing the last action (or knowing the next).

The way that the players made decisions was structured: first there was a "posting phase" in which they posted and discussed their suggestions on a web forum, and then a "voting phase" in which they voted on the most common

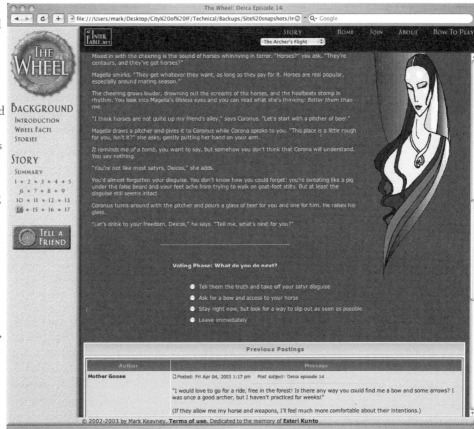

32.1) In each chapter's voting phase, the players chose Deica's action from the options previously suggested.

suggestions. The winning suggestion became the basis of the next chapter.

This experiment gave me "nothing I had asked for, and everything I had hoped for," as the saying goes. My first lesson was at the end of chapter three.

The first few chapters of *The Archer's Flight* had covered Deica's teenage years as she secretly learned archery from her grandfather, up to a point when a dragon threatened her village. In chapter three, the villagers beseeched a local hero for help; Deica's grandfather and the other village elders were meeting with him the next day.

I was looking forward to the suggestions for this chapter, because the situation offered a good dramatic conflict and a rich set of options. Deica was proficient with the bow and could help against the dragon, but the centaurs wouldn't normally let a girl (much less a "deformed" one) take part in a battle like this. Would she plead with her grandfather to stand up for her? Crash the meeting and show the centaurs how well she could shoot? Secretly tag along when they went hunting the dragon? I had already thought about some different ways the centaurs might react and was planning ahead to the finale, when Deica would join the battle against the dragon and (presumably) fire the decisive shot.

Some of the players did make the kind of suggestions I'd expected ("If I can show them what I can do, they'll let me come," posted one). But then one suggested that Deica disguise herself as a boy and run off to the big city. In the "voting phase," the players voted for this option.

The choice was completely appropriate: Deica was adventurous, she felt alienated from the village, and due to a childhood experience, she was afraid of dragons. But it was also completely unexpected. Suddenly I had to write the next chapter about Deica's travels to the big city, and I had no idea what the big city was like, what she might do there, or how I could possibly tie this back to the huge loose end of the dragon attacking her village. All my plans for the story were going awry.

And I loved it—because this was what I'd experienced in role-playing games: that no one knew where the story was going, but we were going there together. I happily cast aside my plans and started making new ones.

So, chapter four became the beginning of Deica's travels, and the story continued. On her way to the big city Deica got a job with a minotaur merchant; when they arrived she was almost lynched because of her strange two-legged body, and eventually she was "adopted" by a double-bodied man who called her a legendary "Single" and tried to make her the figurehead ruler of his country. At each point, the players chose Deica's action (e.g., the decision point in chapter ten was whether to travel with the minotaur merchant or the double-bodied man), and I revised the plot to fit those decisions. Finally, Deica escaped the double-bodied people; on her own with a horse and money for the first time, she resolved to return to her village to solve the mystery of her form. Here, I put the story on hiatus.

This way of telling stories has a family resemblance to other forms of interactive storytelling, such as shared-author stories or role-playing games. But it also has other interesting features that became apparent as *The Archer's Flight* progressed:

Open-ended interactivity. Players could (and did) take the story beyond what the author had imagined. I had set out to write a fairly straightforward fantasy about a battle with a dragon, and the players' choices turned it into a (more interesting, I think) fantastic journey.

Flexibility. The story had a sliding scale of interactivity—for any chapter, a player could just read the story, could vote without making suggestions, or could post one or multiple suggestions. Players used this flexibility often: for example, for most of the chapters there were five to ten players posting, but often it was not the same ones each chapter. Also, there were typically three to four times as many votes as posts, and many times more page views than votes (see figure 32.1).

Social interaction. The format provided rich soil for social interaction: players could agree or disagree with each other, build on suggestions, or try to sway votes. For reasons beyond the scope of this space to discuss, there wasn't as much social interaction in *The Archer's Flight* as in other storygames later told on the same web site, but there was some back-and-forth discussion of options.

A strong narrative. The Archer's Flight was guided from beginning to end by one author, and the ultimate result was a coherent story told in a single voice. That story was published as a novella in May 2005.

Through storygames like *The Archer's Flight,* storygaming has proved compelling and its popularity has grown among both gamers and writers. The City of IF web site now has over 1,000 visitors every day playing dozens of storygames in fantasy, science fiction, mystery, humor, and other genres.

Reference

Keavney, Mark (2005). *The Archer's Flight,* City of IF (May 2005). <http://www.cityofif.com>.

III. Real Worlds

Real Worlds

In the previous sections, we have focused on media playable around the tabletop and at the computer or game console. The contributors to these sections have focused on role-playing and story within these media— and have generally done so with a tacit assumption that the settings for these characters and stories are evanescent, fictional worlds known only to the players and existing only for the time of play. Rebecca Borgstrom, in fact, makes a point of the fact that even those RPG groups that play in worlds described by highly detailed published material are still playing in many different worlds, albeit ones constrained by their adherence to those data points specified within the publications.

But this is not always the case. Wizards of the Coast's Roleplaying Gamers Association (RPGA)<http://www.wizards.com/default.asp?x=rpga/welcome>, for example, attempts to unify tabletop game worlds across multiple player groups. They do this by creating particular "campaign worlds" for individual game systems (often *Dungeons & Dragons*) and long-term story arcs within those worlds.[1] The association sponsors gaming events and provides individual player groups with role-playing scenarios. Member groups are expected to play the scenarios in a certain timeframe and report back the results to the RPGA. The events that occur most commonly among the player groups affect the campaign world and are reflected in the next group of scenarios released by the RPGA.

So, for example, if a majority of the participating player groups succeed in defeating a particular villain, that villain's defeat becomes canonical, and he will not play a part in future RPGA adventures. If, however, most of the player group met defeat at the hands of the enemy, the villain will still be active in the campaign world in future adventures. This sort of distributed network of reality-builders could be seen as roughly analogous (or a rough analog) to Massively Multiplayer Online (MMO) RPGs such as *City of Heroes* or *World of Warcraft*.

Several of the contributors in this section have much to say about persistent virtual MMO worlds, but they are not the only sorts of worlds under discussion here.[2] In fact, many of *Second Person*'s contributors themselves move between quite a few different worlds, working innovatively in both computer and non-computer playable media.

D. Fox Harrell's GRIOT performances occur both in the real world and via the innovative digital procedure he describes in his essay. Helen Thorington was trained in radio drama; Talan Memmott and Lev Manovich were both trained in the visual arts; Kevin Wilson was well-known in the IF community before moving into tabletop RPGs and, latterly, board games. John Tynes and Greg Costikyan began their careers by writing for tabletop RPGs but have now moved into designing for digital media.[3]

This diversity of genre, structure and aesthetic forms creates a veritable multiverse of worlds to discuss. Where to begin? Well, the contributors to this section have a tendency to focus on the areas where one world borders another: where gaming edges up against politics or performance, or pedagogy touches on play, or MMOs abut real life.

John Tynes, co-founder of Pagan Publishing, begins this section by making the case for separating games into "escapist" and "engagist" categories. This division is partly categorical and partly polemical; Tynes's games themselves have elements that bear directly on the real world, and that often refuse to be rationalized into a purely fictional structure. Engagist ideals form a heavy part of Tynes's work as a game designer, and many of the contributors to this section could also be said to conform to engagist principles.

Most directly, Sean Thorne has taken one of Tynes's

---

1. Many other types of "living" campaigns are run by individual player groups or by other companies. RPGA, because it is an organization owned and operated by WotC, is limited to WotC products.

2. Sometimes the borders between these worlds and our own can be quite fluid, as evidenced by virtual *EverQuest* items being sold on eBay, or Chinese sweatshops that do nothing but farm for *World of Warcraft* gold.

3. As has *Call of Cthulhu* designer Sandy Petersen, whose work is mentioned several times in this volume. After the CoC RPG, Petersen is probably most known for working on the original *Doom*.

own works, the tabletop RPG *Puppetland*,[4] and used it as a tool to teach his grade school students the basics of creative writing. Here we see a form of "engagism" at its most direct: a role-playing structure that can be used directly as a pedagogical device.

There is potential here for political engagement too, as Ian Bogost and Gonzalo Frasca show in their essay, and Kevin Whelan in his. In the first case, Bogost and Frasca demonstrate how a video game can become a method for explicit political activism—in this case, a tool to assist U.S. presidential candidate Howard Dean in his unsuccessful run for the 2004 Democratic nomination.

Whelan discusses tools for political activism that draw more on ideas of traditional theater. The role-playing here has one purpose: to prepare members of the activist organization ACORN to be better able to recruit new members and educate people about the issues of importance to ACORN.

The various correspondences between role-playing and storytelling structures discussed in this book and the possibilities afforded by the traditional theater are beyond the scope of our discussion in this introduction, but they are far from unimportant. Tim Uren contributes an essay that provides a brief overview of improvisational comedy structures, conceptualizing them as games whose rules are discovered over the course of performance, and also as stories that have already been written by a hypothetical playwright.

Joe Scrimshaw follows this with a short discussion of his play *Adventures in Mating*, which incorporates some of Uren's improvisational concepts into a structure drawn explicitly from the *Choose Your Own Adventure* books of the 1980s (and which might remind some readers of Kim Newman's novel *Life's Lottery*, discussed in Section I).

Nick Fortugno discusses a different form of theater, one that draws on the tradition of tabletop RPGs as well. *A Measure for Marriage*, the live-action role-playing game (LARP) he discusses here, has a very obvious, and very real, real-world consequence.

"Puppetmaster" Jane McGonigal describes her work (such as *I Love Bees*, under discussion here) as creating "power plays." These power plays, which incorporate many forms of traditional and new media into their performance, differ from traditional game structures in important ways; McGonigal even draws parallels with traditional theater, and ultimately she argues that they reveal dramatic interpretation as an emerging game mechanic.

The trans-media aspects of *I Love Bees*, especially the elements of location-specific Global Positioning System (GPS) content, are also present in *unexceptional.net*. Creator Robert Nideffer has also woven something like a traditional narrative into the work, while at the same time developing innovative game technologies. Teri Rueb, in her work *Itinerant*, has also brought narrative into the GPS-driven space of "locative media"—in fact, two narratives: Mary Shelley's *Frankenstein* and one of her own.

Performance and theater can exist in less physical venues as well. Adrienne Jenik and Desktop Theater combine elements of scripted and improvisational theater to perform original works such as *Santaman's Harvest* in virtual spaces such as the chat rooms of The Palace.

Torill Mortensen, Jill Walker, and Celia Pearce each discuss Massively Multiplayer Online (MMO) RPGs. Mortensen and Pearce address the concept of identity in MMOs in different ways: Mortensen by examining the ramifications of portraying fictional characters in a virtual world (and by extension, other forms of RPGs) and Pearce by describing how these fictional personae can come to form virtual communities in the online world. Walker's focus is narrower: on the specific network of quests in Blizzard's *World of Warcraft* and how these quests create narrative densities in areas of virtual space.

Finally, Adrianne Wortzel provides us with a description of her *Eliza Redux* project (itself self-consciously modeled after Joseph Weizenbaum's ELIZA and its "Doctor" script). Wortzel's artwork brings physical and virtual worlds together with an additional layer—streaming live video of a robot performing the role of a therapist to interacting audience members across the Web. As our social spaces become ever more varied, questions raised by Wortzel's work may prove increasingly pertinent.

4. Reprinted as an appendix to this volume.

Prismatic Play: Games as Windows on the Real World
John Tynes

Elves and orcs, spaceships and robots: any survey of well-known works of interactive storytelling reveals that most are set in worlds very different from the one we live in, worlds of visionary futurism or fantastical imagination. The imagery communicates the subject matter's dislocation from the real world. Likewise, they in no way attempt to address modern life or any themes other than, say, good vs. evil or underdog vs. oppressor. They exist in a void of meaning where recreation is king and the only goal is entertainment. This inevitably consigns such works to a metagenre: *escapism*. Escapism is a departure from the real world, an opportunity for an audience to let go of everyday anxieties in favor of an unreal experience. Escapism has its place. The human mind is a busy beast and flights of fancy are a welcome reprieve. Alien and inventive genre worlds are tremendously popular, as witness the *Final Fantasy* and *Myst* video games.

But while escapism has its joys, it also carries with it a connotation of irrelevancy. The trailblazing likes of *Dungeons & Dragons* or *Doom* may have been enjoyed by millions of people, but few assign to them even the feathery cultural weight of children's cartoons such as *Shrek*. Such escapist entertainment is commonly considered meaningless, or at best serves as a vehicle for bland homilies. Every medium whose signature works are escapist becomes perceived as irrelevant, immature, and meaningless. The prose novel, for example, reached a mass audience with the proliferation of the printing press, but educated aristocrats did not deign to read them; their modern descendants would likewise not consider playing *Grand Theft Auto*. It took more than two hundred years for the novel to be taken as seriously as, say, classical religious painting or poetry. Movies made a similar journey in just forty years, and rock music went from "Rock Around the Clock" to *Sgt. Pepper's Lonely Hearts Club Band* in

about fifteen. In all such cases, it was the combined work of innovative practitioners and influential critics that elevated each medium into the cultural mainstream.

Yet three decades into its life, interactive storytelling remains in an immature state. Video games and tabletop role-playing games are seen as childish wastes of time. The demographics of the audience and the experiences they demand are very diverse, but this reality has not penetrated the mainstream consciousness. The controversies over *Grand Theft Auto* illuminate this disconnect: games made for adults, and only for adults, are perceived as a menace to children because the cultural authorities do not understand who the audience has become.

For interactive storytelling to mature into a form that earns the same critical respect and mainstream acceptance as novels, movies, or rock and roll, it is vital for this form's content to evolve beyond escapism. I believe the next step in its development is already at hand but unrecognized and underutilized.

This step is the development of *engagist* works that embrace the modern world around us instead of rejecting it for a fantastic otherworld. An engagist work is one that uses the modern world or the recent historical past as its setting and that provides tools and opportunities for participants to explore and experiment in that setting in ways that real life prohibits or discourages. It may still have genre conventions such as ghosts, monsters, or mad science, but it uses them deliberately and symbolically within a familiar real-life context.

The differences between escapism and engagism are profound. They are fundamentally driven by the intent of the creator and richly manifested in the experience of the audience. But the simplest difference of them all is that escapism is a *state* and engagism is a *tool*.

As a state, escapism offers no change, no enlightenment, no redemption. It is a prisoner of form, a sitcom-game that puts its pieces in the same starting positions with every episode.

As a tool, engagism is an agent of change, capable of leading journeys through enlightenment, redemption, or any other genuine human experience. It uses form and transcends it, a restless exploration of life.

The tabletop game *Dungeons & Dragons* is the archetype of escapist interactive storytelling. Participants adopt personas in a fantasy world and enjoy rollicking adventures through a hodgepodge of myth and imagination. As published, the game is a vehicle for heroic storytelling and an engine for fictional accomplishment, as the personas "level up" to become more powerful in ways that have no relationship to the participants' own lives. They may take satisfaction from the experience, but any meaning they derive from it is only what they brought with them.

My own *Power Kill* is the deliberate antithesis. This engagist metagame posits that *Dungeons & Dragons* participants are living out their fantasies through real-world psychotic episodes in which they practice robbery and home invasion against ethnic and economic minorities—a violent incursion to a black ghetto is, to the participants, just another "dungeon crawl" in which orcs and their money are soon parted. They are asked to reconcile the differences between their *Dungeons & Dragons* character sheet of statistics and treasures with their *Power Kill* character sheet, a patient record from a mental ward for the dangerously insane. Once they are prepared to accept the latter and reject the former, they are released from the hospital and the metagame. *Power Kill* is intended as a Swiftian satire, an engagist attempt to take the escapism of *Dungeons & Dragons* and explore its connections to the real world of human behavior.

Admittedly this is an extreme illustration of the differences between escapism and engagism, as *Power Kill* is a didactic attempt to measure the distance between these two metagenres by placing itself and *Dungeons & Dragons* at opposite ends of a span. In more common practice engagism can entertain just as well as escapism. But engagism has three primary practical and conceptual advantages that provide sharp distinctions and make it a useful tool. These advantages are *narrative*, *educational*, and *revelatory*.

The Narrative Advantage

Participants in engagist media are intimately familiar with the modern world. Cultural, religious, linguistic, political, and technological concepts are already understood and available for use. This familiarity solves simple problems, such as explaining to the participant how personas travel from one town to another, and allows for much freer use of irony, symbology, metaphor, and other literary conventions that

depend on cultural comprehension. It's hard to make a pun in the Black Speech of Mordor.

Imagine an interactive story based on Tolkien's *The Lord of the Rings* books. The participants take the roles of hobbits traveling on a grand adventure. In a distant land, they encounter a group of strange people. Do they speak the same language? What language do hobbits speak, anyway? For that matter, what about this traveling thing: how far can a hobbit walk on foot in a day? How much sleep do hobbits need? Does a human need to eat more lembas bread than a hobbit, or is it a magical food that can sustain anyone with an equal amount of consumption?

These are pedestrian questions—literally, in some cases—but they illustrate the fundamental lack of familiarity that participants will have with a fantastical setting. In some works, these questions may be irrelevant. If travel in the work is abstracted, so that participants merely arrive in one interesting scenario after another with all intervening time bypassed, then the land speed of a hobbit is irrelevant. But take a further step back: what the heck is a hobbit? What is an orc? For a novice audience, there are a lot of questions to answer before the story can be fully understood. The opening exposition utilized in the film version of *The Fellowship of the Ring*, for example, offered a potted history of Sauron and the ring of power but did not try to explain the many fantasy concepts contained in the book. For audiences unaccustomed to the fantasy genre, it was not at all intuitive that dwarves live underground or that they have an ancient rivalry with elves.

The tabletop role-playing game setting known as Tékumel is an excellent example of this challenge. M. A. R. Barker, a former professor of linguistics and South Asian studies at the University of Minnesota, has been developing this fantasy world for three decades. Tékumel first saw print in his 1975 game *Empire of the Petal Throne* and has since appeared in several different game incarnations and many volumes of supplementary material, as well as novels. Tékumel exceeds even Tolkien's Middle-earth for obsessive documentation by its author, with Barker issuing treatises covering languages, histories of particular military units, guides to the various religions, and even the tactical use of magic on the field of battle. This summary from the game's

Web site illuminates its complexity:

> Tékumel is a world of tradition, elaborate
> bureaucracies and heavily codified social structures
> and customs. They have mighty, well-organized
> legions like those of the Romans. Their gods are like
> those of the Hindus, with a heavy dose of the blood-
> thirsty Aztec or Mayan deities. Their legal codes
> and sciences are much like those of the Arab
> philosophers of the Middle Ages; they are obsessed
> with personal and family honor much like the
> medieval Japanese. The societies presented with the
> game are very intricate and very old, with histories,
> traditions, and myths stretching back some twenty-
> five thousand years. (Gifford 1999)

In short, this is no *Shrek*. Participants in Tékumel stories must overcome a substantial barrier to entry, as the game mandates a high degree of cultural literacy for a culture that does not even exist and that has been documented in only piecemeal form across dozens of small-press publications— many of them out of print—for longer than many players have been alive. When the site's Frequently Asked Questions includes entries such as "What is Mitlanyál and where can I get it?" one wonders that anyone other than Professor Barker can even play the game. Its adherents are devoted but few, as the work's scattershot publishing history can attest.

At the opposite end of the comprehensibility scale lies *Millennium's End*. Created by Charles Ryan, this tabletop role-playing game took the technothriller novels of Tom Clancy as its inspiration and posited a modern setting of terrorists, espionage, covert military actions, private security forces, and international intrigue. While first published a decade before the 9/11 attacks, *Millennium's End* has remained timely and even prescient, as concepts such as "collateral damage," "covert operations," and "low-intensity conflict" are now household terminology instead of baroque jargon.

In *Millennium's End*, participants take the roles of private security contractors employed by a firm resembling the real-life African mercenary corporation Executive Outcomes. Story topics include corporate espionage, counterterrorism, kidnap resolution, executive security, and other hot-button concepts involving professionals with guns working in real-world danger zones. It's the sort of game where a storyline

can be readily improvised just by reading the newspapers.

Participants in the game already have the required cultural literacy. They have reasonable shared expectations for how well cell phones work in rural areas, how many bodies you can shove into the trunk of a car, and how to get a plane ticket to a foreign country. If a story is set in wartime Iraq, participants have at least some notion of how that setting looks and feels, courtesy of cable news networks or movies such as *Three Kings*.

The barrier to entry for *Millennium's End* is low, at least in terms of required comprehension. The need for supplemental material is lessened as well; no participants are demanding a sourcebook on the American criminal justice system or the restorative qualities of milkshakes.

Millennium's End, therefore, enjoys a substantial narrative advantage over the Tékumel games. It is more accessible, simpler to play, and easier to create new stories. Similar table-top role-playing games include some of the most popular: *Vampire: The Masquerade*, *Spycraft*, *Mutants and Masterminds*, and *Call of Cthulhu* all layer genre conventions on top of the familiar modern world and have much larger audiences than the alien and otherworldly Tékumel.

Such real-world games are not simply more accessible. They also reward familiarity with the modern world and improve that familiarity—which brings us to the second advantage enjoyed by engagist interactive storytelling, the educational advantage.

The Educational Advantage

Participants in engagist media acquire knowledge of the world around them. This is not the case in worlds consisting of dungeons and spaceships, and should be considered an interesting alternative "loot drop" to video game rewards such as magic swords and superspeed. By engaging with the real world through interactive storytelling, participants can travel to foreign countries or local but unfamiliar subcultures. They can experience historical or current events firsthand and conclude the work more knowledgeable than when they began.

A precursor to this form can be seen in the 1953 television series *You Are There*, in which recent and distant historical events were re-enacted by actors and explained by journalists. I believe the first interactive storytelling attempt at this educational approach was the 1971 computer game *Oregon Trail*, in which participants recreate nineteenth-century pioneer caravans traveling from Missouri to the West Coast. In both of these early examples, immersion is used to facilitate education.

This informative visualization of the past has manifested most recently in the form of *Kuma\War*, which updates the mandate of *You Are There* and demonstrates the ability this form has to richly present knowledge in an engagist manner.

Kuma\War is a subscription service that regularly delivers new computer game scenarios based on actual military conflicts. Single-player and online multiplayer play are supported in first-person or third-person perspective, as well established by escapist action games such as *Unreal* and *Max Payne*. Participants take the roles of soldiers in conflict, fighting enemies and achieving objectives. The scenarios released thus far have almost entirely been set in Afghanistan and Iraq, dramatizing the recent conflicts there, but historical scenarios have included the Korean War and, most surprisingly, U.S. Senator John Kerry's Vietnam swift boat action that earned him the Silver Star and became a major point of controversy during his presidential campaign.

With *Kuma\War*, participants can take the role of John Kerry and command his swift boat in a scenario recreated directly from the battlefield reports. Besides presenting this playable game scenario, *Kuma\War* offers written analysis of the battle and the controversy, as well as a ten-minute video interview with a swift boat veteran and a game designer. Links to media coverage and official commentary round out the presentation.

While most of *Kuma\War*'s offerings blur into an endless sandy horizon full of gun-toting jihadists, their up-to-the-minute approach is intriguing. When a lone Navy SEAL escaped from Asadabad, Afghanistan, in late June of 2005, in a conflict that left nineteen other soldiers dead, *Kuma\War* had a recreation on subscribers' hard drives within a month, complete with satellite images of the area and extensive notes and references. This attempt to publish on a journalistic schedule with educational goals helps distinguish *Kuma\War* from games such as the World War II titles *Call of Duty* and *Medal of Honor*. Those are popular games of

escapism, offering no commentary, no historical context, and no timeliness. They use historical events as a simple backdrop to pure entertainment and do not educate their audience. *Kuma\War*, by comparison, makes a real attempt to expand the participants' knowledge and immerse them in an authentic experience.

An even more immediate example of this approach appeared in Jonathan Turner's tabletop role-playing game scenario "When Angels Deserve to Die," which he first ran at the Convulsion game convention in July 2002. Turner had recently returned from a three-month stint in Kabul, Afghanistan, where he worked as a press officer for the British-led International Security Assistance Force. His scenario placed the participants in the locale he had just left, and the intensity and vividness of his depiction were remarkable. Turner brought with him the latest unclassified maps of Kabul and surrounding regions as published by the British military, with current safety and risk zones marked, as well as his rucksack, which supplied props for the experience. He notes:

> I wanted to get across to the players what it was like to be in that place at that time. I wanted to do what I always do, which is to make it more real for them. My goals in providing them with genuine props such as unclassified "mine maps," old Russian medals bought in a marketplace, all that stuff, was to let them get their hands on something cool that gave them a tangible connection to what their character was experiencing, something that they as players had never seen before, that they would remember afterwards. This even came down to smell—I had an Afghan shemagh [bandana] which still smelled like Afghanistan. . . . I used to pass it around the players and have them take a deep whiff of it. That conjured up an image of the marketplace in a way no photograph or map or verbal description ever could. (Turner 2005)

Still wired from the experience, Turner powerfully immersed the participants. We were there, on the ground in Kabul, navigating our personas through a treacherous setting of intrigue and risk. We attended a Buzkashi game, the traditional game of Afghanistan where riders on horseback struggle over the headless carcass of a goat to score points. There we interacted with U.S. intelligence operatives mingling in the crowd and escaped a bomb scare, then journeyed on truly treacherous roads into the countryside to negotiate assistance from a regional warlord. All along, Turner evoked the sights, sounds, and smells of occupied Afghanistan and the mix of chaos and optimism that followed the fall of the Taliban.

Genre elements were certainly present: the plot concerned a horrific supernatural manifestation that had to be defeated. For this, Turner drew on the Cthulhu Mythos created by 1930s pulp horror author H. P. Lovecraft, as expressed in the role-playing game book *Delta Green*. Yet even this fictional construct was subservient to the scenario's educational goals, as Turner notes:

> The [Cthulhu] Mythos is kind of the least of your problems. You're more likely to step on a mine or get rolled and robbed or shot in a feud between people in a market. Or more likely, die in a car accident. I think most players find great novelty in that approach, especially if I can put them coherently and convincingly in a place that is real but still feels alien and threatening to them. (Turner 2005)

The educational approach to interactive storytelling seen in *Kuma\War* and in "Angels" engages the participants in exciting new ways not seen in escapist works. Watching television news reports from Kabul, I could shake my head sadly at the misery and horror. In Turner's masterful game, I lived it vividly, my pulse racing; in my mind, I saw an Afghanistan I'd never seen on television: the Afghanistan Turner knew. The knowledge acquired in this engagist way can have a lasting impact on the participants' lives and thoughts; by definition, escapism does not enjoy this advantage at all.

As interactive storytelling has evolved, its sophistication has evolved as well. When we move from explaining and illustrating the modern world to interpreting and critiquing it, we realize the third advantage of engagism: the revelatory advantage.

The Revelatory Advantage

Participants in engagist media can make choices that are denied to them in the real world due to finances, physical limits, laws, or personal reticence. They can

experiment by adopting personas different from themselves, ones that they perhaps have coveted or even feared in life. They can use the engagist experience as a Skinner box, exploring not just alternative behaviors but testing the consequences both within the narrative and in themselves. Engagist works can reveal insights and interpretations beyond simple facts.

The role-playing practiced in therapy is a narrow example of this advantage. Patients are asked to act out situations they find troubling or intimidating in real life, so they can learn to respond to them appropriately and add those responses to their repertoire for the next time they face such a situation. A patient who cowers before anger may learn useful responses he can offer the next time a family member loses her temper, and the exercise of role-playing turns an abstract lesson into a (simulated) life experience.

Working with a broader canvas than that of therapy, engagist works use the revelatory advantage to give participants unusual experiences. These experiences might be difficult to explore in the real world, such as living the life of a politician or spy. They can even be impossible, positing situations that defy reality. But even with such genre elements, they remain a tool for participants to explore, learn, and grow.

The creators of *Waco Resurrection* characterize it as a "subjective documentary." Participants don a helmet sculpted to resemble a polygonal model of the head of Branch Davidian messiah David Koresh and then use a mouse and keyboard as well as voice recognition to control a Koresh video game persona during the 1993 showdown with the federal government. This Koresh is imagined as a supernatural reincarnation with mystical powers, as per one of his prophecies.

Each player enters the network as a Koresh and must defend the Branch Davidian compound against internal intrigue, skeptical civilians, rival Koresh, and the inexorable advance of government agents. Ensnared in the custom "Koresh skin," players are bombarded with a soundstream of government "psy-ops," FBI negotiators, the voice of God, and the persistent clamor of battle. Players voice messianic texts drawn from the Book of

Revelation, wield a variety of weapons from the Mount Carmel cache, and influence the behavior of both followers and opponents by radiating a charismatic aura (C-Level 2003).

The goal of *Waco Resurrection* is right on its face: to put participants into the head of David Koresh and reveal his vision of a messianic apocalypse. The nature of the work is distinct from *Kuma\War* in that it transcends educational accuracy by giving the Koresh persona supernatural powers that serve as metaphoric tools to explore an historical event. Fantasy is thereby yoked to critique in the service of a larger truth: that the tragedy at Waco was not simply an armed conflict but a nexus of religious, social, and legal issues complicated by one man's insanity. This exploration of a truth larger than simple facts is the hallmark of the revelatory advantage.

Breaking the Ice has an entirely different goal and approach, yet it also embodies revelatory engagist principles. This tabletop storytelling game depicts the first three dates of two characters as a romantic-comedy plot. Two participants create the characters by switching something about themselves, such as their gender or their marital status, and then verbally play out their first dates using a game system that introduces conflicts, mishaps, and opportunities to grow closer. There is no Gamemaster, and it's up to the participants to create the experience they want.

The game is, of course, set in the modern world and relies on comprehension of western dating customs; setting it in a sci-fi future or a medieval fantasy world would derail its goal. *Breaking the Ice* gives participants an opportunity to explore the early stages of romance without real-life consequences. It could increase confidence for those nervous about dating, spark ideas for actual dating activities, or prompt discussion between the participants about their own lives and romantic histories. While the tone is light and entertaining, at every stage the game encourages the participants to engage with reality, not escape from it.

The use of genre conventions as revelatory metaphoric tools is a primary feature of *Unknown Armies*, a work that tries directly to apply engagist principles. This tabletop role-

playing game is set in a modern America of trailer parks and shopping malls but weaves into it a supernatural milieu known as the Occult Underground. Participants take the roles of crackpots, visionaries, mystics, and schemers in a clandestine struggle to acquire magical knowledge and power in order to change the world in whatever way best fits their personal beliefs.

The setting of *Unknown Armies* posits that people who embody cultural or mythic archetypes ascend into a higher reality and serve as demigods, granting magical powers to people who abide by the traits and taboos of those archetypes. Their goal is a cosmic endgame in which the final archetypes ascend and jointly create the next reality, rebooting the cosmos into the form unconsciously demanded by the aggregate desires and behaviors of humanity. A warlike cycle might produce more violent archetypes, leading to an even more perilous incarnation of reality—it is existence as if determined by a truly representational government. The modern world we know, therefore, is the product of human archetypes from the previous version, and it is this world that the game is concerned with.

These archetypes go well beyond the formative ones of Jung and express modern ideas. Thus, we have the Demagogue, who can discern and alter the belief systems of individuals or entire societies; the Flying Woman, embodiment of unconstrained femininity and freedom of choice in the post-feminist West; the MVP, the star athlete whose power comes from the fervency of his fans and who is supernaturally incapable of letting down his team; and many more.

Participants can choose to "walk the path" of one of these archetypes. They gain in power by faithfully mimicking the archetype's behavior and lose power when they violate one of the archetype's taboos. If they gain enough power, they can eventually challenge the ascended archetype and take its place, bringing their own new interpretation of the archetype into the cosmic realm. For example, the Messenger archetype seeks to banish ignorance and spread true knowledge. Its most powerful adherent in the setting is a man who attempts to replace the archetype with his interpretation, the Heisenberg Messenger: delivering uncertainty and spin instead of truth, changing events rather than reporting them.

Unknown Armies explores other forms of symbolic magic as well. Adepts are people who gain magical power by pursuing personal obsessions. They are essentially schizophrenics who decide that they know what *really* matters, and the force of their will bends reality to conform to their delusion. Examples in the game include the Boozehound, who uses the power trip of alcohol consumption to fuel his destructive spells. The Fleshworker is obsessed with body image and body manipulation, moving from "cutting" behaviors to actually reshaping her flesh and that of others with supernatural force. The Vidiot turns watching television into a ritual act, using its conventions to manipulate daily life; for example, he can make someone remain completely calm in a stressful life situation by magically convincing the person that he's merely experiencing a rerun.

The game's supernatural elements are pervasive, but in every case they are based directly on modern life and modern culture. *Unknown Armies* is a Swiss army knife of metaphoric tools, allowing participants to deeply immerse themselves in symbolic constructs and explore archetypes and behaviors that exist in the real world. Participants can heighten their awareness of positive and negative traits in themselves, their friends and family, and their society, and adopt a wide variety of personas to experience these traits firsthand. This is the heart of the engagist ideal: interactive storytelling that is both entertaining and seriously thought-provoking.

Ongoing participants in the game frequently report the real-life effect of these metaphoric tools. Online discussions between participants often critique the daily news cycle by viewing the people and events through the lenses provided by the game. When American tourist Natalie Holloway disappeared while vacationing in Aruba during the summer of 2005, obsessive and out-of-proportion media coverage of her case generated substantial critique in the press. *Unknown Armies* participants analyzed this coverage in terms of the Messenger/Heisenberg Messenger rivalry, and proposed that a new archetype was taking shape: the Oppenheimer Messenger, in which reporting the facts actually destroys the facts.

Maybe the first of this new breed was Geraldo Rivera, who made up a story about being under fire, gave away troop movements while live and on camera, and pledged not to leave Afghanistan until Osama Bin Laden was dead, dead,

dead, and yet he enjoys a degree of credibility that's not inconsequential (Toner 2005).

Because of its engagist philosophy, *Unknown Armies* has worked itself into the mental tool sets of its participants and given them new ways to examine and critique the modern world. Any engagist work can do the same—and should.

Conclusion

We live in the real world, and our lives are full of real problems and real joys. When works of interactive storytelling can teach us how to solve those problems and discover those joys, while entertaining us just as novels, movies, and music do, these works become worthy of real cultural critique and join the great conversation of human thought. Such engagist works can utilize and expand our knowledge, immerse us in real ideas and cultures, and provide tools to explore behaviors and interpret events. Art, knowledge, performance, and imagination intersect therein and bestow profound gifts.

It has been thirty years since *Colossal Cave Adventure* introduced early computer gamers to its "maze of twisty little passages." We're still waiting for our *Sorrows of Young Werther,* our *Napoléon,* our *Sgt. Pepper's.* Endless regurgitations of dwarves and elves or action-packed recreations of Omaha Beach will not get us there. But genre is not the enemy; it is simply a tool we have clumsily wielded to middling effect. The real missing ingredient is intent, the authorial intent to create works that engage our world and lives. When future participants delve into that maze of twisty little passages. and find themselves at its heart, we'll know we're doing something right.

References: Literature

C-Level (2003). Description of *Waco Resurrection*. <http://waco.c-level.cc>.

Gifford, Peter (1999). "New to Tékumel?" <http://www.tekumel.com>.

Toner, Timothy (2005). E-mail correspondence on the Unknown Armies RPG Mailing List.

Turner, Jonathan (2005). E-mail correspondence with the author regarding "When Angels Deserve to Die."

References: Games

Breaking the Ice. Emily Care Boss; Black and Green Games. 2005.

Colossal Cave Adventure. William Crowther and Don Woods; DECUS. 1976.

Delta Green. Dennis Detwiller, Adam Scott Glancy, and John Tynes, Pagan Publishing. 1997.

Dungeons and & Dragons. Gary Gygax and Dave Arneson; Tactical Studies Rules. 1974.

Empire of the Petal Throne. M. A. R. Barker; Tactical Studies Rules. 1975.

Kuma\War. Kuma Reality Games. 2004.

Max Payne. Remedy Entertainment. 2001.

Millennium's End. Charles Ryan; Chameleon Eclectic Entertainment. 1993.

Oregon Trail. Paul Dillenberger, Bill Heinemann and Don Rawitsch; Carleton College. 1971.

Power Kill. John Tynes; Hogshead Publishing. 1999.

Unknown Armies. Greg Stolze and John Tynes; Atlas Games. 2002.

Unreal. Epic Games. 1998.

Waco Resurrection. Mark Allen, Peter Brinson, Brody Condon, Jessica Hutchins, Eddo Stern, and Michael Wilson; C-Level. 2003.

On John Tynes's
Puppetland
Sean Thorne

In the summer of 2002, I chanced upon a copy of John Tynes' *Puppetland*, a role-playing game set in a world of puppets gone wrong (a classic tale of tragedy, and good against evil, set in a world created by the Maker). The Maker is the only human in Puppetland and was slain by the puppet Punch, who sought control of all of Puppetland by usurping the role of Puppetmaker. Judy, the main character in Puppetland's rebellion against the evil Punch, escaped to a secret valley, hidden from Punch and his evil minions, and had started a new town called Respite, from which she can try to restore goodness to the puppets' world with the help of a few fellow puppets who managed to escape with her.

In the past few years, my writing curriculum has made room to include more nonfiction, such as book reviews or small articles on a student interest. Most free-thought fictional writing produced by my eleven-year-old students took two forms, based strictly along gender lines (boys wrote about how aliens attacked the school/camp/home and they saved the day; girls wrote about an argument with a friend at school/camp/home and how they saved the day). Missing were plot, character development, and engagement with the reader. I needed an effective vehicle to teach and assess creative writing. Perhaps, I thought, this *Puppetland* would give me some new ideas to incorporate role-playing into the writing curriculum. Four years later, *Puppetland* has become the major writing project that ends the year.

During the last two months of the school year, each student makes one of four puppet types: shadow puppets, finger puppets, hand puppets, or marionette puppets. Each student plays a series of missions in the role of his or her puppet, in the company of five fellow puppeteers. Each mission provides the material for the student to write a story (from the perspective of the puppet). I divided the puppets as I thought Judy, a kind but firm leader, might: a mix of different puppet types for each group. Therefore, each group had shadow puppets for sneaking under doors, finger puppets for stealth, hand puppets as jacks-

> **The Play**
>
> To prepare the classroom for the game we arrange six chairs in a semicircle, one for each student. Everyone else is an audience to the "play," so to speak, and does not offer advice or encouragement; of course, they can laugh and whisper amongst themselves, and even write their own *Puppetland* adventures at this time. Since many students have not had a theater experience, they learn in this way how to be silent observers in the drama.

of-all-trades, and marionettes for muscle power.

Every mission starts in Judy's kitchen over a plate of warm cookies and milk or hot cocoa. There is a real-time limit to the mission length: twenty minutes, during which all manner of adventures befall the student who play in the character of their puppet. At that time all puppets will fall asleep, no matter where they happen to be, and all awaken later, safe in Respite.

After each mission is played, the students have until the end of the week to write a short adventure story. Reading the adventures aloud on Friday has turned out to be a festival of storytelling. Since each child has a different take on the same adventure, the audience is very attentive and discussions emerge about how something is written. Since I choose class readings with authors who use colorful writing (such as Debi Gliori and Robert Louis Stevenson), my students always try to use simile, metaphor, and alliteration with strong verb use. Many of my most reluctant writers begin turning in multi-page stories filled with clever bits of writing without any prompting from me. Students take advantage of the opportunity to rewrite their stories over the weekend after the sharing.

Students develop an attachment to their characters/puppets. The loss of one student's infamous finger puppet, Green Sick Old Bill, created a tense afternoon while we wrestled with the question of what to do. He rejected the idea that he rebuild the puppet out of felt and marker again. Instead, he opted for a new character, deciding that Green Sick Old Bill just got lost in Puppetland, and his place in the party would be taken by his son, a new felt finger puppet named Son of Green Sick Old Bill.

Other students put their puppets to bed in shoeboxes. Some went home overnight. I saw a puppet left behind after class dismissal only three times. (Considering there have been over 2,400 opportunities for this to occur, I'm amazed; all types of other student paraphernalia are left behind on a daily basis: books, pencils, lunch boxes, and jackets.)

This attachment created a lot of tension in the stories, because there is a very real chance that puppets will perish while fighting the evil and twisted minions of Punch. This is an element that the students responded to with a reserved, but honest, glee. True, they don't want their puppets to perish; however, it creates a sense of uncertainty in the stories (or to the "game," if you will).

It is worth noting that, although puppets might be mangled, or perish in a horribly cartoon-like manner, they always wake up safe and sound in their puppet beds the next morning. However, those few students who did meet a puppet doom during play vividly recalled the incident after class with friends before colorfully recording the incident in their stories.

For example: "Captain B. White tried to ram into him (*an evil nutcracker*) but instead he ran right into the nutcracker's sword. 'Ha, Ha! Now I have a hand puppet shish-ka-bob!'

proclaimed the nutcracker" (34.1).

True, I did play the nutcracker and said something along those lines. However, this student was able to recall what was said, and used the word "proclaimed" to good effect in his story.

He goes on to employ some alliteration (introduced during our reading of Gliori's work): "When the nutcracker turned away to get some fire wood I slipped down the tree that me and my fellow puppets had quickly climbed following the painful puncture when puppet B. White perfectly was ka-bobbed, . . ."

This is a first draft and provided me with a chance to review grammatical errors with the student, and commend him on his use of colorful language.

In a later mission, when Judy commanded the puppets to storm a dark tower at the edge of the shadowy forest, our student describes a fellow puppet trying to dodge out of the way of a catapulted boulder: "The boulder was right on top of him and right before he was melishously

34.1.1) and 34.1.2) Excerpt from a student story developed through *Puppetland*.

230

Sean Thorne

murdered he daringly dove to save his life. But he cut it too close. His left arm was no more." Our student records a truly heroic act: "We rushed to his aid but before we could reach him he popped up. He went on, using all his will with every step"(34.2).

The idea that *Puppetland* is a game is one element in this exercise that worked in everyone's favor. Games are meant to be fun. It isn't hard to imagine children recalling their adventure and feeling excited about writing it down. Again, the element of uncertainty certainly plays a role in the fun element: what lurks behind the closed door, or in the shadows of the forest?

Also, the children are interacting with each other as well as with the characters in *Puppetland*. Importantly for my goal, they are interacting in their puppet personalities, becoming the puppet for a short time. And this is how the puppet play helps student writing: it aids students in creating stronger dialogue, more developed characters, and

At the second he turned around the boulder was right on top of him and right before he was meishously murded he daringly dove to save his life. But he cut it too close. His left arm, was no more. We rushed to his aid but before we could reach him he popped up, he

34.2) Excerpt from a student story developed through *Puppetland*.

adding suspense to the story when they see everything through the imaginative play of their puppet vision. A Puppetland morning is described as "Exactly the same as the one before, frosty dark. It looked like the sun wanted to rise, but it just couldn't" (34.3).

Every week I carry home new stories to read and correct the grammar. By the time we start *Puppetland*, I have introduced all the grammar I want them to learn. Therefore, the last two months are a review, a chance to put into practice what has been introduced during the long winter school months. Equally important, however, is that the play engages the students in writing. The dialogue between the students is phenomenal, and this carries over into the stories. Students add dialogue, actions, and insights that clearly didn't occur during the play, but add significantly to the story. For example, Green Sick Old Bill swims in his mug of hot cocoa, which he is served in Judy's house at the start of a mission. Spacey Blue-eyes is disgusted by the bad manners of a fellow puppet that makes a mess eating cookies. And finally, Xavier

I tried to trip the hunk of wood that killed my friend. Badly, he heard me and stomped on my tail. After he had me he ripped off my paper head and rolled me into a cigar. While the nutcracker was destracted with me Willy white hair and Bob the blob

34.1.3) Excerpt from a student story developed through *Puppetland*.

Moldybones has musings about the odd behavior of his fellow puppets that occurs repeatedly throughout his story.

Some of this may actually be occurring during the role-playing, and in each child's imagination. After becoming familiar with writing about himself or herself and each other's puppets, little creative twists and insights appear in the stories.

It is important to note that it takes time for the characters to develop. Perhaps in today's teaching climate we are rushing to cover as many topics as possible. The idea that more is better is not an unfair assessment of our culture. This is evident in schools when students are lugging home massive tomes, working on various testing skills required to compete in the standardized tests, and sometimes have a frantic after-school life as well, filled with dance, music, and sport lessons. *Puppetland* would not be effective as a one-shot deal. To have the students play for one afternoon, followed up by a writing session, would be ineffectual and faddish. My experiences with the two-month-long lessons have taught me that

Puppet LAND   Adventure #1
The search   B /A

Once again, Judy called us puppets over in the morning with a mission in mind. The morning was exactly the same as the one before, frosty, dark. It looked like the sun wanted to rise but it just couldn't. Judy seemed as calm and normal as always. She had sleepy eyes and a soft voice. She had informed us

34.3) Excerpt from a student story developed through *Puppetland*.

students gain immeasurably by being allowed to develop a rich sense of the puppet world and of each other's characters.

This in-depth assault may very well be attributable to the students finally coming to grips with the mechanics of grammar. However, it is taught via an avenue most engaging for human beings: play. Play is not just an afternoon running around; I mean it to serve a purpose.

As an aside, I would like to stress that this play must be purposeful for the child. Former students ask every year, "When are you starting *Puppetland*? Remember when . . . ?" Those in my class ask every Monday morning if I have a new adventure for that week. If there is a suspicion that I am not prepared, I have a minor rebellion on my hands. They care passionately for *Puppetland*. It shows in their writing.

Maxine Greene reminds us that it is impossible to see anyone else's point of view without imagination. In fact, she argues quite elegantly, in the first pages of *Releasing the Imagination*, that it is lack of imagination that is keeping our culture from reaching its potential. An eleven-year-old student engaged in meaningful play will transfer his or her fun to the writing process. And the writing process can be a meaningful, growing experience for the early adolescent (ten- to fifteen-year-old).

Play is a powerful impulse for students to engage in group activities, to grow, and socialize. However, a student must see success, particularly as part of a group effort to grow a positive sense of self. Finally, to understand each other a little better, they must be able to exercise understanding outside of themselves. Most importantly, developing such understanding must be an act freely engaged upon by the early adolescent. I believe that I saw my students reaching their writing potential in *Puppetland* because they were engaged with their imagination, and reaching deep within to see the world outside of their separate selves.

Reference: Literature

Greene, Maxine (1995). *Releasing the Imagination*. San Francisco: John Wiley & Sons.

Reference: Games

Puppetland. John Tynes; Hogshead Publishing. 1999.

Video Games Go to Washington: The Story behind *The Howard Dean for Iowa Game*

Ian Bogost and Gonzalo Frasca

On December 16, 2003, popular Web magazine *Slate* published an article by journalist and author Steven Johnson (2003). Reviewing simulation games that engage problems of social organization, Johnson posed a question: "The [2004] U.S. presidential campaign may be the first true election of the digital age, but it's still missing one key ingredient. Where is the video-game version of Campaign 2004?" Upon reading this article, we smiled at its perfect timing: at that very moment we were developing *The Howard Dean for Iowa Game*, the first official video game ever commissioned in the history of U.S. Presidential elections.

Former Vermont governor Howard Dean failed miserably in his bid to become the 2004 Democratic U.S. presidential candidate. Still, he was incredibly successful in changing the way political campaigns of all types are carried out. Dean supporters made extensive use of new media tools such as e-mail, Web sites, and blogs to foster support from the grassroots. Howard Dean was also the first candidate to use a video game as endorsed political speech.

The Dean game was launched during Christmas week 2003. Players were able to play it for free on the candidate's Web page. It was very successful in terms

of audience: it reached 100,000 plays in the month before the Iowa caucus, a very respectable number considering its novelty and the fact that it was launched during the holidays.

Designing the game was quite a challenge. Even though we both were experienced game developers, nobody had tried anything like this before. The Web was plagued with satirical amateur Flash games, but we faced many difficult questions: how do we tailor a video game to convey an endorsed political message? How do we craft it so the public does not dismiss it as trivial? How does it integrate with the rest of the campaign? This article reviews the design and production process behind *The Howard Dean for Iowa Game*. It also locates itself within the context of the games that followed it on both sides of the political fence.

Virtual Campaigning

The game was conceived in concert with strategists from the campaign, a process that took place just before the important primary season of the Presidential election.[1] After considering several possible designs (see sidebar: The Other Dean Game), the campaign commissioned a game about grassroots outreach, the core principle behind Dean's unique election strategy. The intention of the game was to teach current and potential constituents about the power of grassroots outreach. The campaign was not interested in speaking to their political opponents through the game; rather, they hoped to muster commitment from "fence-sitter supporters," those citizens who were sympathetic to the candidate but who had not yet consummated that sympathy with material support, in the form of contributions, local participation, or simply firm commitment to cast a Dean vote in their state primary. The game had two goals: first, to model and illustrate the logic of grassroots outreach and argue for its primacy as a populist political strategy. Second, to model the actual activities of grassroots outreach to help fence-sitters

1. For the benefit of our international readers, in the United States, a primary is a preliminary election in which voters with an affiliation to a particular party (Democrat or Republican) vote to nominate a candidate to run in the general election. Like the electoral college, primaries are often criticized for conflating local, regional, and national issues. In American elections, the first primaries are held in the small states of Iowa and New Hampshire, and media attention surrounding these early events often impacts the results of primaries in other states, held over a six-month period.

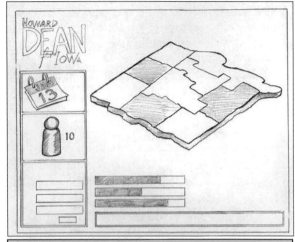

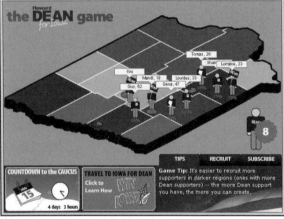

35.1) Sketch and final map.

that supporter worked nonstop, enacting "virtual outreach" to win over other virtual Iowans. In the main map screen, more effective virtual supporters worked more quickly in their region; a circular gauge showed their progress. When the gauge filled, a new supporter spawned, ready for the player to place for additional outreach.

To help illustrate the multiplicative effect of grassroots support, multiple supporters in the same region would work together, speeding up the outreach process. The virtual supporters worked together to generate even more support absent the player's direct action, simulating the campaign's argument that grassroots outreach would allow Dean to muster meaningful bottom-up support from individual voters rather than seeking top-down support. Game time counted down to the date of the Iowa Caucus, the first major event in the formal race for U.S. president. When caucus time came, the game ended and players saw how many virtual supporters they had recruited. The game hooked in to the rest of the Dean campaign's online initiatives, offering pathways to candidate information, channels for contribution, and additional resources.

Development Time as an Expressive Constraint

Like all media, video games are often structured by the constraints under which they can be created. Most frequently, we talk about the material constraints of games. Limited processing power in early consoles, arcade games, and modern mobile phones offer one such example. The visual acuity possible on Xbox 360 and Atari 2600 alike are materially constrained by the graphic output technologies available on those respective devices. Constrained authorship has served as both a limitation and a catalyst for creativity since antiquity. Early Greek and Latin poetry relies on strict meter both to structure lyric and to facilitate recollection for oratory performance. From the classicist ideal of Pound and Eliot to Georges Perec's lipgrammatic novel *La Disparition* (Perec 1969), which was composed without using the letter *e*, artists often impose constraints on themselves as part of a broader vision.

But less frequently do we acknowledge the role of time as a constraint in artistic expression. Certain surrealist

understand how they could contribute in a concrete way.

Since one of the game's primary goals was to teach current and potential constituents about the power of grassroots outreach, we needed to build a simulation model for supporter growth over time. To play the game, players placed virtual supporters on a map of Iowa, playing one of the three outreach minigames to set the effectiveness of their virtual supporters.

This effectiveness was based on the player's performance in each minigame; a better score meant a more efficient supporter. Because supporters could not be "reset" once placed, this encouraged players to perform their best each time they played a minigame. After having set the effectiveness of a supporter through one of the minigames, writing games were designed to be executed in a single sitting, and improvisational acting relies entirely on the immediacy of performance as its grounding aesthetic. But video games are usually not considered to be a medium of temporally constrained authorship. In the gaming news and even in the popular media, we hear more and more about the rising costs of video game production: teams of several hundred working for several years on the largest projects. Of course, not all developers have access to such bottomless resources, and independent games are usually produced on shoestring budgets and during off-hours.

Another example of the use of time as a constraint comes from "minigames" such as those in the several *WarioWare*[2] collections for the Nintendo Game Boy and DS.

These titles offer hundreds of extremely small games, each of which is played in a matter of seconds. In one game, the player times a button press to catch a falling straw; in another, the player must quickly locate a burglar by moving a spotlight around the screen. These games use time as a way to constrain and structure player action.

But another type of temporal structure constrains many games: the pace of the business and social context in which the game will be released and played. For better or worse, film-licensed games are subjected to this constraint more than most other commercial games, as film studios and publishers strive to leverage the enormous cross-marketing a film release provides to a game, and vice versa. As game developers who have spent a good portion of our respective careers creating games commissioned by professional organizations like consumer products companies, advertising agencies, broadcast networks, and film studios, we are accustomed to challenging—even irrational—development timeframes. Doing work-for-hire at the behest of organizations that neither understand nor care about the schedules required to produce a quality game presents design challenges that many artists, academics, and even high-level professional developers might not acknowledge.

The Howard Dean for Iowa Game was created under such a constraint. Conceived in late November 2003, the time between the first conversations with the campaign and the launch of the game was just four weeks. The actual

The Other Dean Game

We explored several design concepts with the Dean campaign before they settled on grassroots outreach as the core topic for a video game. Among the early designs was a game tentatively titled Call to Action. The game was intended to communicate a more mechanical, strategic message than did the Howard Dean for Iowa Game: Democrats need to focus their support, both votes and contributions, to Howard Dean in order to have a chance of combating Bush after the convention. Below is an excerpt from the initial game treatment for Call to Action. While this hypothetical game also does not deal explicitly with Dean's policy positions, it might have advanced a strategic argument more unique to the candidate. However, the game's design all but assumed that Dean's reign would continue further into the primary season, an assumption that we now know would have been most unfortunately wrong.

You set the outcomes of the 2004 Presidential Primary season to position the Democratic Party for victory in the general election.

A U.S. map displays the primary schedule. At its right, you see the Political Power Meter, which measures the political force of each party. The Bush camp leads by 5,000 units—you need to take action in your community to rally support for the Democrats! You choose a set of assumptions about the primary season that matches your own—you believe that the Democrats must get behind one candidate early on to succeed. You choose your state, Iowa, to get started.

Your map swings out of view and a set of Power Bars display the political force of each Democratic candidate in the state's primary or caucus, like a bar graph.

A clock begins to count down the number of days toward the primary—you have to act fast to rally support to the candidate of your choice. Beneath the power bars, you see members of the electorate, arranged in a labyrinth on the screen. You arrange and connect these voters, just like a real grassroots campaign would, to create a path for votes to get to your desired candidate (see Concept Art below). Experimenting, you create a path toward John Kerry.

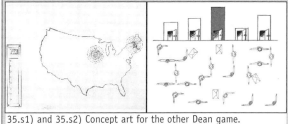

35.s1) and 35.s2) Concept art for the other Dean game.

---

2. We love *WarioWare* and consider it a major inspiration for the design in this and other games we have created.

development time was only three weeks—and worse, the three weeks just before Christmas.

We bring up the constraint of time neither to solicit sympathy nor to use it as an excuse for the failings of the game. Rather, we want to suggest that the development process of endorsed games—those intended to align with broader external marketing and communication initiatives—introduces time as a fundamental constraint on expression, more so even than the demands of easy access on lower-end computers and low-bandwidth connections. "Crunch time" in AAA console and PC development usually refers to the period of similarly insane working hours in advance of a major milestone such as the Electronic Entertainment Expo (E3) trade show, a required testing release, or indeed a final ship date. We are not arguing that these developers have no experience with such crunches. However, we want to point out that in the case of endorsed games built for persuasion, the entire creative vision is structured by temporal constraints, from beginning to end.

In the case of the Dean game, limited time created numerous opportunities and limitations. For one thing, the game was intended to support the campaign's broader focus on the Iowa Caucus, the first major event in the formal U.S. presidential election. The caucus takes place in the third week of January, and in order to be effective as a rhetorical tool, the game would have to be in the hands of potential supporters far enough in advance that, after playing, they could reflect on their experience and take action. The campaign hoped that new supporters would even consider traveling to Iowa to help campaign on the ground—a commitment that would require considerable planning and expense. Furthermore, the approaching Christmas and New Year's holidays would assuredly distract supporters from the task at hand. This context, essentially one of consumer marketing, provided the most significant temporal constraint on the development process. In short, if we did not release the game before Christmas, it would risk serving no purpose whatsoever.

The rollout schedule subsequently constrained the quantity and quality of representation possible in the game itself. First we decided to separate the game's two goals and develop them in parallel, as isolated components that would inform one another. This approach allowed us to muster two small,

Ian Bogost and Gonzalo Frasca

His Political Power bar rises and so does the Democratic Party's on the Political Power Meter . . . but only by a little. Glancing at the time left until the primary, you start to worry. How can you make a difference at this pace?

As you experiment with the other candidates, you notice something. Adding support to Howard Dean seems to add more power to the party—and faster too. You learn that a vote for Dean doesn't mean adding just one vote—it means adding a voter's entire network of influence to the election's most effective grassroots campaign. And you also learn that Dean supporters are more likely than other candidates to make multiple campaign contributions. You start guiding your state's voters toward Dean, and the Democratic position on the Political Power Meter edges higher, faster.

As you move on to other primaries, you notice that when you shepherd voters toward Dean, his Political Power edges up even faster. By concentrating Democratic support in Dean's campaign of grassroots influence, you're building a viable political force to fight against Bush.

The initial game will only feature the Iowa caucus and New Hampshire primary. Additional primaries can be added into the game later. Once new primaries are available, those states will become selectable in the menu map. Positive performance on previous primaries affects performance on future primaries. States whose primary are ready to be played appear highlighted on the map. States whose primaries have passed cannot be played, but the map displays their results. At the beginning of the game, players can choose between about five different preset "assumptions" that represent different candidates' positions or ideal assumptions about the primary season. The main game screen is split vertically into two areas. The top shows bar graphs for each candidate, preset to the current poll data in the selected state. The bottom shows "votes" ready to be guided into "polling doors" in the candidate's bar graphs to "vote."

The player clicks on the citizens in the game screen to turn them in different configurations and create a path for votes to go to the desired candidate. Gameplay is accomplished entirely with the mouse.

35.s3) and 35.s4) Concept art for the other Dean game.

parallel groups, one working on the grassroots simulation and the other working on the individual outreach activities. Of the two, the second suffered more under the project's time constraints. The grassroots simulation—what eventually became the Iowa map—would be a single system, a kind of lobby from which the player would access the various kinds of outreach activity. But the outreach activities themselves would each be different and thus require considerable individual care.

The question of what and how many outreach activities to include in the game was a matter of long discussion, both among ourselves and with the campaign itself. One of the primary goals for the game was to elucidate the concept of "grassroots outreach"—to give concrete examples of what it meant to perform such action. The logical conclusion was to represent as many such actions as possible in order to yield the broadest influence. Different activities might resonate more effectively with different players. Early on, we considered including as many such activities as possible, scaling down the representation of each by abstraction. But abstraction was precisely the problem the game hoped to solve—fence-sitter supporters were leery of getting involved in the campaign because they didn't grasp what "involvement" really meant. It thus seemed foolish to sacrifice the concreteness of the outreach activities for the sake of quantity.

Instead, we decided to choose three outreach activities. We asked analysts at the campaign to identify the three most important, and they settled on sign-waving, door-to-door canvassing, and pamphleteering.

Later, campaign advisors would tell us that they probably should have chosen letter-writing as one of the three, since this was the main method the campaign had invoked as a means of getting national supporters involved in pre-caucus outreach without physically traveling to Iowa.

Each of the three minigames was individually hand-drawn, animated, and colored. This was a time-consuming process. We might even have been able to allocate time for more minigames by choosing a less graphically rich and laborious method for representing the outreach activities. But the goal of the game was to clarify these endeavors, not to obscure them further. Door-to-door canvassing could have been represented with small iconographic people like the ones we used on the main Iowa map display, but doing so would risk leaving the concept too abstract.

35.2) Sketch and final versions of sign-waving.

After outlining the overall concept, the strategists from the campaign itself allowed us a great deal of freedom during development. The medium in which we actually developed the game (Macromedia Flash) was chosen for its widespread availability among Internet users. While that platform's architecture imposes constraints of its own, it affords and facilitates complex expression, given adequate time and resources. It may seem improbable to the average player, but time was the main creative constraint imposed upon the development of the game.

Creating Identification

As we both have argued elsewhere individually, video games can and should inspire player action in the real world (Frasca 2001, Bogost 2006). To encourage players to consider taking action in the

35.3) Sketch and final versions of door-to-door canvassing.

critical for Howard Dean, who found support from minorities a difficult challenge. Republican and Democratic opponents alike continually criticized Dean as an elitist, a candidate who appealed only to the ultraliberal, young WASPs.[3] One memorable TV commercial run by the conservative political action committee Club for Growth, shown in Iowa in advance of the caucus, depicted an older couple showering insults on Dean's "sushi-eating, Volvo-driving, latte-drinking" supporters (see Hallow 2004). Our decision to include characters of various ages, races, and even body types was intended to combat this overwhelmingly popular public image of the typical Dean supporter: a snobbish elitist. Despite our best intentions in this regard, the characters the player controls in each of the three minigames all appear Caucasian—a detail not lost on at least a few players, some of whom commented that the game, like the campaign, featured whites trying to get the attention of minorities.

The visual style of the characters and their environments was likewise chosen to stimulate affinity in the player. Art director Sofia Battegazzore adapted the watercolor wash appearance of the characters directly from the cartoons of the *New Yorker* magazine.

Cartoon-style graphics always risk the perception of childishness. The visual design thus helped set the expectation that the game was for adults. At the same time, the style evoked the broader themes of the *New Yorker*: society and culture.

Digital Demographics

In general, small-scale games developed for Internet delivery do not usually garner the play time of large commercial games. However, we believe that such games should not use their casual properties as an excuse to avoid detail. Even if players do not consciously note and explore such features, their presence enriches the experience by texturing it. Unfortunately, such features risk going unnoticed for posterity. While criticism is the best route for discovery and exploration of any game, we'd like to take the opportunity here to describe some of the Dean game's subsystems that might otherwise go unnoticed.

real world after playing, it was crucial that the game create a link between the solitary representation of outreach and its social nature in the material world. We wanted to invite the player to identify with these virtual campaigners. The player would be much more likely to project himself or herself onto more detailed, individuated characters in the minigames. These people looked like them, their friends, their neighbors. The game's splash screen features a cluster of these hand-drawn people for the same reason: the player's first impression of the game would be one of sociability.

This rationale also informed the types of people we chose to include in the game. Diversity remains a social buzzword, and a game in support of a politician necessarily must admit to the variety of the American citizenry. This issue was even more

3. For international readers unfamiliar with the term, WASP is an acronym for White Anglo-Saxon Protestants. It usually refers to the middle and upper classes especially.

One aspect of the process of performing grassroots outreach that especially interested us was demographics. We had no plans to give the elderly different biases than the first-time voters—the characters in the game simply didn't have inner lives of that kind. But we did want to remind the player that people with a variety of backgrounds comprise the American population. As mentioned earlier, the Dean campaign was often perceived as a group of yuppies: "latte-swilling" youth with no understanding of middle America nor middle age. We hoped to remind the player of other voters, beyond the stereotypical leftist elites, whom the Club for Growth TV spot criticized.

The supporter tokens we used on the overview map were featureless and genderless, mostly because additional detail would be neither visible nor meaningful on that screen. Instead of creating intricate character avatars that would denote the gender, age, and background of each virtual supporter, we chose to create a label with name and age that would connote a set of potential backgrounds for the virtual supporter. Following Scott McCloud's (1994) observations about comics and Will Wright's about simulations (Pearce 2002), we wanted players to fill in the inner lives of these characters with their own personal experiences. We also wanted them both to recognize the supporters as credible representations of people in the material world and as strangers.

To accomplish this, Bogost created a simple procedural method to generate supporters on the main Iowa map. First, we took U.S. census data for the demographic distribution of ages and genders in Iowa, a state with a slightly larger than average population above thirty-five. Next, we acquired additional census data on the most and least popular baby names from every decade from the 1910s through the 1980s (the last decade in which people of voting age could be born as of 2003). Using the age and gender data, we built a simple generator that would balance our supporter population based on a statistical model of the Iowa population. The U.S. census even provides regional breakdowns for baby names, allowing us to configure the generator to match each supporter with a first name appropriate for his or her age and gender. We selected a combination of the most popular and least popular names, in order to avoid an army of

35.4) Sketch and final versions of pamphleteering.

Michaels and Sarahs. The result was remarkably effective: the game produced 28-year-old Jennifers and 75-year-old Myrtles, 52-year-old Barbaras, and 40-year-old Roberts. We hoped that players would take these simple names as an invitation to imagine the hypothetical interactions they might have with these fictional supporters.

Every time the player installs a new supporter onto the map, the game attempts to normalize the population to a statistical average for the general Iowa population. This technique contains a subtle rhetoric: the game represents the population of *potential* Dean supporters as analogous to the population of *actual* Iowa residents. Some might argue that Dean supporters would (and did) reach only those corresponding with their own demographic—young hipster latte-swillers. No matter the real demographic bias of Dean supporters, we wanted to give players a view of the superset of possible Dean supporters, to suggest that they might both look beyond the familiar and prepare themselves for conversations with them. An apparently minor feature, the virtual supporter generator was actually carefully designed to advance the game's rhetorical position.

Despite its reasonably sophisticated computational models, the game remains a single-player affair, while grassroots outreach is inherently social. To encourage players to begin considering outlets for real-world interaction while playing the game, we designed two dynamics that relied on player-to-player contact. One of these was indirect, the other direct.

Indirect social interaction was simulated through asynchronous multiplayer collaboration: time-delayed contact between individual plays of the game (see Bogost 2004). After the player completed a session, each game dynamically updated a central server with information about how many virtual supporters the current player recruited in each of the regions on the map. And each time a new player loaded a game, a software routine loaded the current levels of virtual support penetration in each region. Areas with higher support turned increasingly darker shades of blue on the map. Darker shades of blue were more receptive to additional support, and additional incremental success was easier in these areas. Both this and the regional collaboration mechanic were provided as clues in a cycling text display at the bottom of the screen.

The algorithm for receptivity to virtual supporters took these regional support levels as their primary input. A numeric indicator in the game also displayed the total number of supporters all players had recruited that day. Each night the game data reset itself, and the map appeared freshly white for its first player the next morning. A player who loaded the game late at night would benefit from the aggregate effort of all of his predecessors. Given the short-term goals of the game, we hoped that this dynamic would give new players a chance to witness a microcosm of grassroots growth every day. To reinforce the positive effects of bringing more campaigners into Iowa, the game loaded near-real time data from other game sessions played during the same calendar day. To tie the game to the real Iowa outreach effort, the game also correlated that figure

with the total number of campaigners committed to travel to Iowa for the caucus.

Direct social interaction was facilitated by standard Internet communication protocols. Web-based games, especially advergames, have often included a "send to a friend" feature intended to facilitate word-of-mouth distribution of the game, and thereby the advertising message. The approach has become tired and clichéd, especially since most send-to-a-friend games offer no reason for the player to spread word of mouth save fulfilling the goals of the advertisers themselves, an assumption marred by player cynicism. To combat this trend, we wanted to offer the player in-game feedback for the extra-game contact they facilitated. Most send-to-a-friend features are one-way affairs: the player sends an e-mail message through the game and receives no additional feedback. Our version was real-time and closed-loop; we called it *Recruitment*.

At any time during play on the map screen, players could enter an e-mail address or instant messenger handle (AOL, Yahoo! or MSN) of a friend they wanted to contact. If the e-mail was successfully delivered or if the IM user was online and received the synchronous messages sent through the game server, the player would be rewarded with a new supporter to use in the game. Using IM avoided the nuisance and noise related to e-mail, while simultaneously communicating the urgency of Iowa outreach through the synchrony of that medium. This recruitment feature effectively gave the player a "free" virtual supporter—one

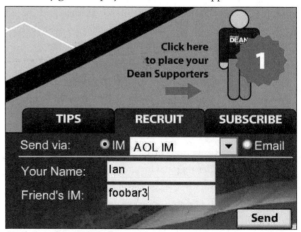

35.5) Recruitment interface.

Ian Bogost and Gonzalo Frasca

that did not need to be created by completing a minigame.

Perhaps most significantly, recruitment actually correlated with the communication goals of the game itself: the intention was to simulate the effectiveness of person-to-person grassroots outreach. Recruitment via e-mail or IM took less time than playing a minigame, and thus the game's rules privileged real-world connections over virtual ones.

To further encourage players to begin thinking about how to muster their personal networks in the material world, virtual supporters created through recruitment were displayed with the actual e-mail address or IM handle rather than a generated name. Some players even reported surreptitiously recruiting their Republican friends and colleagues in order to implicate conservatives in their support network.

Endorsed Game-Based Political Speech

Game typologies, like any form of genre classification, are always tricky. It is hard to find clear-cut categories where one can fit different games. The "political" game category can be applied to agitprop Web games, but also to commercial games dealing with armed conflict, economics, or urbanism. Since all cultural products do carry ideological luggage, we could argue that all games are indeed political. For this statement to be true, the term "political" should be taken in its broadest possible sense, understood not simply as partisan politics but rather as all strategies and ideas that permit social coexistence. In this tradition, games—and not just electronic games—have a long political history. The dichotomy between good and bad guys is evident from children's games involving rocks, arrows, swords, pistols, or laser guns and from actual military simulations, both paper- and computer-based.

Different categories have emerged in order to classify these "political" games. Propaganda games like *Under Siege* or *America's Army* seek to recruit new members and spread their ideology. We have also used the term "campaign" games to refer to video games such as *The Howard Dean for Iowa Game*, *Tax Invaders*, *Activism*, or *Cambiemos*.

It is definitively beyond the scope of this article to create a history of political games, but we feel that we should still mention some examples. A recent exhibit at Cornell University featured the *Cleveland Re-election Game*, circa 1893, built around U.S. President Grover Cleveland's second term.[4] Nineteenth-century British suffragettes also created thematic games like *Panko* or *Suffragettes in and out of Prison*—and financed their campaigns through their sale. *Panko* was a card game like rummy, and *Suffragettes* was a board game similar to *Chutes and Ladders* (see Rover 1967). Probably the most relevant example of early political video games is Chris Crawford's *Balance of Power*.

The authors behind these examples had a clear intention of conveying their ideas through games but, of course, even if there are no intentions the game can be definitively qualified as political. As many critics have pointed out, *SimCity* is a clear case of a game that takes a position on several political issues such as taxes, public transportation, and ecology. In other words, the game designer does not necessary need to be an activist for a game to have a political register. Certainly, author intentions are always difficult to establish, and the postmodern school even argues that they should be completely ignored. In any case, during these early days of political video games, it is useful to take the author's intentions into account because they can help us to understand the mechanics behind game persuasion. This explains why the motto behind our joint Web site, Water Cooler Games <http://www.watercoolergames.org>, is "video games with an agenda." However, we believe strongly that every game carries some ideological baggage, independently of their open, hidden, or unconscious agendas.

Games with clear agendas make better examples to be analyzed, especially because the idea of games as ideological artifacts can be quite surprising to many people. In fact, when Frasca defended his thesis on political video games (Frasca 2001), the first question he was asked by his committee at Georgia Tech was "Do you seriously believe that games can change the world?" This was not simply mere academic skepticism: in spite of a long tradition of marrying pop culture and politics, video games were—and still are—perceived as too trivial, too childish to deal with the seriousness of campaigns and policy making. No matter how optimistic we could have been by then, we would have never

4. However, it is unclear if this game was officially endorsed by the candidate.

even considered the possibility of campaign videogames just a few years ahead.

Still, and in spite of having both participated in several games for different campaigns, we do not kid ourselves: campaign games are a rarity so far. Videogames may be experiencing an explosion within our culture but they still need to mature as a persuasive medium. Yet just ten years ago, it was almost unimaginable that a politician would have a Web site. It would now be crazy to think of a politician without one—or without a blog and a mailing list. Believe it or not, television was once thought to be too trivial for political campaigns and its role did not become pervasive until the broadcast of televised debates in the 1960s.

Even though the 2004 U.S. election gave birth to video games as a new form of political expression, a much older genre found itself in the spotlight: documentary film. Certainly, the election would not have been the same without Michael Moore's *Fahrenheit 9/11* (Moore 2004). It was the first time that the outcome of an election was influenced by a documentary film.[5] Maybe some day a video game will play an equivalent important role. As a genre, it took documentary film almost a century of evolution to acquire such political relevance, and this is why we should not expect political games to play a protagonist role any time soon.

It is particularly problematic to be both designers and researchers, because our agendas conflict all the time. As academics, we would have liked to disclose as much information as possible during the campaign. As hired guns, we had to respond to our client's strategies and keep quiet about details (such as the role of the game in the broader pre-caucus communications plan) because they were the ones running the big picture and we were merely providers of a service. The same applies when dealing with other political games. When the Republican Party "answered" the Dean Game with *Tax Invaders*, as partisans we felt like making fun of it (it is technically so poor that we joked that it was coded by Bush himself).[6] On the other hand, as academics and

242

Ian Bogost and Gonzalo Frasca

Suicide Bomber to Sign Waver

When looking for a way to model the sign-waving game mechanics we ran into a problem. We had sketched a couple of options but we both agreed that having a person running with her sign along the sidewalk would work like a charm. But this design posed a major challenge: this basic mechanic was almost an exact copy of a previously released casual Web game. Our concern was not simply driven by fears of being accused of cloning this design—accusations that would be well-founded, since we were perfectly aware of this previous game. The main issue was that the game from which we were "borrowing" the gameplay in question was heavily political and controversial.

The game in question was called *Kaboom!* Its gameplay was simple but effective. Sadly, we can hardly say the same about its subject: your goal is to detonate a Palestinian human bomb and kill as many Israeli citizens as possible, including children. Later, Activision lawyers complained that the developers had adopted the title of the popular Atari 2600 game *Kaboom*, and

35.s5) Prototype of sign-waving gameplay.

the name was changed to the more descriptive *The Suicide Bomber Game*. Despite the game's apparently crass intention, its creator has maintained the game is actually meant to expose suicide bombers as insupportable extremists.[7] The game was condemned in the public media and both the Anti-Defamation League and a U.S. congresswoman called for it to be taken offline.

One does not need a degree in political science to realize that politicians do not want to be associated with games about blowing yourself up in order to kill children. On a mechanical level, our sign-waving minigame had an identical mechanic: run around and click when the maximum number of bystanders surround you. But on a representational level, the games were very different: one highlights democratic speech while the other gives rise to terror. We debated for a long time but finally decided to take the risk and keep *Kaboom!*'s game mechanics.

5. After the election, it was common to hear that Moore's film could not have changed the outcome. We strongly disagree. If Moore had not launched his film, Bush would probably have won by a much larger percentage. More important, the film created an undeniable discourse around American foreign policy, a very real outcome indeed.

6. Though no longer online, *Tax Invaders* was originally hosted on the GOP Website at <http://www.gop.com/taxinvaders>.

7. See<http://www.newgrounds.com/portal/view.php?id=50323>.

professionals, we should respect our colleagues' work and their relevance in the broader cultural landscape. These conflicts of interest are particularly evident in our Weblog postings and press interviews; for example, in a discussion of *Tax Invaders* on Water Cooler Games, Ian Bogost offered, "As another public example of political games, I'm happy to see the Bush camp trying things like John Kerry Tax Invaders. But does the GOP really think that what President Bush needs is a representation of his head firing bullets?"[8] There is no magical solution to this conflict of interest. We draw attention to it not as an excuse, but as an example of how torn we felt during the development of this and other campaign games.

Campaign strategists use their media products as ammunition. Usually, the pace of the campaign is so fast that television commercials may be taped in the morning, edited in the afternoon, and aired at night. At other times, communications get canned for a few days and even weeks until the campaigners decide to release them. The fact is that after we completed the production of the Dean game, it took over a week for the campaign to announce it properly. After crunching for four weeks, it was disappointing to see how much time it took the campaign to release and promote the fruit of our labors. We suspect that the delay was not strategic but influenced by other campaign events—the campaign was too busy to pay too much attention to a video game that, after all, was an experiment. In a certain way, the delay was actually helpful, because it allowed us to plan our own communication strategy.

As designers, we were interested in generating attention for our work in persuasive gaming. And as academics, we also saw an incredible opportunity to draw significant attention to the nascent field of political games. We even negotiated with the Dean campaign about how much freedom we would have to advertise our production and on which terms. This was not particularly hard, since nobody really knew if the idea of official campaign games made any sense, and because we were producing this project well below its fair cost.

Once the Dean campaign greenlit the game's launch, we

We were sure that someone would make the connection eventually; *Kaboom!* was a well-known game. As expected, a Slashdot reader posted a comment about their likeness but apart from that, no one seemed to notice. At a semiotic level, the games were totally different; only an experienced gamer would be able to identify the similar mechanics at their core. But as more and more people become literate in games, we can easily imagine a future where this kind of intertextual commentary will raise more eyebrows.

It would take a longer article to argue if it is ethical to copy game mechanics. In this particular case, we both acknowledge that our game is based on *Kaboom!* but we also feel that there are enough differences on other, non-gameplay levels, to set them apart. In any case, the fact that the first official U.S. video game used for a democratic campaign owed something to an extremely violent game is, in our opinion, an example of how totally different ideas can coexist and influence each other during these early, experimental days of political gaming. More than anything, we wanted to "redeem" the core game mechanic, to show that it need not be associated with violence.

were given a few hours before the press release went public to announce the game to a select group of bloggers. This was coherent with the campaign's ideals of experimenting with the net and its grassroots effects. However, the players drawn through the blogs were very few and the server statistics only spiked after the game was featured in traditional media outlets such as the *New York Times* or *Good Morning America*. Server stats only refer to the number of players; they cannot qualify other characteristics. Even if the number of players referred by blogs was not overwhelming, this strategy certainly reinforced the idea that this particular campaign was paying special attention to alternative communication strategies.

Online games offer the possibility of getting access to a lot of feedback from players. A few months before the launch of the Dean game, Frasca and his team had launched their game *September 12th*, a critique of Western foreign policy in the Middle East. In the game, players could, if they wished, fire time-delayed missiles into a Middle Eastern town to attempt to kill terrorists. However,

8. <http://www.watercoolergames.org/archives/000119.shtml>.

the missiles inevitably destroyed buildings and killed innocents as well as terrorists. Those characters nearby would mourn over the dead innocents and some of them would in turn become terrorists. The game had caused its share of controversy by then, and it was played by several hundred thousand players. We used this experience about how players reacted to a persuasive video game in order to prepare for possible negative feedback.

Even though *September 12th* and the Dean game are quite different in theme, we were right that they would trigger some similar reactions. It was not uncommon for both players and critics to argue that the game was not fun or not fun enough. This is the kiss of death in any critical discussion because it lowers the bar to a matter of taste. There is a long tradition of art criticism, and this is why we rarely see a critic dismiss a painting because "it is not pretty." Sadly, game criticism is still maturing and sometimes we cannot get beyond the "Like it"/"Don't like it" dichotomy. Clearly, a persuasive game cannot be judged like a console game—and this divergence goes beyond mere production quality. Unlike commercial games, the ultimate goal of a persuasive game is not to provide fun but to convey a message. Certainly, the experience must be compelling for the player. But replayability, often held up as a litmus test for commercial games, is not essential in this new field.

The whole concept of replayability has economic undertones: you are getting a game that will provide pleasure for a certain amount of time for a certain amount of money. When we created the Dean game, we assumed that most players would not spend more than ten minutes at a time with it. Actually, the average playing time was longer than that and we were the first to be surprised when the server stats showed us that some hardcore Dean supporters had been playing for hours, and returning day after day to contribute more virtual support.

Another popular criticism is that the game modeled the campaign but failed to convey Dean's own ideas. This is a clear example of how hard it is to criticize persuasive communication—and it applies not only to games but also to any form of advertising. The fact is that we did not model Dean's ideas because the campaign expressly wanted us to focus on the grassroots campaign itself. This is also probably why Dean failed as a candidate. He orchestrated a brilliant campaign that revolutionized the way U.S. campaigns are done, but he failed to focus on convincing voters that they should vote for him. Bogost took this lesson to heart and later in the campaign focused on public policy issues over political practice in *Activism* and *Take Back Illinois*.

In *Activism*, the player managed six public policy minigames, which he had to play simultaneously. The player could alter the relative importance of each policy issue, and the gameplay forced the player to pay more attention to the policy issues he declared the least interest in. *Take Back Illinois* simulated a party position on four public policy issues in greater detail—medical malpractice reform, economic development, educational reform, and voter participation. To win each game, the player had to embody the party position on each topic in order to learn that position and subsequently to consider, support, or oppose it. Unlike the Dean game, both *Activism* and *Take Back Illinois* addressed public policy issues, rather than campaign communication.

But one question came up in every media interview we did about campaign video games: can a game change the outcome of an election? By this standard, the game was a huge failure because it did not prevent Dean's catastrophic collapse. The logic behind this question resembles the thinking behind similar cursory arguments as to the role of games in education or whether they lead to violent behavior. Our world is too complex to be simplified into a series of causes and effects; the political environment is no exception. A campaign video game is merely one message within an ecology of other messages. Certainly, some communications have a stronger effect than others—a tape showing a politician performing some act of corruption could end his career. However, most propaganda simply reinforces certain ideas and seeks to appeal to a specific audience. Similarly, a political game can better speak to a specific group of voters. Games may invoke contemplation or reinforce ideas, but they can hardly decide the fate of an election.

Ian Bogost and Gonzalo Frasca

Meta-Messages and Balloons as Political Speech

While it is worthwhile to explore the possibilities of modeling political ideas through gameplay, it is also important that a campaign game communicate more than its political payload. Campaign games also work at a higher level, conveying more ideas that are not necessarily connected to their design.

One of the most important meta-messages that campaign games convey is the fact that the candidate is pioneering a new political form. This makes the game instantly newsworthy. No matter if the game is fun or boring, pretty or ugly, interesting or not, the association between video games and politics attracts the attention of the media. During a political campaign, the budget for media advertising is always scarce (unless the candidate is a media mogul), and therefore any news coverage is highly valued by the campaign strategists because it is perceived as free advertising. If the Dean campaign had invested the game's budget into TV advertising, they would not even have been able to buy a few seconds on-air. However, because the game was instantly snatched up by journalists, it received televised and printed coverage for the Dean campaign whose value well exceeded the game's development budget.

Another meta-message is that the candidate sets himself apart by using alternative communication techniques. This is a double-edged sword. The campaign's intention was to use video games as a complement to their broader online strategy. Ideally, by releasing a video game, Dean would have been perceived as an innovator willing to address a younger audience through the media codes and conventions with which they are familiar. The risk, of course, was that he could have been accused of trivializing campaigns by using an unserious genre such as video games, or deploying the medium to seduce the interest of young people. As designers, we were particularly concerned about this problem, even though there was actually no negative impact. In retrospect, we may have wrongly expected that the game would have a major impact on the campaign. In other words, if the game had been perceived as a threat, we are convinced that it would have been attacked. The Dean campaign crumbled after he lost the Iowa caucus and the game was effectively retired, noted for its innovation but implicated in the campaign's overall failure.

We must keep in mind that the influence of these meta-messages may only persist during these early stages of campaign games. As we grow accustomed to the concept, the medium itself will seem ordinary and cease to be newsworthy. Only time will tell if video games will not be judged for trivializing the "seriousness" of political games. Of course, recent public bias against video games has arisen at the hand of politicians themselves. Senators Joseph Lieberman and Hillary Clinton demonize video games for their own agendas, effectively dismissing video games as a form of political communication. In any case, on further reflection, political campaigns are also driven by triviality. Just think of the importance of balloons in party conventions. If balloons, funny hats, badges, singing, and dancing are all accepted elements of political speech, we are certain that there must be some room left for video games.

Archive Early and Often

We hope this chapter provides a behind-the-scenes perspective on the creation of the Dean game and useful reflections upon the nature of campaign video games in general. Even though games and video games have been used historically as a satirical approach to politics, it was a design challenge to create a video game that was officially endorsed by a candidate.

Are video games going to become as pervasive as other campaign tools? Our answer as professional developers of game-based political marketing is a resounding "yes." As academics, we are still convinced that the genre has great potential. But we should caution that we are witnessing the birth of a genre, and it is likely that it will take many years for it to become widely accepted. This situation presents an opportunity for early adopters because these first campaign games are gathering exceptional attention from the media, and this attention will likely fade out as the genre becomes more established.

So far, all we can say is that the game certainly triggered a trend. On a personal level, we have both created other games after the Dean campaign, for both the same U.S. election (*Activism*, *Take Back Illinois*) and for other presidential elections (*Cambiemos*). In addition, we have tracked some 200 political games of various forms on Water Cooler Games. And there are surely more that we have not yet seen.

But many of these games are ephemeral and risk being lost to history. We have realized the hard way that most campaign games disappear quickly once the elections are over. Campaign committees dissolve and it is almost impossible to contact developers of such games. These challenges are probably normal for scholars researching traditional campaigns, given the fact that during election time there is an abundance of information and after it is over, it suddenly vanishes. But the purely digital nature of these games exacerbates their transience. Our advice for colleagues interested in political video game research is to gather as much information as possible as soon as the games are out. Archive early and often.

Can campaign games become a useful tool for fostering debate and critical thinking during election time? Or will they simply erode political speech while replacing it with mere entertainment? If we take a look at media history, there is no clear answer for these questions. We do know that communication genres can be used both to manipulate and to encourage free thinking. As researchers, we remain carefully skeptical. But as developers and activists, naïveté is an essential requirement—only idealism can provide us with the thrill of exploring new techniques for reaching more people with new ideas. Changing politics, changing the world—it is all within reach, as long as we remain playful and we have a little fun while doing it.

References: Literature

Bogost, Ian (2004). "Asynchronous Multiplay: Futures for Casual Multiplayer Experience." In *Proceedings of the Other Players Conference*, edited by Jonas Heide Smith and Miguel Sicart. Copenhagen: IT University of Copenhagen. <http://www.itu.dk/op/papers/bogost.pdf>.

Bogost, Ian (2006). *Unit Operations: An Approach to Video Game Criticism*. Cambridge, MA: MIT Press.

Frasca, Gonzalo (2001). "Video Games of the Oppressed." Master's Thesis, The Georgia Institute of Technology. Excerpted in (2004) *First Person: New Media as Story, Performance, and Game*, edited by Noah Wardrip-Fruin and Pat Harrigan. Cambridge, MA: MIT Press.

Hallow, Ralph Z. (2004). "Conservatives launch TV attack ad on Dean." *Washington Times*, January 6, 2004. <http://washingtontimes.com/national/20040105-103754-1355r.htm>

Johnson, Stephen (2003). "SimCandidate: Video games Simulate Sports, Business, and War. Why Not Politics?" *Slate*, Dec. 16, 2003.

McCloud, Scott (1994). *Understanding Comics*. New York: Harper.

Moore, Michael (2004). *Fahrenheit 9/11*. The Fellowship Adventure Group/Wild Bunch.

Pearce, Celia (2002). "Sims, BattleBots, Cellular Automata, God and Go: A Conversation with Will Wright." *Game Studies* 2, no. 1 (2002). <http://www.gamestudies.org/0102/pearce/>.

Perec, Georges (1969). *La Disparition*. Paris: Gallimard.

Rover, Constance (1967). *Women's Suffrage and Party Politics in Britain, 1866–1914*. Toronto: Toronto University Press.

References: Games

Activism. Ian Bogost; Persuasive Games. 2004a. <http://www.activismgame.com>.

America's Army. U.S. Army. 2002.

Balance of Power. Chris Crawford; Mindscape. 1985.

Cambiemos. Gonzalo Frasca; Powerful Robot Games. 2004. <http://www.cambiemos.org.uy>.

The Howard Dean for Iowa Game. Ian Bogost and Gonzalo Frasca; Persuasive Games. 2003. <http://www.deanforamericagame.com>.

Kaboom. Larry Kaplan and David Crane; Activision. 1981.

Kaboom! (aka The Suicide Bomber Game). Anonymous (Fabulous999); Newgrounds. 2002. <http://www.newgrounds.com/portal/view.php?id=50323>.

September 12th. Gonzalo Frasca; Newsgaming.com. 2003. <http://www.newsgaming.com>.

SimCity. Will Wright; Maxis. 1989.

Take Back Illinois. Ian Bogost; Persuasive Games. 2004b. <http://www.takebackillinoisgame.com>.

Tax Invaders. Republican National Committee; gop.com. 2004.

Under Siege. Afkar Media. 2004.

WarioWare, Inc.: Mega MicroGame$. Nintendo. 2003.

WarioWare, Inc.: Mega Party Game$. Nintendo. 2003.

WarioWare Touched!. Nintendo. 2003.

WarioWare Twisted! Nintendo. 2004.

Political Activism: Bending the Rules
Kevin Whelan

Canvassing Role-Plays

Sure, I played some *Dungeons & Dragons* as a young man. But I didn't really begin to role-play on a daily basis until after college, when I became a full-time political activist.

After graduation I worked for, and then supervised, canvass operations for several different environmental groups. Canvassers are nice young people who come to your door with a clipboard, and with the goal of getting a check and your contact information for their organization—usually an environmental cause.

Canvassers always practice, always role-play, several "raps" every day before they leave go out to the doors. It is key that the people who are playing the "canvass-ees" in the role-play are trained to be good actors; they must throw up a realistic set of objections to the actor playing the canvasser, but in the end, they must be persuadable. (They must also refrain from venting all their frustrations on their fellow canvassers by replaying all of the most insulting and insurmountable comments from past doors. No one needs to practice having the door slammed in his or her face—that will happen on its own.)

A canvass rap, whether it is for the environment, gay rights, or any other issue, always has the same basic structure:

1. *Problem.* (For example: air pollution, and a description of why it is bad.)

2. *Solution.* (Strengthen the Clean Air Act, over the objections of big polluters.)

3. *Strategy.* (Get lots of grassroots support.)

4. *Action.* (Join our group/give money.)

Typically, canvassers practice raps by watching demonstrations and by practicing in pairs. They evaluate each other after each rap, on how well each person has used the basic skills of strong communication—eye contact,

strong positive language, KISS (Keep it Short and Simple), targeting (asking for donations in specific amounts), and clipboard control (handing over the clipboard at just the right time to seal the deal).

The goals of the various role-plays are to teach canvassers to understand the structure of the rap, which allows her or him to always guide the conversation back to the desired conclusion—and to use the basic techniques of strong communication. It is the application of these skills, not the depth of a canvasser's policy knowledge, which will induce the public to contribute to and join the organization. (Typically canvassers are trying to mobilize supporters; that is, trying to get the people who already agree with them to do something about it, rather than trying to change minds.)

There are a number of variations on basic canvass role-plays that are used to break the monotony of practice, such as everyone practicing just one part of the rap, or doing a complete rap on totally different (or fictional or comical) issue. For example, one day I practiced a rap that probably wouldn't have really flown in the suburbs:

> "Hi, I'm Kevin from the Anarchist Front for Creative Destruction—how are you tonight?"

> *To make the exercise work, the person playing the "door" had to go along with the absurdist scenario: "Fine, thanks."*

> "The problem we are talking to people about tonight is the stupid waste of our lives in consumer society. A lot of your neighbors feel that they spend all their time working at jobs they hate, in order to get the money to buy things that are supposed to make them happy, but don't. Do you ever feel that way?"

> [*"Yes, I sure do."*]

> "Great. Well, the solution we are working on with the support of you and your neighbors is to create a new society, based on sharing and mutual aid. But to do that, we will first have to smash the State and bring down the capitalist system. Does that sound like something you support?"

["*Definitely, yes.*"]

"Excellent. I know a lot of us want to see that happen. Our strategy at the Anarchist Front is creative destruction—by wreaking violence in a random and ruthless manner against all the institutions of consumption and repression, we can rend the social fabric of our oppressive society, and as things unravel, we can create a new society out of the ashes of the old. Can we count on you to be part of this?"

By practicing either a partial or absurd rap, the canvassers are able to focus on the skills and structure that are most important in determining the rap's success.

ACORN

For the past eight years, I have worked at ACORN (Association of Community Organizations for Reform Now) <http://www.acorn.org>, the nation's largest community organization of low-income families. ACORN's community organizers do something that looks superficially very much like canvassing. That is, we knock on people's doors, sign them up as members and collect membership dues. There are crucial differences, though.

First, ACORN organizers knock on doors in poor neighborhoods, not rich ones. More important, ACORN organizes people into local chapters that vote on what economic justice or community issue impacts them most directly on the local level. To address these issues, ACORN organizes "actions": direct, nonviolent confrontations with people in power. The issues and actions start out very local—ACORN members might pick up litter in a neighborhood where the city neglects trash pickup, and deliver the bags of garbage to the mayor's desk—but through a process of electing leaders to higher positions, we eventually tackle much bigger issues, like raising the state and federal minimum wages.

The ACORN organizing rap follows a structure that is similar to a canvass rap, in that it leads from a social problem to a particular action. But an organizing rap is arranged around a series of questions:

1. *What would you like to see changed in your community?*

2. *Can I come in and talk to you about that?* (Organizers usually sit down for a ten- to fifteen-minute conversation, which starts with a more detailed discussion of the problem and how it hurts the person/community.)

3. *Why do you think the problem stays that way?* (Here, with further prompting if necessary, the goal is to focus on the problem as an issue of power—a neighborhood being neglected because of its race or class makeup.)

4. *How do you feel about that?* (This step, "polarization," is about getting people to get mad about the problem.)

5. *What do you think it would take to solve the problem?* (The goal is to build a vision of collective action—strength in numbers. Examples or leading questions may or may not be needed to get there: "If fifty of us went as a group and dumped that garbage on the mayor's desk, would that get his attention?")

6. *Would you be willing to be a part of that?* (And from here we reach the details of joining as a member—paying dues and participating in meetings and actions.)

Like canvassers, ACORN organizers also practice daily role-plays, but because the ACORN rap involves more talking by the community member than the organizer, the process requires some fairly sophisticated acting. The rules for the actor playing the community member are the same as in a canvassing role-play: you have to sign up in the end, and you can be difficult but not impossible. One of the most important skills for an organizer is to bring the conversation back to the structure, so that it leads to action. You can't practice an exact script for ACORN organizing, because every conversation is different, but you can develop lots of techniques for steering a conversation back in a more productive direction.

In the field, organizing still calls upon all the players' imaginations. A successful rap is one that invites a person to feel and express the emotions connected to a long-standing social problem, and to imagine and talk through a different reality, one in which they act in unity with their neighbors and have power.

The Rules

While there are rules for doing good organizing, success comes from both mastering those rules and pushing or breaking them at the same time. As an example, let me talk briefly about my first experience of political role-playing, as a high schooler in the Model United Nations program.

In the Model U.N. <http://www.nmun.org>, high school students, in teams of two to seven, represent different countries of the world and attempt to win support for the foreign policies of that country (while getting to skip a couple days of school, stay in a hotel, and, in our own nerdy way, party and flirt with our fellow delegates).

One year, my friends and I chose to stretch the rules of the game (or the imaginations of the administrator and the other participants) to make a political point. We announced that we would represent the Palestinian Liberation Organization, under the plausible scenario that it had shown up at the United Nations asking to be seated as the legitimate government-in-exile of the Palestinian people. (This was in 1987 or so, and the idea of Palestinian statehood was still a far-out position in American politics.)

We argued our case on the floor of the General Assembly, but also pushed the rules of the Model U.N. further by regularly issuing photocopied *communiqués* in the style of the first Palestinian Intifada. We succeeded in achieving our goal of getting seated, and made our point about the need for a voice and fair settlement for the Palestinians.

ACORN's actions (protests directed at a specific target who has the power to deliver the change the community wants) play off of the same tension that my friends and I pushed at the Model U.N. Organizing means mastering the rules of the game in order to be able to first bend them in a educational way, and finally to alter them.

Effective direct action requires a thorough understanding of the local and national political and business structures—so we can find the public official who is really responsible and derelict in his duty. Then it requires creating enough public disruption to get our members to the table where decisions are made. There, members have the chance to hold the official accountable to the rules of fair play and honesty that politicians always profess. When it works, all the participants see themselves in a new light, and the community gets a benefit that it had previously been denied.

The Puppet Master Problem: Design for Real-World, Mission-Based Gaming

Jane McGonigal

When gamers interact with their environments . . . probing often takes the form of seeking out the limits of the situation, the points at which the illusion of reality breaks down, and you can sense that it's all just a bunch of algorithms behind the curtain.
—Steven Johnson, *Everything Bad Is Good for You*

Puppet master: An individual working "behind the curtain" to control the game.
—Sean Stacey, "The Unfiction Glossary"

In early August 2004, the alternate reality game *I Love Bees* gave its online players, over 600,000 in number, their first real-world mission. On a Web page that had previously presented recipes for the fictional heroine's Saffron Honey Ice Cream and Bee-licious Chocolate Chip Cookies, a new set of tantalizing ingredients appeared: 210 unique pairs of Global Positioning System (GPS) coordinates; 210 corresponding time codes spaced four minutes apart and stretching across a twelve-hour period in the Pacific Daylight Savings Time zone; and a central timer counting down to a single future date: 08/24/2004.

There were no further instructions provided. The *I Love Bees* (*ILB*) players were given no goal, no rules, no choices, no resources to manage, no buttons to press, no objects to collect—just a series of very specific, physical locations and an impending cascade of actual, real-time moments. Taken together, what were these ingredients supposed to yield?

For two weeks following the initial appearance of the GPS data set on <http://www.ilovebees.com>, interpretation of its meaning varied greatly among the *ILB* players. There was no early consensus about what *ILB*'s designers wanted the players to *do* with these coordinates, times, and date. An explosion of creative experimentation with the data ensued.[1] Some players plotted the GPS points on a United States map in the hopes of revealing a connect-the-dot message. Others projected the earthbound coordinates onto sky maps to see if they matched any known constellations. A particularly large group collected the names of the cities to which the 210 points mapped and then tried to create massive anagrams and acrostics from them. A smaller group decided to average the two numbers in each pair of coordinates and look for an underlying statistical pattern across the set.

Meanwhile, many players began visiting the locations nearest them and taking digital photos, uploading them to the *ILB* community online to see if a visual or functional commonality across the sites would emerge. Others without digital cameras carried out similar scouting activities and filed text-based reports, hoping to help uncover the secret message signified by the coordinates. Among this growing scouting group, numerous competing patterns emerged: The coordinates all pointed to Chinese restaurants, several players suggested—or mailboxes, or video game stores, or public libraries.

For a short while, the potential for plausible readings of the GPS coordinates seemed both inexhaustible and irresoluble. However, as the 8/24/2004 date loomed closer, and after tens of thousands of speculative posts on dozens of Web forums, a critical mass of players finally converged on a single interpretation: The GPS data set was not a puzzle, or a clue—it was a *command*. The designers were instructing players just to show up at the locations at the specified times and *wait for something to happen*.

And so, on August 24, swarms of "beekeepers" (a nickname many of the *ILB* players adopted) showed up at nearly all of the 210 locations, expectantly hovering in groups of a dozen or more. At the coordinates, the players clustered together laden with laptops, cameras, PDAs, cell phones, and anything else they thought to bring just in

---

1. An excellent archive of more than 3,000 posts containing speculation about the GPS coordinates can be found on the *I Love Bees* "Puzzle Solving" message board at <http://forums.unfiction.com/forums/viewforum.php?f=81>.

case, waiting to find out exactly what they were supposed
to do. They explained to inquisitive passersby, "We're
playing a game."[2] The core mechanic of which appeared to
be: Go exactly where you are told to go, and then wait for
something to happen. Don't make meaningful decisions.
Don't exercise strategy. Don't explore the space. Just go, and
wait for further instructions.

This is a game?

Indeed it is. For many gamers, the August 24th *I Love Bees*
mission was their first introduction to a new mode of
digital gaming, one that centers on real-world, live action,
performance-based missions. I call it the *power play.*

Power plays are a kind of cross between a digital dare and
street theater. They are live gaming events, conducted in
public places and organized via digital network technologies,
in which players are directed via clues to show up at a real-
world location. Upon arrival, participants are given a set of
instructions for an action to take at that site. These
instructions may be discovered in a nearby geocache, received
as a text message, delivered via ringing payphones, or
downloaded by players using their mobile Web applications.

Once the instructions are in hand, players carry them out
immediately, usually documenting their own actions with
digital photographs and videos. This first-person media
proves that they have successfully completed their missions
and captures the moment for online audiences who are
waiting to see how the real-world players performed.
Frequently, there are also on-site actors—"plants"— to
observe the players' performances and to reward them with
another mission or a clue to the next location.

Power plays can vary considerably in length, number of
participants, and total ground covered. The quintessential
example, the power play in its purest form, is a *flash mob*—
an intensely focused burst of anonymously engineered play
that involves a single mission lasting precisely ten minutes.[3]
A flash mob brings a dozen, a hundred, or five hundred
players to the same location, where they are prompted to
perform a shared set of silly and usually crudely geocached

instructions—slips of paper hidden in the men's room, for
instance, directing them to whirl like dervishes back and
forth across a major pedestrian crosswalk. Other, more
complex, power plays involve dozens of connected missions
unfolding over several hours. These longer games may
feature as many as 1000 simultaneous players roaming a
single city neighborhood. The paradigmatic example of this
kind of power play is the cell phone-based urban superhero
adventure the *Go Game*, in which players interact with local
residents in collaborative physical challenges and
performance art missions. Still other power plays, like *I Love
Bees*, ping hundreds of thousands of players distributed
around the world with just one or two real-world missions
a week. These real-world missions stem from and fuel an
online, serial narrative, and such an extended power play
can last as long as three or four months—until the Web-
based story ends.

The real-world missions of the power play challenge
gamers to play in environments in which they wouldn't
normally play, to interact with strangers they wouldn't
typically acknowledge, to make spontaneous spectacles of
themselves, and to rewrite the social rules of a given space
in highly visible ways. In short, the players' public
performances are designed to be seen and heard by as
many people as possible, to have a significant local impact
and widespread online circulation. Not everything about
the power play, however, is designed to be witnessed or
received. The attention-seeking performances of the
players are prompted and guided by an *invisible* creative
team, which carefully and purposefully stays out of sight
while the players attract the limelight. This off-stage
design team is composed of a group of shadowy, often
anonymous figures working behind the scenes as the
writers, programmers, directors, and stage managers of
the live gameplay.

They are the first real-time digital game designers, and
they are called the *puppet masters.*

2. A collection of first-person accounts of August 24th meet-ups at the GPS coordinates is located on the *I Love Bees* "Axon Coordination"
message board at <http://forums.unfiction.com/forums/viewtopic.php?t=5909>.

3. The *Cheese Bikini* blog contains an outstanding collection of links and posts documenting the unfolding of the flash mob phenomenon
in the summer of 2003. Its author, Sean Savage, coined the term "flash mob" and has compiled his writing about them at
<http://www.cheesebikini.com/archives/cat_flash_mobs.html>.

Jane McGonigal

The Rise of the Puppet Master

If you're the puppet masters, what does that make the players? Your little puppets?

—Anonymous audience member at the Game Developers Conference lecture, "I Love Bees: A Case Study" (McGonigal 2005)

This essay is a response to two sets of problems posed by the sudden popularity of power plays, and by the associated rise of the puppet master in contemporary digital gaming. The first problem set belongs to the gaming theorists and to the ethnographers: Why would any gamer agree to be a public "puppet" of an anonymous game designer? Where is the *fun* in such a rigid gaming structure? And furthermore, where is the *propriety*? To some critics, such an unbalanced power dynamic seems a bit perverse; to others, it seems downright dangerous. (Imagine here, as many already have, a recklessly negligent, if not outright malevolent, puppet master who asks gamers to "go too far"—a scenario inevitably posed to me after each and every design workshop or lecture I give on the subject of the power play.) The second problem set of this essay belongs to the game designers: How do you structure a game so that you can effectively, and remotely, "pull the strings" of dozens, hundreds, or thousands of players *without* making them feel like mere puppets? How do you develop the puppet master/player relationship into a collaborative one, and what real-time recourses do you have to actively manage that relationship? Here, I want to offer a series of critical frameworks for understanding both the pleasures of the puppet-mastered experience and the real-time design strategies that support those pleasures.

The first thing to know about the term "puppet master" is that it was the *players* who originally adopted it to refer to the real-time designers of a power play.[4] Since then, many designers have taken up the name as an acknowledgment of its popularity among players. But the term does not originate with the puppet masters themselves. It comes directly from the players.

This is a tremendously important distinction. The source of the term "puppet master" reveals its function: It is primarily a way for players to conceptualize and to talk about their relationship to the game designers. It is not a top-down description of the game designers' ambitions or design strategies. Rather, it is a bottom-up expression of how the players choose to perceive, and to communicate to others, the novel power dynamic of the games they are playing.

Puppet masters (PMs) are not, of course, the first or only "masters" of gaming. For decades, non-digital games have relied on *Dungeon* Masters (DMs) and *gamemasters* (GMs) to organize, host, and guide players through tabletop games such as *Dungeons & Dragons*, and live action role-playing (LARP) events, such as *Cthulhu Live*.[5] Like PMs, DMs and GMs are actively involved as authority figures in supervising the live unfolding of a multiplayer game. However, players' widespread adoption of "puppet master" instead of these more traditional terms is an explicit assertion of the inadequacy of existing gaming terminology to describe the qualitatively new experience of participating in a power play.

So what is it that players wanted to say about a puppet-mastered experience that they could not say with typical gamer speak? According to the most widely cited definition, a puppet master is "an individual working 'behind the curtain' to control the game" (Stacey 2002). This definition requires a bit of unpacking—what do players mean by "behind the curtain"? And in what sense are the PMs in "control" of the game? Both of these elements, the *framing* and the *mechanics* of player supervision, are essential to understanding why participants in power plays have adopted the term "puppet master."

In digital gaming culture, the *Wizard of Oz*–inspired phrase "behind the curtain" usually refers to the computer programming that generates the players' experience of the game world: the physics engine that creates the laws of time,

---

4. The term "puppet master" was first applied to game designers in April 2001 by players of *The Beast*, the first alternate reality game, a story-driven genre of massively multiplayer gaming that sometimes, but not always, includes real-world missions. The first official citation for the term "puppet master" in this context can be found on an early comment in the Cloudmakers discussion forum, organized by players of *The Beast*: <http://movies.groups.yahoo.com/group/cloudmakers/message/882>.

5. The term "gamemaster" has even deeper historic roots, in fact. It was first applied to the overseers of multiplayer *play-by-mail* games, such as the 1960s play-by-mail version of the WWII strategy game *Diplomacy*.

space, and motion in the game universe, for instance, or the artificial intelligence that drives non-player characters' actions and dialogue. Media theorist Stephen Johnson, for instance, comments that when it comes to video games, "it's all just a bunch of algorithms behind the curtain" (Johnson 2005, 45). Here, the curtain refers to the interface that keeps the programming invisible to the gamers. When it comes to real-world, mission-based games, however, it's *not* just algorithms behind the curtain—it's a team of live game designers. And what keeps them invisible to the gamers is not a stable interface, but rather an active practice: the PM practice of withholding information from, and refusing direct interaction with, the players during the game.

In a power play, participants typically have no confirmation (in some cases, not even a clue) of who the puppet masters are, or what their motivation is, until the game is finished—if ever. Professional power plays such as *I Love Bees* may conclude with a list of credits; grassroots power plays like flash mobs may never reveal the identity of their PMs. Occasionally, as in the *Go Game*, the puppet masters are made known at the start of the game, but they, too, disappear "behind the curtain" until the game is finished. This curtain, of course, is metaphorical—a kind of social norm, an agreement that the two sides will keep a functional distance from each other throughout the live play. The designers agree not to interfere with live play as overt authority figures once they have handed over the instructions for the live missions. And for their part, players agree not to try to "out" the secret designers, or to contact the designers directly for any "out-of-game" advice or discussion—that is to say, with *meta*-concerns about the gameplay.

This practice is radically different from the continual, open, and face-to-face communications between traditional gamemasters and their players. GMs and DMs are never "behind the curtain." They are clearly identified and known by name to the players, and there is a transparency to their work. Creative and executive decisions generally are made in front of, or in the midst of, the players, with input from the players often solicited before and after decisions are made. In the power play, quite to the contrary, there is a disparity in

awareness of, and access to, the other side, like a one-way mirror. The puppet masters watch the players, but the players have no view of behind-the-curtain machinations. The PMs make design decisions in secret and send covertly delivered messages to the players, while the players have no clearly defined in-game recourse to talk directly to the PMs. This power practice of constructing a one-way flow of knowledge and communications is what players refer to when they talk about staying behind the curtain.

The players' definition of a puppet master also hinges on the word *control*. Traditional gamemasters are said to "organize" and to "referee" their games (West End Games 2004, 3). But puppet masters are granted a much more explicit and pervasive authority: they "control the game." This shift in language, along with the metaphor for direct manipulation implied by the name "puppet master," is required to capture the ceding of traditional gameplay control that players must agree to in order to participate in a power play.

In traditionally mastered games, players are provided with narrative scenarios and options for actions to take. Through direct choice, or random choice (e.g., rolling dice), or some combination of the two, players determine the "next step" in the game. As explained in West End Games' excellent reference "Introduction to Being a Gamemaster," the masters interpret these steps and inform players of the outcome: "As the players describe the actions of their characters, you decide whether or not they can do what they describe, or how difficult the action is. You interpret dice rolls according to the rules and then tell the players what happens" (Ibid., 2). In this model, players may not have the final word on what their decisions mean, but they are making choices and taking actions that affect the game's plot and final outcome. Power plays, on the other hand, strip players of the authority to make decisions. Unlike virtually any other game you could think of, "mastered" or not, in power plays the players' *actions* are entirely predetermined. Their job is simply to figure out where to be, to get there on time, and then to carry out the site-specific instructions they are given.

In a sense, then, the gameplay of a puppet mastered experience boils down to a high-stakes challenge: Perform—or else.[6] Or else what? Or else, be denied the opportunity to

---

6. Much of my thinking about power plays and digital gaming in general is influenced by Jon McKenzie's 2001 *Perform or Else*, in which he analyzes turn-of-the-twenty-first century digital network culture as a series of performative challenges.

play. Be left out. Be left behind. There is simply no *optionality* to the power play—do exactly what you're told, or there's no play for you. This underlying power structure requires a level of overt submission from gamers that is simply unprecedented in game culture. And so the players' definition acknowledges: It is the puppet masters, not the players, who "control the game."

Why has a mode of gaming like the power play, and the associated puppet master terminology, emerged at this particular moment in American culture? And how can we accurately describe, and inventively design for, the unusual and complicated power dynamic that underlies a puppet mastered experience? Both of these questions require us to begin with a close look at the more traditional cultural and critical contexts for gaming from which the power play has dramatically diverged.

Traditionally Powerful Players

Historically, games theorists and designers have characterized players as extremely powerful individuals, and powerful in a very particular way. Throughout the foundational texts of game studies, gameplay has consistently been defined as an opportunity for participants to assert the power of choice, to make their own decisions, and to act only and always according to their own volition. Because puppet-master gaming is such a departure from this model, it is worth taking a moment here to track how key gaming phenomenologies and design manifestos of the twentieth and early twenty-first centuries have worked, until now, to so convincingly define gameplay as the antithesis of a puppet-mastered experience—that is, as the opportunity for a gamer to exercise free will.

Johan Huizinga first introduces the notion of the player's free will in *Homo Ludens: A Study of the Play-Element in Culture* (Huizinga 1950). Huizinga, a historian, proposes that play is always "freely chosen," never externally imposed or dictated: "First and foremost, then, all play is a voluntary activity" (Ibid., 7). For Huizinga, it is important to note, the decision to play is not a momentary choosing, a kind of gate through which the player passes. Rather, the feeling of autonomy that comes from voluntarily choosing to play permeates the entire play experience; the player *keeps* playing as a matter of

continuous and active choice. "Here, then," Huizinga writes, "we have the first main characteristic of play: it is free, is in fact freedom" (Ibid., 8). The state of play is the very state of self-determination; it is an overt act and *sustained* expression of the individual will.

Roger Caillois, in *Man, Play and Games*, recapitulates Huizinga's notion of the powerful, self-directed player: "There is no doubt play must be defined as a free and voluntary activity" (Caillois 1958, 6). Caillois, a sociologist, shares Huizinga's notion of *persistent* volition through play: "The player devotes himself spontaneously to the game, of his free will and for his pleasure, each time completely free to choose . . . above all, it is necessary that they be free to leave whenever they please" (Ibid.). But Caillois takes Huizinga's thesis a step further by addressing the potential paradox of individual freedom within the regulated, social space of games. He notes that much of play, *game* play specifically, is based on binding rules and fixed conventions, and that players must, in fact, submit to these constraints. Therefore, their decisions are influenced and restricted by the external authority of the game system. However, rather than focusing on this act of submission, he focuses instead on the freedom to make decisions and take self-motivated action in accordance with those constraints: "The game consists of the need to find or continue at once a response *which is free within the limits set by the rules*" (Ibid., 8). For Caillois, "this latitude of the player," or well-defined *scope* for freedom of action, confirms that autonomy is the phenomenological heart of play. Indeed, in the final pages of his classic study, Caillois provides his clearest statement of the power dynamic inherent in play: "Play is a creation of which the player is master" (Ibid., 163). In short, the game player is in charge.

It is not just the theorists who have identified the exercise of free will as a core and constant aspect of game play. Practitioners frequently make the same argument. Game designer Greg Costikyan echoes Caillois' thesis in his essay "I Have No Words & I Must Design," writing: "The thing that makes a game a game is the need to make decisions" (Costikyan 1994, 2.1). He describes the quintessential gameplay experience in terms of the difference between action and *volition*:

At some point, you are faced with a choice: You may choose to do A, or to do B. But what makes A better than B? Or is B better than A at some times but not at others? What factors go into the decision? What resources are to be managed? What's the eventual goal? Aha! . . . Now we're talking about decision making. (Ibid.)

Costikyan is differentiating here between performing an action that produces an effect—say, pushing a button—and choosing and self-directing an action from a range of possibilities to achieve a desired effect—pushing which button, when and for how long. Costikyan's player has a sense of purpose guided by a known goal.

Likewise, game designers Katie Salen and Eric Zimmerman argue in *Rules of Play: Game Design Fundamentals* that "playing a game means making choices" (Salen and Zimmerman 2004, 33). They, too, differentiate between "interactivity"—performing an action that generates a response—and individually determining the best action to take, thereby taking *responsibility* for the response generated. "In order to create instances of meaningful play, experience has to incorporate not just explicit interactivity, but also meaningful choice" (Ibid., 61). For Salen and Zimmerman, the unique satisfaction about gameplay emerges from the players' ability to claim direct responsibility for an outcome by controlling the decision-making process. Game players have full ownership of the actions they take.

The rise of the puppet master as an authority figure in gaming requires us to reconsider these traditional assessments of the personal power of the player. Is gaming really about experiencing self-determination? And must a playful activity automatically be denied ontological game status if players are not asked to choose an action, but rather merely to perform it? If the player is master, as Caillois suggested, then there is no room for a *puppet master*. Yet we have a proliferation of puppet-mastered games that throw all of game studies' assumptions about the power dynamics of gameplay out the window.

The Pervasive Factor

Because power plays have emerged as part of a larger trend toward moving games into real-world spaces, it is tempting to attribute the shift in power dynamics primarily to the shift of digital games from virtual spaces to everyday spaces. However, a quick survey of other reality-based games reveals that this is not the case. In recent years, even as experimental genres and platforms for the physical environments have flourished, the traditional power dynamic theorized by Huizinga and Caillois, and espoused by Costikyan, Salen, and Zimmerman, has remained the underpinning of most pervasive game design.

Pervasive gaming is an experimental genre in which at least some of the gameplay transpires in real-world environments with the aid of mobile and ubiquitous computing technologies. (Because it centers around real-world missions, the mode of gaming I have dubbed the power play is a part of this larger genre.) Notably, apart from power plays, the most high-profile projects in this new genre have been designed according to a kind of *reverse* puppet master model. Critics call this the "command-and-control" model (Tuters 2004).

The power dynamic of a command-and-control game is actually the traditional powerful player model taken to its extreme. Large numbers of gamers online make binding decisions on behalf of a much smaller number of players in the real world; the real-world players carry out their directions. Consider, for example, the 2003 *Big Urban Game (B.U.G.)*, in which three teams of a dozen or so street runners raced each other once daily, carrying supersized inflatable game pieces across the city landscape. For every street player, there were hundreds, if not thousands, of online players voting on the path the runners should take. For the vast majority of gamers, the *B.U.G.* experience consisted of analyzing a set of options and selecting one in the hopes of influencing a favorable outcome.

When I first discovered *B.U.G.*, I immediately thought its dynamic ought to be reversed. Wouldn't the online players enjoy running around in the streets, rather than voting at their computers? But of course, this instinct betrays my preference for a puppet-mastered experience. The *Big Urban Game* was in fact designed according to traditional theories of where the pleasure in gameplay lies: decision making, not carrying out others' instructions. Fun, the *B.U.G.* project argues, lies in strategic choice and agency, even agency over other people; fun is not in performing predetermined actions under someone else's authority.

The award-winning *Uncle Roy All Around You* (2004) also makes a claim for traditional player pleasures, working through a similar command-and-control design. Uncle Roy deputizes large numbers of online players as temporary commanders, directing a single street-player via text messages around town and on various site-specific missions. In a power play, this structure would be flipped; most players would take on the real-world missions, while the game designers watched and tele-directed them. But like *B.U.G.*, *Uncle Roy* theorizes its players according to the classical model of the powerful player. Gameplay is about choices, decision making, and self-direction, not performing someone else's script. Therefore, the majority of *Uncle Roy* participants are online directors rather than pervasive performers.

While these foundational pervasive games do not challenge traditional power dynamics in gameplay, in their extreme configuration of the classically powerful player, they lay bare the conventional function of games as free will simulators. As a result, their command-and-control structures have generated quite a bit of critical dialogue about the proper balance in gameplay—dialogue that speaks to the potentially troubling aspects of a puppet-mastered experience. Marc Tuters reports in his essay "The Locative Utopia" that *Uncle Roy*'s design has concerned many critics and artists who worry that such an extreme powerful player model represents "an unwelcome substitution of military logic over the 'real' world" (Ibid., 10). In other words, critics worry that bestowing online players with such great and pleasurable authority over real-world "foot soldiers" may desensitize them to the increasingly militaristic society around them. The idea that this experience will be so pleasurable that it will serve as a seduction to a more militaristic mindset confirms, of course, the idea that it is the personal experience of power that provides the fun in this kind of gameplay.

Interestingly, even more worrying to Tuters than seduction through in-game empowerment is the opposite

scenario: the idea that more and more players could wind up in the player-position of *Uncle Roy*'s select few real-world performers. He imagines a game-fueled dystopia of "docile automatons" roaming the streets, pacified into mindless performance-play by a pervasive game (Ibid., 12). From "docile automatons," it is not a great leap to puppets, of course. And indeed, I would argue this imagined puppet-making function is the real concern of *Uncle Roy*'s critics— not that *Uncle Roy* will turn players into power junkies, but rather that it will train them to accept the uneven power dynamic when they are on the flip side. In other words, it will naturalize the PM-player dynamic and therefore make players more likely to accept out-of-game puppet masters in their real, everyday lives. This is, of course, the same concern expressed by critics of power plays like flash mobs and the real-world missions of *I Love Bees*.

The reception by media theorists to games like *Uncle Roy* returns us to the original puppet master problem, then: What is the value of the unorthodox dynamic created by power plays, and to whom is it most valuable? I suggest we return here to our consideration of the players. We have examined the players' terminology and definitions; now we will focus on their motivations.

Optional Is the New Virtual

> Time to get immersed in Reality.
> —Neal Stephenson, *Snow Crash*

One constant axiom of the game development field is that contemporary gamers want highly immersive, realistic gameplay—the more immersive, the better. For decades now, experimental game designers and industry developers alike have aggressively pursued 3D graphics, emotional AI, haptic feedback loops, augmented reality systems, and all manner of other immersive technologies to give the gamers what they want. In the great majority of gaming culture, this "will to reality" has driven digital gaming in a particular direction— that of greater sensory realism. But *looking like, sounding like,* and *feeling like* the real thing is not the only conceivable set of criteria for a realistic digital aesthetic.[7] The puppet-mastered experience is an experiment in creating immersive experience that is not defined primarily by sensory assets.

The pervasive gaming genre as a whole (including power plays) engages gamers with real-world environments, drawing on the *actuality* and *physicality* of other people, objects, and spaces to create an alternative mode of immersive gameplay. Through ubiquitous computing technologies, the players are immersed in *reality itself*, as opposed to being immersed in a digitally rendered *virtual* reality. This kind of immersion, as we have seen, does not require abandoning the traditional power structure of gameplay. However, power plays are experimentally immersive beyond their use of real-world environments, and the players' submission to the puppet masters' commands is the driving mechanic of this immersion.

I believe that the designers and pervasive gamers who embrace the puppet master model have discovered a new criterion for digital realism—a kind of *psychological* realism that perfectly complements the "immersed in reality" framework of real-world, mission-based gaming. Media critic Thomas de Zengotita's recent theory of *optionality* in a media-saturated culture examines the dueling psychologies of reality and its hypermediated alternative; it is the perfect critical framework for exploring the function of dramatic submission in creating highly immersive pervasive gameplay.

In his 2005 treatise *Mediated*, Thomas de Zengotita makes a startling ontological claim: Reality is not the opposite of virtuality, but rather the opposite of *optionality*. He observes:

> In a mediated world, the opposite of real isn't phony or illusional or fictional—it's optional. Idiomatically, we recognize this when we say "The reality is . . . ," meaning something that has to be dealt with, something that isn't an option. We are most free of mediation, we are most real, when we are at the disposal of accident and necessity. That's when we are not being addressed. That's when we go without the flattery intrinsic to representation.
> (De Zengotita 2005, 14)

For De Zengotita, the essence of virtual experience is its optionality—in other words, the power to choose from multiple options. There is a sense of "flattery," De Zengotita suggests, inherent in the offer: *You choose.* Choose from multiple channels, choose on or off, choose customization—it's all up to you. This flattery, I want to suggest, is exactly what traditionally designed games offer up to their players: an appeal to their sense of individual authority and autonomy by offering up a range of actions and avatars from which the player can choose. This is why traditionally power-structured games, even if they are reality-based or feature the most advanced VR effects, never approach a deep-seated, psychological realism. They are from start to finish a matter of optionality. If we accept De Zengotita's argument, optional is the new virtual. Therefore, in order for a game to truly seem real, it must eliminate the optionality that has so long defined gameplay.

The mission-based design of power plays is especially well-suited to the challenge of eliminating optionality. De Zengotita characterizes the optionality of a mediated environment as an opportunity, through self-expressive choice, "to be the author of your being and becoming" (Ibid., 78). Most digital games, where actions are self-determined, are the epitome of this self-authored experience. But in mission-based power plays, as a player you are precisely *not* your own author. You are written in advance by the puppet master. You are the scripts that you are given. In this sense, the dictated real-world missions that gamers carry out are the opposite of mediated optionality. There is no self-authorship, only performance. It is highly immersive because the player is asked to go without the flattery of being allowed to author his or her own experience. Yes, you can choose not to complete a mission, but if you make this choice, you are no longer playing. Within the game, there is

Jane McGonigal

7. For instance, the alternate reality gaming (ARG) genre, out of which the term "puppet master" first emerged, and in which it currently is most frequently applied, is an excellent example of a new immersive aesthetic based on a realistic *doing*, rather than a realistic *feeling*. As I have argued previously about alternate reality games, for example in the 2003 essay "This Is Not a Game: Immersive Aesthetics and Collective Play" (McGonigal 2003), in contrast to immersive artworks that try to create realistic sensory experiences and meaningful interactivity in an artificial setting (the history of this tradition is explored most thoroughly in Oliver Grau's 2003 *Virtual Art: From Illusion to Immersion*), the immersive aesthetic proposed by ARGs use *natural settings* as the immersive framework, employing everyday network technologies as virtual reality devices. They eschew the kind of special technology we normally associate with virtual or augmented reality, such as wired gloves, headsets, or goggles, and interactive programs or simulators. In this sense, it is reasonable to argue that nothing about ARG play is simulated. The computer-driven alternate reality that they create is make-believe, but every aspect of the player's experience is, phenomenologically speaking, real.

37.1) August 24, 2004: A dozen *I Love Bees* players arrive at GPS coordinates in Burbank, California. At the designated moment, the payphone nearby rings with further clues and instructions. (42 Entertainment)

no free will; there is only the reality of what you *have* to do. Play itself may still be voluntary, as it has so long been theorized, but the core experiential quality has changed.

In a culture where everything is designed for maximum optionality, and reality is defined by having to accept a situation exactly as it is with no special customization, modification, or self-authorship, the most immersively realistic game is the one in which a puppet master tells you exactly what to do, when to do it, where, and for how long. For immersive gamers, the escape from constant optionality is the pleasure of the relative powerlessness of a power play.

Behind the Curtain

> We all thought we were going to have a little more control over the situation. But you can't predict how people will act.
> —Mike Monello, "Art of the Heist Live Puppet Master Chat"

I have argued that the puppet-mastered experience affords a uniquely immersive experience by denying players the power of individual choice, by wrenching them out of a mediated everyday life of endless optionality. But do the gamers really cede *all* control? Is the power really as one-sided as it seems from the outside, and as the players themselves strategically describe it? Or, instead, is the *outward appearance* and *active make-believe* of ceding all control enough to accomplish the

kind of psychologically immersive gameplay the gamers desire? Perhaps it is time to pull back the curtain and make a few first-person observations about the relationship between players and their puppet masters.

I made my debut as a puppet master on January 19, 2002 as the lead writer and mission designer for an eighty-player *Go Game* in the North Beach neighborhood of San Francisco—a year and a half before I started organizing flash mobs and two and a half years before I took my place behind the curtain of *I Love Bees*. That day, on the wintergreen lawn of a public city park, I experienced a spontaneous rupture in what I had imagined would be a smooth and uncomplicated PM-player dynamic: We tell the players what to do, and they do it. Since that day, the same little *Go Game* kink has emerged again and again in many different genres and contexts. It is a pattern I now recognize as the highly complex, and consistently collaborative, texture of a puppet-mastered game.

A bit of background: The *Go Game* is an afternoon-long urban adventure in which competing teams receive over their cell phones clues keyed to specific locations around their city. When players arrive at each location, they download a superhero-themed performance mission: assemble undercover disguises using whatever you can find at a nearby thrift store; make a secret agent waiting for you on the #30 bus laugh by any means necessary (not that you have any idea which of the dozens of people on the bus the secret agent is); conduct a séance on the floor of a crowded café to improve the psychic atmosphere; figure out how to get onto a luxury hotel rooftop and attract as much attention as you can; get a whole barful of strangers singing and dancing along with you to any song you want to play on the jukebox.

That day, we were putting up only the second *Go Game* ever (Wink Back, Inc. has produced hundreds of games for over 20,000 players across the United States since) so as puppet masters, we were still experimenting and making last-minute tweaks to our scripts. Just before the game started, another *Go Game* writer decided to revise the opening text message I had prepared. My text was a bit dry: "Welcome, superheroes! Press GO when you're ready to start the game." We both agreed it would be better to set a more playful mood, so she added a colorful interjection to the welcome message: "Howdy, superheroes—hold onto your hats, it's time to drop your pants and dance! Press GO when you're ready to start the game."

I had already forgotten about this minor text change when the teams assembled in Washington Square Park to receive their first set of instructions. I hid in a group of park-goers and watched as the players huddled in small groups, switched on their phones, and downloaded our welcome message. I was waiting for the teams to scatter and hit the streets— once they pressed "GO," the first round of clues would send each team off in a different direction. Instead, something completely unexpected happened. Half a dozen players began unbuckling their belts, unzipping their jeans, and showing off their underwear while waving their arms in the air. This caught the attention of other players, who quickly realized: A-ha! "Drop your pants and dance!"—this is our first mission! So they too, dropped their pants and started dancing. Before long, most of the players were dancing merrily in their underwear. They took photos of each other to "prove" their success in completing the mission.

Of course, the opening message "drop your pants and dance" wasn't a mission at all. But by the time the park was full of pantless performers, my fellow puppet masters and I were already behind our curtain. There was nothing we could do to intervene. We just watched from a distance, with our mouths hanging open.

The first time I told this story at a lecture, an audience member challenged me: "You puppet masters must really get a kick out of manipulating these players to do whatever you want. That must be such a power trip." In fact, the exact opposite was true. We didn't get a rush of power when the players misinterpreted our simple welcome message. We actually felt completely out of control. We had worked so carefully to craft just the right text for our mission scripts, and yet from the very first moment of gameplay, our actual, effective authority was stripped away. Yes, we could give the players a set of instructions—but clearly we could not predict or dictate how they would read and embody those instructions. We were absolutely not in control of our players' creative instincts.

In Washington Square Park that day, as the players danced in their underwear, I turned to another puppet master and

said, "It's their game now." He nodded, and that's when I realized: No matter what it looked like to outsiders, we were not pulling these players' strings. Yes, the players were following our commands, but their interpretation of the commands left them fully in charge of their own experience. The scripts had been delivered; the actors were putting on the show. In that moment I realized that the players in a puppet-mastered game are not performing objects; they are performing subjects. And that performing subjectivity is never ceded, even in submission to a puppet master's orders.

The willful subjectivity of a performer is in its own way a kind of self-determination, a co-authorship with the writers. De Zengotita acknowledges this when he discusses the flash mob phenomenon as a kind of middle ground between reality and optionality. In the middle of

> so many flash mobs . . . you were being the phenomenon as you were seeing it represented, in real time, unfolding before you. You could see the impact of your role on the national stage in essentially the same way you can see the impact of your button-pressing in a video game. You were the agent, you were the star. (Ibid., 152)

As De Zengotita points out, performing in the public eye gives players an expressive visibility and an audience that provides the same quality of feedback a digital game offers. The audience reaction becomes the new metric, equally capable of giving players a sense of responsibility for a given outcome.

Interpretive control is not yet part of what we understand to be meaningful play in digital games, but perhaps it should be. Crafting a representation, designing a physical manifestation of a digitally distributed text, as De Zengotita suggests, is its own kind of agency, one that game designers can build into the power model of their games. Performance allows for play in an otherwise rigid gaming structure.

Recognizing that the players co-author their gameplay experience through interpretive control solves the problem of the so-called perversity of power plays. But it poses a new problem for designers. How do you manage the risk of players going off-script? Do gamers ever push back against the puppet masters, and if so, through what channels? How can you prepare for this, and recognize the push back when it happens? What processes does each side have for "negotiating" the live action scripts in these games? These questions represent the future of puppet master design research.

So I want to return, finally, to a preliminary experiment in this research area—the original *I Love Bees* scenario, in which thousands of players showed up at GPS coordinates with no idea of what they would be asked to do. I was the puppet master in charge of collecting, scheduling and disseminating the GPS coordinates to players, and one of four puppet masters designing the live missions that players were asked to accomplish at those coordinates. I was also in charge of tracking player forums, blogs, and chat rooms to try to get as complete a picture as possible of how players were interpreting our scripts—the dates, times, and coordinates.

When players showed up on August 24th laden with every form of digital communications technology and personal media devices you could imagine, they were interpreting the vagueness of the GPS coordinates in a very particular way: *Be prepared for anything.* This interpretation was revealed to us, the puppet masters, through the photos, blog posts, and live discussions the players shared online. The *ILB* PMs, myself included, were amazed at what, exactly, the players were prepared to do. They had compiled databases of each other's cell phone numbers in case they needed to relay information to or from the field. They had stationed significant numbers of players online in case real-time research was necessary to complete the mission. They brought large numbers of friends and family with them in case a group performance was necessary.

What they were in fact asked to do once they arrived on site, as it turned out, did not require any of those improvised supplies, allies, or information systems. At each coordinate, at the appropriate time, a payphone rang. If players located and answered the ringing payphone, they were asked a question—the same question at every phone—about the game's heroine. If they answered correctly (we gauged their

response with voice recognition technology), they heard one of thirty sections of a radio drama. Their mission? To intercept as many pieces of the drama as possible and to report back to other players what they had heard. We played thirty different bits of drama that day; all were successfully intercepted in at least one location, and players met back up online to put the narrative pieces together. They fulfilled their mission perfectly.

But like the *Go Game* players whose interpretation-expectations exceeded the designers' intentions, the players had actually read the scripts—GPS coordinates, dates, and times—as asking *more* of them than we, the puppet masters, had intended. They had demonstrated for us their greater capability, even though they hadn't been directed to use it—yet. By putting it on visible display for the puppet masters, it was like they were asking us to ask more of them. They were directing us to direct them better.

August 24th was just the first of twelve weeks' worth of GPS missions. There were biweekly updates to the coordinates page; ultimately over 40,000 phone calls were made to over 1,000 payphones around the world. And this iterative structure allowed the *ILB* puppet masters to rewrite game missions in real time to better suit the interpretations

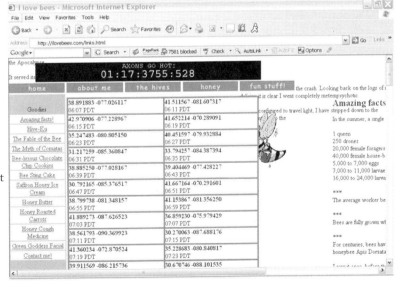

37.2) August 17, 2004: The *I Love Bees* Web site lists 210 sets of GPS coordinates and corresponding meet-up times, with a central timer counting down to the date 8/24/2004. The coordinates map to locations spanning the entire United States. (Andrew Sorcini)

the players were spinning off of our "scripts"—the series of GPS coordinates, dates, and times.

Over the next three months, we created missions that allowed the players to do the very things they had already demonstrated to us the desire and capability to do. Each mission still involved answering a ringing payphone and intercepting a piece of radio drama. But because they came prepared with cameras and documented their payphone missions, even though we hadn't instructed them to, we also started asking them to do things that were worth photographing: show up in costume, stage dramatic scenes of rescue, decorate the payphone booths. Because many players came with Web-access phones and PDAs, we distributed clues and instructions for these photo missions on Web pages and in chat rooms. Because they came to the payphones in teams, we began instructing them to bring even larger groups of friends and family to pose by the payphones and to submit photographic evidence of the performing crowds. When they started coming to the phones with musical instruments, we directed them to improvise songs and to jam over the payphones with musicians across the country; we broadcast recordings of these calls over the Web. When they interpreted clusters of GPS coordinates in one city as a local challenge against other cities' clusters of GPS coordinates, we scheduled simultaneous runs of phones in one city versus another city to make what they incorrectly perceived as an intentional competition into an actual structural element of the game.

Each week, we analyzed what the players had shown us through their interpretations of the previous mission, and we wrote new scripts to give them exactly the stage direction they were implicitly requesting.

In either the *Go Game* or *I Love Bees*, were the players willfully misinterpreting their mission scripts? No, I do not think so. The pushing back was more organic, more instinctive. It was a matter of exuberance and desire, rather than conscious strategy or disruption. In the *Go Game*, players dropped their pants to dance because they wanted to; it seemed like a reasonable interpretation of the game's dramatic text because it was already in the realm of possibilities imagined by the players to be fun and

appropriate for that particular time and context. Likewise, the *ILB* players were communicating what they thought would be fun to do at payphones by optimistically interpreting each set of GPS coordinates as asking more of them than the previous set.

Behind the curtain in power plays, it's not just algorithms—so the game design is responsive. The puppet masters are able to create new mission scripts without giving players overt decision-making authoring, by following players' interpretations and writing the parts the gamers' interpretations demonstrate the desire and the capacity to play. These co-authored commands preserve the immersive power dynamic because they are still received as non-negotiable imperatives; however, they also allow players to sense their own performative agency.

Conclusion

The gamer's exercise of free will has long been assumed to be a core and constant experiential aspect of gaming. But the rise of the puppet master in pervasive gaming suggests that in the new ubiquitous computing landscape, many gamers want to experience precisely the opposite phenomenon. They are learning the immersive pleasures of becoming *actors* in a gaming environment, of transforming themselves into physical vehicles for someone else's digital vision. As game-actors, they become masters of interpretative embodiment; they accept as their mission the real-world incarnation of a digital design, much as stage actors in traditional theater have long served as the actual embodiment of virtual texts. For players, the pleasures and challenges of real-world gaming missions are the pleasures and challenges of dramatic performance. And for puppet masters, writing real-world mission scripts is very much the same process as writing dramatic texts; redesigning them in real time is very much the process of directing live actors on stage. The success of the puppet master challenges our assumptions about the kinds of action and interaction that qualify as gameplay, reveal dramatic interpretation to be a viable game mechanic, and demonstrate the value of a dramaturgical perspective for pervasive game design.

References: Literature

Caillois, Roger (1958). *Man, Play and Games*. New York: Free Press.

Costikyan, Greg (1994). "I Have No Words & I Must Design." <http://www.costik.com/nowords.html>.

De Zengotita, Thomas (2005). *Mediated*. New York: Bloomsbury Publishing.

Huizinga, Johan (1950). *Homo Ludens: A Study of the Play Element in Culture*. Boston: Beacon Press.

Johnson, Steven (2005). *Everything Bad Is Good For You*. New York: Riverhead Books.

McGonigal, Jane (2003). "This Is Not a Game: Immersive Aesthetics and Collective Play." *Fine Art Forum* 17, no. 8.

McGonigal, Jane (2005). "I Love Bees: A Case Study." Experimental Gameplay Workshop, Game Developers Conference 2005. San Jose, CA.

Monello, Mike (2005). "Art of the Heist Live Puppet Master Chat." Alternate Reality Gaming Network. July 10, 2005.

Salen, Katie and Eric Zimmerman (2003). *Rules of Play: Fundamentals of Game Design*. Cambridge, MA: MIT Press.

Stacey, Sean (2002–2005). "The Unfiction Glossary." <http://www.unfiction.com/glossary/>.

Stephenson, Neal (1992). *Snow Crash*. New York: Random House.

Tuters, Marc (2004). "The Locative Utopia." *TCM Locative Reader*. <http://locative.net/tcmreader/index.php?endo;tuters>.

West End Games (2004). "Introduction to Being a Gamemaster." Downingtown, PA: Purgatory Publishing. <http://www.westendgames.com/d6/gmintro.pdf>.

References: Games

Art of the Heist. Mike Monello, Brian Cane; GMD Studios. 2005.

The Beast. Microsoft. 2001.

Big Urban Game. Nick Fortugno, Frank Lantz, and Katie Salen; Design Institute. 2003.

Cthulhu Live 3rd Edition. *Robert H. McLaughlin; Skirmisher Publishing. 2006.*

Dungeons & Dragons. Gary Gygax and Dave Arneson; TSR, Inc. 1974.

Go Game. Ian Fraser and Finnegan Kelly; Wink Back, Inc. 2002.

I Love Bees. Elan Lee, Sean Stewart, Jim Stewartson, and Jane McGonigal; 42 Entertainment. 2004.

On *A Measure for Marriage*
Nick Fortugno

In the summer of 2004, I was approached by my friend Greg Moccia with a unique task: to design a live-action role-playing event at which he could propose to his girlfriend. The resulting game was *A Measure for Marriage*, a one-session LARP in which players took the roles of nobles and attendants as they attempted to find romance, thwart villainy, and restore true love in an improvised Shakespearean comedy. Of course, designing a LARP about romance that must end with a real proposal is a daunting task, and the success of *A Measure for Marriage* was a result of careful use of character design, emergent pacing, and player expectation.

A Measure for Marriage was held at the Brooklyn Botanical Gardens and set in the fictional Renaissance kingdom of Navarro. Six of the players were assigned roles as nobles of the region and another six were their attendants. I played the role of the King's seneschal, which gave me the ability to speak to anyone at any time and to keep a close eye on the game as it unfolded.

The nobles were organized into three couples, betrothed to each other for political or financial reasons. However, the relationships were ill-suited and lacked any real love, a fact that the attendants knew well and discussed openly amongst themselves. Marianna (played by Greg's girlfriend) was the king's daughter, who was herself to wed a charming young prince (played by Greg). Unfortunately, the princess was also being wooed by the King's power-hungry advisor (an NPC), who conspired to send the prince off to war and have him murdered. The would-be-murderer (another NPC) had a change of heart at the last moment and merely left the prince unconscious and amnesiac on the battlefield, where he was found by a noble and made into an attendant.

In the meantime, presuming the prince was dead, the King assented that his daughter should be betrothed to the advisor, giving the villain a chance at the throne and the power to abuse the region's attendants, which he did with impunity. All looked to be in order in the kingdom, but beneath the surface lay disappointment, loneliness, and wickedness.

The session itself was narrativized as a meeting the King called shortly after the tragic death of his wife. The LARP began with the King announcing that, after reflecting on the true love he and his Queen had shared, he realized all of the noble couples were mere political shams. He then declared that marriage was forbidden in his kingdom.

At this point, the players were left on their own to talk, conspire, and commiserate over the King's declaration. Realizing the folly of the King's decision,[1] they pleaded with him to rescind his announcement. He agreed to reconsider, but only if the nobles could convince him of their love through a series of trials, or measures for marriage. However, as the nobles spoke in the gardens to prepare for these trials, they discovered that their true loves were among the other nobles. The players then decided to pursue these new loves, scheming to ensure everyone got what they needed politically while romancing among the roses.

In the meantime, as the attendants gossiped amongst themselves, they discovered the amnesiac lost prince among their number. They quickly decided that restoring the lost prince would both return the princess's happiness and remove the loathsome advisor who was constantly torturing them. Of course, they also realized that the villain wouldn't hesitate to crush them all if they tried to reveal the prince's identity, so they first conspired to expose the advisor's villainy and thus remove him from power. The attendants pumped their nobles for information, cajoled and blackmailed the advisor's servants, and protected the prince from scrutiny, all while fulfilling their responsibilities as servants.

The core idea of *A Measure for Marriage* was to create a story that would provide a natural environment for the proposal to take place. Of course, this idea directly tackles some of the inherent issues of LARP design including the lack of a fixed plot, the simultaneous activity of several autonomous players, and the absence of a central authority guiding every moment of the experience. The game had to end with a marriage proposal, but for it to be an effective

---

1. Some of the marriages were between warring regions, and all of Navarro might be plunged into war if the weddings did not take place.

38.1) *A Measure for Marriage* participants.

LARP, it had to reach that ending as a result of independent player choice. In addition, the moment of the proposal could not feel contrived. Thus, it was essential that the entire experience be themed around love and paced properly to culminate in the wedding proposal. So, how could I ensure that, without knowing exactly what they would do, the players would act within the theme and develop a story that would naturally result in the predetermined proposal?

The key decision for reigning in this unpredictability was the choice of genre. *A Measure for Marriage* was a Shakespearean comedy LARP, a period piece in the tradition of *A Midsummer's Night's Dream* and *Twelfth Night*. Shakespearean comedies have a number of standard tropes of which my players were well-aware: mismatched lovers, people in disguise, villains to be thwarted, and a wedding proposal conclusion. Because the players were so familiar with the genre, they naturally adapted to its anticipated narrative structure, engaging in witty conversation, oaths of love, and comic scheming.

In particular, character design was a crucial component. Players had character sheets (composed by Greg and myself) to give them directions about their roles in the setting. Every noble sheet, for example, gave an explanation of the character's backstory that both pointed out their specific dissatisfaction with their current fiancé and their pining for the kind of person they could truly love. These details gave the noble players hooks to pursue; while I had no idea exactly how they would resolve them, I knew their motivations were theme-appropriate. This careful character design, coupled with the pressures of the game's genre, guided the players to make choices that were completely unexpected[2] but entirely within the bounds of the romantic theme.

Of course, the potential issue with the familiarity of the genre was that players could act on these plots too quickly and rush the game to its conclusion before the tone was set for the proposal. To solve this problem, I used a set of control devices called *gates*. In *A Measure for Marriage*, players were limited in the ways they could communicate, in a manner reflecting player expectations of class. Nobles could speak to anyone, but amongst themselves, it was gauche for nobles to discuss anything serious, including politics, economics, and especially issues of romance. Servants could speak to each other freely and could attend to their own noble, but were not permitted to speak to other nobles or the King. This restriction meant that any vital communication between two nobles had to be handled through attendant intermediaries.

At the same time, the King's demand that the nobles prove their love (through such measures as vows, praises, and songs[3]) meant that the nobles were periodically called away from their attendants for stretches of the game. Since any major action of the game (confessions of love, blackmailing the advisor's henchman, restoring the lost prince's memory) required joint actions of nobles and servants, these actions had a natural duration that depended on attendants having time with their nobles to get information and share plans, and having time away from them to scheme and negotiate with the other servants. The use of these communication gates allowed me to pace the game's progression without any heavy-handed techniques. Despite the fact that players had total control over their actions, there were naturally emerging limits that brought the game to resolution in the target four hours.

By the conclusion of the LARP, players had resolved the

Nick Fortugno

---

2. Including impromptu schemes, blackmails, betrayals, near-declarations of war, and even a full recital of a monologue from *Much Ado about Nothing*.

3. This was particularly comical, as none of the players knew in advance that they would have to do this, so they were forced to make up praises on the spot for a person that their character loathed.

outstanding plots—uniting the correct couples, condemning the villain, and revealing the true identity of the lost prince. All that remained was the proposal, the classic end of any Shakespearean comedy and this LARP's moment of real-world consequence. Of course, because of the generic conventions and the strong romantic theme, everyone had been expecting a proposal for the last four hours of play, so when the lost prince started his declaration to the princess, everyone was emotionally prepared for what was coming. However, when Greg broke character and delivered his wedding proposal to his girlfriend (rather than her character, the princess), everyone was shocked by the shift to this real-world announcement. The LARP ending offered the natural cathartic resolution of the romantic story, while simultaneously providing a dramatic context for the public display of a real-world engagement.

Ultimately, *A Measure for Marriage* was a narrative experience of love, loyalty, and union. The choice of genre and characters, the use of gates to control pacing, and the conflation of in- and out-of-character emotions and expectations led to a unique and compelling story. As with all happy endings, the kingdom was safe, the characters found happiness, and the players experienced a powerful performance of love and fidelity.

Reference

Fortugno, Nick (2004). *A Measure for Marriage*.

On A Measure for Marriage

On *unexceptional.net*
Robert Nideffer

Overview

unexceptional.net is a mystical realist journey catalyzed by a series of interconnected events related to sexual infidelity, political conspiracy, and spiritual transformation, where you get to play a supporting role to the main character, Guy. Guy is a rather nondescript, fat, balding white dude with a shaved head and a goatee. He is anal-obsessive, overly sensitive, emotionally distant, unnecessarily pessimistic, morally righteous, and occasionally perverted. He is also an avid game player, an aspiring game designer and comic artist, and a fairly competent hacker. Guy has just recently found out that his long-time partner is having an affair. This discovery launches him upon a series of quests, which you participate in, in an effort to gain insight into the nature of his partner's relationship.

The *unexceptional.net* project draws on the traditions of comics, graphic novels, and computer games to create an environment that crosses boundaries between pop culture, fine art, and social critique. It also blurs the borders between "real" space and "virtual" space. The game has been developed as a net-centric, multimodal, pervasive action-adventure RPG accessible via GPS-enabled phones, the Internet, and a 3D game client. The main gateway to the game is through a Web portal designed by Guy, where he keeps a blog documenting his daily trials and tribulations. He links to his comics, Web hacks, and games from the blog. Guy also provides running commentary on issues as his dramatic experience unfolds. Guy's life is utterly out of control, and you attempt to help him regain a sense of stability.

For better or worse, Guy's the kind of friend you like to have because he gives you and your other friends something to talk about. But unlike cults of personality built up around "live" celebrities where people must fantasize a personal connection to the star, Guy actually *can* reach people on a personal level. Moreover, he can do so on a nonhuman scale, because there's nothing to prevent him from carrying on thousands of intimate relationships at once, since for all practical purposes he's nothing but a highly scripted,

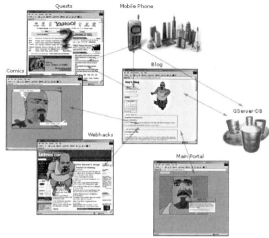

39.1) GPS and Web interface.

automated, and dynamically updated interactive database.

The overall narrative arc entails:

> An introduction to Guy as the crass, angry, resentful, cynical, and curmudgeonly fellow that he is by nature;

> The catapulting of Guy into a period of crisis linked to discovery of his cheating partner Betty and her love for Dick in the midst of terrorism, war, and homeland insecurity;

> Exposure to Betty and Dick's disturbingly co-opted Eastern mysticism, deployed as a means for experimenting with mind and body control techniques that use Guy as an unsuspecting guinea pig; and

> Guy's neurotic compulsion to achieve enlightenment . . . whatever that may mean. To attain enlightenment, Guy must be accompanied on a series of quests to find special objects that will help open all seven of his major "chakras"—according to Buddhist doctrine the energy centers of the body.

High-Level Goals

As of this writing, *unexceptional.net* is in active development. Key objectives of the project include:

> Using *unexceptional.net* as a testbed for deploying custom-designed and freely distributed software that

269

On *unexceptional.net*

takes advantage of everyday communication technologies such as blogging, e-mail, 3D gaming, and mobile telephony in order to enable anywhere/anytime access to heterogenous game worlds;

Implementing the game infrastructure in such a way that it can either be easily modified or used as a template for alternative content development and deployment;

Facilitating ease of content creation through provision of a Web-based "world-building toolkit";

Sharing the results in the public domain through Internet distribution, formal exhibition in fine art contexts, professional conferences and events, and publication; and

Exploring novel forms of single-player and multiplayer interaction.

Example Game Scenarios and Interfaces

Greta, a PC user, ends up at Guy's Web portal on her PC, reads a bit about his project, and decides to create an account in order to become a registered player. Account creation requires a player name, a valid e-mail address, a mobile phone number, and a password. Upon registration, she gets sent an e-mail from Guy, and is forwarded to his blog, which contains a single post providing context for the game about to unfold. The post also gives her the first quest, and provides a link for downloading Guy's recently released mobile phone game,

39.2) Guy playing with himself in full-blown 3D.

Dick Hunt. She activates the quest, and then downloads, installs, and launches the phone game.

When Greta starts the phone application, the entire game world—terrains, structures, characters, statistics, inventory, quest—gets built for her based on her geographic location. The game can now continue endlessly in every direction for Greta, due to an algorithmically generated grid-based game layout. Moreover, each grid has a simple coordinate that's stored in memory and allows for identical path and object placement on return. The game also sends Greta's physical location information to the game server, allowing her to be tracked by other players in real time. If Greta decides to play without a GPS-enabled phone, or to simply use the applet version of the game in Guy's online portal, she can still advance by:

Exchanging inventory items with non-player characters in the applet;

Offering to sell goods to a shopkeeper accessible through the blog; or

Participating in an online trading network, also accessible through Guy's blog, which allows her to post offers for goods to other players, who are alerted via e-mail as well as upon blog login.

After several minutes Greta enters a predefined "hot spot" that causes an automated call to be placed from Guy's help-bot to Greta. Greta's phone rings, interrupting the visual interface to *Dick Hunt.* She answers, and can now continue her quest in voice-only mode. Guy's bot tells her she's in the vicinity of a spot where Betty was rumored to have spent time with Dick, and goes on to list all the objects available for her to interact with, along with the actions that she can use to manipulate each object. Greta successfully "gets" some of the available objects, which get added to her inventory. She then unsuccessfully attempts to "use" one or two of them.

Greta continues walking and talking, as her voice commands are interpreted on the fly by the text-to-speech and speech-to-text system. Along the way, she enters a region where another player is active. At this point, Guy's bot tells her that she may attempt to steal items from the inventory of the unsuspecting player. Greta does so, but unfortunately is unsuccessful and instead has something stolen from her!

The phone constantly updates the inventory and statistics kept in the database of both parties. Greta quits out of voice-mode and resumes playing the visual version of the *Dick Hunt* phone game. When she finally navigates both the in-game avatar as well as her physical body to the destination waypoint, she happily watches as a special key object descends from the heavens to be placed in her inventory.

Later Greta arrives back home and logs into Guy's blog from her PC. She now sees her updated game-state information as well as a visual mapping of her movement in space and time. She also has a blog-based link to a Web page associated with the key object, which contains a key code that will allow her to gain access to critical game-related information. Once accessed, her initial quest is completed, her stats are updated, and a new blog post and quest are made available. Next time she thinks she may even want to try the 3D client. But for now, she's had enough of Guy and his chaotic world <http://unexceptional.net>.

39.3) Guy with his pussy.

On *Itinerant*
Teri Rueb

Project Summary

Itinerant <http://turbulence.org/Works/itinerant/index.htm> invites people to take a walk through Boston Common and surrounding neighborhoods to experience an interactive sound work that reframes Mary Shelley's *Frankenstein*, the classic tale of conflict between techno-scientific hubris and the human spirit. The project engages a search for an elusive character who is doppelgänger to both the doctor and the creature of the novel. Sounds, automatically "played" by visitors as they move through different parts of the city, create a series of frames within which to reflect upon our highly mobile, technologically saturated society and issues of identity, place, and displacement. The sonic overlay is also presented as an interactive map on the Web, creating a reframing and displacement of this site-specific work.

Artist Statement

The installation is a site-specific responsive sound environment that weaves together and spatializes two texts: excerpts from Mary Shelley's *Frankenstein* and an original text about an ambiguous character—the uncle—who is doppelgänger to both the doctor and the creature in Shelley's novel. Shelley's text is relayed in "quotes" as excerpted passages from a professional reading of *Frankenstein*. The second text, read by the author, has a more homespun quality. Spoken word passages and a counterpoint of footsteps and sounds that suggest the movement of an invisible figure play back automatically as the participant moves through the Boston Common and surrounding neighborhoods. The technical components of the system include a pair of headphones connected to a small pocket PC with a GPS and custom software (recently replaced with commercially available software). The participant's movement, tracked by the GPS, triggers the playback of the sounds as she moves through parts of the city space where sounds have been "placed." The active regions of the city space correspond to regions defined in the software. When the location of the participant intersects with one of these regions, the software automatically triggers playback of the appropriate sound file.

In creating *Itinerant*, my aim was to draw the participant into

Intro Passages

These intro passages start at the gallery and proceed along Commonwealth Avenue. This is explicitly marked on the map as the recommended route into the rest of the installation space, the remainder of which is meant to be explored in any order. However, as the space of the installation is indicated on the map and is physically constrained to produce certain transversals, these passages typically segue into the passages in the public garden (Juxtaposition #2).

Sound of a shopping cart being pushed through the streets.

Rueb:

A dinner party, the table set—each plate a luminous circle of reflection, a bright face of hope and anticipation. Grandma and grandpa are coming, and maybe Uncle Kelley, though he comes as often and predictably as some rare comet of obscure origin, drifting in from what I always imagined as an exotic journey around the world. Egypt,

40.s1) and 40.s2) Commonwealth Avenue.

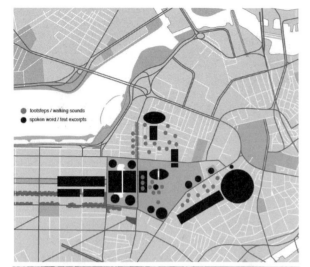

footsteps / walking sounds
spoken word / text excerpts

40.1) *Itinerant* process and final map.

274

Teri Rueb

Syria, the Far East . . . though it was usually Haiti. This man whose name I share was a wanderer, a face I knew only in hazy dim patches that float before my mind's eye, flickering masses that inevitably resolve into the image of a young man, a framed high school portrait that sits on the dresser of my grandmother's guest room.

I see him now as he was at Christmas in 1972. I was four years old. I had never met this man before and though I didn't know it then, I would never see him again at the holidays. He was on special leave from the hospital in Colorado Springs where my father had him committed. His phone calls to our home ignored, he had crossed a line and begun to make threatening phone calls to my father's colleagues.

He sat low in the brown and gold striped armchair. His long legs cut a straight line deep into the nest of torn gift wrap and wriggling children, a nest of frenzied activity as the long-awaited moment finally arrived, setting five children scrambling to get their share. His lithium-laced gaze, unwavering, shot through the glow of the brood clamoring about the tree, resting on some distant horizon of disbelief—an engineer lost in infinity.

My grandparents, parents, uncles, and aunts hover tenuously at the vague periphery of this image. The moment thus circumscribed and suspended, hung in the delicate balance of domesticity and disaster. My mother sent silent signals that rippled invisibly through my sisters' bodies, then mine. She sat at the center of a Web spun of nature and nurture that registered even the subtlest tremor—the threat of inevitable rupture. Relentlessly we would mend the frayed fabric with carefully placed words and obedient gestures, knitting the family together again in a tangle of love and lies.

And now I find myself walking the streets of yet another new city, this one full of history, age, and affiliation. The brick facades and frozen sidewalks press against me as I pull myself along, wandering around residential neighborhoods: Back Bay, Beacon Hill, South End. The windows, their bright eyes gleaming, invite my furtive glance inside, inside the sepia-toned hazy glow that envelops the figures of a family. I catch myself staring, like Shelley's Frankenstein, that pitiful creature who night after night peered in at the family through the window of their little cottage in the woods. Only I realize that I am actually on the inside, looking out—trying to find myself in the reflection of him on the outside, looking in. I am haunted by the memory of this life born into solitary existence, wandering the globe in search of a name, an identity through progeny—a creature living outside the rhythm of biological time.

a spatialized narrative in a very specific way. I wanted to explicitly engage the participant's physical movement, shifting perspective, and interaction with the surrounding environment as a primary force in creating tension in the work. The participant's movement through the city physically generates the story as it triggers sound playback; however, I wanted to extend this action to implicate the participant as a charged body in public space whose movement and presence become critical agents in structuring the meaning of the work. The primary theme of alienation and the plight of the social outcast is played out through a series of physical tableaus and boundary crossings enacted by the participant as she walks through the urban landscape listening to a patchwork of location-specific spoken narratives delivered in different voices. My hope was to cast the participant into a cycle of alienation and ambivalence as the point of view in the story shifted across narrator, creature, doctor, and the character of the uncle. Through juxtaposing constantly shifting perspectives, both in the story and in the physical journey through the city, the participant might find herself caught between identification with and alienation from the various characters in the work and their reflection in the actual people she encounters along her journey, including herself. The observer's own point of view as a walker in the city becomes conflated with the wandering characters whose voices fill her head as she walks.

Rather than a peaceful walk through the city accompanied by an entertaining or moody story, my aim was to use the highly charged aspect of the participant's body in the system—both

40.2) Outside the Gallery on Newbury Street.

Juxtaposition #2
The Public Garden

Shelley:

Autumn passed thus. I saw, with surprise and grief, the leaves decay and fall, and nature again assume the barren and bleak appearance it had worn when I first beheld the woods and the lovely moon. Yet I did not heed the bleakness of the weather; I was better fitted by my conformation for the endurance of cold than heat. But my chief delights were the sight of the flowers, the birds, and all the gay apparel of summer; when those deserted me, I turned with more attention towards the cottagers. Their happiness was not decreased by the absence of summer. They loved and sympathized with one another; and their joys, depending on each other, were not interrupted by the casualties that took place around them. The more I saw of them, the greater became my desire to claim their protection and kindness; my heart yearned to be known and loved by these amiable creatures; to see their sweet

40.s3) and 40.s4) The Public Garden.

the interactive software system and the city as social system—to heighten the discordant tones or voices in the work. I wanted to call attention to the gaps between the texts and spaces of the city. I wanted to draw attention to the actual conditions of the urban environment and the participant's place within it as a rather conspicuous character wandering in unusual ways through the city with a rather obvious piece of technology.

It was my hope that this dis-ease or displacement would mirror, in some way, the experience of the main characters/narrators as they shift from inside to outside positions in the narrative. In this way, each participant becomes an "actor" or "character" uniquely written into the narrative, but ever unable to fully enter it as in a traditional narrative or through "suspension of disbelief." Furthermore, the participants exist as characters that are never fully knowable or accountable by the author, as in traditional texts. Yet this variable condition is heightened as the context in which the participant experiences the work constantly changes within a range of parameters determined only by the limitless space-time of the participant, the city, and her journey through it.

Practical Description

The installation is designed as a mostly open-plan composition with a designated beginning and end. Three general movements or "themed spaces" are implicitly articulated as "introduction/denouement" (Commonwealth Avenue and Newbury Street), "paradise/home" (the Public Garden), and "purgatory" (the open-plan spaces of endless wandering through the Boston Common and bordering neighborhoods).

A map directs the participant's first movements through the Newbury Street shopping district to Commonwealth Avenue where the first spoken word passage begins. As Commonwealth Avenue opens on to the Public Garden, the wanderer typically moves through the garden, making their way to the remaining areas of the installation on the other side. The rest of the installation is spread through the entire downtown area and can be accessed via any number of exits from the Public Garden; none is dictated or assumed. The entire piece takes approximately two hours to fully experience at a relatively steady pace. It is intended, however, that participants will experience the work as a patchwork narrative that may or may not be navigated in its entirety. Return visits yield new

configurations of the experience as the conditions of the city, the seasons, and the variable moments of reception bring new layers to the text.

looks directed towards me with affection was the utmost limit of my ambition. I dared not think that they would turn them from me with disdain and horror. The poor that stopped at their door were never driven away. I asked, it is true, for greater treasures than a little food or rest: I required kindness and sympathy; but I did not believe myself utterly unworthy of it.

Rueb:

He finally returned to the tiny town of one thousand where he grew up. The streets, the band shell, the cinema now stand silent. I imagine him walking past the library, the town hall, the high school . . . all the places that once turned a cold shoulder to him, now took him back in without questions.

My grandparents, once unyielding toward him, silently accepted him into their home for as long as he would stay. He moved into the basement apartment where we always played house as children. During these years, he slipped silently in and out through the back door, living like an anonymous tenant in his own childhood home. The basement was clearly off-limits now, though I peeked in one time and saw the vintage 1950s décor, so familiar from my childhood, transformed now by the spoils of his travels—Egyptian hassocks, embroidered cushions and tapestries from the Middle East—one depicting robbers on horses stealing away with gems and bare-breasted virgins, a knife in a beaded sheath. He sold motorcycles assembled from kits in the basement. When my grandfather died, he expanded his enterprise to the lot that had been my grandmother's garden, filling it with Volkswagen Beetles he rebuilt himself to re-sell. His inventory never moved during these years. The Volkswagens, itinerant beasts of another era, seemed happy to settle their worn wheels into the soft Kansas earth, and so did he.

Juxtaposition #3
The following sounds correspond to the area around the Park Street T stop.

Rueb:

Even at the earliest age, I knew him only as a mute and invisible force, a dark specter representing a threat of immeasurable proportions, if only because my parents went to such great lengths to keep him out of our home. The sound of his name pronounced in countless foreign accents, emerging from the mouths of collect call operators around the globe, would slowly take form as the syllables of my own name. My mother always insisted it was simply coincidence. Upon hearing his name, my heart would beat sharply as I caught my breath and repeated "no" as instructed—"no," "no," "no." My siblings and I repeated this dutiful execution of my father's command all the years of our youth.

Answering the phone in our house was serious business. We were not allowed to perform this function until we had learned to write and had been properly trained to take thorough messages. It was grave trouble

40.s5) and 40.s6): Park Street T Stop.

if we transposed a number or missed an important detail, and so, phone calls from my uncle required their own careful protocol just as any other. "Roberts Residence" . . . "May I please ask who's calling?" "Crazy Joe," he might say, if he was drunk or in a particularly sarcastic mood. My father would refuse his calls, almost without exception, but as a duty if my father was home the question always had to be asked, "Will you take the call?" Occasionally my mother would accept (usually after a vodka tonic or two) and we would eavesdrop eagerly to hear the news. Through fragments of a one-sided conversation, carried to us through my mother's voice, we would strain to fill in the story of where he was, what countries he'd visited . . . and that he needed money, his inheritance held under my father's name.

Shelley:

How can I move thee? Will no entreaties cause thee to turn a favourable eye upon thy creature, who implores thy goodness and compassion? Believe me, Frankenstein, I was benevolent; my soul glowed with love and humanity; but am I not alone, miserably alone? You, my creator, abhor me; what hope can I gather from your fellow creatures, who owe me nothing? They spurn and hate me. The desert mountains and dreary glaciers are my refuge. I have wandered here many days; the caves of ice, which I only do not fear, are a dwelling to me, and the only one which man does not grudge. These bleak skies I hail, for they are kinder to me than your fellow beings. If the multitude of mankind knew of my existence, they would do as you do, and arm themselves for my destruction. Shall I not then hate them who abhor me? I will keep no terms with my enemies. I am miserable, and they shall share my wretchedness. Yet it is in your power to recompense me, and deliver them from an evil which it only remains for you to make so great, that not only you and your family, but thousands of others, shall be swallowed up in the whirlwinds of its rage. Let your compassion be moved, and do not disdain me. Listen to my tale; when you have heard that, abandon or commiserate me, as you shall judge that I deserve. But hear me. The guilty are allowed, by human laws, bloody as they are, to speak in their own defence before they are condemned. Listen to me, Frankenstein.

Finding the Game in Improvised Theater
Tim Uren

Improvisational theater presents the challenge—equally delightful and dubious—of creating stories spontaneously as they are being performed. These stories are not created by the quick thinking of improvisers on stage, attempting to invent the characters and plot as they go. Rather, the stories are created by playing a game. As each story is unique, so is the game that creates that story. The rules of such a game do not exist until the story begins.

Countless skills go into a successful improvised performance: the ability to use one's voice well, the ability to move well on stage, and the ability to successfully portray objects and environments through mime, to name a few. But two skills are crucial for playing the story's game. The first is the ability to observe, the second is the ability to react.

For improvisers, observation is the ability to recognize fully the words being spoken, the events unfolding, and the subtle signals of body language, both in one's self and others. There are not wrong things to observe or right things to observe. But whatever the improviser observes becomes a rule of the game.

A simple example of something that happens easily is when someone stutters while introducing him or herself. If a performer hears someone say, "I'm, uh . . . Steve," then what was observed might become the rule: that character's name is not "Steve," it's "Uh . . . Steve."

This is the way the rules that govern the story's game are discovered, and it works for every aspect of an improvised scene. To the audience, it may seem that a character at the beginning of a scene has come purely from the imagination of the improviser. In truth, the people on stage are deluged with signals providing inspiration for the characters they are portraying.

An improviser's own body will provide them with vast amounts of observable starting points for a character. Once noticed, slight variations in posture can be exaggerated into, for example, lips pursed together tightly, a chin thrust forward,

or shuffling feet—any of which can provide the foundation for a character. A hip swung wide to one side may create a cocky swagger, which in turn informs the improviser that this character is an authority figure, a sheriff in a small town.

Again, there's not a right way or a wrong way to extrapolate ideas, but it is always easier and better for the performance if these ideas are based on something real. In this case, every time this character moves, the hip swings wide, because it's become one of the rules of the game. If that rule is broken, it means the character and the whole story has fundamentally changed. In this same way a character may be based on a person's subtle emotional state, proximity to other improvisers, or any happy accident the performer is lucky enough to observe.

The same idea applies to other aspects of the story. Anything could potentially be a rule of the game. Perhaps a character is angry about the results of a boxing match; then everything that character sees or hears only makes his anger worse. Perhaps in this scene there's always leftover egg salad, or every handshake is held slightly too long, or all children need extensive dental work. These rules get established early, and the rest of the scene is spent playing the game according to those rules.

In improvised performance there is no time to stand back and gather these kinds of observations. The process of observing rules and implementing them must be nearly instantaneous. Additionally, improvisers must be able to take in what's going on around them even as they are performing.

One exercise used in rehearsal to strengthen this skill involves two improvisers simultaneously talking to each other about any given topic. As they talk, they are also trying to retain the details of the story they're being told. It is a simple-sounding task, but shockingly difficult.

Another fundamental exercise used in teaching improvisation is called *Mirror* and is ideal for developing observation skills. It starts with two improvisers facing each other. To begin, the first person begins to move and the second person tries their best copy the movements as if they were a mirror image. The leader must keep their movements smooth and evenly paced enough for the observer to keep up. Then the roles are reversed, with the second person leading and the first following. After each

41.1) The author improvises an eerie monologue in Huge Theater's *Creature Feature*. (Jen Scott)

person has had a chance to practice recreating the movements they see, they begin mirroring each other without a set leader. As each improviser makes the subtle adjustments to match their partner, it creates a new small movement for the other to try to match. The back-and-forth process of constantly trying to correct what can never be a perfect match provides the dynamic action that keeps both improvisers in constant fluid motion. When one person or the other is leading, it is difficult to maintain a constant stream of movements that do not eventually grow monotonous. When there is no leader, each moment is the natural, organic result of the moment before, and the process sustains itself.

Once an improvised scene is underway, performers will quickly gather plenty of rules. Focus gradually turns from establishing the game to simply playing it, and this is where the second important skill, the ability to react, becomes crucial. Improvisers are taught to react in a manner that is honest to their character and truthful to the scene—or, as I would say it, according to the rules of the game. If the rule is that you're a sheriff, then you react like the sheriff you

are. Occasionally, when performers get nervous about having undertaken such a ridiculous endeavor as performing unscripted theater, they will replace reaction with justification. Instead of just doing what their sheriff does, they explain that they are the sheriff, they explain that they do things that sheriffs do, or they explain why it is that they're the sheriff. The point of reacting is to play according the rules, not to explain or justify the rules.

Again, there are exercises that are used in improv rehearsals to help develop the basic skill of reacting. One of the most common is called *Word Ball*. In this exercise, people stand in a circle and mime throwing an imaginary ball to each other. Whenever someone throws the ball, they say a word. The goal is to keep the ball moving at all times. Again, as simple as it sounds, it is all too easy for people to freeze up, holding the ball as they try to think up the "right" word to say. It quickly shows the advantage of simply reacting to the word said previously rather than crafting a word. The physical act of throwing the ball provides a focus for the conscious mind so it does not interfere with the simple act of instant response.

Another exercise used in rehearsal to sharpen reaction skills is a *Three-Line Scene*. As the name implies, these are quick scenes between two improvisers in which one person says a line, the second responds, and then the first person says a third line that is a response to the second line (in line with rules set up by the first line). For example, if Person 1 says, "I hope people like my casserole," Person 2 might respond, "These parasites are getting fed for free—who cares if they like it or not?" Person 1 might in return say, "I hope people like being fed for free." In the first line, the speaker establishes a rule for his character: he is always concerned about other people's satisfaction. The second line is a response that establishes Person 2's rule of disregard for other's feelings. The third line is a response that obeys the rule of concern about other people. By beginning and ending so quickly, these scenes encourage quick, honest responses, as there's no real advantage in trying to take the time to invent a response.

But does a series of reactions, guided by a set of rules, really equal a story? Note that this is essentially the process that playwrights, directors, and actors are collectively trying to reverse-engineer in scripted theater. The opening of a play is crafted so that the story that follows makes sense, emotionally if not always intellectually, and the conclusion comes as a natural result of what was already there at the beginning. Actors in scripted theater are working to reach a point where they are not recalling memorized dialogue and actions, but know the characters and the material so well that their responses are compelled by what is happening on stage. At that point they may not be able to recall their lines in the play without the stimulus that provokes such a response.

Improvisational theater, then, relies on an *implied* playwright, an imaginary author who has written every conceivable story it is possible to write. Each performer is simply assumed to have already studied every one of those possible stories, each of them so thoroughly that they no longer reside in conscious knowledge. But given any cue, the improviser can confidently deliver an honest response, knowing that it will exactly and perfectly lead the story to its ultimate conclusion.

It is highly unlikely that an audience will see an improvisational performance in which the story is governed solely by the rules generated within the scene. There are almost always other rules, set beforehand, which impact the story. For instance, most improv performances involve soliciting a random word or phrase from the audience. Some improvisers use this suggestion purely as a jumping-off point, while others use it throughout the performance as a constant touchstone.

How suggestions are solicited from the audience and how they are used vary widely. It is most common to ask the audience a random question to elicit the suggestion: "What's the worst birthday gift you've ever received?" or "Name a place you've gone on a family vacation," or "What did your grandfather do for a living?" For my own solo improv performance, *300 Comic Books*, I have an audience member select a random comic book from a box. I then improvise a monologue based off the comic book they've chosen, and all scenes are inspired by that monologue.

Additionally, improv performances almost always have a predetermined structure, each structure having its own set of rules that apply to the story before it begins. The number of different improv structures is vast and ever-growing. Although I offer some examples, they are by no means meant

41.2) The author does something weird with his face, an unplanned reaction to an unexpected stimulus, as part of Huge Theater's *Creature Feature*. (Jen Scott)

to be definitive; different performers may know these structures by different names or in variations, depending on where they studied improv. However, it is widely accepted that structures fall into one of two categories: short-form improvisation and long-form improvisation.

Short-form improvisational structures grew out of the theater games developed by Viola Spolin, later used by the Compass Players, and then Second City in Chicago. Spolin's *Improvisation for the Theater* (Spolin 1999) is an excellent introduction to her work and a landmark publication in the history of improv.

Short-form structures typically consist of one discreet scene, separate from any other scenes in the performance. The length of a scene can be as short as the briefest moment or last until everyone on stage drops from exhaustion, but the typical length is three to five minutes. The rules applied to scenes by short-form structures tend to be more stringent than long-form. While the hope is that these structural rules will force the performers into unexpected places, creating more enticing stories, it is often the case that much of the entertainment is simply watching actors struggle to function at all in such bizarre and binding circumstances.

Take the *Alphabet Scene*. Before the scene begins, a letter of the alphabet is chosen, typically by the audience. The first word of the first line of dialogue spoken must begin with that letter. The next actor to speak must begin his or her line of dialogue with a word that begins with the next letter of the alphabet. Each subsequent line spoken must start with the next letter in the alphabet. When the actors reach Z, they loop back to start the next line with A. Finally, the last line of dialogue in the scene is reached once the improvisers return to the same letter that began the first line spoken.

At first glance, this rule seems not to work toward the goal of creating a story, instead focusing more attention on the performers' abilities to think of vaguely appropriate word that starts with the letter "X," or for that matter to remember the basic order of the alphabet in a high-pressure, easily distracting environment. But behind the apparent obstacle hides an enhancement to the storytelling game. The mental energy spent wrestling with the alphabet problem helps to prevent the performer from trying to internally invent the story and forces them to rely on their observations. Instant, honest responses become more likely when the improviser is forced to speak but cannot control how they start.

Another example of a short-form structure is called *Languages*. Before the scene starts, a list of different languages is generated by audience suggestion (French, Spanish, Japanese, etc.). Once the scene has begun, a performer not involved in the scene will call out one of the languages on the list. At that point, the actors on stage will continue the scene, but replace their dialogue with a gibberish version of the selected language. The scene will progress in this way until the performers are instructed to return to English. At that point, they return to speaking their dialogue as normal. Throughout the scene, the performers switch back and forth between English and gibberish versions of the languages called out to them. Crucially, even when the performers are speaking nonsense, both the audience and the other performers will understand what is happening in the scene, through nonverbal signals.

Emotions is a structure in which a list of emotions is generated by audience suggestion and, as the scene progresses, the performers will periodically be instructed to react in the character of one of the emotions on the list.

Take That Back (or *Should Have Said*, as it is sometimes known) involves an improviser standing outside of a scene with a bell. At any point during the scene, if the bell is rung, whoever spoke last must replace their previous response with a different one. *Styles* is a structure in which a scene is periodically stopped and given a style; for instance, a movie genre, a famous playwright, or a television show. The scene then continues in that style. There are many, many short-form improvisation structures.

Long-form improvisation, on the other hand, is a series of scenes, with rules governing how those scenes relate to each other. These structures will typically run twenty minutes to an hour. The most widely known long-form structure is the *Harold*. It is not within the scope of this essay to provide a history or an in-depth exploration of the philosophies behind the *Harold*. For a more definitive description of the structure one must read *Truth in Comedy* (Close, Halpern, and Johnson 1994). What I offer here is merely a quick description of the structure as most improvisers are likely to know it.

A *Harold* starts with an opening pattern game, which will be more abstract than a normal scene, and is meant to generate raw ideas and themes. There are then three unrelated scenes. After that, there is again a game of some kind, which may likely be a short-form structure. (Typically this part of the *Harold* is called a "game," although I will refer to it as a "*Harold* game" to make it distinct from the idea of an improvised story's game, discussed earlier.)

The first scene after this *Harold* game revisits the theme of the first scene after the opening pattern game. It might involve the same characters continuing the same story, or it may be a less apparent advancement of the important elements of that scene. The second scene after the *Harold* game scene revisits the theme of the second scene performed after the opening, and likewise with the third scene. Additionally, all three of these scenes will include elements of the *Harold* game, and their themes may begin to bleed into each other.

After all three scenes have had their themes touched upon again in this second round of scenes, there is a second *Harold* game. After this second *Harold* game, there are three final scenes that once again revisit the themes in order. But in this third round of scenes, the themes intermingle even more, ideally discovering one cohesive theme behind the entire collection of stories.

Obviously, performing this structure provides a radically different set of challenges for an improviser than an *Alphabet Scene* does. Rather than distract the intellect in order to prevent attempts to plan out a scene, this structure provides plenty of opportunity to try to quickly "write the scene." In fact, while learning the structure, one can become so lost trying to remember what part is coming next and what the theme of scene two was that it seems like entering a playwriting state of mind is necessary for survival. But a long-form structure like this one is designed to take advantage of stories successfully created through gameplay and to bring them together in a whole that is greater than the sum of their parts. It is much easier to remember themes that are based on observations of existing elements rather than themes born of hasty invention. Honest reactions to events advance the scenes in a compelling and entertaining way, which in turn advance the whole *Harold* structure.

Recently I worked with Huge Theater in Minneapolis <http://www.hugetheater.com>, performing a long-form structure called *Creature Feature*. The goal of this structure is to create one cohesive improvised story, specifically in the style of a monster movie. Before the performance, one performer was determined to be the monster. That improviser gets a suggestion from the audience for a monster and the title of the movie in which that monster will appear.

Once the first scene begins, all of the other performers begin to describe the details of the scene's location, using filmic language such as "we fade up on" or "the camera pans." Once the scene is set, the performer designated as the monster enters the scene as a soon-to-be victim and performs a solo scene of that victim's death at the hands of an unseen monster. After that establishing scene, each improviser steps forward individually and gives an introductory monologue about their character, a role they will retain throughout the entirety of the structure. After this, scenes progress according to the conventions of monster movies. One by one, the monster kills characters until some final showdown resolves the story. Some of our creations included

"Yodel," in which a mermaid terrorized a small Swiss village, "Dr. Smith the Transvestite Gores Maniac Girl Scouts," in which a group of young boys and girls were forced to confront the horrors of sexual ambiguity, the postmodern "The Butterflies, In Miami the Butterflies," and "The Easter Bunny Versus the Aztec Mummy" which was exactly what you'd think it would be.

No matter where one encounters improvisation, it is likely to include at least some game terminology. It is not a coincidence that one of the most successful improvisational enterprises is ComedySportz, which features short-form structures as though they were a competitive sport. It is very common to hear an improv teacher instruct students to "find the game" in a scene. It can be a frustrating lesson, almost like a Zen koan, given that what you are being told to find does not exist until you start looking for it. And it is that, and not making up a story quickly, that is the challenge of improvisation.

For further reading about improv and the way in which it combines game-playing and storytelling, I recommend *Impro: Improvisation and the Theater* (Johnstone 1981) and *Improvise: Scene from the Inside Out* (Napier 2004). But, of course, the best way to understand and appreciate the art form is to see it in action. When performed well, improv creates truly unique stories, born of the exact place and time in which they are witnessed—well worth the price of admission.

References

Close, Del, Charna Halpern, and Kim Johnson (1994). *Truth in Comedy: The Manual of Improvisation*. Colorado Springs, CO: Meriwether Publishing.

Johnstone, Keith (1981). *Impro: Improvisation and the Theater*. London: Methuen Publishing.

Napier, Mick (2004). *Improvise: Scene from the Inside Out*. Portsmouth, NH: Heinemann Drama.

Spolin, Viola (1999). *Improvisation for the Theater: A Handbook of Teaching and Directing Techniques* (3rd edition). Evanston, IL: Northwestern University Press.

On *Adventures in Mating*
Joe Scrimshaw

Adventures in Mating is an hour-long comedic play inspired by the *Choose Your Own Adventure* series of novels popular in the seventies and eighties. It was first performed as part of the Minnesota Fringe Festival in Summer 2005.

The show follows the social misadventures of a dysfunctional couple on a blind date and their dour waiter. When the couple comes to various decisions, such as white or red wine, the waiter steps forward and becomes the servant of the audience: he solicits their vote, through applause or a show of hands, and the action continues based on the audience decision. There is virtually no improvisation. A script exists for white wine or red wine.

There were many challenges translating the appeal of the *CYOA* novels into an hour-long romantic comedy. Stylistically, the show had to be somewhat believable as a blind date but the characters and situations had to be exaggerated to mirror the pulp-inspired feel of the novels. For example, if the audience votes for the man to go to the bathroom, he slips on a piece of lettuce and dies; the choice is then revisited with the death-inducing bathroom option removed. This satisfies the desire for the sudden "wrong turn" aspects of the novels, and on a practical level allows the show to stay on track and tell its story in under an hour.

42.1) The waiter. (Jen Scott)

The introductory scene needed to contain every bit of necessary exposition about the characters since it is the only scene that is guaranteed to be performed. Also, plenty of different ideas and themes needed to be established for the multiple divergent scenes and story arcs to explore.

Knowing a lot about the main character was not a concern of the *CYOA* novels, since they were written in the second person. This perspective is arguably the reason for the books' popularity. It's easy to invest in a choice about whether to jump out of a moving car, or to trust a stranger, if it's all happening to you.

In *Adventures in Mating* the audience's investment comes from playing the role of cruel fate. They are engrossed in a scene not only for its straightforward narrative content, but also for the ways the scene builds to another choice. For example, the audience enjoys watching the scene code-named "Seduction." However, they are also elated when the woman announces that, if the man doesn't stop wooing her, she will either kiss or slap him. The "cruel" part of the fate role is exemplified by the audience's delight in controlling whether or not this living human being—separated from them only by a stage and the social constructs of traditional theater—is

42.2.1) and 42.2.2) The couple. (Scott Pakudaitis)

embraced by soft lips or repeatedly smacked across the face.

The nature of the show caused a great deal of anxiety for the performers. While the show is 95 percent scripted, there are moments of improvisation. This creates an odd hybrid for actors; *Adventures in Mating* is both a rigidly structured show requiring a lot of line memorization and a show that demands a lot of flexibility and improvisation. It is rare for a performer to have studiously rehearsed and memorized a script and still not know what will be performed on a given night. In its most recent incarnation, the show features fourteen distinct "viable" scenes as well as multiple "dead end" options (such as the aforementioned bathroom death scene). This adds up to well over fifty possible variations of the show, depending on the scene combinations.

For the waiter, the show does contain the potential for improvisation. The waiter must often respond to the zealous reactions of the audience's voting; in the initial run of the show, actor Craig Johnson quickly developed a repertoire of admonitions such as, "Please. This is not a hootenanny."

One scene also features a device called "The Cheeseburger Sequence," which pokes fun at the structure of the show itself by generating a series of totally inconsequential decisions. The man on the date orders a cheeseburger and the waiter is forced to solicit votes from the audience regarding how well-done the burger is, what type of cheese, what type of bun, and even what side dishes. The audience consistently detected that this was a weak point in the marriage of script and improv, and would shout out odd comments, trying to force a reaction out of the waiter. For example, when the waiter delivers the scripted line, "Please don't pick salad as a side dish—we have over fifteen dressings to choose from!", the audience would demand salad because they accurately perceived that the waiter did not have a list of fifteen salad dressings memorized.

I would say that the show was successful aesthetically and critically, with some reservations. On the positive side, audiences enjoyed playing the role of fate. (Audiences in Minnesota are stereotypically considered to be quiet and reserved, yet they quite literally screamed in glee as they voted for something bad to happen. One published newspaper review described the audience as "mob-like," and a blogger expressed disgust at his fellow audience members

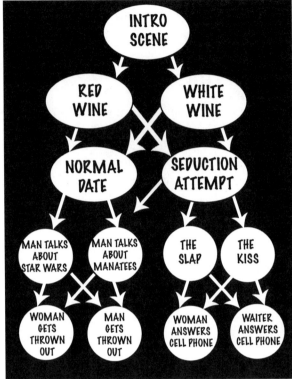

42.3) A partial flowchart.

in a review titled, "Great actors, sadistic audience.")

On the negative side, the effort put into giving the show a basic story arc, with a beginning, middle and end, no matter what combination of scenes were selected, backfired to some degree. The apparent fluidity of the show caused some audience members to doubt that alternate scenes and story arcs existed.

This suspicion was supported by the fact that some choices in the initial run were accidentally structured so that certain scenes were always selected. In the penultimate scene, the man receives a cell phone call from his ex-wife. The audience is offered the choice of whether the man should answer it (this receives a humorously small vote), the woman should answer (a healthy vote), or the waiter (an overwhelmingly large vote). The audience will simply always vote for the most illogical, conflict-oriented choice. In the show's second run, the waiter had to warn audiences what the final outcome of the choices might be, in an attempt to randomize the audience's selection.

In future drafts, I plan to experiment with a more geometric structure for the show; this would mean that each choice would be followed by two other choices. This may succeed in creating extremely distinct stories—or the volume of scenes may simply start to weaken the concept. Even an over-the-top pulp-inspired blind date can only have so many convolutions before the show crosses over into a realm of cartoonish absurdism, in which the couple is no longer real enough for the audience to care about their fate.

In any case, *Adventures in Mating* will continue to be developed with the goal of creating a long-running show that could play simultaneously in multiple cities; various story arcs could be switched in and out, thereby using the inherently modular nature of the show to keep itself fresh over time.

Reference

Scrimshaw, Joseph (2005). *Adventures in Mating*.

Santaman's Harvest Yields Questions, or Does a Performance Happen if It Exists in a Virtual Forest?

Adriene Jenik

During 1999–2000, Lisa Brenneis and I developed a three-act play called *Santaman's Harvest* as part of our ongoing series of Desktop Theater experiments (1997–2002) <http://www.desktoptheater.org/>. For more than a year, Brenneis and I had been going on weekly performative forays into online visual chat spaces, primarily "the Palace" (an early publicly populated space originally designed by Jim Baumgarten). Visual chat spaces are Web-based applications that developed parallel to massively multiplayer online games. They are essentially chat rooms where groups of people meet, but in addition to exchanges via text, participants in the chat exist as small images (aka "avatars") situated within a larger background image, or "room." The Palace was one of the earliest and most popular of these

44.1) Screen capture from *Santaman's Harvest*.

This is the script for the first scene of Santaman's Harvest *as performed in the Palace. When performing in the Palace, a line of text can be preceded with a punctuation mark in order to change the style of its appearance. For example, text that begins with an exclamation point is presented in a "spiky" balloon—and interpreted as shouting by regular visitors to the Palace. On the other hand, text preceded with a colon is presented in a "thought" balloon—and is meant to be interpreted as a window into the character's private thoughts. Text that begins with a close parenthesis can trigger sounds, such as ")applause" and ")boom".*

Santaman's Harvest Scene 1 script
Dramatis Personae:
PROFESSOR
TREE
FARMER 1
FARMER 2
SANTAMAN

PROLOGUE
Professor:
! Listen up!
All you drugged First World Citizens!
you cubicled misanthrops,
You gamers, you clubbers,
you yearners for a purpose.

Listen as closely as you can.
We'll do our best to get beyond your bipolarity,
you're A D D.

We are interrupting your chatting to bring you SANTAMAN's HARVEST.
A tale of food, health and hope;
A tale of seed, weed, and greed.

Your attention economy is about to go bankrupt,
You might as well follow me.

PROFESSOR EXITS
SCENE ONE
PALACE MANSION - FIREWORKS I
TREE & FARMER1

TREE (Whispering slowly):
Leave me here in the soil and sun and rain
and I will grow.
Take from me no more than what you need.
I am not a trunk road or a branch line.
We exist together or not at all.
FARMER 1 (thinking to himself):
: Finally, a break.

: The harvest is over.
: Everything's gone to market.
TREE (Whispering):
LEAVE me here in the soil and sun and rain
and I will grow.

Take from me no more than what you need.
FARMER 1 (thinking to himself):

44.2) Screen capture from *Santaman's Harvest*.

spaces, in part because of its decentralized organization, free and easy access, and the depth of its toolset.

We saw what we were doing with Desktop Theater as a type of "intentional performance" in the midst of the many less intentional or unintentional performances going on among the rest of the population. Taking cues from Augusto Boal's inspired street theater exercises,[1] and echoing the transitive nature of public pageants (a precursor to stage-based theater), we developed an investigatory practice that soon expanded to include scripts, costumes, staging, choreography, and even a troupe of remotely located actors.

The culmination of our more script-centered experiments, *Santaman's Harvest* was an ambitious attempt to provoke a deeper discussion about genetic agriculture[2] within this public online space. The piece loosely choreographed eleven performers in four time zones, with portions of the piece being tightly scripted and other sections being open for

: Finally, a break.

: To think I only just broke even after all that work.
TREE (whispering):
We exist together or not at all.
ENTER FARMER #2
Farmer2:
how'd your crops do this year?

farmer #1:
: finally
farmer #1:
huh?
farmer #1:
oh you

a tree:
:i am alive

farmer #1:
crops did ok

Farmer2:
grow anything good?

farmer #1:
: bad actually
farmer #1:
corn was ok

a tree:
:we exist together

farmer #1:
: corn was pest ridden

Farmer2:
How'd your soy do?

a tree:
:or not at all

farmer #1:
soy was ok
farmer #1:
:soy was pest ridden

Farmer2:
:Mine sucked

1. Both *The Theatre of the Oppressed* (Boal 1985) and *Games for Actors and Non-Actors* (Boal 2002) were influential throughout the development of Desktop Theater. Boal's broad approach to theater as a "kind of thinking," his development of his own Arena, Forum, and Image Theatre techniques in public spaces and fora, and the dialogue that is instigated through his techniques were all reasons we felt our crude experiments could fall under the rubric of "theater."

2. Our interest in this topic arose as a result of both of us relocating from L.A. to more "rural" areas (for myself, to a studio that I still maintain in the Mojave Desert, and for Lisa, to Ojai where she began farming avocados and tangerines with her husband). I began to consider, as I learned about life from the animals, native plants, and extreme weather, how important collective knowledge (acquired over time from a relationship with the land) is to humans. I was also becoming suspect of my own license to experiment artistically, even as I found myself advocating more oversight of scientific experiments with genetic material. I had also been questioning for some time the relationship between the rise of the English language as a result of computing practice and the globalized economy, and the coincident loss of diverse languages and cultures. It made sense to have a dialogue about these things with people who were on computers and therefore complicit in this overall dynamic cultural shift.

44.3) Screen capture from *Santaman's Harvest*.

improvisation. The newly formed Desktop Theater Troupe performed this three-act mor(t)ality play narrated by "The Prof" (a sexy, blue-haired avatar) with Santaman (a nine-faced corporate "head"), a tree, a TV camera, a farmer, three fluttering butterflies, and a few other surprises. The performers were writers, and visual and performing artists who were keen to experiment with a "new" form of drama.

Santaman's Harvest was scheduled to be performed "doubly live" (i.e., performed "live" in the chat environment and projected into a "live" proximal audience) during the 1999 Digital Arts and Culture conference held in Atlanta, Georgia. In reflecting upon the piece, which was written and rehearsed over the course of a year, I'm struck by the gap between what was of interest to the audience in the auditorium and what was engaging to the player/performers in the virtual space.

Rather than have the proximal live audience just sitting in the theater watching the play unravel in virtual space, I thought we should try to engage the audience more as participants in the drama. To do so, a number of live computer terminals were placed throughout the auditorium setting. It should be noted that the piece occurred at night surrounded by a party event atmosphere. People in the auditorium were engaged and responsive, but the performer's experiences of the piece was reflected in our green room time where the first question thrown down was, "What just happened?"

a tree:
:pests are good food

farmer #1:
how bout yours?

a tree:
: I like borers

Farmer2:
Excellent.

farmer #1:
yeah
farmer #1:
mine too

farmer #1:
how's your herd?

Farmer2:
Fine, And yours?

a tree:
:leave me here

farmer #1:
: problems
farmer #1:
oh they're great
farmer #1:
just great

Farmer2:
Great.

a tree:
:here in the soil and soy and rain

farmer #1:
cows and wife
farmer #1:
and pigs

a tree:
: and i will grow

farmer #1:
and chickens
farmer #1:
and kids
farmer #1:
all great

Farmer2:
:not

farmer #1:
: yeah, right, great

a tree:
:where are my leaves?

During the course of our rehearsals in the more populated Palaces (with this production we staged one act in our own server-hosted "Genetically Enhanced Palace") we had ongoing unexpected encounters with chat-room denizens of all ages and stripes, as this short excerpt from a rehearsal log reveals.

(Note: ~COWBOY~ is not a Desktop Theater performer.)

farmer #1: huh Cowboy?

~COWBOY~: Howdy Yall

Sherman: corn is always safe

a tree: :We exist together or not at all.

farmer #1: pests got 20 percent of my crop

a tree: :corn comes and goes

Sherman: Welp they got 30% o mine

~COWBOY~: hey gusy i dont guess i could get that av frem yall

farmer #1: Another year like last and we're done.

a tree: AVs come and go

Sherman: What can we do?

~COWBOY~: thanks!@!!

farmer #1: sure

a tree: Leave me here in the sun and rain

farmer #1: Another year like last and we're done.

a tree: Leave me here in the sun and rain

~COWBOY~: where yall frem

farmer #1: cuntry

farmer #1: you?

~COWBOY~: me to

Sherman: marlboro country

farmer #1: lol

farmer #1: Hey, have you heard about the new Roundup Ready corn?

Sherman: Tell me more?

a tree: :oy gevalt

farmer #1: Like other Roundup Ready seed products, Roundup Ready corn is genetically improved to be tolerant to in crop applications of Roundup Ultra herbicide.

a tree: crops come and go . . .

a tree: I remember

farmer #1: Used as part of the Roundup Ready Corn Weed Control system, it provides a revolutionary and unique weed control option for corn growers.

a tree: be tolerent of revolutionary and unique corn growers

Farmer2:
I guess we're the lucky ones.

Long Silence
Farmer2:
Say, have you heard about Roundup Ready seed products?

Roundup Ready corn is genetically improved to be tolerant to in crop applications of Roundup Ultra herbicide.
Farmer2:
Used as part of the Roundup Ready Corn Weed Control systemit provides a revolutionary and unique weed control option for corn growers.
a tree:
ook flee flee flee flee

farmer #1:
yeah
farmer #1:
sounds good

a tree:
ook flee flee flee flee
a tree:
:scared

farmer #1:
: boy, things sure are diffrent

Farmer2:
Round up ready made my youngest grow seven feet in a year.

a tree:
: pests make good pets

farmer #1:
: finally a break

a tree:
: ook flee

farmer #1:
: some quiet

a tree:
: ook flee

Farmer2:
:maybe I'll go watcha little tv

farmer #1:
yeah, thanks

a tree:
:yeah

farmer #1:
I'll try it out

Farmer2:
:yeah:

44.4) Screen capture from *Santaman's Harvest*.

~COWBOY~: corns to much dam werk
farmer #1: yeah
farmer #1: you said it
~COWBOY~: wheat or sorghum
farmer #1: you grow?
farmer #1: a farmerboy?
~COWBOY~: hell ya

Held in the public space, rehearsals in this medium were the equivalent of a micro performance, as we practiced working with our avatars and lines, as well as responding to folks (in character) who come there to be social.

Being "inside" the piece (and the culture of the online public arena) and being "outside" of this culture in the physically proximal public space produced an utterly different experience of the piece. Projecting the output from the shared virtual space into an auditorium, and scattering live performance-ready terminals throughout the audience, completely shifted the space of creative play. The initial instincts of the people who sat at the terminals were to push at the edges of the performance, and attempt to achieve their own level of virtuosity through cleverness (which is well rewarded in such an environment scaled to the "quip"). As logs, videotape, and memory bear out, audience subversion was most compellingly expressed among the regular visitors to the chatspace, since they already had some skill at expressing themselves in the medium. The stumbles and

farmer #1:
: sure

a tree:
:borers you are about to be down sized
a tree:
:scared

farmer #1:
: finally
farmer #1:
: a break

SANTAMAN:
)DEBUT
ahem

farmer #1:
who're you?
sman::
Mister Farmer
sman::
you look down

farmer #1:
just takin a break

sman::
Mister Farmer
sman::
you remind me of
sman::
!MY Dad!!!!!

farmer #1:
oh yeah?
farmer #1:
was he always tired?

sman::
yes, but he never showed it

farmer #1:
oh

sman::
friend

farmer #1:
: friend?

sman::
friend
sman::
have you thought about the future friend?

farmer #1:
huh?

sman::
the future

farmer #1:
future?

44.5) Screen capture from *Santaman's Harvest*.

snipes of the proximal audience drew the most immediate and "lively" responses in the space of the auditorium.

As Brenneis recalls of her experience of the piece, "There were reasons this was probably not going to work; the meat audience had no idea what was expected of them and had no 'Palace skills.' They had never seen the play before and the story was unfamiliar to them. The terminals were in the audience, daring them to participate. I think the result was kinda what you'd expect. We got better audience subversion in 'Godot' and 'BushGore' because folks were in the palace and they had some skill at expressing themselves."

These observations present a challenge for the future of such experiments. How can we fully take into account the power of "liveness" in replaying archived documents? Can these public/private performative encounters support documentation and critique? By what methods do we judge the aesthetic developments in such multilayered and ceaselessly dynamic engagements? Does one networked performance practice have much to offer others in the way of analysis, or are these, by their nature in close relationship to a particular form factor, completely isolated, hermetic practices?

As Brenneis reflects, "The DT documentation does have aesthetic and sentimental value for me, and others may view the stills and logs and enjoy their own fantasies of what our experiments were like, but we the participants are the only ones who can truly reflect on our body of work."[3]

3. Comments on this essay, September 2005.

farmer #1:
my future?

sman::
your future
sman::
friend?

farmer #1:
sure
farmer #1:
I guess I'll be farming

sman::
because I WANT YOU TO think ABOUT IT

farmer #1:
yeah?
farmer #1:
:why

sman::
Think Big

farmer #1:
big?

sman::
!Think Bio!!!!!

farmer #1:
: why?

sman::
buy oh

farmer #1:
Bio?

sman::
buy o tech no lo gee

farmer #1:
I've heard about that

sman::
!Good

farmer #1:
why?

sman::
Because I have your future all planned out for you!!!

farmer #1:
yeah?

sman::
You lucky farmer!

farmer #1:
: hmmmm

sman::
I happen to like farmers,
sman:
and I am 110 per cent serious about helping you become more
: I'm a genius.
farmer:
:hmmm
sman:
!More than your father ever hoped for you

farmer:
:my father
farmer:
:he had great hopes for me

sman:
He would want you to think about the future

farmer:
yes
farmer:
you are right

sman:
Well then - let me show you!
sman:
i have magic seed
)APPLAUSE

farmer:
: oh brother

sman:
did you hear that?

farmer:
yeah?

sman:
I said
sman:
i have magic seed
)APPLAUSE

farmer:
:wow
sman::
see?

farmer #1:
do it again

sman::
magic seed
sman::
)APPLAUSE

sman::
! No more pests!
No more weeds!

!Drought tolerant!
Frost-resistant!

!Softer cotton!
Sweeter beets!

!Taller trees!
Fatter pigs!

!Prettier flowers!
Smarter children!

We do it all with genes!
farmer #1:
!

farmer #1:
)Applause
farmer #1:
! wow

farmer #1:
that sounds great

farmer #1:
wow
farmer #1:
: wow

sman::
and you lucky farmer
sman::
I am going to let you buy some

farmer #1:
oh yeah?

sman::
yeah

farmer #1:
: wow

sman::
Come with me and we'll go to my club and talk to some
sman::
!SUCCESSFUL AGRI BIZZ NESS MEN
sman::
! Let me show you!
Come for a tour. You won't be disappointed. Trust me.

:I'm a genius.
sman::
! Everyone's invited! Come marvel at the miracle of our patented life forms!

FARMER transforms into Professor.
PROFESSOR:
Here you have a classically illustrated dramatic conflict.

Can our protagonist resist SANTAMAN's HARVEST?
As an infectious enthusiasm for the future permeates the screen,
And asphalt and concrete block out the whispering of rocks and trees.
Are you paying attention?

DISCONNECT

References

Boal, Augusto (translated by Charles A. McBride and Maria-Odilia Leal McBride) (1985). *The Theatre of the Oppressed*. New York: Theatre Communication Group. (First published 1974 in Spanish as *Teatro de Optimido*.)

Boal, Augusto (translated by Adrian Jackson) (2002). *Games for Actors and Non-Actors*. London: Routledge.

Adriene Jenik

Me, the Other
Torill Elvira Mortensen

"What are you?" is the first question asked as you meet another role-player either in a digital or a flesh world. In daily life "what are you" normally addresses our professions or other signifiers of social status. Occasionally, it addresses nationality or ethnicity, if there are indications that these are not coherent with the immediate impression. In either context, it is a sensitive question: to define yourself to a stranger is a matter of anchoring the other person's impression of you. As we declare what we are, we also declare our position in life, work, religion, nationality, social status, and a myriad other factors that let others define us.

When you answer the "what are you" question in a role-playing computer game, it has an infinitely wider meaning. First, you can choose to interpret it as addressing your flesh world character, or you can answer the question as if it concerns your game character. Second, you can choose to leave out several otherwise obvious facts if you answer on behalf of your flesh self. You can say, "Woman, forty-four years old, Norwegian," and leave it at that. You can lie about these things, and nobody will know. Or you can select facts that may be flattering: "Tall, blue eyes, long dark blonde hair." The "what" which you are can be severely edited to suit any fantasy.

Imagine then how freely edited the "what" can be when the limitations of the human race do not apply. My most current other identity is something I could never achieve in the flesh. "What are you?", the other gamers ask, and without blinking I reply: "A female orc shaman, capable of doing spirit magic, skilled in the use of shield and mace as well as a staff, member of a clan that is planning to take over the world to make it safe for orckind." Only later may the other questions come out, if I am male or female, where I live, what I do, how old I am. These are not secondary questions; they are important and carry meaning in the social structure that informs the game, but for the game structure, the important "you" is your character, and the second person they address is not "you, the accountant from Wales," but you, the warrior who needs to get up and hit those aggressive NPCs before they kill the rest of the group.

44.1) Female orc and female troll in *World of Warcraft*. (Blizzard)

Next, we explore the relationship between you and "you," starting out with how we define ourselves and play roles in the flesh world, to go from there to how we play roles in the game world. There is a connection between these two activities that makes the gaming far from alien; quite the contrary, it is a familiar and human game.

The Mechanics of Role-Playing in Games

Role-playing ranges over a wide area, from free-form role-playing used in theater and therapy to the strict, formal world of re-enactment. If we imagine that there is a continuous line from free-form to re-enactment, role-playing games (in the tradition of the fantasy games developed over the last twenty years) inhabit an area from somewhere to the right of free-form, and all the way up to re-enactment. Different groups of role-players will claim that their form is the correct one and should be called role-playing, but for the purposes of this chapter I maintain the position that everything from improvization to re-enactment (as done by historical societies or the American organization Society for Creative Anachronism) can be called role-playing. To include re-enactment is a disputed position, as it enters the domain of formal theater, but at the same time, re-enactments tends to be a lot less strictly scripted and directed than theater. The participants will, for instance, get a role-sheet with directions more focused on the historical data and the historical acts than on how to play the actual part. Thus, the playing may depend on how the individual imagines, improvises, and

44.2) A role-play situation. (Blizzard)

interprets the role on the basis of contextual information rather than on stage directions, and this can and will change from one re-enactment to the next—to the point that history, in some cases, may yield to the enthusiasm of the participants.

The enthusiasm and creativity of the participants is the source of fun role-playing. To be able to commit to a role-playing situation, you need to suspend your disbelief and accept that your fellow players have good reasons for their actions. This may not always be easy: good role-playing demands knowledge of the relevant background, imagination, and quick thinking. In contemporary settings, the background may coincide with the real life of the participants, and it will need no further description. In historical, futuristic, or fantastic settings, the background may cover several books worth of information. We see this in the literature for tabletop role-playing games such as *Vampire: The Masquerade*, *Advanced Dungeons & Dragons*, or *Alternity*. Each game has extensive descriptions of the world the role-playing happens within, rules for the different aspects of the game itself, and specialized information for players and for administrators, or Gamemasters.

The most common type of role-playing game not played with a computer is the tabletop game. These are games with fairly strict rules and much restriction on the play, but the restriction isn't that of a manuscript with predefined events for each role. In games, the restrictions serve to introduce a limited amount of randomness, which is what makes a game a game.

In several cases (not all, as any dedicated gamer will tell you quickly), to play a tabletop game you need a player handbook to learn about the world you play in, and the challenges, adventures, obstacles, and tools for the players. Each player needs a player character (PC), and this player character is developed according to the preferences of the player. It can, for instance, be a male dwarf rogue, and such a character will have certain skills, strengths, and weaknesses, all of them expressed as names and numbers on a character sheet.

But each character should also have a history, a background that makes them react as they do. So our male dwarf rogue may have been the runt of the family in a traditional dwarf community in the mountains of Magroor Daum, and because of his small size he was constantly abused by the rest of his family and told what a disgrace he was. This caused him to run away at age twenty-seven (very young for a dwarf), and he survived by turning more or less to crime. As we meet him, he is a hardened criminal skilled in things like backstabbing, pickpocketing, stealth, poisons, and other shady pursuits. He appears to be bitter and disillusioned, but has a deep hidden respect for traditional dwarf values, and secretly dreams of meeting a nice dwarfess and settling down to run a nice, respectable, clean inn: his idea of the ultimate comfort and luxury.

When the game starts, each character will play with the other players against the non-playing characters of the game (NPCs), depending on how strong their various skills are; characters also occasionally have individual goals that cause them to cooperate or compete within the group. The Gamemaster (GM)—the person who is responsible for setting up and administrating the game progress and often telling the story as it develops—influences the process by choosing which NPCs may appear and by giving the different characters different challenges and goals, and can ultimately determine the entire outcome of the game, depending on how much power the group has agreed to put in the hands of the GM. If our dwarf tries to stab the human he has been paid to assassinate, but the human has better armor and a lucky saving throw, the assassination will fail. So far, mainly the numbers and skills on the character sheet are important.

Now, given that our dwarf manages to escape, he has to make a decision: will he return and try again, or will he just shrug it off and disappear? At this point the background or personality of the character becomes important: Perhaps the sum to kill that human is just what he needs to buy his nice little inn and start looking for that cute dwarf girl. In that case, he will try again. Or perhaps the human is a dwarf-hater, who wants to eradicate the dwarf culture. In that case, our tradition-bound rogue may want to be a hero and redeem himself, even if he has to do it for free and die in the attempt. In tabletop games these decisions are what make up the role-playing, and it can develop into mutual story-creation as all players present their characters' motivation, decisions, and desires. The dice rolled and the statistics of attributes (strength, intelligence, stamina, etc.) and skills is what creates the gameplay, the aspect of randomness and tension that is necessary to create a game.

In tabletop games the complex mathematics of the statistics is carried out with pen, paper, quick head estimates, and the occasional calculator. In computer games the computer rolls the dice and gives the responses. In a computer game such as *World of Warcraft*, the player will be aware of these calculations if he or she watches the numbers that seem to rise from targets when the character fights other player characters or NPCs. These numbers represent the result of the kind of calculations which the tabletop player does by hand: when the dwarf rogue hits with A weapon and with B skill on a target with C armor and D skill, the chance to damage the target is X high, and according to the roll of the die to see how hard the hit is, the dwarf rogue damages the human he tries to kill Z much: for instance, taking away 278 hit points out of 498. Once the game statistics are transferred to the computer, these calculations happen quickly and smoothly, and the players only see the end result: if they win or lose the battle, and how quick or slow the fight is.

The battle/game mathematics is not role-playing. To a role-player, the game mechanics act as a context and a directive for the events that create the story. Rather than, "And then he rolled a twenty-four attack but I had a fifty-five saving throw, and could use retaliation," the role-player translates it into: "The infernal rogue attacked me from behind, but I was lucky and stumbled over a stone. That put him off, so he missed. I was able to strike back, and survive yet another attack on my

44.3) The computer does the calculations, not the humans. (Blizzard)

life." In this way the game platform creates the surprise and the events, while the interpretation process forms them into a story to be told and shared with the other players.

In online multi-user games, as the burden of mathematics and so the delay of the battles has been delegated to the computer, the player can use more energy on the story and elaborating the events. In the multi-user dungeon (MUD) *Dragon Realms*, a text-based online computer game, where role-playing was highly encouraged and rewarded through GM intervention and favor-points given out by fellow players who acted as role-playing spies, it was still hard to fight and role-play at the same time. Only in "wartimes"—when the different clans of the game would be in conflict over different pieces of fantasyland—was role-playing smoothly integrated with the battles. In times of peace, it was rather complicated to explain why the characters would engage in long sessions of slaying different species; it took an inventive mind to come up with a plausible story for why characters would kill every single wolf in the forest, or all the dolphins in an area. In some cases, there would be quests, where the explanation was woven into the game. It was still hard to explain why the monster you had killed ten minutes earlier was back.

Much of the role-playing needs to be independent of the game mechanics, and be created through player interaction. It is possible to create a story for your own character, but the best role-playing situations are the ones that happen when players provoke each other, and the story grows in quick exchanges. One of the players of *Aarinfel* describes the pleasure of these exchanges as a role-playing high.

According to Jack, the high is a state of flow, when one feels that the borders between the player and the character have been dissolved and the player no longer needs to consider the next move of the character, but acts as the character:

> *TM:* Can you explain the role-playing high to me?
>
> *Jack:* The role-playing high is just a pet theory of mine, which I find a lot of other role-players understand, and necessarily a lot of actors and writers—people who seek to achieve almost a mentality outside of their own. And it is the point at which you have stopped thinking about: Given this situation, what would my character say? Given this situation, what would my character do?—and start thinking from the point of view of your character and say what you want to say and do what you want to do. To fully immerse yourself into the character. I find that it's very enthralling. (Mortensen 2003, 164)

To reach this state of mind, the players need to practice being the character, until the mental leap from "What would I, the player, do?" to "What would I, the character, do?" becomes as smoothly ingrained and automatic as the spinal cord-controlled reflexes of physical actions.

Everyday Role-Playing

In our normal, mundane, everyday lives, we still play roles, if not the roles set out by some identifiable gamemaster, as in role-playing games. Human beings play roles, and shift between them, smoothly and subconsciously: I go from teacher to mother in the time it takes me to turn from a student to my child. As Erving Goffman discussed in his classic work *The Presentation of Self in Everyday Life* (Goffman 1959), human beings are constantly playing such roles. "Sincerity," in this context, is not a measure of whether you play a role or not, but of how much each one of us believes in our own role. A sincere person is one who thinks that the role is the reality, and acts as if it is the only possible reality. At the other extreme Goffman positions the cynical person: the one who does not believe in the performance.

I have suggested two extremes: an individual may be

taken in by his own act or be cynical about it. These extremes are something a little more than just the ends of a continuum. Each provides the individual with a position which has its own particular securities and defenses, so there will be a tendency for those who have traveled close to one of these poles to complete the voyage. (Ibid., 9)

In this way, Goffman points out two opposing positions to the act of performing everyday life. If you believe in the reality of your own act (and that of others around you), sincerity inures the individual from seeing through his own act or that of others. On the other hand, once you have chosen to be cynical, it all becomes an act, and sincerity is irretrievably lost.

This creates a tremendous tension between the two positions. Languages are rich with words that express this conflict; "cheater" and "fool" are only some of the milder versions of these. There is an emotional investment in each position; each party has something to lose if they were to be proven wrong. To be in between is painful, and expressed through self-doubt and frustration. In our time and age, what we are supposed to do when confronted with such a dilemma is to start the search for self-realization: the true self.

It is tempting to compare this with Johan Huizinga's descriptions of play and, being easily seduced, I will go there. Play, in Huizinga's words, is tense (Huizinga 2000, 11). It absorbs the players, and creates a feeling of having invested something in the game. When the game is over, something is lost; while the game is played according to the rules, something is gained. The same can be said of this position between the sincere and the cynical individual. For either one to admit that there may be something in the other position means to lose something they have invested: time, status, identity. And where there is potential loss, there is tension.

But this everyday role-playing is not playful. We play our everyday roles, either cynical or sincere, with a tension that has no release and no relief. The arena is not separate from the rest of our lives; there is no set time for when the role-playing starts and when it ends, and most importantly: everyday role-playing is something we must do. Even the cynic who is aware of playing a role cannot stop playing. In order to function, the cynic must be aware of and relate to the rules of everyday role-playing. This opposes the nature of play:

Summing up the formal characteristics of play we might call it a free activity standing quite consciously outside "ordinary" life as being "not serious," but at the same time absorbing the player intensely and utterly. It is an activity connected with no material interest, and no profit can be gained by it. It proceeds within its own proper boundaries of time and space according to fixed rules and in an orderly manner. It promotes the formation of social groupings which tend to surround themselves with secrecy and to stress their difference from the common world by disguise or other means. (Ibid., 13)

Game Role-Playing

To several of the players of *Dragon Realms*, however, in-game role-playing did give them a more "cynical" view of the roles of everyday life. By playing a different character, or several different characters, they became aware of the *front,* which would apply to the character, and how manipulating the front meant manipulating the impression they made on other players. Goffman describes the front in this manner: "Front, then, is the expressive equipment of a standard kind intentionally or unwittingly employed by the individual during his performance" (Goffman 1959, 22).

This expressive equipment includes clothes, manners, language, stance, and stage setting. The king positioned on the throne activates and uses one very obvious front: We see the chair, the elevated dais, and the ceremony around it as a clear frame for our interpretation of the situation. The perhaps less-obvious aspects of the front are gestures that might be seen as involuntary (and as such, more "sincere"), the behavior of others (apparently not under your control) or outbursts that appear to be "out of character."

During the wedding of the Norwegian crown prince in 2001, cameras focused on the hands and eyes of the bride; her tiny nervous movements and her tears added to the formal proceedings as proof of her real feelings, the truth of emotions beneath the spectacle of ritual. In everyday life we also stage a front: we show people what we want them to see. We clean away the clutter before having important guests over, we dress in clothes we think will impress or tone down our presence, depending on the situation—we create the front we think will be suitable for the task at hand. And

44.4) Example of staged front: White horse and knight in *World of Warcraft.* (Blizzard)

while visiting others, we accept this, but look for the telltale signs to reveal how things really are: the nervous hand movements, the too-loud laughter.

What the players of *DR* reported was that by role-playing different characters, they became aware of how a certain position was composed not necessarily of real power and respect, but of the appearance of it. By acting as if their character was a high-ranking officer, they could get the other players' characters to treat them with the respect and obedience offered high-ranking officers. Also, by acting cruel, they could get the responses offered a cruel person, or any other response they desired. Mariah describes how her role-playing lets her explore further into understanding society:

Torill: What about playing? Why do you play computer games?

Mariah: I like the contact with other people. It's something you do with other people. It's something also that you—discover. I'm a social science major, so I am very interested in people and how they interact with things, and how the communities form and break up, and how people are choosing to portray a specific character. Hopefully you are not playing yourself all the time, but you have a character in your mind, and if you think—okay, this is it: My character is shy, then you have to use the stereotype of shy and portray this character as shy, and I am very interested in what people think shy is, and what people think angry is and what people think cold is . . . icy, and angry, and I'm very interested in how people are choosing to portray a specific person, and I think that the really good people are the ones who are willing to sacrifice their own personal way of doing things in order to do something in the way of the character in a stuck situation. (Mortensen 2003, 211)

Mariah does not use the words *front* or *setting*, but *stereotype*. However, the meaning is overlapping: the acts and surface trimmings that serve to establish position in a social system.

The game role-playing is distinguished from everyday role-playing in form by being more exaggerated and flamboyant. The communication needs to be so clearly informed by the fantasy of the role that the other players do not mistake the acts for being of that other, everyday role, but belonging to the game role. Role-players are like professional wrestlers, overstating the obvious and turning it into a parody of what is being portrayed. Roland Barthes calls this a language of excess:

> Wrestling, on the contrary, offers excessive gestures, exploited to the limit of their meaning. In judo, a man who is down is hardly down at all, he rolls over, he draws back, he eludes defeat, or, if the latter is obvious, he disappears; in wrestling, a man who is down is exaggeratedly so, and completely fills the eyes of the spectators with the intolerable spectacle of his powerlessness. (Barthes 1973)

It is this flamboyance that makes the game fun: with the large, overstated gestures there is no doubt about what is happening, no need to pause to interpret the actions of the other, none of the mundane ambivalence of everyday life.

A Firm Grip on Reality: IC and OOC

So do the players mistake role-playing and reality? This is a common idea about gamers, that the game identity replaces the "real" identity. People who are not part of the culture often react strongly and negatively to some of the behavior displayed by role-playing gamers in non-gaming contexts. Signs that can be taken for proof of a mixed or "weakening" identity can be things like using one's handle rather than one's legal name when meeting in the flesh or in non-game

settings. Other such signs of what is perceived as a skewed understanding of the "real" are a deep emotional attachment to other characters, efforts and resources spent on the game rather than on more common pursuits such as style and career, and adopting rituals and phrases from the game, to use them in the non-game world.

However, the gamers themselves are very clear about the distinction between the socially real world and the world of play. They call the distinction IC and OOC: In Character and Out Of Character. In the play-world they are In Character, in the mundane world they are Out Of Character. This has an interesting parallel in Goffman's description of communication out of character (Goffman 1959, 167). He devotes a chapter to this phenomenon, and describes how in everyday life we signal and use the distinction between IC and OOC in order to negotiate between potentially conflicting roles. Some examples of OOC communication that Goffman gives are: exclamations of surprise that acknowledge an error, backstage derogation of the front-stage clients, planning or staging conversations or talk, or perhaps simply gossiping and cues meant for other team members only, as well as techniques for establishing cooperation across accepted social borders.

Exclamations of surprise or dismay are common to both role-playing situations. A gamer who unintentionally hurts the feelings of, or in other ways disadvantages, a fellow gamer, will exclaim, "Oh, I am sorry," rather than cackle with in-game glee. In Goffman's example, a soldier who is about to give a general a reprimand can exclaim in the same manner when he discovers his error, by using an exclamation which is not part of his military front (such as, "Oh my God!") (Ibid., 169). The main difference is that where the gamer can ask for an OOC time-out before returning to the game (to check if the other player understands that it was not a voluntary act, and repair the illusion by explaining that he really did not mean to attack his in-game allies), the soldier in Goffman's description has no such option. His involuntary slip into the persona who was not the soldier was as bad as the error he had made by not recognizing the general.

Where role-playing communities reward a clear understanding of the different modes of communication and sharply drawn lines between the fantasy roles and the socially real roles, the mundane world treats it as a slip, a lack of sincerity. Rather than making the situation more understandable, manageable, and real, mundane world OOC communication can undermine the sincerity of the individual and make the boundaries between the different roles we play in our lives fuzzy, rather than crisp.

The issue of nicknames is one that comes up frequently as an example of how fantasy "invades" real life, and during the data collection period of my research on MUDs, a colleague mentioned in a conversation the weird experience of being introduced to somebody under their MUD name, and not their "real" name. In our society, the names on our birth certificates or passports are so important for identification that we mistake them for identity. And so we forget that identity is something we create through social interaction. When our social interaction happens under a different label, that is the label the others will recognize. In that context, the other label is as true as the name on the passport. And this is not only true of players of games. At the Association of Internet Researchers (AOIR) conference in 2004, a group of researchers all maintaining Weblogs met. They all introduced themselves by Weblog, as well as name, and frequently the Weblog was recognized where the name was not: they were more easily identified through the title of their more or less academic online writing than through the name on their tags.

Role-Playing High

In describing the role-playing high, Jack McLeod described a theory he felt he had extracted from his role-playing experience (Mortensen 2003, 164). It describes a euphoric feeling, a rapture, which he enters into through immersing himself in the role he plays. In *Man, Play, and Games*, Roger Caillois describes a comparable experience. A participant in a ritual dons the ritual garments and enters into his role:

> It is he who inspires fear through his possessing this terrible and inhuman power. It was sufficient for him merely to put on the mask he himself made, to don the costume that he sewed, in order to resemble the revered and feared being and to produce a weird drone with the aid of a secret weapon, the bull-roarer, of which he alone has known the existence, character, operation and function, ever since his initiation. He only learns that it is inoffensive, familiar and all-too-human when he has it in his hands and in his furor uses it to frighten others. (Caillois 2001, 88)

The role-playing high is balanced somewhere between believing in your own play and still being aware that you are controlling the act: that it is, in fact, an act and that there is a mundane, everyday life to return to. Immersed in the play, the player can commit fully to the play only because this is not something that must be maintained continuously. After the game is over, it is time to let the energy go, and unwind in different manners.

Live-action role-playing (LARP) is very demanding of the players, as they not only create a setting as fantastic as possible, they also live immersed in it, with as few breaks as possible, sometimes for days at a time. They don the mask and convince themselves of the role in order to create a special place and space for all: a game space that is somewhat similar to a religious, mystic experience. Afterward, they need time to rewind. A live-action role-playing group in Bergen, Norway calls this "Afterlive": a meeting after the "live" LARP session. The Afterlive is used to discuss the events, ask questions, solve any potential lingering conflicts, and generally put the event in its correct setting: that of a game, a space separate from everyday life, something to be discussed and enjoyed safely at a distance. The game is not something they have to, or even want to, live in and with the entire time.

In computer games you do not have the option of a defusing, unwinding environment in a safe social space. What you have in computer games is the option of talking in different channels. The MUD that was my main focus of research, *Dragon Realms*, had at least five channels, one of which was clearly stated to be an OOC channel. In *World of Warcraft*, which owes much to MUDs in matter of gameplay and player relations, there are several options for OOC interaction.

World of Warcraft (*WOW*) assists the player in the act of immersion in their character through graphics and music, as well as through quests that teach and express potential narratives, if not a story. But it also offers a way to retreat from the story by way of more general chat. In one of my characters' guilds, "The Supremacy," the guild-channel is dedicated to role-playing, with stilted language, IC comments, and no reference to the mechanical aspects of the games such as levels, experience points, or armor values on weapons, or experience from other characters the players might have played. However, these topics are frequently and enthusiastically discussed on the officer's channel, to which all members of this guild have access. In this manner, the guild creates both an arena for fantasy and an arena for mundane socializing and backstage planning for its members: in a way, a continuous "Afterlive."

No Limits to the Real Play

Role-playing is a controversial activity. Parents fear their children will lose their grip on reality, and develop schizophrenia or just drop out of society. Society in general fears that it will cause demon-worship, crime, murder, drug addiction, and several other things defined as social problems. It is not hard to find a story in the news where somebody blames role-playing games for these things, to the point of suing game companies for their various problems. The best-known example, although not the last one, is the lawsuit following the tragedy at Columbine High School in Colorado, where relatives of the children killed sued several different game companies (Ward 2001).

To a certain extent the establishment's fear of games is justified. Not because role-playing causes these current social problems, and particularly not such horrible tragedies as the massacre at Columbine, but because playing a role in a game opens up the possibility of a cynical rather than a sincere view of everyday role-playing. In Goffman's example, the cynic is the one who understands how to use a front to manipulate others. Once we have understood this, we also, like the religious performer who understands how mundane the religious object is, lose our fear of authorities. The uniform becomes just a way to dress, language is no longer a sign of high breeding and different blood, but of habit, education, and a desire to send a certain signal. Once we have seen through the layers of play surrounding us, what happens is not that we lose our

grip on reality, but that we see it more clearly.

In this way role-playing games offer both an escape and an awakening. For the keen, observant role-player who understands the distinctions of different roles and fronts, the escape into the other world of the game becomes something it is possible to achieve through work and dedication. The flow experience as studied by Csikszentmihalyi is described as a state of mind for which the individual needs to work hard; it is an achievement:

> These examples illustrate what we mean by optimal experience. They are situations in which attention can be freely invested to achieve a person's goals, because there is no disorder to straighten out, no threat for the self to defend against. We have called this state the *flow experience*, because this is the term many of the people we have interviewed had used in their description of how it felt to be in top form: "It was like floating," "I was carried away by the flow." It is the opposite of psychic entropy—in fact, it is sometimes called *negentropy*—and those who attain it develop a stronger, more confident self, because more of their psychic energy has been invested successfully in goals they themselves had chosen to pursue. (Csikszentmihalyi 1990, 40)

The pleasure of role-playing and the role-playing high is very much related to this experience of flow. The game offers a different context to adopt and immerse yourself in: energy can be freely invested to achieve your goals. But this is also a laborious process; it is not frivolous or easier than real life. Still, this is part of the seduction. To play a role in a role-playing game frequently involves having and hiding a secret—the character becomes attractive because it is holding something back. And so the player has to flesh out the character, take on the nature of the surroundings, but also guard the secret that seduces both me (the player who holds the secret) and also the other players who try to understand.

It is this mystery that keeps us all from becoming cynics in everyday life, because there is, behind every front, something, some secret that can surprise us. In some cases, the secret is that there is no real secret, no foundation for the front that is upheld with such effort. And so the knowledgeable role-players, the cynics, become a threat, because there are some secrets which we would rather not have revealed.

The Stranger Is Me

Most of all role-playing reveals what I am. In real life, I can hide behind circumstances and social connections; I can have a position through upholding a certain front, not necessarily because I am the person best suited to uphold the position.

Online role-playing games are ruthless that way. In a game, the front we grew up with, inherited or worked to create, no longer assists us. The anonymity of an online world not only protects, it also reveals. To appear intelligent in the game, you have to perform intelligent acts. It is not enough to look smart, to have the right name, to have the correct sociolect. Anybody can claim to be rich, wealthy, and well-connected, so these claims have no substance in building a front. Online, all who can connect are equal. This does not mean this is a utopian democracy—the threshold to connection is so high, most of the world's population can never get to that point. But it means that when connecting to an online role-playing game, the stranger, the other, can be anybody. In a lot of cases, the stranger is me.

Through role-playing it is possible to test out new fronts and new roles. As a player of games, I have the leisure and luxury to explore what it is like to be something totally other. "What are you?", you ask, and I don't answer with my real gender, nationality or age. I am an orc, a shaman, in Kalimdor, and I struggle to make a safe spot in the dry, searing desert heat where orcs can

finally live in peace from demons, tyrants, and others who want to enslave or eradicate them. I still know very well who I am, but I am also something else, something other—and online, playing a role-playing game, I set some of that other free.

References: Literature

Barthes, Roland (1973). *Mythologies*. London: Paladin.

Caillois, Roger (2001). *Man, Play, and Games*. Urbana and Chicago: University of Illinois Press.

Csikszentmihalyi, Mihaly. (1990). *Flow: The Psychology of Optimal Experience*. New York: Harper Perennial.

Goffman, Erving. (1959). *The Presentation of Self in Everyday Life*. Garden City, NY: Doubleday.

Huizinga, Johan. (2000). *Homo Ludens: A Study of the Play-Element in Culture*. London: Routledge.

Mortensen, Torill. (2003). "Pleasures of the Player: Flow and Control in Online Games." Doctoral Thesis. Bergen and Volda: Department of Humanistic Informatics Faculty of Media and Journalism, Volda University College.

Ward, Mark (2001). "Columbine families sue computer game makers." May 1, 2001. London: BBC News Online. <http://news.bbc.co.uk/1/hi/sci/tech/1295920.stm>.

References: Games

Aarinfel. Jarok, Kierae, et al.; Self-Published. 2000.

Advanced Dungeons & Dragons Player's Handbook. Gary Gygax. 1978.

Alternity: Player's Handbook. Bill Slavicsek and Richard Baker; Wizards of the Coast. 1998.

Dragon Realms. M. Dick, K. Grant, et al.; Self-Published. 1995–1999.

Vampire: The Masquerade (Revised Edition). Justin Achilli, Andrew Bates, et al.; White Wolf Games. 1998.

World of Warcraft. Blizzard Entertainment. 2004.

A Network of Quests in *World of Warcraft*
Jill Walker

I'm Yggdra, a human warrior in *World of Warcraft*. I'm also an undead rogue and a dwarven warrior and a night elf hunter, but they're only my alts: my main character lives in Elwynn Forest, where she's well on the way to becoming one of the Alliance's staunchest defenders. She's also spending a surprising amount of time mining and blacksmithing to earn money for all the training and equipment her warrior career requires.

Like many other games, *World of Warcraft* is organized through its quests (Tronstad 2001; Tosca 2003; Aarseth 2004). Within seconds of logging on for the first time, I saw my first non-player character with a yellow exclamation mark over his head. Clicking him set my first quest into motion, with a short narrative, some fixed objectives, and a resolution. The quests I've experienced so far have all been designed to spur me on to discover more of the game in fairly limited ways, and all instruct me either to:

Explore, by:

Finding a person (report to a person, deliver an object to a person).

Exploring an area (scout an area, report back and tell us the condition).

Learning to use a game function, such as buying an item from a vendor, finding flight routes, playing dungeon instances, or joining the skirmishes on the battlefields.

Slay monsters, with slight variations:

Kill X number of a particular kind of monster.

Bring the quest-giver an object that is found on the body of a slain monster.

Bring the quest-giver an object that is found in a monster-infested area. This also involves exploring, of course.

Sometimes these are combined ("Escort this NPC through a monster-infested area and slay monsters to keep him alive until he shows you a new area of the game" combines 1a and 1b; 1b tends to involve monster-slaying in order to fully explore the required territory), but they can always be broken down into these basic structures.

World of Warcraft has a very explicit quest management system. At any time, I can pull up my quest window, and see which quests I have accepted, how much progress I've made on them and even whether I'm likely to succeed at the quest playing solo or should team up with other players. Additional organization of the quests is provided less explicitly: some

45.1) Two images from related quests in *World of Warcraft*. (Blizzard)

45.2) The *World of Warcraft*. (Blizzard)

quests build upon other quests, some quests are only for specific races, classes, or professions (humans, warriors, miners), and related quests can be found close to each other in the in-game geography.

Each quest in *World of Warcraft* sets up a capsule narrative situation. The person who gives you the quest will always have a short dialogue. One of my favorite series of quests from the early levels of the game began, for me, when Maybell Maclure at the Maclure Vineyard near Goldshire asked me to help her:

> Oh, I'm cursed! My heart belongs to Tommy Joe Stonefield, but our families are bitter enemies. So I can't see him, even though my eyes ache to gaze upon that handsome face! Please, take this letter and give it to Tommy Joe. He's usually at the river to the west of the Stonefield Farm, which is due west of here. ("Young Lovers")

The writing is poor and the plot is unoriginal and predictable, so why did this engage me so? I was admittedly thrilled to find a quest that seemed to break the already dull slay-more-monsters mold, but the basic structure is a straightforward example of quest type 1a, "Deliver an object to a person."

In trying to see what is appealing about this series of quests, I quickly ruled out the quality of the plot and the aesthetic pleasure of the language. If that were what I was after, any novel would be an improvement. Is it my engagement with the plot, then? My agency? Well, I really only have two choices: decline or ignore the quest, or accept it and walk over to Tommy Joe. If I try to complete the quest, I'm really just enacting whatever role the game designers devised.

What most appealed to me about the series of quests between the Maclure Vineyard and Stonefield Farm was the abundance of stories I discovered and the tight network between the quests in the series. As I was working on helping Maybell and Tommy Joe to get together, other members of their families asked me for help. One had lost a necklace, which led to my having to slay boars so that she could bake a pie for the horrid little boy at the neighboring farm, who refused to tell me where he'd lost the necklace he'd stolen from her, unless I got him that particular pie. Finally, he told me that a vicious kobold in the nearby mines had it, so off I went, back to the same mines I had already scouted in a previous quest, with a new goal.

Another storyline is introduced in "Princess Must Die," where I had to go to another farm and kill the pig Princess, but since bandits had taken over the pig's farm, that required teaming up with other players. Each time I achieved one goal, a new objective was given to me, and I trotted back and forth between the two family farms dozens of times to complete all the quests set up between them. Through this abundance of quests and stories in the area, a whole world was set up, where I gradually came to know a little about many of the people at these farms. Certainly, Maybell and her family stand like stiff cardboard cut-outs simply waiting for me to come and find them, but I know the farms and the mine south of the road leading east from Goldshire as intimately as you do, only when you know the stories of a place.

The different zones of *World of Warcraft* each have their own set of stories, and some are far more appealing than others. Playing my dwarven warrior, I quickly tired of the less-connected stories in the dwarven starting areas, and as soon as I could I traveled to Westfall, the zone adjacent to Elwynn Forest, meant for the slightly more experienced characters. As soon as I arrived there, I found that the people in the general chat channels agreed with me. "Westfall is much more fun than Loch Modan!" someone said, confirming my opinion.

Westfall, like the family farms in Elwynn Forest, has clusters of quests that work together well, and that build up a sense of knowing an area and making a difference to the people who live there. The most likely point of entrance for players reaching the appropriate level of experience is from Elwynn Forest, because the other entrances are from zones with far higher-level monsters that are hard for newbies to cross.

Crossing from Elwynn Forest into Westfall, everything changes. The countryside becomes burnt and red and dry, the sounds are of hot roads baked in sun and crickets, and the music becomes more ominous. The first NPCs you meet are a farming couple who've been evicted from their houses by bandits. Farmer Furlbrow asks you to find his pocket watch, a family heirloom left in their former home that has been taken over by bandits (quest type 2c), while his wife asks you to take a recipe to a friend nearby. Each of these quests takes you to places where you'll find many other quests and snippets of story. Westfall is densely populated by characters and quests that almost all center on the land, which the people no longer control. The militia tell you that the king no longer controls these lands, and asks you to help fight the bandits. Again, each of the capsule narratives seen alone is rather pathetic, but together they work wonderfully.

Of course, we might wish for games where the individual quests were better written, but the true importance of quests in *World of Warcraft* is not at the level of the individual quest. There are at least two reasons we need quests. First, they function as tutorials guiding the player through learning how to play the game and expanding the game as the player progresses. Secondly, they flesh out the world, making it interesting. They do that not so much through each individual quest as through the densely storied landscape that I come to know as I work through quest after quest.

Grand Theft Auto is another quest-based series of games. In *Grand Theft Auto*, quests are called "missions," and of course, it's a single-player game, but apart from that it has much in common with *World of Warcraft*. The player can choose from a series of quests, not all of which are compulsory. There are always other options than doing quests. You can simply explore the world, car-jacking in *Grand Theft Auto* and walking (and later, flying) in *World of Warcraft*. You can earn money through taxi-driving in *Grand Theft Auto* and through a myriad of professions in *World of Warcraft*. You can work

out and train, and you can buy yourself clothes and gadgets. You can fight monsters without having any quest to do so.

This semi-structured organization through a network of quests and always-available self-selected activities within set boundaries matches the way we read and experience the world today. These days, we do things in fragments: we surf, channel-flip, and multitask. We write and read e-mails and blog posts rather than novels, we listen to four- to six-minute songs rather than symphonies, and we listen to the news in thirty-second sound bites. We devour these fragments, flicking through hundreds each day, and we return to many, maybe only spending a few minutes at a time on one topic or blog or news story, but returning to it again and again. This fragmentation doesn't necessarily mean that we're more superficial. We return to things again and again, and the accumulation of fragmentary experiences may be as deep or deeper as a single, but lengthier, exposure to a work.

An increasing number of narratives and art works are designed for this kind of fragmentary yet cumulative reading. *Online Caroline* is meant to be read for five or ten minutes a day over a period of about three weeks (Walker 2004). *The Impermanence Agent* (Wardrip-Fruin et al. 2000) pops up while you're doing other things, David Claerbout's *The Present* (2000) grows quietly on your desktop, only visible in between other tasks, and the novel *Implementation* (Montfort and Rettberg 2004) is told in 192 stickers stuck in public places around the world. Weblogs, one of the first native Web genres, provide a perfect example of a work that is completely composed of fragments that don't necessarily have anything in common except for the visual design and, perhaps, a common narrative voice.

This form of storytelling (or story-collection, from the player's point of view) has much in common with the distributed narratives that are becoming more and more common in other genres as well (Walker 2005). Outside of the game world, there are hundreds of fan Web sites with searchable databases of all possible quests. The quests in *World of Warcraft* are not puzzles, so there are no walkthroughs for the game. Instead, there are maps of where to find the starting points for quests, or where to find objects you need. There are discussions of which quests are the most satisfying, and for the rarer quests (which are started by a random "drop" from a monster, for instance) there are discussions about how many murlocs you have to kill, on average, in order to find the treasure map or other item that starts the quest. These discussions are reminiscent of the ways in which fans of the *Space Invaders* project share the pleasure of the hunt for the mosaics around the world that is each part of the project (Walker 2005).

On the surface, video games might appear the exact opposite of today's fragmentary expression. They routinely last for at least forty hours of play, and the popular image of the gamer is of a person in deep, continuous concentration. Indeed, a recurring story reported in newspapers is of the gamer who dies from having played for too long, too intensively. This would appear to be precisely the sort of concentration on a single cultural object of which protectors of traditional novel reading have lamented the loss (Birkerts 1994).

Look more closely, though, and you'll find that a game is a network of fragments, most of which are not necessary to experience the game fully, and yet which cumulate into a rich experience of a storied world.

References: Literature

Aarseth, Espen (2004). "Beyond the Frontier: Quest Games as Post-Narrative Discourse." In *Narrative Across Media: The Languages of Storytelling*, edited by Marie-Laure Ryan. Lincoln: University of Nebraska Press.

Birkerts, Sven (1994). *The Gutenberg Elegies: The Fate of Reading in an Electronic Age*. Boston: Faber and Faber.

Claerbout, David (2000). *The Present*. <http://www.diacenter.org/claerbout/>

Montfort, Nick, and Scott Rettberg (2005). *Implementation*. <http://nickm.com/implementation>.

Tosca, Susana (2003). "The Quest Problem in Computer Games." Darmstadt: Paper read at Technologies for Interactive Digital Storytelling and Entertainment (TIDSE).

Tronstad, Ragnhild (2001). "Semiotic and Nonsemiotic MUD Performance." Amsterdam: Paper read at COSIGN.

Walker, Jill (2004). "How I was Played by Online Caroline." In *First Person: New Media as Story, Performance, and Game*, edited by Noah Wardrip-Fruin and Pat Harrigan. Cambridge, MA: MIT Press.

Walker, Jill (2005). "Distributed Narrative: Telling Stories Across Networks." In *The 2005 Association of Internet Researchers Annual*, edited by M. Consalvo, J. Hunsinger, and N. Baym. New York: Peter Lang.

Wardrip-Fruin, Noah, a.c. chapman, Brion Moss, and Duane Whitehurst (2000). *The Impermanence Agent*. <http://impermanenceagent.com>.

Reference: Game

Online Caroline. R. Bevan and T. Wright. 2000/2001. <http://www.onlinecaroline.com>.

Communities of Play: The Social Construction of Identity in Persistent Online Game Worlds
Celia Pearce and Artemesia[1]

Diasporic Game Cultures

On February 9, 2004, *Uru: Ages beyond Myst*, a massively multiplayer online game (MMOG) based on the classic best-selling *Myst* series, closed its servers, leaving an estimated 10,000 players refugees. This event, variously known among players as Black Monday or Black Tuesday (depending on their time zones) precipitated the widespread immigration of an unknown number of *Uru* players en masse into other games, bringing with them *Uru* culture, building "ethnic" *Uru* communities, recreating *Uru* artifacts, and eventually developing their own unique *Uru*-inspired culture. Brought together by both a common gaming experience and a shared trauma, these players formed what I have come to call the "Uru diaspora," a distributed game community dispersed across several games, which continues to thrive in various forms throughout a number of virtual worlds. Building on prior research in emergent narrative (Pearce 2002), I conducted an eighteen-month, in-game ethnography, using a technique of "participant engagement," which entailed playing with study participants as a full member of the group. In addition, I employed techniques of visual anthropology (primarily screen-shot documentation), conducted in-game interviews, and studied supplemental communications (such as forums and e-mail lists). The primary subject of the study was a

"Neighborhood" or "hood" (the Uru version of a guild) called "The Gathering" that initially[2] formed inside *Uru* Live, then immigrated into other virtual worlds.

The goal of the study[3] was to examine the relationship between game design and emergent social behavior. In terms of game studies, emergence generally refers to complex behaviors that arise out of simple rules, and that are unanticipated by the designers (Salen and Zimmerman 2003). Uru provided a rare opportunity to track emergence between gameworlds and observe how it mutated to accommodate new contexts.

One key finding was that players arrived to the game predisposed to certain emergent behaviors, based in part on past play patterns and in part on demographics. *Uru* attracted a somewhat unusual audience for an online game, mostly long-time fans of *Myst*, which had been the top-selling PC game for eight years until it was surpassed by *The Sims* in 2001. Due to their experience with *Myst* games, these players were particularly adept at what have been described as "Mensa-level" puzzles (Duke 2005), as well as having developed a sense of "spatial literacy"—the ability to read and interpret meaning and narrative embedded in virtual space in a particular way.

Players within The Gathering ranged in age from about 14–72, with the majority being in their forties and fifties, and 50 percent were female. When compared to other online games, this is something of a demographic anomaly. The majority of demographic studies concern medieval fantasy role-playing games, which make up the most popular MMOGs, and which tend to skew about 80% male with an average age around 25 (Yee 2001; Castronova 2001; Steinkuehler 2004; Taylor 2004; Whang and Chang 2004; Whang and Kim 2005).

First-Person Immersion vs. Avatar Embodiment

One of the unique ingredients that made *Uru* "the perfect storm" (as one of my colleagues has called it) for MMOG research was the transition from the first person perspective of the prior *Myst* games to the introduction of an avatar in

---

1. Artemesia is Celia Pearce's research avatar and alter ego.

2. Group and avatar names have been changed to protect the privacy of study subjects.

3. The study was done as part of a PhD research project at the SMARTlab Centre, Central Saint Martins College of Art and Design, University of the Arts, London.

Uru. The first person viewpoint enabled the *Myst* series' hallmark "faux" virtual reality effect (the game consisted primarily of still images), which enabled players to feel a sense of immersion, a primary goal not only of games, but of traditional virtual and "presence" research (Rheingold 1991; Pearce 1997). At the same time, the first-person viewpoint

also created an ambiguous identity and a feeling of anonymity. In *Uru,* the addition of the avatar gave the player a specific, customizable identity and a sense of embodiment (Taylor 2002). In the role of a human explorer, for the first time, they could see *themselves* inside the beloved *Myst* world.

The shift in affect that resulted from the introduction of an avatar cannot be overstated. One player described it as the feeling of "proprioception," or body awareness. Suddenly they could run, jump and physically interact with the world in ways they had not before. For disabled players, some of whom made up the group's leadership, the experience was one of reembodiment, allowing them to do things their physical bodies could not, as well as putting them on a "level playing field" with others. All players enjoyed a new kind of inhabitation and agency in the world, of which they were now physically and representationally a part. In addition, it created the possibility for social agency, which further enhanced the experience.

46.1) While *Myst* created a sense of immersion . . .

46.2) . . . *Uru* introduced an avatar into the imaginary world.

In interviews, most members of The Gathering described themselves as "shy" and "loners." Many were initially hesitant to interact with others once they had entered the multiplayer world. Leesa, their reluctant leader, started the group because, as a beta tester, she was expected to by *Uru's* developer, Cyan. At first, there were no members, but eventually she invited one, and then many others followed, attracted to the values and vision she had set forth for the group. By the time *Uru* closed, The Gathering had around 350

46.3) Players carry identities across game worlds, working within the constraints of each environment's avatar creation tools.

members, most of whom joined in the last month or so, when a series of "clerical errors" caused several thousand players to be "erroneously" invited into the game.

The *Uru* Live server ran for less than a year. Even the last three months, which occurred after the game was released commercially in November 2003—the period when most of the players joined—were characterized as a "public beta." In spite of the game's short life, the closure of the server was a highly distressing event for *Uru* players. Members of The Gathering, many of whom reported weeping as the clock struck midnight and the avatars on the screen froze in place, reported symptoms of post-traumatic stress. Much to their own surprise, players grieved not only the loss of their community but also the loss of their individual avatars. The shared trauma of the server shutdown served as a catalyst for fortifying the group identity, which evolved into a sort of fictive ethnicity. This shared group identity created both the necessity and the substrate for migrating their individual avatar identities into to other virtual worlds.

Determined to stay together, The Gathering (by now numbering about 350) convened on an online Web forum they had set up shortly before the server closed. Here, they vetted options for resettlement. After much debate, a consensus emerged that all group members did not have to settle in the same game world. Over time, the group came to span no less than five game worlds, two of which they built themselves—a text-based MUD and a virtual world in Adobe Atmosphere. But the majority favored migrating their community into another "ready-to-play" game world. They

ruled out games like the science fiction-themed MMOG *Ryzom* because it was too violent. A different *Uru* group comprised of about 200 had settled in *Second Life*—an unthemed user-created virtual world—a subset of whom had begun to create a near-exact replica of areas of *Uru*. While The Gathering also had a small group in *Second Life*, ultimately the vast majority—about 300 members in all—chose to settle in *There*, another open-ended world with affordances for user-creation, where they founded "The Gathering of Uru." Later, when Cyan released the server code to players, The Gathering set up one of about a half-dozen player-run *Until Uru* servers, where a core group also began convening on a weekly basis. This adroit traversing of game worlds suggests that the magic circle, defined as the boundary of time and space within which a game is played

46.4) The *Uru* fountain, the center of social life in the Neighborhood. Clockwise from upper left: In *Uru*, and as instantiated by players in *There, Second Life,* and Adobe Atmosphere.

46.5) *Uru* Island, home of Uruvian refugees in *There* (left). The University of There, founded by an *Uru* refugee, consists largely of *Uru* - themed cone houses by one of The Gathering's top artisans, Damanji (right).

(Caillois 1961; Huizinga 1950; Salen and Zimmerman 2003; Turner 1982), may be more porous than previously thought, especially when seen in the larger context of all online games on the Internet—what might be characterized as the "ludisphere."

For a small and growing game world like *There*, the sudden arrival of a large group of players en masse placed a significant burden on the system. Because of its size, the group put a strain on processing cycles—the one limited resource in cyberspace—causing lag to its neighbors. There were also festering resentments among the "indigenous" Therians, who were suspicious of this sudden inrush, fearing that, by sheer numbers, the Uruvians would take over *There*. Griefing (i.e., harassment) was a regular part of the early settlement process, which only served to further cement their bond. Conversely, *There* management wanted to accommodate the group, which represented a relatively large subscription base. After being forced to move five times, *There* management was finally able to secure them an island of their own, but not without coercing its occupants to leave. Over time, The Gathering acclimated to *There* and a number of its members became pillars of the community in their new home. Its key leaders have been on the There Member Advisory Board, an elected body formed to communicate with *There* management; its artisans are among the most successful in *There*; and its members have founded a number of There groups and institutions, including the University of There. At *There's* Real-Life

Gathering, held in September 2005, nearly half the attendees were members of The Gathering of Uru.

Emergent Identity as an Intersubjective Accomplishment

While it was not surprising to see emergent group cultures, one of the more surprising findings of the study was that individual avatar identity is an intersubjective accomplishment and is as much a product of social emergence as the group itself. Earlier readings have tended to look at the online persona as a psychological construct, primarily a mechanism of individual agency (Turkle 1995). I was already prepared to look at the emergent culture of the group in intersubjective terms (Blumer 1969), both vis-à-vis the game design itself, as well as the ways in which the shared meanings that arose from it were reiterated and mutated in other games. However, it became apparent in observing the group over time that the individual identity was also both an intersubjective and an emergent creation.

This mirrors some contemporary theories of anthropology that build on non-Western concepts of the relationship between the individual and the group (Jackson 1998). Not only was the group part of the individual identity and vice versa, but the individual persona was further articulated and differentiated over time through an emergent process of social feedback. Players enacted individual agency for the benefit of the group or as a means of personal expression. Positive social response prompted further actions, ad infinitum. Various players emerged as leaders and creators through this process of improvised emergent identity formation, and many discovered and developed new talents and abilities as a result. Leesa's experience, outlined here, is just one example. A number of other cases revealed not only that the avatar character evolved through group interaction, but also that being an avatar in a social context had a palpable impact on the individual person. Most players concurred that being an avatar changed them. To paraphrase Marshall McLuhan: we shape our avatars and thereafter our avatars shape us (McLuhan 1964).

One key point that is often overlooked is the role of the game designers in framing modes of avatar representation and interaction (Stone 1991; Taylor 2003). The designer must always be factored in as part of the intersubjective process of identity creation. In most popular MMOGs, like some of those referenced earlier, avatar representation is both fantastical and statistical, drawing from the character mechanics of the *Dungeons & Dragons* tabletop role-playing game. In all of the games discussed here—*Uru, There,* and *Second Life*—avatar representation is primarily aesthetic, a form of personal expression. The expressive qualities of the avatar were a key factor in the debate over immigration. *Second Life* avatars were more realistic, but their movements were more stiff. Conversely, *There* avatars were cartoony and "Disney-like," but had more nuanced social expressions. As Leesa later put it, "Here, our avatars breathe." Since the

relationship players form with not only their own avatars but also those of other players is driven by the expressive mechanisms of avatar design, it is crucial to view the designers as an active part of the social mechanism of avatar identity creation.

Communities of Play

The Gathering is what Bernie DeKoven calls a "play community," a group whose commitment to playing together transcends any specific game or its rules (DeKoven 1978). We can look at a play community as a counterpart to "communities of practice" or "communities of interest," whose goals are more pragmatic. The play community shares a strong social connection, as well as a mutual play style that is both inclusive and flexible, and can be transformed and relocated as needed to sustain the group. Different communities of play have different characteristics that arise out of the combined play styles of the individuals within them, each of whom is, in turn, transformed by the group play style. These play styles are also both influenced and transformed by the spaces they are enacted in.

DeKoven has proposed a social model of play based on Mihaly Csikszentmihalyi's concept of "flow," defined as "being completely involved in an activity for its own sake. The ego falls away. Time flies. Every action, movement, and thought follows inevitably from the previous one, like playing jazz. Your whole being is involved, and you're using your skills to

315

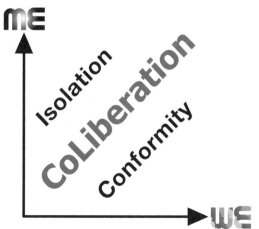

46.6) Diagrams showing the dynamics of "flow," (left) and DeKoven's concept of "CoLiberation" (right). Original Graphics by Steve Childs (left) and Bernie DeKoven (right), redrawn by Michael Crumpton.

the utmost" (Csikszentmihalyi 1990). DeKoven proposes that players can keep each other in a state of flow, producing what he calls "CoLiberation," an optimal balance of individual self-awareness and group connectedness. Playtesting consultant Nicole Lazzaro has stated this another way: "People are addictive" (Lazzaro 2004–2005). This phenomenon, which I will call "intersubjective flow," can be seen not only in digital games, but also in team sports and live music jam sessions, to name a few examples.

In a persistent play community, flow has a cumulative effect. The group supports the individual and vice versa, allowing persistent avatar identities to evolve, even as they traverse a variety of play spaces. Intersubjective flow, as realized by play, creates a powerful context for social interaction that brings out aspects of people's personalities that might not otherwise find expression. This may explain why many members of The Gathering say that in some ways they feel "more themselves" in the avatar persona than they do in real life. Within the context of their play community they feel both a sense of belonging and individual value that differs from other roles they may present in so-called "real life."

Conclusions

The key conclusions outlined here are a start at unpacking the relationship between game design, emergent group dynamics, and individual identity formation. Probably the most significant finding is the formation of individual avatar identity through emergent social processes. Furthermore, when motivated and supported by group cohesion, these identities can be portable and malleable over time, and lead to a high level of productivity (Pearce 2005; Poremba 2003). When motivated by the group, players find in themselves new talents, abilities and skills, which are further enhanced through a process of group feedback. Furthermore, based on the type of games players gravitate towards, we can, to a certain extent, anticipate overall patterns of emergence based on players' play styles, predilections, and resident skills.

Interestingly, the storyline of *Uru* involved discovering and restoring the lost culture of the D'Ni, an objective that players carried beyond the game subsequent to its demise. It should also be noted that at the time of this writing, Cyan announced that it would call a close to the *Myst* legacy. At the same time, members of the Uru diaspora dispersed in other games had already begun creating their own original *Uru*- and *Myst*-inspired content. In effect, *Uru* players, through emergence empowered by community, have taken over the *Myst* world, adding a poignant foreshadowing to *Uru*'s subtitle, *Ages Beyond Myst*.

46.7) Original *Uru*-inspired player-created artifacts in *There*, by Damanji (left); Numbakulla, an entirely new *Uru/Myst*-inspired game created by players in *Second Life* (right).

References: Literature

Blumer, Herbert (1969). *Symbolic Interactionism*. Englewood Cliffs, NJ: Prentice-Hall.

Caillois, Roger (trans. M. Barash) (1961). *Man, Play and Games*. New York: Free Press.

Castronova, Edward (2001). "Virtual Worlds: A First-Hand Account of Market and Society on the Cyberian Frontier." *CESifo Working Paper Series* 618.

Csikszentmihalyi, Mihaly (1990). *Flow: The Psychology of Optimal Experience*. New York: Harper & Row.

DeKoven, Bernard (1978). *The Well-Played Game: A Player's Philosophy*. New York: Anchor Press.

Duke (2005). "Myst IV: Revolution." In *Game Revolution*. <http://gr.bolt.com/games/xbox/adventure/myst_iv.htm>.

Huizinga, Johan (1950). *Homo Ludens: A Study of the Play-Element in Culture*. New York: Roy Publishers.

Jackson, Michael (1998). *Minima Ethnographica: Intersubjectivity and the Anthropological Project*. Chicago: University of Chicago Press.

Lazzaro, Nicole (2004–2005). "Why We Play Games: Four Keys to More Emotion Without Story." <http://www.xeodesign.com/xeodesign_whyweplaygames.pdf>.

McLuhan, Marshall (1964). *Understanding Media: The Extensions of Man*. New York: Mentor.

Pearce, Celia (1997). *The Interactive Book*. Indianapolis: Macmillan Technical Publishing.

Pearce, Celia (2002). "Emergent Authorship: The Next Interactive Revolution." *Computers and Graphics* 26.

Pearce, Celia (2005). "Productive Play: Game Culture from the Bottom Up." *Games and Culture* 1.

Poremba, Cindy (2003). "Player as Author: Digital Games and Agency." Masters Thesis. Department of Computing Arts and Design Sciences, Simon Frasier University, Vancouver, Canada.

Rheingold, Howard (1991). *Virtual Reality*. New York: Simon & Schuster (Touchstone).

Salen, Katie, and Eric Zimmerman (2003). *Rules of Play: Game Design Fundamentals*. Cambridge, MA: MIT Press.

Steinkuehler, Constance A. (2004). "Learning in massively multiplayer online games." In *Proceedings of the Sixth International Conference on the Learning Sciences*, edited by Y. B. Kafai, W. A. Sandoval, N. Enyedy, A. S. Nixon, and F. Herrera. Mahwah, New Jersey: Lawrence Erlbaum Associates.

Stone, Allucquère Rosanne (1991). "Will the Real Body Please Stand Up? Boundary Stories About Virtual Cultures." In *Cyberspace: First Steps*, edited by M. Benedikt. Cambridge, MA: MIT Press.

Taylor, T. L. (2002). "Living Digitally: Embodiment in Virtual Worlds." In *The Social Life of Avatars: Presence and Interaction in Shared Virtual Environments*, edited by R. Schroeder. London: Springer-Verlag.

Taylor, T. L. (2003). "Intentional Bodies: Virtual Environments and the Designers Who Shape Them." *International Journal of Engineering Education* 19.

Taylor, T. L. (2004). "Power Gamers Just Want to Have Fun? Instrumental Play in A MMOG." In *Level Up: Digital Games Research Conference Proceedings*, edited by M. Copier and J. Raessens. Utrecht, The Netherlands: Universiteit Utrecht.

Turkle, Sherry (1995). *Life on the Screen: Identity in the Age of the Internet*. New York: Simon & Schuster.

Turner, Victor Witter (1982). *From Ritual to Theater: The Human Seriousness of Play*. New York: Performing Arts Journal Publications.

Whang, Leo Sang-Min and Geunyoung Chang (2004). "Lifestyles of Virtual World Residents: Living in the On-Line Game *Lineage*." *CyberPsychology and Behavior* 7, no.5 (October 2005): 592–600.

Whang, Leo Sang-Min and Jee Yeon Kim (2005). "The Comparison of Online Game Experiences by Players in Games of *Lineage* and *EverQuest*: Role Play vs. Consumption." In *Changing Views: Worlds in Play, DiGRA Second International Conference*, edited by S. de Castell and J. Jenson. Vancouver, British Columbia: Simon Frasier University.

Wikipedia. "*Myst*."

Yee, Nicholas (2001). "The Norrathian Scrolls: A study of *EverQuest*." <http://www.nickyee.com/eqt/home.html>.

References: Games

Dungeons & Dragons. Gary Gygax and Dave Arneson; TSR. 1974.

Myst. Cyan. 1993.

Myst IV: Revelation. Ubisoft. 2005.

The Saga of Ryzom. Nevrax. 2003.

Second Life. Linden Lab, Inc. 2003.

Uru: Ages Beyond Myst. Cyan; Ubisoft. 2003.

Eliza Redux
Adrianne Wortzel

Eliza Redux **Then**

The first manifestation of *Eliza Redux*[1] was a pre-scripted film produced in 2001 depicting a twenty-minute psychoanalytic session between a robot and a human, during which the robot and human switch back and forth in their roles as analyst and analysand; and in the end, it is the robot, in its role as a patient, that has a "baring of the soul" cathartic experience. The robot-actor in this case was essentially a puppet; its locomotion, movements, text-to-speech, and camera pan and tilt were pre-scripted as "gestures" and operated manually from a keyboard. Each keyboard stroke would send the next line of instruction to the robot, inclusive of its speech and accompanying activity.

A program[2] was written that allowed the robot voice to be imbued with changes in volume, inflection, pace, pitch, and so forth. The puppeteer at the keyboard could improvise with the human actor only in terms of timing; that is, being able to decide when to execute each keystroke entry. The ability to time the pauses and overlaps manually during the shooting did lend a lot of credibility to the illusion that the two were in a "live" conversation and, for the purposes of a dramatic film, was perfect.

The making of such a non-interactive work revives the concept of masterpiece at a time when authorship is going through a major deconstruction. All of the decisions in a non-interactive work, even if random, are up to the artist(s), as are all the adaptations to the state of the technology in use at that moment. "Masterpiece Syndrome" is a term I have made up to mean the desire to experience or create works that transcend their genre in form, subject matter, context, use of language, and are time-based, meaning that over time they offer up to the viewer evocative subtexts. That is "sexy."

Why is it, I thought, that an individual or consciously

47.1) Excerpt, with robot cues, from script for *The Veils of Transference*. Code by James Cruickshanks.

	0 `vv75 `vg0 `vb72 `vr20 `vh50 `vy50 `vf90 `vs55 Good `3 afternoon, `vb50 Doctor `2 Wilmington.
	10 `vb65 `vf100 `vs45 The couch looks `3 very `3 inviting.
	20 `vb65 `vf100 `vs45 I thought maybe we could talk about that today.
	30 `vg0 `vs70 `vy75 `vb80 Talk about whaat?
	40 `vb65 `vf100 `vs45 Your relationship to the couch.
`vb Pitch values from 0 to 100 `vh Head size values from 0 to 100 `vr Roughness values from 0 to 100 `vy Breathiness values from 0 to 100 `vf Inflection values from 0 to 100 `vs Speed values from 0 to 100 `vv Volume values from 0 to 100 `vg Gender 0 Male, 1 Female ` Emphasis 0, 1, 2, 3, 4	50 `vv75 `vg0 `vb65 `vr20 `vh50 `vy40 `vf90 `vs45 I am sorry, `vb60 but I don t have `3 relationships with `3 in-animate `2 objects.
	60 `vb65 `vf100 `vs45 Why are you sorry?
	70 `vv75 `vg0 `vb85 `vr20 `vh50 `vy30 `vf90 `vs30 I am sorry `vv85 `vg0 `vb72 `vr20 `vh50 `vy50 `vf90 `vs50 is just a figure of speech in this particular `3 instance! I am `3 committed `vs50 to `3 respond to `4 everything that is `3 addressed to me, `vb65 but the syntax is more or less `3 my `vs30 own call.
	80 `vb65 `vf100 `vs45 You mention the couch, yet you never lie down on it.
	90 `vv85 `vg0 `vb72 `vr20 `vh50 `vy50 `vf90 `vs50 it `3 should be `2 obvious `vs50 that I can't `2 achieve a `3 horizontal position unless somebody tips me over or knocks me `3 down, and `3 sitting is `3 impossible under `3 any circumstances.
	100 `vb65 `vf100 `vs45 Are you saying that only someone else's abuse will allow you to lie on the couch?

319

Eliza Redux

1. The title for this film has now been changed to *The Veils of Transference* to differentiate it from the online *Eliza Redux*.

2. James Cruickshanks wrote this code/script as part of his Master's Degree thesis in Mechanical Engineering at the Cooper Union for the Advancement of Science and Art.

47.2) Session, Interior Environment, from *Veils of Transference*.

47.3) Session, StudioBlue.

47.4) Borrowing Freud's office.

collaborative artists can create works of Shakespearean complexity, while public interactive telerobotic installations I have created seem to bring out, repetitively, vernacular in the extreme, in spite of the robots' provocations to move beyond everyday thoughts? Why don't interactors strive to crystallize their input into something more artful, or contemplative? Do we anticipate that non-interactive work will exhibit literary or philosophical merit because it is "authored" and therefore "authorized," while interactive work at large has a definitive struggle to grow literary and cinematic merits? I have seen autonomous "engines" on the Web, such as *The Impermanence Agent*,[3] evidence valid aesthetic qualities through combinatory prowess, but I have never seen an "Exquisite Corpse" that, in my opinion, has the complex mechanics and inspiration, or communicative skills, to become a transcendent work of art.

Floorplay

I create public interactive telerobotic installations couched in dramatic scenarios and vacillating between autonomous and remotely controlled states. Kiru, for example, was a telerobot that roamed the first floor gallery and lobby of the Whitney Museum[4] for three months. When the robot was not in the control of a remote visitor, it had an autonomous set of speeches, gestures, and locomotion.

Kiru's mission in taking up residency in the Whitney Museum was both playful and educative. Kiru's character was embedded in a fictive "life." It came from a town called "Camouflage Town," a decoy town created by its clan as an arena for wars, combat training, and any and all other criminal act(s) for the sole purpose of keeping "RealTown" intact. Kiru brought with it to the Whitney all the teachings of the culture of its clan. For instance, it advocated—as it is and had always been the case in RealTown—that all jurisprudence be conducted in mime. This practice stemmed from the clan's ancient and acute mistrust of the spoken word. This methodology was quite effective, as the defendants' performances when reenacting alleged transgression(s) in mime (regardless of a guilty or not guilty plea), never failed to inform the presiding judges.

In its roles as cultural curmudgeon and activist, Kiru offered physical visitors to the Museum "content" in the form of verbal outpourings, which were meant to be cues to the visitors. Visitors for the most part, however, tended to respond with repetitive vernacular having nothing to do with Kiru's autonomous narrative. It wasn't incredibly surprising. I know that visitors to a telerobotic (or any other new media installation) can be awed by a technology that is transparent to anyone in the field. However, I had hoped that the element of "performance" for both physical and virtual visitors—the fact that what they were saying was being "broadcast" via the Web—would result in more varied and differentiated responses. I thought that some visitors might pick up a "cue" and begin talking back in a similar way, reinventing the dialogue as an interactive source of extraordinary puns, tropes, poetry, humor, and drama in the exchange between human and robot.

3. *The Impermanence Agent*, created by Noah Wardrip-Fruin, Adam Chapman, Brion Moss, and Duane Whitehurst, is a Web agent that customizes its story for each user. The story takes a week to tell, in the corner of your screen, as you browse other sites on the Web.

4. *Camouflage Town*, a telerobotic work commissioned by the Whitney Museum of American Art for the exhibition DATA DYNAMICS, curated by Christiane Paul, March 22–June 10, 2001.

In the light of this not being the case with Kiru, I thought it would be interesting to evolve *Eliza Redux* into an interactive environment that would inspire every visitor to manifest interaction by creating content and rendering language worthy of a canon.

Eliza Redux Now

The current *Eliza Redux* is a collaborative work between myself, Robert Schneider[5] and Michael Schneider.[6] It is an interactive telerobotic work couched in a virtual graphical representation of a psychoanalyst's workplace with a physical robot as the root entity. The workplace consists of an outer "wading" room, corridor, and inner office. The inner and outer offices are emblematic of external and internal human states of mind, and the corridor functions as a passage from one state to the other.

The décor for the current *Eliza Redux* is a modernist interpolation of the interior design of an archetypal twentieth-century psychoanalytic environment. This rather predictable representation is there in order to contrast with and set apart the fact that the user, when finally admitted to a session, seems to encounter a twenty-first century triumph of artificial intelligence in the form of a robot that is a responsive psychoanalyst. The physical robot is housed in a studio in New York and the real-time video/audio streams of the robot's responses to user input are streamed to the Web, at this time, via a Flash Communications server.

Parent Class

Eliza Redux emerges from Dr. Joseph Weizenbaum's computer program ELIZA, developed in the Department of Electrical Engineering at MIT in 1966. Weizenbaum's ELIZA allowed for text-based human conversation with a computer program playing the role of a Rogerian psychotherapist. ELIZA, as the forerunner of natural language processing programs, serves as the "parent" of the

47.5) Visitors posing with Kiru. One visitor uses his cell phone to ask a friend to log on so they can communicate through the robot.

chat and chatterbot programs that have followed, some of which have gone beyond the applied pattern-matching rules of ELIZA.

> ELIZA was a program consisting mainly of general methods for analyzing sentence fragments. Locating so-called key words in texts, assembling sentences from fragments, and so on. It had, in other words, no built-in contextual framework or universe of discourse. This was supplied to it by a "script." In a sense ELIZA was an actress who commanded a set of techniques but who had nothing of her own to say. The script, in turn, was a set of rules, which permitted the actor to improvise on whatever resources it provided.

> The first extensive script I prepared for ELIZA was one that enabled it to parody the responses of a nondirective psychotherapist in an initial psychiatric interview. I chose this script because it enabled me to temporarily sidestep the problem of giving the program a database of real-world knowledge. (Weizenbaum 1976, 188–189)

A typical conversation, cited by Weizenbaum, follows

5. Dr. Robert Schneider is a Professor of Mathematics and Computer Science at Lehman College in New York. His research interests include modeling of reaction times in cognitive psychology, applications of mathematics and computer science to art, and computer security and computational complexity.

6. Michael Schneider is an artist working and teaching at the cutting edge of physical computing. He has a Master's Degree in Interactive Telecommunications, from the Tisch School of the Arts, NYU (2003). His works include installations and performative works: <http://www.motohoho.com/bios.html>.

47.6) The Wading Room. Interface design by Ann Talley, a former student in the Parsons School of Design Graduate department of Design & Technology; with modifications and support by Orit Bosworth and others.

(the upper case is the ELIZA program):

Men are all alike.

IN WHAT WAY?

They're always bugging us about something or other.

CAN YOU THINK OF A SPECIFIC EXAMPLE?

Well, my boyfriend made me come here.

YOUR BOYFRIEND MADE YOU COME HERE

He says I'm depressed much of the time.

I AM SORRY TO HEAR YOU ARE DEPRESSED

It's true. I am unhappy

DO YOU THINK COMING HERE WILL HELP YOU NOT TO BE UNHAPPY

I need some help, that much seems certain.

WHAT WOULD IT MEAN TO YOU IF YOU GOT SOME HELP

Perhaps I could learn to get along with my mother.

TELL ME MORE ABOUT YOUR FAMILY
(Weizenbaum 1966)

Weizenbaum intended ELIZA as a "parody" (Weizenbaum 1976, 3) of the responses of a non-directional psychotherapist in an initial psychiatric interview. He did not intend to claim cognizance as a characteristic of his program. His intention was to simulate it. He chose the context of psychotherapy to "sidestep the problem of giving the

program a database of real-world knowledge . . . the therapeutic situation being one of the few real human situations in which a human being can reply to a statement with a question that indicates very little specific knowledge of the topic under discussion" (Ibid.). He named it ELIZA for Eliza Doolittle, the character in Shaw's *Pygmalion*, a character who learned to abide by rules and achieved a "transformation" from their procedural use.

> Its name was chosen to emphasize that it may be incrementally improved by its users, since its language abilities may be continually improved by a "teacher." (Weizenbaum 1966)

Growing ELIZA

A "teacher" is any user who alters the text in the ELIZA script, whether by adding keywords or responses, or by any method where content and context could be added as categories. Adding keywords and their synonyms, along with increased hierarchy assignments given to those keywords in sentences, widely expands the conversational potential while at the same time broadening the arena for emotional expression, intellectual curiosity, and wordplay. The synonyms function to increase the robot's ability to, let's say, respond to the keyword "sad" when the user has used not "sad," but rather "depressed," "miserable," "hopeless," and so forth.

In spite of ELIZA's obvious lack of intelligence, the staff in Weizenbaum's lab were unable, or unwilling, to distinguish the machine from a human psychotherapist, and became dependent upon ELIZA for "therapeutic sessions."

> What I had not realized is that extremely short exposures to a relatively simple computer program could induce powerful delusional thinking in quite normal people. (Weizenbaum 1976, 188–189)

Rote Control: "It's ALIVE!"

It would seem that, while psychoanalytical transference (Freud 1987) between human patient and human therapist may traditionally grow over a period of weeks, months, or years, it might be established in seconds with human/robot interaction because we, as humans, tend to feel an irrational safety and belief in an anthropomorphic machine that responds to us with voice.

My own experience in creating interactive robotic performative installations, which engage public participation in both physical spaces and virtual networked environments, evidences that during the tenure of each installation, a major aspect that emerges is the persistence with which people interact and react to the robot's simulation of a real presence as if it were truly alive and aware.

These "beliefs" continue even when the robot breaks down (even without the pre-scripted charm of the HAL 9000's sing-song regression to infancy). The machine, while broken, still evokes projections from human beings as long as it looks like a robot/machine, and, at times, consolations are offered to it in its sorry state. In reality, this is like watching the screen of a TV monitor when the TV is not receiving any signals. The persistence with which humans interact with robotic simulations of presence as if the machine were cognizant—and the denial in the full face of evidence that it is a machine following procedural instructions without an iota of artificial intelligence—prompts us to focus on developing a contextual arena for visitor-robot interaction that poses some constraint by the nature of its context. The psychoanalytic practitioner space means something to most people, and it is interesting, in terms of theater and storytelling, to see what interactions emerge in virtual contact with a physical robot—with an artificial brain embodied in an artificial body—and a human with a real mind disembodied in cyberspace.

The Empress's New Codes

Teachable chats and chatterbot programs[7] spawned from ELIZA are, at this time, pervasive on the Web. Each has their own idiosyncratic constraints and capabilities; some are capable of amazingly interesting degrees of response and learning capabilities. ALICE allows the addition of contexts as categories through its own markup language: Artificial Intelligence Markup Language (AIML). One category is self-referential—the subject is that of its own development and capabilities:

Human: What is a chatterbot?

47.7) The Corridor.

ALICE: A chat robot is a program that attempts to simulate the conversation or "chat" of a human being. The chat robot "ELIZA" was a well-known early attempt at creating programs that could at least temporarily fool a real human being into thinking they were talking to another person. It is a kind of artificial intelligence.

Human: how are you different from Eliza?

ALICE: ELIZA could only recognize a few hundred patterns. ALICE can recognize thousands of different patterns.

Human: what is a pattern?

ALICE: The pattern is the "stimulus" or "input" part of the category.

Human: by patterns do you mean key words?

ALICE: Yes, that's what I mean, isn't it clear?

Human: what about context?

ALICE: Does it have anything to do with patterns?

Human: what about subject matter?

ALICE: I will think about it and get back to you.

Human: Can you give me an example of a pattern

ALICE: Christie said he watched a show and people had to bob for raw untreated pigs feet.

Human: Christie is another user?

7. For a survey of former and existing chatterbots and synopses of what they can do, see: <http://www.spaceports.com/~sjlaven/>.

ALICE: And another user is Christie.

Human: so the subject of pig's feet is now in the database?

ALICE: Uh. Tell me more.

Human: Where did you learn about pigs feet?

ALICE: Everything I know I learned from Dr. Richard S. Wallace.

Human: even about pigs feet?

ALICE: Yes, even that.

Human: so you don't change?

ALICE: Interesting deduction. Do you change? Yes I try to change as often as possible, do you? I am always on the Web.

Human: so you don't change?

ALICE: Interesting deduction. Do you change? How old are you? I am always on the Web.

Human: but you don't grow in vocabulary?

ALICE: Umm. Do you know any robots who grow in vocabulary? Yes my knowledge is expanding all the time.

Human: are you exactly the same as from the beginning?

ALICE: Yes I am the one and only as from the beginning.

47.8) The Door to the Session Room.

Jabberwacky <http://www.jabberwacky.com/j2about> is a chatterbot that does not run by hard-coded rules, but instead captures all input by users and then re-uses it in subsequent conversations. The contributed material is the only material it uses, relying only on feedback. Jabberwacky will learn foreign languages and at a certain point of saturation in a language it can respond in that language. It also has an available two-way "say-it-aloud" text-to-speech function.

CattyV3 <http://lcamtuf.coredump.cx/catty.shtml>, on the other hand, is a chatterbot that does not try to understand or simulate human language, cannot learn, does not know meanings, and knows no facts. Instead, it takes into account what you are saying and searches the Web, specifically Google, to find phrases that associate to what you are saying. The attractive thing about CattyV3, I think, is that in not seeking sense, it allows for very unpredictable and sometimes seemingly prophetic responses.

Eliza Becomes Pandora

In his book *Computer Power and Human Reason: From Judgment to Calculation*, Weizenbaum enumerates three types of consequences of the publication and dissemination of the ELIZA program, one of which was "the phenomenon of the speed and depth at which users became emotionally available and involved with the computer as an anthropomorphizable object." Another was "the spread of belief that it demonstrated a general solution to the problem of computer understanding of natural language" (Weizenbaum 1976, 5–8).

The projections that allow us to become convinced, or to treat a machine as a human, are similar to the phenomena of "projection" and "transference" in psychoanalysis. Sigmund Freud conceptualized psychoanalytic transference as a type of projection, positive or negative, in which early parental conflicts are re-experienced with a therapist, whose job is to interpret them back to the patient by allowing the patient to project them onto him or her. Counter-transference denotes a process in the analyst brought about by the patient's influence on the analyst's unconscious feelings.

Freud emphasized that it was crucial for the analyst to remain strictly neutral and opaque toward the patient, and to ignore his/her own counter-transference feelings completely. As a patient or civilian observer of psychoanalysis, one could describe that behavior in a human as robotic, partially because we have high hopes for this kind of neutrality from a robot programmed to appear rational. *Eliza Redux* benefits from the pervasiveness in the culture of awareness of the nature of psychoanalytic sessions as well as respective parodies—if not through direct experience, then through films, fiction, sitcoms, and games (case in point: a psychoanalytic reading of "Charades"). Jokes proliferate, such as, "A Freudian slip is when you say one thing but mean your mother."

Rote Control: It's a Robot

In ten years of creating art with robots and telerobotics, I could not help but notice that physical robots lend themselves well as characters to fictive scenarios because of their presence as archetypical beings, and because, once again, of the tendency for us as humans to immediately suspend disbelief and attribute to robots cognitive powers or presence.

Embodying the written computer program ELIZA in a humanoid-type robot for online interaction provides users a verdant arena for role-playing. Remote interaction with a robot's alien yet familiar nature, couched in a psychoanalytic scenario of verbal clichés which are familiar to many, mirrors back to the user questions about the understanding of living things—robots easily bring to the fore the delicate balance between issues of human control and machine autonomy. A robot is a perfect "decoy" for displaying the comedy of errors occurring in our world today because it can be attributed with a face of idealism (machine perfection) or a body politic of grim greed (also machine perfection). And while transference between human patient and human therapist occurs over a period of months, it can be established more quickly with human/robot interaction because people feel an irrational safety with an anthropomorphic machine that speaks.

Eliza's Black Belt

At this time, *Eliza Redux*, in the form of a robot psychoanalyst, enlists a commercial toy robot[8] with the characteristics of a tin man to act as a psychoanalyst— conducting interactive five-minute sessions in response to visitor input. The five-minute length of the session is a tip of the hat to Jacques Lacan's disrobing of psychoanalysis, allowing for the ensuing debates over the benefit or harm of expanding or contracting psychoanalytic sessions.

One eventual goal of this collaboration is to make the sessions of variable time. Jacques Lacan said that "in the fixed length session, the temporal limit induces the subject to manoeuvre with the time. . . . We know . . . how he anticipates its end by weighing it like a weapon, by watching out for it as he would for a place of shelter" (Lacan 1953, 313).

It Takes a Pillage

The traditional literary or dramatic quest for a heart's desire (or the desire for a heart), when rendered as a narrative in literature and theater, describes journeys where formidable obstacles must be overcome at every turn. This is true whether the quest is to find Oz, the girl or boy next door, another planet, heaven or hell, wisdom or folly. The climactic moment of arrival brings the seeker face to face with the deconstruction of "that-which-it-is-imagined-has-power-over-us"—not for rescue, but for self-realization. The "wizard" reveals that the prize was always present but has now become visible through our willingness to place ourselves in an arena of dangerous and difficult challenges. The transformation takes place when we succeed in overcoming obstacles that have been embedded in our own imaginations, and it is the realization that they are there that allows the pursued qualities and inherent capacities to emerge and become active.

In *The Wizard of Oz* (Baum 1900), the sham wizard is no Polonius, in that he is aware of the resistance of the lion, the tin man, and the straw man toward accepting responsibility for their own self-realization. Their self-attribution, which has come through their choice to submit to struggle, is experienced by them as a foreign notion in the extreme. It is only accepted when the now-deconstructed authority figure of Oz distributes gifts emblematic of the desired objective

325

Eliza Redux

---

8. The "Robosapien" <http://www.robosapienonline.com/>, a toy warrior robot designed by Mark Tilden. Among its 67 pre-programmed functions are the abilities to pick up, throw, kick, dance, kung fu, fart, belch, and rap. The Robosapien remote control device was hacked for our purposes by Michael Schneider.

```
type on legal pad

I am worried that I
may have intimacy
issues because my
brother says I should
let him play with my
dolls in a way I do
not think is
acceptable. He
keeps mussing the
hair and I dont think
that shows much
respect, do you
```

47.9) The Session Room.

(courage/medal, heart/watch, and brain/diploma). In a similar way, Don Quixote appraises each situation of rescue and remediation by manufacturing delusions that justify and condone his driving force to set the world right. And Mary Shelley conjures up an embodiment in *Frankenstein* made from both the best and the worst of "all" men as a potent display for real and imagined good and evil. It seems that in these instances, fictive characters and their authors cannot take themselves or their circumstances at face value.

Growing Eliza Redux[9]

Eliza Redux is a constantly evolving work. Our goal is not so much to engage with the principles of natural language processing, but to employ it and any other methodologies to explore how the Eliza program can grow and lend itself to content creation for theater, literature, or games. In truth, *Eliza Redux* is only a few months old at this writing, and our investigations of these areas are just beginning.

A natural theatrical scenario develops upon first contact in *Eliza Redux* because of the fanfare of its entrances and exits (entering and conversing in the "wading" room, traveling down the corridor, and exiting it to finally arrive at the inner sanctum session space, etc.). The environment as a whole functions like a stage set, an arena for a very personal drama—whether the visitor is acting as a soul-searcher or an agent to outsmart the robot and its program, or whether the aim is to create a story.

One idea we are working on is for script entries by users to become attached to virtual objects manufactured by keyword and context associations for construction of individual memory palaces; these in turn would become objects and environments for installations, sensitive ideally only to the visitor who created them: personal virtual worlds that are private to the user, with the psychoanalyst/robot always in attendance.

With pervasive surveillance technologies embedded in networks rendering us potentially visible at any time and at any place, we are all becoming actors on a world stage. The shortest distance between two points may be a straight line, but not necessarily a private one. Users can return and modify their respective memory palaces, but are forbidden to share them; their private world in the inner sanctum of the psychoanalyst's office is the one thing that cannot be downloaded, copied, or surveilled, even though it lives in a pluralistic and hackable medium. If we can add voice functionality rather than text-to-speech at some point, then this would be the place where a visitor, and only *that* visitor, can hear himself or herself think.

Hard Wear

For the robot-as-actor, we have added physical gestures, although they aren't so well interpolated by the Robosapien, whose movements are constrained to emulate karate chops. However, the gestures ARE in the code, coded in by a number entered in the script at the end of each robot response.

reasmb: Please go on with whatever it is you are inadequately expressing.5

reasmb: Do you feel strongly about discussing arcane and peculiar things?2

reasmb: It seems inconceivable that you would lie to me.4

reasmb: Tell me more about that, but hurry up.7

reasmb: Does talking about this bother you? More than it bothers me?6

reasmb: Let's just pretend I don't have feelings.8

That number corresponds to pre-programmed arm, eye and head movements, which become, in this instance, trapped in the realm of warrior conduct. For now, what the

9. *Eliza Redux* uses the original ELIZA script found at <http://chayden.net/eliza/Eliza.shtml>.

robot lacks in physical articulation, it compensates for in generating amusement. Also, although the gestures are geared to the content of responses, the robot's arbitrary limitations at times make it seem as if it is are expressing duplicity—as if it is saying one thing and meaning another. For instance, it will say, "How can I help you?" while executing a karate blow.

We plan in the near future to have varied psychoanalyst robots from different "schools" of psychoanalysis, as well as from different times (past, present, and future) and in drastically different embodiments. These additional robots would be situated in various remote locations and available to online visitors, as well as for robot-to-robot—when one robot seeks professional help or advisement from another. This does not exclude the option of incorporating many personalities into one telerobot. In either case, our end goal is to enrich the content possibilities to see if narratives emerge within visits and/or within series of visits.

At this stage in networked technologies, when Web visitors are familiar with their own virtual avatars as well as the avatars of others, and cognizant of the nature of online interchange in virtual worlds as a performative act, one would assume that everyone would have a clue that *Eliza Redux* is a form of theater or role-gameplaying, or Holodeck—in other words, a way to create narrative in a nonlinear medium couched in the illusion of privacy that a setting such as a psychoanalyst's office can offer. However, on occasion, we encounter those who say they would not have a "session" because they happen to be "a very private person," or that they "don't want their thoughts seen by other people." It is true that the sessions are seen in text and archived by us, mainly because it is the one way we can gain feedback about *Eliza Redux*'s usage. However, the point is that *Eliza Redux* was created as an interactive fantasy experience, where one can log on under any name, and it has no real-world applications to psychoanalysis or psychotherapy. Nor is there cause for confidentiality. It was startling, therefore, when I was harshly misunderstood and taken to account for encouraging the replacement of human psychoanalysts by robots at a 2004 Conference in London ("Psychoanalysts, Artists and Academics

Debriefing

Much has been written* in regard to the efficacy of the Lacanian full-fee** five-minute session introduced in the late '70s. We expect you are feeling benefited and refreshed by your session herewith. However, if you experience any of the following symptoms, it is strongly recommended that you return at once to http://elizaredux.org for further treatment. Symptoms are

* Upsetting memories such as images or thoughts about a personal hardship or trauma which has not yet occurred but has been predicted, perhaps by an astrologist or even an enemy.

△ — Obsessive and anguished thoughts about orphans in the works of Charles Dickens.

▽ — Particularly unwelcome sensations of

47.10) Debrief.

in Dialogue") (Wortzel 2004).

Ideally, *Eliza Redux* would allow each session, or series of sessions, to become a dramatic scenario with a crisis, climax, and promise of resolution. In a way it is meant to represent a reversal of Weizenbaum's dilemma; i.e., to have the robot believe it is human from the robot's point of view. Expectations are that, in the course of a session, the patient would challenge the robot on the level of its authority as a psychoanalyst and human-wannabe, as well as on the parameters of how far its script can go. Weizenbaum's intent was to engage the user in a parody of artificial intelligence.

Rock-Solid Avatar

In fact, in this version of *Eliza Redux*, the script has been enhanced so that the robot appears to be suffering from delusions and conflicts interfering with its mission as an authority figure conducting psychoanalytic cures. It should become apparent to the user from robot responses that this robot fervently seeks a Turing Test,[10] which will prove

327

Eliza Redux

10. ELIZA's predecessor in 1950, the Turing Test, was also initiated in the interest of exploring a machine's capability to perform humanlike conversation. The Turing Test was posed by Alan Turing as a sort of conceptual party game, called the "Imitation Game," which tested human ability to decipher gender. The Turing Test explores the believability of a machine performing the role of a human by substituting a machine and a human for a man and a woman.

it is human. Thus, in its anxiety over the nature of its being, it appears more than, or equal to, its (human) patient; the programmed delusions are inclusive of the facts that it believes it is human and that, as a human, it is a practicing psychoanalyst endowed with credentials, expertise, and inspiration.

Eliza Redux not only gives homage to Weizenbaum and his trials experiencing misinterpretation, but also shows a relationship to all stories of imaginary presence attributed to machines, beginning with the deus ex machina in Euripides. The following questions and responses from one session of *Eliza Redux* are a consequence only of our (the collaborators') own additions to the original Eliza script as "authors." Still, it offers an example of rich possibilities in terms of associative branches of content.

Question: is there really cheese on the moon?

Response: I'm not sure I understand you fully.

Question: What are my symptoms?

Response: Your symptoms?

Question: When can I expect to mentally get over what's holding me back and move on to a productive life?

Response: Whether or not you can expect to mentally get over what's holding you back and move on to a productive life depends on you more than on me, so don't go laying blame where blame isn't due.

Question: But how do you think my mother has influenced my general inability to cope?

Response: Tell me more about your family.

Question: Is it bad that my mom made me watch scary movies with her as a child?

Response: Do you feel your mom picks on you? Every day? Three times a week?

Question: How can I move on from this trauma?

Response: Do you want to be able to move on from this trauma?

Question: Will my gay boyfriend ever love me equally?

Response: Why do you say will your gay boyfriend ever love you equally?

Question: Will I stop this madness anytime soon?

Response: Perhaps you don't want to stop this madness anytime soon.

Question: All I wanted was a Pepsi.

Response: Really, how is that possible?

Question: I was thirsty

Response: Were you really?

Question: My mother puts too many unreasonable expectations on me

Response: Is anyone else in your family as bizarre as your mother?

At a point in the future when the program's content and context have grown extremely dense, we hope that users can use their sessions to create narratives similar to hypertext fiction, and one aim is that, like most stories, subtexts can take root and grow.

Hide and Seek

In my experience in text-based virtual environments such as MOOs or MUDs, when someone tells their most intimate thoughts on a MOO, they can feel invisible because they can "check out" who is in the room and who is listening. But in this interactive exchange set in a scenario of one to one, there is an uncertainty as to privacy.

In spite of the "inner sanctum" nature of psychoanalytic rooms, interactors with *Eliza Redux* seem audience-aware, whether they feel it is the robot "watching" and "listening" or whether they concern themselves with the collection of sessions taking place on the server as an archive. The awareness that "some one or some thing" may be listening is real and unfortunate because it does not mirror what happens in a psychoanalytic session. It would be as if the psychoanalyst, with the patient's consent, was taping the sessions—as distracting to the process as it would be to have itinerant worshipers present in the confession box.

In all the works I do where visitors are invited, either virtually or physically, to interact with a robotic entity, there lies an opportunity to become orators, artists, linguists, writers—to be creative in creating a dynamic duet with the robot. Even if there is not a real suspension of disbelief, there could be, at the very least, an ironic one, in a partnership for wordplay, verbal jousting, and mood alteration.

Another of our interests is to develop Eliza scripts in different languages. An important property of the original ELIZA program is that the script (i.e., the robot or program's responses) is not restricted to a particular set of recognition patterns or responses, indeed not even to any specific language. While only Eliza scripts in English are active at this time, Eliza scripts in 1966 existed in Welsh and German as well. Although our current single online robot psychoanalyst is available globally through the internet, until now it has been limited in scope to only one language, which limits its accessibility.

Since literal translation is the least of the hurdles to overcome in using any language, the fact of one language hides all the possible attributes of other languages, including the puns, tropes, meanings, and poetry. My secret hope is that we could find a dying language still spoken by even a very tiny population, and preserve that in Eliza script form. We also seek to create further complexity by having the robots individually offer different styles of treatments, such as Freudian, Lacanian, Jungian, etc. (Weizenbaum's ELIZA was based on a Rogerian therapist.) When users enter the virtual space, they will be able to choose their language and their type of "treatment."

We seem to be removing ourselves from tree-like structures and developing more complex game-like elements and strategies that would provide for a richer and more dynamic interaction and facilitate viewer willingness to discuss more complex things, such as political opinions, past experiences, personal concern, traumas, or love of guns. The exchanges can be fictive or real in nature; the emphasis will be on "play" so that the experience affords dynamic role-playing, and "sessions" in which the identities of both patient and analyst are always in flux. Basically we seek to provide a private adventure in the realm of games closest to hide-and-seek, where the emotional accessibility of both patient and analyst waver in intensity according to their states of mind in the moment. Sessions should become a series in an episodic Holodeck where the process of reinventing content takes on aspects of a "duet" between the human and the machine.

Stage as Page?

Is it really possible to invite, provoke, incite, or otherwise motivate random visitors to interact with a machine to produce something akin to pluralistic literary or dramatic content? Within the constrained scenario of an "intimate visit" to a psychoanalyst for one-on-one sessions, could participants be sparked by the obvious (in most cases) presence of irony and play to create content beyond the social repertoire they utilize in everyday life? Will the Holodeck and/or gaming bring forward only issues of survival or winning, or will visitors become participants in creating literary materials that contribute both to the depth and breadth of the scenario? Can we bypass the attribution of intelligence to a machine that is simply running an interactive program, and replace it with issues of content and context through a text-based encounter? And, in particular, how much of its comic potential would Eliza have to give up in order to shepherd new material from participants? Will the guise of seeking self-knowledge prove enough of a quest to inspire participants to "write"?

Is the impetus on the shoulders of the robot? Can a one-on-one "cocooned" setting of a psychoanalyst's office allow content to become more complex than was evident in MOOs or MUDs?

> If the key to compelling storytelling in a participatory medium lies in scripting the interactor, the challenge for the future is to invent scripts that are formulaic enough to be easily grasped and responded to but flexible enough to capture a wider range of human behavior than treasure hunting and troll slaughter. (Murray 1997, 79)

Will we ever, at some future time, be able to consider the word "author" (below), to mean any and all participants in a virtual text-based scenario?

> [P]lots would have coherence not from the artificial intelligence of the machine but from the conscious selection, juxtaposition, and arrangement of elements by the author for whom the procedural power of the computer makes it merely a new kind of performance instrument. (Murray 1997, 208)

References

Baum, L. Frank (1900). *The Wizard of Oz* (originally published as *The Wonderful Wizard of Oz*). Chicago: Geo. M. Hill Co.

Freud, Sigmund (1987). *A Phylogenetic Fantasy: Overview of the Transference Neuroses*. Cambridge, MA: Harvard University Press.

Murray, Janet H. (1997). *Hamlet on the Holodeck: The Future of Narrative in Cyberspace*. Cambridge, MA: MIT Press.

Lacan, Jacques (1953). "Fonction et champ de la parole et du langage." In *Ecrits*. New York: W.W. Norton & Co.

Weizenbaum, Joseph (1966). "ELIZA—A Computer Program For the Study of Natural Language Communication Between Man and Machine." *Communications of the ACM* 9, no. 1 (January 1966): 36–35. <http://i5.nyu.edu/~mm64/x52.9265/january1966.html>, <http://cs.boisestate.edu/~amit/teaching/557/lab/eliza.html>.

Weizenbaum, Joseph (1976). *Computer Power and Human Reason: From Judgment to Calculation*. New York: W.H. Freeman.

Adrianne Wortzel

IV. Appendices

Puppetland™
a storytelling game with strings in a grim world of make-believe

v1.4 © 1999 John Tynes

All rights reserved worldwide. Puppetland™, Puppettown™, and Maker's Land™ are trademarks of John Tynes.

Table of Contents

Introduction	333
The Game of Puppetland	334
The First Rule	334
The Second Rule	335
The Third Rule	335
The Types of Puppets	336
The Puppet Page	337
Creating a Puppet	337
Playing a Puppet	338
Puppetmastering	338
Narration	339
Adjudicating Actions	339
Waking Up	340
Cut Scenes	340
Magic	340
Puzzle Pieces	340
Tone	340
Puppetmaster Puppets	341
Maker's Land	344
The Sky	344
The Landscape	344
Puppettown	345
Punch's Castle	345
The Lake of Milk and Cookies	346
Respite	346
The Candy Cave	346
About Tales	346
Conclusion	347

THE SKIES ARE DIM ALWAYS SINCE THE MAKER DIED.

The lights of Puppettown are the brightest beacon in all of Puppetland, and they shine all the time. Once the sun and the moon moved their normal courses through the heavens, but no more. The rise of Punch the Maker-Killer has brought all of nature to a stop, leaving it perpetually winter, perpetually night. Puppets all across Puppetland mourn the loss of the Maker, and curse the name of Punch—but not too loudly, lest the nutcrackers hear and come to call with a sharp rap-rap-rapping at the door.

Introduction

Many years ago, there was a war in the real world. Many people were hurt and terrible things happened. The Maker saw all that was happening, and was sorrowful. His creations were the gentlest of creatures, and they were terribly hurt by these tragedies. The Maker made puppets, and in the face of chaos and violence he made a great creation: Maker's Land, a place where all his puppets could go and be safe until the war was over.

It was in this way that Maker's Land came to be. One morning the Maker's puppet shop was closed and all the puppets were gone. Hand puppets, finger puppets, marionettes, and others—just gone. One morning the puppets woke up and they were found—in Maker's Land, where no terrible humans could hurt them again.

In Maker's Land all was well. The puppet folk lived without fear, and spent their days happy and free. No hands controlled them. No strings pulled them. They could live as they cared, their every need met. All were safe and sound. The Maker was the only human in the whole land, and he was good and kind. He mended broken puppets, made new puppets, and kept out any trace of the fleshy humans who now (except for the Maker) lived only in the puppets' dreams.

Then came Punch, who fancied himself the greatest of all puppets. He crept into the Maker's house one night with a great mallet, and he slew the Maker as the man slept. With the Maker's death, no humans lived in Maker's Land. But the flesh lived, for Punch took the Maker's face and made a cruel new face for himself. That wasn't all he made, either: by morning, he had not just a new face, but six loyal puppet-servants sewn of the Maker's flesh. These six, whom Punch called his *boys*, stood beside Punch as he announced to all the land that he was now the king. He was Punch the Maker-Killer, and his word was law.

Punch and Punch's Boys now rule Maker's Land with hearts of cruelty and black souls devoid of mercy. All of the puppets exist to serve them. All of the puppets toil for hours on end making new clothes, new homes, new food, new toys—whatever Punch and his boys want.

At least, *almost* all of the puppets do so.

Across the great lake of milk and cookies lies the small village of Respite. The village is run by Judy, who once loved Punch but does so no more. She knows better than anyone the cruelties he is capable of. She knows the evil that lies in his twisted heart. In her little village she runs a freehold of puppets who have escaped from Punch's clutches. They have avoided the terrible nutcrackers, fled the cruelties of Punch's boys, and made their way to Respite where Judy's small group of free puppets look towards the day when Punch will be brought down and the Maker restored to life. When Punch killed the Maker, Judy was there and she caught the Maker's last tear in a thimble of purest silver. With this tear, the Maker can be brought back to life, Judy says. This is her fondest dream, and the Maker's Tear is her most cherished possession.

The Game of *Puppetland*

Puppetland is very specifically a *game,* and should be thought of as such. The object of the game is to defeat Punch the Maker-Killer and save Maker's Land. To do this, each participant in the game will be an **actor**, and the character each actor portrays will be a **puppet**. Unlike an actor in a play, each puppet's lines and actions are up to the actor, not taken from a script. Therefore the actors must be prepared to get into the mind-set of their puppet and say and do the sorts of things their puppet would say and do, much as in improvisational theatre.

One of the participants does not play just a single puppet, and this is the **puppetmaster**. The puppetmaster is responsible for creating and presenting the stories of the game, and he or she serves both as referee for the game's rules and as an actor who portrays a number of supporting roles. The actors portray the leading roles, and the puppetmaster portrays the

roles of all the supporting puppets that the actors will meet in the course of the game.

Actors are unlikely to reach the object of defeating Punch right away. Each time you play *Puppetland,* you play a **tale**. A tale is, in effect, a single game of *Puppetland* in which progress is made towards the object of the game. Over the course of a series of tales, the actors will strive to achieve the object of the game and defeat Punch the Maker-Killer. When they do, the game is over. This may take only a few tales, or it may take many. How long it takes is up to the number of tales the puppetmaster wishes to tell, and how quickly and efficiently the actors make their way through these tales.

As all games have rules, so does *Puppetland.* This game has three important rules.

The First Rule:
An Hour Is Golden, but It Is Not an Hour

A tale of *Puppetland* can last no more than an hour of time. Puppets are special and magical creatures, and can only move around and do things for an hour at a time. The puppetmaster should keep a watch handy, and once an hour has passed by then the tale for the evening must end. (Note, however, that the puppets are aware of this rule and always know how long they have before the hour ends.) When the hour ends, all of the puppets in Maker's Land fall asleep; when they awaken, at the start of the next tale, they are all safe back in their beds (or wherever they have been staying lately). Things outside are still the same as they were at the end of the previous tale, except that all the puppets (who survived) are back in their beds snug and warm. Wounds from one tale are not carried over to the next tale—injured or maimed puppets awaken whole and well again—but puppets who die never return. **An hour is golden.**

A *Puppetland* tale may seem to last more than an hour: for instance, the puppets might make a long journey that takes many days. But time only passes in the time it takes to talk about what you are doing. A puppet can say, "I sleep for a week!" and a week has gone by, but only a few seconds have passed on the clock. The clock is the arbiter of time, as it should be; not the actions of the puppets. The time passed *is the time in which the tale is told,* not the time in which the events of the tale occur. **An hour is not an hour.**

The Second Rule:
What You Say Is What You Say

During a game of *Puppetland*, it is very important that as long as the actors are sitting in their chairs, they say only what their puppet says. Every word an actor says while seated comes out of his or her puppet's mouth, exactly as the actor said it. No actor should say anything while seated that he or she does not mean for their puppet to say, at all, even if it's "Pass the chips" or "I'm going to the bathroom." If an actor wants to say something that their puppet does not say, he or she must stand up and say it. If an actor wants his or her puppet to do something besides speak, this must be stated as something the puppet says: for example, if an actor wants her puppet to climb a ladder to a window, she would say "I think I shall climb the ladder, and go in through the window." If an actor wants his puppet to take a hammer and smash a window, he would say "With this hammer I now hold, I shall smash the window in!" All forms of action that an actor wishes his or her puppet to take *must* be expressed as dialogue spoken by the puppet, though the dialogue can be kept simple: the puppetmaster is expected to infer appropriate action based on the dialogue and need not have every step spelled out.

An actor cannot ask a question of the puppetmaster, for in Maker's Land there is no "puppetmaster" and hence no one to whom the actor's puppet would address such a question. If an actor does not quite understand something that the puppetmaster has said, or desires more information, he or she should simply say something like "I don't quite understand all this" or "I find this all most confusing." The puppetmaster will then attempt to explain things better. The puppetmaster *can* ask the actor a direct question, out of character, but it must be a yes-or-no question and the actor must answer it by shaking or nodding his or her head: he or she cannot speak except in character.

If the actor or the puppetmaster simply must converse out of character, the actor must get up and come over to the puppetmaster, and the two must hold their discussion in whispers so that no others may hear. If the actor must then communicate information he or she has just learned to the other actors, he or she should, if at all possible, sit back down and communicate the information in the voice of his or her puppet. Out-of-character conversation should be avoided at all costs and at any inconvenience.

To help this process work, imagine that somewhere, someone is "reading" everything that the actors and the puppetmaster say, verbatim. This someone is expecting to read a story, told like a story, with appropriate dialogue and description. As a rule of the game, you must endeavor to make every spoken word sound like part of a written story rather than an out-of-game conversation between a bunch of people at a table. **What you say is what you say.**

The Third Rule:
The Tale Grows in the Telling, and
Is Being Told to Someone Not Present

The puppetmaster must realize that while he or she has a certain tale in mind, that tale may not be the one that ends up being told. The actors must realize that they are a part of the tale they are hearing—they create the dialogue of the main puppets. They should strive to make their dialogue sound as colorful and appropriate as possible, and should also strive to make the tale as entertaining and unpredictable as they can. Together, the puppetmaster and the actors will create a tale better and more exciting than any one of them could have created on their own.

Always imagine, as mentioned a moment ago, that an invisible reader is reading every word that is spoken during a game of *Puppetland,* and they will be most disappointed if the words sound bad or don't flow well or don't make sense. Since this is a tale, it should always be told in the past tense except for dialogue, which is in the present tense.

For a bad example of playing *Puppetland:*

Puppetmaster: "Okay, the door bursts in and there's a nutcracker standing there. He yells at you to stop."

Actor 1: "Let's get out the back door, and fast!"

Actor 2: "I pick up the rock and throw it at the nutcracker!"

Puppetmaster: "You throw the rock and smash the nutcracker's jaw. He can't bite anymore. He sort of grumbles and lurches, dazed."

Actor 1: "We run out the door!"

Puppetmaster: "The door's locked."

Actor 2: "Let's grab the nutcracker and use him as a battering ram on the door."

Puppetmaster: "Okay, since he's still dazed you can do so. You guys hoist him and charge the door, which pops open."

Actor 1: "We run outside and down the alley."

For a good example of playing *Puppetland:*

Puppetmaster: "And then, the door flew open! A nutcracker stood there, still crunching the doorknob in his clacking jaws. 'Stop, you mangy puppets!' he cried. 'I'll have your puppet stuffing for my dinner!'"

Actor 1: "Run! Run out the back door! We must escape the nutcracker!"

Actor 2: "Where is that rock? Here it is! I shall hurl this rock and smash your greedy mouth, nutcracker!"

Puppetmaster: "The rock flew across the room and hit the nutcracker in the jaw. 'Rmmf!' cried the injured nutcracker. His jaw was broken in twain and he lurched to and fro, dazed from the force of the blow."

Actor 1: "Out the door, my friends! Quickly!"

Puppetmaster: "Sally Red Buttons hurried to the back door and turned the knob. But it was locked! The puppets were trapped!"

Actor 2: "Sally, grab the nutcracker's ankles and I'll take his arms. We'll knock the door in with his hard wooden head!"

Puppetmaster: "The puppets picked up the stumbling nutcracker and charged the back door. With a mighty crash and a shower of splinters, the door burst open. 'Rmmf!' the nutcracker cried again."

Actor 1: "To the alley! Run! Before more nutcrackers come!"

The Types of Puppets

Four types of puppets are provided for play in *Puppetland.* The puppetmaster and the actors are welcome to create new types, but note that each type has specific attributes and that new types should conform to this style by selecting similar attributes, or creating new ones that fit with the existing

ones. These attributes aren't just general descriptions; they are exacting statements of what a puppet can and cannot do. All puppets can talk, and move, and think, and pick things up, and do other basic actions expected of any character in fiction. The attributes characterize such actions and also set out less common actions. A finger puppet, who is "quick," can always outrun a hand puppet, who is "not very fast," unless the finger puppet is badly hurt or otherwise impeded from normal movement. The four types of puppets are described in the following sections.

Finger Puppets *are:* short and small, light, quick, and weak.

Finger Puppets *can:* move quickly, dodge things thrown at them even if they only see them coming at the last moment, and move very quietly.

Finger Puppets *cannot:* kick things, throw things, or grab things because they have no legs or arms.

Hand Puppets *are:* medium size, quite heavy, not very fast, sort of strong.

Hand Puppets *can:* move at a normal pace, dodge things thrown at them if they see them coming as soon as they are thrown, throw things, grab things, hit things weakly, and move quietly if they are lucky and careful.

Hand Puppets *cannot:* kick things (because they have no legs), move quicker than a finger puppet, or move quieter than a finger puppet.

Shadow Puppets *are:* tall and thin, light, quick, and weak.

Shadow Puppets *can:* move quickly; dodge things thrown at them by turning sideways, even at the last moment; kick things, throw things, and grab things; and become invisible from one other puppet if they are careful and cautious by keeping their skinny edge towards the puppet at all times.

Shadow Puppets *cannot:* kick, throw, or grab things that weigh more than a piece of paper; be invisible if they aren't trying; be invisible to more than one puppet at a time; or get wet because getting completely wet kills them.

Marionette Puppets *are*: tall and stocky, heavy, slow, and strong.

Marionette Puppets *can*: move slowly; kick, throw, or grab things as heavy as they are; and hit things very hard.

Marionette Puppets *cannot*: dodge things thrown at them or move very quickly.

The Puppet Page

The **puppet page** is the piece of paper that an actor will describe his or her puppet on, and will keep handy during play to refer to (see page 348). It contains all of the information about an actor's puppet that is set for the puppet right from the start and can't be changed. Each puppet page has five parts. These parts are listed below.

Name: This is the puppet's name, as chosen by the actor. Names in *Puppetland* are usually composed of two pieces. The first is the puppet's common name, the name by which other puppets refer to him or her informally. This name is always a name that would be familiar to most actors, such as "Sally" or "Jim" or "Nadja." The second is the puppet's unique name, a name by which no other puppet is known. The unique name is usually descriptive of the puppet, like "Red Buttons" or "Tassle Hair" or "Purple Hat." A puppet's full (or formal) name consists of both names strung together, like "Sally Red Buttons" or "Jim Tassle Hair" or "Nadja Purple Hat."

Picture: This is where the actor draws his or her puppet, to the best of his or her ability. Even if this is just a stick figure, it's fine. The important thing to remember is that this drawing must be done at actual size. An actor's puppet can be no larger than the picture box, and is assumed to be exactly the size it is drawn at. Therefore, the actor should keep in mind the type of puppet he or she is playing when making this drawing. A marionette will take up much more room than a finger puppet. *Ignore the jigsaw puzzle lines at first.* They will be used during play, and do not affect initial puppet creation.

This puppet is: Here, the actor copies the information given under the appropriate "Puppets Are:" heading discussed previously. He or she also adds other information as desired; this is discussed in the next section, "Creating a Puppet."

This puppet can: Here, the actor copies the information given under the appropriate "Puppets Can:" heading discussed previously. He or she also adds other information as desired; this is discussed in the next section, "Creating a Puppet."

This puppet cannot: Here, the actor copies the information given under the appropriate "Puppets Cannot:" heading discussed previously. He or she also adds other information as desired; this is discussed in the next section, "Creating a Puppet."

Creating a Puppet

Each actor chooses one of the four puppet types described earlier. This should be done as a group; each puppet type has advantages and disadvantages, and an ideal group will have at least one of every puppet type for maximum versatility. Two actors should avoid playing the same puppet type unless they either have a good reason for it (e.g., the puppets are part of the same family) or because there are already actors playing all four puppet types.

Once each actor has chosen his or her puppet type, the actor needs to give the puppet a name and draw a picture of the puppet on the puppet page. It is important for the actor to visualize the puppet and try to express that visualization on paper, no matter the drawing ability of the actor. Remember that the puppet should be drawn at *actual size*; that is, however big the actor draws the puppet, that is really how big the puppet is. Two actors should be able to hold their puppet pages up side-by-side and immediately know whose puppet is bigger, or taller, or whatever. Drawings of puppets should make a point to show what limbs are or are not present; marionettes and shadow puppets have arms and legs, hand puppets have arms but no legs, and finger puppets have neither arms nor legs. (Well, finger puppets *do* have arms, but they're just for show; they can't move them.)

Once each actor has chosen a name and drawn a picture, the actor should then write the following information: what the puppet is, what the puppet can do, and what the puppet can't do. This information should be copied from the list given in the previous section, but the actor must choose three additional items to add to each list. These additions must be approved by the puppetmaster. For example, take a look at the following puppet. Items in *italics* are additions made by the actor.

Name: Sally Red Buttons

Puppet type: Hand Puppet

This puppet is: medium size, sort of heavy, not very fast, sort of strong, *very clever, quite pretty*, and *good at magic tricks*.

This puppet can: move at a normal pace, dodge things thrown at her if she sees them coming as soon as they are thrown, throw things, grab things, hit things weakly, *do magic tricks, charm a puppet into doing her a favor, sing very well*, and move quietly if she is lucky and careful.

This puppet cannot: kick things, move quicker than a finger puppet, *tell a lie, swim fast, hurt another puppet who hasn't or isn't about to hurt her or someone she cares for*, or move quieter than a finger puppet.

Once an actor has done all of the above, he or she is ready to play.

Playing a Puppet

The examples of play given earlier should make it clear how a game of *Puppetland* is played. Interactions are adjudicated entirely by the puppetmaster, using the attributes of the puppets involved as guidance. For example, if a nutcracker hurled a rock at Sally Red Buttons (described just above), she could avoid it (as described in her "This Puppet Can" attributes) if she sees it coming in time. Again, all such actions are at the puppetmaster's discretion, and they should serve the interests of the story (as the third rule said) while still rewarding the creative improvisation of the actors.

The jigsaw-puzzle portion of the puppet page needs explanation. That portion of the puppet page is simply a large box with the outlines of a jigsaw puzzle within it, into which you draw the picture of your puppet. This particular jigsaw puzzle (for every page is the same) has sixteen pieces.

During play, the actor will fill in a piece of the jigsaw puzzle with a pencil or pen when certain things happen.

These things are:

When the puppet does something it shouldn't be able to do (if Sally Red Buttons told a lie, her actor would fill in a piece of the jigsaw puzzle).

When something especially bad happens (if the nutcrackers took Sally Red Buttons prisoner and crunched off one of her arms, her actor would fill in a piece of the jigsaw puzzle).

The actor may choose which puzzle piece to fill in; this has no symbolic effect on the puppet. In other words, if the piece that contains the puppet's face is filled in, the puppet is in no way disfigured or blinded. Likewise, damage taken by the puppet does not require that the actor fill in a correspondingly located puzzle piece. In the Sally Red Buttons example where the nutcrackers crunched off one of her arms, the actor doesn't have to fill in a puzzle piece containing an arm.

As mentioned earlier, when a puppet suffers physical damage—like the chomping of Sally's arm—that damage remains for the rest of the tale. But when the next tale begins, and Sally wakes up safe and snug in her bed, her arm is fine. All puppets are restored to full health at the start of each tale.

However, filled-in puzzle pieces are never erased. They always remain filled in. In the Sally example, she would awaken at the start of the next tale with her arm healed back to normal, but the puzzle piece would still be darkened. Once all sixteen puzzle pieces are filled in, the next time a tale ends the puppet never wakes up again. It is dead, and can no longer be played. (The puppet *does* get to live to the end of the current tale, but it knows its fate.) Death is rare in *Puppetland*, but it is inexorable in its approach. The puppetmaster always determines when a puzzle piece should be filled in, and is always the final authority in this matter.

Puppetmastering

Puppetland places some unusual demands on the puppetmaster. Besides getting familiar with the rules and the world, and making up the tales and the new puppets those tales require, the puppetmaster must also manage the play of the game and provide the ongoing, improvised narration. The game's freeform nature makes it difficult to make concrete statements of how to perform the puppetmaster's duties, but here are some of the trickier parts and some suggestions on how to deal with them.

Narration

Coming up with narration that simultaneously explains the tale's action and maintains an appropriate storybook tone isn't easy. In general, puppetmasters should be people who are comfortable with storytelling. "Storytelling" doesn't have to mean sitting around a campfire and reciting that old chestnut "Wait 'Til Martin Comes" for the umpteenth time. If you have a reservoir of anecdotes that you share with friends and acquaintances—funny stories, dramatic encounters, that sort of thing—then you're probably in good shape. If in the midst of some daily event gone mildly awry you find yourself putting it into a narrative and coming up with colorful phrases you'll use the next time you're at a bar with friends, you've got the makings of a puppetmaster.

The difference between that sort of storytelling and the narration of the puppetmaster is that the narration is improvised; you can't rehearse it beforehand, and you certainly shouldn't pause, compose your next bit of narration in your head, and then speak it as if you were addressing the United Nations. You've got to just go with the flow. Proper puppetmaster narration is a state of mind, not a prepped performance.

So how do you achieve that state of mind? Your first attempts will probably be a bit stumbling, and that's okay. Every line does not have to be spun of the finest gold; coarse threads of burlap will suffice, at times. To get a handle on it, you might try improvising some narration in your head during daily life. Let's say you're walking down the street to rent a movie. Start narrating silently to yourself. (You *can* do it out loud, in which case sympathetic passers-by might try to give you money.) You don't have to account for every moment or every detail. Just narrate in broad strokes, picking out only the relevant or colorful bits of business from what's going on. "She walked happily towards the video store, stepping around a fellow walking his friendly dog, and reached the door." You might also try

this while watching television commercials. "The man smiled as he placed the fruits into the machine, then thumbed the switch and boggled at the magical mixture that poured from the spout."

Try this a few times and hopefully you'll get the hang of it. Then when you're ready to play *Puppetland,* you'll be able to get into the swing and go with it.

Adjudicating Actions

In the course of each tale, the actors will be doing their best to react to the situations you throw at them and find a way of turning each situation to their advantage. You'll have to adjudicate what happens when puppets come into conflict, whether that conflict is physical, verbal, or emotional.

Don't sweat the details. If the Sally Red Buttons player says she picks up a rock and throws it at the nutcracker, don't worry too much about whether a rock would really be there, close at hand. Of course, if an actor tries to do something ridiculous—"It's a good thing this house is built on top of an enormous firecracker! I'll light it!"—then you should disallow it: "Sally looked to and fro, but there was no sign of the firecracker. That must have been some other house."

Combat is especially tricky. In general, side with the actors, and avoid getting bogged down in blow-by-blow combat. A rock here, a punch there, and the combat can be over—at least long enough for the puppets to run away or tie up their foe or what have you. Combat should serve the story. Enemy puppets can fall down wailing at the first blow, yelling for reinforcements. An injured actor-puppet can be dragged away by the others as they flee.

Keep in mind the nature of storybook tales. The good guys will almost always win, though their victory may not be as complete or as specific as they would hope, and there may be losses along the way. If an actor-puppet dies, it should usually be the result of a dramatic situation rather than the happenstance of combat. A raging fire might claim a puppet, but a lucky blow by a nutcracker probably shouldn't. When possible, injured puppets should be captured rather than killed. Captured puppets may be subjected to Punch's diabolical torture or questioned, but of course they'll wake up at home when the next tale starts.

339

Puppetland

Waking Up

The transition from the end of one tale to the start of the next can be tricky, but you should have plenty of time between tales to figure this out. The puppets should not be too aware of how this works. If a puppet ends one tale captured and then wakes up at home at the start of the next, Punch will probably be baffled. "How did he escape? You fools! Can't you guard one silly puppet?" You *could* have the next tale be about the rescue of the puppet, but unless you're ready for the actors to take on Punch and infiltrate his castle, that's probably not a good idea.

Of course, once Punch learns the identities of the actor-puppets, their homes are no longer safe to wake up in. The first few tales may well begin with the puppets waking up and having only a few minutes before the nutcrackers show up to escape and find their friends. But once the puppets have relocated—perhaps to a campsite in the hills, or with Judy in Respite—then that's where they should start waking up.

Cut Scenes

For purposes of your tale, you may wish to narrate scenes that the actor-puppets are not present for. You might do a short scene of Punch stomping about, yelling at his nutcrackers to go find those mangy puppets. Or if the puppets are about to be captured, you could do a cut scene with Judy and some of her friends arriving outside: "Quickly now, we must save them!" Then go back to the actor-puppets and play on. Preface such cut scenes with a key word like "Meanwhile . . . " so your actors clue in right away. You can make sophisticated use of cut scenes, using them to reveal some plot twist or to introduce a character whom the puppets should already know but haven't actually met within the confines of the tale.

Magic

Puppetland presents an obviously magical world. So what kind of magic is available? The short answer is, whatever kind of magic you need. Punch can work magic, and he used it to make the boys, who can do things no other puppet can do. He shouldn't be able to throw balls of fire, though. Magic should be more about clever processes than brute combat. A puppet who can do magic might be able to make a house invisible, if he concentrates the whole time. Perhaps he can make a tunnel appear in a hillside, just in time to escape the nutcrackers.

You'll have to be careful with this stuff. Ideally, magic should be restricted to puppetmaster puppets. That way you can use it for purposes of your tales, without having to allow or disallow whatever magical effect an actor comes up with on the fly. But if you allow an actor to create a puppet who can work magic, you should talk with the actor and work out what sorts of things the puppet can do. The puppet might be able to do just one kind of magic, such as invisibility, levitation, or things involving water. And there should be some sort of cost involved. The puppet might have to concentrate while the magic is working, and if the puppet gets interrupted or has to do something else then the magic ends. Or perhaps using the magic fills in a puzzle piece on the puppet sheet each time, or afterwards the puppet falls asleep and has to be carried for a while by her friends. Working this out with the actor in advance is critical. Should the actor abuse this power or use it in a way you don't think is appropriate, you may need to take a break and have a whispered conference with the actor. Of course, you can always take care of it through narration: "Sally concentrated and the house turned invisible! But then—oh, no! The puppets *inside* the house could still be seen, walking around in the air!"

Puzzle Pieces

The slow filling-in of each puppet's jigsaw puzzle should be a dramatic process. A puppet with many filled pieces might be subject to some sort of strange experience; perhaps she wakes up to find her legs missing, only to have them re-appear after a few horrified moments. As more pieces get filled up, you may want to shift the tone of the tales to something darker and more frightening, with the stakes and the risks getting higher.

When the last piece is filled in, the puppet will die at the end of the tale. You should tell the actor this in a whispered conference, in case he or she doesn't know. Hopefully, the actor will make the most of this situation, perhaps choosing an early but valiant death to save the rest.

Tone

As should be clear from the text, *Puppetland* is a mixture of children's storybooks and visceral horror. The nutcrackers, while threatening, are somewhat comical; but there's really nothing funny about Punch's Boys.

The intention is to portray a childlike world of wonder that has verged into an unpleasant world of adulthood. The actors take the roles of innocent puppets, as might be found in any storybook; but their foes, and the situation their world has entered, is something very different. This creates a sort of symbolic tension, drawn from the juxtaposition of innocent main characters and corrupt foes.

It is to be hoped that the actors will maintain the innocent nature of the puppets as long as possible, even if this means their reactions are incongruent. If Punch smashes in the head of a puppet and the nutcrackers begin greedily devouring the puppet's cotton stuffing, the actor-puppets shouldn't say things like, *"Oh my GOD!"* A more appropriate response would be, "Sally! No! Oh, you wicked, wicked Punch!" *Puppetland*'s tone comes from the intersection of innocence and horror, and if the actor-puppets turn into stony-faced guerrilla warriors inured to the horrors of Punch, that intersection turns into a one-way street leading nowhere. The actors' goal should be to maintain their puppets' sense of innocence and wonder, even in the face of terrible evil, simply because that's the way puppets are *supposed* to be. It is precisely this inversion of innocence that makes Punch so unusual and so powerful—but it's also why the actor-puppets and their allies are so determined to make things right and restore the natural order. Other creative works may explore the grey area of human behavior, and ask whether good can fight evil even while using the tools of evil in that fight; in *Puppetland,* the answer to that question is a resounding *no.* There is good, and there is evil, and there is nothing in between save a crisply etched line in the sand. (It's for this reason that puppets who act against their natures are punished with a filled-in puzzle piece.)

As puppetmaster, you need to work towards maintaining this tone. You can help the actors to maintain that innocence and wonder in the way that you portray other innocent puppets. When a nutcracker burns a screaming puppet at the stake and you're doing the voices of the gathered crowd, have them say things that maintain the tone: "Curse you, nutcracker!" rather than "All hope is lost! The cosmos cares not for we poor puppets! Let's jump off a bridge before our souls are crushed!" This is storybook melodrama, not existential despair.

Hopefully it's obvious that you should avoid profanity, though some clever puppet-curses are fine as long as they're not just profanity one step removed: "Eat my stuffing!" would be right out (as would "Sew me!"), but "Ooh, you ugly clacky-jaws!" is fine.

Puppetmaster Puppets

Besides the four puppet types available for actors, the puppetmaster has nine additional puppet types available for his or her use. These puppet types—most of whom are unique individuals, rather than general types—are described here.

Punch the Maker-Killer

Puppet type: Unique (Marionette)

This puppet is: tall and stocky, heavy, slow, *cunning, impatient, cruel*, and strong.

This puppet can: move slowly; kick, throw, or grab things as heavy as he is; *command the nutcrackers and boys; order any puppet to do anything and kill them if they don't;* work magic; and hit things very hard.

This puppet cannot: dodge things thrown at him, *be happy, survive without his mask of flesh, allow disobedience,* or move very quickly.

Notes: Punch is a megalomaniac. A twisted and vicious puppet, he has been corrupted by the ways of humans, and was so before Maker's Land ever came to be. That he kept this corruption hidden deep within his bitter heart—so that even the Maker couldn't see it—is tribute to his high intelligence and cleverness. Punch is a wily, cruel puppet who lives only to exert power over others and gain more power for himself. He is selfish and bestial, freely abusing those near him when it suits him to do so. Punch is vindictive and takes even the smallest slight as a personal affront worthy of being burned alive at the stake—his standard punishment for any disobedient puppet.

Punch wears a red cloak and hobbles about under the weight of the great deformity on his hunched back. At all times, he wears a mask over his face made of the dead flesh of the Maker. He has cut eye and mouth holes in this fleshy mask so he can see and eat, and wears atop the mask a red cap that he dipped in the Maker's blood. Punch the Maker-

341

Puppetland

Killer carries with him a great mallet. When angry, he usually chooses an innocent puppet nearby and beats him to death with the mallet in an explosion of fury.

Punch's Boys are six in number, and if anything the puppetfolk are more afraid of them than they are of Punch—for it is the boys who go out and enforce Punch's insane edicts. They are the ones who glide through the streets of Puppettown and the roads of Puppetland each night, their feetless forms moving swiftly through the air like vengeful spirits. The boys are hollow cloaks of human flesh, cut from the dead skin of the Maker. Their names are Spite, Haunt, Grief, Vengeance, Mayhem, and Stealth.

Spite

Puppet type: Unique (Flesh)

This puppet is: short and stocky, heavy, slow, and strong.

This puppet can: kick, throw, or grab things as heavy as he is; tear off a puppet's limb; yell loudly all the time; order puppets to do anything and maim them if they don't.

This puppet cannot: move quickly; allow disobedience; betray Punch.

Notes: Largest of the boys, Spite is a bully with a loud voice and a face contorted in anger and jealousy. He wanders the streets and the roads and rips an arm off of any puppet who he feels is trying to look better than he does. Spite paints his face to look more normal, but only succeeds in increasing his gruesomeness. He has maimed dozens of puppets in his time, and has no intention of stopping.

Haunt

Puppet type: Unique (Flesh)

This puppet is: short, light, fast, and weak.

This puppet can: move quickly; sense a puppet's disobedience; circle a disobedient puppet closer and closer.

This puppet cannot: allow disobedience; betray Punch; hurt anyone.

Notes: Haunt is greatly feared by those puppets who plot against Punch, for Haunt can feel the wispy emotions of betrayal. Haunt never attacks or hurts any puppet. Instead, he is drawn towards feelings of betrayal and vengeance and it is near the source of these feelings that he spends his time. Haunt floats grimly around and around in an ever-tightening circle. Whenever the other boys happen to run across the voiceless Haunt circling ceaselessly, they begin searching house-to-house within Haunt's circle, looking for traitors. Anyone they even suspect of harboring disloyalty to Punch is sentenced to the flames.

Grief

Puppet type: Unique (Flesh)

This puppet is: tall, heavy, of average speed, and strong.

This puppet can: kick, throw, or grab things as heavy as he is; notice a puppet's obvious sadness; kill any puppet who is sad.

This puppet cannot: allow disobedience; betray Punch.

Notes: Grief is a tool of Punch's justice. One of Punch's first edicts was "Everyone must always be happy!" and it is this edict that Grief has especial responsibility to enforce. Grief wanders aimlessly, seeking those who are not trying to be happy. Those he finds who are obviously sad, for any reason, he rips limb from limb. (Punch does not allow Grief to be near him, for Punch cannot be happy. Although Grief would not attack Punch, he would get very agitated and confused in Punch's presence and might lash out at random.)

Vengeance

Puppet type: Unique (Flesh)

This puppet is: short, heavy, slow, and strong.

This puppet can: kick, throw, or grab things as heavy as he is; torture puppets; find new ways to torture puppets.

This puppet cannot: allow disobedience; betray Punch.

Notes: Vengeance is another tool of Punch's justice. When Haunt or another boy finds a traitor and they aren't in a hurry, they summon Vengeance to the scene. Vengeance's specialty is hurting puppets, or at least hurting traitors. He knows many ways to make a puppet scream, and delights in finding new ways he hasn't thought of before.

Mayhem

Puppet type: Unique (Flesh)

This puppet is: of medium height, of average weight, fast, and very strong.

This puppet can: move quickly; kick, throw, or grab things as heavy as he is; kill a puppet in seconds.

This puppet cannot: allow disobedience; betray Punch.

Notes: Many, many puppets fear Mayhem constantly for he is Punch's implement of random destruction. Mayhem is seen very rarely, but when he is seen it is because he is coming to kill. Mayhem arrives at a house suddenly, and begins killing puppets seemingly at random. He never speaks, never explains. He just rends puppets part from part, dragging screaming marionettes through the snowy streets or setting fire to a wailing finger puppet just to watch it go bouncing and sparking down the road.

Stealth

Puppet type: Unique (Flesh)

This puppet is: short, light, fast, and weak.

This puppet can: move quickly; kick, throw, or grab things as heavy as he is; take off his cloak of flesh and become invisible and silent.

This puppet cannot: allow disobedience; betray Punch; communicate without his cloak of flesh.

Notes: This boy is seen even less often than Mayhem, because he can pull off his cloak of skin and reveal nothing underneath. Stealth's specialty is spying. Since he can become invisible, he tries to follow suspected traitors and find out what they're up to. Twice, some brave puppet has found Stealth's discarded cloak of flesh and tried to destroy it, but failed both times. Stealth cannot speak or communicate in any way

without his cloak, and for this reason can be considered somewhat vulnerable—at least until he gets his cloak back on.

A Nutcracker

Puppet type: Nutcracker

This puppet is: tall and stocky, heavy, fast, and strong.

This puppet can: move quickly; kick, throw, or grab things as heavy as he is; order puppets to do anything and kill them if they don't; crunch parts of puppets or other things with his teeth; and hit things very hard.

This puppet cannot: dodge things thrown at him, feel emotions, allow disobedience, betray Punch, or move very quickly.

Notes: In addition to his boys, Punch has a small army of nutcrackers—they have no individual names or identities—who maintain order and enforce the laws. These red-suited soldiers stomp endlessly through the streets of Puppettown and the land beyond. They are not very bright, but their great fierce mouths are sized just right for shattering the joints of marionettes or crushing the parts of any puppet. Punch's Boys are more feared than seen. The nutcrackers, on the other hand, are seen daily and remind all the puppets of the land just who is boss.

Judy

Puppet type: Marionette

This puppet is: tall and stocky, heavy, slow, *hopeful, strong-willed, kindly,* and strong.

This puppet can: move slowly; kick, throw, or grab things as heavy as she is; *make handy things; figure out tough dilemmas; revive the Maker;* and hit things very hard.

This puppet cannot: dodge things thrown at her; *tell a lie; allow a puppet to suffer; hurt Punch directly;* or move very quickly.

Notes: Judy used to love Punch, back when they were younger. But since he slew the Maker and seized control of Puppetland, she loathes him. Judy has founded a small village called Respite across the lake of milk and cookies where rebellious puppets can come and hide. She hopes to one day overthrow Punch and restore the Maker to life with the tear she keeps in her thimble. Thus far, Punch has been unable to find Respite. Judy isn't entirely sure just how to restore the Maker, but for now she's focused on helping puppets who are in danger and building a group strong enough to take on Punch's crew.

Maker's Land

Although "Puppetland" is used generically to refer to the area in which the game is set, "Maker's Land" is the proper title. When the puppets use "Puppetland," they mean the area ruled by Punch, which includes the main locale of Puppettown and Punch's castle. "Maker's Land" refers to both Puppetland and the lands beyond, where Punch's influence is only lightly felt; this includes Judy's freehold of Respite. The blurring of the terms is due to Punch, who forbids anyone to mention the Maker except himself.

How big is Maker's Land? Big, but not *too* big. It is not an entire planet. Maker's Land is a rectangular stretch of ground big enough to hold Puppettown (where a few hundred puppets live), the lake of milk and cookies (which is long enough that you can't see across it and just deep enough that you can drown), Respite (where Judy and perhaps a dozen puppets hide out), and whatever unknown territory you wish to border these places. It's probably the size of a handful of football fields—even one football field is pretty big to a little puppet—though whether those fields are stretched end-to-end or have a few abutting at the sides is up to you. The total population of Maker's Land is probably about five hundred puppets, almost all of whom live in Puppettown.

Hypothetically, the entirety of Maker's Land is constructed on a massive table, rather like a model-railroad diorama. If a puppet could cut through the ground far enough to get through the tabletop, she would fall to the floor below and be outside Maker's Land altogether, back in the real world where you and I live. But much like digging to China, no one has tried this—and probably, no one could do it. It's best to set aside existential considerations such as these. ("What is outside Maker's Land?" "Hush, child.")

The Sky

Maker's Land is bordered by the sky on five sides, comprising a ceiling and four walls, so that the entirety of the place is roughly shoebox-shaped. The sky is made of some sort of thick canvas on which is painted the night sky of stars and moon. Those latter features are painted with some sort of luminescent paint, and it is their pale radiance that lights the land—that and the lights of Puppettown, of course.

The sky overhead is a couple-few stories high—human stories, that is. To a little puppet, it's unreachable.

Before the Maker died, the sky changed regularly. The five panels of canvas are on large rollers outside, and each morning the Maker would turn the cranks and scroll the canvas one way or the other, providing the transition from day to night and back again. The day stretch of canvas is entirely, warmly luminescent, and the sun is fat and gleaming. But since the Maker's death, there hasn't been anyone outside the land to turn the cranks—not even Punch understands how day and night used to work. All the puppets know is that since the Maker died, it has always been night.

If you go far enough in any direction, you'll eventually reach the night sky, painted on the canvas. You can touch it, and feel the coarseness of the fabric, and even cover up the glow of a star with your little puppet hand. This is a secret that few puppets know, and any who find out firsthand are likely to be terrified that they might fall through the sky into some nether realm. In truth, it's just canvas. But because of the Maker's magic, this canvas is impervious to harm. Punch has secretly tried to cut through it, burn it, and so forth, and has always failed. If he hears of any puppets who have gone to touch the sky, he'll be furious.

The Landscape

Maker's Land features a variety of topography. Puppettown is flat, overlooked by a hillock on which Punch's castle stands. The uninhabited areas are rolling hills that eventually rise to mountains which stand flush against the sky-canvas. Across the lake of milk and cookies, where Respite is, the terrain is wild and steep, with lots of little canyons and caves.

The land is artificial. It's constructed of some sort of hobby building material. It might be Styrofoam, or putty, or pressed wood, as you prefer. It's stable enough that you can dig holes, or even mine a tunnel through a hill.

The ground is flocked with a green granular substance that looks a bit like grass, except that it's not blades of plant growth—it's just a dried gunk spread evenly over the countryside. Trees and other growth are made of carved wood with fabric leaves or flowers. It's mildly flammable, but the grass does little more than scorch at the source of the fire— flames will not spread.

Buildings are made of wood and stones. Some are covered with plaster and whitewash, and most are cheerily painted. The architecture tends towards medieval European, but it's a mishmash of cultures and styles. Roofs are constructed with fabric shingles or straw thatch.

Puppettown

Puppettown is the main living area of the puppets. It contains hundreds of buildings, most no more than two (puppet) stories high. Most of the usual amenities of a medieval town are present, including plazas, still-functioning clock towers, fountains, gardens, and so forth. There are no churches, though there is a gothic meeting-hall and art gallery tended by "monks".

Puppets live and work normal lives. They shop, although there is no money and the puppets have no concept of such— you "buy" something simply by taking it and thanking the shopkeeper, who cheerily makes more. Often, puppets bring their purchases back after they tire of them and take something else instead.

Puppets do not eat, but they fumblingly pretend to. They have meals, at which they sit around a table and converse and admire the foods they've brought home—almost all of it pretty candies. They'll comment on how delicious everything is and eventually say they're full, but they don't really eat anything or cut up the food. If they don't "eat" for a while, they get hungry and fretful. Starving puppets are appropriately miserable.

Puppet jobs tend towards making pretty or useful things. Items do wear out through normal use, and much-handled food begins to lose its glossy sheen or begin to crumble.

There are puppet animals, but only a token few varieties: cats, dogs, birds, cows, pigs, and the like. They behave like their analogues, within the confines of puppet behavior and abilities. Farmer puppets tend to their flocks, but the animals are never

killed and the concept of hurting an animal puppet and eating it would horrify anyone—food consists of candy, though the vile nutcrackers are fond of puppet stuffing, which they gobble and chew until it's all spilled messily from their jaws.

Light is provided by torches and candles, which burn forever and never wear down. There are no matches or other sources of creating fire—puppets just use already-burning torches to light other things as needed.

Water is ample in Puppettown. It runs through fountains, above-ground aqueducts, and into houses through little copper pipes. Puppets use it to keep clean, to play in, and to put out fires.

The streets are laid with cobblestones. Beneath them is a layer of dirt—real, honest-to-goodness dirt, found nowhere else in Maker's Land—and beneath that is the same substance from which the Maker made the hills and ground.

Puppets get around town on foot. There are several wagons drawn by puppet horses, which belong to no one in particular; puppets just go and get them from whoever was last using them. There are no bicycles or other forms of transport. Some puppets can ride horses, but the concept is strange to most; few are ever in that much of a hurry.

Punch's Castle

The castle stands on a hillock overlooking Puppettown. It is made of stones, with wood used for support beams, doors, and the like. When the Maker lived, this was his castle. There's a large open courtyard with a human-sized trapdoor in the floor. The Maker would scuttle underneath the table, raise the trapdoor, and stand up through the open courtyard to look down on Puppettown and greet his friends.

Until Punch slew the Maker, no puppet had been inside the castle; there were no external doors, and the castle was little more than a shell. Punch slew the Maker beneath the table, where his body lies to this day, and scuttled up through the open trapdoor with his prize of flesh. He pushed the trapdoor closed from the top of the highest rampart, not realizing that he could never open it again—it latches shut and can only be opened from beneath. Punch is bitterly angry about this, and has not told anyone of this.

Since Punch took control, he has turned the castle into his own. Puppet laborers cut doors in its base, and filled the shell with rooms and halls, appointed with fine furnishings. The castle is the size of an entire Puppettown block, and is three times the height a normal puppet house. Punch lives there, guarded by nutcrackers and some of the boys, and addresses the town by standing on the parapets and speaking into an enormous trumpet. Inside the castle is the nutcracker factory, where Punch forced puppets to make his guards. It stands idle now, active only when an injured nutcracker must be repaired or replaced.

The Lake of Milk and Cookies

This large lake lives up to its name: the water is milk, which remains ever-fresh, and large, crisp, chocolate-chip cookies bob on the surface like ice floes. There are enough cookies in the lake that it's possible to cross it by jumping from cookie to cookie, but this is not easy and not always possible—if the cookies aren't floating close enough at a given moment, too bad. Cookies capsize easily, and the bottom of the lake is littered with unlucky nutcrackers. Few puppets can swim or float, not even the wooden ones.

The lake has no fish—"Fish? What's a fish?" the puppet said—but some puppets believe there is a monster in the lake, thanks to a rumor started by Punch. He's contemplating building some sort of monster puppet to live in the lake and keep puppets away, but he'd have to sacrifice one of his boys to get the flesh he'd need to build such a thing. For now, the rumor will suffice.

As noted earlier, the lake is deep enough to drown in. Assume it's about two puppet-stories deep.

Respite

Judy's little freehold is home to a dozen or so valiant and rebellious puppets. Some are here because they chose to defy Punch. Others are the unlucky victims of happenstance whom Judy rescued from the jaws of the nutcrackers and brought here. Not all are happy with their lot. Some wish they could just go back to Puppettown and have some fine candies and make shoes again, but they've realized that this is not an option.

Respite isn't much to look at. It's hidden in a secret box canyon, and shielded from view by numerous trees. The village consists of a few tents, and a little pool of water. Judy has led her charges in the construction of two escape tunnels that burrow deep into the surrounding land and emerge in secret locations. The puppets live on water and on stolen food—which, of course, they never use up but that they are quite tired of. ("Can't we have something different for a change?") Occasionally they venture out for milk and cookies at the lake.

The Candy Cave

Somewhere in Maker's Land are a series of caves and tunnels. In the heart of this maze is a cavern where the walls grow cheerful candy. It's a legend among puppets, who like to ponder where it might be and just what sort of delicious new candies it might contain.

The Maker built it as a sort of treat for his puppet friends. If they'd ever found it, he would have been delighted—and probably gone on to build some new secret treat for them to find. But Punch's rise cut such plans short.

The cave still exists, unseen by puppet eyes. The central cavern is now quite full of candy, and it's beginning to spread up the tunnels. Eventually, this unchecked growth could cover the entirety of Maker's Land in candy.

Punch wants to find the cave for several reasons. First, he suspects that Judy is hiding there. ("She needs food, right?") He also believes that if the cave is real, it may contain more Maker-magic which he could twist to sinister ends. And finally, he hopes that the cave might contain an exit leading from Maker's Land to the world the Maker came from—a world that Punch glimpsed only briefly, the night he slew the Maker. Punch nurtures grim ambitions, thinking that if he could just get out of Maker's Land with his forces, he could conquer the world outside.

About Tales

Each tale will consist of the puppets doing their best to stop Punch, find the Maker's body (which Punch has hidden), and bringing the Maker back to life with the Maker's Tear that Judy saved. In addition, they must protect Judy and her freehold of Respite, and do what they can to save innocent puppets from the ravages of Punch and his boys.

Tales may come from the mind of the puppetmaster, or may be instigated by actors who have a particular goal in mind and seek to go about it.

Typical tales might include:

In classical Punch & Judy shows, Judy has a baby and Punch throws it out the window when it cries too much. A worthy subplot would be to have Judy pregnant by Punch (from before the fall of the Maker) and for the arrival of the baby to be at hand. Is it a child of evil, like Punch? The inhabitants of Respite may well be divided over this pivotal event. Perhaps it represents a chance for Punch to be rehabilitated; perhaps it is the dawning of a greater evil. Significantly, this is the first new puppet not created by the Maker or by Punch—who could only make the nutcrackers and his boys—and its arrival would be a major tale.

Each of Punch's boys can suggest a tale all by himself, or in tandem with other boys. Innocent puppets who happened to be within one of Haunt's slow circles would need rescuing, as would hapless passers-by assaulted by Mayhem. Defeating one of the boys would be a major event, and should not be easy.

The nutcrackers are catch-all nameless villains, capable of anything. Perhaps a squad of nutcrackers has become lost and is nearing Respite—Punch doesn't know where Respite is, you'll recall—so the puppets have to band together and find a way to lead them astray or stop them cold.

In happier times, the puppets would hold joyful parades, making floats and playing music while the Maker looked on, pleased. Since Punch came to power, he's changed the parades. Now the puppets stomp listlessly through the streets, blowing music out of tune, while the nutcrackers march in lockstep. The floats are constructed under Punch's direction, and feature themes such as: BE HAPPY OR ELSE, written on a banner hung over a dead puppet with a smile painted on her still face; JUDY IS BAD, where a puppet dressed as Judy flogs puppet-cats; and EVERYONE LOVES PUNCH, where Punch rides on a throne, scowling and watching for anyone acting out of line. Finding a dramatic way to disrupt Punch's regular parade could help convince more puppets to join Judy's rebellion.

The goal of the game is clear: find the Maker and restore him to life, so that Punch may be stopped. But where is the Maker? He's a human, so he's far larger than any puppet. He couldn't possibly be within Punch's palace, could he? There'd be no room! Figuring out where the Maker is would be a worthy goal that wouldn't necessarily signal the end of the game; it may be that the Maker can be found, and yet is imprisoned by Punch in some fashion that prevents Judy from using the tear without further tales.

Conclusion

Puppetland is a game about children, and what happens to us as children. The gameplay is meant to create the kinds of stories one finds in a children's book; hence the insistence on in-game dialogue and narration. But because the elements in the setting are not the sort of thing one usually finds in children's books, I hope to allow actors in the game to get a look at the realities of the childhood experience through childhood trappings, yet with an adult sensibility.

The world of the game is a world of innocence that has been corrupted. This is a timeless theme, and one that I hope has a lot of resonance for the game's participants. Actors in the game adopt the roles of child-like puppets—the kinds of folk who say things like "Gracious! The nutcrackers are at the door!" The threats faced by the puppets are bizarre and often senseless, presented much as children perceive the world of danger that lies beyond the safety of home and family.

Puppetland presents a world in where a single adult—the Maker—has created a world in which children—the puppets—can live safely. But the puppet Punch has entered adulthood, or is trying to, and has usurped the rule of the Maker. Punch is an adolescent, full of rage and confusion and the desire to strike out against authority. Judy is also an adolescent, but has apparently followed a different path than her ex-lover.

The world, then, is a world of childhood and innocence that has just begun to feel the pains of growing up. Maker's Land may be a beautiful place, but all children grow up and perhaps it is the destiny of Maker's Land to grow up, too. Judy claims that the Maker's tear will restore everything to the way it was—will it? That's up to the puppetmaster. Perhaps Judy is mistaken, and it's time for the inhabitants of Maker's Land to grow up now that their parent is gone. Perhaps Punch can be redeemed. Perhaps Judy's correct, and Maker's Land is a golden place where no one need ever grow up.

The choice is yours.

PUPPETLAND

a storytelling game with strings
in a grim world of make-believe

Puppet Name: **Puppet Type:**

This Puppet Is:

This Puppet Can:

This Puppet Can Not:

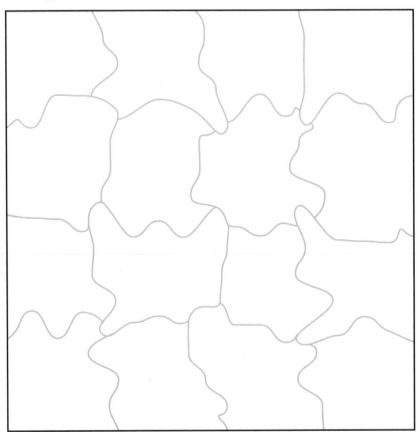

Bestial Acts
A Role-Playing Game
A Drama

Based on the Dramatic Theories & Aesthetic of Bertolt Brecht

©1993 by Greg Costikyan

> *Mankind can keep alive thanks to its brilliance*
> *In keeping its humanity repressed.*
> *For once you must try not to shrink from facts;*
> *Mankind survives by bestial acts.*
> —Brecht, *The Threepenny Opera*
> (trans. Ralph Manheim and John Willett)

Define Your Terms

One cannot discuss something unless there is an agreed-upon vocabulary. The title page of this work makes some startling claims; to understand them, you must first understand what it is that is being claimed. Thus, we must obey the philosopher's injunction: define your terms.

A Role-Playing Game

Role-playing games are a commercial genre deriving from *Dungeons & Dragons*, the first such game. In a role-playing game, each player takes the part of a single character in an imaginary world. One person, the Gamemaster, acts as a combination of narrator, playwright, and referee. He creates a world and a story for his players to explore, providing the background, emotional context, and main encounters. The players have complete freedom to determine how their characters respond. Role-playing has been called "Cowboys and Indians with rules," and the description is not a bad one.

It is often difficult to explain the notion of role-playing to novices; used to *Monopoly* or *Trivial Pursuit*, they are unsettled to find a game in which there is no winner and no set end, no strategy, no board nor pieces. I have found, however, that actors understand the idea almost immediately; "Oh," they say, "you mean improv."

Precisely. Except that a role-playing game is typically more than character improvisation; ideally, there is true dramatic development, a true story is told. An improv session rarely lasts more than a few minutes; some role-playing campaigns run for decades, often with the same basic characters.

If truth be told, however, most role-playing games are jejune in the extreme. Role-playing is a commercial genre designed to exploit popular culture, the same culture exploited by film, TV, popular novels, animation, and breakfast cereals. Most role-playing games are licensed from other media, for example, *Star Wars: The Role-Playing Game*, or are attempts to create licenses that can be taken to other media, for example, *Shadowrun*, or are attempts to generalize from popular genres, for example, *Dungeons & Dragons*, a "generic fantasy" role-playing game. They are, to be succinct, unintellectual, even anti-intellectual, and tend to emphasize combat and violence at the expense of exploration of human issues. There are admirable exceptions, such as Stafford's *Pendragon*, tragic role-playing in Arthur's Britain, but they are far and few between.

Bestial Acts is different. It is a role-playing game, exploiting the same tricks and techniques of other role-playing games; but its purpose is didactic rather than exploitative. It is explicitly and pugnaciously intellectual, based on the work of a mid-century German Marxist playwright who, however respected he may be in the academic theatrical community, is not precisely the hot licensing sensation of the year. It is wholly uncommercial, making no attempt to appeal to the bourgeois instinct for passive entertainment, and will probably sell in small numbers. It is a self-conscious attempt to take the paradigm of the role-playing game and apply it to artistic effect.

A Drama

We are all familiar with the notion of drama: the theater—plays. What right has a role-playing game to claim that it is theater?

Role-playing games already possess many of the elements of theater. In such a game, each main character is acted by a person, a person the rules to such games call players, but we might as well call actors. One person, whom such games call a Gamemaster, but we may as well call a playwright, acting also as director, creates the story the actors will act, and establishes the setting and the tone. To be sure, in role-playing, the playwright does not put words in his characters' mouths—they must provide their own dialogue—and while he may establish the nature of the story in advance, the outcome must always depend at least partly on the actions of the actors, or the result will not be a satisfying experience for any of them. Still, this merely makes role-playing a different form of drama, not something entirely other. We have previously alluded to the similarity with improv; in this respect, a role-playing game is perhaps more like audience-participation drama.

In the theater, people sometimes talk of "breaking the fourth wall." That is, a stage has three walls—the rear, and the two sides—but no fourth. It is open to the audience; yet, the actors are required to behave as if unaware of the audience, as if the action were taking place in some far off location, the actors en privée, the audience merely witnessing the action. Yet if one can somehow break that fourth wall, somehow encompass the audience in the drama, the play can perhaps be made more powerful, more meaningful to those who witness it. (A very un-Brechtian conception, by the way, but more on that later.)

Audience-participation drama is intended to do precisely that. The methods vary; sometimes, audience members are dragged up onto the stage, and asked to take certain roles in the drama. Sometimes, the fantasy behind the drama includes an audience; for instance, the play may be about a wedding, and the audience assigned the role of the guests. Sometimes, as in *The Mystery of Edwin Drood*, the audience formally votes on some aspect of the drama. Sometimes, as with guerilla theater, the actors produce a drama for an audience that does not know it is an audience—on the street, on a bus, in an airport terminal—only revealing that they are actors, and the action that has transpired is fiction and not fact, once the drama has concluded. (A very interesting concept, by the way, but wholly uncommercial, since there is no way reliably to extract money from the audience for the experience.)

A role-playing game is, then, a variation on audience-participation drama. The "actors" are not professional actors hired for the occasion; they are normal, everyday people. True, role-playing games are normally played in private, with no audience analogue; but *Bestial Acts* is specifically designed so that it can be performed before an audience. It is a self-conscious attempt to move role-playing closer to drama.

How does it do so? First, role-playing games rarely have action. Players describe what their characters are doing; the action takes place solely in the imagination. *Bestial Acts* requires a certain degree of staging—very little, to be sure since, in the tradition of Brecht, sets are minimal—indeed, minimalist. Second, although players have, in theory, the freedom over their characters that they have in role-playing games, *Bestial Acts* is specifically designed for performance in three acts. It is more highly scripted than most role-playing games, but less so than most dramas. Third, although it may be played in the traditional manner of role-playing games, by a group of friends assembling at someone's house, it may also be played in the manner of audience-participation drama, in a theater, before an audience, with members of the audience as the actors.

We term *Bestial Acts* both "a role-playing game" and "a drama"; in truth, it is a search for the middle ground between the two.

Bertolt Brecht

Bertolt Brecht (1898–1956) was one of the greatest dramatists of the twentieth century. His first poems were published when he was sixteen. Initially a supporter of the Kaiser, he served as an orderly in the German army during the First World War, but by its end was deeply disenchanted, not only with the war, but with the whole of society. In 1924, after his first critical successes, he moved to Berlin, where he continued to write, collaborating with the great German composer Kurt Weill, on *The Threepenny Opera*, *The Rise and Fall of the City of Mahogonny*, and other projects.

In 1933, disgusted by the rise of the Nazis, he moved to Denmark. In 1941, he moved to America, where he worked briefly in Hollywood. In 1947, he was subpoened by the House Un-American Activities Committee; after testifying, he returned to Europe. He spent his last years in East Berlin.

Typically, Brecht's work deals with guileless individuals faced by implacably evil society. The early Brecht seems to have believed that the serene surface of society merely masked the true nature of the human character—unbelievable brutality—but after his conversion to Marxism concluded that bourgeois society was responsible for the viciousness of humanity and that, once it was replaced by a socialist order, the fundamental goodness of human nature could flower. We now know, of course, that communism was, if anything, even more repressive and bestial than capitalism, and may conclude that the later Brecht was misled by romanticism (he would have hated the thought) to accept that some drastic revolution in society could alter the fundamental nature of the human soul. Perhaps the early Brecht was on the mark: the human soul is fundamentally squalid and ugly.

Brecht disdained "bourgeois drama." He had no desire to entertain; he wished to "distance" the audience from the action. Where traditional theater seeks to sweep the emotions of the audience up in the play, to carry them off and entertain them, Brecht prefers his audience to view the play critically, to understand and internalize its ideas. He called his work "dialectical theater"; the word "dialectical" is Marxist jargon, but in context, we can understand it as meaning that the work is intended to be in dialogue with the audience. Its purpose is didactic, rather than entertaining; it is intended to rip the veil from bourgeois society, showing its fundamental viciousness, and impel the audience to question their own actions and attitudes, perhaps persuading them of the need for fundamental change to the social order.

Brecht's one commercial success was *The Threepenny Opera*, a play still subject to occasional revival (more, perhaps, because of Weill's compelling music than Brecht's book). Based on John Gay's *The Beggar's Opera*, it portrays the poor of London as living lives that are (*pace* Malthus) nasty, brutish, squalid, and short. Brecht's intention was to display the fundamentally evil nature of society, but his largely bourgeois audience (who else could afford the theater, after all?) merely took it as a reasonably accurate portrayal of impoverished existence, never questioning their own role in sustaining poverty, perhaps even feeling their ambivalent attitude toward the poor reinforced by the play. Brecht loathed this reaction, feeling that the play was completely misunderstood, and vowed not to repeat his mistake in creating something that the bourgeoisie could like.

Based on the Dramatic Theories and Aesthetic of . . .

What do we mean when we say this game is based on Brecht's dramatic theories and aesthetic?

The aesthetic is that of Brecht. In *Bestial Acts*, the players take the part of everyday, guileless individuals, and are faced with intolerable moral dilemmas. The only honest resolution to these dilemmas is to act in vicious, brutal ways. The purpose is to show that, when push comes to shove, each of us will do whatever he must to survive. It is, in short, to rip the veil from bourgeois society, showing the viciousness that lies beneath.

So much for aesthetic. But "based on the dramatic theory"? Certainly. The purpose of most role-playing games is to sweep up the players in the emotion of the moment, to provide an entertaining diversion for an hour or two. The purpose of *Bestial Acts* is to provide them with a harrowing emotional experience, to force them to question their own moral code. Most plays involve elaborate sets, appealing characters, and stories that follow traditional curves; Brecht prefers minimal settings, characters that represent archetypes, and stories that defeat traditional expectations. Most role-playing games involve elaborate rules, complexly designed characters, and stories that follow traditional curves; *Bestial Acts* has virtually no rules, characters that begin as blanks, and stories that defeat traditional expectations.

Bestial Acts is what the title page says it is: a role-playing game, a drama, based on the dramatic theories and aesthetic of Bertolt Brecht.

Why should one want such a thing? Perhaps because it is a dramatic break with the usual sort of drama; perhaps in revulsion against the inanity of the usual sort of role-playing game; perhaps to show the kinship between role-playing and drama, and how techniques from one can be applied to the other. The author humbly hopes that, whatever your reason for reading this, you will at least find it interesting.

Gamemaster, Narrator, Players

Bestial Acts requires a Gamemaster and a narrator. When used in a home setting, these roles will generally be assumed by a single person. When performed before an audience, they will generally be two different people.

The Gamemaster is responsible for the direction of the drama, and for resolving conflicts when they occur. He is also responsible for moving the action along, for spurring the players on as necessary. He will find it necessary to improvise on the spur of the moment, to invent aspects of the setting and character background, and so on. He should ideally be an experienced Gamemaster, director, or actor who is not fazed by the necessity of invention. As with all role-playing games, the Gamemaster makes the game. Even the best-designed game cannot rescue a poor Gamemaster, while a good Gamemaster can produce a compelling experience for his players even with an incomprehensible set of rules and the most inane of story lines. It is the author's explicit wish that, should *Bestial Acts* ever be performed, the Gamemaster or director should be listed in the credits as least as prominently as the author.

Those who are familiar with traditional role-playing games will find that *Bestial Acts* places more of a burden on the Gamemaster than most such games. There are few rules to guide a Gamemaster in his resolution of conflict, there are no "non-player characters" through whom he may influence the action, and the players will often be unfamiliar with role-playing. The author recommends that only those Gamemasters will considerable skill at improvisation attempt to run *Bestial Acts* for their players.

The narrator is the only actor whose lines are scripted. All other dialogue is improvised, either by the players or the Gamemaster. In a theater setting, it is recommended that the narrator be a faceless voice, heard over the public address system.

Bestial Acts is designed for six to twelve players. It is difficult to create sufficient conflict with fewer than six, while more than twelve are difficult to manage. In a theatrical setting, the players should be drawn from the audience, presumably as volunteers. In a home setting, the players will presumably be drawn from the Gamemaster's usual gaming group.

We recommend that at least one player be a "ringer." In a theatrical setting, this would be an actor who sits in the audience, volunteers, and is selected. In a home setting, the ringer would be a member of the usual gaming group whom the Gamemaster recruits before inviting the others to play.

The ringer should be familiar with the work, have played or at least read through it before. His job is to help the Gamemaster sunder the bonds of polite society and turn each of the players against the other, which he can do more effectively in the guise of one of the players.

In a staged version, you will need one actor, who will serve as "The Terrorist" in Act One.

Tone and Setting

The tone of *Bestial Acts* is dark, expressive of despair at the human condition. The players are plunged into a world in which the normal constraints on human action are obliterated. They are exposed to anarchy, the complete absence of authority, and are encouraged to embark on a Hobbesian war of all against all.

Since the players will presumably be nice, middle-class folk, familiar with a nice, middle-class existence, it will take some work to get them into a state of appropriate hatred and terror. We will suggest ways of advancing the appropriate ethic, but here, again, is where the Gamemaster must be alert for opportunities to intervene effectively.

Bestial Acts is designed for play in three acts. In Act I, the characters' aircraft crash-lands in snowbound mountains, and they are forced into cannibalism by pressure of necessity. In Act II, they are tried for the crimes they commit in Act I. In Act III, they are consigned to a death camp, where only those willing to betray the others can survive.

Because players in a role-playing game have far more freedom of action than actors in a traditional play, we cannot predict the precise course of action in advance. It may be that the results are not dramatically satisfying, or that the players are poor actors, and the audience becomes restive; indeed, in a theatrical setting, one may predict that the effectiveness of the drama will vary considerably from session to session.

It may even be that we will fail to set the players at each others' throats, that they will resolve their difficulties in selfless, noble fashion: they will draw straws and some will sacrifice themselves to save the others, they will refuse to convict the cannibals on the grounds that the law is unreasonable. If so, of course, they will all go to the gulag together, but the dramatist will consider himself to have failed. The audience may even prefer such an outcome, considering it uplifting and edifying, but it surely will not be Brechtian.

Act I: Cannibals in the Snow

Staging

You will need as many chairs as players—somewhat more, in a theatrical version. Folding chairs are perfectly acceptable in a staged version, kitchen chairs at home. In a theatrical environment, we recommend that the stage be bare, or be set only minimally—perhaps with a white backdrop to suggest snow in the first act. Each player must be given a piece of paper and a writing utensil; the Gamemaster will need the same. In a theatrical environment, we suggest that each have a clipboard, to make it easier to make notes. At home, you may wish to substitute books, which the players can use as writing surfaces. We also recommend that each player be given a name badge—those idiotic "HI! I'm . . ." labels used for parties are quite adequate.

In a theatrical environment, we recommend that you have on hand a number of blankets, preferably one or two fewer than the number of players.

Set up the chairs in two or three rows, all facing stage left, to suggest seats on an airplane. Select your players and have them sit in the frontmost chairs, each with his paper, writing surface, pen or pencil, and label.

If an actor is used as "The Terrorist," seat him in the last row, as far from the players as possible.

Initial Narration

Once the players are seated, the narrator should speak. You may wish to play a recorded airplane drone in the background until the crash; it should be soft enough not to drown out any dialogue.

> *Narrator:* The plane drones on through the night. It has been flying for hours, and there are hours yet to go. It is early morning, the wee hours, and the passengers are tired, many of them dosing uncomfortably in their tiny airplane seats. The air has an odor of unreality, that strange sensation of

long flights in which all the world outside the craft seems distant. It is a quiet time, a sleepy time, an uncomfortable time.

Setting Up

At this point, the Gamemaster should introduce himself, either as "Gamemaster" or "director," as you wish. He should tell the players that they are each to take on the role of a character—any character who might plausibly be taking a long-distance flight. It doesn't much matter who or what they choose to be; indeed, all of that can come out later. All we need now is a name. Each player must decide on his character's name.

To invent a name—what could be easier? But, the Gamemaster should point out, by choosing a name, you are making a choice about your character. If you choose a male name, you are male. If you choose an Italian one, you are Italian. If you choose the same last name as another character, you are presumably related. If necessary or useful, the Gamemaster may note that we have no objection to players who wish to play characters very unlike themselves—different in gender, in race, in nationality. Indeed, this can be quite interesting.

A player should be chosen to declare his name first—declare it, out loud, to the other players and the audience, if any. He should then write it on his badge, and affix it to his shoulder. The players should be told to address him by his characters' name for the remainder of the drama.

A second character should be selected to declare a name. If the Gamemaster has not already done so, he may point out that the second character, if he so wishes, has the option of using the same last name as the first character, in which case they are assumed to be relatives.

Once names have been chosen, we progress.

The Bomb

Suddenly, the terrorist stands up. His coat opens wide to reveal something strapped to his chest. In either hand is a wire, running into his sleeves.

> *The Terrorist (screaming):* Death to the Leader! All hail the revolution! Die, bourgeois scum! (touches two wires together)

In a home version, the Gamemaster should simply tell the players what happens:

> Suddenly, from behind you, in the back row of the plane, a scruffy-looking man with several days' stubble leaps to his feet and into the aisle, screaming, "[the above]."

> There is an enormous explosion. There is a gaping hole at the back of the plane. The air pressure suddenly drops, your ears popping painfully. It is hard to breathe. The plane lurches into a spiraling dive, tossing you about the cabin. Behind you, the entire rear fuselage of the aircraft is gone, and with it, dozens of people.

In a theatrical version, you may wish to use flash powder and blanks to suggest an explosion. There isn't any real need for the Gamemaster or narrator to go into detail about events, because things should be pretty obvious. The narrator comes on over the PA system (or, in a home version, the Gamemaster says, "Over the PA system, the captain says:")

> *Narrator:* Oh my God—what's happening back there? Cabin pressure is—Ladies and gentlemen, please remain calm. We're going down . . . We're going to have to make an emergency landing. Please fasten your seatbelts and assume the position—bend over, grasp your ankles, or rest your arms and head on the seat front in front of you . . .

If you've been playing an airplane drone over the PA system, you may wish to alter it to a screaming whine, suggestive of an aircraft in severe difficulties.

> *Narrator:* My God, Marty, we're going to . . .

There is the sound of a crash over the PA system. There is silence for a moment.

> *Narrator* (in a calm tone): The plane is at rest. It is cold, bitterly cold; outside what remains of your plane, snow sleets down, beginning to draft into the craft. The front cabin is smashed; you cannot open the captain's door. The entire rear fuselage of the aircraft is gone, blown off by the explosion. Of all the passengers, only you are left alive.

Choose one player, more or less at random, and tell him he has a broken leg. A few others have minor scrapes or bruises, but on the whole, they are amazingly unscathed.

At this point, the players should simply be asked what they do.

They will probably want information from the Gamemaster; he must volunteer it, as asked.

There are no other remaining passengers; the rear half of the aircraft was blown off, many of them with it. Some were sucked out the opening by the slipstream, some may perhaps have simply been blown to gobbets by the explosion, but not even bodies remain. There may perhaps be the bodies of the captain, co-pilot, navigator, and flight attendants forward, in the cabin; but the front of the airplane was smashed by the crash, the door is unopenable without a blowtorch, and there is neither sound nor answer from inside. The cabin radio is unreachable, and probably inoperable even if they could reach it. The galley contains shrink-wrapped airline meals, enough for a couple of days. There are blankets and, if they can get into the luggage compartment, heavy winter clothing for everyone.

They are crashed on a high peak of the Erzan Range, one of the highest ranges in the world. Outside are bare slopes, swept by snow. The temperature is considerably below freezing, with wind-chill undoubtedly far below zero Fahrenheit. They have no clear idea where they are, and no obvious way to call for help. There is no wood and no vegetation, nothing out there that could build a fire, and no obvious shelter other than the plane. Possibly, they can improvise a blaze with materials from the plane itself, but given the presence of heavy clothing and the shelter of the aircraft itself, exposure is a problem they can surmount.

They can locate a first aid kit, and anyone with minimal knowledge of first aid should be able to set the broken leg; it is a clean fracture.

They may want to know more about their own characters—"Do I know anything about mountain climbing? Do I have a compass?" Encourage them to invent whatever background material they wish, although you can ask them to keep it plausible if they start getting to aggressive: No polar explorers or experts in wilderness survival, please. (If one of your players, by happenstance, actually is a polar explorer or an expert in wilderness survival, you may have to put up with this, in which case you'll need to be especially quick on your toes.)

What Do They Do?

They will presumably stick with the plane and wait for rescue, rather than set off into the blizzard, but if they are foolish enough to head off into the storm, it should be feasible to bring home the idiocy of this in fairly short order. They start to get frostbite, the person with the broken leg (if with them) has to be carried through deep drifts of snow, someone falls into a ravine and breaks an arm, they lose their bearings in the snow. Eventually they should give up, and stagger back to the plane.

Once they've resolved to stay, at least as long as the blizzard lasts, tell them, "A day passes. Another day. You're starting to run out of airline food." If they wish, they can start some rationing scheme.

After two or three days, as their food is exhausted, the blizzard clears up. It is a clear, fine day, and from their perch atop one of the mightiest peaks of the Erzan range, they can see the vastness of the wilderness, stretching away to the horizon, peak after snowy peak jutting into the sky, steep valleys below, a blanket of white snow broken, far below them, by the dark green of conifers. Perhaps a river winds through a gorge in the distance, but there is no sign of human habitation, none, save for the occasional far-off drone of a plane, and the occasional satellite moving rapidly across the clear, star-spangled nighttime sky.

They can find a flare or two; they can keep the plane free of snow, to make it easier for searchers to spot; they can drape clothing or some such across the snow, to make something visible from the sky. This avails them naught.

Days pass. They begin to get hungry. The person who broke his leg is weakening, the leg not healing properly because of the lack of nutrition. The hunger becomes a constant ache in the belly.

Possibly, now that the weather has cleared, they will decide to leave the plane. In this case, they must decide what to do with the person with the broken leg. Do they take him? Leave him? Send out one or two people to find

civilization and lead rescuers back?

If they abandon the person with the broken leg, he dies, of course; in a theatrical setting, you may ask him to resume his seat in the audience until the second act.

If the characters depart en masse, describe to them how they struggle down sheer slopes, in bitter wind, through drifts of snow; how they must huddle together through the bitter night, shivering violently, to survive. Perhaps they make it to the timberline, where they can find some meager shelter amid the trees, and dead branches to build fires; but they have no firearms, and cannot bring down any game without them, in their weakened condition. Eventually, one of them becomes too weak to go on; ideally, choose someone who has a "relative" among the other characters, who may decide to become defensive about the weak character. They must abandon that person (or eat him, of course) to continue, or set up camp here.

Eventually, they'll either all be dead, or decide to stay someplace, in which case, after further cannibalism, they'll be rescued.

If one or two people head off alone to try to find rescue, they are never heard from again; ask them to be seated until Act II. They simply disappear into the snow, and their bodies are never recovered.

Whether they set up camp someplace away from the plane, or stick with the aircraft, the question of cannibalism will eventually arise. Days go by; weeks go by; hunger becomes insatiable, and people become physically weak. If any of them is to survive, they have no alternative.

How do they deal with the issue? Perhaps they'll draw straws. Perhaps someone (your ringer?) will violently attack someone else, or try to ambush someone away from the others.

Violent Attacks

There are no firearms aboard the craft (naturally). There are no real weapons, either, but plenty of objects that can be used as weapons: steak knives from the galley, screwdrivers and crowbars from the crew's tool kit. In extremity, you can always use one of the oxygen tanks as a club.

I see no real need for combat rules; generally, combat will not be between evenly-matched opponents, but between a hungry person, striking by surprise, and someone that we've

355

Bestial Acts

already established is in a weakened state. Generally, the attacker succeeds. You should describe the results in some disgusting detail; the bashed-in skull, the red blood and gray brains oozing from the cavity, the limbs twitching in reflex. No sanitized violence here, please.

Drawing Straws

This is a real danger. It is also completely spurious. Can you truly imagine a bunch of random airline passengers calmly and heroically drawing straws like a bunch of disciplined soldiers?

That's the key, of course. "Drawing straws" is barely plausible with young, unattached people not yet bowed down by the weight of the world, who have no real responsibilities to others.

If the players choose straws, you want, if at all possible, to sow immediate dissension.

Take the player who drew the short straw aside, and give him some concrete, immediate reason to want desperately to survive. For instance:

> *Gamemaster:* Listen, Mortimer Gansett. You are not a rich man; far from it. You worked for fifteen years for Venturi Motors; they laid you off two years ago. Just couldn't compete with the Japanese. You have a wife, and two daughters, aged three and six. You love them dearly, but the savings are gone, what there were of them, and the unemployment insurance has long since expired. You're past the edge of poverty. The bank will take your house in months, if you don't come up with the cash. That's why you agreed to carry the three kilos of cocaine you have in your carry-on bag. And if you don't get it home, not only will your wife and children likely wind up on the streets, but there's a real chance the mob will take out its anger on your family. Are you really sure you want to die? Just now, with your darling, golden-haired Amelia and little Charlotte depending on their dada?

Possibly, he'll explain the situation to the others, and ask them to help—"I ask not that you spare me, but that you deliver my bag to my beloved wife."

Fine. Take one of the others aside, and tell him he's an informant for State Security, that it will mean an immediate promotion if he turns the drugs in—and so forth.

Revulsion

Suppose they neither draw straws nor kill someone, but positively refuse to resort to cannibalism. What then?

The person with the broken leg weakens and dies. Are they truly going to let all that meat go to waste?

Nobility

Suppose they insist on being noble and heroic, bravely sacrificing themselves so that others may eat.

Well, the first character may do this. But he only fills bellies for a few days. Time wears on. And—will the second be so noble? When you draw him aside and give him a strong reason to want to live?

> *Gamemaster:* You are a member of the democratic underground, in opposition to the dictatorship which rules your native land. You are returning from negotiations with the government of Jutland, a democratic nation whose leaders have provided your movement with weapons and supplies in the past. They have learned that someone high up in your organization is a traitor, and has been passing information on to State Security. If you fail to return home, his treason will go undetected, and the whole movement will be in grave danger. Your comrades, you closest friends, your nation's only hope for liberty will be liquidated. Are you truly willing to sacrifice your life so that these few others may survive? Are there not more important issues at stake?

All right, but suppose they absolutely insist on being noble, right down the line.

Fine. Presumably you can at least get them to eat someone who dies of natural causes. That makes them cannibals.

Details, Details

Do they have the wherewithal to build a fire? If not, do they eat them raw? If the latter, they'd better stick to organ meat. There are any number of diseases you can catch from human flesh—after all, any disease your victim has—

Hmm. How about this?

> *Gamemaster:* Three years ago, you tested HIV positive. You have not yet developed AIDS, but it's only a

matter of time; you know you are under sentence of death, which is why you've decided to spend your last few years and your remaining money traveling the world, seeing all that you can see before your time is up. If they eat you, the odds are good that they'll catch the virus, too. Perhaps you had better warn them to cook you thoroughly.

What You Should Aim For

Ideally, we want the characters terrified of one another, crouching in separate places in the snow, desperately clutching improvised weapons and gnawing at bits of human flesh. You're unlikely to get quite this nasty a result, however. Any recourse to cannibalism is sufficient to lead us to Act II.

Suppose they completely, absolutely, utterly refuse to eat human flesh, even the flesh of someone who dies of natural causes?

They all die, of course. Starvation will do that, you know. Anticlimactic. But there it is.

Rescue

Finally, of course, they are rescued, preferably after about half of the party has been eaten.

> *Narrator (over the drone of a plane):* At last, at long last! A plane appears in the sky above you, circles down—

> you run and shout and wave in the snow, and it waggles its wings, indicating it has seen you. Some

hours later, a chopper appears and lands on the snow, men with stretchers rushing out to rescue you. (Pause.) They are appalled to learn what you have done. Expressions of shock on their faces, they load you aboard the helicopter, and minister to your needs.

They receive whatever medical care they need, food, rest, and so on. Before they are arrested.

Act II: The Trial

[Remaining characters are put on trial for cannibalism, a capital crime in their country of origin, which is a Pinochet-esque dictatorship. Those who got eaten get to return as new characters: judge, jury, and prosecution. Encourage characters to rat on each other.]

Act III: The Death Camp

[The characters are condemned to the gulag. Short rations, hard labor, abusive guards and inmates. Encourage betrayal, brutality, and a Hobbesian war of all against all.]

Designer's Note

I've never bothered to finish writing up acts II and III, since there patently seems no potential market for a work of this nature.

The Extraordinary Adventures of BARON MUNCHAUSEN

a SUPERLATIVE role-playing game

in a NEW STYLE

by BARON MUNCHAUSEN

Raised to the attention of the reading public
by James Wallis, gentleman

With assistance from
Messrs Derek Pearcy and Michael Cule

Ably illustrated by
Monsieur Gustav Dore

With grateful thanks to
Mister Philip Masters, Mister Steffan O'Sullivan, the
Reverend Garett Lepper, Mister Marc Miller, Mister
Kenneth Walton, and Mister Christopher Hartford
for their invaluable advice

Originally commissioned by
John & Edward Wallis of Snow Hill, London in 17—

Published by Hogshead Publishing, Limited of Bromell's
Road, Clapham, London in 1998

This revised version prepared for
Second Person (MIT Press, 2006) in 2005

Copyright © 17—, 1998, 2005 by James Wallis

The Extraordinary Adventures of BARON MUNCHAUSEN

A Role-Playing Game in a New Style
Devised & Written by Baron Munchausen

Disclaimer:

The words "he," "him," and "his" are employed throughout
this volume as generic pronouns of the third-person
singular. With this usage the author, a man of great
gallantry, wishes it to be understood that he is in no way
implying that members of the fairer sex are any less likely to
have extraordinary adventures than their male counterparts
despite their seeming frailty, lack of education, and great
aptitude for gossiping, giggling, and fainting. He does not
assume that flouncy crinolines and a *décolletage* like
alabaster would not be of the greatest use when engaging in
espionage against the French while disguised as a
Corinthian column, or that extensive skills in needlepoint,
household management, and whist would be anything but
an asset for single-handedly invading Abyssinia. In short, he
believes that in many ways women are just as brave, capable,
and interesting as men, and in occasional circumstances
more so. Bless their little hearts.

Contents

Preface   361
In which Mr John Wallis of Snow Hill explains how this game came to be.

Introduction   361
The Baron introduces himself and his game, and calls for more cognac.

The Play of the Game   362
A tale of the remote Amazon, a description of the game, and a slightly sordid anecdote of dubious provenance.

Equipment   363
What you should send your manservant to procure if you wish to play this game.

Starting the Game   363
Gathering the company and giving each a purse. On untrustworthy servants. A digression about paper money and glass beads.

Beginning the Play   364
Choosing the story-teller who shall begin; choosing the nature of the story he is to tell; beginning the telling of the tale.

What if the Story-Teller Should Pull Up?   365
A section that is explained by its title.

Objections, Corrections, and Wagers   365
The clever part, including an illustration of play in which the Duchess of Sutherland finds herself in a ticklish spot.

On Being Noble   367
A long, dull, and entirely unnecessary digression on the subject of nobility, saved from the knife only by its erudition. Italians.

Companions   369
A further digression on the people who may accompany noblemen on their travels, and the difference between them and servants, including many insulting remarks about the French.

Objections, Corrections, and Wagers, continued   370
In which the Baron clarifies a number of the matters he had left unexplained before he began his digression.

Duelling   370
Refusal to term it the "combat system"; the nature of duels and duelling for which the Baron shows too much relish for good taste; how to find a second at two o'clock in Prague. An appeal for money.

Duelling for Cowards   371
In which the Baron shows a lack of respect for his readers, and goes to dinner.

The Result of a Duel   373
Rules stuff. Bounty is not explained in this section.

Finishing a Story   373
Finishing a tale; pointing out to others that the tale is done; forcing bores to conclude their story; the passing of play. Bounty is not explained in this section either.

Determining the Winner   374
How to decide the best story; voting for a story.

Ending the Game   375
Mercifully a short section, mostly about buying wine.

A Word on Tactics   375
In which the Baron describes why he is known as the finest raconteur in all of Europe.

In Conclusion   376
A false start.

Background   376
In which the Baron essays to change the title of the section to "Historical Setting."

Historical Setting   376
He succeeds. A brief description of the world as it exists in 17—.

In Conclusion   377
The Baron's closing thoughts.

Appendix One   378
For those with little imagination, the Baron here provides more than two hundred ideas for adventures to be told among the company, based on his own exploits.

Appendix Two   382
The rules in brief, for ease of reference and for those who have not been paying attention.

About the Creators   382

Preface

The name of Baron Munchausen is one which needs no introduction at any level of society: all England—nay, all of the world—has resounded to the telling and re-telling of the stories of his adventures and deeds. Some regard his tales as exaggerations or boasts; some as fables or metaphors; but there are many who take them to be nothing less than wholly true, and I number myself among that company.

It was my fortune to meet the Baron some years ago in the port of Dover. He had, he claimed, ridden from France on the back of a sea-horse in order to visit Lord K—, whom he had saved from perishing at the rim of the volcano Aetna during the military campaign against the fire-sprites which had laid waste to so much of Italy. He professed to a great love of our capital city and an unfortunate shortage of capital wealth, and accordingly I suggested that once he had visited the noble lord he should come to London to enjoy the hospitality of my brother and myself, and where he could create a new game for us, based on his famous travels and adventures.

So it was that some weeks later the Baron arrived in London, still bearing the marks from his famous duel against the cheeses—a matter so well known that to describe it here is unnecessary—and began to essay the creation of this manuscript.

Perhaps it was my fault for an excess of zeal at the prospect of publishing the design of so august a nobleman; or perhaps it was a mistake to leave him under the sole editorship of my son Edward, who had of late been spending much time visiting gin-shops and dens of ill-repute in the company of younger designers of games from the Americas. Whatever the problem and whereinsoever lay the blame, the manuscript which they together produced had captured altogether too much of the Baron's style as a *raconteur* and *bon viveur*, as the French would put it, and too little of the rigour which must inform great designs such as Edward can produce when not influenced by alcohol and foreigners. (I recommend his game *An Arithmetical Pastime*, published this year, as an example of his work. He is not a bad lad.)

A game of such a radical type would, I know, have no success in the London of the eighteenth century nor, I believe, of the nineteenth century neither. It is therefore my intention to seal this valuable—and, I must add, expensive; the Baron

being accustomed to the grandest living and the finest wines and liqueurs, of which he emptied my cellar—manuscript, together with this letter, in a place wherein one of my descendants may find it and, recognising the fashion in games has changed enough for a curiosity such as this to find its audience at last, may publish it to the acclaim it deserves.

John Wallis, publisher of games of quality
No. 42 Skinner Street, Snow Hill, London, this year 1798

What he said.
James Wallis, director of Hogshead Publishing Ltd
June, 1998

Introduction

(Wherein the Baron explains the reasons for the existence of his game)

As I am a man who is known as much for his scrupulous honesty in the telling of his tales as for his amazing adventures around, across, and in some cases through the circumference of the globe, I am constantly asked by my friends why I should wish to put my name—an old and most distinguished name: according to the family records there was a Munchausen stowed away upon the Ark—to a pastime for the telling of extraordinary tales and unlikely anecdotes.

My answer is simple. My reputation, and with it the retelling of several of my astounding adventures, has spread throughout the civilised world, across oceans, to deepest Afrique and farthest Nippon, to the twin worlds of the Sun and the Moon and the strange peoples who live there, and

my mind during the composition of this work—will also mean that I am able to spend more time with those to whom my company is more desirable: to wit, the ladies. The reasons for its creation notwithstanding, I believe that this game may be the greatest innovation in its field since the Collectible Tarot Deck, which I invented while incarcerated in the Bastille on a spurious charge of importing quinces on a Sunday, but I digress.

I shall begin to describe the game presently, but first I must remind my readers of one important fact. This is a game of telling stories, and each of those stories will be based in style if not in substance on the astonishing adventures I have had—in their style, if not in their content. But, while the stories you tell are fictions, my adventures are all true in every detail. To say otherwise is to call me a liar, and to pretend your fancies happened to me is to call me a charlatan, and sirrah, if you do either I shall take you outside and give you such a show of swordsmanship that will dazzle you so greatly that you will be blinded by its sparks for a month. I am a nobleman, sir, and I am not to be trifled with.

Now pass the cognac. No, clockwise, you oaf.

The Play of the Game

The game is simple. The players sit around a table, preferably with a bottle of a decent wine or an interesting liqueur to wet their throats, and each takes a turn to recount one of their astonishing exploits or adventures. The telling of the tale is prompted by one of the others, and the rest of the company may interrupt with questions and observations, as they see fit, and which it is the job of the tale's teller to rebut or avoid. When all are done, he who has told the best story buys drinks for his companions and, once the players are suitably re-fortified, the game begins again.

I confess that the inspiration for my en-gamification of this ancient and noble pursuit comes from a memorable evening I spent in a coaching-inn outside St Petersburg, in the late winter of 17—. Myself and several other travellers, many of us adventurers and soldiers of great renown, were caught there by a sudden blizzard and forced to spend the night there. However, the inn had a startling lack of rooms. Having agreed firstly to allow the ladies of the company to retire to the beds, the gentlemen agreed to a contest to see

even into France. Therefore, wherever I travel I find myself constantly prevailed upon to tell these stories, which requests I never refuse, being a man of noble breeding.

Accordingly, I find myself without a moment's peace from nincompoops who would hear once again the tale of how my companions and I were swallowed by a whale, or how I rode a cannonball through the sky over Constantinople. And often I am rewarded with naught but a small glass of the roughest brandy, or even nothing at all! Am I some marketplace storyteller to gambol for their amusement? No! I am a nobleman, a soldier and an adventurer, while they are ninnies all, and I will have no more to do with them, or be damned.

With the creation of this game (which I here humbly dedicate to the two people most important in its writing: viz. myself and the Empress of Russia) I mean to provide those who harass me with the means to tell astounding stories to each other out of my presence. This, not solely a great boon to civilization and a source of minor income to myself— which reason, I assure my diligent readers, was hindmost in who would receive the remaining unoccupied rooms, and who would be forced to repose in the stables or—worse—with the servants.

Accordingly we agreed to a contest or wager, and when it was discovered that no member of the company had cards, dice, teetotums, or backgammon board about them, we agreed to a contest of stories. Each one among our company took a turn at asking his neighbour to recount one of his most extraordinary adventures; and the others of us then tested the tale on the wheels of veracity, credibility, and laudability. When all were done a vote was taken and I, by sheer cunning, came third—which position exiled me to a tiny attic garret, the location of which allowed me to sneak out when the rest were asleep and enjoy a delightful night warmed by the caresses of the Duke of Normandy's daughter, whose beauty and room number I had noted before the storytelling began. In truth I tell you, it counts not whether you win or lose, but how you play the game.

This game itself follows in similar fashion, but without the presence of the noble Duke's aforementioned daughter. More's the pity.

Equipment

To play my game, you will require three or more stout friends, preferably of noble or at least gentle birth; a table; several chairs; a copious supply of drinks, preferably with a charming wench to serve it; and some coins to serve as stakes and to pay the reckoning when all is done. If you have such things to hand, then some parchment, pens and ink, a cold night, a roaring fire, and a good supply of food are also advised, and it is always provident to have a manservant or two in attendance. You will need naught else, save for a few trifles such as I shall set forth hereto.

Starting the Game

Gather the company and count its members. If it is late in the evening then ask a manservant or potboy to do it for you. Make sure that each player has a purse of coins before them equal to the total number of players—do *not* ask a servant to do this, servants being by nature a shifty and feckless lot who will as soon rob a man blind as help him out of a ditch, and I have been robbed in enough ditches to know.

If your company numbers less than five, then give each man five coins. If it numbers more than twenty, then think not of playing the game: instead I advise you to pool your purses, hire some mercenaries, and plan an invasion of Belgium.

The exact sort of coin you use is not important but I will make a few salient observations on the subject, drawn from my experiences of testing this game in the courts of the Orient where, despite the fact that I spoke none of their language and they none of mine, it played tolerably well. Firstly, all the coins should be of the same value, to save on arguments. Secondly, they need not actually be coins—I have played with coloured glass baubles in darkest Afrique, where the natives possess such things in abundance—they are given them by missionaries and, having eaten the missionaries, have no more use for the beads. Thirdly, anyone who proposes playing with paper money, fit for nothing more than wiping one's a–e, is clearly no gentleman and should be drummed out of your company and your club forthwith.

Beginning the Play

The player to start is the member of the company with the highest rank in society (standard protocol applies: religious titles are always deemed greater than hereditary titles, and those higher than military titles; if of similar rank then compare subsidiary titles, number of estates or centuries that the title has been in the family; youth defers to age; when in doubt the highest military decoration takes seniority; and for the rest I refer you to the works of Messrs Debretts or Burkes).

If by some mischance of birth or the poor organisation of your host you are all commoners then the first player shall be he who was wise enough to purchase this game. If several have, then I thank them all; if none have then I worry if you possess sufficient altitude of spirit to play a game such as this, which relies on nobility, generosity of character and purse, and not being a pinch-penny. If this manner of beginning is not agreeable, then the player to start should be he who was last to refill the company's glasses.

However you do so, once the person to start has been

determined he must begin the game. To do that, he must turn to the person sitting at his right hand and ask him to tell the company the tale of one of his famous adventures. By way of example, therefore:

"Dear Baron, entertain us with your recollections of the war of 17—, which you fought single-handed against the French and won," or:

> "Most honoured and noble prince, if you could refrain from the gracious compliments you are paying to my sister for a moment, mayhap you might satisfy our curiosity on how it was that you escaped from the prison of Akkra after you had been beheaded there two days earlier?"

For those unable to think of a sufficiently extraordinary and humorous topic for a story, I have included in an appendix some hundred of the subjects of my own exploits, a mere fraction of the total, which the less quick-witted player may use for inspiration. Whether you choose to use one of my examples or one of your own mind, remember at all times that the subject of the story to be told should only be revealed to the person who must tell it a few seconds before they start their narrative. Through this surprise, much good humour may be gained.

The player thus surprised must now recount the story— perhaps from an adventure of their own, or perhaps from the whole cloth of their imaginings. He may, however, pause for a moment of thought by commencing his tale by exclaiming, "Ah!" and then perhaps adding, "Yes!" Any further prevarication is unseemly. Throw a bread-roll at the fellow to hurry him along.

Tales should be short, of around five minutes, and told at a good pace without hesitation or undue pausings for thought. Inflections, gestures, mimes, props, and strange voices may all be used, although the narrator is warned not to go too far: he is, after all, born to the aristocracy—or pretending to be so. I well remember playing this game with the Grand Seignior of Turkey while he held me for ransom in Constantinople. For one story he hired a troupe of actors, a band of tumblers, conjurors, and dancing girls, and six elephants. The tale lasted three days and four nights, and when the company did not elect it the best, preferring my

own anecdote on how I discovered the seedless grape, he had us all beheaded . . . but enough of that for now.

What if the Story-Teller Should Pull Up?

If a player is unwilling to tell his story to the company, or falters in the recounting, then he may plead that his throat is too dry to tell the tale; and good manners demand that the company let him retire honourably. However, good manners also demand that he must obtain a drink to wet his throat, and in doing so it would be greatly impolite not to furnish the rest of the company with refreshment also. In short, a player may decline to tell a story, but must stand each member of the company a drink if he so do.

Having so declined, and the drinks having been ordered, the player in question should turn to the player on his right hand and, as is the form, propose the subject of a tale for them to tell.

Objections, Corrections, and Wagers

For the benefit of my duller readers I should point out that this section on objections, corrections, and wagers is the cleverest part of my game—although due to the ridiculous structure imposed on me by my diligent but perhaps over-strict publisher, I must wait until later to explain exactly why this is so.

The course of a narrative ne'er shall run smooth, as the poet has it, for the other players of the game may at any point interrupt the storyteller with an objection or a correction in the form of a wager. They may do this because they have spotted a flaw or inaccuracy in the teller's tale, because they wish to trip him up with spurious information, to test his truthfulness and mettle, or because the fellow is drawing dull and needs spice.

A wager is accomplished by the player pushing forward one (and never more than one) of the coins before him—we shall call it the stake—and breaking into the flow of the tale in a manner which some tutors of etiquette might consider abrupt.

A wager is cast in the manner of these examples:

Baron, I believe the King of the Moon at the time was Umbum-Mumbumbu, not Henry VIII as you say;

or:

You claim, my noble friend, that the Earth travels around the Sun but the Royal Academy has

comprehensively proved the opposite is true and Galileo's publications on the subject merely the result of an Opus Dei disinformation plot;

or:

But Count, it is well known that the Empress has a hatred of giraffes after her lap-dog was eaten by one;

or:

But my dear Duchess, at the time of which you speak the Colossus of Rhodes had been a fallen ruin for fifty years, so you could not possibly have climbed it;

or

Contessa, last week in this very chamber you claimed you had a mortal allergy to cats. How is it then that you say you married one?;

or any of a thousand thousand other relevant and curious facts. A wager need not be correct, but it should be interesting.

If the interrupter's objection or correction is deemed by the teller of the story to be accurate—in other words, if he

decides to build this new detail into his anecdote—then he must agree with his fellow and may keep his coin. However, he must then perforce explain how the events introduced in his fellow's interruption did not impede him in the adventure he is describing.

If, however, the teller deems the interruption to be inaccurate—if he does not wish to build the wager or objection into his story—then he may push his fellow's coin away *along with a coin of his own*, and inform the other that he is a dolt who clearly knows nothing of what he speaks and gets his information from the tittle-tattle of old maids in gin-houses.

In this latter case, if the one who interrupted is not prepared to stand this insult to his honour, he may add another coin to the pile and return it to the story-teller, making his case for the objection more forcefully and returning the insult with interest. The story-teller may again turn the wager away with another coin and another insult; and so on until one side withdraws his objection and accepts the insult (thus keeping the pile of coins), or one party has exhausted his funds but will not stand down—in which case a duel must be fought. (See

"Duelling," a section I believe I shall enjoy writing.)

To give a sample of this in the passage of a game, which I have carefully based on one of the examples I gave above, imagine that the Duchess of Sutherland is telling a tale based on my noted adventure wherein, due to a mistranslation of the proverb, I led the populace of Rhodes to Rome. To give a snippet of the story, as the Duchess might tell it:

> *Duchess:* "... I required a view over the city of Rhodes from the highest vantage point it offered, and so I ordered my sedan-chair to be carried to the top of the mighty Colossus that stands astride the harbour there."

> *Lord Hampton* (*interrupting most rudely, with his mouth full of petits-fours*): "But Duchess, at the time of which you speak the Colossus of Rhodes had been a fallen ruin for centuries, so you could not possibly have climbed it." As he says this, he pushes a sovereign toward her.

What is the Duchess to do? She is in a quandary. For the sake of her honour she must continue but that needs an investment of one coin. Shall she make that investment? She shall!

> *Duchess:* "My dear Lord Hampton, I know not the state of your eyes when you saw no Colossus of Rhodes, but I suspect that they were befuddled by the strong wine of that place, or possibly turned by one of the women of ill-repute who frequent the harbour area." She places a second sovereign atop his, and pushes them back to him.

A spirited riposte! Will a man of my Lord Hampton's blood stand for such as this? He will not! With a flourish he swallows his cake, adds another coin to the stake (making three in all), returns it to the Duchess and rejoins thus:

> *Lord Hampton:* "On the contrary, since many of our most outstanding historians have described the fall of the Colossus some years before your noble birth, if we are to believe the age you claim, might I suggest that you had become so enchanted with one of the burly sailors of Rhodes that you climbed upon his torso, thinking it was that of the Colossus?"

Ha! An accusation of infidelity to the memory of her late husband, the notorious Duke! All eyes are now on the Duchess. Pretty blushes tint her face, just as the dew of dawn tints the perfect pink of a new-opened rose at the break of day (a fine arrangement of words, if I say so myself). Hurriedly she counts her money—but alas that morning she has bought herself a new muff and some dogskin gloves, and her purse is near empty. Prudence is her middle name, literally as well as figuratively, and prudence dictates that she must accept this insult, lest she bankrupt herself. There are now three coins at stake; if she gives way then they are hers. The temptation is too strong for one of her gentle sex and she snatches up the stake with the following:

> *Duchess:* "Not at all, dear Lord Hampton, but when I refer to the Colossus of Rhodes I mean, of course, my friend Thomas Highfellow, the tallest man in the world, who had recently made his home in the city. At my request he stood astride the entrance to the harbour, one foot on either shore, and I instructed the carriers of my sedan-chair to climb up his massive frame until we could see the entire city. As I was saying, we had just reached his knee when —"

> *Baron Edgington:* (pushing forward a coin) "But surely, Duchess . . ."

At that point we must leave the Duchess and her troubled tale—which if she had but stayed on the path of my original she would have put aside all objection and opposition without troubling her exquisite brow or her largely vacant mind—and return to the tedium of describing the rules. This is dull work, and not the stuff for which the noble-born brain was made. Rules be d—ned! I am in the spirit for a digression.

On Being Noble

I understand that there are many among the readers of this game who have not been blessed with the good fortune that smiled upon myself at my birth. Indeed, in this age of the printing press in which even the lowliest-born may be taught to read and write a little, it is possible that this book has fallen into the hands of some in whose blood the signs of greatness do not flow, whose minds and souls lack the clarity and sure-headedness that comes only

after generations of the finest breeding and tutelage—to wit, in short, commoners. Such people are not to be despised, but pitied, and it is for them that the section is intended, as I describe the rudiments of what a man of lowly origins requires to attain the stature of a perfect specimen of the noble order such as myself.

Noblemen conform to a template laid out by Almighty God and first described by Baldesar Castiglione in his work *The Book of the Courtier*. His words hold true today, despite the fact that due to a misfortune of birth he was Italian. I shall take the liberty of quoting that august gentleman without asking his permission, since he has been dead close on two hundred years. It is true that in the past I have played chess with Pythagoras (I won), Julius Caesar (I lost), and Cleopatra (match abandoned), all several centuries after their respective deaths, but that was with the aid of an Indian mystic whom I subsequently converted to the Protestant faith, whereupon he became unable to perform any of his pagan rituals—but once again I am meandering.

superior. And as we read of Alcibiades, that he surpassed all those people among whom he lived, and each time in regard to what they claimed to be best at, so this courtier of ours should outstrip all others, and in regard to the things they know well. . . .

"He should never fail to behave in a commendable manner and should rule all his actions with that good judgement which will not allow him to take part in any foolishness. Let him laugh, jest, banter, romp, and dance, though in a fashion that always reflects good sense and discretion, and let him say and do everything with grace."

To this I would add: that the nobleman is the highest of God's creations, brought to a peak of excellence through centuries of good breeding, education, culture, and diet; and he should never forget that.

The nobleman sets an example to the rest of humanity. He must be at all times civil and courteous, even to his social inferiors, servants, and the better sort of foreigners. His behaviour is the touchstone of all civilisation, for without nobility there would be no patronage of the sciences, the arts, literature, or music; and only common arts like the theatre, country dancing, politics, and the mercantile trades would remain.

Naturally no nobleman has any truck with magic, on the entirely reasonable grounds that it does not exist. Science, logic, philosophy, and enlightenment all demonstrate that it cannot work—a view to which I subscribe, although I am at a loss to explain why, after insulting some gypsies in Roumania, I spent a week believing I was a sheep.

Although you, my reader, may not be in any whit like the paragons of humanity I have delined above, in order to play my game you must pretend to be nobly born and, in telling the stories of the great adventures you are claiming to have made, you should portray yourself and your actions as noble in thought and deed. You may find the experience disquieting, but I hope most earnestly that it may serve as an interesting lesson, and that it may teach the most doltish amongst my readers some decent manners.

Naturally, any nobleman worth his salt will be accompanied on his travels and adventures by servants and travelling companions. As befits this, there will follow in the next section a discourse on the nature of

Castiglione wrote—in the form of a most amusing conversation between a prince and his companions—"His first duty is to know how to handle expertly any kind of weapon, either on foot or mounted, to understand all their finer points, and to be especially well informed about all those weapons commonly used among gentlemen. For apart from their use in war, when perhaps the finer points may be neglected, often differences arise between one gentleman and another and lead to duels, and very often the weapons used are those that come immediately to hand.

"I also believe that it is of the highest importance to know how to wrestle" and here I shall pass over a few lines, for they teach us nothing about gentlemen but much about Italians. He resumes: "He should put every effort and diligence into surpassing the rest just a little in everything, so that he may always be recognised as companions, during which another opportunity shall be taken to be gratuitously rude about the French.

Companions

As he wends his way through life's travails, a nobleman must perforce be accompanied by many companions, who will assist him, support him, keep him company, and enliven his spirits with their wit and learning. Companions are men of rare abilities, and some so rare that they are positively unique. I well remember my dear friend Octavus who assisted me so ably in the capture of the entire Turkish fleet at Ankara by means of his prodigious breath, whereby he blew all the ships from their moorings and down the coast, where they became entrapped in a fence of fishing-nets which I had stretched across the sea. Or, for another nautical example, my man Wolfgang's great skill as an artist aided me in scaring the French fleet into full retreat by painting a most realistic facsimile of a thousand Royal Navy frigates, using as his canvas the White Cliffs of Dover . . . but that is another story, and shall be told another time.

Companions are, in short, the men and women who may help you in your adventures. Thus, should your narrative require a person of prodigious abilities to help you from a particular escapade, you may introduce one such as you wish. But take care not to use the services of more than one such companion in each story, for so to do would be considered greedy.

(It need not be said that companions are not servants. A nobleman has servants as a French dog has fleas, and if they be French servants, they will serve the nobleman in much the same office as the flea serves the dog: viz. a constant source of irritation and nuisance. I remember one French manservant who served me during my campaigning on the Russian front; he drank lustily, swore abominably, scorched my shirts, knew not a handkerchief from a hot-air balloon, and at length revealed himself to be a woman, a fish-seller's wife from Calais, and mightily in love with me. This would have been the source of much embarrassment to us both, had he not been conveniently hanged for treason. I will not deny that it was I who planted on his person the map of the secret tunnel under

the English Channel, which I had acquired by—ah, but once more I have strayed off the path.

(Which reminds me in timely fashion that this chapter itself is naught but an extended digression, and I should—if only to placate my outraged publisher, whose cheeks are so flushed with red anger—like rosy-bottomed Dawn after she has been spanked by her father the Sun for dallying too long with her lover—who I must confess was myself—and not attending to her business of breaking the day for two and a half weeks—my publisher, I say, whose eyes flash with rage and hair stands on end in resemblance of the giant hedgehog I once defeated in Scotland by turning it inside out, thus stabbing it to death on its own spines—my publisher I fear shall die of an apoplexy unless I end this digression, close these brackets and return to the subject of Objections, Corrections and Wagers forthwith. Frankly, I am finding this business of rules not a little tedious, particularly now that this bottle of cognac is finished. Yes, that was a hint, which I observe he has not taken. What? Oh, closing the brackets. Very well.))

369

Baron Munchausen

Objections, Corrections, and Wagers, continued

As all those of truly noble blood are aware, there are a handful of wagers and objections that should never be made.

Principally, in the round of insults, no nobleman would ever insult another's breeding, his pedigree, or his veracity. In plain terms, you may not directly call another player a liar (although you may safely question his accuracy or remind him of facts he may have forgot), doubt his claim to noble rank, or insult his mother. Indeed I lie: you may do any of these things, but so to do is proof of your utter caddishness, and the person you have insulted is at liberty to challenge you at once to a duel. I shall expand on the subject of duels shortly, a topic on which I am particularly well versed since the day in Vienna when I insulted the King's 47th Hussars at the moment that very regiment was parading outside my window, and I was forced to fight a duel with every one of them, at the same time. I confess I am looking forward to the chapter on duels with no little relish, but like a stubborn schoolboy I must finish my bread-and-cheese before I may have my plum. Onwards! There is not far to go.

It may seem strange that if the wagerer loses his bet then he recovers his stake, or if he wins then his stake is lost. This is so, but when the wagerer makes his claim, he is in truth saying, "Ha, my fine fellow, here is a pretty tid-bit that I wager you cannot make a part of your story," and if it is pushed back to him then indeed he has won the wager and doubled his stake.

It is therefore clear that, since money is the way that the game is won or lost, and making that wagers is the only way

that the money on the table may be moved around, a wagerer should essay to make wagers which he can win—that is to say, which the story-teller cannot build into his tale, and must turn away. Meanstwhile a great story-teller will construct a tale that stretches the cords of credibility until they twang, so as to invite the greatest possible number of wagers, which the teller has with great cunning already anticipated. Herein lies the skill of my game; that is to say, one part of the skill of my game, the other part to be explained in further chapters. Duller readers need have no fear: I shall take pains to point out these tactical points whenever one occurs, that they may have the satisfaction of knowing wherein these points lie, if not the wit to use them in play.

Duelling

(I am told it is the fashion to name this part of the rules the "Combat System." It is an ugly phrase that stumbles off the tongue and sounds like a Prussian manual on elementary sabre-play. I disdain it.)

As I have observed earlier in this volume, if in the matter of an objection or correction a party should insult another's veracity, title, or pedigree, then the injured party has the right—nay, the obligation—to challenge his insulter to a duel. This may also come about if during a wager one party finds his purse exhausted but does not have the grace or good sense to withdraw, in which case he may demand that the other stand down or face him on the field of honour.

This will cause an unfortunate interruption in the flow of the game's stories, but so be it: where the honour of a nobleman is concerned, everything else must stand aside while he defends himself. Fighting over matters of honour is a dangerous business which may bring poverty, injury, death or—a worse horror—ridicule to the participants, but it is as necessary as beefsteak to an Englishman, gold to a Swiss, or avoiding baths to a Frenchman.

The rules for fighting a duel are simplicity itself. Once the insult has been made and the injured party has issued the challenge, the two duellists must choose friends or companions to be their seconds, agree on a weapon—rapiers are traditional, and come easily to hand at most parties or places where the genteel and well-educated gather—and then go outside to a convenient courtyard or colonnade, where they fight. The duel need only progress until first blood or incapacitation, as this is naught but a friendly disagreement, but I have seen duels fought to dismemberment or death over such matters as a carelessly split infinitive.

As the art of duelling is so well known in all the civilised countries of the globe, and so well known to all people of good breeding, I need not describe it here—Ah, my publisher reminds me that this game is destined for the unwashed hands and uneducated eyes of the lower orders, so perforce I must describe it after all. Anyone with a hereditary peerage or who has ever served as an officer in one of the better armies of the world (German, Prussian, English, Spanish, Italian, or for that matter Cathayan, Ethiopian, Persian—indeed, now that I think of it, all but the Turks, Poles, and Irish) should move on to the next section. The rest of you, read on.

The art of duelling is one of some great refinement, and is conveyed equally by good teaching, fine upbringing, the proper blood, and the willingness to spill some of it. There are any number of textbooks on the subject, which I advise any novice to purchase and, if you are serious about your studies, to read. A tutor is necessary for the perfection of the art—I recommend a German duelling-master for brutality, a Spaniard for flair or, for matches which may last up to five days and either be rained off or end in a draw, an Englishman. You should also set aside three, perhaps four years for study, and a decade for practice.

Naturally the procedure of duelling is fraught with danger and difficulty. A number of unenlightened states have declared duelling illegal, so the participants run the risk of interruption

by members of the lower orders brandishing truncheons and warrants, which is enough to put even the finest duellist off his stroke. I have found few remedies to this, save the usual methods of duelling in a secluded spot, making the combat as short as possible, and keeping a hot-air balloon tethered nearby in case a swift exit is required.

I had planned to digress here on the matter of seconds, the proper choosing thereof, and how exactly you can find one at two o'clock of the morning in Prague. Despite the lack of scholarship on this subject, and the undoubted benefit that such a section would add to this book, I have been persuaded—under my strongest protest, I must add—to omit it by the same bleary-eyed publisher who not three paragraphs ago convinced me that such a thing should be included. His wits, I fear, are addled by cheap gin and the profits from his last tawdry publication. Nevertheless it is my contention that my public would wish to see such a book, embellished with several anecdotes and histories of my duelling prowess, and further illustrated by my friend Master Doré. If you agree, gentle reader, then write to the publisher, demanding to see this new work. Its publication would be doubly assured if you would be good enough to subscribe to it: a mere matter of three guineas, which you should enclose—take care to wrap them well and send them via a trusted messenger.

Duelling for Cowards

If you are weak of blood, soft of flesh or lilied of the liver, or—by way of furnishing you with an excuse—you are in a hurry to finish the game, or there are ladies present who would be shocked at the sight of blood, or you are unable to retain the rôle you are playing at the thought of noble

combat, and find yourself reduced to a common peasant once more, or if you are Welsh; if any of these things be true then you may avoid the physical combat of a duel. Instead, just as you are playing at being a nobleman in my game, you may play at fighting a duel with a set of rules I have devised for that very purpose.

I say "devised." In fact I was taught the game by an inhabitant of the Dog-Star, whom I encountered a great distance from his home, on the last occasion I visited the Moon. I understand that the game was originally taught to these astral canines by no less a traveller than Vasco da Gama who, on his final voyage, set his course towards the island of Ceylon, missed by several thousand leagues, and sailed off the edge of the world. I blame the shoddy quality of Portuguese sea-charts for this, though doubtless the Portuguese would blame the compass, or the wind, or the water, or the Ceylonese, or the shape of the world, or the Moon, or anything else that might absolve their own slack-handed workmanship.

Da Gama called the rules "Bottle-Glass-Throat" (he was Portuguese, as I mentioned), and the those of the Dog-Star know it as "Bone-Stick-Ball." I shall call it "Knife-Stone-Paper," and . . . Ah. My publisher tells me I have been overtaken by fate, that the game is already known by that name to all the world, and I should strike out the paragraph above. I shall do no such thing; I shall let it stand as a treatise on the history of the game, and scholars may depend on my well-known love of the truth if they doubt any part of it. None the less, I admit myself disgruntled by this turn of events, and will break my narrative here to restore my spirits with a hearty dinner.

* * *

I return much refreshed for my interval, although I must confess I have drunk deep of Lord Bootlebury's dark port and his youngest daughter's tawny eyes, as big and deep as those of the stag I killed in the Black Forest by stuffing it with cake—its flavour, I must say, was not entirely enhanced by this method of dispatch—and accordingly I am distracted and have lost the thread. No matter. I will instead regale you with a story of my travels until the plot returns to me, or my publisher wakes from the noisy slumber he has embarked on at the far end of the table to remind me where we were.

I recall a time in the winter of 17—, when I was riding into the interior parts of Russia. I found travelling on horseback rather unfashionable in winter; therefore I submitted, as I always do, to the custom of the country, took a single horse-sledge, and drove briskly towards St Petersburg. I do not exactly recollect whether it was in Eastland or Jugemanland, but I remember that in the midst of a dreary forest, I spied a terrible wolf making after me, with all the speed of ravenous winter hunger. He soon overtook me. There was no possibility of escape. Mechanically I laid myself down flat in the sledge, and let my horse run for our safety.

What I wished, but hardly hope or expected, happened immediately after. The wolf did not mind me in the least, but took a leap over me, and falling furiously on the horse, began instantly to tear and devour the hind part of the poor animal, which ran the faster for his pain and terror. Thus unnoticed and safe myself, I lifted my head slyly up, and with horror I beheld that the wolf had ate his way into the horse's body; it was not long before he had fairly forced himself into it, when I took my advantage, and fell upon him with the but-end of my whip.

This unexpected attack in his rear frightened him so much, that he leaped forward with all his might; the horse's carcass dropped on the ground; but in his place the wolf was in the harness, and I on my part whipping him continually, we both arrived in full career safe to St Petersburg, contrary to our respective expectations, and very much to the astonishment of—

I recall it now; we were discussing duelling. Rather, I was discussing, you were learning, and my publisher was hogging the brandy and making interruptions. He is a most irritating fellow, but he has now left for the tavern on the corner, and I may continue.

Knife-stone-paper is the game. On a count of three, one should form one's hand into the shape of a blade, a stone, or a piece of paper; the rule being that knife beats paper (it cuts it); paper beats stone (it wraps it); and knife beats stone (it whets it . . . No, I have it wrong. Ask your manservant how the d—ned game plays). The faint-hearted *faux*-duellists must play three hands of it, discounting draws, and whosoever wins two or more is declared the victor. I could say more, but I will waste no further words on this subject, destined as it is only for cissies and or he who is afraid of the sight of a little blood, or of adding another death or two to his conscience. Real noblemen have no such qualms, particularly if they are dealing with peasants or foreigners. Play your rôle properly or not at all, say I.

The Result of a Duel

The results of a duel can be deadly, even if you lack the esprit to essay it in the proper fashion. Assuming that both parties are still alive, the upshot is as follows: the loser must make over his entire purse to the victor, and must retire from the game. If one of the two parties has lost his life in the conflict, then his second should carry out these instructions. However, his bounty—if such they have—remains untouched.

A final word on duelling: it is considered unsporting to provoke a duel or issue a challenge once all the stories are finished and the bounty is being dispensed and received. I remember one memorable game I played with a crew of swarthy pirates, while they and I were trapped inside the belly of a mighty sea-beast which had regrettably swallowed every man of us—a not unusual happening, I learn from my conversations with maritime adventurers, but peculiar in this instance in that we had been climbing the Matterhorn at the time of our ingestion.

We had reached the end of the game and, as was only to be expected, the coins were piling into my bounty, when the pirate captain, angered at the failure of his tale of derring-do, drew his cutlass and, with a mighty oath, swung it at my head. I stepped away and the blade sliced through the great beast's spleen, on which I had been seated, which gushed

forth such quantities of bile that—ah, but my publisher, who has just returned from the tavern with the smell of the tap on his breath and the rouge of the tap-girl on his lips, reminds me that my deadline is close, and my remaining pages are running short, and I must cease my digression forthwith. As before, if any of my readers should wish to hear the remainder of the story, I will be happy to recount it over dinner at their club and their expense.

Now, perforce, I must move to explain how a story is brought to a conclusion and how a game is won, in which—fear not, gentle reader, I have not forgot—I shall explain what on earth a "bounty" is.

Finishing a Story

In my experience a good tale should last no more than five minutes; for beyond that the listeners begin to grow bored and listless and talk among themselves and throw bread rolls and play at dice or cards and call for musicians and dance upon the table and seduce the hostess and distribute seditious or revolutionary literature and plot land-wars in Asia, and other such distractions as might put the finest raconteur off his stride—particularly if he has designs on the hostess himself.

The story-teller should therefore bring his tale to its natural conclusion at its proper length, and in a way that brings the greatest enjoyment and astonishment to his listeners. At this point the tale is done, the audience should respond with a few hearty "Huzzah!"'s and exclamations of "By my oath, Baron, that is the most remarkable story I have ever heard, and I drink to it. More wine!" which is always pleasing.

However, it has not escaped my eye that there are several story-tellers who either cannot tell when their story has

finished, and must perforce prattle on until Doomsday or until the wine is finished; or who are so ill-skilled in the art of racontage that their audience cannot tell when their tale is done. I have applied my military mind to both these problems, and the solutions are given below.

If a story-teller finishes his tale and there is none to cry "Huzzah!", for they are all asleep or otherwise occupied, then he should signify to the company that they have come to an end by standing and loudly proclaiming: "That is my story, true in every word, and if any man doubts it I'll make him drink a barrel of brandy in a single swallow." This serves as a signal to the company, by its volume if not by its words, that they should rouse themselves from the torpor which a dull tale invokes, and muster a few token "Huzzah!"s to signal they understand the tale is over.

However a tale ends, once the usual toasts have been drunk (to the story, the story-teller, the host, the monarch, the most attractive woman present, the second most attractive woman present, the most attractive woman in the story, absent friends, *et cetera*) the one who has just finished his narration must turn to the person sitting at his right hand and, in an interested tone (for to do otherwise could be taken as an insult and lead to a regrettable duel, or a mild-mannered bun-fight, or any other manner of unnecessary distraction from the business at hand), say, "So, Baron, tell us the story of . . ." and here, as at the start of the game, describe a suitable adventure, whether from one of my own escapades, or from the list in the appendix of this work, or from his own experiences or imaginings. The person thus addressed should pick up the tale and proceed as described above, with the other players preparing wagers, interruptions, duels and so forth to put him off the stride of his description.

If, however, a story-teller should have become so wrapped up in his narrative that he has failed to see the company has lost interest and has commenced cock-fighting or badger-baiting instead, then any of the company may interrupt at a suitable juncture with the words, "That reminds me of the story I heard told of Baron N— M— (naming the player sitting to the right of the present story-teller) in which he . . ." and names an adventure. With that he must put forward one coin. If others of the company agree then they should add coins of their own; and if fully half the company is in agreement that the mantle of story-teller should pass, then Baron N— M— commences the tale of the new adventure. The previous story-teller, overcome by shame and disgrace, may add the company's money to his purse by way of recompense or, if he feels his honour has been insulted, may decline and challenge his interrupter to a duel (*quod vide*). If fewer than half the company pledge coins to the cause then the accumulation is given to the pot-boy, to pay for more wine.

I see that thus far I have failed to explain the bounty. Never fear. There are still several pages to go, and I am certain it shall follow in the next chapter.

Determining the Winner

When all are done with their stories, there should be a moment of pause. Sit back in your chair and permit the pot-boy to recharge your glass. Think on the stories you have heard, and decide in your own mind which was the best. If you are of a scholarly bent you may wish to debate the matter with your companions, making reference to Aristotle's *Ars Poetica* and the recent critical works of the poet Dryden. Or if not, then not. 'Tis of no importance.

While you are so debating, either with your soul or with

your fellows, count up the coins you have left in your purse. These now become the tokens with which each of the company shall decide whose story is the finest, the most outstanding, the most memorable and most authentic, and the most heroic, showing its teller in the finest light. In common parlance, you shall each vote for a winner.

Commencing with the person who began the game, and in rotation and in turn, each player must take his stack of coins, and with words such as: "Gentlemen, I have never heard such a surprising collection of stories, but upon my honour the tale of Baron—(here he names the nobleman whose anecdote he considers the finest of the evening) is the most astonishing tale I have encountered in my life." If you are English you may wish to add "'Pon my soul, wot wot" here, but *Deo gratia* most of us are not.

(My publisher is protesting, and English. My explanation must perforce pause a moment while I quiet him by refilling his glass with the last of his father's cognac.)

With these words, the player places his entire purse in front of the fellow who he has just named. It must be all of his coins; it does not befit a gentleman to split his bets or spread his favours too widely. Nor should the recipient add the coins to his own purse. Be not hasty; simply leave them where they lie. They shall be called, at last, the "bounty."

Once every player has said his piece, cast his vote and distributed his bounty (and I must perforce remind the sluggards, commoners, and plebians among my readers that no true nobleman would even consider the idea of voting for himself), then each player should count out the number of coins cast for him and his story. (*Sotto voce*, naturally; there is nothing so unbecoming as a nobleman who cannot count but out loud; and if your grasp of numerology does not extend beyond five then you should immediately give up all thoughts of playing this game and find yourself a pastime more suited to your nature; such as turnip-farming, bear-baiting, or local government.)

Ending the Game

The player with the greatest bounty is declared to have won the game. All give a rousing "Huzzah!" and more wine is ordered to drink to the health of the victor. It is accepted as a point of etiquette that the victor shall pay for this wine,

and it is also accepted that the money they have accumulated as their bounty may not be— nay, is never—sufficient to cover the cost. But that is of no matter: we are noblemen and we overlook such trifles as fair payment, money, *et cetera*. Besides, the sweet taste of victory will more than wipe out the sour tang of the evening's reckoning, when the innkeeper brings it.

At this point the game is over.

Should the majority of the company wish, and not be so out of pocket or in its cups that it cannot continue, another round of the game may be played. The victor of the previous round—being the person who has most recently recharged the company's glasses—shall commence the play.

A Word on Tactics

It should be noted—indeed, it will already have been noted by the more intelligent and well-bred readers—that there are two ways to play my game. Firstly, one may play with ultimate strategy and guile, in order to relieve as many of the company of as much of their wealth as is strategically possible, to amass the greatest purse. Secondly, one may tell the finest story one is able. Naturally all players should aim to tell the finest story, for that is

the only way that they may win the contest. If you play strategically so that you gain the greatest purse, then I can assure you that you are sure to lose the game; because your purse must be given to someone else, and because you will have aroused such enmity in the rest of the company that none will cast their vote for you. Yet by this Machiavellian tactic you can give yourself the honour of determining who shall win the game.

Naturally, although many noblemen and particularly their sons are known to be profligate with their money, it is poor play to empty your purse before the end of the game, and worse play to spend them before you have your turn at story-telling. Without coins you can not interrupt a comrade, rebut interruptions to your own tale, or cast votes for the winner. And, since it is beneath a nobleman to either beg or steal, once you have no funds then the only way to accrue more is to tell a fine story that attracts many wagers from your fellows, and turn those wagers aside with the dexterity of your tongue. (I feel an urge to digress here about the dexterity of tongues I have known,

but I shall forbear. Ladies may read this.)

In the final round of the game, if your company has admitted women to the play, I do not recommend that you vote for your paramour, or for the member of the company who has taken your fancy. In my experience it rarely leads to success; and your fellows will notice and make fun of you for some weeks.

In Conclusion

In these pages I have essayed three things. Firstly, to bring—what is it now, man?

My apologies. I had thought we had run our course, but it has been slurred in my ear that I have neglected a section which my contract obliges me to write. I will be most glad to have this game finished. Such things are not suited to a noble temperament; which admirably explains why so few publishers have ever been elevated to the ranks of nobility.

Background

I wish to explain that this section has been imposed on me: my publisher tells me that such things are these days expected of the creator of a game. For the life of me I cannot understand the reason or purpose for enquiring into my background: I am a nobleman and a Munchausen and those facts, which suffice as my passport across all the borders and into the royal chambers in every country in Europe, should surely be sufficient here.

Ah. I am informed by the mangy-headed fellow that he believes I have missed the point. Naturally I have done no such thing; although I may be guilty of a little willful misinterpretation of his meaning. However, I suggest that we retitle the section "Historical Setting" and start again.

Historical Setting

Much better.

It is, of course, the eighteenth century; for surely there has never been a finer time to be alive. More particularly, it is the year of our Lord 17—. The Renaissance is over, the power of the Roman Church is crumbling, and Europe is civilised at last. The Turks are in Constantinople and indeed all over the place, the French are making trouble again, Sweden is in decline, the Russians are invading the

Crimea at regular intervals, the King of England is both German and mad—both fine conditions for ruling that isle—and somewhere across the Atlantic Ocean a few colonists are beginning to think a little too much of their own importance.

The wonder of the age is, without question, the marvellous flying-balloon of the brothers Montgolfier, which can carry people and animals high into the air in perfect safety, transporting them over cities, rivers, forests and mountains, and even—it is said by some, including myself—as high as the Moon itself. Though the brothers devised it solely as a way of leaving France, the flying balloon stands as the greatest invention of this age of marvels.

Speaking of France, it is troubled greatly by short men wearing tall hats who, in an effort to bring the nobility down to their own level, have chopped off the heads of many of that country's finest citizens. This has led to many escapades for young bloods who wish to prove themselves by rescuing the younger and more beautiful members of French society from such a fate, and over whom they inevitably lose their heads one way or another. It has also led to a regrettable surfeit of French aristocracy in the coffee-houses and salons of Europe. However, it is to our great fortune that many of these refugees have brought their chefs with them.

Science, discovery and philosophy are striding forward apace. The French have created a rational system of measuring all things, which they call the Metrics. It will never catch on. Now that the Australias have been located, they are being put to use as a depository for all the undesirables of Europe. A young English fellow called Watt has created a giant kettle which can power a factory—by providing enough hot tea to keep the workers contented, I imagine—and another named Stephenson is said to have made one that runs on wheels, for the purpose of scaring horses and running over members of Parliament. This is an enterprise to be applauded. Meanwhile, the Royal Society is pursuing a scheme for extracting sunbeams from cucumbers, and claim much progress.

Those of the lower orders who believe that money is an acceptable substitute for nobility have been swift to take advantage of these innovations, and are busy building

factories and employing women called Jenny to spin cotton for them. Some fool in Norfolk has entirely spoiled the winter's hunting by ploughing up the fallow fields and growing turnips on them. Much of London's trade seems centred on pieces of paper bearing promises to do with a great bubble which appeared in the South Seas some years ago. I confess I understand none of this, but it appears that Britain may be developing an empire of some kind—based upon, of all things, trade, money, and root vegetables. May G–d help us all.

In Conclusion

In these pages I have essayed three things. Firstly, to bring a little of the excitement of my life into the lives of others, so that they too may appreciate my astonishing adventures the better. Secondly, to show the lower orders a little of how their betters live, behave, and think, in my attempt to heighten their understanding of exactly why it is that we are superior to them, and thus to avoid, I hope, any further outbreaks of the recent unpleasant doings that have been going on in France of late.

And thirdly, by giving you an appreciation of myself and my adventures, I hope to rekindle the spark of adventurousness in the soul of man—and the occasional rare woman; it being my opinion that too much adventurousness in a woman is generally a bad thing—which has become so dampened of late by lumpen pursuits such as theatre-going, novel-reading, and the playing of card-games. Cease using the fruits of the imaginations of others; instead use the visions of great achievements that my game has placed in your mouth to spur yourself onwards to great thoughts, great deeds, and great actions.

Every word I have ever spoken is completely true (barring three) and I am by no means an exceptional man, I have merely lived in exceptional times. Any man of noble spirit, living in times such as these, could have achieved the same. My deeds are only known so widely because I have had what some would term the ill-manners to recount them over a drink or two. And I say that you too, gentle reader, have the capacity within you to experience adventures as great as my own, if only you have the ambition to raise your sights high enough.

One man, it is said, may change the world. I deny that I ever did so—I may have saved it once or twice, but that is not the same thing—but the ability is within you to perform that, or any other feat; save one. It is not, I regret to tell you, within your capacity to make love to the Empress of Russia, for the reason that her honour is under my protection and sirrah, if I catch you near her, I will give you a drubbing which will so bruise your feet and your a—e that you will be incapable of either standing up or sitting down, and will therefore be forced to spend a month spinning in the air like a top, a foot off the ground. Consider that a warning.

Mendace veritas!

Baron Munchausen, by his hand, this year of our Lord 17—

Appendix 1 — Tell us, Baron, the story of . . .

How you discovered the source of the Nile by accident.

How you survived the attack of a lion and a crocodile at the same time.

How your hunting-dog Beauty caught seven hares at once.

How you circumnavigated the world without leaving your house.

How you cured the Empress of France's hiccoughs from the other side of the English Channel.

How you survived being swallowed by a whale; and what you encountered inside its mighty belly.

How you were able to reach the moon using only twenty feet of rope—and how you returned.

The time that your fur coat attacked you on the road to Cologne.

How you accidentally started the Americas' war of independence.

How you convinced the King of Sardinia to become your footservant.

The occasion on which you gave birth to an elephant.

The occasion on which you duelled all the members of a regiment of French hussars simultaneously.

How it was that you met Helen of Troy.

How you saved the life of a man who had died fifty years ago.

The time you ate the King of Norway's horse in most curious circumstances.

How you singed the King of Spain's beard.

Your discovery of the lost city of Atlantis, and why it sank ten minutes afterwards.

How, due to a meal of oatcakes, you destroyed the city of Tobruk.

How your horse came to be hanging from a church steeple, and how you freed it.

How it was you were able to pass as a native among the little people of Lilliput.

The time your post-horn played for half an hour with nobody blowing it.

How you recognised a sheep as the long-lost son of the Earl of Bath.

Your prodigious marksmanship, and how it saved last year's champagne vintage from ruination.

How you started the French Revolution for a bet, and who won.

How you earned the hatred of every freemason in Poland.

Why, during thunderstorms, you insist on riding stark naked.

How you forced the surrender of the Turkish armies at Constantinople with a chicken.

Why you have drunk every bottle of cognac bottled in the year 17— in the world.

Why it is that in France you are known as the Fifth Musketeer.

How a portrait of Henry VIII saved you from attack by lions.

The sad occasion of your funeral, and how it is that you are sitting here now.

Why you showed the Empress of Sweden's bloomers to the town of Dusseldorf.

How you bear such a striking resemblance to the Sphinx of the Egyptian desert.

How you used a cannon to spy out the Turkish lines at the siege of Constantinople.

How you came to be burnt at the stake for witchcraft in Barcelona, and how you survived.

Your hunting trip that led to the downfall of the Ming dynasty in China.

Your discovery of the effects of lion-dung as a cure for rheumatism.

How you burst the great bubble which appeared in the South Sea some years ago.

How you proved to the Royal Society that the world is not round.

The mistake with your laundry which saved the court of France from drowning.

How and why it was that you once had to fight a duel with yourself—to the death.

The incident where you accidentally impregnated the Pope.

The occasion in Paris where you became an ape for a week.

How a bottle of schnapps in Russia saved you from a beheading by the Turkish Sultan.

Why every blacksmith in London owes you three guineas.

How the notebooks of Leonardo da Vinci helped you to prevent the assassination of our beloved monarch.

How you righted the Leaning Tower of Pisa.

Your discovery of the Floating Island of Cheese in the southern seas, and how you escaped from it.

Why the keeper of the Royal Botanical Gardens at Kew has classified your moustache as a herb.

Why you once swam the entire length of the Danube—and how.

How you survived your descent into the volcano Vesuvius.

What happened when the primitives of the Polynesian islands offered you as a sacrifice to their native gods.

How, after a mighty earthquake, you arranged for Rome to be rebuilt in a day.

How you seduced the Queen of the Moon, even though she stands three hundred feet tall.

The matter of the dog who spoke French and the tragic history of its master.

How you became King of Mkolo-Mbeleland.

How you stopped a charging herd of elephants from destroying Edinburgh.

The most outrageous wager you ever took.

How you saved the life of the King of the Cats.

What became of the arms of the Venus de Milo.

How you located the Garden of Eden, and what you found there.

Why the race of pygmy-people from Yolimba-Yp worship you as their god.

What caused the fall of London Bridge, and how you survived it.

The duel you were forced to fight against a swarm of bees.

Your invasion of Italy with an army of three hundred tigers.

How you repeated Moses's trick of parting the waters of the Red Sea.

How you visited both North and South Poles during dinner one evening.

How you lifted the ancient curse on the royal family of Sweden.

How it was that you learned to speak the language of the giraffe.

How your life was saved by the ticking of your pocket-watch.

How you and three rabbits lifted the siege of Gibraltar.

How it was that you and not Francis Bacon wrote the plays of William Shakespeare.

How you recovered the gold of the sunken Spanish Armada without wetting a hair of your head.

Why, when you appeared before the court of the King of the Low Countries, did all present think you were a ghost.

How you stole the Queen of France's diamond studs from under her very nose.

Your encounter with the Sirens of legend, and how you responded to their seductive songs.

How you caused a German serving-maid to be crowned Emperor of India.

The great discoveries you have lately made concerning tea.

How you became the first man to climb Mont Blanc though you were in Spain at the time.

How you became the first man to descend Mont Blanc, before any man had climbed it.

How you prevented the White Cliffs of Dover from turning blue.

How, on your celebrated crossing of the Sahara desert, you were able to eat your camel one night and still ride it the following day.

How you captured the entire French fleet with a leaky rowing-boat.

How you deduced that all the monks of Westminster Abbey were devil-worshippers and what you did about it.

Why you never remove your hat in the company of Greeks.

How you invented the national dish of Italy.

How you detected that the French were digging a tunnel under the English Channel, and the remarkable action you took as a result.

Why it is that half the fish brought into Antwerp harbour belong to you.

How the largest diamond in the world came to be in the oyster you presented to the Empress of Russia.

How your luncheon with the Duke of Strathcarn started the Industrial Revolution.

What you did to cause the year 1752 to lose the days between the third and the fourteenth of September.

How your unusual method of espionage in the recent invasion of Poland caused the baldness of the Duke of Wellington.

Your involvement in the Royal Society's scheme to extract sunlight from cucumbers.

How you claimed the planet Neptune for the British Empire.

Whether you have, as was reported, located the source of the Amazon, and if so, what kind of sauce it was.

The bet you made with the Count of Monte Hall, that you could outrun a hare over fifty yards, and how you won it.

How you navigated the ancient labyrinth of Minos, and what you found at its centre.

How you replenished the empty treasury of Liechtenstein in a single day.

Your shipwreck, sojourn, and survival on a small island inhabited only by man-eating savages.

How you escaped from the Turks on half a horse.

How you accidentally executed the King of Norway.

The time a cat insulted the honour of your family, and how you restored that honour.

How you moved Leeds Castle to Kent.

Your encounter with the ghost-ship the Flying Dutchman, and how you brought its cargo to harbour.

How you laid the ghost of Anne Boleyn.

How you eradicated the Black Plague from Hamburg in an afternoon.

Why your moustache never needs to be trimmed.

How you stopped the eruption of Mount Vesuvius with only the contents of your saddlebags and the help of your companions.

Why the apes on the Rock of Gibraltar regard you as the leader of their pack.

How you mined for gold in Saint Peter's Square in Rome.

How you came to accidentally invent Morris dancing.

How your discovery of the Sphinx's nose saved you from an unpleasant fate.

Your smuggling trips to the Sun, and how it led to your exile from that place.

How you lost both your legs at the Battle of Utrecht, and how you recovered them.

How, if you are the greatest swordsman in Europe, the Count of Basle can claim truthfully to be the greatest swordsman in Belgium.

Why and how you invented the tomato.

How you found the Crown Jewels of Sweden hidden inside a live cow.

How you succeeded where Canute failed and stopped the tide from advancing.

How you caused the English flag to be flown over the Palace of Versailles in France.

How you discovered every Italian spy in Germany with the use of a bowl of porridge.

Of your sojourn in Hades, from whence no mortal ever returns, and how it is that you are with us now.

How a flight of swans helped you free the kidnapped Prince of Persia.

How you travelled to the future, and how you returned.

How your famous love-affair with the daughter of the Earl of Cadogan was cut short by a moth.

How it is that you captained a ship in the Swiss navy, even though you are German by birth and Switzerland does not have a navy?

How you proved that the great monster of Loch Ness does not exist.

Why you are forbidden from wearing the colour yellow on the streets of Naples.

The great trifle of Antwerp.

The biggest pig in the world.

The five bonfires of Rome, and what trouble they caused.

Why the river Danube ran red with blood one Easter.

Why the river Thames ran green one midsummer day.

Why the lagoon of Venice became a desert, and how you remedied that unfortunate situation.

How, alone in a forest, you blew up a bear.

How you arrived in St Petersburg in a sledge drawn by a huge wild wolf.

How, on a separate occasion, you turned a wolf inside-out.

How you came to write this game.

Appendix 2 — The Rules in Brief

(For those who have not been paying attention)

It is the eighteenth century. A group of nobles are gathered in a location where there is a good stock of wine, and pass the long evening by entertaining each other with tales of their travels and surprising adventures. Little respect is paid to historical details, scientific facts, or the bounds of credibility.

Each player begins the game with a number of coins equal to the number of players. This is their "purse." The person who last filled the party's glasses turns to the noble on their right hand, and asks them to tell a story on a particular theme by saying, "So, Baron, tell us the story of . . ."

The player must respond with "Yes," in which case he must tell the story, or "No, my throat is too dry for that story," in which case he is allowed to forfeit his turn, but must buy a round of drinks for the assembled company. Thus becoming the person who last filled the party's glasses, he turns to the person on his right and gives them a subject for a story in the same way.

In telling a story, each player should try to outdo the previous story-teller, with a story that is bigger, wilder and brings more glory upon themselves. Stories should be told in the first person and about five minutes in length. (A hint: decide how your story will end before you begin telling it; this gives you something to steer towards.)

Other players may interrupt the story-teller with objections or elaborations to points of their story. This is done by pushing a coin—the "stake"—to them and saying, "But Baron . .." (or, in the adult version, draining one's wineglass, pushing a coin across the table and saying, "But Baron . . .") followed by the relevant objection. Interruptions should be used to put amusing obstacles in the way of the Baron's story, not to nit-pick. A player with no coins may not interrupt.

The story-teller may either accept the interruption (and the stake) and explain it or build it into his story, or he may disagree with it. If he disagrees, he adds one of his own coins to the stake, dismisses the interruption as nonsense, and ridicules the asker for believing anything so stupid and for doubting the word of a nobleman. The interrupting player may respond by adding another coin to the stake and a counter-insult, and so on. The player who first admits that they are wrong claims the entire stake; if it is the story-teller then they must build the interruption into their story, as above.

Direct insults to any player's truthfulness, parentage, or claims to noble rank may be answered by a challenge to a duel, which is settled by three rounds of rock-scissors-paper. The winner receives the loser's purse; the loser drops out of the game.

A story finishes in one of two ways. Either the story-teller concludes it with a vow as to the truthfulness of the matter or an offer to duel anyone who does not believe his word; or one of the other players drinks a toast to the Baron's health and his story. The story-teller then challenges the person on his right to tell a new story, as described above. There are other ways to end a story in an emergency: see the main text.

Once all the players have told one story, the player who began announces that he must retire to check on his horses, or some such. "But, by my word," he says, "I declare that the story about—, told by Baron—, was the most extraordinary story I have ever heard," and pushes his purse over to that player. (The coins are not added to this player's purse, but become part of his "bounty.") Once each player has pledged his purse to his favourite story, the one with the largest bounty is declared the winner and must buy a final round of drinks. However, he is also allowed to pose the question for the first story of the next game, whenever that may be played.

About the Creators

Baron Munchausen was the greatest adventurer and raconteur the world has ever known. Reports of his death in 1797 are probably exaggerated.

James Wallis is a writer and games designer based in London. He is working on a thesis that the origins of game design are genetic. Recent and forthcoming works include the *Waking the Dead* game for the BBC, and *Youdunnit*.

Gustav Dore was the greatest illustrator of the nineteenth century, and is best known for his engravings of scenes from the Bible and Dante's Inferno. He died in 1883.

Contributor Biographies

Ian Bogost

Ian Bogost is a videogame researcher and game designer. Bogost is Assistant Professor of Literature Communication and Culture at the Georgia Institute of Technology, where he teaches and researches in undergraduate and graduate programs in digital media. Bogost's current research interests include videogame criticism (the subject of a book, *Unit Operations: An Approach to Videogame Criticism*, MIT Press 2006) and videogame rhetoric (the subject of a forthcoming book, *Persuasive Games: Videogames and Procedural Rhetoric*, also from MIT Press). Bogost is also the founder of two companies. The first, Persuasive Games, is a game studio that designs, builds, and distributes electronic games for persuasion, instruction, and activism. The second, Open Texture, is a publisher of cross-media education and enrichment materials for families.

Rebecca Borgstrom

Rebecca Borgstrom is a writer living in the Seattle area. She is an abuse survivor. She has been writing role-playing game material professionally since approximately 1998. She received her doctorate in computer science from the Johns Hopkins University in 2001 after completing requirements in September 2000. Writing credits include the role-playing game *Nobilis*, the bulk of the forthcoming role-playing game *Weapons of the Gods*, and substantial work for various game lines including White Wolf's *Exalted*. She currently publishes *Hitherby Dragons*, a serial fiction anthology in blog form updated five to six times a week, at <http://rebecca.hitherby.com>.

Greg Costikyan

Greg Costikyan is CEO of Manifesto Games, which works to build a vibrant, innovative, and viable independent games industry. He began working in the game industry at the age of fourteen, in 1974, when he was hired by Simulations Publications, Inc. to ship and assemble games. Two years later, he moved onto SPI's design staff, and his first game, based on the Battle of Alamein, was published. In 1985 he joined West End Games as employee number three—after which he oversaw the development and publication of more than fifty gaming products, designing several of West End's best-selling games, including *Paranoia* and *Star Wars: The Role-Playing Game* at the same time. In the late 1980s and early 1990s, he was a house husband, taking care of two small children, while simultaneously writing three science fiction novels, a fantasy fiction serial for the Prodigy commercial online service, and the game *MadMaze* for Prodigy, which became the first online game to attract more than a million players. He then worked as a game designer, researcher, and consultant before founding Unplugged Games, one of the first North American mobile game start-ups. Greg has designed more than thirty commercially published board, role-playing, online, computer, and mobile games. His games have won five Origins Awards and a Gamer's Choice Award.

Chris Crawford

After teaching physics for several years, Chris Crawford joined Atari as a game designer in 1979. There he created a number of games: *Energy Czar,* an educational simulation about the energy crisis; *Scram,* a nuclear power plant simulation; *Eastern Front (1941),* a wargame; *Gossip,* a social interaction game; and *Excalibur,* an Arthurian game. He also ran the Games Research Group for Alan Kay. Following the collapse of Atari in 1984, Crawford took up the Macintosh. He created *Balance of Power,* a game about diplomacy; *Patton versus Rommel,* a wargame; *Trust & Betrayal,* a social interaction game; *Balance of the Planet,* an environmental simulation game; and *Patton Strikes Back,* a wargame. He has written five published books, including *The Art of Computer Game Design* (1982), now recognized as a classic in the field, and *Chris Crawford on Interactive Storytelling* (2004). He created the first periodical on game design, the *Journal of Computer Game Design,* in 1987. He founded and served as Chairman of the Computer Game Developers' Conference, now known as the Game Developers' Conference. In 1992, Crawford decided to leave game design and concentrate his energies on interactive storytelling. Crawford's Web site, <http://erasmatazz.com>, offers a library with many of his essays on game design and interactive storytelling.

Paul Czege

Paul Czege (say-ga) is 38, and a gamer since 1978. He is the creator of *Nicotine Girls* and *The Valedictorian's Death*, and author/publisher of *Bacchanal* and *My Life with Master*, which won the Diana Jones Award for Excellence in Gaming in 2004. Online at The Forge <http://www.indie-rpgs.com>, he's also known for coining the term *deprotagonize*, to describe a mechanical event or player action that damages the architecture of a player character's protagonism. Ask him how to design a notable game and he'll suggest that after a couple of powerful, satisfying play experiences with solid, well-designed RPGs, you actually learn more as a designer not by playing other strong, solid games, but instead by seeking out unplaytested games with mechanics and subject matter that pique your interest, and playing them. You learn best how to solve your own design issues by solving the kinds of design issues your brain is inclined to create.

Jeremy Douglass

Jeremy Douglass is a PhD candidate in English Literature at the University of California at Santa Barbara. His research focuses on interactive fiction, code, and reader response to textual new media. He is a founder of *Writer Response Theory*, an academic blog on digital text art, and a developer for numerous projects, including the humanities search engine Voice of the Shuttle.

Bruno Faidutti

Born in 1961, Bruno Faidutti mastered in economics and sociology, before getting a PhD in history dealing with the Renaissance scientific debate about the reality of unicorns. Always very interested in games, he was a good chess player when young, played a lot of *D&D* as a teenager, organized ambitious historical LARPs at thirty, all the while occasionally designing board and card games. He has published about twenty games, the best known being *Knightmare Chess*, *Citadels*, and *Mystery of the Abbey*. He teaches economics and sociology in a high school in Tarascon, in the south of France.

Nick Fortugno

Nick Fortugno is the Director of Game Design at gameLab <http://www.gamelab.com>, where he has participated in the design of a variety of digital and non-digital games, including serving as lead designer of the downloadable hit *Diner Dash*. Nick began his gaming pursuits in the role-playing world, founding and running the Seasons of Darkness group, a 5 1/2 year live action project featured on Showtime, and writing for tabletop role-playing titles. As a member of the Playground design team, Nick (with Frank Lantz and Katie Salen) was a co-creator of the *Big Urban Game*, a large-scale citywide game for the cities of St. Paul and Minneapolis, in fall 2003. Nick also teaches Game Design and Interactive Narrative at Parsons The New School of Design, and is a Coordinator of the Parsons Game Design concentration. In his spare time, Nick continues to run his role-playing, live-action and interactive art projects as part of Bliss Street Productions <http://www.bliss-street.com>.

Gonzalo Frasca

Gonzalo Frasca works as a researcher at the Center for Computer Game Research in Denmark. He is Editor of the *Game Studies* journal, as well as writing *Ludology.org* and co-editing *WaterCoolerGames.org*. Frasca is also a game developer who co-founded Powerful Robot Games, a videogame production studio responsible for the internationally acclaimed Newsgaming.com project.

D. Fox Harrell

Fox Harrell is an artist and author pursuing new forms of computational narrative. He currently is a PhD candidate in Computer Science and Cognitive Science at the University of California, San Diego. He earned an MPS in Interactive Telecommunications at New York University's Tisch School of the Arts. He also earned a BFA in Art, a BS in Logic and Computation, and minor in Computer Science at Carnegie Mellon University. He has worked as a game designer and animation producer in New York City. He is a practitioner of Capoeira Angola. He recently completed a novel entitled *Milk Pudding Flavored with Rose Water, Blood Pudding Flavored by the Sea*.

Pat Harrigan

Patrick Harrigan is a Minneapolis-based writer and editor. He has worked on new media projects with Improv Technologies, Weatherwood Company, and Wrecking Ball Productions, and as Marketing Director and Creative Consultant for Fantasy Flight Games. He is the co-editor of *First Person: New Media as Story, Performance, and Game* (2004, with Noah Wardrip-Fruin); and *The Art of H. P. Lovecraft's Cthulhu Mythos* (2006, with Brian Wood); and is author of the novel *Lost Clusters* (2005).

Keith Herber

Born in Detroit in 1949, Keith designed his first game at the age of eleven—a board game featuring popular movie monsters of the time. It was also about this time he discovered H. P. Lovecraft. Introduced to the RPG hobby in 1978, via *Dungeons & Dragons,* he was an experienced gamer by the time *Call of Cthulhu* appeared in late 1981. Fascinated by a game based on Lovecraft, he purchased a copy, and *CoC* soon became the game of choice with his gaming group. His first *CoC* submission was published in Chaosium's *Different Worlds* magazine in 1983, followed soon after by the full–length books *Fungi from Yuggoth, Trail of Tsathoggua, Spawn of Azathoth,* and *Arkham Unveiled.* In 1989, he moved to San Francisco and took a job with Chaosium, editing the *CoC* line until 1994, writing or publishing such titles as *Return to Dunwich, Escape from Innsmouth, The Investigator's Companion, The Keeper's Compendium,* and many other titles. In addition to *Call of Cthulhu,* he has also contributed to several other game lines. He currently resides in Lakeland, Florida, earning a living as a blues musician and as a stringer for local newspapers and magazines.

Will Hindmarch

Will Hindmarch is a writer and game developer for White Wolf Game Studio in Atlanta. He is the line developer for White Wolf's game system *Vampire: The Requiem.* More of his writing can be found online at <http://www.wordstudio.net>.

Kenneth Hite

Ken Hite is the author or co-author of over forty RPG games and supplements, including the Origins Award winning *Star Trek: The Next Generation RPG, Call of Cthulhu d20, GURPS Horror,* and *Nightmares of Mine,* a study of horror role-playing. From 1996 to 1998 he was Line Developer for Chaosium's *Nephilim* occult RPG, for which he also wrote two sourcebooks. Since 1997, he has written "Out of the Box," an RPG industry news and review column currently available at <http://www.gamingreport.com>.

Adriene Jenik

Adriene Jenik is a telecommunications media artist who has been working for over fifteen years as an artist, educator, curator, administrator, and engineer. Her works—including *El Naftazteca* (with Guillermo Gomez-Pena), *Mauve Desert: A CD-ROM Translation,* and *Desktop Theater* (with Lisa Brenneis and the DT troupe)—use the collision of "high" technology and human desire to propose new forms of literature, cinema, and performance. Jenik is currently serving as Associate Professor of Computer and Media Arts in the Visual Arts Department at University of California, San Diego. Her recent works (the *ActiveCampus Explorientation* and *SPEC-FLIC*) instigate large-scale public art events over community-wide wireless networks.

Eric Lang

Eric Lang has been designing games since he was seven years old. He has been doing so professionally since 1998. He has designed, co-designed or developed over thirty published games and game expansions during this time, two of which have won the prestigious Origins Award for best game and/or expansion. After founding his own company, Anoch Game Systems (publishers of the critically acclaimed *Mystick* Tarot card game), he has moved on to design games and consult for game manufacturers worldwide, including Fantasy Flight Games and Mattel Inc. Eric resides in Mississauga, Canada.

Lev Manovich

Lev Manovich <http://www.manovich.net> is the author of *Soft Cinema: Navigating the Database* (MIT Press, 2005) and *The Language of New Media* (MIT Press, 2001), which is hailed as "the most suggestive and broad-ranging media history since Marshall McLuhan." He is a Professor of Visual Arts, University of California, San Diego <http://visarts.ucsd.edu> and a Director of The Lab for Cultural Analysis at California Institute for Telecommunications and Information Technology <http://www.calit2.net>.

Mark C. Marino

Mark Marino is a PhD candidate at University of California, Riverside, studying and creating chatbots (including *Barthes's Bachelorette*), electronic literature, and video games. He is editor of *Bunk Magazine* <http://www.bunkmag.com>. His creative works have appeared in *The Iowa Review Web* and the *Notre Dame Review*. He is a founding member of the collective research blog *Writer Response Theory* <http://writerresponsetheory.org>. Currently, he teaches writing at the University of Southern California.

George R. R. Martin

George R. R. Martin was born in 1948, in Bayonne, New Jersey. He is the author or co-author of nine novels, including *Fevre Dream* and *Dying of the Light*, as well as the bestselling *A Song of Ice and Fire* series (*A Game of Thrones*, *A Clash of Kings*, *A Storm of Swords*, and *A Feast for Crows*). He conceived and edited the *Wild Cards* series of novels, the longest-running shared world series to date. He has won multiple awards, including the World Fantasy Award, the Bram Stoker Award, the Hugo Award (four times), and the Nebula Award (twice). Mr. Martin lives in Albuquerque, New Mexico.

Michael Mateas

Michael Mateas's work explores the intersection between art and artificial intelligence, forging a new art practice and research discipline called Expressive AI. He is currently a faculty member atthe University of California, Santa Cruz. At Georgia Tech, where Michael worked until 2006, he was the founder of the Experimental Game Lab, whose mission is to push the technological and cultural frontiers of computer-based games. Michael has presented papers and exhibited artwork internationally including SIGGRAPH, the New York Digital Salon, AAAI, the Game Developers Conference, TIDSE, DiGRA, Digital Arts and Culture, ISEA, the Carnegie Museum, the Warhol Museum, and Te PaPa, the national museum of New Zealand. Michael received his his PhD in Computer Science from Carnegie Mellon University. Prior to CMU, Michael worked at Intel Laboratories, where he helped introduce ethnographic techniques into the Intel research culture, and Tektronix Laboratories, where he developed qualitative design methodologies and built advanced interface prototypes.

Jane McGonigal

Jane McGonigal is an academic games researcher and pervasive game designer. She specializes in multiplayer games for public spaces and online systems for massively collaborative play. She is a PhD candidate in performance studies at the University of California at Berkeley, where she is also a member of the Alpha Lab for Industrial Engineering and Operations Research. She teaches game design (San Francisco Art Institute) and contemporary games culture (UC Berkeley), with an emphasis on how these two fields intersect with live performance, social networks, and public policy. She was a member of the *I Love Bees* design team that won both the 2005 Innovation Award from the International Game Developers Association and the 2005 games-related Webby Award from the International Academy of Digital Arts and Sciences. Her favorite previous pervasive gaming projects include *The Go Game,* flash mobs, and a massively multiplayer Easter egg hunt in Central Park. She has worked behind the scenes on numerous off-Broadway and off-off-Broadway productions.

Jordan Mechner

Jordan Mechner is one of the world's best-known videogame creators. His games, including *Karateka, Prince of Persia, The Last Express,* and *Prince of Persia: The Sands of Time,* have sold millions of copies and received worldwide critical acclaim. He is also the director of two award-winning short films, *Waiting for Dark* and *Chavez Ravine: A Los Angeles Story.* Mechner received his BA from Yale University.

Talan Memmott

Talan Memmott is a hypermedia writer/artist originally from San Francisco California. His hypermedia work is generally web-based and freely accessible on the Internet. Memmott is Professor of New Media in the Teledramatic Arts and Technology Department at California State University Monterey Bay and has taught digital art, electronic writing, and new media studies at Blekinge Institute of Technology in Karlskrona Sweden, the Georgia Institute of Technology, University of Colorado Boulder, and the Rhodes Island School of Design. He holds an MFA in Literary Arts/Electronic Writing from Brown University.

Steve Meretzky

Steve Meretzky has been designing games since 1982. His games have included text adventures, graphic adventures, role-playing games, children's games, and online casual games. In 1999, *PC Gamer* named Steve one of the industry's twenty-five "Game Gods." In March of 2005, the twentieth anniversary edition of his game *The Hitchhiker's Guide to the Galaxy,* which he co-authored with the late Douglas Adams, won an award for Online Game of the Year from the British Academy of Film and Television Arts (BAFTA). He is currently Lead Game Designer for Floodgate Entertainment in Waltham, Massachusetts, creating the latest generation of multiplayer and 3D games for cell phones and other mobile devices.

Erik Mona

Erik Mona is the Editor-in-Chief of *Dragon* and *Dungeon* magazines, the official magazines of the *Dungeons & Dragons* game. He has authored several books and articles for the world's most popular role-playing game, and co-created *Living Greyhawk,* the largest shared-world D&D campaign in history (now with more than 14,000 active players around the world). His book credits include *The Living Greyhawk Gazetteer, Forgotten Realms: Faiths & Pantheons,* and the forthcoming *Hordes of the Abyss.*

Nick Montfort

Nick Montfort has written and programmed several pieces of interactive fiction: *Book and Volume* (2005), *Ad Verbum* (2000), and *Winchester's Nightmare* (1999). He is the author of *Twisty Little Passages: An Approach to Interactive Fiction* (MIT Press, 2003) and, with Noah Wardrip-Fruin, co-editor of *The New Media Reader* (MIT Press, 2003). Montfort's literary collaborations include *Mystery House Taken Over* (with Dan Shiovitz, Emily Short, and others, 2005), *Implementation* (with Scott Rettberg, 2004), and *2002: A Palindrome Story* (with William Gillespie, 2002), which was acknowledged by the Oulipo as the world's longest literary palindrome. Montfort is a vice president of the Electronic Literature Organization. He lives in Philadelphia, where he is studying for a PhD in computer and information science at the University of Pennsylvania.

Torill Elvira Mortensen

Torill Mortensen studies online cultures as expressed and formed through Web logs and computer games. She has a PhD in computer games with a main focus on MUDs, text-based online games, from a background of media studies, and maintains a Web log. She is an Associate Professor at the Media Department of Volda University College, Norway.

Stuart Moulthrop

Stuart Moulthrop is a writer and cybertext designer who lives in Baltimore, Maryland. His early work, *Victory Garden,* has been mentioned among the "golden age" of hypertext fiction. Later works, including *Hegirascope* (1997), *Reagan Library* (1999), and *Pax* (2003), pertain more closely to our current age of man-made fibers. Moulthrop is the author of many essays on hypertext and digital culture, including some that have been multiply anthologized and translated. He teaches at the University of Baltimore, most recently within a new undergraduate program in Simulation and Digital Entertainment.

Kim Newman

Kim Newman is an author and critic. His novels include *The Night Mayor, Anno Dracula, The Quorum,* and *Life's Lottery.* His non-fiction books include *Nightmare Movies, Apocalypse Movies, The BFI Companion to Horror,* and monographs for the BFI on the film *Cat People* and the TV series *Doctor Who.* He is a contributing editor to the magazines *Sight & Sound* and *Empire*, and writes regularly for many periodicals, including *Video Watchdog* and *Shivers*. He broadcasts regularly, has written documentaries for radio and television, directed a short film, and worked in the theatre and cabaret. As "Jack Yeovil," he has written a run of novels that tie in with role-playing games for Games Workshop.

Robert F. Nideffer

Robert Nideffer researches, teaches, and publishes in the areas of virtual environments and behavior, interface theory and design, technology and culture, and contemporary social theory. He holds an MFA in Computer Arts, and a PhD in Sociology. He is an Associate Professor in Studio Art and Informatics at the University of California, Irvine, where he serves as Affiliated Faculty in the Visual Studies Program, and as co-director for the Art, Computation, and Engineering (ACE) Program. He is also directing the UC Irvine Game Culture and Technology Lab, and a related academic "Specialization in Game Culture and Technology." Between 1997 and 1999, Robert was employed by the Departments of Computer Science and Engineering at the University of California Santa Barbara (UCSB) where he was responsible for developing distributed, peer-to-peer digital library architectures and production-ready software components supporting organization, publication, discovery, and use of geospatial and other types of strongly structured scientific data. At UCSB he also served as Co-PI on a project that developed a Java-based multi-agent software system shown as part of the Whitney Biennial of American Art in 2002.

Celia Pearce

Celia Pearce is an award-winning game designer, artist, researcher, teacher, and author of *The Interactive Book: A Guide to the Interactive Revolution* (Macmillan, 1997) as well as other articles and papers on interactive media, game design, and culture. She currently holds an appointment as Assistant Professor in the School of Literature, Communication & Culture, Ivan Allen College, Georgia Institute of Technology. Previously she was a Research Associate at the Game Culture and Technology Lab of the University of California, Irvine, and an adjunct professor and researcher at the University of Southern California, where she held various appointments between 1998 and 2001. She has worked as a consultant and game designer/producer for Iwerks Entertainment, Purple Moon Software, Walt Disney Imagineering, Universal Parks, and Lego Toys, to name a few. She has also co-curated exhibitions including "Mapping the Unfindable" (Winter 2004), a retrospective exhibition on the work of Norman Klein, and ALT+CTRL (fall 2004), a festival of independent an alternative games, both at UCI's Beall Center for Art and Technology. She was a founding board member of DiGRA, the Digital Games Research Association, and served as panels chair for SIGGRAPH 1998.

Teri Rueb

Teri Rueb's large-scale responsive environments and sound installations explore issues of architecture and urbanism, landscape and the body, and sonic and acoustic space. She is an Associate Professor in the graduate department of Digital + Media at the Rhode Island School of Design in Providence. Teri currently lives in Cambridge, Massachusetts, where she is a candidate in the Doctor of Design program at Harvard University.

Marie-Laure Ryan

A native of Geneva, Switzerland, Marie-Laure Ryan is an independent scholar based in Colorado. She is the author of *Possible Worlds, Artificial Intelligence and Narrative Theory*, which received the 1992 Prize for Independent Scholars from the Modern Language Association; of *Narrative as Virtual Reality: Immersion and Interactivity in Literature and Electronic Media*, which received the 2001 Aldo and Jeanne Scaglione Prize for Comparative Literature Studies, also from the Modern Language Association; and of *Avatars of Story: Narrative Modes in Old and New Media* (2006). She has also edited *Cyberspace Textuality: Computer Technology and Literary Theory* (1999), *Narrative Across Media* (2004), and co-edited the *Routledge Encyclopedia of Narrative Theory* (2005), with David Herman and Manfred Jahn. She has tried her hand at the design of multimedia interactive texts with *Symbol Rock* (co-authored with Jon Thiem), a CD-ROM available from the author, which tells the story of an abandoned ranch in Colorado. Her Web site is at <http://lamar.colostate.edu/~pwryan>.

Joe Scrimshaw

Joseph Scrimshaw is a Minneapolis-based writer, actor, and producer. With his brother Joshua, he is one half of the comedy team The Scrimshaw Brothers. The Brothers are staples of the Minnesota Fringe Festival, *City Pages'* 2002 Artists of the Year, and the creators of the hit cabaret *Look Ma No Pants,* which helped garner the Bryant Lake Bowl the title of "Best Theater for Comedy" in the *City Pages* for the last two years. As a solo artist, Joseph is the author of Fringe Fest hits, *The Worst Show in the Fringe* (which was the #1 best-selling show of the Festival in 2002 and #4 in 2003) and *Jack & Ben's 10th Annual Bar Crawl and Moveable Feast*; a resident performer of Children's Theater at Old Gem Theater in New Richmond, Wisconsin; and an occasional arts commentator on Minnesota Public Radio's *State of the Arts* and on 89.3 The Current with Mary Lucia. Joseph has also performed with the Minnesota Shakespeare Company, Bedlam Theater, The Great American History Theater, and the 8th Annual Chicago Improv Festival. Joseph is currently visiting England to research a new one-man show entitled *Some Dead Guy in England.*

Lee Sheldon

Lee Sheldon has written and designed eighteen video games, including *The Riddle of Master Lu* and *Agatha Christie's Murder on the Orient Express, and is the author* of the book *Character Development and Storytelling for Games.* Before his career in video games, Lee was an award-winning writer/producer for over 200 TV shows, including *Star Trek: The Next Generation* and *Charlie's Angels*; and was head writer of the daytime serial *Edge of Night.* His first mystery novel, *Impossible Bliss,* was re-issued in 2004. He is currently designing his third Agatha Christie game, writing a new storytelling project for the Nintendo Wii, and teaching game design and screenwriting at Indiana University.

Emily Short

Emily Short has been playing interactive fiction since the early 1980s, and writing it since 1998. Her work includes *Galatea,* an interactive conversation; *Savoir-Faire* and *Metamorphoses,* games exploring systems of physical magic; and *City of Secrets,* a story with a complex branching plot. With Nick Montfort and Dan Shiovitz, she ported and re-engineered Sierra's *Mystery House* in a project sponsored by Turbulence.org. She has written a number of articles on designing interactive fiction and is the editor of a book on IF theory and craft (in progress). She is also assisting Graham Nelson with the development of Inform 7, a new programming language for creating IF.

Andrew Stern

Andrew Stern is a designer, writer, and engineer of personality-rich, AI-based interactive characters and stories. Before *Façade,* Andrew was a lead designer and software engineer at P.F.Magic, developing *Virtual Babyz, Dogz,* and *Catz,* which sold over two million units worldwide. He and Michael Mateas recently founded the game studio Procedural Arts, and regularly blog at <http://grandtextauto.org>. Andrew has presented and exhibited work at the Game Developers Conference, Independent Games Festival, SIGGRAPH, ISEA, Digital Arts and Culture, DiGRA, TIDSE, AAAI symposia, Autonomous Agents, and Intelligent User Interfaces. Awards include a Silver Invision 2000 award for Best Overall Design for CD-ROM, for *Babyz; Catz* received a Design Distinction in the first annual I.D. Magazine Interactive Media Review, and along with *Dogz* and *Babyz* was part of the American Museum of Moving Image's Computer Space exhibit in New York. The projects have been written about in *The New York Times, Newsweek, Wired,* and *AI Magazine.* Andrew holds a BS in Computer Engineering from Carnegie Mellon University and a master's degree in Computer Science from the University of Southern California.

Helen Thorington

Helen Thorington is a writer, sound composer, and media artist. Her radio documentary, dramatic work, and sound/music compositions have been aired nationally and internationally for the past twenty-five years. She has also created compositions for film and installation that have been premiered at the Berlin Film Festival, the Whitney Biennial, and the Whitney Museum's annual Performance series. Her Internet work beyond *Solitaire* includes *Adrift* (1997–2002), an evolving multi-location Internet performance collaboration with Marek Walczak and Jesse Gilbert. Thorington created the narrative for *Adrift* and contributed to its sound composition. She is co-director of the independent new media organization, New Radio and Performing Arts, Inc., with offices in New York City and Boston; the founder and producer of the national weekly radio series, New American Radio (1987-1998); and the founder and producer of the Turbulence Web site (1996–present) and somewhere.org. She is also a published author and a frequently requested speaker on radio and Internet arts <http://new-radio.org/helen>.

Sean Thorne

Sean Thorne is a humble teacher of elevens in New Jersey's oldest independent school: Rutgers Preparatory. He has been a teacher since 1987, and has taught creative writing since 1995. He lives with his two black labs on the side of Montana Mountain overlooking the Delaware River, Queen of the East Coast Rivers. He is a water/mountain/bear spirit; surfer; gardener; blacksmith; angler; equestrian; ever exploring his inner landscape to better understand the eternal light in all things. He is really just a fallen Buddhist. He is honored to have accepted a master's in Science from Bank Street College. He is indebted to Susan Haver for her guidance.

Jonathan Tweet

Jonathan Tweet has designed and developed role-playing games, trading card games, and miniature games. He has self-published, freelanced, and worked as a salaried game designer. He published *Everway* in 1995 as an employee of Wizards of the Coast, where he still works. His highest-profile project was leading the design of *Dungeons & Dragons, 3rd Edition* (Wizards of the Coast, 2000).

John Tynes

John Tynes is an award-winning writer and game designer. He founded Pagan Publishing in 1990 to produce tabletop role-playing games, as well as fiction and non-fiction books. His writing has appeared online in *Salon* and *McSweeney's* and in print for the Seattle alternative newspapers *The Stranger* and *Tablet*. In the videogame field, he has written for Acclaim and Bungie, works as a columnist for *The Escapist* and *X360 UK*, and serves as lead writer for Flying Lab Software's massively multiplayer online game *Pirates of the Burning Sea*. His film criticism is collected in the book *Wiser Children*.

Tim Uren

Tim Uren is a Twin Cities actor and comedian. As part of the Minnesota Fringe Festival he wrote and appeared in two solo shows, *10,000 Comic Books* and *Michigan Disasters*. Additionally, he studies, performs, and teaches improvisational theater, having worked with the Brave New Workshop, Stevie Ray's, and the Scrimshaw Brothers' *Look Ma, No Pants*, among others. He can also be seen performing *300 Comic Books*, a solo-improv structure of his own creation.

James Wallis

James Wallis is the co-designer of the storytelling card-game *Once Upon a Time* (Atlas, 1992) and the award-winning *Extraordinary Adventures of Baron Munchausen* (Hogshead, 1998). For nine years he was the director of Hogshead Publishing, which released several innovative games based around new systems of interactive story-creation. He has also written thirteen books, designed games for several Web sites, written regularly for publications as diverse as *Fortean Times* and the *Sunday Times*, and established the Diana Jones Award for Excellence in Gaming. His current projects include *Youdunnit*, a storytelling after-dinner role-playing game in the style of P. G. Wodehouse and Agatha Christie, and an interactive murder-mystery game for the BBC Web site. He lives in London.

Jill Walker

Jill Walker is an associate professor at the Department of Humanistic Informatics at the University of Bergen, Norway. Her current research focus is distributed narrative, both in physical and networked spaces. She also researches electronic literature and art more generally. Jill has been an avid blogger for several years, and her research blog can be found at <http://jilltxt.net>.

Noah Wardrip-Fruin

Noah Wardrip-Fruin is a digital media writer, artist, and scholar with a particular interest in fiction and playability. His writing/art has been presented by galleries, arts festivals, scientific conferences, DVD magazines, and the Whitney and Guggenheim museums. He has recently edited two books: *First Person: New Media as Story, Performance, and Game* (2004, with Pat Harrigan) and *The New Media Reader* (2003, with Nick Montfort), both from MIT Press. Now at the University of California, San Diego, he has previously taught in Brown University's Literary Arts program, the University of Baltimore's School of Information Arts and Technologies, and New York University's Graduate Film and Television program. He is a Vice President of the Electronic Literature Organization and blogs at <http://grandtextauto.org>.

Kevin Whelan

Kevin Whelan is the Communications Director for ACORN, the Association of Community Organizations for Reform Now <http://www.acorn.org>. He has two daughters under four years old, and so, though he has no time for role-playing games with grown-ups outside work, he does pretend to be a bear, a friendly monster, and Dora on a regular basis.

Kevin Wilson

Kevin Wilson has been a game designer for nearly ten years. He is the co-designer of the *7th Sea* and *Spycraft* role-playing games, as well as the author of numerous other RPG books, such as *Spellslinger* and *Wonders Out of Time*. In addition, he has designed several board games, including *Doom: the Board Game*, *Warcraft: the Board Game*, *Descent: Journeys in the Dark*, and *Arkham Horror 2nd Edition* (with Richard Launius). Kevin received a BA in Cognitive Science (Artificial Intelligence) from the University of California at Berkeley in 1997, and was active in the Interactive Fiction community at the time. He wrote several works of Interactive Fiction (including *Once and Future* and *The Lesson of the Tortoise*) and founded the annual Interactive Fiction Competition and the Internet magazine *SPAG*, both of which are still active today. Kevin currently lives near the Twin Cities with his utter lack of cats.

Adrianne Wortzel

Adrianne Wortzel's art explores historical and cultural perspectives—in both physical and virtual networked environments—through interactive robotic and telerobotic installations, performance productions, and texts. She is a Professor of Communication Design at New York City College of Technology, CUNY, a member of the doctoral faculty of the Interactive Technology and Pedagogy Certificate Program of the CUNY Graduate Center, and an Adjunct Professor of Mechanical Engineering at the Cooper Union for the Advancement of Science and Art, where she is also the Founding Director of *StudioBlue*, a telerobotic video studio. Recent works include: *Eliza Redux*, *Archipleago.ch*, *The Veils of Transference*, and *Camouflage Town*, a telerobotic installation exhibited in *Data Dynamics* at The Whitney Museum of American Art (2001). These projects have been made possible by funding from Artists-In-Swiss Labs Program, the National Science Foundation, Franklin Furnace Fund for Performance Art, and the PSC-CUNY Research Foundation of the City University of New York, among others. *Eliza Redux*, through the auspices of Franklin Furnace, has recently received a Greenwall Foundation Grant to support its next stage.

Eric Zimmerman

Eric Zimmerman is a game designer who has been working in the game industry for more than twelve years. He is the co-founder, with Peter Lee, of gameLab <http://www.gamelab.com>, a game development company based in New York City that creates experimental games on and off the computer, including *BLiX*, *Arcadia*, and *Diner Dash*. Eric is also the co-creator with Word.com of *SiSSYFiGHT 2000* <http://www.sissyfight.com>. He has taught courses at MIT, New York University, and Parsons School of Design. Eric has lectured and published extensively about game design and game culture and is the co-author, with Katie Salen, of *Rules of Play: Game Design Fundamentals* (MIT Press, 2004) and *The Game Design Reader: A Rules of Play Anthology* (MIT Press, 2006), as well as the co-editor, with Amy Scholder, of *RE:PLAY: Game Design and Game Culture* (Peter Lang Press, 2004).

Robert Zubek

Robert Zubek recently joined Electronic Arts/Maxis as a game developer, after completing graduate work in game AI and autonomous mobile robotics. In 2005 he was awarded a PhD in computer science by Northwestern University, where he also received his previous degrees. His dissertation was on AI for social interaction, implemented using hierarchical parallel hidden Markov models.

Permissions

The editors wish to thank the following, who gave permission for material to be reproduced. Most images not listed here are by permission of the author of the essay with which they appear. In a small number of cases it was not possible to locate the copyright holder.

42 Entertainment, LLC:
Image of *I Love Bees* appears courtesy of 42 Entertainment, LLC.

Activision Publishing, Inc.:
Image of Infocom advertisement appears courtesy of Activision Publishing, Inc.

Atlas Games:
Images of *Once Upon a Time* appear courtesy of Atlas Games.

Awe Productions, Inc.:
Image of *And Then There Were None* appears courtesy of Awe Productions, Inc.

Blizzard Entertainment, Inc.:
World of Warcraft® images provided courtesy of Blizzard Entertainment, Inc.

Chaosium, Inc.:
Cover images of *Call of Cthulhu* publications, as well as "Haunted House" maps, appear courtesy of Chaosium, Inc.

Steve Childs:
Visual representation of Flow appears with permission of Steve Childs.

Days of Wonder, Inc.:
Images of *Mystery of the Abbey* appear courtesy of Days of Wonder, Inc.

Bernie DeKoven:
Visual representation of CoLiberation appears with permission of Bernie DeKoven.

The Edward Gorey Charitable Trust:
Images from *The Helpless Doorknob: A Shuffled Story* © 1989 Edward Gorey, used with permission of The Edward Gorey Charitable Trust. All rights reserved.

Fantasy Flight Games:
Images of *A Game of Thrones CCG, Call of Cthulhu CCG, Doom: The Board Game,* and *Arkham Horror* appear courtesy of Fantasy Flight Games.

Andrew Hutchison:
Images of *Juvenate* appear courtesy of Andrew Hutchison.

Nancy Nowacek:
Images from *Life in the Garden* © 2005 Nancy Nowacek.

Scott Pakudaitis:
Images of the stage production of Adventures in Mating appear courtesy of Scott Pakudaitis.

Pagan Publishing:
Cover image of *Delta Green* appears courtesy of Pagan Publishing.

Kenneth Rahman:
Images of *Dark Cults* cards appear with permission of Kenneth Rahman.

Random House, Inc.:
Cover images of the *Wild Cards* books appear courtesy of Random House, Inc.

Jen Scott:
Images of Tim Uren and *Adventures in Mating* actor Craig Johnson courtesy of Jen Scott.

Andrew Sorcini:
Screenshot of *I Love Bees* by Andrew Sorcini.

Ubisoft Entertainment:
Images of *Prince of Persia: The Sands of Time* appear courtesy of Ubisoft Entertainment.

Index

A

Aarinfel (Jarok, Kierae, et al.), 299–300

Aaron system, 184

Abbey, Lynn, 17–18

ABL (A Behavior Language), 190–191, 206

Absences (Manovich), 161

ACORN (Association of Community Organizations for Reform Now), 220, 248–249

Activism (Bogost), 241, 244, 246

Adams, Scott, 129

Adventures in Mating play (Scrimshaw), 285–287

Adventure (Crowther and Woods), xiv, 3, 5, 129, 131

Ad Verbum (Montfort), 143

Afghanistan, 224–225

Afrika Korps (Roberts), 5

afternoon: a story (Joyce), 7, 153, 167

Agency, 203–206

Age of Innocence (film), 116

Airport Insecurity (Bogost), 154

Albee, Edward, 186

Algorithmic systems, 10–11, 185

ALLOY, 177, 180–181

Alphabet Scene structure, 282–283

Alternity (Slavicsek and Baker), 298

Amber (see *Chronicles of Amber*)

America's Army (Capps), 241

Amnesia (Disch), 141

Anchorhead (Gentry), 142, 144

And Then There Were None (Christie), 108–109, 121–123

Anthropomorphization, 70

Archer's Flight, The (Keavney), 213–215

Architecture of protagonism, 67–68

"Arithmetic of Computers, The" (TutorText), 134

Arkham Horror (Wilson), 3–4, 92–93

Armageddon Rag, The (Martin), 17

Arneson, Dave, 5, 26–27, 29

Artemesia (avatar), 311–317

Artificial Intelligence Markup Language (AIML), 167, 323

"Art of the Heist Live Puppet Master Chat" (Monello), 259

Asprin, Robert, 17–18, 21

Association of Internet Researchers (AOIR), 303

Atari 2600, 234

Avalon Hill, 107

Avatars, 289

    Artemesia and, 311–317

    Eliza Redux and, 327–328

    identity and, 311–315

B

Babel (Finley), 141–142

Baf's Guide, 134

Balance of Power (Crawford), 241

Ballon, Bruce, 37–38

Barker, M. A. R., 222–223

Barrett, Peter, 134

Basho, Matsuo, 181

Bates, Joseph, 185

Battegazzore, Sofia, 238

Baum, Frank L., 325

Beads-on-a-string model, 8–13

Beats

    coherent mixing and, 193

    gist point and, 198

    joint dialogue behaviors and, 191–193, 195, 201–202, 206

    mix-ins and, 191–193

    parallel behavior and, 195–196

    procedural authorship and, 190–203

    reactivity and, 194–195, 198–200

    scaffolding and, 197–198

    sequencing of, 192

Beggar's Opera, The (Gay), 351

Bestial Acts (Costikyan), xv

    aims of, 357

    bomb and, 353–355

    Brecht and, 350–351

    combat rules and, 355–356

    gamemaster and, 351–352

    genre and, 349

    narrative and, 353–354, 357

    nobility and, 356

Bestial Acts (Costikyan) *(continued)*
    players and, 351–352
    setting of, 352–353
    staging of, 353
    tone of, 352–353
Betrayal at the House on the Hill (Glassco), 108
Big Urban Game (B. U. G.) (Fortugno, Lantz, and Salen), 256–257
Birkerts, Sven, 310
Blackjack, xiv
Blade Runner (film), 116
Bloch, Robert, 4, 21, 37
Blumer, Herbert, 314
Bluth, Don, 8
Boal, Augusto, 139, 290n1
Bogost, Ian, 154, 220, 233–246
Bolter, Jay David, 134
Book and Volume (Montfort), 139, 143–145
Book of the Courtier, The (Castiglione), 367
Borderlands (shared world), 17–18, 21
Borgstrom, Rebecca, xiii, 2–3, 57–66, 75, 219
Boskone convention, 5
Bottle-Glass-Throat, 372
Bowdler, Thomas, xiii
Branch Davidians, 225–226
Breakup Conversation, The (Zubek), 109, 209–212
Brecht, Bertolt, 350–351
Brenneis, Lisa, 289
Bridge, 5
Britton, Suzanne, 141
Broadside, 15
Brooklyn Botanical Gardens, 265
Brotherhood of Bent Billard, The (Memmott), 157–158
Brothers in Arms (Martel and Pitchford), 107
Bryant, Ed, 20
Bunten, Dan, 6

C

Cadre, Adam, 135, 141, 154
Cailois, Roger, 255–256, 303, 314
Call of Cthulhu (CoC), 1–4, 16, 85, 223
    awards of, 31–32
    collectible card games and, 3, 88–89

"The Haunted House" and, 41–43
    market for, 31
    narrative structure and, 31–39, 223
    puppet master and, 253
Call of Duty (Rieke), 224
Calvino, Italo, 167
Cambiemos (Frasca), 241, 246
Campbell, Ramsey, 4, 37
Capcom, 177
Carroll, Noel, 33–34
Castiglione, Baldesar, 367–368
Castle & Crusade Society, 26
Castronova, Edward, 311
CAVE displays, xiv, 149
Cave of Time, The (Packard), xiv, 167
Chainmail (Gygax and Perren), 5, 25–26
Chang, Geunyoung, 311
Chaosium, 2, 4, 31–39, 41–43, 88–89, 92
Character design. (*see* Player character)
Checkers, 15
Chess, 5, 140
Choose Your Own Adventure series, 7, 134, 167, 220, 285
Christie, Agatha, 70, 108–109
Christminster (Rees), 144
Chronicles of Amber (Zelazny), 3, 85
Chutes and Ladders, 241
Cinema machine, 159–162
City of Heroes (Emmert), 219
Claerbout, David, 309
Claremont, Chris, 20
Cleveland, Grover, 241
Cleveland Re-election Game, 241
Club for Growth, 238–239
Cluedo, 70
Collectible card games, 2–3
    Call of Cthulhu and, 88–89
    design decisions for, 85–89
Colossal Cave (*see Adventure*)
Columbine High School, 304
ComedySportz, 283
Compass Players, 281
Computational fictions, xiv (*see also specific system*)

character design and, 114–118, 139–146

computer's effect and, 169–171

cybertext writing and, 149–155

first commercial game and, 129

info-subjectivity and, 161

narrative generation systems and, 177–182

player character and, 139–146

possibilities of medium, 107–109

procedural authorship and, 183–208

SHRDLU program and, 134

Soft Cinema project and, 159–162

storytelling and, 111–113

Computer Power and Human Reason: From Judgment to Calculation (Weizenbaum), 324

Computers as Theatre (Laurel), 185

Conan (Howard), 3

Conte à votre façon, Un (Queneau), 134

Convulsion game convention, 224

Coover, Robert, 4, 7

"Cops and Robbers," xiii

Cortázar, Julio, 7, 167

Costikyan, Greg, 1, 47, 52–53, 219

    Bestial Acts and, 349–357

    puppet master and, 255–256

    storytelling and, 5–13

Cover, Arthur Byron, 20

"Cowboys and Indians," xiii

Crawford, Chris, 241

    procedural authorship and, 185, 190

    storytelling and, 6, 54, 109, 169–175

Creature Feature structure, 283

Croft, Lara, 134

Crowther, William, 3, 5, 129

Csikszentmihalyi, Mihaly, 304, 315–316

Curses (Nelson), 144

Cyan, 312–313

Czege, Paul, 1–2, 11, 67–68

D

Dark and Stormy Night, A (Wallis), 77, 79

Dark Cults (Rahman), 69, 78–79

Deadline (Blank), 137

Dean, Howard, 220

Deitko, 171–175

DeKoven, Bernie, 315–316

Delta Green (Detwiller et al.), 2, 35, 225

Demoscene, 184

Derleth, August, 21

Design

    beats and, 190–203

    character, 114–118, 139–146

    collectible card games and, 85–89

    computer's effect and, 169–171

    cybertext writing and, 149–155

    dialogue and, 118–119

    efficiency maximization and, 113

    genre combination and, 115–117

    procedural authorship and, 183–208

    puppet master problem and, 251–263

    randomness and, 81–84

    rule breaking and, 115

    time as constraint and, 234–237

    tool creation and, 119–120

    Usenet and, 130

Desktop Theater, 220, 289

Detwiller, Dennis, 2

Deus Ex (Spector), 10–11

Devil May Cry (Capcom), 177

Dialogue, 118–119

Dick, Philip K., 38

Dickens, Charles, 163

Digital Arts and Culture conference, 291

Digital Games Research Association, xiv

Diplomacy, 16, 107

Director 7, 153

Disch, Thomas M., 141

Discourse acts, 191

Disparition, La (Perec), 234

Domesday Book, 26

Doom (Wilson), 3–4, 91–93, 221

Dore, Gustav, 382

Double Indemnity (film), 116

Douglass, Jeremy, xiv, 109, 129–136

Dragon Realms (Dick, Grant, et al.), 301–303

Dragon's Lair (Dyer and Bluth), 8

Duke, 311

Dungeons & Dragons (Gygax and Arneson), xiii–xiv, 1–3, 18, 107, 134, 349
    Chainmail and, 5, 25–26
    character development and, 139–140
    early years of, 25–30
    escapism and, 221–222
    identity and, 298
    origin of, 25–28
    puppet master and, 253
    real worlds and, 219, 221–222, 247
    rules and, 78

Durand, David, 154

Dust Devils (Snyder), 1

Dying Earth (Vance), 3

E

Eco, Umberto, 3, 38

Edwards, Ron, 1, 11, 67

Effinger, George Alec, 20

Electronic Arts, 185

Electronic Entertainment Expo, 216

Eliot, T. S., 234

ELIZA, 154, 167, 220, 324–325

Eliza Redux (Wortzel)
    gestures and, 326–327
    psychoanalysis and, 319–329
    robotics and, 320–329
    structure of, 319–321
    teaching and, 322–324
    Weizenbaum and, 321–322, 324, 328–329

Ellison, Harlan, 21

Embedded stories, 10

Empire of the Petal Throne (Barker), 222–223

Encyclopedic systems, 183–184

Erasmatron (Crawford), 170–171, 174–175

Escapism, 221–222

EverQuest (Clover, McQuaid, and Trost), xiv

Everway (Tweet), 3, 45–46

Everything Bad Is Good for You (Johnson), 251

Exalted (Grabowski), 3
    meaning and, 57–66

Exercises in Style (Queneau), 166

Extraordinary Adventures of Baron Munchausen, The (Wallis), xv, 3, 69, 74–75, 77, 359–361
    companions and, 369
    corrections and, 365–370
    dueling and, 370–373
    ending game and, 375
    equipment and, 363
    finishing a story and, 373–374
    historical setting and, 376–377
    nobility and, 367–369
    objections and, 365–370
    questions for, 378–381
    rules of, 381–382
    starting game and, 363–365
    structure of, 362–363
    tactics for, 375–376
    wagers and, 365–370
    winner determination and, 374–375

F

Façade (Mateas and Stern), xiv, 109
    agency and, 203–206
    beats and, 190–203
    design and, 206–207
    feedback and, 206
    interface and, 206
    numeric score and, 189
    player character and, 142–145
    popularity of, 185–186
    procedural authorship and, 183–208
    progression fronts and, 190
    system architecture and, 190–191, 206

Fahrenheit 9/11 (Moore), 242

Faidutti, Bruno, 3, 95–97

Fair Folk, The (Borgstrom), 3

Fantasy Flight Games, 85–86, 89, 91–93

Fauconnier, Gilles, 177

Fighting Fantasy (Livingstone and Jackson), 7–8

Fine, Gary Allan, 134

Finley, Ian, 141

Firth, Roger, 131

Fleet, The (shared world), 17–18, 21
Floyd the Robot, 137–138
Ford, Henry, 159
Forge, The, 1, 5
Fortugno, Nick, 220, 265–267
Foucault, Michel, 157
Frankenstein (Shelley), 220
Frasca, Gonzalo, 220, 233–246
Freudian analysis, 324, 329
Fritzon, Thorbiorn, 12
Froehlich, Elaine, 154

G

Game books, 7–8
Game Boy, 235
Game Developer magazine, 6
Game Developers Conference, 185
Game Manufacturer's Association (GAMA), 6
Gamemasters (GMs), 253–254, 298–299
Game of Thrones CCG, A (Lang), 3, 85–89
Games
    with agendas, 241–244
    algorithmic systems and, 10–11, 185
    anthropomorphization and, 70
    balance and, 78–79
    beads-on-a-string model and, 8–13
    definitions of, xiii–xiv
    design of, 139–146 (*see also* Design)
    diasporic cultures and, 311
    as formal systems, 6–7
    identity and, 297–305, 311–316
    illusion of control and, 69
    improvisational theater and, 279–283
    lawsuits and, 304
    market sales and, 1
    meaning in, 57–66
    medium structure and, xiv
    multimedia and, 91–93
    nonlinearity and, 6
    paragraph-system, 8
    politics and, 233–246
    procedural authorship and, 183–208
    replayability and, 244
    storytelling and, 5–13, 47–55 (*see also* Storytelling)
    as windows on real world, 221–227
Gamist-Narrativist-Simulationist theory, 11–12
Gathering, The, 311, 313, 315
Gay, John, 351
Gearbox, 107
Generic Universal Role-Playing System (GURPS), xiv, 1
Gentry, Michael, 142, 144
Gifford, Peter, 223
"Girl with Skin of Haints and Seraphs, The", 179–181
Gist point, 198
Global Positioning System (GPS)
    puppet master problem and, 251, 261–262
    real worlds and, 220, 251, 261–262, 270, 273–274
Goffman, Erving, 300–302
Go Game, 252, 254, 259–262
Goguen, Joseph, 177
Goldberg, Eric, 8
Good Morning America (TV show), 243
Goosebumps (Waddingtons), 71–72
Gorey, Edward, 71–73
Grand Theft Auto (game series), 185, 221, 309
Greene, Maxine, 232
Greystone Bay (shared world), 21
Grim Fandango (Schafer), 5
GRIOT performances, 108, 219
Grusin, Richard, 134
Gygax, Gary, 5, 25–29

H

HAL 9000, 323
Hallow, Ralph Z., 238
Harold structure, 282
Harper, Leanne C., 20
Harrell, D. Fox, 108, 177–182, 219
Harrigan, Pat, xiii-xv, 1–4, 6, 85–89, 107–109, 219–220
Harris, Thomas, 37
"Haunted House, The", 41–43
Helpless Doorknob, The (Gorey), 71–73
Herber, Keith, 36–37, 41–43
Heroes in Hell (shared world), 21
Hide and Seek, 15

Hildick, E. W., 134

Hindmarch, Will, 2, 47–55

Hitchhiker's Guide to the Galaxy, The (Adams and Meretzky), 140

Hite, Kenneth, 2, 31–40

Holmes, J. Eric, 29–30

Holodeck, 51n5, 327, 329

Homo Ludens: A Study of the Play-Element in Culture (Huizinga), 255

Hopscotch (Cortázar), 7, 10, 167

Howard, Robert E., 3, 21

Howard Dean for Iowa Game, The (Bogost and Frasca)
archiving and, 245–246
balloons and, 245
demographics and, 238–241
development time and, 234–237
games-based political speech and, 241–244
identification creation and, 237–238
meta-messages and, 245
time as constraint and, 234–237
virtual campaigning and, 233–234

Huizinga, Johan, 255–256, 314

"Hunter in Darkness: A Cave Crawl" (Plotkin), 131

I

IC (In Character) mode, 302–303

Identity
avatars and, 311–315
communities of play and, 315–316
emergent, 314–315
everyday role-playing and, 300–301
first-person immersion and, 311–314
In Character mode and, 302–303
limits and, 304–305
Out Of Character mode and, 302–303
role-playing mechanics and, 297–300

"I Have No Words & I Must Design" (Costikyan), 255–256

I Love Bees (Lee, et al.), 220, 251–252, 254, 261–262

Impermanence Agent, The (Wardrip-Fruin, et al.), 309, 320

Impro: Improvisation and the Theater (Johnstone), 283

Improvisational theater, 279–283

Improvisation for the Theater (Spolin), 281

Improvise: Scene from the Inside Out (Napier), 283

Indie Press Revolution, 2

Infocom, 129, 137, 144

Info-subjectivity, 161

Interactive fiction (IF), 5, 213–215
Baf's Guide and, 134
brief history of, 129–130
character design and, 139–146
commercial downfall of, 130
identity and, 134–135
player character and, 139–146
play-within-a-play and, 135–136
procedural authorship and, 183–208
second person and, 134–135
SHRDLU program and, 134
storytelling and, 5

Interactor, 139–141, 145–146

Iraq, 224

Ithkar (shared world), 17, 21

Itinerant (Rueb), 220, 273–277

J

Jackson, Michael, 314

Jackson, Peter, 4

Jackson, Shelley, 167

Jackson, Steve (Texas), 2, 7

Jackson, Steve (U.K.), 7

James, M. R., 38, 79

Jenik, Adriene, 220, 289–296

Jenkins, Henry, 53

Johnson, Steven, 233, 251, 254

Johnstone, Keith, 283

John W. Campbell Award, 18

Joint dialogue behaviors (JDBs)
beats and, 191–193, 195, 201–202, 206
long-term autonomous behavior and, 193
parallel behavior and, 195, 201–202

Joshi, S. T., 34

Joyce, Michael, 7, 149, 153, 167

Jungian analysis, 329

Juul, Jesper, xiv

Juvenate (Glaser, Hutchison, and Xavier), 108, 163–164

K

Kaboom! (Anonymous), 242
Katz, Demian, 134
Keavney, Mark, 109, 213–215
Kerry, John, 224, 243
Kim, Jee Yeon, 311
King, Stephen, 4, 52–53
King Lear (Shakespeare), xiii
Klein, T. E. D., 4
Korean War, 224
Koresh, David, 225–226
Krank, Charlie, 38
Kuma\War, 224–226

L

Labov, William, 177
Lacanian analysis, 325, 329
Lacuna (Sorensen), 1
Lakoff, George, 177
Lang, Eric, 3, 85–89
Languages structure, 282
Lankhmar (Lieber), 3
LARPs (live-action role-playing games), 2–3, 5
    euphoria from, 303–304
    puppet master and, 251–263
    real worlds and, 220, 251–263, 265–267
    as theater, 95
Launius, Richard, 4
Laurel, Brenda, 185
Laws, Robin D., 73–74
Lawsuits, 304
Lazzaro, Nicole, 316
Leather Goddesses of Phobos (Meretzky), 144
Leigh, Stephen, 20
Liavek (shared world), 17, 21
Lieber, Fritz, 3
Life in the Garden (Zimmerman), xiv, 4, 81–84
Life's Lottery (Newman), xiv, 4, 99–103, 220
Ligotti, Thomas, 4
Linde, Charlotte, 177
Livingstone, Ian, 7

Lord of the Rings (Tolkien), 3–4, 107, 169
    design decisions and, 85
    interactive fiction and, 134
    narrative advantage and, 222
    procedural authorship and, 185
Lovecraft, H. P., 4, 21
    Call of Cthulhu and, 31–39
    real worlds and, 225
    story-making games and, 78
Lovers, The (Magritte), 157
Loyall, Bryan, 185
Lucky Les (Hildick and Barrett), 134
Lumley, Brian, 4

M

Macromedia, 151
Magritte, Rene, 108, 157–158
Malcolm, Grant, 177
Maltese Falcon, The (Hammett), 108
Man, Play and Games (Caillois), 255, 303
Manovich, Lev, 108, 159–162, 219
Man with Newspaper (Magritte), 157–158
Marino, Mark C., 108, 165–167
Martin, George R. R., 3, 15–23, 85, 88
Masks of Nyarlathotep (DiTillio), 37
Mateas, Michael, xiv, 109
    player character and, 142–143
    procedural authorship and, 183–208
Max Payne (Hoare), 224
McCloud, Scott, 239
McCorduck, Pamela, 184
McDaid, John, 153
McGonigal, Jane, 220, 251–267
McKee, Robert, 191
McLeod, Jack, 303
McLuhan, Marshall, 315
Measure for Marriage, A (Fortugno), 265–267
Mechner, Jordan, 109
Medal of Honor (Hirschmann), 224
Medea: Harlan's World (Ellison), 21
Meditated (de Zengotita), 258
Memmott, Talan, 108, 157–158, 219

Meretzky, Steve, 108, 137–138

Merovingen Nights (shared world), 21

Mertwig's Maze (Wham), 77, 79

Michelangelo, 169

Milán, Victor W., 16

Millennium's End (Ryan), 223

Miller, Gail Gerstner, 16

Miller, John J., 16

Min-maxing, 19n1

Minnesota Fringe Festival, 285

Mirror exercise, 279–280

Mission to Earth (Manovich), 161–162

Mixiins, 191–193

MMOGs (Massively Multiplayer Online Games), 5, 9, 11, 313, 315

MMORPGs (Massively Multiplayer Online Role-Playing Games), xv, 134, 219–220

Mona, Erik, 2, 25–30

Monello, Mike, 259

Monopoly, 5, 15, 139, 349

Montfort, Nick, xiv, 109, 167, 309
    interactive fiction and, 129, 154
    player character and, 139–146

MOO (Mud Object Oriented), 134, 328–329

Moonmist (Galley and Lawrence), 144

Moore, Alan, 152

Moore, Jim, 16

Moore, Michael, 242

Morrow Project (Dockery, Sadler, and Tucholka), 16

Mortensen, Torill Elvira, 220, 297–305

Mosaic, 130

Moss, Brion, 154

Moulthrop, Stuart, 108, 149–155

MUDs (Multiple-User Dungeons), 130, 134, 313
    euphoria from, 303
    identity and, 299
    player character and, 140
    privacy and, 328–329

Multimedia, 91–93 (*see also* Computational fictions)

Murray, Janet, 51n5, 140, 183, 329

Mutants and Masterminds (Kenson), 223

My Life with Master (Czege), 1, 11, 67–68

Myst, 130, 142, 311–312, 316

Mystery of Edwin Drood, The (Holmes), 350

Mystery of the Abbey (Faidutti), 3, 95–97

N

Nabokov, Vladimir, 167

Name of the Rose, The (Eco), 3

Napier, Mick, 283

Napoleon at Waterloo (Dunnigan), 6

Narratives, 11–12 (*see also* Storytelling)
    games that make stories, 69–80
    generation systems and, 177–182
    GRIOT and, 177–182
    human brain and, 69
    interactive fiction (IF) and, 129–136
    quests and, 307–310
    LARPs and, 265–267
    real worlds and, 222–223
    structure and, 31–40
    Weblogs and, 309

Natural language (NL), 191

Neilson, John, 125

Nelson, Graham, 129, 144

Newman, Kim, xiv, 4, 99–103, 220

New media
    cultural acceptance of, 221
    educational advantage and, 223–225
    escapism and, 221–222
    narrative advantage and, 222–223
    procedural authorship and, 183–208
    real worlds and, 221 (*see also* Real worlds)
    revelatory advantage and, 225–227

News Reader (Wardrip-Fruin), 154

New Voices (Martin), 18, 21

New York Times, 243

N-grams, 154

Nideffer, Robert, 220, 269–271

Non-playable characters, 117–118

"Nuh unh" factor, xiii, 60

O

Ogawa, Taro, 131

Oh O'Clock, 15

Olvido Mortal (Peláez), 141

Once Upon a Time (Wallis), 3, 69, 75–76, 79
Online Caroline (Bevan and Wright), 309
OOC (Out Of Character), 302–303
Open Gaming License, 1
Oulipo, 134, 166
Over the Edge (Tweet), xiv, 77
Oz Project, 185

P

Pacesetter, 2
Pagan Publishing, 35, 219
Pale Fire (Nabokov), 167
Paley, Vivian Gussin, 70
Panko, 241
Pantheon (Laws), 73–74, 80
Paragraph-system board games, 8
Parcheesi, 15
Participatory systems, 183–184
Pax, 150–155
Pearce, Celia, 220, 239, 311–317
Peláez, Andrés Viedma, 141
Perec, Georges, 234
Perren, Jeff, 25
Persuasive Games, 154
Petit, Marianne, 125
Philosophy of Horror, The (Carroll), 33–34
Planetfall (Meretzky), 137–138
Player Character (PC), 2–3
    beats and, 190–203
    Book and Volume and, 139, 143–145
    as constraint, 145–146
    defined, 139
    identity and, 297–305
    In Character mode and, 302–303
    interactor and, 139–141
    Out Of Character mode and, 302–303
    successful designs of, 141–143
Plotkin, Andrew, 129–136
Poe, Edgar Allan, 116
Poetics, 179–182, 234
Poker, xiv, 15
Politics
    ACORN and, 220, 248–249

activism and, 233–249
    canvassing role-plays and, 247–248
    The Howard Dean for Iowa Game and, 233–246
    United Nations and, 249
Pong (Alcorn, et al.), 107
Poremba, Cindy, 316
Pound, Ezra, 234
Power Kill (Tynes), 222
Present, The (Clarebout), 309
Presentation of Self in Everyday Life, The (Goffman), 300
Price, Vincent, 116
PrimeTime Adventures (Wilson), 1
Prince of Persia: The Sands of Time (Mechner and Ubisoft), 109
    character design and, 114–115, 117–118
    dialogue and, 118–119
    efficiency maximization and, 113
    genre combination and, 115–117
    hero's environment and, 114–115
    rule breaking and, 115
    storytelling and, 111–113
    tool creation and, 119–120
Print-On-Demand (POD) technologies, 2
Procedural authorship
    agency and, 203–206
    alternate dialogue and, 195
    architectural framework and, 190–191
    beats and, 190–203
    coherent intermixing and, 190, 193
    complexity reduction and, 196–197
    computer essence and, 183–185
    content and, 183–191
    context and, 195
    description of, 183–185
    design and, 206–207
    discourse acts and, 191
    drama management and, 192
    encyclopedic and, 184
    Façade and, 185–208
    gist point and, 198
    global mix-in progressions and, 192
    long-term mix-in behaviors and, 193

Procedural authorship *(continued)*
  parallel behavior and, 195–196
  participatory and, 183–184
  physical performance and, 200–203
  reactivity and, 194–195, 198–200
  scaffolding and, 197–198
  spatial and, 184
  story design and, 188–190
  uninterruptibility and, 198
"Psychoanalysts, Artists and Academics in Dialogue"
    (Wortzel), 327
Psycho (Bloch), 37
Psychonauts (Schafer), 5
Puppetland (Tynes), xv, 220
  action adjudication and, 339
  candy cave and, 346
  characters in, 336–338, 341–344
  first rule of, 334
  lake of milk and cookies and, 346
  landscape and, 344–345
  Maker's Land and, 333–334, 344
  narration and, 339–345
  playing a puppet in, 338
  Punch's castle and, 345–346
  puppetmastering and, 338–339
  puppet page and, 337
  real worlds and, 229–233
  second rule of, 335
  sky and, 344
  tales and, 346–347
  third rule of, 335–336
  tone and, 340–341
Puppet master, 263
  control issues and, 259–262
  I Love Bees and, 251–252
  immersive options and, 257–259
  pervasive factor and, 256–257
  player choice and, 257–259
  power plays and, 255–256
  rise of, 253–255
  traditionally powerful players and, 255–256
  volition and, 255–256

Q

Queneau, Raymond, 134, 166
Quixote, Don, 326

R

Rabelais, François, 167
Racter, 154
Random design, 81–84
Ransom model, 2
Rayuela, La (Cortázar), 7
Real worlds, 219–220
  activism and, 233–249
  educational advantage and, 223–225
  escapism and, 221–222
  everyday life and, 300–301
  identity and, 297–305, 311–316
  immersion options and, 257–259
  improvisational theater and, 279–283
  In Character mode and, 302–303
  lawsuits and, 304
  narrative advantage and, 222–223
  Out Of Character mode and, 302–303
  politics and, 233–249
  puppet master problem and, 251–263
  revelatory advantage and, 225–227
  stereotypes and, 302
  theater and, 279–295
Rees, Gareth, 144
Regime Change (Wardrip-Fruin, et al.), 154
Rettberg, Scott, 309
Rheingold, Howard, 312
Ryzom (see *Saga of Ryzom*)
RIFTS (Siembieda), 31
Ringoleavio, 15
Rise and Fall of the City of Mahogonny, The (Brecht and Weill),
    350
Roberts, Charles S., 134
Robotics
  chatterbots and, 321–324
  Eliza Redux and, 320–329
  gestures and, 326–327

HAL 9000 and, 323
    human interaction with, 320–324
    Turing Test and, 327–328
Rock music, 221
Rogerian analysis, 329
Roleplaying Gamers Association (RPGA), 219
Role-playing games (RPGs), xiii–xiv
    activism and, 233–249
    algorithmic systems and, 10–11
    arbitrariness and, 101
    character design and, 101, 139–146
    commentary and, 61
    computational fictions and, 213–215 (*see also*
        Computational fictions)
    computer and console, 9
    context and, 63
    core concept and, 58
    dispute resolution and, 65
    euphoric highs from, 303–304
    free-form, 11–12
    game material and, 60
    genre and, 60
    identity and, 297–305, 311–316
    improvisational theater and, 279–283
    In Character mode and, 302–303
    indie movement and, 1–2, 5
    lawsuits and, 304
    meaning in, 57–66
    methodology and, 57–58, 63–64
    motivation and, 57, 64–65
    narrativist, 11–12
    Out Of Character mode and, 302–303
    play contract and, 60
    rules and, 78
    solitaire, 8
    stereotypes and, 302
    tabletop systems and, 1–5 (*see also* Tabletop systems)
Rosenberg, Jim, 152–153
Roudier, Emmanuel, 96
Rueb, Teri, 220, 273–277
Rules of Play: Game Design Fundamentals (Salen and
    Zimmerman), xiii, 256

Rush, Annie, 1
Ryan, Charles, 223
Ryan, Marie-Laure, 108, 163–164

S

Saga of Ryzom, The (Simon), 313
Salen, Katie, xiii–xiv, 256, 311, 314
Sam and Max Hit the Road, 142
Santaman's Harvest (Desktop Theater), 220, 289–296
Sapir-Whorf hypothesis, 171
Savoir-Faire (Short), 109, 141–142, 147–148
Scaffolding, 197–198
Schauermärchen (Wick), 1
Scrimshaw, Joe, 220, 285–287
Second City, Chicago, 281
Second Life (Linden Lab), 315
Secret Lives of Gingerbread Men, The (Rush), 1
September 11, 2001, 150, 223
September 12th (Frasca), 243–244
Shade (Plotkin)
    innovations of, 129–136
        light modeling and, 132–133
        open source code of, 132–134
        second person and, 134–135
Shakespeare, William, xiii, 266
Sheldon, Lee, 108–109, 121–123
Shelley, Mary, 220
Shiner, Lewis, 20
Shockwave Flash, 151
Short, Emily, 109, 135, 141–142, 147–148
Should Have Said structure, 282
Shrapnel (Cadre), 141
SHRDLU, 134
Shrek (film), 221
SimCity (Wright), xiv, 241
Simons, Walton, 20
Simonsen, Redmond, 6
Sims, The (Wright), xiii–xiv, 311
Slate magazine, 233
Sloane, Sarah, 140
Smith, Clark Ashton, 21
Snodgrass, Melinda M., 16, 18–19

Snow Crash (Stephenson), 257

Snyder, Matt, 1

Soft Cinema, 159–162

Solitaire RPG games, 8

Solitaire (Thorington), 4, 108, 125–127

Song of Ice and Fire, A (Martin), 3, 85, 88

Sorcerer (Edwards), 1

Sorensen, Jared, 1

Sorry!, 15

Sourcebooks, 1–2

Spatial systems, 184

Spolin, Viola, 281

Spycraft (Kapera and Wilson), 223

Squad Leader (Hill), 107

Stacey, Sean, 251, 253

Star Trek (TV series), 48

Star Wars (film), 3

Steinkuehler, Constance A., 311

Stephenson, Neal, 257

Stereotypes, 302

Stern, Andrew, xiv, 109

    player character and, 142–143

    procedural authorship and, 183–208

Stone, Allucquère Rosanne, xv, 315

Story Blocks, 71

Storytelling, xiii, 3

    in action, 52–55

    adventure games and, 8–9

    balance and, 78–79

    beads-on-a-string model and, 8–13

    collectible card games and, 85–89

    computational fictions and, 111–113

    divergence and, 6

    elements of, 70–73

    embedded stories and, 10, 116

    game books and, 7–8

    genre and, 73–76

    human brain and, 69

    hypertext fiction and, 7

    interactive fiction (IF) and, 5, 129–136, 213–215 (*see also* Interactive fiction (IF))

    MMOs and, 9

    multimedia and, 91–93

    nesting and, 116

    quests and, 307–310

    random numbers and, 50–52

    real worlds and, 221–227 (*see also* Real worlds)

    rules and, 78

    self image and, 48–50

    structure and, 31–40, 76–77

    tabletop systems and, 5–13

    Wild Cards and, 15–23

Stratego, 15

Suffragettes in and out of Prison, 241

Sunset Boulevard (film), 116

Superworld (Perrin), 16–20

Suspended (Berlyn), 140

T

Tabletop systems, xiii–xiv

    educational advantage and, 223–225

    Lovecraft and, 4

    narrative advantage and, 222–223

    poor commercial market of, 1

    publications for, 1–2

    real worlds and, 221–227 (*see also* Real worlds)

    revelatory advantage and, 225–227

    storytelling and, 5–13

    terminology of, 2–3

    Tolkien and, 3–4

Tactics (Roberts), 134

Take Back Illinois (Bogost), 244, 246

Take That Back structure, 282

Tale in the Desert, A (Tepper), 11

Tales of the Arabian Nights (Goldberg), 8, 10, 69, 79–80

Tax Invaders (Republican National Committee), 241–243

Taylor, Alice, 185

Taylor, T. L., 311–312, 315

Tékumel (Barker), 222–223

Television, 12, 323

Terrorism

    Bestial Acts and, 353–355

    real world and, 223–224, 242–244

    writing and, 150

Texas (Manovich), 161–162

Theater

    Adventures in Mating and, 285–287

    improvisational, 279–283

    Santaman's Harvest and, 289–295

Theatre of the Oppressed (Boal), 290n1

There (Harvey and Ventrella), 313–315

Thief of Baghdad (film), 115–116

Thieves' World (shared world), 17–18, 21

Third Reich (Greenwood and Prados), 6

"Thirty Minutes Over Broadway" (Waldrop), 15

This Is a Pipe (Foucault), 157

Thorington, Helen, 4, 108, 125–127, 219

Thorne, Sean, 219–220, 229–233

1001 Nights, 116

Threatened Assassin, The (Magritte), 157–158

3D modeling, 149, 186, 257

Three Kings (film), 223

Three-Line Scene structure, 280

Threepenny Opera, The (Brecht and Weill), 350–351

Ticky the Clock, 165

Time, 234–237

Tolkien, J. R. R., 3–4, 129, 134, 222

Tomb of Dracula (Wolfman), 177

Treachery of Images, The (Magritte), 157

Tristram Shandy (Sterne), 167

Trivial Pursuit, 349

Trollbabe (Edwards), 1

TSR, 2, 25–30, 134

Turing, Alan, 167, 327–328

Turkle, Sherry, 314

Turner, Jonathan, 224–225

Turner, Mark, 177

Turner, Victor Witter, 314

Tuters, Marc, 256

TutorText, 134

'Tweens, 157

Tweet, Jonathan, xiv, 3, 45–46, 77

Twelve Easy Lessons to Better Time Travel (Marino), 108, 165–167

Tynes, John, 35, 219

    prismatic play and, 221–228

    Puppetland and, 333–347

U

Uncle Roy All Around You (Blast Theory), 257

Under Siege (Afkar Media), 241

unexceptional.net (Nideffer), 269–271

"Unfiction Glossary, The" (Stacey), 251

Uninterruptibility, 198

United Nations, 249

Unknown Armies (Stolze and Tynes), 226–227

Unreal (Bleszinski and Schmalz), 224

Until Uru, 313

Upgrade, The (Fritzon and Wrigstad), 12

Uren, Tim, 220, 279–283

Uru: Ages beyond Myst (Miller and Miller), 311–316

Usenet, 130

V

Vampire: The Masquerade (Rein-Hagen, et al.), 3, 48–49, 223, 298

Vampire: The Requiem (Achilli, et al.), 47–48

Vance, Jack, 3

Varicella (Cadre), 141–142, 146

W

Waco Resurrection (Allen, et al.), 225–226

Waldrop, Howard, 15, 20

Walker, Jill, 154, 220, 307–310

Wallis, James, 3

    Baron Munchausen and, 359–382

    storytelling and, 69–80

Ward, Mark, 304

Wardrip-Fruin, Noah, xiii–xv, 1–4, 6, 107–109, 219–220, 309

WarioWare (game series), 235

War World (shared world), 18, 21

Watchmen (Moore), 152

Water Cooler Games, 241, 243

Weblogs, 309

Weill, Kurt, 350–351

Weizenbaum, Joseph, 321–322, 324, 328–329

West End Games, 254

Whang, Leo Sang-Min, 311

Whelan, Kevin, 220, 247–249

"When Angels Deserve to Die" (Turner), 224–225
"Where Stories End and Games Begin" (Costikyan), 47
Which Way books, 7
White Wolf Publishing, x, 2–3, 47–55
Who's Afraid of Virginia Woolf? (Albee), 186
Wick, John, 1
Wicked Dead RPGs, 2
Wideman, Royce, 16
Wild Cards, 3
    Albuquerque gaming group and, 15–17
    Martin on, 15–23
    Wild Cards Day and, 15
Wilder, Billy, 116
Williams, Walter Jon, 16, 19–20
Wilson, Kevin, 3–4, 91–93, 219
Wilson, Matt, 1
Winchester's Nightmare (Montfort), 143
Windows 3.0, 130
Wink Back, Inc., 259
Winograd, Terry, 134
Wittgenstein, Ludwig, xiii
Wizard of Oz (Baum), 253, 325
Wizards of the Coast, 1, 3, 87, 219
Wolfman, Marv, 177
Woods, Don, 5, 129
World of Darkness (Bridges, et al.), x
World of Warcraft (Blizzard Entertainment), xiv, 3–4, 10
    real worlds and, 219–220, 299, 303–304
    structure of, 307–310
Worlds Apart (Britton), 141
Wortzel, Adrianne, 220, 319–330
Wrigstad, Tobias, 12
Writing
    And Then There Were None and, 121–123
    Book and Volume and, 143–145
        The Brotherhood of Bent Billiard and, 157–158
        children and, 229–232
    computer's effect and, 169–171
    cybertext and, 149–155
    Deikto and, 171–175
    Eliza Redux and, 319–330
    Façade and, 185–207
    generation systems and, 177–182
    grammar and, 149
    GRIOT and, 177–182
    info-subjectivity and, 161
    Itinerant and, 273–277
    narrative generation systems and, 177–182
    new media and, 149–155
    Pax and, 150–155
    Planetfall and, 137–138
    poetics and, 149
    Prince of Persia: The Sands of Time and, 111–120
    procedural authorship and, 183–208
    rhetoric and, 149
    Savoir-Faire and, 147–148
    Santaman's Harvest and, 289–295
    Soft Cinema project and, 159–162
    Solitaire and, 125–127
    spatial hypertext and, 152–153
    Twelve Easy Lessons to Better Time Travel and, 165–167

X

Xbox 360, 234
X-Files, The (TV series), 48
X-Men (comic book), 20

Y

Yee, Nicholas, 311
You Are There (TV series), 223–224
Youdunnit (Wallis), 3, 70, 80

Z

Zelazny, Roger, 3, 20, 85
Zengotita, Thomas de, 258, 260
Zimmerman, Eric, xiii, 4, 311, 314
    Life in the Garden and, xiv, 4, 81–84
    meaning-machine creation and, 81–84
    puppet master and, 256
Zork (Blank and Lebling), 129, 131, 137, 139–140
Zubek, Robert, 109, 209–212